TheMen Who Made

the

Law

During the time of Justinian's compilation
and Blackstone's Commentaries.

Charles E. Harman, M.D., J.D.

OLD COURT PRESS
BROOKINGS, OREGON
2002

The Men Who Made the Law

Old Court Press

For Information, write to
Old Court Press, P.O. Box 4031
Brookings, Or 97415

Library of Congress Cataloging-in-Publication Data

Harman, Charles E., 1931-
    The Men Who Made the Law : during the time of Justinian's
compilation and
    Blackstone's commentaries / Charles E. Harman.
        P. cm.
    Includes bibliographical references and index.
    ISBN 0-9649391-1-8 (alk. paper)
        1. Law--Great Britain--History. 2. Roman law--History. I. Title.

    KDS540 .H37 2002
    340.5'4--dc21

                                                    2002020023

Printed in the United States of America

Contents

Preface
Introduction

iv

Preface

What a change the passage of years can make. As a youth my most hated and neglected subjects were history and those associated fields of politics, law and government. It was only perhaps by accident that I would spend my last remaining years in the study first of law and of necessity that of history and government. Having first developed a love of mathematics and the sciences, I later pursued the study and practice of medicine, specializing in neurology and psychiatry. It was only after three legal or quasi-legal encounters that I would take up the study of law, obtaining a J.D. degree in October 1997.

This work represents my own attempt to understand the justice system as it functions in the United States today. The *Men Who Made the Law* goes back to the sources of western law, starting with the Romans and concluding with the English kings, at least to the time of George III. This book is written for the student, for those who wish to pursue the basic question— Where does the law come from? What are the sources of law? It is written for those whose lives, or the lives of their families, have been impacted by the law and who wish to know more about the legal establishment and who is behind it. It is written for all citizens who have responsibilities towards others in this country.

The writer is grateful to the translators, editors and publishers of the many marvelous historical books listed in the bibliography such as the works of Cicero, Plutarch's *Lives*, the works of Tacitus, *The History of England* by David Hume, *The Short History of the English People* by J. R. Green and the historic plays of Shakespeare. The publications of The Library of America such as the *Jefferson Writings* and the *Debate on the Constitution* are much appreciated and valued. Quotations from these works and others will be found throughout the book and can be readily discerned by italics compared to the text originated by the writer. The rather extensive use of quotations in this book has a long established precedent in the *cases and materials* books used by law students. The liberal use of quotations from David Hume, a contemporary of Blackstone, for the history of England to William III and John Richard Green for the modern period to George III are justified by their neglect by modern historians, even though acclaimed as literary and historical masterpieces. It is hoped the reader will be motivated to turn to the sources here used and listed in the bibliography. [1]

This work would not have been possible without the unfailing love and sense of truth and justice always forthcoming in a most beautiful way from my wife Mary.

---

[1] For this text see Addendum following Index for conversion of page numbers for references to H in *Critical Commentaries on Blackstone*.

Introduction

There is a need today for all citizens to understand the justice system and the operations of government at all levels. Everyone in the United States lives in a county, or even near or within a city. Everyone lives in a state, with its own laws and government. All people in the United States have responsibilities to others in this country. Today, as was the case when this nation was founded, there is a great need for study and debate about the events of today involving government and law. All have the responsibility to do whatever they can to improve their knowledge and communicate with others. Parents have the responsibility of doing whatever they can to insure that this nation remains free. The warning of Thomas Jefferson, written over two hundred years ago, applies to us today.

I am persuaded myself that the good sense of the people will always be found to be the best army. They may be led astray for a moment, but will soon correct themselves. The people are the only censors of their governors. --- If once they become inattentive to the public affairs, you and I, and Congress and Assemblies, judges and governors, shall all become wolves.[1]

There can be no doubt that fear even in today's democracy and land of freedom prevents most people from a free and open discussion of the most important issues of government and law. The urgency today is most readily apparent from the recent supreme court decision Bush v. Gore in which chief justice Rehnquist and the supreme court decided the presidency, not the people or the voters. The abdication of congress is unsettling. Nevertheless, we should remind ourselves of the admonition of Cicero written over two thousand years ago.

Of injustice there are two types: men may inflict injury; or else when it is being inflicted upon others, they may fail to deflect it, even though they could. --- But also, the man who does not defend someone, or obstruct the injustice when he can, is at fault just as if he had abandoned his parents or his friends or his country.[2]

Cicero asked in his dialogues, *The Republic,* and *The Laws,* '*What is the source of law?*' How can we understand the operations of

---

[1] Jefferson, Writings, pp 880-881.

[2] Cicero, On Duties, p 10.

government and law today? It is this question that is the reason for writing this book. The study of law was difficult and disturbing to me since there was lacking the answer to the question raised by Cicero in any of my law courses or required readings. The only guide I had was my own sense of right and wrong, which I had learned in childhood from my mother. No doubt most people have developed a sense of right and wrong. This remains the best bulwark against injustice and unfairness. Unfortunately, until recently my only education was a high school civics course. All my life I had believed that the justice system in this country was the best in the world, and that truth and justice prevailed.

It was a shock to me to experience first hand the operations of the law courts. Most people have no idea what it is like to be involved in a lawsuit. From these experiences I learned first hand about the operations of the justice system. I learned from the first case that knowledge is the key. First, one must not only focus meticulously on the facts but also must obtain documentation and subject all possible witness to intense questioning by depositions. Practice guides are available. One must follow the procedures of the court. Lawyers have information about the peculiarities of each court. Those who have had experiences in the courts are the best judges of how the justice system operates. It remains their task, and those of their families, to use their minds and spirit to understand just what happened to them and why. To be able to discuss and even write about disturbing events is very helpful to overcome negative or even harmful effects to one's body and soul. Court watch or justice watch group discussions are helpful and may even give notice that people are interested and are watching what goes on in the courts.

What are the sources of law? It was not until my third year of law studies that I took the course on constitutional law. It should have been taught in the first year. Yet all law schools in the United States today do the same. They wait until the third year before presenting that which is the basis of all law in the United States.

Article VI of the Constitution of the United States, second paragraph, reads:

This Constitution, and the laws of the United States which shall be made in pursuance thereof; and all treaties made, or which shall be made, under the authority of the United States, shall be the supreme law of the land, and the judges in every state shall be bound thereby, anything in the Constitution or laws of any State to the contrary notwithstanding.

That law or justice is the foundation of government is clearly stated in the opening words of the *Constitution of the United States: We the people of the United States, in order to form a more perfect union, establish justice.*

It is therefore quite clear that the starting point for understanding where the law comes from is our constitution, the first written constitution to appear among nations. The discussions and debates by the founding fathers before the constitution and first ten amendments were written provides a valuable source of information to anyone interested in justice in the United States today.[3] The Declaration of Independence and its historic foundations are not subjects taught in law schools. All Americans should read this document, which provides the reason for the foundation of our country.

Few are aware that Jefferson and four others, in 1776, met to decide the question whether American law or English law should be the law of the land. Instead of establishing American law based on American principles of justice, three of these men decided on the easier course. Jefferson, of English and Welsh parentage, had learned his law from William Blackstone's *Commentaries on English Law*. American lawyers read Blackstone as a primary source for their education in the law for the next one hundred years. Blackstone was even referred to in the Bush v. Gore debate in the year 2000. John Marshall, who is regarded today as the most important chief justice in the history of the U.S. Supreme court, read Blackstone's *Commentaries* and attended only six weeks of lectures at the college of William and Mary.[4] There were no law schools until Harvard established the first law school in 1817. The case method was started in 1871. Up to then lawyers were self-taught. There is no reason why a motivated person should not learn a great deal about the justice system today by self-study.

That Blackstone and English law, not American law, is the foundation of our justice system today is taught by a professor of legal history at a New York law school. *It is not surprising that as late as the 1830's Blackstone's Commentaries continued to be seriously studied as a legal textbook in the United States. --- The common law today is what it has been since it crystallized in the fourteenth century. A London barrister of 1500 would need only a few months of remedial education to step into an American courtroom today. If he were brought back today, Blackstone would not be at all surprised by the common law in either Britain or the United States. He would applaud it. But led by the prominent law schools, the symbolic and totemic recognition of English common law endures.*[5]

There is no doubt that study of the laws of England are necessary in order to understand how the law functions in the United States today. Blackstone made commentaries on English law, but it is the men who made the law in England that we must study. The source of law is human beings. Therefore, it is necessary to study what kind of

---

[3] The Debate on the Constitution, vols 1 and 2.

[4] The Debate on the Constitution, Part 2, p 1001.

[5] Cantor, pp 365 and 373 .

persons these laws came from. The source of English law is Roman law. England was occupied and ruled by Romans for nearly five hundred years. Roman law was not only the basis of the laws which ruled England, but of the Roman Church, which became dominant after the Romans left. Shortly after the discovery of Justinian's compilation of Roman law in 1130 A.D., lectures on Roman law were given at Oxford. Therefore we have the daunting task of studying the history of the Romans as well as the English, to George III. This will necessarily include study of the ancients from the Romans to the time they left England. Then we must study medieval history from the time the Romans left England to the time of Richard III. There follows the early modern period of English history from Henry VII to George III, who was king at the time of the Revolutionary war. The study of history can be a very dull, tedious undertaking. As with law, an attempt to survey everything written on the subject is impossible. Therefore it becomes crucial what sources of information one should rely on, and yet maintain an interest in the subjects of study.

My approach to the study the men who made the law was the way I had been trained and had learned during my years of practice as a physician, neurologist and psychiatrist. Unfortunately, there are no records of accurate medical histories, physical and neurological examinations, or laboratory data for any of the men under study. I began, however, my psychiatric residency by focusing on the life history of each patient referred to me. I was interested not only in what patients said or how they behaved, but what they had accomplished in life and what they could do at present. It was by reading *Plutarch' Lives* that I became interested in history, especially by his stated objective. *It must be borne in mind that my design is not to write histories, but lives. And the most glorious exploits do not always furnish us with the clearest discoveries of virtue or vice in men; sometimes a matter of less moment, and expression or a jest, informs us better of their characters and inclinations, than the most famous sieges, the greatest armaments, or the bloodiest battles whatsoever. Therefore as portrait-painters are more exact in the lines and features of the face, in which the character is seen, than in the other parts of the body, so I must be allowed to give my more particular attention to the marks and indications of the souls of men, and while I endeavor by these to portray their lives, may be free to leave more weighty matters and great battles to be treated of by others.*[6]

There followed the discovery, for the first time to me, of other great historians of the ancient world such as Tacitus and Seutonius. But all histories are biased from the person and the culture from which such histories are written. The anti-Semitism of the ancient Greek and Roman historians had to be balanced by Josephus, the eminent Jewish historian.

---

[6] Plutarch, Lives, vol 2, p 139.

The history of the middle ages had always been something I had never expected to be interested in. *The History of England,* volumes 1-6, by David Hume was another fascinating discovery. This history was noted by Jefferson, and most likely read by him, but has scarcely been referred to in modern times. Hume, during his last twenty years, was the librarian at the Edinburgh library and had directed his brilliance and his energies in this final work. Yet Hume's anti-clerical sentiments had to be balanced at least by the venerable Bede with his *Ecclesiastical History of the English People.* Hume's bias against the Irish had to be countered by Cusack's *History of Ireland.* Cicero, however, became the best authority for answering the question where does the law come from. Cicero also gave us perhaps the best account of the men who made the law at the time. An equally fortuitous discovery for me, which enlivened the study of medieval history, were the historic plays of Shakespeare, from Richard II to Henry VIII. Who better than Cicero, Plutarch, Tacitus, Hume and Shakespeare could best describe the character and mentality of the tyrants?

Few references will be made to modern historians. It was, however, necessary to rely on John Richard Green's *A short History of the English People* for the period between the Stuarts and George III. Green also provides great insights into people and the times, but unfortunately is out of print, but available in many libraries. There are also historic novels such as Robert Graves' *I Claudius* and histories written like novels such as Carolly Erickson's *First Elizabeth,* which can enliven the study of the ancients and modern men under study. The writer recommends that the reader have at hand one or more modern Histories of England as well as access to a set of encyclopedias to help follow the stories and events.[7]

The Men Who Made the Law, includes the men, Romans and English, whose laws are found in the two major compilations of Law which exist in the Western world, the *Digest of Justinian* and the *Commentaries on the Laws of England* by Blackstone.

Perhaps the most important reason for presenting *The Men Who Made the Law* is that it may provide a preliminary survey for a study of tyrants in the past as well as in the present. There is no danger greater than man himself as documented by tyrants who have wrecked havoc upon this earth and who have destroyed or maimed untold millions of good people. A study of these men is necessary to understand the origins of tyranny and the degradations of government, laws and societies in nations today.

---

[7] Works by Morgan, Editor, and Trevelyan, listed in the bibliography, provide a contrast to the works cited.

Chapter 1

Coriolanus

Introduction

Historians and literary critics have acclaimed Edward Gibbon's work *The Decline and Fall of the Roman Empire,* the first volume published in 1776, a masterpiece. Gibbon's conclusion on the fall of the Roman Empire was that it was plagued by internal and external enemies. The internal enemies were the Christians, a radical revolutionary group who were a threat to the traditions and beliefs of the Romans. The external enemies were the barbarians who invaded Rome in A.D. 408-410.

Oddly Gibbon began his work during the second century A.D. Arnold Toynbee, whose ten volume work, *A Study of History,* comes to an entirely different conclusion on the reason for the fall of the Roman Empire. Toynbee believed that the Romans sowed the seeds of their own destruction long before the second century. Toynbee attributed the fall of the Roman Empire to corruption and the enormous military expenses and costs to maintain the vast Roman Empire.

Our concern here is an understanding of the character of the men who rule. We shall begin the story of the Romans long before the second century with the story of Coriolanus. This was the time when Rome was just beginning as a small nation. We shall then go to the story of Pompey followed by the story of Julius Caesar, which was the end of the Republic and the beginning of rule by Emperors.

In between Coriolanus and Julius Caesar there was hardly the semblance of a Republic. Rome struggled for its mere existence. The near sack of Rome, by Coriolanus and the Volscians, in 491 B.C., was averted only by the mother of Coriolanus. There followed the victory of Rome over the Volscians, and the major victory over the Etruscans in 474 B.C. There were more wars with the Gauls in 382 B.C., with the Greeks in Italy from 280-275 B.C., and more wars with the Carthaginians with defeat of Hannibal in 202 B.C., and the destruction of Carthage in 146 B.C. We shall continue the story of the expansion of the Roman Empire after presenting the story of Coriolanus.

Coriolanus

The story of Coriolanus is found in Plutarch's Lives and was featured in Shakespeare's play, *Coriolanus*. The name Coriolanus was a third name added to Caius Marcius in honor of his conquest of the City of Corioli in his successful war against the Volcians in 493 B.C. Coriolanus was a member of the patrician nobility. His story is that of a military commander and an aristocrat, who also ran for consul. At the time in Rome, about 500 B.C., there were three political entities. The senate included the nobility or the patricians. Menenius Agrippa, a friend of Coriolanus, was a leader in the senate. One or sometimes two consuls were appointed by the senate to rule for one year. Coriolanus attempted to run for consul, but the peoples' assembly forced his banishment from Rome. In retaliation, Coriolanus joined up with the Volcians and threatened Rome, but was dissuaded by his mother, wife and children.

The people's assembly included citizens of Rome, who were involved in the politics of the day. They elected leaders known as tribunes, and at times proposed and passed laws. The tribunes in the story of Coriolanus were Junius Brutus and Siccinius Velutus.

The story of Coriolanus is a story of the rich, or the elite, vs. the poor, or the people. The lines are clearly drawn with Coriolanus representing the rich and Brutus and Siccinius the poor, or the people. As the story unfolds, the senate is forced, by public opposition, to the role of mediator between Coriolanus and the people. Our focus here in this story will be on the kind of mentality shown by Coriolanus.

Family and upbringing

From Plutarch we read that Marcius, as we shall call him before the name Coriolanus is bestowed upon him, descended from the patrician house of his name. But his father died when Marcius was a child. He was raised by his mother Volumnia. The mother of Coriolanus therefore is a large part of the story from the beginning to the end, when the Romans erect a statue on her behalf for saving Coriolanus and Rome from his own vengeance. That she was a large part of his development and character is apparent from reading Plutarch's account. Even after marriage, he chose to continue to live with her, and she figured large in encouraging all his activities.

Marcius (Coriolanus), as a boy, *having more passionate inclination than any of that age for feats of war, began at once, from his very childhood, to handle arms; and feeling that adventitious implements and artificial arms would effect little, and be of small use to such as have not their native and natural weapons well fixed and prepared for service, he so exercised and inured his body to all sorts of activity and encounters, that besides being a racer, he had close wrestlings with an enemy; so that his competitors at home in displays of bravery, loth to own themselves inferior in that respect, were wont to ascribe their deficiencies to his strength of body, which they say no resistance and no fatigue could exhaust. Those were times at Rome, in which that kind of worth was most esteemed which displayed itself in military achievements; one evidence of which we find in the Latin word for virtue, which is equivalent to manly courage. As if valor and all virtue had been the same thing, they used as the common term the name of the particular excellence.*

The first time he went out to the wars, being yet a stripling, --- The armies met and engaged in a decisive battle, in the vicissitudes of which Marcius, while fighting bravely in the dictator's presence, saw a Roman soldier before him, and slew his assailant. The general after having gained the victory, crowned him for this act.[1]

From Plutarch's account, the mother of Marcius (Coriolanus) encouraged his physical training and military exploits, as a youth. *Marcius, having a spirit of this noble make, was ambitious always to surpass himself, and did nothing, how extraordinary soever, but he thought he was bound to outdo it at the next occasion; and ever desiring to give continual fresh instances of his prowess, he added one exploit to another, and heaped up trophies upon trophies, so as to make it matter of contest also among his commanders, the latter still vying with the earlier which should pay him the greatest honor and speak highest in his commendation. --- But Marcius, believing himself bound to pay his mother Volumnia all that gratitude and duty, which would have belonged to his father, had he also been alive, could never satiate himself in his tenderness and respect to her. He took a wife, also, at her request and wish, and continued even after he had children, to live still with his mother, without parting families. [2]*

Civil disturbances in Rome

There were growing civil disturbances in Rome. *There had been frequent assemblies of the whole senate, within a small compass of time, about this difficulty, but without any certain issue; the poor commonality, therefore, perceiving there was likely to be no redress of their grievances, on a sudden collected in a body, and encouraging each other in their resolution, forsook the city, with one accord, and seizing the hill which is now called the Holy Mount, sat down by the river Anio, without committing any sort of violence or seditious outrage, but merely exclaiming that for a long time they had been, in fact, expelled and excluded from the city by the cruelty of the rich; that Italy would everywhere afford them the benefit of air and water and a place of*

---

[1] Plutarch's Lives, v 1, pp 292-293.

[2] Ibid, p 293.

burial, which was all they could expect in the city, unless it were, perhaps the privilege of being wounded and killed in time of war for the defense of their creditors.[3]

The senate sent Menenius Agrippa to negotiate with the people, who demanded five tribunes to represent their interests with Junius Brutus and Sicinius Vellutus selected as leaders. But the Volcians, whose principal city was Corioli, were aware of the civil disturbances in Rome, and had already assembled their forces under the command of Aufidius. The consul Cominius was the Roman Commander who commanded one army, and Titus Lartius was appointed command of the other army.

Corioli taken

Marcius achieved great fame in battle, entered the city of Corioli with only a few that accompanied him, and held it open so that Lartius could follow. The Volcians were defeated and Marcius was greatly praised. From Plutarch: *Corioli being thus surprised and taken, the greater part of the soldiers employed themselves in spoiling and pillaging, while Marcius indignantly reproached them, and exclaimed that it was a dishonorable and unworthy thing when the consul and their fellow-citizens had now perhaps encountered the other Volscians, and were hazarding their lives in battle, basely to misspend the time in running up and down for booty, and under a pretense of enriching themselves, keep out of danger. Few paid him any attention.* As to the distribution of the spoils of war, Marcius stated *one special grace to beg, and this I hope you will not deny me. There was a certain hospitable friend of mine among the Volscians, a man of probity and virtue, who has become a prisoner, and from former wealth and freedom is now reduced to servitude. Among his many misfortunes let my intercession redeem him from the one of being sold as a common slave.[4]* The Roman commander, Cominius, proposed a vote that due to his virtuous conduct as well as his valor in the war that Marcius should henceforth have the name Coriolanus as a third name to Caius Marcius.

Coriolanus, as we shall now call him, excelled in leading his troops in battle. Plutarch earlier warned of the severity of Coriolanus's nature, *which lacked the education, humanizing and civilizing lessons, which teach us to submit to the limitations prescribed by reason and to avoid the wildness of extremes. While his vigor and perseverance led him successfully into many achievements, yet, on the other hand, by indulging the vehemence of his passion and through an obstinate reluctance to yield or accommodate his sentiments to those of a people about him, he*

---

[3] Ibid, p 294.

[4] Ibid, p 296.

became incapable of acting and associating with others. Those who admired his tendency to refrain from pleasures, and to bear hardships, fortitude, and firmness; yet the average citizen and statesman could not be but disgusted at his severity and ruggedness, and his overbearing, haughty, and imperious nature.[5]

Coriolanus vs the people

Marcius (Coriolanus), *even before the war against the Volcians, had clearly expressed his disfavor of the people and the tribunes who represented them and opposed the senate who tried to accommodate them. When the consuls thought it most advisable to comply a little in favor of the poor, Marcius, with more vehemence than the rest, alleging that the business of money on either side was not the main thing in question, urged that this disorderly proceeding was but the first step towards open revolt against the laws, which it would become the wisdom of the government to check at the earliest moment. [6]*

The popular uprisings were a real threat to the rulers of Rome, the senatorial nobility and the consuls. The oratory of the tribunes blamed the wealthy for the growing misery of the people; and the shortages of food due to the inability to raise and harvest their own crops while the men were away fighting wars at the demand of the senate.

The war against the Volscians was no sooner at an end, than the popular orators revived domestic troubles, and raised another sedition, without any new cause or complaint or just grievance to proceed upon, but merely turning the very mischiefs that unavoidably ensued from the war into a pretext against the patricians. The greatest part of their arable land had been left unsown and without tillage, and the time of war allowing them no means or leisure to import provisions from other countries, there was an extreme poverty. The movers of the people then observing that there was no corn to be bought, and that if there had been they had no money to buy it, began to calumniate the wealthy with false stories and whisper it about, as if they, out of their malice, had purposely contrived the famine.

At this time there was a *pestilential disease,* which led to the loss of nine out of ten people in the city of Velitrae, not far from Rome. The senate found this to be an opportunity to get rid of many of Rome's *superfluous members, in order to dissipate the gathering sedition by ridding themselves of the more violent and heated partisans. --- The consuls, therefore, singled out such citizens to supply the desolation at Velitrae, and gave notice to others, that they should be ready to march against the Volscians, with the politic design of preventing intestine*

---

[5] Ibid, p 291.

[6] Ibid, p 294.

broils by employment abroad, and in the hope that when rich as well as poor, plebeians and patricians, should be mingled again in the same army and the same camp, and engage in one common service for the public, it would mutually dispose them to reconciliation and friendship.[7]

But Caius Marcius (Coriolanus), who began now to bear himself higher and to feel confidence in his past actions, conscious, too, of the admiration of the best and greatest men of Rome, openly took the lead in opposing the favors of the people. Marcius had made inroads to a neighboring city where, finding a considerable quantity of corn, and collecting much booty, both of cattle and prisoners, he reserved nothing for himself in private, but returned safe to Rome, while those that ventured out with him were seen laden with pillage, and driving their prey before them. This sight filled those that had stayed at home with regret for their perverseness, with envy at their fortunate fellow-citizens, and with feelings of dislike to Marcius, and hostility to this growing reputation and power, which might probably be used against the popular interests.[8]

Popular revolt

In the midst of these disturbances, a large quantity of corn reached Rome, a great part bought up in Italy, but an equal amount sent as a present from Syracuse, from Gelo, then reigning there. Many began now to hope well of their affairs, supposing the city, by this means, would be delivered at once, both of its want and discord. A council, therefore, being presently held, the people came flocking about the senate-house; but Marcius, standing up, sharply inveighed against those who spoke in favor of the multitude, calling them flatterers of the rabble, traitors to the nobility. --- Completing Marcius' address: *Concession is mere madness; if we have any wisdom and resolution at all, we shall, on the contrary, never rest till we have recovered from them that tribunician power they have extorted from us; as being a plain subversion of the consulship.[9]*

Marcius appears in the forum

But when the day of election was now come, and Marcius appeared in the forum, with a pompous train of senators attending him,

---

[7] Ibid, p 299

[8] Ibid, p 300.

[9] Ibid, p 302. Note. This was an important declaration of Marcius. In one simple statement, he proposed that all representation of the people be abolished; and that rule, and power, would be the exclusive province of the aristocrats.

and the patricians all manifested greater concern, and seemed to be exerting greater efforts, the commons then fell off again from the kindness they had conceived for him, and in the place of their late benevolence, began to feel something of indignation and envy; passions assisted by the fear they entertained, that if a man of such aristocratic temper and so influential among the patricians should be invested with the power which that office would give him, he might employ it to deprive the people of all the liberty which was yet left them. In conclusion, they rejected Marcius. Marcius, straightforward and direct, and possessed with the idea that to vanquish and overbear all opposition is the true part of bravery, in these ulcerations of anger, retired, full of fury and bitterness against the people. [10]

The peoples' assembly

The assembly met and soon became tumultuous. The sum of what Marcius had spoken, having been reported to the people, excited them; to such fury, that they were ready to break in upon the senate. The tribunes presented this, by laying all the blame on Coriolanus, whom, therefore, they cited by their messengers to come before them and defend himself. And when he contemptuously repulsed the officers who brought him the summons, they proposed to carry him away by force, and accordingly, began to lay hold on his person. The patricians, however, coming to his rescue, not only thrust off the tribunes, night approaching, but put an end to the contest. But, as soon as it was day, the consuls, observing the people to be highly exasperated, and that they ran from all quarters and gathered in the forum, were afraid for the whole city, so that, convening the senate afresh, they desired them to advise how they might best compose and pacify the incensed multitude.

The majority of the senators giving way proceeded to pacify the people, but the tribunes standing up, declared, in the name of the people, that since the senate was pleased to act soberly and do them reason, they likewise, should be ready to yield in all that was fair and equitable on their side; they must insist, however, that Marcius should give in his answer to the several charges: first, could he deny that he instigated the senate to overthrow the government and annul the privileges of the people? And in the next place when called to account for it, did he not disobey the summons? And lastly, by the blows and other public affronts had he not done all he could to commence a civil war? [11]

Marcius came to make his apology and clear himself, in which belief the people kept silence, and gave him a quiet hearing. But when, instead of the submissive language expected from him, he began to use

---

[10] Ibid, p 301.

[11] Ibid, p 303.

not only an offensive kind of freedom, seeming rather to accuse than apologize, but as well by the tone of his voice as the air of his countenance, displayed a security that was not far from disdain and contempt of them, the whole multitude then became angry, and gave evident signs of impatience and disgust; and Sicinnius, the most violent of the tribunes, after a little private conference with his colleagues, proceeded solemnly to pronounce before them all that Marcius was condemned to die by the tribunes of the people, and without delay take him to the Tarpian rock and throw him headlong from the precipice.[12]

The patricians responded to Sicinnius. *Rather, how came it into your minds, and what is it you design, thus to drag one of the worthiest men of Rome, without trial, to a barbarous and illegal execution? Very well,* said Sicinnius, *you shall have no ground in this respect for quarrel or complaint against the people. The people grant your request, and your partisan shall be tried. We appoint you, Marcius,* directing his speech to him, *the third market-day ensuing, to appear and defend yourself, and to try if you can satisfy the Roman citizens of your innocence, who will then judge your case by vote. The senators were divided on whether to permit the tribunes to pass sentence on one of their patricians, or to concede the power requested by the tribunes as a mark of respect and kind feeling and the mere possession of this power of voting would at once dispossess them of their animosity.*

When, therefore, Marcius saw that the senate was in pain and suspense upon his account, divided, as it were, betwixt their kindness for him and their apprehensions from the people, he desired to know of the tribunes what crimes were they intended to charge him with. He was told by them that *he was to be impeached for attempting usurpation, and that they would prove him guilty of designing to establish arbitrary government. Let me go then, he said to clear myself from that imputation before an assembly of them; I freely offer myself to any sort of trial, nor do I refuse any kind of punishment whatsoever; only, he continued, let what you now mention be really made my accusation, and do not you play false with the senate.* On their consenting to these terms, he came to his trial.

But when the people met together, the tribunes, contrary to all former practice, extorted first, that votes should be taken, not by centuries, but by tribes; a change, by which the indigent and factious rabble, that had no respect for honesty and justice, would be sure to carry it against those who were rich and well known, and accustomed to serve the state in war. In the next place, whereas they had engaged to prosecute Marcius upon no other head but that of tyranny, which could never be made out against him, they relinquished this plea, and urged instead, his language in the senate against an abasement of the price of

---

[12] Ibid, p 304.

corn, and for the overthrow of the tribunican power; adding further, as a new impeachment, the distribution that was made by him of the spoil and booty he had taken from the Antiates, when he overran their country, which he had divided among those that had followed him, whereas it ought rather to have been brought into the public treasury; which last accusation did, they say, more discompose Marcius than all the rest, as he had not anticipated he should ever be questioned on that subject, and therefore was less provided with any satisfactory answer to it on the sudden. And when, by way of excuse, he began to magnify the merits of those who had been partakers with him in the action, those that had stayed at home, being more numerous than the other, interrupted him with outcries.

Banishment

In conclusion, then, they came to vote, a majority of three tribes condemned him; the penalty being perpetual banishment. The sentence of his condemnation being pronounced, the people went away with greater triumph and exultation than they had ever shown for any victory over enemies, while the senate was in grief and deep dejection. [13]

Marcius appeared composed, however, *he was wholly possessed with a profound and deep-seated fury, which passes with many for no pain at all. And pain loses every appearance of depression and feebleness; the angry man makes as show of energy, while in fact, all this action of the soul is but mere diseased palpitation, distension, and inflammations. That such was his distempered state appeared presently plainly enough in his actions. On his return home, after saluting his mother and his wife, who were all in tears and full of loud lamentations, and exhorting them to moderate the sense they had of his calamity, he proceeded at once to the city gates, whither all the nobility came to attend him.* [14]

Revenge

He then departed and he continued solitary for a few days in a place in the country. With his rage and indignation he considered for himself no honorable or useful end, but only how he might best satisfy his revenge on the Romans.

Marcius then traveled to the city of the Volscians, Antium, and located his old enemy Tullus Aufidius. He proposed to lead an army of Volscians *to seek vengeance on those that expelled* him. Tullus, on hearing this, was extremely rejoiced, and giving him his right hand, exclaimed, *Rise Marcius, and be of good courage; it is a great happiness*

---

[13] Ibid, p 306.

[14] Ibid, p 307.

you bring to Antium. Marcius was given command of the army, which was to invade Rome, while Tullus commanded the defense of Antium.

Marcius, finding no army to oppose him had taken by force Toleria, Lavici, Peda, and Bola, not ten miles from Rome, where he found great treasure, and put almost all the adults to the sword. The other Volscians ordered to stay behind and protect their cities, heard of his achievement and success. They had not the patience to remain any longer at home, but hastened in their arms to Marcius. They said that he alone was their general and the sole commander they would own; with all his name and renown spread throughout all Italy.

All at Rome were in great disorder; they were utterly averse from fighting, and spent their whole time in cabals and disputes and reproaches against each other; until news was brought that the enemy had laid close siege to Lavinium. --- The people now were for repealing the sentence against Marcius, and calling him back into the city; whereas the senate, being assembled to reconsider the decree, opposed and finally rejected the proposal. --- Marcius himself, who was bringing distress upon all alike, though he had not been ill-treated by all, was become a declared enemy to his whole country. --- This resolution of theirs being made public, the people could proceed no further, having no authority to pass anything by suffrage, and enact it for a law, without a previous decree from the senate.[15]

When Marcius heard of this, he was more exasperated than ever, and, quitting the siege of Lavinium, marched furiously towards Rome, and encamped at a place call the Cuilian ditches, about five miles from the city.

Negotiations

It was agreed unanimously by all parties, that ambassadors would be despatched to offer him return to his country. They desired that he would free them from the terrors and distresses of the war. *The persons sent by the senate with this message were chosen out of his kindred and acquaintance, who naturally expected a very kind reception at their first interview. Being led through the enemy's camp, they found him sitting in state amidst the chief men of the Volscians, looking insupportably proud and arrogant. He bade them declare the causes of their coming, which they did in the most gentle and tender terms, and with a behavior suitable to their language. When they had made an end of speaking, he returned them a sharp answer, full of bitterness and angry resentment, as to what concerned himself and the ill-usage he had received from them. He demanded restitution of the cities and the lands which had been seized upon during the late war, and that the same rights and franchises should be granted them at Rome, which had been before*

---

[15] Ibid, p 312.

accorded to the Latins (Volscians); since there could be no assurance that a peace would be firm and lasting without fair and just conditions on both sides. He allowed them thirty days to consider and resolve.[16]

When the ambassadors had come back, and had acquainted the Senate with the answer, seeing the whole state now threatened as it were by a tempest, and the waves ready to overwhelm them, they were forced, as we say in extreme perils, to let down the sacred anchor. A decree was made, the whole order of their priests, those who initiated in the mysteries or had the custody of them, according to the ancient practice of the country should go in full procession to Marcius with their pontifical array and should urge him, as before, to withdraw his forces. He consented so far, indeed as to give the deputation an admittance into his camp, but granted nothing bidding them once for all to choose whether they would yield or fight, since the old terms were the only terms of peace.[17]

Coriolanus's Mother and family sent to negotiate

With the failure of the high priests to negotiate with Coriolanus, Volumnia, the mother of Coriolanus, along with Vergilia, his wife, and their children went to the camp of Coriolanus. In the words attributed to Volumnia by Plutarch: *I and Vergilia, my countrywomen, have an equal share with you all in the common miseries, and we have the additional sorrow, which is wholly ours, that we have lost the merit and good name of Marcius, and see his person confined, rather than protected, by the arms of the enemy. Yet I account this the greatest of all misfortunes, if indeed the affairs of Rome be sunk to so feeble a state as to have their last dependence upon us. For it is hardly imaginable he should have any consideration left for us, when he has no regard for the country, which he was wont to prefer before his mother and wife and children. Make use, however, of our service; and lead us, if you please, to him; we are able, if nothing more, at least to spend our last breath in making suit to him for our country.*

Having spoken thus, she took Vergilia by the hand, and the young children, and so accompanied them to the Volscian camp. So lamentable a sight much affected the enemies themselves, who viewed them in respectful silence. Marcius was then sitting in his place, with his chief officers about him, and, seeing the party of women advance toward them, wondered what should be the matter; but perceiving at length that his mother was at the head of them, he would fain have hardened himself in his former inexorable temper, but, overcome by his feelings, and confounded at what he saw, he did not endure they should approach him

---

[16] Ibid, p 313.

[17] Ibid, p 314.

sitting in state, but came down hastily to meet them, saluting his mother first, and embracing her a long time, and then his wife and children, sparing neither tears nor caresses, but suffering himself to be borne away and carried headlong, as it were, by the impetuous violence of his passion. [18]

There follows, from the Shakespeare historic drama *Coriolanus* the exhortations of the mother of Coriolanus, Volumnia, who came to the camp of Coriolanus and the Volscians in mourning habits with Coriolanus' wife Virgilia and their two children, young Marcius and his daughter Valeria.

Volumnia: *Should we be silent and not speak, --- Are come we hither: since that thy sight which should make our eyes flow with joy, hearts dance constraints them weep, and shake with fear and sorrow; Making the mother, wife, and child to see the son, the husband, and the father tearing his country's bowels out.*

Virginia: *Ay, and mine, that brought you forth this boy, to keep your name living to time.* Boy: *'A shall not tread on me; I'll run away till I am bigger; but then I'll fight. ---*

Volumnia: *That, if thou conquer Rome, the benefit which thou shalt hereby reap is such a name, whose repetition will be dogg'd with curses; whose chronicle thus writ, --- The man was noble, but with his last attempt he wip'd out: destroy'd his country; and his name remains to the ensuing age abhorr'd. ---*

Coriolanus: *O my mother, mother! O! You have won a happy victory to Rome; but for your son, — believe it, O, believe it, most dangerously you have with him prevail'd if not most mortal to him But let it come. — Aufidius, though I cannot make true wars, I'll frame convenient peace.* [19]

Rome saved but Coriolanus slain

Marcius never did see his mother, wife and children again. He broke up his camp and led the Volscians homeward. *When Marcius had come back to Antium, Tullus Aufidius, proceeded at once how he might immediately dispatch him. Having suborned several partisans against him, he required Marcius to resign and give the Volscians an account of his administration. An assembly was called, and popular speakers, as had been concerted came forward to exasperate and incense the multitude; but when Marcius stood up to answer, the more unruly and tumultuous part of the people became quiet on a sudden, and out of reverence allowed him to speak without the least disturbance. Tullus, therefore, began to dread the issue of the defense he was going to make*

---

[18] Ibid, p 317.

[19] Shakespeare, Coriolanus Act V, Sc 4.

for himself; for he was an admirable speaker, and the former services he had done the Volscians had procured and still preserved for him greater kindness than could be outweighed by any blame for his late conduct. Indeed, the very accusation itself was a proof and testimony of the greatness of his merits, since people could never have complained or thought themselves wronged, because Rome was not brought into their power, but that by his means they had come so near to taking it. For these reasons the conspirators judged it prudent not to make any further delays, nor to test the general feeling. But the boldest of their faction crying out that they ought not to listen to a traitor, nor allow him still to retain office and play the tyrant among them, fell upon Marcius in a body, and slew him there, none of those that were present offering to defend him. But it quickly appeared that the action was in no wise approved by the majority of the Volscians, who hurried out of their several cities to show respect to his corpse; to which they gave honorable interment, adorning his sepulcher with arms and trophies, as the monument of a noble hero and a famous general.

In Rome, the senate passed a decree that a temple might be erected to Female Fortune, the expense of which they offered to defray out of their own contributions. The senate caused the temple to be built, set up a statue and made up a sum among themselves for a second image of Fortune. The Romans uttered, as it was put up, words to this effect, 'Blessed of the gods, O women, is your gift.' [20]

---

[20] Plutarch, v 1, pp 320-321.

Chapter 2

Pompey

Introduction

In the introduction to Coriolanus the events of the Roman Republic with the expansion of Rome concluded with the defeat of Hannibal by the Romans in 202 B.C. From 200 to 189 B.C. Roman armies had reduced two of the three empires of Alexander, Macedonia and Syria, to vassal states of Rome. Corinth was burned in 146 B.C., as was Carthage in 133 B.C. Egypt became an ally of Rome. In a century and a quarter, from 265 to 133 B.C., wars with Carthage in the west and Greek states in the east had enlarged Roman conquests from the Italian peninsula to a world empire with provinces along the Mediterranean and Aegean seas in southern Europe, northern Africa and western Asia.

The conquests brought wealth to Rome and Italy. The military commanders gained enormous wealth from confiscations and booty, a good part of which was to support the costs of the military ventures. The rest went to the state as well as the coffers of a growing class of the rich. Large estates grew up in Italy. Slave labor became increasingly abundant. Military conquests involved slaughter of people who were regarded enemies of Rome, their lands and peoples vanquished. Captives were brought back to Rome and henceforth served as slaves. The small farmers had their properties destroyed during the wars. The senate was interested in protecting the large estates.

By this time the Roman Empire had become totally corrupt, well before the time of Pompey, Caesar and Cicero. Corruption and misrule characterized the government. A group of businessmen and loan sharks called publicans were all in on the plunder of the provinces. A wealthy class emerged. Competition as to who had the most wealth became a singular preoccupation. Single combats had been introduced during the wars with Carthage. Gladiatorial combats became popular entertainment.

The Republic of Rome was not a republic in our sense of the word. The common people of Rome were debased and poverty was rampant. The state had to arrange distributions of grain to feed the people. Only those who had great wealth could run for office. Bribery of public officials and the people who could vote greatly expanded the costs of running for office. The senate did nothing to alleviate the distress of the farmers. Tiberius Gracchus, elected tribune in 133 B.C., brought before the assembly a bill for the reassignment of public lands and the protection and support of the farming class. He addressed the people *'You who fought and die for Italy enjoy only the blessings of air and light. These alone are your heritage. Homeless, unsettled, you wander to and fro with your wives and children. You fight and die to give wealth and luxury to others. There is no clod of earth that you can call your own.'* Gracchus was slain by the senators. His younger brother took up the struggle and was elected tribune. He attempted not only land reforms but reform of the senate. He wanted to give those who lived outside of Rome full citizenship. He was murdered, in 121 B.C.

Meanwhile, two men of great importance emerged. Gaius Marius represented the popular party, while Cornelius Sulla represented the aristocrats. The assembly passed a law appointing Marius military commander. In 88 B.C. Sulla led an army into Rome and expelled Marius. The senate selected Sulla to command a war in Asia Minor. During his absence Marius and his people's army returned with vengeance and slaughtered the leading senators. Sulla, victorious in Asia Minor, returned to Rome and defeated the popular army. He established a dictatorship and then slaughtered the leaders of the assembly and tribunes, leaving the state power in the hands of the senate.

Pompey's background

Pompey, (b. 106 B.C., d. 48 B.C.), was a member of the aristocracy, the Roman senatorial nobility, and followed Sulla as a great military commander. He served with Marcus Licinius Crassus as consul in 70 B.C. He was a member of the triumvirate from 61 to 54 B.C., and was appointed by the senate in 50 as sole consul. Pompey's army was defeated in battle by Caesar at Pharsalus August 9, 48 B.C. On September 28, 48 B.C. he was murdered on the shores of Egypt at Pelusium by order of King Ptolemy's advisors.

Plutarch began his account of Pompey with a quote from a Greek poet, after which he lauded great praise on Pompey. *Never had any Roman the people's good will and devotion more zealous throughout all the changes of fortune, more early in its first springing up, or more steadily rising with his prosperity, or more constant in his adversity than Pompey. In his youth, his countenance pleaded for him, seeming to anticipate his eloquence, and win upon the affections of the people before he spoke. His beauty even in his bloom of youth had something at once of gentleness and dignity; and when his prime of manhood came, the majesty and kingliness of his character at once became visible in it.*[1]

---

[1] Plutarch, Lives, p 70

Pompey's father Strabo was a Roman general, a formidable warrior. People were awed by his military power, but never did the Romans give demonstrations of such hatred against any of their generals as they did against Strabo, father of Pompey. Strabo's greed was especially notable, but the immense wealth he had accumulated from plunder of Rome's enemies and his estates in eastern Italy gave Pompey a start in life as a very wealthy man, and a member of the nobility.

Pompey, as a very young man accompanied his father in military expeditions, even intervening successfully in an uprising by the troops against his father. No further information is given about Pompey's youth and upbringing, but like Coriolanus he was gifted physically, even still showing more strength and skill than others in combat at the age of 60. After the death of his father he was accused of complicity in embezzlement of the public treasury, a few items found in Pompey's possession. Pompey defended himself successfully and the praetor and judge in the case, Antistus, *took a great liking to him, and offered him his daughter in marriage. Pompey was married to Antistia.*[2]

Pompey Joins Sulla

Pompey joined up with Sulla while vacationing in Picenum, Italy when he saw that all the nobles went over to Sulla's camp. At age 23 he mustered three legions and granted himself full power of command. At this time in Rome the cost of armies was born largely by very wealthy commanders such as Pompey. In 83 B.C, there were campaigns to recover Rome and Italy from control by Marius. *Three commanders of the enemy encountered him at once, --- and drew up their forces. --- Pompey was collecting all his troops into one body, and placing his horse in the front of the battle, where he himself was in person, he singled out and bent all his forces against Brutus, and when the Celtic horsemen from the enemy's side rode out to meet him, Pompey himself encountering hand to hand with the foremost and stoutest among them killed Brutus with his spear. The rest seeing this turned their backs and fled, --- and the towns round about came in and surrendered themselves to Pompey.* Pompey then defeated consul Scipio's troops. *Scipio's soldiers saluted Pompey's, and came over to them, while Scipio made his escape by flight.* He then put Carbo's troops to flight. *He forced them in the pursuit into difficult ground, impassable for horse, where, seeing no hopes of escape, they yielded themselves with their horses and armor, all to his mercy.*

Sulla was very impressed by these victories as well as Pompey's army, *so well appointed, his men so young and strong and their spirits so high and hopeful with their success, he alighted from his horse and,*

---

[2] Ibid, p 73.

being first as was his due, saluted by them with the title of Imperator. He returned the salutation upon Pompey, in the same term and style of Imperator, which might well cause surprise, as none could have ever anticipated that he would have imparted, to one so young in years.[3]

Sulla dispatched Pompey to Gaul where he achieved *wonderful exploits of himself.* When Sulla was proclaimed dictator by the senate, he began to reward his followers. For Pompey he offered Aemilia his own step daughter in marriage, providing that Pompey divorce his wife Antistia. Aemilia happened to be married and pregnant. The marriage did take place, but was followed shortly thereafter by the death of Aemilia during childbirth.

Pompey was next dispatched to Sicily, where his enemy, Perpenna immediately departed, leaving the whole island to him. The citizens of Messena protested against Pompey's rule citing an ancient charter or grant of the Romans. Pompey replied sharply *What! Will you never cease prating of laws to us that have swords by our sides?[4]* Pompey commanded a man who was three times consul of Rome to be brought in fetters to stand at the bar, and sitting at the bench in judgment, he afterward ordered him to be taken away and put to death.

Pompey next received a decree of the senate and a commission from Sulla in 82-81 B.C. to sail to Africa and make war upon Domitius, formerly a general under Marius who caused a revolution in Rome and who had become a fugitive outlaw and a tyrant. No sooner than Pompey had landed in Carthage that seven thousand of the enemy revolted and came over to Pompey, who had six legions of his own. After weathering a bad storm affecting both forces the enemy was routed and the camp was taken, and among the rest Domitius was slain. In forty days Pompey had overthrown the enemy, had reduced Africa and established all the kingdoms of that country.

Sulla had ordered Pompey to disband his forces but his troops supported him and when the whole city of Utica received Pompey with every display of kindness and honor, Sulla had a change of mind and saluted Pompey with the title of Magnus— Pompey the Great. Pompey returned to Rome in great splendor, and hoped to have his chariot drawn by four elephants, however they could not enter the gates and had to be replaced with horses. Pompey used his influence to get Lepidus elected as consul in 78 B.C. over Sulla's choice, who remarked to Pompey: *Well, young man, I see you rejoice in your victory. And, indeed, is it a most generous and worthy act, that the consulship should be given to Lepidus,*

---

[3] Ibid, pp 74- 75.

[4] Ibid, p 76.

the vilest of men, in preference to Catulus, the best and most deserving in the city, and all by your influence with the people?[5]

Appointed general of army by senate

Lepidus gathered up the dangerous remains of the faction opposing Sulla and was a threat to the nobility. The senate appointed Pompey general of the army with the command to oppose Lepidus, who held cisalpine Gaul in subjection with an army under Brutus. Pompey was victorious without a battle. Brutus surrendered himself to Pompey, but was slain the next day by a centurion under Pompey's command. Pompey was censured for the murder of Brutus, father of the famous Brutus who assassinated Caesar. Lepedius *fled to Sardinia where he fell sick and died of sorrow, not for his public misfortunes, but upon the discovery of a letter proving his wife to have been unfaithful to him.*[6]

Proconsul of Spain

The senate decreed Pompey to be proconsul of Spain. Pompey brought his army to Spain where Sertorius was in possession of Spain and had become very formidable to Rome. *Pompey gained a great reputation among the soldiers with his good will, and his example of frugality, and temperance, and no ways inordinate in his desires. Sertorius had taken advantages over Mellitus, by his quickness and dexterity, by hovering about and coming upon him unawares, disturbed him perpetually with ambuscades and light skirmishes, whereas Metellus was accustomed to regular conduct and fighting in battle array with full-armed soldiers. Pompey had kept his army in readiness, but found himself all of a sudden encompassed; and could not move out of his camp while the city, Lauron, was taken and burned.*[7] Pompey gained two victories over Sertorius' lieutenants, however in battle, Sertorius gained the upper hand. Pompey himself was almost made a prisoner, but he released his horse, which had richly adorned golden trappings and the soldiers quarreled among themselves for the booty. While they were fighting with one another, Pompey made his escape.

Pompey, having made use of and expended the greatest part of his own private revenues upon the war, sent and demanded monies of the senate.[8] The senate granted his request. Meanwhile Sertorius was

---

[5] Ibid, p 81.

[6] Ibid, p 82.

[7] Ibid, p 83.

[8] Ibid, p 84.

murdered by some of his own party. Perpenna took command, but he was defeated in battle by Pompey. Perpenna was taken captive. He had in his possession *all of Sertorius's papers, including several letters from the greatest men in Rome, who desired a change and subversion of the government, and who had invited Sertorius to return to Italy. Pompey, fearing worse wars, thought it advisable to put Perpenna to death and burnt the letters.*[9]

Spartacus

After allaying the disorders in the provinces of Spain, Pompey returned to Italy where he helped Crassus defeat an uprising by Spartacus. *Accordingly, upon his arrival, Crassus, the commander in that war, at some hazard, precipitated a battle, in which he had great success and slew upon the place twelve thousand three hundred of the insurgents. Nor yet was he so quick, but that fortune reserved to Pompey some share of honor in the success of this war, for five thousand of those that had escaped out of the battle fell into his hands; and when he had totally cut them off, he wrote to the senate that Crassus had overthrown the slaves in battle, but that he had plucked up the whole war by the roots.*

Consul

Pompey disbanded his army and returned to Rome to run for consul and was declared consul in 70 B.C., *yet this honor did not seem so great an evidence of his power and glory as the ascendant which he had over Crassus, wealthiest among all the statesmen of this time,* who asked Pompey if he could appear as a candidate for consul. Pompey granted the request and both served as consuls. *Crassus prevailed in the senate, and Pompey's power was no less with the people, he having restored to them the office of tribune, and having allowed the courts of judicature to be transferred back to the knights by a new law.*[10]

After the expiration of Pompey's term as consul *he withdrew himself totally from the forum, showing himself but seldom in public; and, whenever he did, it was with a great train after him. Neither was it easy to meet or visit him without a crowd of people about him; he was most pleased to make his appearance before large numbers at once, as though he wished to maintain in this way his state and majesty, and as if he held himself bound to preserve his dignity from contact with the addresses and conversation of common people. And life in the role of peace is only too apt to lower the reputation of men that have grown great by arms, who naturally find difficulty in adapting themselves to the*

---

[9] Ibid, p 85

[10] Ibid, p 86.

habits of civil equality. They expect to be treated as the first in the city, even as they were in the camp.[11]

Subdues pirates in Mediterranean

Pompey was next given the task to subdue the pirates in the Mediterranean who had ravaged the cities of Italy *whilst the Romans were embroiled in their civil wars, being engaged against one another even before the very gates of Rome, the seas lay waste and unguarded, --- to seize upon and spoil the merchants and ships upon the seas, but also to lay waste the islands and seaport towns. The people's assembly appointed Pompey, in 67 B.C., supreme commander of all the Mediterranean, given absolute power and authority in all the seas within the pillars of Hercules, and in the adjacent mainland for the space of four hundred furlongs (fifty miles) from the sea, the sole sovereign over all men.*[12] The senate looked upon this as exorbitant power and opposed the bill; and all went against it except Julius Caesar who gave his vote for the law.

Pompey, provided with an army of 125,000 men and 500 vessels for the Mediterranean campaign, took within three months ninety men-of-war and twenty thousand prisoners restoring commerce and availability of grain. *He determined to give the pirates a taste of an honest and innocent course of life by tilling the ground, transporting them to towns who were willing to receive them or which were depopulated.*[13]

Eastern provinces

Pompey was given command in the east against Mithridates, but had to gain supremacy over Lucullus. *Pompey and Lucullus contended for power and the two met in Galatia,* modern central Turkey. *Pompey encamping not far distant from him, sent out his prohibitions, forbidding the execution of any of the orders of Lucullus, and commanded away all his soldiers. After this Lucullus went away, and Pompey having placed his whole navy in guard upon the seas betwixt Phoenicia and Bosphorus, himself marched against Mithridates, who had a phalanx of thirty thousand foot, with two thousand horse, yet durst not bid him battle.*

Pompey followed the king into the next camp and found water by sinking wells that Mithridates failed to take advantage of. Pompey's

---

[11] Ibid, p 87.

[12] Ibid, pp 88-89.

[13] Ibid, pp 90-92.

army reached Mithridates forces at night and in the dark: The Romans ran upon them with a great shout; but the barbarians, all in a panic, unable to endure the charge, turned and fled, and were put to great slaughter, above ten thousand being slain; the camp also was taken.[14]

Pompey thereafter planned the consolidation of the eastern provinces. He extended the borders of Rome, and conquered Syria, Armenia, Albania, Cilicia, Mesopotamia, Phoenicia, Palestine, Judea, and Arabia. *Most of the time that he spent there was employed in the administration of justice. --- For the reputation of his power was great; nor was the fame of his justice and clemency inferior to that of his power.[15]*

Returned to Rome

Pompey now having ordered all things, and established that province, took his journey homewards in greater pomp and with more festivity. --- So that now by these acts he well hoped to return into Italy in the greatest splendor and glory possible to man, and find his family as desirous to see him as he felt himself to come home to them. He was to have a sad welcome. *For Mucia, his third wife, during his absence had dishonored his bed. Whilst he was abroad at a distance he had refused all credence the report; but when he drew nearer to Italy, where his thoughts were more at leisure to give consideration to the charge, he sent her a bill of divorce; but neither in writing, nor afterwards by word of mouth, did he ever give a reason why he discharged her.*

The splendor and magnificence of Pompey's triumph was such that though it took up the space of two days, --- In the first place, there were tables carried, inscribed with the names and titles of the nations over whom he triumphed, Pontus, Armenia, Cappadocia, Paphlagonia, Media, Colchis, the Iberians, the Albanians, Syria, Cilicia and Mesopotamia, together with Phoenicia and Palestine, Judea, Arabia, and all power of the pirates subdued by sea and land. And in these different countries there appeared the capture of no less than one thousand fortified places, nor much less than nine hundred cities, together with eight hundred ships of the pirates, and the foundation of thirty-nine towns. Besides, there was set forth in these tables an account of all the tributes throughout the empire.[16]

Pompey faced opposition from the senate and Lucullus. When Lucullus *returned out of Asia, where he had been treated with insult by Pompey; he was received by the senate with great honor, which was yet*

---

[14] Ibid, pp 95-96.

[15] Ibid, p 101-102.

[16] Ibid, pp 104-105.

increased when Pompey came home; to check whose ambition they encouraged him to assume the administration of government. --- However he began for the time to exert himself against Pompey, attacked him sharply, and succeeded in having his own acts and decrees, which were repealed by Pompey, re-established. With the assistance of Cato, he gained the superiority of the senate. [17]

Alliance and marriage to Caesar's daughter Julia

Pompey was forced to fly to the tribunes of the people for refuge. Pompey had also alienated Cicero, who left Rome. Caesar, returning from military service was elected consul, *and began at once to take an interest with the poor and meaner sort, by preferring and establishing laws for planting colonies and dividing lands, lowering the dignity of his office and turning his consulship into a sort of tribuneship.* Then he turned to Pompey and asked him if he would back Caesar's new laws with military force, to which Pompey replied *'I shall be ready, and those that threaten the sword, I will appear with sword and buckler.'* Pompey formed thus an alliance with Caesar, to the dismay of his friends, and he married Caesar's daughter, Julia, to enhance their relationship. *Pompey, filing the city with soldiers, carried all things by force as he pleased. And thus having cleared the forum of all their adversaries and got their bills established for the division of lands and passed into an act.* [18] Caesar resolved the conflict between Crassus and Pompey and the first triumvirate of Pompey, Caesar, and Crassus was formed in 60 B.C.

Pompey retired to his estate and passed his time in consulting with his friends by what means he might best allay the displeasure of the senate and nobles against him. He was advised to call Cicero back from banishment and was easily persuaded. *No sooner had Cicero returned to Rome that he used his efforts to reconcile the senate to Pompey; and by speaking in his favor of the law regarding the importations of corn, did again, in effect make Pompey sovereign lord of all the Roman possessions by sea and land.*

Pompey, in his final time of glory sailed himself into Sicily, Sardinia and Africa and filled the markets with vast stores of corn. He was just ready to set sail upon his voyage home, when a great storm arose upon the sea, and the ships' commanders doubted whether it were safe. Upon which Pompey himself went first aboard, and bid the mariners weigh anchor, declaring with a loud voice that there was a necessity to sail, but no necessity to live. So that with this spirit and

---

[17] Ibid, pp 106-107.

[18] Ibid p 108.

*courage, and having met with favorable fortune, he made a prosperous
return, and filled the markets with corn, and the sea with ships. So much
so that this great plenty and abundance of provisions yielded a sufficient
supply, not only to the city of Rome but even to other places too,
dispersing itself, like waters from a spring, into all quarters.*[19]

The relationship between Pompey and Caesar took a decided
turn for the worse. *Meantime, Caesar grew great and famous with his
wars in Gaul --- in truth he was working craftily by secret practices in
the midst of the people, and countermining Pompey in all political
matters of most importance --- his gold and silver and other spoils and
treasure which he took from the enemy in his conquests, he sent to Rome
in presents, tempting people with his gifts, and aiding aediles, praetors,
and consuls, as also their wives, in their expenses, and thus purchasing
himself numerous friends. --- Insomuch, that when he passed back again
over the Alps, and took up his winter quarters in the city of Luca, there
flocked to him an infinite number of men and women, striving who should
get first to him, two hundred senators included, among whom were
Pompey and Crassus.*[20]

Conference at Luca

The conference at Luca in 56 B.C. extended the triumvirate of
Pompey, Caesar and Crassus. At the conference Pompey and Crassus
were to be elected consuls for 55. Caesar's command in Gaul was to be
extended another five years. Crassus received command in Syria while
Pompey would receive command of Africa and Spain. But Cato and the
senate would contest the consulship of Pompey and Crassus. *Most of the
candidates nevertheless abandoned their canvass for the consulship;
Cato alone persuaded and encouraged Lucius Domitius not to desist,
'since,' he said, 'the contest now is not for office, but for liberty against
tyrants and usurpers.'*

Pompey and Crassus ruled by force. *To this end, therefore,
they sent in a band of armed men, who slew the torchbearer of Domitius,
as he was leading the way before him, and put all the rest to flight; last
of all, Cato himself retired, having received a wound in his right arm
while defending Domitius. Thus by these means and practices they
obtained the consulship.*[21]

*Crassus, upon the expiration of his consulship, departed
forthwith into his province; but Pompey spent some time in Rome, upon
the opening or dedication of his theater, where he treated the people with*

---

[19]   Ibid, pp 109-110.

[20]   Ibid p 111.

[21]   Ibid, p 111-112.

all sorts of games, shows, and exercises, in gymnastics alike and in music. There was likewise the hunting or baiting of wild beasts, and combats with them, in which five hundred lions were slain; but above all, the battle of elephants was a spectacle full of horror and amazement.

These entertainments brought him great honor and popularity; but on the other side he created no less envy to himself, in that he committed the government of his provinces and legions into the hands of friends as his lieutenants, whilst he himself was going about and spending his time with his wife in all the places of amusement in Italy.

Death of Julia

It once happened in a public assembly, as they were at an election of the aediles, that the people came to blows, and several about Pompey were slain, so that he, finding himself all bloody, ordered a change of apparel; but the servants who brought home his clothes, making a great bustle and hurry about the house, it chanced that the young lady, who was then with child saw his gown all stained with blood; upon which she dropped immediately into a swoon, and was hardly brought to life again; however, what with her fright and suffering, she fell into labor and miscarried. The young lady referred to was Pompey's wife, Julia, who was the only daughter of Caesar. *Afterwards she was great again, and brought to bed of a daughter, but died in childbed. Pompey had prepared all things for the internment of her corpse at his house near Alba, but the people seized upon it by force and performed the solemnities in the field of Mars, --- the people seemed at that time to pay Caesar a greater share of honor in his absence, than to Pompey, though he was present.* [22]

The death of Caesar's daughter in childbirth was an important factor in the enmity, which grew between Caesar and Pompey. The conflicts between Caesar and Pompey were to grow into one of the worst civil wars of Rome. *For the city now at once began to roll and swell, so to say, with the stir of the coming storm. Things everywhere were in a state of agitation, and everybody's discourse tended to division, now that death had put an end to that relation which hitherto had been a disguise rather than restraint to the ambition of these men.*

Besides, not long after came messengers from Parthia with intelligence of the death of Crassus there, by which another safeguard against civil war was removed, since both Caesar and Pompey kept their eyes on Crassus, and awe of him held them together more or less within the bounds of fair-dealing all his lifetime. [23]

---

[22] Ibid, p 112

[23] Ibid, p 113.

In the growing chaos and civil disorder in Rome, and fears of Caesar not discharging his forces, members of the senate proposed *that Pompey should be created consul alone; alleging, that by these means either the commonwealth would be freed from its present confusion, or that its bondage should be lessened by serving the worthiest, --- adding, that any form of government was better than none at all; and that in a time so full of distraction, he thought no man fitter to govern than Pompey. This counsel was unanimously approved of, and a decree passed that Pompey should be made sole consul,* in 50 B.C. [24]

Marries Cornelia

Pompey then married Cornelia, his fifth wife, a woman who had been married to Publius, the son of Crassus, and who had been killed in Parthia. *Pompey attempted to govern Rome, never considering that his very consulship was a public calamity, which would never have been given him, contrary to the rules of law, had his country been in a flourishing state. Afterwards, however, he took cognizance of the cases of those that had obtained offices by gifts and bribery, and enacted laws and ordinances, setting forth the rules of judgment by which they should be arraigned; and regulating all things with gravity and justice, he restored security, order and silence to their courts of judicature, himself giving his presence there with a band of soldiers. But when his father-in-law, Scipio, was accused, he sent for the three hundred and sixty judges to his house, and entreated them to be favorable to him; whereupon his accuser, seeing Scipio come into the court, accompanied by the judges themselves, withdrew the prosecution.*

Upon this Pompey was very ill spoken of. --- Such partiality was looked upon as a great fault in Pompey and highly condemned; however he managed all things else discreetly, and having put the government in very good order, he chose his father-in-law to be his colleague in the consulship for the last five months. His provinces were continued to him for the term of four years longer, with a commission to take one thousand talents yearly out of the treasury for the payment of his army.[25]

Caesar's power and threat

Caesar was gaining in power and influence while in Gaul and was always at hand about the frontiers of Italy, sending his soldiers continually into the city to attend all elections with their votes. There were debates in Rome as to whether Caesar should deserve a second consulship. Many, however, considered Caesar a threat with his forces. Pompey was seemingly becoming more unfit to realize the threat of

---

[24] Ibid, p 114

[25] Ibid, pp 115-116.

Caesar. *For Pompey, yielding to a feeling of exultation, which is the greatness of the present display of joy lost sight of more solid grounds of consideration, and abandoning that prudent temper which had guided him hitherto to a safe use of all his good fortune and his successes, gave himself up to an extravagant confidence in his own contempt of Caesar's power. --- Besides this, Appius, under whose command those legions which Pompey lent to Caesar were returned, coming lately out of Gaul, spoke slightingly of Caesar's actions there. Appius at the same time told Pompey that he was unacquainted with his own strength --- for such was the soldiers hatred to Caesar, and their love to Pompey so great, that they should all come over to him upon his first appearance. By these flatteries Pompey was so puffed up, and led on into such a careless security, that he could not choose but laugh at those who seemed to fear a war; and when some were saying, that if Caesar should march against the city, they could not see that forces there were to resist him, he replied with a smile, bidding them be in no concern, 'for,' said he, 'whenever I stamp with my foot in any part of Italy there will rise up forces enough in an instant, both horse and foot.'* [26]

Caesar crossed Rubicon

But the die was cast and Caesar crossed the Rubicon on January 11, 49 B.C. *No sooner was the news arrived, but there was an uproar throughout all the city, and a consternation in the people even to astonishment, such as never was known in Rome before; all the senate ran immediately to Pompey, and the magistrates followed. And when Tullus made inquiry about his legions and forces, Pompey seemed to pause a little, and answered with some hesitation that he had those two legions ready that Caesar sent back, and that out of the men who had been previously enrolled he believed he could shortly make up a body of thirty thousand men. On which Tullus crying out aloud, 'O Pompey, you have deceived us: --- Favonius, a man of fair character,--- bade Pompey stamp upon the ground, and call forth the forces he had promised.'* [27] *Thus all Italy in a manner being up in arms, no one could say what was best to be done. For those that were without came from all parts flocking into the city; and they who were within, seeing the confusion and disorder so great there, all good things impotent, and disobedience and insubordination grown too strong to be controlled by the magistrates, were quitting it as fast as the others came in.*

Pompey, at length, seeing such a confusion in Rome, determined with himself to put an end to their clamors by his departure, and

---

[26] Ibid, p 117.

[27] Ibid, p 119.

therefore commanding all the senate to follow him, and declaring that whosoever tarried behind should be judged a confederate of Caesar's. About the dusk of the evening he went out and left the city. The consuls also followed after in a hurry.

Some few days after Pompey was gone out, Caesar came into the city and made himself master of it. It is clear from this, that Pompey did not have the forces required to prevent Caesar from marching down the east coast of Italy and take command of Rome. *Pompey fled Rome and reached Brundisium,* at the southeast tip of Italy, *in time to dispatch his forces to* the west coast of Greece, *before Caesar's arrival. But Pompey arriving at Brundisium, and having plenty of ships there, bade the town consuls embark immediately, and with them shipped thirty cohorts of foot, bound before him for Dyrrhachium,* on the west coast of Greece.

And now Caesar having become master of all Italy in sixty days, without a drop of bloodshed, had a great desire forthwith to follow Pompey; but being destitute of shipping, he was forced to divert his course and march into Spain, designing to bring over Pompey's forces there to his own.

In the meantime Pompey raised a mighty army both by sea and land. As for his navy, it was irresistible. For there were five hundred men-of-war, besides an infinite company of light vessels, --- and for his land forces, the cavalry made up a body of seven thousand horse, the very flower of Rome and Italy, men of family, wealth, and high spirits. [28]

Caesar, repassing the Alps and making a running march through Italy, came to Brundisium about the winter solstice. He crossed the sea and landed at the port of Oricum on the west coast of Greece below Dyrachhium. There followed the battle at Dyrachhium in which Pompey was victorious over Caesar. Caesar then marched eastward into Thessaly, and Pompey followed, *firmly resolved with himself not to give him battle, but rather to besiege and distress him, by keeping close at this heels, and cutting him short.* [29] Caesar defeated Pompey, at Pharsalia, August 9, 48 B.C. The details of this battle will be presented in the next chapter on Julius Caesar, but will be summarized in the few words of Plutarch which follow: *Common arms, and kindred ranks drawn up under the selfsame standards, the whole flower and strength of the same single city here meeting in collision with itself, offered plain proof how blind and how mad a thing human nature is when once possessed with any passion.*

Pompey fled to Cilicia, Cyprus and Egypt hoping that King Ptolemy would honor his previous service. Pompey was slain on the

---

[28] Ibid, pp 121-122.

[29] Ibid, p 124.

shores of Egypt, at Pelusium, September 28, 48 B.C. by Pothinus, vizier of Cleopatra's young brother Ptolemy XII.

These were Pompey's final words: *He turned about to his wife and son, and repeated those iambics of Sophocles.*

> *He that once enters at a tyrant's door*
> *Becomes a slave, though he were free before'*

He, therefore, taking up his gown with both hands, drew it over his face, and neither saying nor doing anything unworthy of himself, only groaning a little, endured the wounds they gave him, and so ended his life, in the fifty-ninth year of his age, the very next day after the day of his birth.

Cornelia, with her company from the galley, seeing him murdered, gave such a cry that it was heard on the shore, and weighing anchor with all speed, they hoisted sail, and fled. [30]

---

[30] Ibid, p 134.

Chapter 3

Julius Caesar

After Plutarch wrote the story of Pompey, he continued with the stories of Alexander and Julius Caesar. He began with a clear statement of his objective. *It being my purpose to write the lives of Alexander the king, and of Caesar, by whom Pompey was destroyed, the multitude of their great actions affords so large a field that I were to blame if I should not by way of apology forewarn my reader that I have chosen rather to epitomize the most celebrated parts of their story, than to insist at large on every particular circumstance of it. It must be borne in mind that my design is not to write histories, but lives. And the most glorious exploits do not always furnish us with the clearest discoveries of virtue or vice in men; sometimes a matter of less moment, and expression or a jest, informs us better of their characters and inclinations, than the most famous sieges, the greatest armaments, or the bloodiest battles whatsoever. Therefore as portrait-painters are more exact in the lines and features of the face, in which the character is seen, than in the other parts of the body, so I must be allowed to give my more particular attention to the marks and indications of the souls of men, and while I endeavor by these to portray their lives, may be free to leave more weighty matters and great battles to be treated of by others.*[1]   Julius Caesar does give us in his commentaries, *The Gallic War* and *The Civil War* details of the many wars he commanded. By the details of war he presents with his own pen, one may get an idea of the kind of man Julius Caesar was. In addition, we are indebted to Plutarch for his own commentaries about these events.

Background

---

[1] Plutarch, Lives, v 2, p 139.

To begin, Gaius Julius Caesar was born about the year 100 B.C. in Rome. Caesar was a patrician, of the oldest aristocracy of Rome, a member of the gens Julia. The Julii Caesars claimed to be descendants of Venus. Caesar was to be called Julii, the divine. His father Gaius Caesar died, when Julius was fifteen years old. His mother Aurelia came from a noble family. He was born by Cesarean section, however there is no apparent documentation to support this. Despite the patrician status and divine origins of Caesar, one might wonder why there is so little information available about his parents. Caesar's aunt Julia, his father's sister, had married Marius, and their son Marius was a first cousin of Caesar.[2]   Several uncles or near relations had been elected consuls. Caesars father, Gaius Caesar, served as praetor and achieved the governorship of Asia. He died when Caesar was fifteen years old. Caesar had two sisters, both with good marriages.[3] Why is so little information available about Caesar's family and early upbringing?

Plutarch, in the story, which follows, mentions the important family history of Caesar's paternal aunt Julia's marriage to Marius. Sulla and Marius were the military dictators that came before Pompey and Caesar. Pompey had been a general under Sulla, while Caesar was to follow in the footsteps of Marius. The story began with conflict, first between Marius and Sulla and then Sulla against Caesar for his affiliation with Marius. Marius had married Julia, Caesars paternal aunt. In 84 B.C., when sixteen years old, Caesar married Cornelia, who was the daughter of the Marian leader, Cinna. Caesar performed military service in Asia and then Cilicia fleeing from Sulla who thought Caesar even as a boy resembled Marius.

From Plutarch we read that Caesar *had been an expert rider from his childhood; for it was usual with him to sit with his hands joined together behind his back, and so to put his horse to full speed. For he was distempered in the head and subject to epilepsy, which it is said, first seized him at Corduba.* [4]

The first time Caesar was in Corduba was about 60 B.C. when he was governor of Spain. After he was dictator for the third time, he set out for Spain to conquer the remains of Pompey's forces now under his son's command. He reached Cordoba in December of 46 B.C. He would have been as young as forty years or as old as fifty-four years at the time when he first developed seizures, most likely the latter. The cause of his epilepsy was not something he acquired during birth or childhood but had acquired later in life. One might speculate that head trauma may have

---

[2] Plutarch, v 2, p 199.

[3] Grant, pp 5, 6.

[4] Plutarch, v 2, pp 210-211.

been related, however, any number of other conditions could have led to a seizure disorder? *His contempt of danger was not so much wondered at by his soldiers because they knew how much he coveted honor. But he did not make the weakness of his constitution a pretext for his ease, but rather used war as the best physic against his indispositions; whilst by indefatigable journeys, coarse diet, frequent lodging in the field, and continual laborious exercise, he struggled with his diseases and fortified his body against all attacks.[5]*

Sulla died in 78 B.C. and it was safe for Caesar to return to Rome. Caesar began his career as a prosecutor against some of Sulla's men and lost his first case against Dolabello to Hortensius, the leading advocate of the time.

Caesar left Rome for study in oratory at Rhodes, an island off the southeast coast of Turkey. Caesar had training from a famous rhetorician, professor Molon, and had Cicero for one of his scholars. Caesar was admirably fitted by nature to make a great statesman and orator, *and to have taken such pains to improve his genius this way but his choice instead was to be first rather amongst men of arms and power.* Caesar in 74B.C., twenty-six years old, raised an army from his family's wealth, to go to war against Mithridates VI, king of Pontus. On his return to Rome he gained an elective military tribuneship.

In Rome his pleading in a prosecution of Publius Antonius for corrupt practices demonstrated his eloquence and obtained him *great credit and favor. He won no less upon the affections of the people by the affability of his manners and address, in which he showed a tact and consideration beyond what could have been expected at his age; the open house he kept, the entertainments he gave, and the general splendor of life contributed little by little to create and increase his political influence. --- Cicero was the first who had any suspicions of his designs upon the government, and as a good pilot is apprehensive of a storm when the sea is most smiling, saw the designing temper of the man through this disguise of good humor and affability, and said that in general, in all he did and undertook, he detected the ambition for absolute power.[6]*

Affiliation with Pompey

Caesar then began his political career by affiliation with Pompey and to reverse the edicts of the military dictator Sulla who decreed that the senate must approve any of the laws proposed by the people's assembly, or their elected tribunes. Roman government and law thus lacked a foundation that would persist from one military dictator to

[5] Ibid, p 201

[6] Ibid p 201

another. Reference to a constitution was as meaningless as we shall later find in England, where Kings, not military dictators (except Oliver Cromwell) or Emperors ruled. Neither Rome nor England had a written constitution. Thus, whoever had power from military forces determined what the law was and what kind of government prevailed.

In 68 B.C. Caesar's wife Cornelia died. He next married Pompeia, a distant relative of Pompey and the granddaughter of Sulla. In that same year Caesar was elected quaester, which is the first step in the career of Roman politics. Plutarch describes his approach to winning popular support. *The first proof he had of the people's good-will was the time when he received by their suffrages a tribuneship in the army— A second and clearer instance of their favor appeared upon his making a magnificent oration in praise of his aunt Julia, wife to Marius, publicly in the forum, at whose funeral he was so bold as to bring forth the images of Marius, which nobody had dared to produce since the government came into Sulla's hands.*

Elections to office

Caesar was elected aedile in 65 and elected to pontifex maximus in 63. Plutarch describes his methods of gaining political influence. *When he was made surveyor of the Appian Way, he disbursed, besides the public money, a great sum out of his private purse; and when he was aedile, he provided such a number of gladiators, that he entertained the people with three hundred and twenty single combats, and by his great liberality and magnificence in theatrical shows, in processions, and public feasts, he gained so much upon the people, that every one was eager to find out new offices and new honors for him in return for his munificence.*[7]

The senate began to be fearful of Caesar's popularity with the people. Caesar's relationship to Catiline was questioned. Cicero convinced the senate into sentencing to death two of Catiline's men who remained in Rome, while Catiline was banished. What was Caesar's role in the Catilinarian conspiracy? Catilina's supporters *Crassus and Caesar had been scared off by Catilina's increasing tendency to adopt a policy of abolition of debts and redistribution of land, which threatened property owners.*[8] More of this story about the Catiline conspiracy appears in the chapter on Cicero, from Plutarch's account as well as from Cicero's writings.

Caesar, who was then a young man, and only at the outset of his career, but had already directed his hopes and policy to that course by which he afterwards changed the Roman state into a monarchy. Caesar

---

[7] Plutarch, v 2, p201-2

[8] Cicero, Selected Political Speeches, pp 72-3

gave his opinion proposing *that the conspirators should not be put to death, but their estates confiscated, and their persons confined in such cities in Italy as Cicero should approve, there to be kept in custody till Catiline was conquered.* But Cicero *delivered Lentulus to the officer, and commanded him to execute him; and after him Cethegus, and so all the rest in order, he brought up and delivered up to execution.*[9]

After the conclusion of the Catiline conspiracy Caesar was elected a praetor in 62 B.C. He divorced his second wife Pompeia after a scandal involving Publius Clodius in his house during a celebration of rites for Bona Dea (a Roman god of fruitfulness) for women only, administered by his wife.

Caesar gained the governorship of Farther Spain in 61-60 B.C. and pursued a military campaign gaining booty and loot to pay back his indebtedness to his creditors in Rome for which the wealthy Crassus had supplied bail for a portion of Caesar's debts. Crassus was one of the most important rivals of Pompey. Caesar returned to Rome and ran for consul in 60 B.C., and was elected, along with his opponent Bibulus, also as consul for the year 59 B.C. Pompey had returned to Italy after his successful campaign in Asia, defeating Mithridates forces. Pompey disbanded his army but the senate would not allow allotments for his soldiers.

The first triumvirate was formed by an alliance of Caesar, Pompey and Crassus in 59 B.C. These men were descended from the nobility. They were extremely wealthy and powerful. Each had military commands. Crassus had opposed Pompey, but Caesar intervened to form a reconciliation. Pompey sealed his alliance with Caesar by marrying Caesar's daughter, and only child, Julia. In this manner the first triumvirate was formed. Caesar introduced a bill in support of the veterans and used some of Pompey's soldiers to force the senate to approve the provision for Pompey's veterans. At the same time Caesar was assigned the province of Gaul. The story of Caesar in his commentaries on *The Gallic War* is unique as an historical source. His own words tell us what kind of person he was.

The Gallic War

Caesar began with the phrase remembered by the beginning Latin student-*All Gaul is divided into three parts-* Belgic, Aquitanian, and Celtic Gaul. The three parts of Gaul referred to in Caesar's opening remarks are all north of the Province, and include territory from the Garonne River in southern France to the Rhine and the Atlantic, with the Belgae north and many ancient peoples within these borders. There was no such thing as a nation of Gaul and most of the peoples were not combined in defense. Caesar commented: *they all differ among*

---

[9] Ibid, p 422

themselves in respect of language, way of life, and laws. Caesar also commented: *Of these the Belgae are the bravest, for they are furthest away from the civilization and culture of the Province. Merchants very rarely travel to them or import such goods as make men's courage weak and womanish.*[10]

Caesar left Rome for his first encounter with the Helvitii who Caesar refused passage through the Province. Caesar had to reinforce his troops by returning to Cisalpine Gaul by forced marches returning to fight the Helvitii, who had now engaged Rome's allies to the northwest of the Province. Caesar's armies defeated the Helvitii in 57 B.C. Caesar described the battles in detail. He estimated from tablets written in Greek characters that of 368,000 men only 100,000 were to return home. Caesar congratulated himself by the following: *At the end of the war with the Helvitii the leaders of almost all the Gallic states came as envoys to congratulate Caesar. They were aware, they said, that Caesar's aim had been to exact punishment in return for outrages long ago inflicted on the Roman people by the Helvetii (Caesar avenged not only a national but also a private injury: for the grandfather of his father-in-law Lucius Piso was a legate killed by the Tigurani in the same battle as Cassius).*[11]

The next battle was against Ariovistus who had crossed the Rhine with Germans and had defeated the Gauls. After failure of negotiations and the spread of fear of the Germans among Caesar's forces a council was ordered and Caesar gave a prolonged speech to his men. *At the end of this speech the change of attitude was quite remarkable, and there arose an immense enthusiasm and eagerness to start the campaign.*[12] Caesar reported his success: *So the battle swung back in our favor, and all the enemy turned tail and did not stop running until they reached the Rhine, nearly five miles away from the field of battle. There a very few trusted in their own strength and aimed to swim across, or found boats and thus ensured their own safety. Ariovistus was of their number.*[13] Caesar was in Cisalpine Gaul, or nearer Gaul, when he heard that *the Belgae were hatching a plot against the Roman people and exchanging hostages.* Caesar discovered that *most of the Belgae were of German extraction, and had long ago crossed the Rhine and settled on the western side because of the fertility of the soil.* Caesar described the outcome of a battle between Roman and Belgaec forces

---

[10] Caesar, The Gallic War, First Book, first page.

[11] Ibid, p 19, and p 9.

[12] Ibid, p 27.

[13] Ibid, p 34.

separated by a marsh. *There a fierce battle was fought. Our men attacked the enemy while they were stuck in the water and killed a large number of them. The rest struggled with great daring to make their escape through the midst of the bodies but were forced back by a shower of missiles. Those who had crossed first were surrounded by our cavalry and cut down. --- The result was that our men, without any risk, killed as many of the enemy as time allowed. Caesar accepted leading citizens as hostages, including two sons of King Galba himself; all the town's weapons were handed over.*[14] The remaining wars with the Belgae were fought with difficulty, with one state, the Nervii, *who were almost wiped out, --- from 60,000 men capable of active service to a mere 500. Another neighboring state, the Aduatuci, surrendered themselves and all their possessions to the Roman's control.*[15] The editor noted that *the usual fate of the inhabitants of a captured town was to be sold into slavery. A great part of Roman war profits came from the sale of people, as well as of property.*[16] After these wars Caesar took his legions to their winter quarters in central Gaul and set out for Italy.

It is of interest in this narrative, that the first reference Caesar made of Britain is that some of those who had opposed Caesar living in the region between present day Belgium and Normandy fled to Britain. Caesar also refered to the Belgae who *within living memory they had a king --- who was the most powerful in the whole of Gaul, and controlled a large portion of that region and also of Britain.*[17] The Belgae were defeated in 57 B.C. Two years later Caesar crossed the channel in his first invasion of Britain.

Caesar left Servius Galba to winter where he could keep the passage through the Alps open and he fought several battles successfully. The Gauls decided to renew hostilities and attack the legion since they believed the legion was below full strength, that they could have superior ground position. *There was also the fact that they were aggrieved because their children had been taken from them as hostages, --- and that the Romans were trying to take control of them forever, and to annex the lands bordering the Province.* Again, Caesar related the gory details of battle concluding: *The total number of Gauls who had come to the camp was reckoned at more than 30,000; more than a third of them were killed, and the rest were terrified and put to flight.*[18]

---

[14]Ibid, pp 40-42.

[15] Ibid, pp 50-51.

[16] Ibid, p 227.

[17] Ibid, p 38.

[18] Ibid, pp 55, 56.

Meanwhile, Caesar was wintering at Lucca as related by Plutarch. *He now, after settling everything in Gaul, came back again, and spent the winter by the Po, in order to carry on the designs he had in hand at Rome. All who were candidates for offices used his assistance, and were supplied with money from him to corrupt the people and buy their votes, in return of which, when they were chosen, they did all things to advance his power. But what was more considerable, the most eminent and powerful men in Rome, including Pompey and Crassus, came to visit him at Lucca. --- In deliberations here held, it was determined that Pompey and Crassus should be consuls again for the following year; that Caesar should have a fresh supply of money, and that his command should be renewed to him for five years more.*[19]

Other Military expeditions

Caesar thought that Gaul had been subdued and set off for Illyricum, or today's Dalmatia, Bosnia and Montenegro across the Adriatic Sea from Italy. But suddenly war broke out in Gaul now involving the entire north coast of France, Brittany and Normandy, extending to the north coast of present day Belgium. The coastal states had a large navy. *Not only do they have a large navy, which they used for voyaging to Britain; but they also excel in nautical matters, both theoretical and practical.*[20] Caesar then described the difference between the ships of these people, which were sailing vessels compared to the Roman ships, propelled by oars. Their ships had shallow drafts so they could navigate shallow coastal harbors and rivers compared to the deep drafts of the Roman ships. This difference is significant and will become apparent in Caesar's later invasion of England.

It is of interest that English forces were allies of these states and that by Caesar's time there must have been considerable exchange of trade and people between southern England and the north coast of France. This was given as a reason for Caesar's later invasion of England. Even more of interest to us was Caesar's description of these people. *They urged the other states to choose to maintain the liberty they had been given by their ancestors, rather than enduring enslavement to the Romans.* One of the reasons Caesar gave for the uprisings in the coastal states of Gaul is that they wanted to retrieve hostages taken by the Romans including their wives and children. Caesar commented that *almost all Gauls are eagre for political change and, because of their fickleness, are soon roused to war; and also that all men naturally long for liberty and despise a state of servitude.*

---

[19] Plutarch, V 2, p 214.

[20] Caesar, The Gallic War, p 57.

Roman ships disabled the Gallic sailing ships by using long grappling hooks to seize the rigging and break the ropes that supported the masts removing the advantage of sail. Roman ships surrounded the disabled Gallic vessels. The other Gallic ships could not escape the Romans since the wind had died. Caesar described the end of this campaign: *now that the ships were all lost they had no way of retreat left to them, nor any means of defending their towns. They therefore surrendered themselves and all their property to Caesar. Caesar decided that their punishment must be severe, to make these barbarian peoples uphold the law of nations more carefully in future. So he executed all the senate of the Veneti, and sold the rest of the people into slavery.* [21]

The people on the north coast of present day Belgium, however, in this same year of 56 B.C., could not be subdued by winter and the Germans invaded this region. Caesar, learning of this, returned to Gaul and his armies. Caesar defeated these forces in 55 commenting: *He (Caesar) arranged his forces— and swiftly reached the enemy camp before the Germans could be aware what was happening. The Germans had departed from their homes and crossed the Rhine with all their possessions. The crowd of women and children who remained began to flee in all directions. Caesar sent the calvary to hunt them down.*

Next, Caesar crossed the Rhine into Germany: *Once the German campaign was over Caesar decided that for a number of reasons it was imperative he should cross the Rhine. The most compelling of these reasons was that now he had seen how easily the Germans were induced to invade Gaul, he wanted them to experience fear on their own account, — when they realized that the army of the Roman people was both capable of crossing the Rhine and brave enough to venture it.* [22] Caesar built a bridge across the Rhine and accomplished his objectives, namely *terrorizing the Germans. So after spending a total of eighteen days on the other side of the Rhine he judged that he had achieved enough in terms of both honor and advantage, returned to Gaul, and tore down the bridge.*

Caesar next prepared for the first invasion of England in 55 B.C. His second invasion of England was in 54 B.C. Caesar gave his own impressions of the geography and the customs of the people. We will review this subject in Chapter 11, which focuses on early England and the Romans.

Caesar's next campaigns in 53 B.C. were in northeastern Gaul, and for the second time his forces built a bridge across the Rhine to pursue the Germans who had again aided the Gauls. Caesar wrote about one of his generals Labienus (and reference to himself) who gave his

[21] Ibid, p 62.

[22] Ibid, p 77.

troops the following pep talk: *Soldiers, he said, you have the chance you have been looking for: you have the enemy on uneven ground. Now show the same courage under my leadership as you have often shown to our commander, Caesar. Imagine that he is present and looking on in person.*[23]

Caesar ended his commentaries about these campaigns: *After ravaging the region in this manner Caesar took his army— back to Durocortorum, a town of the Remi* (in central Belgium). *There he called a Gallic assembly and held an inquiry into the plot of the Senones and Carnutes. The ringleader of the plot, Acco, was condemned to death and was punished in accordance with ancestral custom.* [24]

This is a prelude to the seventh and final book of *The Gallic War* by Caesar inasmuch as he was to face the most extensive uprising of the Gauls: *The Gallic leaders called an assembly in a remote forest location. There they deplored the execution of Acco, and declared that the same fate could befall them.* Revenge was a recurrent motivation for the Gauls as well as the Romans.

Vercingetorix

The Gauls proclaimed Vercingetorix king and leader of the states throughout Gaul who were recruited against the Romans. While Caesar had campaigned against individual peoples and states he was now confronted by the coalition of Gallic forces raised by Vercingetorix, who was many centuries later to become a symbol of Gallic resistance to threats of invasion, even in the twentieth century, symbolizing the struggle of the Resistance against Hitler, the imperialist aggressor.[25]

The first strategy of Vercingetorix was to send a general to Narbo to cut off Caesar, who had set out from Rome to Transalpine Gaul, from contact with his armies. This policy failed and Caesar marched north to quell rebellion of Gallic states while Vercingetorix brought his army to Gorgobina, about ten miles south of present Nevers in central France, where Caesar next brought his forces. *Vercingetorix had suffered one setback after another. --- He summoned his supporters to an assembly, and told them of the need to continue the war according at a totally different strategy from the one they had adopted until now. They must now concentrate their efforts on cutting the Romans off from food and supplies, by every means possible. --- They must burn down their buildings and settlements, which seemed likely to be within reach of the foraging parties. --- They themselves would have sufficient store of the*

---

[23] Ibid, p 123.

[24] Ibid, p 141, p 236

[25] Ibid, p 237.

necessary supplies, because they would receive material support from the Gallic peoples in whose territories the war was going on. They must *remember that it was far worse to have their children and wives dragged off into slavery, and themselves be killed: and this was sure to be their fate if they were defeated.* [26]

Fires were burning all over Gaul but the people of Avaricum did not want to burn their city, *what was nearly the finest city in the whole of Gaul.* In the battle against Caesar: *The Gauls had tried everything, and everything had failed. The next day they took the decision to flee from Avaricum, at Vercingetorix's prompting and instructions.* --- *They were making ready for their nocturnal escape when suddenly the married women rushed out and threw themselves weeping at the feet of their men. They begged and pleaded with the men not to abandon them and the children they had together to the enemy's torments, just because their natural physical weakness made it impossible for them to join the flight.* --- *The Gauls were so stricken with fear of the Roman cavalry overtaking them on the road that they abandoned their plan.* --- *This unexpected action panicked the enemy.* --- *So they threw their weapons away and with a concerted effort made for the furthest reaches of the town. Some of them found themselves crushed in the narrow opening of the gates, and were killed by our soldiers; others got through the gates and were killed by the calvary.*

Not one of our men gave a thought to booty. They were so severely provoked by the massacre at Cenabum and the effort that had put into the siege that they spared neither the elderly, nor the women, nor even the little children. In the end, of a total number of about 40,000, barely 88 reached Vercingetorix safely. [27]

Once again we have Caesar's own unflinching admission of the barbarism of his armies. The next confrontation of Caesar with Gallic forces was at Georgovia, near present Clermont-Ferrand, where Caesar was to experience his first major defeat. Caesar blamed his men, not himself for their defeat: *The following day Caesar called an assembly and upbraided the soldiers for their impudence and over-eagerness in deciding for themselves where to advance and what action to undertake, and for not halting when the signal for retreat was given.* [28]

Caesar withdrew his troops and marched north to prevent former allies from capitulating to Vincengetorix and to retrieve supplies. Gallic forces, however, reached first the town of Noviodunum, present Nevers

---

[26] Ibid, p 150-1.

[27] Ibid, p 158-9.

[28] Ibid, p 172.

in central France, and burned the city after taking stores of supplies and corn. Caesar crossed the Loire and found enough cattle and corn.

Vincengetorix gathered large forces and Caesar's armies were reinforced for the remaining battles in Gaul. The Romans were marching their entire force in front of the enemies camp *to strike fear into the enemy.* Vincengetorix withdrew to Alesia, northwest of present Dijon, which was nearly impregnable. Caesar killed 3,000 of the enemy's rearguard and pitched camp outside the city. Vincengetorix levied more forces throughout Gaul and Caesar obtained reinforcements from the good offices of *Commius in Britain.* Roman forces defeated the Gauls, and *Vincengetoix was handed over and weapons were thrown down.*

The final years of Caesar in Gaul

The final years of Caesar in Gaul were related in Book eight by Aulus Hirtius, who states in the preface to this chapter: *Because of the gap which existed between his earlier and later writings, I have composed a continuation of our friend Caesar' commentaries on his campaigns in Gaul.* Caesar's forces contained the uprisings, which occurred throughout Gaul, during the years from 52 to 50 B.C. The Biturges, in central Gaul, were overcome by the surprise arrival of Caesar. Caesar next subdued the Carnutes, a state less than 100 miles to the north. The major campaign involved the Bellovaci in present Normandy east of the Seine. The Bellovaci were led by Commius, whom Caesar had crowned king of the Atrebates, on the northern coast of France near present Calais; and whom Caesar had sent to Britain as his envoy, and who had assisted him in the Roman assault on Alesia as we have reviewed above. The battles between the reinforced Gallic forces of the Bellovaci and augmented Roman legions ended with the defeat of the Gauls. *The enemy lost heart and tried to flee in all directions, to no avail. They were overcome and beaten and fled in confusion with the loss of more than half their force. Some made for the forest, some the river, and even these were dispatched by our men, who pursued them keenly. --- When they realized that the Romans were approaching they blew a trumpet to summon an assembly at once, and sent envoys and hostages to Caesar. --- The following night the envoys reported his reply to their people and collected the hostages. The envoys of the other nations, which were awaiting the fate of the Bellovaci, hastily assembled. Except for Commius, who was too afraid to entrust his own safety to anyone's good faith, they gave hostages and obeyed Caesar's orders.*[29]

We next read that there were reasons why Commius wanted to avoid the Romans at all costs. *The previous year, while Caesar was dispensing justice in Nearer Gaul, Titus Labienus had caught Commius in the act of inciting revolt among the Gallic nations and plotting against*

---

[29] Ibid, pp 206-7.

Caesar; but he had judged that Commius' treachery could be suppressed without any breach of a safe conduct. Labienus did not believe, however, that Commius would come to his camp if summoned, and was unwilling to put him on his guard by attempting it. So he sent Gaius Volusenus Quadratus to feign interest in holding talks, and have him killed; and assigned to him a picked group of centurions well fitted for the task. When the parley took place and Volusenus seized Commius by the hand as arranged, a centurion --- troubled by the unusual nature of the task, perhaps, or quickly obstructed by Commius' friends --- failed to finish him off. Nevertheless, he did inflict a serious wound to Commius' head with a first stroke of his sword. After this it was said that Commius had resolved never to come within sight of a Roman again.[30]

Caesar left his questor, Mark Antony, with fifteen cohorts with the Bellovaci to prevent the Belgae from a fresh revolt, and went to Uxellodunum, which was west of the Province in the southwest corner of Gaul. With difficulty Caesar cut off the water supply to the city. *The townspeople now lost all hope of saving themselves. Caesar decided upon making an example of the townspeople in punishing them, so as to deter the rest. He allowed them to live, therefore, but cut off the hands of all those who had carried arms against him. This made the punishment for wrongdoers plain to see.*[31]

Caesar spent the year 50 B.C. administering the newly conquered territory, leaving four legions under Mark Antony in Belgium, and legions throughout Gaul in winter quarters, after which he joined his forces in Belgium. Caesar learned how Commius the Atrebatian had clashed in battle with the Roman cavalry. Antony had reached winter quarters and *found the Atrebates staying loyal, but Commius, after being wounded as I related earlier, had habitually kept himself in readiness — and who in battle wounded the Roman commander who escaped thanks to the speed of his horse. But Commius had lost too many of his men and surrendered hostages. He begged for one condescension to his fear— not to be obliged to come within sight of any Roman. Antony judged that his request sprang from a legitimate fear, so he pardoned him as requested and accepted the hostages.*[32]

We will return to Mark Antony at the end of this chapter, however, it is likely that Caesar was close to Antony when he remained with him in Belgium during winter quarters. But now we enter a new period of Roman history with Caesar's return to Italy: *Once winter was past, in a change from his usual practice Caesar set out at top speed for*

---

[30] Ibid, pp 207-8.

[31] Ibid, p 217.

[32] Ibid p 219.

Italy, to address the communities and colonies— he had already recommended to them the candidature of his quaestor Mark Antony for a priesthood.

The Civil War

We have a problem in continuing with Caesar's commentaries *The Civil War*, in that it becomes difficult to believe what he says. Not so with Caesar's *The Gallic War* which we have reviewed above. Why can we believe that the commentaries in *The Gallic War* have any credibility? The inhuman, barbarous acts he relates with equanimity could hardly be fabrications. Caesar frequently attempted to glorify himself, and even bragged about the barbarous acts he and his armies committed.

It is not surprising that Julius Caesar later became a model for the German people who thought they could rule the world. From J. W. Hartmann's *Mantle of Caesar*, London, 1929: *Today, when the need of the strong man is felt, and --- when, particularly in Germany, the guidance of the people is entrusted to any striking talent in the military-economic field --- we would like to recall --- the great man --- Caesar.*[33]

It was Caesar who was responsible for starting the civil war by crossing the Rubicon. Caesar summarized the deliberations of the senate: *Thus the majority, browbeaten by the consul, frightened by an army on the doorstep, and threatened by Pompey's friends, voted unwillingly and under duress for Scipio's motion: that Caesar should dismiss his army before a certain date, and if he did not, he would be judged to be committing an act hostile to the state.*[34]

Caesar, still at Ravenna in the authorized region of Cisalpine Gaul, gave an address to his soldiers. *He detailed all the wrongs done him in the past by his personal enemies, complaining that out of malice and jealousy of his own renown they had alienated Pompey from him and twisted his judgment, while he himself had always supported and promoted Pompey's prestige and position.* Caesar described his crossing the Rubicon simply as: *Having discovered the feelings of his men, he set out with his legion for Ariminum*, which is south of the Rubicon River.[35]

Plutarch gave a more likely explanation for Caesar crossing the Rubicon and starting the civil war: *Caesar had long ago resolved upon the overthrow of Pompey, as had Pompey, for that matter, upon his. For Crassus, the fear of whom had hitherto kept them in peace, having now been killed in Parthia, if the one of them wished to make himself the*

---

[33] Ibid, p xxxvii.

[34] Caesar, The Civil War, p 4.

[35] Ibid, p 7.

greatest man in Rome, he had only to overthrow the other, --- but Caesar had entertained this design from the beginning against his rivals, and had retired, like an expert wrestler, to prepare himself for the combat. Making the Gallic wars his exercise ground, he had at once improved the strength of his soldiery, and had heightened his own glory by his great actions, so that he was looked on as one who might challenge comparison with Pompey.

One of his (Caesar's) *captains who was sent by him to Rome, standing before the senate house one day, and being told that the senate would not give Caesar longer time in his government, clapped his hand on the hilt of his sword and said, "But this shall".*

Yet, the demands, which Caesar made, had the fairest colors of equity imaginable. For he proposed to lay down his arms, and that Pompey should do the same, and both together should become private men, and each expect a reward of his services from the public. --- But Scipio, Pompey's father-in-law, proposed in the senate, that if Caesar did not lay down his arms within such a time he should be voted an enemy; and the consuls putting it to the question, whether Pompey should dismiss his soldiers, and again whether Caesar should disband his, very few assented to the first, but almost all to the latter. --- At last, in a sort of passion, casting aside calculation, and abandoning himself to what might come, and using the proverb frequently in their mouths who enter upon dangerous and bold attempts, 'The die is cast', with these words he took the river. Once over, he used all expedition possible, and before it was day reached Ariminum and took it. [36]

Seutonius summarized the reason for Caesar crossing the Rubicon and starting the civil war: *It has also been suggested that constant exercise of power gave Caesar a love of it; and that, after weighing his enemies' strength against his own, he took this chance of fulfilling his youthful dreams by making a bid for the monarchy.*

Plutarch summarized why Caesar crossed the Rubicon and started the civil war. He dismissed the improbable notion that Anthony was a primary cause, as promulgated by Cicero in one of his Phillippics. Plutarch made it clear that Caesar, and only Caesar, had made the decision. *This was to him, who wanted a pretense of declaring war, a fair and plausible occasion; but the true motive that led him was the same that formerly led Alexander and Cyrus against all mankind, the unquenchable thirst of empire, and the distracted ambition of being the greatest man in the world, which was impracticable for him, unless Pompey were put down.* [37] Some of Cicero's commentaries on Caesar will be presented in the next chapter.

---

[36]   Plutarch, Lives, V 2, pp 218-221.

[37]   Ibid, p 485.

Retreat of Pompey

Pompey and the consuls fled Rome, after Caesar had crossed the Rubicon. About a week later, Caesar, even after crossing the Rubicon into territory, which he was not authorized to enter, occupied four other cities south of the Rubicon. He invaded the east coast of Italy and went as far as 100 miles west into central Italy. Caesar sent envoys to Capua, about 100 miles below Rome just north of Naples, where Pompey and the consuls had fled. Caesar, fully aware that he was a threat to all in Rome, made demands that if Pompey were to go to Spain, and the forces gathered by Pompey in Italy be dismissed, that two other commanders would take over nearer and farther Gaul, and he would canvass in person and present himself a candidate for consul. This cynical and improbable proposal of Caesar was rejected by Pompey and the consuls, who sent a written message to Caesar *which in brief was this: Caesar was to return to Gaul, withdraw from Ariminum, and disband his armies; and if he did this, Pompey would go to Spain; in the mean time, until guarantees had been given, the consuls and Pompey would go on levying troops.*[38]

Regardless of Caesar's proposals and the reactions of the senate his armies marched down the east coast of Italy, and occupied all the cities on his way to Corfinium. He sent Marcus Antonius with five cohorts of the thirteenth legion while Caesar met him days later with the Eighth legion, and twenty-two cohorts from new recruiting in Gaul. Domitius, who hoped to get help from Pompey, held the city of Corfinium. Pompey wanted Domitius to join him with his forces in Luceria. Domitius was surrounded by Caesar's forces and sent his envoy to Caesar who told him *it was not to do him harm that he had crossed the boundary of his province, but to defend himself from the insults of his enemies, to restore to their proper dignity the tribunes who had been expelled from Rome in the course of this affair, and to assert his own freedom and that of the Roman people, who were oppressed by an oligarchic clique.* After more negotiations, Caesar *ordered Domitius's soldiers to take the oath of loyalty to himself, and on that day moved camp and completed a normal day's march.*[39]

With Caesar advancing, Pompey retreated from Luceria, about 100 miles south of Corfinium, and reached Brundisium, which is further south on the east coast of Italy, on the heel of the boot. Caesar's forces marched toward Brundisium. *The consuls had left Brundisium for Dyracchium,* across the Adriatic on the west coast of Greece, *with a large part of the army, while Pompey remained at Brundisium.* In the consul's absence, Caesar claimed he could not negotiate any kind of

---

[38] Caesar, The Civil War, p 9, p 274.

[39] Ibid, p 15.

settlement with Pompey. *So Caesar concluded that the objective he had so often and fruitlessly tried to attain could not be indefinitely pursued, and that he must proceed with war.*

After Caesar had built siege works around the city, Pompey left Brundisium with his troops and went to Dyracchium. But Caesar could not follow *because Pompey had requisitioned all the ships and removd any immediate chance of pursuit. It remained to wait for ships from the more distant regions of Gaul, Picenum, and the Straits of Messina.* He sent his officers to Sardinia and Sicily but the officer he sent to Africa was repelled by one of Pompey's generals.

Caesar to Rome and Spain

Caesar dispersed his soldiers to rest from their exertions, while he himself made his way to Rome. --- There he argued his cause --- He spoke of the bitterness of his enemies, who refused to do in their own case what they demanded of a rival (disband their armies) --- their injustice in taking his legions, their savagery and arrogance in restricting the tribunes' freedom of action.

Caesar needed funds to support his armies. Caesar implied that Metellus had already opened the treasury. Plutarch gave a different story than Caesar about the treasury: *Afterwards, when Mettelus, the tribune, would have hindered him from taking money out of the public treasure, and adduced some laws against it, Caesar replied that arms and laws had each their own time; 'If what I do displeases you, leave the place; war allows not free talking.' --- Having said this to Mettelus, he went to the doors of the treasury, and the keys being not to be found, sent for smiths to forced them open. Mettellus again making resistance and some encouraging him in it, Caesar in a louder tone told him he would put him to death if he gave him any further disturbance. 'And this', said he, 'you know, young man, is more disagreeable for me to say than to do.'* [40]

Caesar left Rome and led an army into Spain, and achieved in 49 B.C. victory over Pompey's forces, but his general Curio was defeated in Africa. Caesar reorganized his forces in Gaul and returned to Rome in December, 49 B.C. Caesar was created dictator by those in the senate who remained. *He then appointed himself consul: For within eleven days he resigned his dictatorship, and having declared himself consul, with Servilius Isauricus, hastened again to the war.*

Victory of Pompey at Dyrachhium

Caesar marched so fast that he left all his army behind him, except six hundred chosen horse and five legions, with which he put to sea in the very middle of winter, --- and having passed the Adriatic, took Oricum and Apollonia, on the west coast of Greece, *and then sent back*

---

[40] Plutarch, Lives, v 2, p 223.

the ships to Brundisum, to bring over the soldiers who were left behind in the march. [41]

Anthony crossed over from Brundisium with battle weary troops to Apollonia to join Caesar, who had attempted to cross back over to Brundisium in a small boat but had to return in a storm. Caesar's forces led an assault against Pompey at Dyrachhium, about 75 miles up the coast from Apollonia, but were defeated by Pompey at Dyracchium in 49 B.C., Caesar narrowly escaping. Pompey was criticized for not pursuing a victory over Caesar. *But Pompey was afraid to hazard a battle on which so much depended. --- For these reasons Pompey had no mind to fight him, but was thanked for it by none but Cato, who rejoiced at the prospect of sparing his fellow-citizens. For he, when he saw the dead bodies of those who had fallen in the last battle on Caesar's side, to the number of a thousand, turned away, covered his face, and shed tears. But every one else upbraided Pompey for being reluctant to fight.* [42]

Caesar defeated Pompey at Pharsalia, August 48 B.C.

After his defeat at Dyrrachium, Caesar gathered his army together and withdrew from the coast and marched to Thessaly. Pompey followed a few days later and brought all his forces into one camp not far from Caesar's forces near Pharsalia. According to Plutarch, *Pompey's calvary numbered five thousand against one thousand of Caesar's. Nor were the numbers of the infantry less disproportionate, there being forty-five thousand of Pompey's against twenty-two thousand of the enemy.* [43]

Whilst the foot was thus sharply engaged in the main battle, on the flank Pompey's horse rode up confidently, and opened their ranks very wide, that they might surround the right wing of Caesar. But before they engaged, Caesar's cohorts rushed out and attacked them, and did not dart their javelins at a distance, or strike at the thighs and legs, as they usually did in close battle, but aimed at their faces. For thus Caesar had instructed them, in hopes that young gentlemen, who had not known much of battles and wounds, but came wearing their hair long, in the flower of their age and height of their beauty, would be more apprehensive of such blows, and not care for hazarding both a danger at present and a blemish for the future. And so it proved, for they were so far from bearing the stroke of the javelins, that they could not stand the sight of them, but turned about, and covered their faces to secure them. Once in disorder, presently they turned about to fly; and so most shamefully ruined all. For those who had beat them back at once

---

[41] Ibid, p 224.

[42] Ibid, p 227.

[43] Plutarch, Lives, v 2, pp 228

*outflanked the infantry, and falling on their rear, cut them to pieces.
Pompey, who commanded the other wing of the army, when he saw his
cavalry thus broken and flying, was no longer himself, nor did he now
remember that he was Pompey the Great, but, like one whom some god
had deprived of his senses, retired to his tent without speaking a word,
and there sat to expect the event, till the whole army was routed and the
enemy appeared upon the works which were thrown up before the camp.
--- Then first he seemed to have recovered his senses, and uttering, it is
said only these words, 'What, into the camp too?' He laid aside his
general's habit, and putting on such clothes as might best favor his flight,
stole off.* [44]

Pompey's flight to Egypt and murder

*When Pompey had got a little way from the camp, he
dismounted and forsook his horse, having but a small retinue with him;
and finding that no man pursued him, walked on softly afoot, taken up
altogether with thoughts, such as probably might possess a man that for
the space of thirty-four years together had been accustomed to conquest
and victory, and was then at last, in his old age, learning for the first
time what defeat and flight were. And it was no small affliction to
consider that he had lost in one hour all that glory and power which he
had been getting in so many wars and bloody battles.* [45]

Pompey gained passage on a merchant ship to Mitylene, on a
Greek Island just off the west coast of Turkey, and there joined his wife
Cornelia and son. Pompey decided to seek refuge in Egypt, thinking
young Ptolemy would be indebted to him for the favor he had shown to
his father. During his journey across the sea, *Pompey began to complain
and blame himself to his friends that he had allowed himself to be driven
into engaging by land without making use of his other forces, in which he
was irresistibly the stronger and had not kept near enough to his fleet,
that failing by land he might have reinforced himself from the sea.* [46]

Pothinus and Theodotus, Ptolemy's advisors, decided to take
away his life. *Only four days later Caesar arrived from Rhodes, and
sailed into Alexandra harbor with his small force of three thousand two
hundred infantry and eight hundred cavalry. The king's tutor, Theodotus,
a professor of rhetoric from Chios, came out to meet his flagship, and
offered him welcoming gifts: the signet-ring of Pompey and also his
head, which, he explained, had been embalmed on the young king's*

---

[44] Ibid, p 229

[45] Ibid, p 129.

[46] Ibid, p 131

order.[47] Caesar's reactions were likely those of disgust at this royal practice, but it is possible his remorse may have been in the remembrance of his daughter, Julia. Not certain is his reactions to the slaughter of fellow Romans by his own hand. From Plutarch: *Caesar, when he came to view Pompey's camp, and saw some of his opponents dead upon the ground, others dying, said, with a groan, 'This they would have; they brought me to this necessity. I, Caius Caesar, after succeeding in so many wars, had been condemned had I dismissed my army.'* [48]

Pompey recognized his own fatal mistakes of judgment. His reactions of grief and depression at the end of his life were appropriate. There is no example in Caesar's commentaries I believe, in which Caesar admitted he made errors or mistakes.

Caesar and Cleopatra

However, pursuit of Pompey was by no means Caesar's only reason for coming to Egypt. He also needed money. His politic moderation to the eastern provinces after Pharsalus made it all the more necessary to lay hands on Egyptian funds, which, since they were foreign, could be seized with less delicacy. The vast wealth of the kingdom was the magnet, which had brought Pompey to Egypt, and so it was with Caesar. In particular, he maintained that the country owed him an extremely large sum. --- Moreover, Caesar maintained that there existed a highly altruistic justification for his intervention in the internal affairs of this ostensibly autonomous state. For the late king was reported to have called upon the Roman government to see that his will proclaiming the joint heirs was carried out; and the story is not improbable, for he may have felt this as the best way to avoid Roman annexation, which his own predecessor was said to have actually requested. Caesar, therefore, to use his own rather disingenuous phrase, 'was most anxious, as a friend of both sides and as arbitrator, to settle the disputes in the royal family'. [49]

Ptolemy's advisor Pothinus told Caesar that he should leave Alexandria and attend to more important matters: *Caesar replied that he did not want Egyptians to be his counselors, and soon after privately sent for Cleopatra from her retirement. She took a small boat, and one only of her confidants, Apollodorus, the Sicilian, along with her, and in the dusk of the evening landed near the palace. She was at a loss to get in undiscovered, till she thought of putting herself into the coverlet of a bed and lying at length, whilst Appolodorus tied up the bedding and carried*

[47] Grant, Julius Caesar, p 119.

[48] Plutarch Lives, vol 2, p 231.

[49] Grant, p 120.

it on his back through the gates to Caesar's apartment. Caesar was first captivated by this proof of Cleopatra's bold wit, and was afterwards so overcome by the charm of her society that he made a reconciliation between her and her brother, on the condition that she should rule as his colleague in the kingdom. Caesar discovered a plot by Achillas, general of the king's forces, and Pothinus. *Caesar, upon the first intelligence of it, set a guard upon the hall where the feast was kept and killed Pothinus. Achillas escaped to the army, and raised a troublesome and embarrassing war against Caesar, which it was not easy for him to manage with his few soldiers against so powerful a city and so large an army. The first difficulty he met with was want of water, for the enemies had turned the canals. Another was, when the enemy endeavored to cut off his communication by sea, he was forced to divert that danger by setting fire to his own ships, which, after burning the docks, thence spread on and destroyed the great library.*[50]

Caesar spent the winter of 48 B.C. and early 47 in Alexandria. *At last, king* Ptolemy, *having gone off to Achillas and his party, Caesar engaged and conquered them. Many fell in that battle, and the king himself was never seen after. Upon this he left Cleopatra Queen of Egypt, who soon after had a son by him, whom the Alexandrians called Caesarion, and then departed for Syria.*[51] Cleopatra and Caesarion came to Rome three years later during the celebration of Caesar's victory in Spain. This was only months before his assassination.

Caesar returned triumphant to Rome

In Syria, Caesar marched against Pharnaces, son of Mithridates, drove him out of Pontus, and totally defeated his army. He returned to Rome where he was proclaimed dictator for the second time in 47 B.C. In keeping with his primary occupation as a military commander he left Rome for Africa and his forces defeated what remained of Pompey's forces and his ally king Juba, at Thrapsus in April, 46 B.C. Cato, who was to defend Utica, committed suicide.

Caesar returned to Rome, in July 46 B.C., with his triple triumphs, Egypt, Syria and Africa. *After the triumphs, he distributed rewards to his soldiers, and treated the people with feasting and shows. He entertained the whole people together at one feast, where twenty-two thousand dining couches were laid out; and he made a display of gladiators, and of battles by sea, in honor, as he said, of his daughter Julia, though she had been long since dead. When these shows were over, an account was taken of the people who, from three hundred and twenty thousand, were not reduced to an hundred and fifty thousand. So*

[50] Plutarch, Lives, v 2, p 231.

[51] Ibid, p 232.

great a waste had the civil war made in Rome alone, not to mention what the other parts of Italy and the provinces suffered.[52]

Instead of trying to solve the horrendous problems in Rome, Caesar left Rome for Spain to seek out and destroy Pompey's sons, *who had gathered together a very numerous army. --- The great battle was near the town of Munda, in southern Spain, in which Caesar, seeing his men hard pressed, and making but a weak resistance, ran through the ranks among the soldiers, and crying out, asked them whether they were not ashamed to deliver him into the hands of boys? At last, with great difficulty, and the best efforts he could make, he forced back the enemy, killing thirty thousand of them, though with the loss of one thousand of his best men. --- The younger of Pompey's sons escaped; but Didius, some days after the fight, brought in the head of the elder son to Caesar. This was the last war he was engaged in. The triumph which he celebrated for this victory displeased the Romans beyond anything, for he had not defeated foreign generals or barbarian kings, but had destroyed the children and family of one of the greatest men of Rome.*[53]

Dictator for life

Caesar became, nonetheless, dictator for life and consul for the fourth time. *This was indeed a tyranny avowed, since his power now was not only absolute, but perpetual too.* With this new power Caesar set out with grandiose plans, resolving to make war upon the borders of the entire Roman Empire *completing the whole circle of his intended empire, and bounding it on every side by the ocean.*

While preparations were being made for this expedition, he proposed to dig through the isthmus on which Corinth stands; and appointed Anienus to superintend the work. He had also a design of diverting the Tiber, and carrying it by a deep channel directly from Rome to Circeii, and so into the sea near Tarracina, that there might be a safe and easy passage for all merchants who traded to Rome. Besides this, he intended to drain all the marshes by Pomentium and Setia, and gain ground enough from the water to employ many thousands of men in tillage. He proposed further to make great mounds on the shore nearest Rome, to hinder the sea from breaking in upon the land, to clear the coast at Ostia of all the hidden rocks and shoals that made it unsafe for shipping.[54]

Caesar was to accomplish none of these things. Plutarch and other historians gave him, or the best of his philosophers and

---

[52]   Ibid, p 234.

[53]   Ibid, p 235.

[54]   Ibid, p 236.

mathematicians, credit for establishing a new and more exact method of correcting the calendar, the Julian calendar, which is used to this day.

But the die was cast: *that which brought him the most apparent and mortal hatred was his desire of being king; which gave the common people the first occasion to quarrel with him, and proved the most specious pretense to those who had been his secret enemies all along.* [55]

The assassination of Julius Caesar
Everyone knows the story, memorialized in Shakespeare's play, *Julius Caesar*, of the conspiracy of those in the senate, chiefly Brutus and Cassius. On the Ides of March, which is simply the date of March 15, Caesar was assassinated in the chambers of the senate in the year 44 B.C.

---

[55] Ibid, p 237. Note. See next chapter Cicero's history, in Book 2 of The Republic, of the early kings of Rome. This explains the Romans', fear of a monarchy.

Chapter 4

Cicero

Marc Anthony

Cicero, in his First Philippic against Marcus Antonius, makes it clear to Anthony what he thinks of him: *But what frightens me more --- is the possibility that you yourself may disregard the true path of glory, and instead consider it glorious to possess more power than all your fellow-citizens combined, preferring that they should fear you rather than like you.*[1]

Cicero would later be slain by assassins who were dispatched by the second triumvirate, Anthony, Caesar Octavius (later Augustus), and Lepidus. Cicero's head was cut off by the centurion, *and by Anthony's command his hands also, and who ordered that his head and hands were to be fastened up over the rostra, where the orators spoke; a sight which the Roman people shuddered to behold, and they believed they saw there, not the face of Cicero, but the image of Anthony's own soul.*[2]

It is fitting to begin the story of Cicero with the end of his life and a brief presentation of Anthony who ordered his execution. The dismal end of Cicero is seldom presented to students in contrast to Cicero's glorified orations. Nor are his brilliant comments about the mentality of tyrants passed on to members of the legal profession as found in his Republic: *As soon as the king takes the first step towards a more unjust regime, he at once becomes a tyrant. And that is the foulest and most repellent creature imaginable, and the most abhorrent to God and man alike. Although he has the outward appearance of a man, he outdoes the wildest beasts in the utter savagery of his behavior.*[3]

---

[1] Cicero, Selected Political Speeches, p 315.

[2] Plutarch, Lives, V 2, p 441.

[3] Cicero, Republic, Book Two, p 50.

Plutarch presents a poignant characterization of the triumvirate's order to kill Cicero: *Thus they let their anger and fury take from them the sense of humanity, and demonstrated that no beast is more savage than man when possessed with power answerable to his rage.*[4]

Cicero's declarations in his speech against Anthony were based on correct observations and conclusions about Anthony's life long course, which Plutarch provides fitting commentary throughout his story of the life of Anthony (82-30 B.C.). He began as a young man a friendship *with Curio, a man abandoned to his pleasures, who, to make Anthony's dependence upon him a matter of greater necessity, plunged him into a life of drinking and dissipation, and led him through a course of such extravagance that he ran, at an early age, into debt to the amount of two hundred and fifty talents. For this sum Curio became his surety; on hearing which, the elder Curio, his father, drove Anthony out of his house. After this, for some short time he took part with Clodius, the most insolent and outrageous demagogue of the time, in his course of violence and disorder; but getting weary, before long, of his madness, and apprehensive of the powerful party forming against him, he left Italy and traveled into Greece, where he spent his time in military exercises and in the study of eloquence.*[5] Anthony first served as a commander in Judea and Egypt, 57- 54 B.C., and was with Julius Caesar, as noted above in the Gallic wars in 54-50 B.C. Plutarch commented that although Anthony was popular with the soldiers: *He was too lazy to pay attention to the complaints of persons who were injured; he listened impatiently to petitions; and he had an ill name for familiarity with other people's wives. In short, the government of Caesar got a bad repute through his friends. And of these friends, Anthony, as he had the largest trust, and committed the greatest errors, was thought the most deeply in fault.*[6]

Anthony's performance as master of the horse, (second in command) during Caesar's absence, in Rome, 48-47 B.C. was a disaster according to Plutarch. *Dolabella* (Cicero's son-in-law), *however, who was tribune, being a young man and eager for change, was now for bringing in a general measure for canceling debts, and wanted Anthony, who was his friend, and forward enough to promote any popular project, to take part with him in this step. --- Anthony suspected that Dolabella was too familiar with his wife; and in great trouble at this, he parted with her --- and came to open hostilities with Dolabella, who had seized on the forum, intending to pass his law by force. Anthony, backed by a vote of the senate that Dolabella would be put down by force of arms, went*

[4] Plutarch, Lives, v 2, p 439.

[5] Ibid, p 482.

[6] Ibid, p 485.

down and attacked him, killing some of his, and losing some of his own men; and by this action lost his favor with the commonalty, while with the better class and with all well-conducted people his general course of life made him, as Cicero says, absolutely odious, utter disgust being excited by his drinking bouts at all hours, his wild expenses, his gross amours, the day spent in sleeping or walking off his debauches, and the night in banquets and at theaters, and in celebrating the nuptials of some comedian or buffoon.[7] Caesar removed Anthony from being second in command and he remained unemployed until 44 B.C., the year of Caesar's assassination.

We all know the story from Shakespeare's play *Julius Caesar*—the attempts of Anthony to crown Caesar three times, the conspiracy among the senators, chiefly Cassius and Brutus, and the slaying of Caesar at the senate house. Caesar's funeral was Anthony's finest hour and he played the part. His speech at Caesar's funeral as artfully created by Shakespeare: *Friends, Romans, countrymen, lend me your ears* has been memorized and given in speech classes by countless thousands of students, yet the Big Lie of the speech is seldom if ever discussed. Throughout the speech Anthony was trying to claim that Caesar was not ambitious! Historians also concede that the will, which Anthony read in this speech, was a complete fabrication. Anthony was successful by his orations to cause the people to become agitated and hateful toward those who planned and carried out Caesar's death.

There followed the formation of the second triumvirate of Anthony, Caesar Octavius (later Augustus) and Lepidus, which led to the slaughter of one hundred senators and the defeat of the armies of Cassius and Brutus at Philippi, and the assassination of Cicero.

Caesar Octavius, in 33 B.C., declared war against Cleopatra and defeated the forces of Anthony and Cleopatra in 31, followed by the suicides of Anthony in 31 and Cleopatra in 30.

Background of Cicero

Now to the life of Cicero, who was born in 106, the same year as Pompey, and six years before Julius Caesar. Cicero was murdered, in December 43 B.C., when he was 63 years old. Cicero came from a wealthy family, a social group at the time called the knights or equites, in contrast with Pompey and Caesar, who came from the nobility, also known as the patricians. Members of his family were aristocrats and were well educated, landed, leisured, and involved in local politics. Cicero would become a consul in 63 B.C, the highest position in government held ordinarily by members of the nobility. As such he was called a 'new man', the first in his family to occupy such a high position in government. Cicero considered this his greatest achievement, however,

---

[7] Ibid, p 486

his role in history has far surpassed his own assessment. The prolific output of his creative mind can hardly be noted here. His greatest achievements went far beyond the courtrooms or even the halls of the senate during his latter years with his writings *The Republic*, *The Laws* and his final work *On Duties*. He was also gifted as an historian, especially transmitting the knowledge of the Greeks to the Romans. The reader's attention will be directed in particular to his last work, which may be his greatest work, *On Duties,* which was completed after the assassination of Caesar in 44. This was Cicero's final contribution to his son's education and includes a lifetime of his own experiences in guiding his son to pursue a life of honor.

Cicero's remarkable talents were noted early in life when he pursued his studies according to Plutarch. *For as soon as he was of an age to begin to have lessons, he became so distinguished for his talent, and got such a name and reputation among the boys, that their fathers would often visit the school that they might see young Cicero, and might be able to say that they themselves had witnessed the quickness and readiness in learning for which he was renowned.* [8]

Cicero then became an auditor of Philo the Academic and received training while in Rome from eminent statesmen and leaders of the senate, and acquired a background in rhetoric, philosophy and law. The teachings of Philo and the academics based on the dialogues of Plato formed a foundation, which lasted his entire lifetime. Plato's dialogues became the models for his late works *The Republic* and *The Laws*. But Sulla was at this time a threat to Cicero, since he had already acquired fame in defending a former slave of Sulla. Cicero left Rome for Greece, and continued his studies in Athens from 79-77 B.C. Cicero sailed from Athens to Asia (Minor) and Rhodes, just off the south west coast of Turkey where he studied oratory, philosophy and became quite fluent in Greek. Apollonius remarked, according to Plutarch: *You have my praise and admiration, Cicero, and Greece my pity and commiseration, since those arts and that eloquence which are the only glories that remain to her, will now be transferred by you to Rome.*

Rome

After Sulla's death Cicero returned to Rome where *his friends at Rome earnestly soliciting him to return to public affairs, he again prepared for use his orator's instrument of rhetoric, and summoned into action his political faculties, diligently exercising himself in declamations and attending the most celebrated rhetoricians of the time. But when his own desire of fame and the eagerness of his father and relations had made him take in earnest to pleading, he made no slow or gentle advance to the first place, but shone out in full luster at once, and*

---

[8] Plutarch, Lives, v 2, p 409.

far surpassed all the advocates of the bar.[9] Cicero was elected to his first public office as quaestor, or deputy governor, for the province of Sicily in 76. Plutarch described Cicero's fame which he acquired in Sicily: --- *After they had experience of his care, justice, and clemency, they honored him more than ever they did any of their governors before. It happened, also, that some young Romans of good and noble families charged with neglect of discipline and misconduct in military service, were brought before the praestor in Sicily. Cicero undertook their defense, which he conducted admirably, and got them acquitted. So returning to Rome with a great opinion of himself for these things --- Meeting an eminent citizen in Campania, --- he asked him what the Romans said and thought of his actions, as if the whole city had been filled with the glory of what he had done. His friend asked him in reply, 'Where is it you have been, Cicero?' This for the time utterly mortified and cast him down to perceive that the report of his actions had sunk into the city of Rome as into an immense ocean, without any visible effect or result in reputation. --- Nevertheless, he was always excessively pleased with his own praise, and continued to the very last to be passionately fond of glory; which often interfered with the prosecution of his wisest resolutions.*[10] Plutarch thus gives us a forecast of Cicero's character, which was always fond of glory and praise from others.

Cicero succeeded in getting Verres condemned, *who had been praetor of Sicily, and stood charged by the Sicilians of many evil practices during his government there. --- Verres was thus convicted; though Cicero, who set the fine at seventy-five myriads, lay under the suspicion of being corrupted by bribery to lessen the sum. But the Sicilians, in testimony of their gratitude, came and brought him all sorts of presents from the island, when he was aedile (in 69); of which he made no private profit himself, but used their generosity only to reduce the public price of provisions.*[11] Cicero became praetor in 66 B.C. *Numerous distinguished competitors stood with him for the praetor's office; but he was chosen before them all, and managed the decision of causes with justice and integrity.*[12]

Praise of Pompey

It was Manilius, a tribune of the people, who proposed to the Assembly that Pompey should be appointed to the command against

---

[9] Ibid, p 411.

[10] Ibid, p 412.

[11] Ibid, p 413.

[12] Ibid, p 414.

Mithridates, of Pontus, in Asia Minor, the northern most section of Turkey. Cicero, as praetor, brought the motion before the Assembly in his famous oration, *On the Command of Cnaeus Pompeius.* This was perhaps the most important speech of his political career. It would solidify his endorsement of Pompey, and paved the way to his later appointment of consul in 63. The rise of military rule in the Roman republic with Marius, Sulla, Pompey and Caesar, with the defeat of Pompey by Caesar in 48 B.C., would lead to the end of the Roman republic as well as his own political career. His speech also gives us a clear indication of his own political acumen and skill in oratory by the way he introduced himself to the senate, whose forces had been defeated by king Mithridates, and the way he reviewed the history of previous generations of Romans who gloriously established empires in Asia and elsewhere. By his oratory he impressed the members of the senate with the horrible massacres of Mithridates against Roman citizens in Asia. He gave a clear account of the economic impacts of failure to protect Roman investments in Asia, the need to establish military dominance and defeat of Mithridates, by the senate's selection of Pompey to do the job. Cicero presented his praise of Pompey to the Senate as follows.

I think I have said enough to explain, first, why the character of this war means that it is inevitable, secondly, why its dimensions make it dangerous. Next, I feel I should speak about the commander whom we ought to choose to conduct the campaign and assume responsibility for all the major issues involved. Gentlemen, I only wish the supply of brave and honest generals at your disposal was so large that the selection of a man to put in charge of these major operations and all that they involve presented some problem. In fact, however, Cnaeus Pompeius is in the unique position of not only exceeding all his contemporaries in merit, but also even eclipsing every figure recorded from the past. That being so, surely there is no reason whatever to feel the slightest misgivings about such a choice. After describing the qualities of the ideal general and reviewing Pompey's experiences and success in the African, Transalpine, Spanish wars, the war against Spartacus and the war against the pirates in the Mediterranean Cicero concludes with the following. *The abilities of Cnaieus Pompeius are too vast for any words to do them justice. No imaginable compliments would be worthy of him, or new to you, or unfamiliar to any single person.* [13]

Not content to rest in this praise, Cicero continues at length in his speech detailing Pompey's achievements and the characteristics of not only a *perfect general* but by *a variety of other notable talents. Well, throughout the whole history of the world, no name has ever been more illustrious than the name of Pompey; and indeed, in his case, this renown is based on achievements that have never been equaled. --- Nowhere on*

---

[13] Cicero, Selected Political Speeches, pp 48-49.

earth, believe me, is there a region so desolate that news has not reached it or that solemn day when the entire Roman people packed the forum, and crammed every available corner in each of the temples which overlook this platform, in order to demand that a war involving all the nations in the world should be placed under the charge of Cnaeus Pompeius alone.[14] Cicero next argued against his rival orator Hortensius, who had opposed Pompey's command in 67 against the pirates. *--- And yet if the people of Rome had on that occasion paid more attention to our authoritative advice than to their own welfare and true interests, heaven know, our glorious renown and our world empire would not be in existence today. --- In former times we not only protected the whole of Italy but also succeeded, through the prestige of our imperial name, in securing the safety of all our allies right to the very ends of the earth.* [15]

Historians have not only commented on Cicero's tendency toward repeated self-praise, but point out the inconsistencies, which will become apparent in his political and courtroom oratory and his writings. Cicero, in all fairness, contrasts the praise he gives Pompey with the ignominy, which he directs toward Caesar. Thus, Cicero chose the better of two evils, Pompey rather than Caesar. He favored a tribune of the people, Manilius, instead of the Optimates, or aristocrats, about twenty families, which controlled the senate, in the hope that somehow the Roman republic could be saved. These were times in Rome when government was in shambles. In the words of Plutarch: *Only a spark was needed to set everything on fire, and since the whole state was rotten within itself, it was in the power of any bold man to overthrow it.*

Cicero's consulship and the Catiline conspiracy

Cicero's greatest achievement, so he always believed and repeatedly proclaimed, came three years later in 63 B.C., when he was promoted to the highest office of consul. *Yet he was preferred to the consulship no less by the nobles than the common people, for the good of the city; and both parties jointly assisted his promotion.* The senate however conceded to the choice of Cicero, and feared his opponent Catiline, who proposed land reform and had a private army at his disposal. Catiline attempted to gain the consulship in 63 when Cicero was presiding officer. Catiline was defeated and he ventured to gain the consulship by illegal means using strong-arm force in what has been called the Catiline conspiracy. The suppression of the Catiline conspiracy was Cicero's claim to a position of glory and honor in saving Rome from disaster. From Plutarch's account of the Catiline conspiracy: *Pompey being at this time employed in the wars with the kings of Pontus and*

---

[14] Ibid, p 56.

[15] Ibid, p 60-61.

Armenia, there was not sufficient force at Rome to suppress any attempts at a revolution. These people had for their head a man of bold, daring, and restless character, Lucius Catiline, who was accused, besides other great offences, of deflowering his virgin daughter, and killing his own brother. He corrupted many of the young men of the city. He provided for every one pleasures, drink, and women, and profusely supplying the expenses of these debauches. But Rome itself was in the most dangerous inclination to change on account of the unequal distribution of wealth and property, those of highest rank and greatest spirit having impoverished themselves by show, entertainments, ambition of offices, and sumptuous buildings, and the riches of the city having thus fallen into the hands of mean and low-born persons. So that there wanted but a slight impetuous to set all in motion, it being in the power of every daring man to overturn a sickly commonwealth.[16]

That Catiline was a threat to the government of Rome is clear from Plutarch's account. The old soldiers of Sulla were Catiline's chief stimulus to action and there were plots to assassinate Cicero before the election. *Not long after this, Catiline's soldiers got together in a body in Etruria, and began to form themselves into companies, the day appointed for the design being near at hand.* Senators went to Cicero's home with letters warning of the danger. Cicero, as consul, called for a meeting of the senate. Catiline, with others of his group, came to the senate intending to make his defense but none of the senators would sit near him. There followed Cicero's first speech to the senate against Catiline which led to his exile.

Cicero had delivered four speeches *Against Lucius Sergius Catilina*, two to the senate and two orations to the people. Only a few excerpts can be given from these lengthy written accounts. From the first speech, with Catiline present in the senate, he starts: --- *In the name of heaven, Catilina, how long do you propose to exploit our patience? Do you really suppose that your lunatic activities are going to escape our retaliation for evermore?* After reviewing the history of the murders of Tiberius Gracchus and his son C. Sempronius Gracchus who favored land reforms and was considered a threat to members of the Senate. Cicero stated: *Members of the Senate, my desire is to be merciful. Yet in this grave national emergency I also do not want to seem negligent; and as things are I blame myself for culpable inaction. Inside Italy, within the passes of Etruria, there is a camp occupied by men who plan the destruction of the Roman people. The number of these enemies increases every day. But as for the real commander of that camp, the leader of the hostile force, he is to be seen within our own walls and even inside the Senate itself, plotting every day, from his interior vantage point, some form of ruin for our country.*

---

[16] Plutarch, Lives, v 2, p 416

Cicero continues his oration and makes the recommendation that Catiline leave the city of Rome. *Since that is the position, Catilina, I call upon you to leave for the destination you already have in mind. Depart, at last, from our city! The gates are open; be on your way. Your camp run by Manlius has been waiting all too long for you to take over its command. And take all your friends with you, or as many as you can clean the city up. Once there is a wall between you and ourselves, you will have delivered me from grave anxiety. With us, you can remain no longer. I find it unendurable that you should still be here: unendurable, intolerable and impermissible.*[17] Catiline did leave Rome with several hundred of his men and the Senate declared him a public enemy. Catiline joined his confederates in Etruria but some of his supporters remained in Rome.

In Cicero's last two speeches Against Catalina, the third speech to the people and the fourth before the senate, the oratory is directed against the primary supporters of Catiline who remained in Rome after Catiline's departure. Cicero directed his invective primarily against Publius Cornelius Lentulus, a patrician who was a member of the senate and who held a second praetorship in 63 B.C., the year of Cicero's consulship. Another Catiline conspirator, Gaius Cornelius Cethetus was a patrician and a member of the senate.

Cicero began his speech before the people as follows: *First of all, when Catilina broke out of town a few days ago, he left behind him at Rome the associates in his odious designs, the ferocious leaders of this horrible war. Since then I have continually been on the watch, citizens, planning how we may best be saved from these deadly clandestine intrigues. --- But I soon saw that, instead, we still had with us in Rome a collection of men whose madness and malignancy knew no limits.*[18] Cicero then described a plot by Catilina with Lentulus as his envoy to enlist Gallic troops as allies to overthrow the Roman government. Cicero's men, two praetors and a force intercepted letters from Catilina and other conspirators to the Gauls. *The plan was to set fire to all quarters of the city, - defined according to their allocation and distribution among his supporters - and to massacre an enormous number of citizens. Meanwhile Calilina himself was to be at hand, in order to intercept the fugitives and effect a junction with his leading representatives in the capital. --- Now, gentlemen, these letters and seals and handwritings and uniformly repeated confessions seemed to me, at least, the most convincing possible evidence and proof of these men's culpability. Then, citizens, after the evidence had been reviewed and recited, I requested the Senate to direct that steps should be taken for the*

---

[17] Cicero, Selected Political Speeches, pp 78-81.

[18] Ibid, p 111.

safety of the state. --- The Senate unanimously adopted their proposals. --- The Senate also decreed that Publius Lentulus, when he had resigned from his praetorship, should be placed under arrest, and that Gaius Cethegus, Lucius Statlius and Publius Gavinius, all of whom were present, should likewise be taken into custody. --- The Senate leniently limited its sentences to this small number of defendants, gentlemen, because in spite of the formidable character of the plot and the large number of traitors involved it was believed that the country could be saved by the punishment of only the nine worst offenders, and that the rest could be recalled to their right minds. --- What had to be done first was done and completed. That is to say, Publius Lentulus, although on the strength of the evidence and his own confession the Senate had judged him deprived of the rights not only of a praetor but also even of a Roman citizen, nevertheless resigned from that office.[19]

Cicero then decreed a thanksgiving at every place of worship and told the people that he had *saved them from a miserable and horrible death. You have been saved without slaughter, without bloodshed, without an army, without a battle.*

In his last speech, before the senate, now that the conspirators were arrested by order of the Senate, Cicero debated the opposing views as to the disposition of Catiline's conspirators. Execution was favored by Cato and supported by Cicero, while others including Caesar favored life imprisonment. The Senate voted for execution. Cicero ended his oration before the Senate with self-praise:

My claims to a military command, to an army, to a provincial governorship— I have renounced them all. I have declined the opportunity of a triumph and other honors, in order to devote myself to the protection of this city and yourselves. --- I ask nothing of yourselves except that you cherish the memory of this time and of my sole consulship. For as long as that memory remains implanted in your hearts, I shall feel securely encompassed by the strongest of protective walls. --- I commend to you my little son. He will have enough protection, without a doubt, no only for his continued existence but for his whole career, if you will just remember that his father was the man who, at his own risk, and his alone, preserved the entire Roman world.[20]

The men were executed. The act was justified by the Emergency Decree, which had been passed by the Senate as well as the reasoning that the imprisonment of the men for life would have been short lived and their release would have endangered the state again. There were no prisons in ancient Rome that could contain those arrested. A month later Catilina was killed at Pistoia, about 20 miles northwest of Florence.

---

[19] Ibid, pp 116-118.

[20] Ibid, p144.

After leaving the consulship Cicero became active in the courtroom. In 61 B.C. he testified against Clodius in a case involving the profanation of the rites of the Bona Dea, a rite of women at the house of Caesar, which Clodius entered dressed as a music-girl, to gain the favors of Caesar's wife Pompeia. Not only did Cicero testify against Clodius *but many other good and honest citizens also gave evidence against him, for injuries, disorders, bribing the people, and debauching women. Clodius was acquitted and bribery was reported to have been employed. --- And when Clodius upbraided Cicero that the judges had not believed his testimony, 'yes', said he, ' five-and-twenty of them trusted me and condemned you, and the other thirty did not trust you, for they did not acquit you till they had got your money.*[21]

Cicero's Exile

Clodius got his revenge by his influence in enacting a law that anyone who had put a Roman citizen to death without trial was to be outlawed. Caesar agreed with Clodius. Cicero, without waiting for trial, left for Brundisium, and then sailed to Dyracchium on the west coast of Greece. Pompey did not intervene on Cicero's behalf. Plutarch described Cicero's life in Greece as follows: *Although many visited him with respect, and the cities of Greece contended which should honor him most, he yet continued disheartened and disconsolate, like an unfortunate lover, often casting his looks back upon Italy; and indeed, he was become so poor-spirited, so humiliated and dejected by his misfortunes, as none could have expected in a man who had devoted so much of his life to study and learning. And yet he often desired his friends not to call him orator, but philosopher, because he had made philosophy his business, and had only used rhetoric as an instrument of attaining his objects in public life. --- Clodius, having thus driven away Cicero, fell to burning his farms and villas, and afterwards his city house.*[22]

Meanwhile in 59 B.C., the first triumvirate would be formed, with Caesar, Pompey, and Crassus now in command of all Rome. Cicero would decline to have anything to do with the autocratic rule of the triumvirate, which now threatened the Republic. *The senate, also, striving to outdo the people, sent letters of thanks to those cities which had received Cicero with respect in his exile, and decreed that his house and his country— places, which Clodius had destroyed, should be rebuilt at the public charge.*

---

[21] Plutarch, Lives, v 2, p 428.

[22] Ibid, p 430.

Returned to Rome

Cicero, upon his return to Rome, resumed legal practice and took on the defense of Marcus Caelius Rufus in 56 B.C. against Clodia, the sister of Clodius. Cicero's orations in defense of Rufus are as pointed as is his summary statement: *The indictment (against Rufus) is supported by not the slightest ground for suspicion. Proofs of the alleged facts just do not exist. The dealings which are supposed to have taken place have left not a trace of what was said or where or when. No witness has been named; nor has any accomplice.*

The whole accusation emanates from a house that is malevolent, disreputable, merciless, crime-stained and vicious. Cicero also lambasted the prosecutor as follows: *All the other matters raised are not really accusations in any proper sense of the word, but only slanders, more appropriate to some vulgar shouting-match than to a national court of justice.*[23]

The conference at Lucca in 56 B.C. restored the first triumvirate. Pompey and Crassus became consuls in 55 B.C. Disorders in Rome however were out of control and Clodius, who was responsible for much of the disturbances, was killed by Milo. Cicero would now provide the defense of Milo in 52 B.C. at his trial, which was closely guarded by Pompey's military guards. *Whenever my eyes turn, they look in vain for the customary sights of the Forum and the traditional procedure of the courts. The usual circle of listeners is missing; the habitual crowds are nowhere to be seen. Instead you can see military guards, stationed in front of all the temples. They are posted there, it is true, in order to protect us from violence, but all the same they cannot fail to have an inhibiting effect on oratory. This ring of guards is, I repeat, both protective and necessary, and yet the very freedom from fear, which they are there to guarantee, has something frightening about it.*[24] Milo was convicted and was exiled, his property sold to pay his debts.

Retirement from law practice

Cicero had already begun a new career which was to be his greatest triumph. He completed *De Republica* in 52 B.C., *De Legibus* (The Law) which he wrote in 52 B.C., and his greatest work *De Officiis* (On Duties) completed in 44 B.C. after Caesar's assassination.

In 51 B.C. Cicero was given the province of Cilicia, in south east Turkey, and for one year governed the province admirably according to Plutarch. *And perceiving the Cilicians, by the great loss the Romans had suffered in Parthia, and the commotions in Syria, to have become*

---

[23] Cicero, Selected Political Speeches, p 199, p 183.

[24] Ibid, p 217.

disposed to attempt a revolt, by a gentle course of government, he soothed them back into fidelity. He would accept none of the presents that were offered him by the kings; he remitted the charge of public entertainments, but daily at his own house received the ingenious and accomplished persons of the province, not sumptuously, but liberally. His house had no porter, nor did any man ever find him in bed; but early in the morning, standing or walking before his door, he received those who came to offer their salutations. He is said never once to have ordered any of those under his command to be beaten with rods, or to have their garments rent. He never gave contumelious language in his anger, nor inflicted punishment with reproach. He detected an embezzlement, to a large amount, in the public money, and thus relieved the cities from their burden, at the same time that he allowed those who made restitution to retain without further punishment their rights as citizens. --- On leaving his province, he touched at Rhodes, and tarried for some length of time at Athens, longing much to renew his old studies. He visited the eminent men of learning, and saw his former friends and companions; and after receiving in Greece the honors that were due to him, returned to the city, where every thing was now just as it were in flames, breaking out into a civil war. [25]

When one of Caesar's envoys asked Cicero to join his party, *Cicero gave an angry reply, 'that he should not do anything unbecoming his past life.'* After Caesar crossed the Rubicon in January 49 B.C., Cicero supported Pompey and helped recruit his forces in Italy. Cicero unsuccessfully tried to intervene by proposing in the Senate that Caesar should not engage in war with Pompey. Caesar's victory over Pompey at Pharsalia, in August of 48 B.C., was the end of Cicero's hopes that Caesar could be contained. Thereafter, Pompey could no longer work with the senate and continue government without a military dictatorship. The dismal end of Pompey was reviewed in both previous chapters of Pompey and Julius Caesar.

After Pharsalia

Caesar pardoned Cicero for his support of Pompey. Cicero returned to Rome from Brundisium and before the Senate delivered an oration in support of Caesar. Cicero began his speech *In Support of Marcus Claudius Marcellus*, a member of the Senate whom Caesar had also pardoned, with the following: *During this recent period* (Cicero had not spoken in the Senate for two years), *Senators, I have maintained a long silence, due not to fear but to a combination of sorrow and diffidence.* Cicero then lauds praise of Caesar, in as glorious a manner that he had given in his speech *On The Command of Cnaeus Pompeius* twenty years earlier in 66.

---

[25] Plutarch, Lives, v 2, p 432.

And so now, Gaius Caesar, what you have done is to allow my old occupation, from which I had been severed, to be thrown open to me again; and to all other Senators, likewise, you have raised aloft a signal of hope for the future of Rome. For one thing has become very clear to me from the experiences of numerous people and most of all from my own; and it has of late become universally apparent, now that after explaining your grievance against him you have vouchsafed Marcus Marcellus to the Senate and commonwealth of Rome. --- As for your own deeds, Gaius Caesar, no genius could be abundant enough, no pen or tongue sufficiently eloquent and fluent, to embellish them or even to describe them. Nevertheless I maintain, with all deference, that the glory you have gained today is greater than any you have ever won before. I am continually aware, and I constantly tell others, that all the exploits of Roman generals and foreign powers combined, all the achievements of the most potent nations and illustrious monarchs in the world, fall short of what you have achieved: so enormous was the magnitude of your enterprises, and the number of your battles, and the lightning rapidity with which you acted, and the immense diversity of the military operations involved. No one else upon this earth could have traversed all those widely separated lands with the amazing speed with which you marched— or rather, I would say, with which you conquered.

For all this it is hard not to agree with the editor that *It is easy, and right, to be shocked at this fulsome praise of the autocrat against whom Cicero had sided and on whose death he was shortly to gloat.*[26] There are numerous references in Cicero's writings describing Caesar as a tyrant who was the gravest threat to the Roman Republic.

Cicero withdrew from public life once more and according to Plutarch: *Henceforth, the commonwealth being changed into a monarchy, Cicero withdrew himself from public affairs, and employed his leisure in instructing those young men that would, in philosophy; and by the near intercourse he thus had with some of the noblest and highest in rank, he again began to possess great influence in the city. The work and object to which he set himself was to compose and translate philosophical dialogues and to render logical and physical terms into the Roman idiom. --- He had a design, it is said, of writing the history of his country, combining with it much of that of Greece, and incorporating in it all the stories and legends of the past that he had collected. But his purposes were interfered with by various public and various private unhappy occurrences and misfortunes; for most of which he was himself in fault. For first of all, he put away his wife Terentia, by whom he had been neglected in the time of the war; neither did he find her kind when he returned into Italy, for she did not join him at Brundisum where he stayed a long time, nor would allow her young daughter, who undertook*

---

[26] Cicero, Selected Political Speeches, pp 280-281.

so long a journey, decent attendance, or the requisite expenses; besides, she left him a naked and empty house, and she had involved him in many and great debts. These were alleged as the fairest reasons for the divorce.

Cicero married a young woman *for the love of her beauty, as Terentia upbraided him, or as Tiro, his emancipated slave, has written, for her riches, to discharge his debts. For the young woman was very rich, and Cicero had the custody of her estate, being left guardian in trust; and being indebted many myriads of money, he was persuaded by friends and relations to marry her, notwithstanding his disparity of age, and to use her money to satisfy his creditors.*

Not long after this marriage, his daughter Tullia died in childbed at Lentulus's house, to whom she had been married after the death of Piso, her former husband. The philosophers from all parts came to comfort Cicero; for his grief was so excessive, that he put away his new-married wife, because she seemed to be pleased at the death of Tullia. And thus stood Cicero's domestic affairs at this time.[27]

Assassination of Caesar

Caesar was assassinated March 15, 44 B.C. Cicero would complete his greatest and most original work, *De Officiis* for his son later that year. He would not write the histories of Greece and Rome. Plutarch wrote his *Lives of the Noble Grecians and Romans* almost 150 years later. The importance of childbirth as it has influenced events in history has never been properly appreciated. Caesar was reportedly born by Caesarian section. The world would have been different without him. Caesar's daughter Julia, who was married to Pompey in an alliance with Caesar, died in childbirth. This led to the alienation and growing enmity between Caesar and Pompey. Would the civil war, the end of the Republic, and the course of the Roman Empire have been different had Julia not died in childbirth and Caesar crossed the Rubicon?

Two days after Caesar's assassination, Cicero addressed the Senate and spoke in favor of a general amnesty. *I reminded members of the ancient precedent created by the Athenians, making use in my oration of the Greek term which that state then employed to calm down civil strife— and I moved that every memory of our internal discords should be effaced in everlasting oblivion.*[28] He intended to visit his son who was studying in Athens, but instead returned to Rome and delivered his Phillipic orations against Anthony, which would lead to his demise. The first oration against Anthony was in September of 44 and the last in April of 43. His final orations against Anthony, thirteen speeches given before

---

[27] Plutarach, Lives, v 2, p 436.

[28] Cicero, Selected Political Speeches, p297.

the Senate, were possibly suicidal, knowing the person of Anthony who he so artfully portrays. Was this a symptom of an extremely depressed state of mind in his old age following the death of his daughter and the domestic turmoil in recent years? Was he dreaming that his oratory could save Rome from the impending disaster of Anthony and the other two triumvirs? Or was Cicero a true patriot who was willing to sacrifice his own life to the inevitable?

Cicero was murdered December 7, 43 B.C. at the command of Anthony on the shores of Italy at Formia, about half way between Rome and Naples.

Creative writings on government and law

There can be no doubt however of the remarkable abilities of Cicero, which, despite grave threats to his own life and terrible tragedies involving his family and personal life, he would during the last ten years of his life continue to be creative. Cicero surpassed his previous achievements by writing such books as *The Republic, The Laws* and *On Duties,* which we can here provide only a few excerpts and commentary.

The Republic, Book 1

Cicero used Plato's *Republic* as a model for his own dialogues on government. Unfortunately, there are only fragments remaining of *The Republic* as well as from *The Laws*. Nevertheless, these two works influenced the development of government and law. Therefore it is important to review these works of Cicero.

The Republic was started in 54 B.C., which was two years after the renewal of the triumvirate at Lucca. *The Republic* would be completed two years later, in 52. This was the year of his defense of Milo under military guard. Cicero uses a number of persons in *The Republic* taking part in the conversations while he is a participant in *The Laws*.

In the preface to this work, half of which is missing, Cicero raised the basic questions which are as important today as then: *What is the source of law, either the law of nations or this civil law of ours? From where did justice, good faith, and fair dealing come?* [29]

The dialogues focus on one of the participants, Scipio, who defines a republic as a *numerous gathering brought together by legal consent and community of interest*. He then described three forms of government— monarchy, aristocracy and democracy.

Scipio next discussed the defects of each form of government. *Nevertheless, in monarchies the rest of the populace plays too small a part in the community's legislation and debate; in aristocracies the masses can have hardly any share in liberty, since they are deprived of any participation in discussion and decision making; and when the*

---

[29] Cicero, The Republic, p 4.

government is carried on entirely by the people (however moderate and orderly) their equality is itself unequal, since it acknowledges no degrees of merit.

In defense of democracy Scipio states: *So liberty has no home in any state except a democracy. Nothing can be sweeter than liberty. Yet if it isn't equal throughout, it isn't liberty at all.*

With much of the text missing, Scipio continues: *We are told that, when one or more exceptionally rich and prosperous men emerge from the populace, (a despotism or an oligarchy) comes into being as a result of their arrogance and contempt; for the faint-hearted and the weak give way and succumb to the haughtiness of wealth. But if the people would hold fast to their rights, nothing, they say, would be superior in power, liberty, or happiness, inasmuch as they would be in charge of laws, courts, war, peace, treaties, individual lives, and wealth. They maintain that this form of government is the only one that deserves the name of 'republic'; and that for this reason the republic tends to be restored to freedom from the domination of a king or senate.*

More leaves of the manuscript were lost. Scipio continued: *When --- a few with money, not worth, have gained control of the state, those leaders seize the name of 'aristocrats' with their teeth, although lacking any right to it in fact. Money, name, and property, if divorced from good sense and skill in living one's own life and directing the lives of others, lapses into total degradation and supercilious insolence. And indeed there is no more degenerate kind of state than that in which the richest are supposed to be the best. But what can be more splendid than a state governed by worth, where the man who gives orders to others is not the servant of greed, where the leader himself has embraced all the values which he preaches and recommends to his citizens, where he imposes no laws on the people which he does not obey himself, but rather presents his own life to his fellows as a code of conduct?* [30]

Scipio then spoke of the instability of the three forms of government. *But the first and most inevitable of all changes is that which overtakes a monarchy. As soon as a king begins to rule unjustly, that kind of government vanishes on the spot, for that same man has become a tyrant.*[31] Tyranny is the perversion of a monarchy, oligarchy of an aristocracy, and mob rule of a democracy.

Scipio introduced the subjects we have just quoted by referring to the best type of *constitution* and how one kind of *constitution* can pass into another. The use of this word is by no means the same as we in

---

[30] Ibid, pp 19-24.

[31] Ibid, p 31. We have quoted Cicero' comments, p 50, in The Republic regarding a tyrant in the first page of this chapter.

America have learned to understand it since we have in the United States a written constitution, the first ever to be established. This constitution is unchanged other than amendments to it, which are established by the vote of two thirds of the members of both houses of congress and ratification by two thirds of the states. This written constitution is the foundation of government and is the law of the land; however the meaning of constitution among the Roman and English writers is the form of government existing at a particular time and place. The discussion in Cicero's dialogues reflects the instability of this form of government and law, changing from one assembly, Senate, consul, or dictator to the next only to be upbraided by another tyrant or king.

Book 2 of The Republic

In book 2 of *The Republic*, Cicero presents an account of the early Roman kings: *Accordingly in my discourse I shall go back, as Cato used to do, to the origin of the Roman people (I gladly borrow his actual word). Moreover, it will be easier to carry out my plan if I describe for you the birth, growth, and maturity of our state, which eventually became so firm and strong, than if I deal with some imaginary community, as Socrates does in Plato.*[32]

Cicero began his account of the formation of Rome by recounting the mythology of Romulus, the first king, who supposedly ruled in the eight century B.C. (Cicero says that he reigned *less than six hundred years ago*). Romulus, together with Tatius of the land of the Sabine women, *chose a royal council made up of leading citizens*, an early Senate of Rome. Romulus ruled but was protected by the Senate. Romulus divided up the populace into three tribes, each of which *he divided into thirty voting districts which he named after the Sabine girls and appealed for a peace treaty.*[33]

Numa Pompilius was the next king of Rome and he ruled for thirty-nine years. *The people had already held an Assembly of Voting Districts to appoint him king, he still had a law passed by that same body to confirm his regal powers.* He appointed *five priests from among the leading citizens to take charge of the various religious rituals.*

He also *instituted fairs and games and all kinds of other occasions for crowded gatherings. By organizing these activities he won over to mild and civilized behavior characters, who were fierce and brutalized by their enthusiasm for warfare.*

On the death of King Pompilius (Numa), the people made Tullus Hostilius king at a meeting of the Assembly of Voting Districts chaired by the interrex. And Tullus, following Pompilius' example, had

---

[32] Ibid, p 35.

[33] Ibid, p 39.

his position officially ratified by each district in turn. He was a man with a brilliant military reputation, earned by his great feats on the battlefield. From the sale of his plunder he built and enclosed a Senate house and a place of the people's assembly. He also drew up a legal procedure for declaring war. To be more precise, he formulated the procedure himself in very fair terms and then, by incorporating it in the fetials' ceremonies (priests responsible for the rituals of declaring war and concluding peace treaties), he enacted that every war which had not been declared and proclaimed should be deemed unjust and unholy. Note how firmly our kings already grasped the point that certain rights should be granted to the people.[34]

The next king was Ancus Marcius, the son of Numa's daughter, who was appointed king by the people, and had a law passed in the Assembly to ratify his position. He reigned for twenty-three years. Cicero then digressed from the subject of kings and focuses on the introduction of Greek culture, *a rich culture of moral and artistic thinking to Rome.*

When Marcius died the monarchy passed by the unanimous vote of the people, to Lucius Tarquinius. After having his position ratified by law, he first doubled the original number of the Senate, --- *Then he organized the knights in the system, which has survived to our own day* (Cicero's family was from the knights, or equites). *We are told that Lucius Tarquin was the first to hold the great games, which are called 'The Roman Games'.*[35]

Tarquin was killed as a result of a conspiracy hatched by the sons of Ancus and Servius (sons of the two previous kings). Tullius began to rule, *the first to rule without being formally chosen by the people, but not without their consent and goodwill. After Tarquin's burial he asked the people to endorse his position. He was pronounced king by acclamation and had the decision legally ratified by the Assembly of Voting Districts.* Cicero commented about the division of the people by the previous king Servius into classes from rich to poor. He gave the rich more voting power than the poor. *Thus Servius' system ensured that the mass of the people was neither excluded from the right to vote, nor given too much power, which would have been dangerous. He called the rich 'assudui' and those who had no more than fifteen hundred sestertii or nothing at all to count towards their assessment except their heads, he called them 'proletarii', conveying the idea that they were expected to contribute children [proles], that is to say the country's next generation.*[36]

---

[34] Ibid, p 44.

[35] Ibid, p 46.

[36] Ibid, p 47.

The last king in Rome

The last king in Rome was Tarquinius Superbus who turned into a tyrant and was expelled along with his sons and the entire Tarquin family. Cicero gave a description of this king.

Now this king I'm speaking of had, right from the start, an uneasy conscience; for he was stained with the blood of an excellent king. Terrified, as he was, of paying the ultimate penalty for his crime, he was determined to terrify others. Later on, buoyed up by his conquests and wealth, he allowed his insolence to run riot, being quite unable to control his own behavior or the lusts of his family. Finally his elder son violated Lucretia; and that modest and noble woman punished herself for the outrage by taking her own life. Whereupon, Lucius Brutus, a man of exceptional courage and ability, struck the cruel yoke of harsh servitude from the necks of his fellow-Romans. Though just a private citizen, Brutus took the whole country on his shoulders, and he became the first in this state to show that, when it comes to preserving the people's freedom, no one is just a private citizen. Following his example and leadership, the country was roused by this new complaint on the part of Lucretia's father and relatives, as well as by the memory of Tarquin's arrogance and the many injuries done by him and his sons in the past. As a result, the king himself, along with his sons and the entire Tarquin family, was sent into exile. You see, then, don't you, how a king turned into a despot, and how, by the wickedness of one man, that type of government swung from good to the worst possible. This latter type is represented by the kind of political master, which the Greeks call a 'tyrant'. As soon as the king takes the first step towards a more unjust regime, he at once becomes a tyrant. And that is the foulest and most repellent creature imaginable, and the most abhorrent to God and man alike. Although he has the outward appearance of a man, he outdoes the wildest beasts in the utter savagery of his behavior. He then defines a king: *Our own countrymen have applied the word 'king' to all who have held absolute power over their people on a permanent basis.* [37]

When the two hundred years of monarchy were over (or perhaps a little more, if one takes account of the interregna), and when Tarquin had been expelled, the Romans were gripped with a hatred of the name of king, just as strong as the sense of longing which had gripped them after the death, or rather the departure of Romulus. Then they could not do without a king; now after getting rid of Tarquin, they could not bear the word.

This is the historic basis of the conspiracy by members of the Senate to assassinate Caesar. It should also be pointed out, that despite the sons of two kings assassinating the king who followed their fathers,

---

[37] Ibid, pp 49-50.

that there wasn't a hereditary basis for selection of the Roman kings such as existed in Asia, Egypt and later in England. Tarquinius Superbus, the last king of Rome, was exiled in 509 B.C., a few decades before the time of Coriolanus.

The remaining books 3-6 of *The Republic* are so incomplete it is difficult to read them let alone follow what Cicero intended to communicate. Only the subjects of his remaining books give us a clue. For book 3 the subjects are primarily the 'ideal statesman', and 'justice'. Books 4, 5 and 6 are in a *pitiable state*, according to the editor. We will turn to *The Law,* by Cicero and his final work *On Duties* to find more on the subjects of government and law.

The Law, Book 1

Cicero began his discussion of justice in Book 1 as follows: *But in our present analysis we have to encompass the entire issue of universal justice and law; what we call civil law will be confined to a small, narrow, corner of it. We must clarify the nature of justice, and that has to be deduced from the nature of man. Then we must consider the laws by which states ought to be governed, and finally deal with the laws and enactments, which peoples have compiled and written down.* Cicero continued, (Marcus in the dialogue) --- *For all these reasons I shall look to nature for the origins of justice. She must be our constant guide as our discussion unfolds.*[38]

Marcus spoke of the importance of reason: *law is the highest reason, inherent in nature, which enjoins what ought to be done and forbids the opposite.* Marcus finds the basis of justice in reason, which is related to a divine providence in the universe shared by all men. *Hence this whole universe must be thought of as a single community shared by gods and men. --- Again, the same moral excellence resides in man and in God, and in no other species besides. And moral excellence is nothing other than the completion and perfection of nature.*[39]

Marcus continued: *Nature, too, has not only equipped him with mental agility; she has provided him with senses, which act as his servants and messengers. She has given him as a preliminary outline, dim and not fully developed perceptions of very many things, which form a foundation, as it were, of knowledge. And she has blest him with a versatile physique in keeping with the human mind. For whereas nature made other animals stoop down to feed, she made man alone erect, encouraging him to gaze at the heavens as being, so to speak, akin to him and his original home. She also shaped his facial features so as to express his innermost character. Our eyes tell our emotional state very*

---

[38]   Ibid, p 103-104.

[39]   Ibid, pp 103, 105.

clearly; and what we call the expression, which cannot exist in any creature except in man, indicates our character. I need not mention the faculties and abilities of the rest of the body, such as the control of the voice and the power of speech, which is above all else the promoter of human fellowship.

Marcus continued to express the belief that man is born for justice and that all men are alike and the logical outcome is that they share in not only knowing what justice is but that justice should be applied in the same manner to all people— a concept that has not even yet been realized. He said: *Yes the points which I am now briefly touching on are important but of all the issues dealt with in philosophical debates surely nothing is more vital than the clear realization that we are born for justice, and that what is just is based, not on opinion, but on nature. This will at once become clear if you examine the society of men and their relations to one another. --- Thus, however one defines man, the same definition applies to us all. This is sufficient proof that there is no essential difference within mankind.*[40]

Continuing with the theme that all men share common beliefs in justice*: What community does not love friendliness, generosity, and an appreciative mind which remembers acts of kindness. What community does not reject the arrogant, the wicked, the cruel, and the ungrateful --- yes, and hate them too? So, since the whole human race is seen to be knit together, the final conclusion is that the principles of right living make everyone a better person. --- My whole thesis aims to bring stability to states, steadiness to cities, and well being to communities. So I am anxious not to make a mistake by laying down first principles, which have not been well considered and carefully examined.*[41]

Marcus argued against the idea that fear of punishment is the foundation for good behavior, or that *everything is to be measured by self-interest. If justice is a matter of obeying the written laws and customs of particular communities, and if, as our opponents allege, everything is to be measured by self-interest, then a person will ignore and break the laws when he can, if he thinks it will be to his own advantage. That is why justice is completely non-existent if it is not derived from nature. --- If laws were validated by the orders of peoples, the enactments of politicians, and the verdicts of judges, then it would be just to rob, just to commit adultery, just to introduce forged wills, provided those things were approved by the votes or decrees of the populace. --- Just as true and false, logical and illogical, are judged in their own terms and not by some external criterion, so a consistent mode*

---

[40] Ibid, p 107.

[41] Ibid, pp 108, 110.

of life (which is right) and likewise inconsistency (which is wrong) will be tested by their own nature.[42]

Cicero ended book 1 with a discussion of the 'highest good' based on a review of the ancient philosophers, and follows with the duty of man to know himself: *the person who knows himself will first of all realize that he possess something divine, and he will compare his own inner nature to a kind of holy image placed within a temple. --- And, when that same mind examines the heavens, the earth, the sea, and the nature of all things, and perceives where those things have come from and to where they will return, when and how they are due to die, what part of them is mortal and perishable, and what is divine and everlasting; and when it almost apprehends the very God who governs and rules them, and realizes that it itself is not a resident in some particular locality surrounded by man-made walls, but a citizen of the whole world as though it were a single city; then, in the majesty of these surroundings, in this contemplation and comprehension of nature, great God! How well it will know itself.*[43]

The Law, Book 2

Cicero began Book 2 with a recapitulation of the subject of justice based on natural law and then the dialogues focus on the subject of religion: *I note, then, that according to the opinion of the best authorities,* (the stoics) *law was not thought up by the intelligence of human beings, nor is it some kind of resolution passed by communities, but rather an eternal force which rules the world by the wisdom of its commands and prohibitions. In their judgment, that original and final law is the intelligence of God, who ordains or forbids everything by reason.* The next pages seems to develop a more direct relationship between religion and law, and its relation to reason *fully developed in the wise man,* and the *laws which were devised to ensure the safety of citizens, the security of states, and the peaceful happy life of human beings.*

Well then, as the divine mind is the highest law, so, in the cases of a human being, when reason is fully developed, that is law; and it is fully developed in the mind of the wise man. Those laws, however, which have been formulated in various terms to meet the temporary needs of communities, enjoy the name of laws thanks to popular approval rather than actual fact. We are taught that every law (or at least those which are properly entitled to the name) is praiseworthy by arguments such as these: it is agreed, of course, that laws were devised to ensure the safety of citizens, the security of states, and the peaceful happy life of human

---

[42] Ibid, p 112.

[43] Ibid, p 118, 119.

beings; and that those who first passed such enactments showed their communities that they meant to frame and enact measures which, when accepted and adopted, would allow them to live happy and honorable lives; provisions composed and endorsed in this way would, of course, be given the name of laws. From this it is reasonable to infer that those who framed harmful and unjust rules for their communities, acting in a way quite contrary to their claims and promises, introduced measures which were anything but laws. So when it comes to interpreting the word, it is clear that inherent in the very name of law is the sense and idea of choosing what is just and right. [44]

What of the fact that many harmful and pernicious measures are passed in human communities— measures which come not closer to the name of laws than if a gang of criminals agreed to make some rules? If ignorant unqualified people prescribe a lethal, instead of a healing treatment, that treatment cannot properly be called 'medical'. In a community a law of just any kind will not be a law, even if the people (in The Laws *spite of its harmful character) have accepted it. Therefore law means drawing distinctions between just and unjust, formulated in accordance with that most ancient and most important of all things— nature.*[45]

Book 3 of *The Law* is left for the reader. Most of the content of Book 3 refers to the duties of the magistrates or Roman rulers. These include consuls, praetors, aediles, questors, as well as tribunes, and military dictators at different periods of Roman history as well as some of the laws enacted. At the time *The Republic* was written, Rome was in great turmoil, government was in shambles, and Caesar would soon cross the Rubicon. We shall leave the dialogues of Cicero. One of the nice things about dialogues is that the reader may enter himself into the discussion as a party with a different background than the participants; Marcus, his brother Quintus and Atticus, a patrician favoring the aristocracy. Only Marcus has been quoted from the dialogues. It would be an error to take all of his statements claiming this was Cicero's viewpoint or what he recommended—for Rome or anywhere or anytime somewhere else. Those who favor monarchy or aristocracy will naturally select the content from the dialogues, which support monarchy or aristocracy or some form of a 'mixed constitution' or the need of a military dictator in times of social upheaval. The same is true for the dialogues of Plato, which are a conversation among friends, teacher and students. Dialogues are conversations to stimulate thought and rational discussion of issues, not meant as a final edict or proclamation. What is remarkable with *The Republic* and *The Laws* is that Cicero has presented

---

[44] Ibid, p 125.

[45] Ibid, p 126.

at a time of great disturbances, issues in government and law in support of a democracy, which are relevant even today.

De Officiis (On Duties)

Even greater was Cicero's contribution to the wellspring or the origins of law as we find in his last and perhaps his greatest work, *De Officiis*, On Duties. For Caesar it was sufficient that law came from a supreme commander who was victorious in battle. For Pompey and Caesar the one who held the sword gave the law. In the Preface to *The Republic*, Cicero asked: "What is the source of law? From where did justice, good faith and fair dealing come from?" The answers to his own questions which are highly relevant today, are found in *De Officiis*.

Duty is defined by the entire content of Book 1 of *De Officiis* and is explained by the entire life of an honorable man, as he wishes his son to be by presenting a lifetime of his learning, knowledge and experiences.

The English word for duty does not fit the Latin word officiis as pointed out by the editor of *The Republic* and *The Law*. The English word duty means obedience, compliance to law (as in Blackstone's Commentaries), and payment of taxes. Officium carried the idea of kindly service as well as obligation, as the editor defines it. However, there is much more to it as found in *De Officiis*.

Book 1 starts as a letter from Cicero to his son, whom he had planned to visit before his fateful return to Rome where he delivered his Phillipic orations against Anthony. *Marcus, my son, you have been a pupil of Cratippus for a year already, and that in Athens. Consequently, you ought to be filled to overflowing with philosophical advice and instruction, through the great authority of both teacher and city: the former can improve you with his knowledge, the later by her examples. However, since I myself have always found it beneficial to combine things Latin with things Greek, (something I have done not only in philosophy, but also in the practice of rhetoric), I think you should do the same, that you may be equally capable in either language. --- I strongly urge you, therefore, assiduously to read not only my speeches, but also the philosophical works, which are now almost equal to them.*[46]

Cicero advised his son to follow a life of honor. To determine whether a certain course is honorable, it is necessary to use reason. *Man, however, is a sharer in reason; this enables him to perceive consequences, to comprehend the causes of things, their precursors and their antecedents, so to speak; to compare similarities and to like and*

---

[46] Ibid, p 1-2. De Officiis was written just before the Philippic orations. His son would not follow in his footsteps as he wished. The Roman republic, the occupations of orator in the courts and before the senate, public service as a magistrate would all be eliminated as a result of the military dictators Pompey, Julius Caesar, Anthony and Caesar Augustus. His son Marcus would work in one of the bureaucracies of the Roman Empire.

combine future with present events; and by seeing with ease the whole course of life to prepare whatever is necessary for living it.

Man's relationships to others was stressed: *The same nature, by the power of reason, unites one man to another for the fellowship both of common speech and of life, creating above all a particular love for his offspring. It derives him to desire that men should meet together and congregate, and that he should join them himself; and for the same reason to devote himself to providing whatever may contribute to the comfort and sustenance not only of himself, but also of his wife, his children, and others whom he holds dear and ought to protect. Furthermore, such concern also arouses men's spirits, rendering them greater for achieving whatever they attempt. The honorableness that we seek is created and accomplished. --- The search for truth and its investigation are, above all, peculiar to man. An impulse towards pre-eminence* is related to a *greatness of spirit.* Related is the capacity of man to appreciated beauty: *No other animal, therefore, perceives the beauty, the loveliness and the congruence of the parts, of the things that sight* (and sound) *perceives.* Justice and kindliness are essential to the relationship of man to others.[47]

Justice

Justice is the basis for honor as Cicero commented in Book 2: *For justice is the foundation of lasting commendation and repute. Without it nothing can be worthy of praise*[48]

Justice is a subject which occupies much of De Officiis. *Of justice, the first office is that no man should harm another unless he has been provoked by injustice; the next that one should treat common goods as common and private ones as one's own.* Property law is fundamental to Cicero: *Now no property is private by nature, but rather by long occupation (as when men moved into some empty property in the past), or by victory (when they occupied it by war), or by law, by settlement, by agreement, or by lot. --- What becomes each man's own comes from what had in nature been common, each man should hold onto whatever has fallen to him. If anyone else should seek any of it for himself, he will be violating the law of human fellowship.* Cicero failed to note here that wars lead to taking whatever belongs to others, or booty. The use of the phrase *provoked by injustice* would also justify harm to others. It would be difficult to find where injustice did not prevail in Rome, and in the provinces.

---

[47] Ibid, pp 6-9.

[48] Cicero, On Duties, p 92.

Failing to do anything about known wrongs

Of injustice there are two types: men may inflict injury; or else when it is being inflicted upon others, they may fail to deflect it even though the man who does not defend someone, or obstruct the injustice when he can, is at fault just as if he had abandoned his parents or his friends or his country. The duty to come to the aid of others is further elaborated. Those who retire in intellectual pursuits or private life and ignore the plight of other men are criticized. *For neglecting to defend others and deserting one's duty there tend to be several causes of this. For some men do not wish to incur enmities, or toil, or expense; others are hindered by indifference, laziness, inactivity or some pursuits or business of their own, to the extent that they allow the people whom they ought to protect to be abandoned. --- They observe one type of justice, indeed, that they should harm no one else by inflicting injury, but they fail in another --- they abandon those whom they ought to protect. --- Such men abandon the fellowship of life, because they contribute to it nothing of their devotion, nothing of their effort, nothing of their means. --- In most cases, however, men set about committing injustice in order to secure something that they desire: where this fault is concerned avarice is extremely widespread. In men of greater spirit, however, the desire for wealth has as its goal influence and the opportunity to gratify others.*[49] As for injustice: *There are two ways in which injustice may be done, either through force or through deceit; and deceit seems to belong to a little fox, force to a lion. Both of them seem most alien to a human being; but deceit deserves a greater hatred. And out of all injustice, nothing deserves punishment more than that of men who, just at the time when they are most betraying trust, act in such a way that they might appear to be good men.*

Greed

Cicero continues to enlarge on the theme of greed and avarice. *The result of such things is that desire for money has become unlimited. Such expansion of one's personal wealth, as harms no one is not, of course, to be disparaged; but committing injustice must always be avoided.* Cicero used Crassus and Caesar, who, along with Pompey, were self-appointed members of the triumvirate, as examples. *The rash behavior of Gaius Caesar has recently made that clear: he overturned all the laws of gods and men for the sake of the pre-eminence that he had imagined for himself in his mistaken fancy.*[50] Plutarch in his chapter on Marcus Crassus begins as follows: *People were wont to say that the many virtues of Crassus were darkened by the one vice of avarice, and*

---

[49] Ibid, pp 10-11.

[50] Ibid, p 11.

indeed he seemed to have no other but that; for it being the most predominant, obscured others to which he was inclined. The arguments in proof of his avarice were the vastness of his estate, and the manner of raising it.[51] The biographical notes to *De Officiis* cite a number of references to Cicero's scathing criticism of Crassus' greed- in *De Finibus* (written in 45), attributing his desire for command to greed, which for Crassus was a means to political influence. The same applied even more to Caesar whose political fortunes came from bloodshed and plunder.

Do no harm

Cicero elsewhere sums up man's relationship to others by the principle *do no harm:--- the fundamentals of justice that I laid down at the beginning: first that one should harm no one; and secondly that one serve the common advantage.*[52]

The final rule in providing kind services and personal assistance is to fight neither against fairness, nor on behalf of injustice. For justice is the foundation of lasting commendation and repute. Without it nothing can be worthy of praise.[53]

Public service

Cicero returned often to the relationship of man to the community. *First is something that is seen in the fellowship of the entire human race. For its bonding consists of reason and speech, which reconcile men to one another, through teaching, learning, communicating, debating and making judgments, and unite them in a kind of natural fellowship. For since it is by nature common to all animals that they have a drive to procreate, the first fellowship exists within marriage itself, and the next with one's children. Then, there is the one house in which everything is shared. Indeed that is the principle of a city and the seedbed, as it were, of a political community.* The political community extends from parents, children, brothers and other family and marital relations to people of similar backgrounds and interests. *--- Important also are the common bonds that are created by kindnesses reciprocally given and received, which, provided that they are mutual and gratefully received, bind together those concerned in an unmistakable fellowship.*

But when you have surveyed everything with reason and spirit, of all fellowships none is more serious, and none dearer, than that of each of us with the republic. Parents are dear, and children, relatives

---

[51] Plutarch, Lives, v 1, pa 724.

[52] Cicero, On Duties, p 13.

[53] Ibid, 92.

and acquaintances are dear, but our country has on its own embraced the affections of all of us.[54]

Cicero appealed to the loftiness of spirit, the man who will enter public life in the service of his community or country. He cautioned against desire for fame and glory as a motivation to enter politics. *Beware of the desire for glory, as I have said. For it destroys the liberty for which men of great spirit ought to be in competition.* Cicero advocates that the politician should not work for and support only some of the *citizens and neglecting others,* since *they bring upon the city the ruinous condition of unrest and strife. Few are Champions of everyone. --- He will devote himself entirely to the republic, pursuing neither wealth nor power, and will protect the whole in such a way that the interest of none is disregarded.* [55]

Those who are equipped by nature to administer affairs must abandon any hesitation over winning office and engage in public life. For only in this way can either the city be ruled or greatness of spirit be displayed. But Cicero advises: *Before you approach any business, thorough preparations must be made.* And at a time in Rome when the only way to obtain political office was to serve as a military commander he told his son that *many achievements of civic life have proved greater and more famous than those of war.* At a time when physical prowess and strength was regarded as a prerequisite to glory Cicero advised his son: *That honorableness that we seek from a lofty and magnificent spirit is in general produced not by bodily strength, but by strength of spirit.*

Cicero continued: *It is the mark of a truly brave and constant spirit that one remain unperturbed in difficult times, and when agitated not be thrown, as the saying goes, off one's feet, but rather hold fast to reason, with one's spirit and counsel ready to hand. That is the mark of a great spirit; but his is the mark also of great intellectual talent: to anticipate the future by reflection, deciding somewhat before hand how things could go in either direction, and what should be done in either event, never acting so that one will need to say, 'I had not thought of that'. Such is the work of a spirit not only great and lofty but also relying on good sense and good counsel. ---*

In general those who are about to take charge of public affairs should hold fast to Plato's two pieces of advice: first to fix their gaze so firmly on what is beneficial to the citizens that whatever they do, they do with that in mind, forgetful of their own advantage. Secondly, let them care for the whole body of the republic rather than protect one part and neglect the rest.[56]

---

[54] Ibid, pp 21,23

[55] Ibid, p 34.

[56] Ibid, pp 29,31, and 32.

Book II of De Officiis

Cicero began book II with personal reflections: *Next I must pursue the classes of duties that relate to civilized living and to the availability of the influence and wealth that men find beneficial. ---For my part, when the republic was being run by the men to whom it had entrusted itself, I devoted all my concern and all my thoughts to it. But then a single man (Caesar) came to dominate everything, there was no longer any room for consultation or for personal authority, and finally I lost my allies in preserving the republic, excellent men as they were. Then I did not surrender to the grief that would have overwhelmed me had I not fought it, nor to pleasures unworthy of an educated man.*

I only wish that the republic had remained in its original condition, rather than fall into the hands of men (Antony and Caesar's supporters) greedy not merely for change, but for revolution. For first I would be devoting myself to action rather than writing, as I used to when the republic was standing. Secondly, it would be my own speeches rather than my present subject matter that I would be putting on paper, as I have often done before. All my care, all my thought, all my effort, used to be directed towards the republic; when that ceased completely to exist, than inevitable legal and senatorial speeches ceased to flow from my pen.

But my mind could not be entirely inactive. Therefore, as I was versed in such studies from my youth, I thought that I could most honorably set aside my troubles by turning to philosophy. I had spent much time on this as a young man for the sake of education. Later I began to take up the honorable burden of public office, and gave myself completely to public life. Now the only time I had for philosophy was that which I could spare after seeing to the needs of my friends and of the republic. All of that was used up in reading; I had no leisure for writing.

From the greatest of evils I seem still to have salvaged a little good: I now have the chance to put into writing ideas that were not familiar enough to my countrymen, but most worthy of knowing. In heaven's name, what is more desirable, what more distinguished than wisdom? What is better for a man, what more worthy of a man? Those who seek it are called philosophers, and philosophy, if you want to translate it, is nothing other than the pursuit of wisdom. Wisdom, according to the definition of the philosophers of old, is the knowledge of everything divine and human, and of the causes which regulate them. If anyone despises the pursuit of that, it is difficult to see what on earth he would see fit to praise.[57]

---

[57] Ibid, pp 63-65.

From Book 2, Cicero portends the results of a tyrant's rule. *But there is nothing at all more suited to protecting and retaining influence than to be loved, and nothing less suited than to be feared. --- Indeed no amount of influence can withstand the hatred of a large number of men. --- Fear is a poor guardian over any length of time; but goodwill keeps faithful guard forever. --- For those who wish to be feared cannot but themselves be afraid of the very men who fear them. --- Nor is there any military power so great that it can last for long under the weight of fear.*

Cicero, after noting the tyrannical rule of Sulla and Caesar, and that only the walls of the city remain standing, provides the result of the rule of tyrants by fear. *The republic we have utterly lost. And we have fallen into this disaster - for I must return to my proposition - because we prefer to be feared than to be held dear and loved.*

Book III

From book III, Cicero portends his ultimate fate resulting form his open approval of Caesar's assassination and especially after he had delivered his Philippics against Antony: *For I pursue leisure because I am barred from public life and from legal business by the force of accursed arms, and for the same reason I have left the city. Wandering around the countryside now, I am frequently alone. --- But my leisure was determined by scarcity of business, not by my eagerness to rest; for when the senate has been suppressed and the law courts destroyed, what is there worthy of me that I can do in the senate house or in the forum? Thus I, who once lived surrounded by crowds and under the gaze of the citizens, now hide myself as much as possible, fleeing the sight of wicked men, with whom every place overflows; I am often alone. --- Therefore I make use of my leisure - though it is not the leisure that a man deserves who once secured repose for the city - and I do not allow my solitude to grow idle, although necessity rather than willingness brought it upon me. --- I have directed all my devotion and concern towards this type of literary work. As a result, I have written more in the short time since the overthrow of the republic than in the many years while it stood.*[58] He delivered his First Philippic Oration against Anthony September 2.

The murder of Cicero

This chapter began with the barbarous end to the life of Cicero, at the command of Anthony, Caesar Octavius, and Lepidus. It ends with the gruesome murder of Cicero. From Plutrarch: *After passing through a variety of confused and uncertain counsels, at last he let his servants carry him by sea to Capitae, where he had a house, an agreeable place to retire to in the heat of summer, when the Etesian winds are so*

---

[58] Ibid, pp 101, 102. Note. Cicero completed *De Officiis* in 44 B.C. Cicero returned to Rome August 31, 44 B.C.

pleasant. --- But in the meantime the assassins were come with a band of soldiers, Herennius, a centurion, and Popillius, a tribune. --- And Cicero, perceiving Herennius running in the walks, commanded his servants to set down the litter; and stroking his chin, as he used to do, with his left hand, he looked steadfastly upon his murderers, his person covered with dust, his beard and hair untrimmed, and his face worn with his troubles. So that the greatest part of those that stood by covered their faces whilst Herennius slew him. And thus was he murdered, stretching forth his neck out of the litter, being now in his sixty-fourth year. Herennius cut off his head, and, by Anthony's command, his hands also, by which his Philippics were written; for so Cicero styled those orations he wrote against Anthony, and so they are called to this day.[59]

And so ended the life of Cicero, who in this writer's opinion was a remarkable human being the Romans and all could be proud of. Not so with the men presented in the next six chapters, from Augustus including a continued account of Antony, to Nero and the Civil Wars.[60]

---

[59] Plutarch, vol 2, p 440, 441.

[60] The reader may opt to avoid these next six chapters and turn to Chapter 11 to the history of England, from its ancient sources to George III.

Chapter 5
Augustus

Gaius Octavianus, or Octavian, later named Augustus by the senate, (b. 63 B.C, d. 14 A.D.) was the first emperor of Rome. He ruled from 31 B.C. to 14 A.D. Julius Caesar adopted Octavian as his son and made him heir to the empire. He was only eighteen years old at the time when news then came that Caesar had been assassinated. As Caesar's heir Octavian had the support of the veterans who served under Caesar. The senate made Octavian a senator and favored his participation in the war against Anthony. With the defeat of Anthony at Mutina, Octavian's soldiers forced the senate to make Octavian consul. There followed a triumvirate of Octavian, Anthony and Lepidus. The civil wars continued from 43 B.C. to the final victory over Anthony in 31 B.C. Octavian then became the undisputed ruler of the Roman Empire. After 27 B.C. he was called Caesar Augustus by proclamation of the Roman Senate. Perhaps no one has had more illustrious titles or a more elaborate mythology. The precedents of Augustus would influence emperors and the Roman Empire for the next 300 years.

Plutarch did not include Augustus in his *Lives of the Noble Grecians and Romans*. Tacitus, from the *Annals of Imperial Rome*, provided an introduction to his brief history of Augustus. *Famous writers have recorded Rome's early glories and disasters. The Augustan Age, too, had its distinguished historians. But then the rising tide of flattery exercised a deterrent effect.[1] The reigns of Tiberius, Gaius, Claudius, and Nero were described during their lifetimes in fictitious terms, for fear of the consequences, whereas the accounts written after their deaths were influenced by still raging animosities. So I have decided to say a little about Augustus, with special attention to his last period, and then go on to the reign of Tiberius and what followed. I shall write without*

---

[1] Note. Perhaps Tacitus is referring to men like Virgil, Livy, and Horace who in their literary works were supporters, or even propagandists of Augustus.

indignation or partisanship: in my case the customary incentives to these are lacking.[2]

Family history, Birth, early life

Gaius Octavius, later Octavianus, then Augustus, (b. 63 B.C., d. A.D. 14), was born at Veltrae, his family's estate. Seutonius provided the paternal ancestry of Gaius Octavius. *The grandfather of Augustus, Gaius, was the first Octavian elected to office by the popular vote— he won a questorship. His sons Gnaeus and Gaius fathered two very different branches of the family. Gnaeus descendants held all the highest offices of state in turn, but Gaius' branch, either by accident or choice, remained simple knights until the entry into the Senate of Augustus' father. This information is given by others; it is not derived from Augustus' own memoirs, which merely record that he came of 'a rich old equestrian family', and that his father had been the first Octavian to enter the Senate.* His mother Atia was the daughter of Julius Caesar's sister Julia, which we shall henceforth call Julia I, to distinguish between others named Julia in this family.[3]

Octavian was born, 63 B.C., at Velitrae, Italy, which is located about 25 miles southeast of Rome. His father died in 59 when Octavian was only four years old. *Gaius died suddenly on his return to Rome, before he could stand as a candidate for the consulship. He left three children: Octavia the Elder, Octavia the Younger and Octavian; the Mother of Octavia the Elder was Ancharia; the other two were his children by Atia, daughter of Marcus Atius Balbus and Julius Caesar's sister Julia.*[4] The cause of death of his father is not stated. Little is said about his mother Atia, except that she died when Octavian was 20 years old. Only hints of his education are mentioned by Seutonius: *Even in his boyhood Augustus had studied rhetoric with great eagerness and industry, and during the Mutina campaign, busy though he was, is said to have read, written, and declaimed daily.*[5] No dates are given for the following: *He had ambitions to be as proficient in Greek as in Latin, and did very well at it. His tutor was Apollodorus of Pergamum, who accompanied him to Apollonia, though a very old man, and taught him elocution. Afterwards Augustus spent some time with Areus the philosopher, and his sons Dionysius and Nicanor, who broadened his general education; but never learned to speak Greek with real fluency,*

---

[2] Tacitus, The Annals of Imperial Rome, Chapter 1, *From Augustus to Tiberius* pp 31-32.

[3] See table, The Julian House

[4] Seutonius, The Twelve Caesars, p 55.

and never ventured on any Greek literary composition. He greatly enjoyed the Old Comedy, and often put plays of that period on the stage.[6]

Early Military Career

At sixteen, having now come of age, he was awarded military decorations when Caesar celebrated his African triumph, though he had been too young for overseas service, Caesar then went to fight Pompey's sons in Spain; Augustus followed with a very small escort, along roads held by the enemy, after a shipwreck, too, and in a state of semi-convalescence from a serious illness. This action delighted Caesar, who, moreover, soon formed a high estimate of Augustus' character quite apart from the energetic manner in which he had made the journey. Having recovered possession of the Spanish provinces, Caesar planned a war against the Dacians and Parthians, and sent Augustus ahead to Apollonia, in Illyria, where he spent his time studying Greek literature.

Accession

News then came that Caesar had been assassinated. Caesar had made him *his heir, and Augustus was tempted, for a while, to put himself under the protection of the troops quartered near by. However, deciding that this would be rash and premature, he returned to Rome, and there entered upon his inheritance, despite his mother's doubts and the active opposition of his step-father, Marcius Philippus, the ex-Consul.* He was only eighteen years old. Caesar had adopted Octavian as his son in 44 B.C. As Caesar's heir Octavian had the support of the veterans who served under Caesar. Octavian was Caesar's man, having been adopted by him and learning early in life the traditions of the military establishment, which Caesar had established in his foreign and civil wars. Octavian would also ally himself with the Senate initially to contest Anthony. The senate made Octavian a senator and asked him to join the campaign of Mutina against Anthony. From Seutonius: *The senate awarded him praetorian rank, gave him the command of this army, and instructed him to join Hirtius and Pansa, the two new Consuls, in lending aid to Decimus Brutus. Augustus brought the campaign to a successful close within three months, after fighting a couple of battles. However, when Augustus heard that Mark Anthony had been taken under Lepidus' protection and that the other military commanders, supported by their troops, were coming to terms with these two, he at once deserted the senatorial party.*[7]

---

[5] Ibid, p 100.

[6] Ibid, p 100.

[7] Ibid, p 59.

The Tiumvirate and the Civil Wars

Octavian reached an agreement with Anthony and Lepidus on November 27, 43 B.C. They were given five-year appointments as dictators and triumvirs. One of their first acts of revenge was the murder of 300 senators and 2000 knights, equestrians. The brutal murder and disposition of Cicero by Anthony has been told in the previous chapter. With the recognition of Julius Caesar as a God, Octavian was recognized as the son of a God, in January 42 B.C. The forces garnered by the triumvirate were then directed at the assassins of Julius Caesar— Brutus and Cassius at Phillipi.

As a member of a triumvirate consisting of Anthony, Lepidus, and himself, Augustus defeated Brutus and Cassius at Philippi, though in ill health at the time. In the first of the two battles fought he was driven out of his camp, and escaped with some difficulty to Anthony's command. After the second and decisive one he showed no clemency to his beaten enemies, but sent Brutus' head to Rome for throwing at the feet of Caesar's divine image; and insulted the more distinguished of his prisoners. When one of these humbly asked for the right of decent burial, he got the cold answer: 'That must be settled with the carrion-birds'. And when a father and his son pleaded for their lives, Augustus, it is said, told them to decide which of the two should be spared, by casting lots or playing morra (a game). The father sacrificed for the son, and was executed; the son then committed suicide; Augustus watched them both die. His conduct so disgusted the remainder of the prisoners, including Marcus Favonius, a well-known imitator of Cato's, that while being led off in chains they courteously saluted Antony as Imperator, but abused Augustus to his face with the most obscene epithets.

The victors divided between them the responsibilities of government. Antony undertook to pacify the eastern provinces if Augustus led the veterans back to Italy and settled them on municipal lands. At the treaty of Brundisium Octavian received control of the west and Italy while the east went to Anthony. Lepidus was allowed to retain control of Africa.

There followed war against the brother of Anthony at Perusia, approximately 85 miles north of Rome. *After the fall of the city* (Perusia) *Augustus took vengeance on crowds of prisoners and returned the same answer to all who sued for pardon or tried to explain their presence among the rebels. It was simply: 'You must die!' According to some historians, he chose 300 prisoners of equestrian or senatorial rank, and offered them on the Ides of March at the altar of the God Julius, as human sacrifices.*[8]

Octavian waged war against Sextus Pompey. Disaster followed. Historians concur that Augustus was not a good commander. *The Sicilian*

---

[8] Ibid, p 59-60.

war, one of his first enterprises, lasted for eight years (43-36 B.C.). It was interrupted by two storms that wrecked his fleets - in the summer, too - and obliged him to rebuild them; and by the Pompeians' success in cutting his grain supplies, which forced him to grant a popular demand for an armistice. At last, however, he built an entirely new fleet, with 20,000 freed slaves trained as oarsmen, and formed the Julian harbor at Baiae by letting the sea into the Lucrine and Avernan lakes. Here he exercised his crews all one winter and, when the sailing season opened, defeated Sextus Pompey off the Sicilian coast between Mylae and Naulochus. Credit for the victory has been awarded to Agrippa, rather than Octavian. --- *It would be safe to say that the Sicilian was by far his most dangerous campaign.*[9]

Octavian arranged the marriage of his sister Octavia to Anthony, who had spent the previous winter with Cleopatra in Egypt. *However, Augustus failed to satisfy either the landowners, who complained that they were being evicted from their estates; or the veterans, who felt entitled to better rewards for their service.*[10] The triumvirate ended with the exile of Lepidus, leaving Anthony and Octavian contending for the supreme command. *Lepidus, the third member of the triumvirate, whom Augustus had summoned from Africa to his support, thought himself so important as the commander of twenty legions that, when Sextus Pompey had been beaten, he demanded the highest place in the government with terrible threats. Augustus deprived him of his legions and, though successfully pleading for his life, Lepidus spent what was left of it in permanent exile at Circeii.*

Defeat and Death of Anthony and Cleopatra

Soon Octavian would contend with Anthony, but first he would become victorious in three military campaigns in Illyricum and Dalmatia, (presently Bosnia, Croatia, Montenegro and Yugoslavia) between 35 and 33. Anthony divorced Octavia, and Octavian obtained Anthony's will, which contained damaging evidence of Cleopatra's influence over Anthony. In 32 Octavian declared war, with support from the senate, not against Anthony, but against Cleopatra. *Eventually Augustus broke his friendship with Mark Anthony, which had always been a tenuous one and in continuous need of patching; and sought to prove that his rival had failed to conduct himself as befitted a Roman citizen, by ordering the will he had deposited at Rome to be opened and publicly read. It listed among Anthony's heirs the children fathered by him on Cleopatra.*[11]   From

---

[9] Ibid, p 61.

[10] Ibid, pp 59-60.

[11] Ibid, p 62.

Plutarch: *Caesar Octavian made preparations for declaring war against Cleopatra and depriving Anthony of his authority over Cleopatra. Anthony was so dependant on Cleopatra, that although knowing of his superiority of land forces, he agreed with Cleopatra to engage in a naval contest with Caesar. While Anthony lay with his fleet near Actium, Caesar seized upon this opportunity to engage him in combat. Several important commanders of Anthony and Cleopatra deserted to Caesar Octavian or were in favor of a land battle rather than rely on the naval forces, which were unready. But for all this, Cleopatra prevailed that a sea-fight should determine all, having already an eye to flight, and ordering all her affairs, not so as to assist in gaining a victory, but to escape with the greatest safety from the first commencement of a defeat.[12]* Cleopatra's ships left the scene of battle and Anthony followed. *But at Actium, his* (Anthony's) *fleet, after a long resistance to Caesar, and suffering the most damage from a heavy sea that set in right ahead, --- gave up the contest, with the loss of not more than five thousand killed, and three-hundred ships taken, as Caesar himself has recorded. Only a few had known of Anthony's flight; and those who were told of it couldn't at first give any belief to so incredible a thing as that a general who had nineteen entire legions and twelve thousand horse upon the seashore, could abandon all and fly away.[13]* Caesar Octavian defeated Anthony's forces at Actium, on September 2, 31 B.C. on the west coast of Greece. Anthony, by his own hand, thrust a sword into his belly. The wound was not immediately fatal. Cleopatra, and two of her women, hoisted Anthony into her quarters. Anthony breathed his last, as one of Caesar's men arrived. Cleopatra's made elaborate preparations for her own suicide. The stories vary regarding the cause of her death, but Caesar, disappointed with her death, *in his triumph, carried a figure of Cleopatra, with an asp clinging to her.* Cleopatra died in August 30 B.C. *She lived thirty-nine years, twenty-two of which she had reigned as queen, and for fourteen had been Anthony's partner in his empire.[14] Augustus had Caesarion, Julius Caesar's son by Cleopatra, overtaken, and killed him when captured. --- Augustus turned the kingdom of Egypt into a Roman province; and then, to increase its fertility and its yield of grain for the Roman market, sent troops to clean out the irrigation canals of the Nile Delta which had silted up after many years neglect. To*

---

[12] Plutarch, vol 2, p 520.

[13] Ibid, p 523.

[14] Ibid, 533, 534.

*perpetuate the glory of his victory at Actium, he founded a city close to
the scene of the battle and named it Necropolis- or 'City of Victory.'*[15]

Summaries of the triumvirate and civil wars

Tacitus provided a brief summary of the triumvirate at the
beginning of his Chapter *From Augustus to Tiberius* as follows: *The
violent deaths of Brutus and Cassius left no Republican forces in the
field. Defeat came to Sextus Pompeius in Sicily, Lepidus was dropped,
Antony killed. So even the Caesarian party had no leader left except the
'Caesar' himself, Octavian. He gave up the title of Triumvir,
emphasizing instead his position as consul; and the powers of a tribune,
he proclaimed, were good enough for him— powers for the protection of
ordinary people.*

*He seduced the army with bonuses, and his cheap food policy
was successful bait for civilians. Indeed, he attracted everybody's
goodwill by the enjoyable gift of peace. Then he gradually pushed ahead
and absorbed the functions of the senate, the officials, and even the law.
Opposition did not exist. War or judicial murder had disposed of all men
of spirit. Upper-class survivors found that slavish obedience was the way
to succeed, both politically and financially. They had profited from the
revolution, and so now they liked the security of the existing arrangement
better than the dangerous uncertainties of the old regime. Besides, the
new order was popular in the provinces. There, government by Senate
and People was looked upon skeptically as a matter of sparring
dignitaries and extortionate officials. The legal system had provided no
remedy against these, since it was wholly incapacitated by violence,
favoritism, and, most of all, bribery.*[16]

From Seutonius: *For ten years Augustus remained a member of
the Triumvirate commissioned to reorganize the Government, and though
at first opposing his colleagues' plan for proscriptions, yet, once this had
been decided upon, carried it out more ruthlessly than either of them.
They often relented under the pressure of personal influence, or when the
intended victims appealed for pity; Augustus alone demanded that no one
was to be spared, and even added to the list of proscribed persons the
name of his guardian Gaius Toranius, who had been an aedile at the
same time as his father Octavius. Julius Saturniunus has more to say on
this subject: when the proscription was over and Marcus Lepidus, in an
address to the house, justified the severe measures that had been taken
but encouraged the hope that greater leniency would now be shown,
since enough blood had been shed, Augustus spoke in a quite opposite*

---

[15] Seutonius, p 63.

[16] Tacitus, Annals, p 32.

sense, "I consented to close the list,' he said, 'on the condition that I should be allowed a free hand in future.' [17]

Emperor

As emperor Augustus was the sole ruler in 31 B.C. to 14 A.D. He was commander in chief of the army, had the sole right to make war and peace, controlled the grain supply of Rome, spoke first in the Senate and nominated or approved the candidacy of Roman citizens for high public office. After the death of Lepidus in 12 B.C. he was Pontifex maximus or high priest. Augustus had now become the sole ruler of the Roman world and established the Greco-Roman principate, a system of government, which gave him complete control. Augustus controlled the senate and the members of the extensive bureaucracies in the provinces. Part of his success, according to historians was his marriage to Livia in 38 B.C., a significant link to the aristocracy.

Tacitus provides two opinions regarding the person of Augustus and his methods of gaining and retaining power. *Then there was much discussion of Augustus himself. Most people were struck by meaningless points such as the coincidence between the dates of his first public office and his death, and the fact that he died in the same house and room at Nola as his father, Gaius Octavius. There was also talk about his numerous consulships- which equaled the combined totals of Marcus Valerius Corvus and Gaius Marius - of his tribune's power continuous for thirty-seven years, of the twenty-one times he was hailed as victor, and or his other honors, traditional or novel, single or repeated. Intelligent people praised or criticized him in varying terms. One opinion was as follows. Filial duty and a national emergency, in which there was no place for law-abiding conduct, had driven him to civil war— and this can be neither initiated nor maintained by decent methods. He had made many concessions to Anthony and Lepidus for the sake of vengeance on his father's murderers. When Lepidus grew old and lazy, and Anthony's self indulgence got the better of him, the only possible cure for the distracted country had been government by one man. However, Augustus had put the State in order not by making himself king or dictator but by creating the Principate. The empire's frontiers were on the ocean, or distant rivers. Armies, provinces, fleets, the whole system was interrelated. Roman citizens were protected by the law. Provincials were decently treated. Rome itself had been lavishly beautified. Force had been sparingly used— merely to preserve the peace for the majority.*

The opposite view went like this. Filial duty and national crises had been merely pretexts. In actual fact, the motive of Octavian, the future Augustus, was lust for power. Inspired by that, he had mobilized ex-army settlers by gifts of money, and raised an army. He was only a

---

[17] Seutonius, p 68.

half-grown boy without any official status, and won over a consuls's brigades by bribery. He pretended to support Sextus Pompeius, and by senatorial decrees usurped the status and rank of a praetor. Soon both consuls, Gaius Vibius Pansa and Aurlus Hirtius, had met their deaths— by enemy action; or perhaps in the one case by the deliberate poisoning of his wound, and in the other at the hand of his own troops, instigated by Octavian. In any case it was he who took over both their armies. Then he had forced the reluctant senate to make him consul. But the forces given him to deal with Anthony he used against the State. His judicial murders and land distributions were distasteful even to those who carried them out. True, Cassius and Brutus died because he had inherited a feud against them; nevertheless, personal enmities ought to be sacrificed to the public interest. Next he had cheated Sextus Pompeius by a spurious peace treaty, Lepidus by spurious friendship. Then Anthony, enticed by the treaties of Tarentum and Brundusium and his marriage with Octavian's sister, had paid the penalty of that delusive relationship with his life. After that, there followed the disasters of Marcus Lollius and Publius Quinctillius Varus; and there were the assassinations, for example, of Aulus Terentius Varro Murena, Marcus Ignatius Rurus and Iullus Antonius.

And gossip did not spare his personal affairs— how he had abducted the wife (Livia) *of Tiberius Claudius Nero, and asked the priests the farcical question whether it was in order for her to marry while pregnant. But Livia was a real catastrophe, to the nation, as a mother and to the house of the Caesars as a stepmother. Besides, critics continued, Augustus seemed to have superseded the worship of the gods when he wanted to have himself venerated in temples, with god-like images, by priests and ministers.*[18]

Military operations

Augustus introduced many reforms into the Army, besides reviving certain obsolete practices, and exacted the strictest discipline. He grudged even his generals home-leave to visit their wives, and granted this only during the winter. --- He gave the entire Tenth legion an ignominious discharge because of their insolent behavior, and when some other legions also demanded their discharge in a similarly riotous manner he disbanded them, withholding the bounty, which they would have earned had they continued loyal. If a cohort broke in battle, Augustus ordered the survivors to draw lots, then executed every tenth man, and fed the remainder on barley bread instead of the customary wheat ration. Centurions found absent from their posts were sentenced to death.[19]

---

[18] Tacitus, Annals, pp 37-39.

[19] Seutonius, p 66.

After Augustus became emperor, there continued wars and military operations in the frontier provinces. In 23 B.C. Alpine tribes were laid waste. Galatia (in Asia Minor) was annexed. Augustus completed the conquest of Spain, in 23 B.C. but became ill. In 19 B.C. Agrippa completed the subjugation of Spain. He visited Gaul, and the near conquest of Germany to the Elbe was accomplished. After the defeat in 9 A.D. of Quintillus Varus in Germany, the possibility of an Elbe frontier was abandoned, and the Rhine and Danube became the Roman boundaries. Tiberius and his brother Drusus senior were commanders. Tiberius was successful in Armenia, Parthia, Germany, Spain, Dalmatia, the Alps, and France. Drusus was successful in the Alps, France, the Low Countries, and especially in Germany. The provinces of Rhaetia, Noricum, Illyricum, and Pannonia were annexed to the empire. After the deaths of Anthony and Cleopatra, Egypt was annexed and reorganized. An agreement was reached with Parthia in 20 B.C. and the legionary standards captured from Crassus 33 years earlier were returned. Judea was annexed in 6 A.D.

Julia, daughter of Augustus

The only child of Augustus acknowledged by historians was Julia, with the designation Julia III to differentiate between Julia I, Julius Caesar's sister, and Julia II, daughter of Julius Caesar and Cornelia. Julia II, as noted in the chapter on Julius Caesar, had died in childbirth when married to Pompey.

Augustus' daughter Julia III had previously married her cousin Marcellus. Marcellus was the son of Augustus's sister Octavia and her first husband. Marcellus and Julia had no children by this marriage. After the death of Marcellus, Julia married M. Agrippa. Augustus *singled out Marcus Agrippa, a commoner but a first-rate soldier who had helped to win his victories, by the award of two consecutive consulships. After the death of Marcellus, Agrippa was chosen by Augustus, as his son in law.*[20] There were three sons and two daughters by this marriage, all grandchildren of Augustus.

Julia III bore Agrippa three sons, Gaius, Lucius, and Agrippa Posthumus; and two daughters, Julia IV, the younger, and Agrippina the Elder. Augustus married Julia IV to Licius Paulus whose father, of the same name, was Censor; and Agrippina to Germanicus, the grandson of his sister (Octavia). *He then adopted Gaius and Lucius, and brought them up at the Palace; after buying them from Agrippa by a token sale. He trained his new sons in the business of government while they were still young, sending them as commanders-in-chief to the provinces when only Consuls-elect.*

---

[20] Tacitus, Annals, p 32.

The education of his daughter Julia and grand-daughters included even spinning and weaving; they were forbidden to say or do anything, either publicly or in private, that could not decently figure in the imperial day-book. He took severe measures to prevent them forming friendships without his consent, and once wrote to Lucius Vinicius, a young man of good family and conduct: 'you were very ill-mannered to visit my daughter at Baiae.'

His satisfaction with the success of his family and its training was, however, suddenly dashed by Fortune. He came to the conclusion that the Elder and the Younger Julia had both been indulging in every sort of vice; and banished them. When Gaius then died in Lycia, and Lucius eighteen months later at Massilia, Augustus publicly adopted his remaining grandchild, Agrippa Postumus and, at the same time, his stepson Tiberius; a special bill to legalize this act was passed in the Forum. Yet he soon disinherited Postumus, whose behavior had lately been vulgar and brutal, and packed him off to Surrentum, on the Italian west coast below Naples, near Capri. Tacitus implicates Livia in his own account: *There were Agrippa's sons Gaius Caesar and Lucius Caesar. --- After Agrippa had died, first Lucius Caesar and then Gaius Caesar met with premature natural deaths— unless their stepmother Livia had a secret hand in them. Lucius died on his way to the armies in Spain, Gaius while returning from Armenia incapacitated by a wound. --- Livia had the aged Augustus firmly under control— so much so; that he exiled his only surviving grandson to the island of Planasia,* modern Corsica.. *Though devoid of every good quality, he had been involved in no scandal.*[21]

Continuing with Seutonius: *When members of his family died, Augustus bore his loss with far more resignation than when they disgraced themselves. The deaths of Gaius and Lucius did not break his spirit; but after discovering his daughter Julia's adulteries, he refused to see visitors for some time. He wrote a letter about her case to the Senate, staying at home while a quaestor read it to them. He even considered her execution; at any rate, hearing that on Phoebe, a freedwoman in Julia's confidence, had hanged herself, he cried: 'I should have preferred to be Phoebe's father!' Julia was forbidden to drink wine or enjoy any other luxury during her exile; and denied all male company, whether free or servile, except by Augustus's special permission and after he had been given full particulars of the applicant's age, height, complexion, and of any distinguishing marks of his body— such as moles or scars. He kept Julia for five years on a prison island before moving her to the mainland, where she received somewhat milder treatment. Yet nothing would persuade him to forgive his daughter; and when the Roman people interceded several times on her behalf, earnestly pleading for her recall,*

---

[21] Ibid, p 33.

he stormed at a popular assembly; 'If you ever bring up this matter again, may the gods curse you with daughters and wives like mine!' While in exile Julia the Younger gave birth to a child, which Augustus refused to allow to be acknowledged or reared. Because Agrippa Posthumus' conduct, so far from improving, grew daily more irresponsible, he was transferred to an island, and held there under military surveillance. Augustus then asked the Senate to pass a decree making Postumus' banishment permanent; but whenever his name, or that of either Julia, came up in conversation he would sigh deeply, and sometimes quote a line from the Iliad:

'Ah, never to have married, and childless to have died!'²²

In his will: *He had given orders that 'should anything happen' to his daughter Julia, or his grand-daughter of the same name, 'their bodies must be excluded from the mausoleum.'²³*

Health of Augustus

Augustus was not a physically well man. He reportedly suffered from a number of disorders, which would be difficult to understand today from the ancient descriptions.

His body is said to have been marred by blemishes of various sores— a constellation of seven birthmarks on his chest and stomach, exactly corresponding in form, order, and number with the Great Bear; and a number of hard, dry patches suggesting ringworm, caused by an itching of his skin and a too frequent and vigorous use of the scraper at the baths. He had a weakness in his left hip, thigh, and leg, which occasionally gave him the suspicion of a limp; but this was improved by the sand-and-reed treatment. Sometimes the forefinger of his right hand would be so numbed and shrunken by cold that it hardly served to guide a pen, even when strengthened with a horn finger-stall. He also suffered from bladder pains, which, however, ceased to trouble him once he had passed gravel in his urine.

Augustus survived several grave and dangerous illnesses at different periods. The worst was after his Cantabrian conquest, when abscesses on the liver reduced him to such despair that he consented to try a remedy which ran counter to all medical practice: because hot fomentations afforded him no relief, his physician Antonius Musa successfully prescribed cold ones. He was also subject to certain seasonal disorders, which recurred every year: in early spring a

---

²² Seutonius, Twelve Caesars, pp 89-90.

²³ Ibid, p 112.

tightness of the diaphragm; and when the sirocco blew, catarrh. These so weakened his constitution that either hot or cold weather caused him great distress.

In winter he wore no fewer than four tunics and a heavy woolen gown above his undershirt; and below that a woolen chest protector; also underpants and woolen gaiters. In summer he slept with the bedroom door open, or in the courtyard beside a fountain, having someone to fan him; and could not bear the rays even of the winter sun, but always wore a broad-brimmed hat when he walked in the open air, even at home. He preferred to travel by litter, at night, and his bearers kept so leisurely a pace that they were two days in arriving at Praeneste or Tibur; yet whenever it was possible to reach his destination by sea, he did so. Indeed, he pampered his health especially by not bathing too often and being usually content with an oil rub, or with a sweat-bath beside a fire, after which he took a douche of water either warmed or allowed to stand in the sun until it had lost its chill. When hot brine or warm Albulan water (from the sulphur springs) was prescribed for his rheumatism he did no more than sit on a wooden bath-seat calling it by the Spanish name dureta— and alternately dip his hands and feet into the bath.[24]

Augustus died from an illness at age 76, on August 19, A.D. 14. The nature of his terminal illness is not described. It would not be one of Julia and Agrippa's sons who would follow Augustus. It would be Tiberius, his stepson.   All four emperors following Augustus were descendants of Livia and Tiberius Claudius Nero, who were cousins. According to Seutonius: *Tiberius was doubly a Claudian: his father having been descended from the original Tiberius Nero, and his mother from Appius Pulcher, both of them sons of Appius the Blind.*[25]

Livia had two children by Tiberius Nero who figured large in the inheritance of the empire, Tiberius (who followed Augustus) and Drusus senior. Drusus senior was the father of Claudius (who followed Caligula) and Germanica. Livia's grandson Germanica married Agrippina the elder, youngest daughtrer of Julia III and Agrippa. Their son Caligula followed Tiberius. The youngest daughter of Germanicus and Agrippina the elder was Agrippina the younger, whose husband was Ahenabarbus and whose son Nero would follow Claudius. Nero would marry his aunt Octavia, daughter of Claudius. There were many inter-marriages among the children and grandchildren of Livia and Tiberius Claudius Nero. The reader may find the genealogy of the Julio-Claudian emperors in Table 1 helpful.

---

[24] Seutonius, The Twelve Caesars, p 98-99.

[25] Ibid, p 115.

Precedents of Augustus

Augustus, the first emperor, set precedents for others emperors to follow, with other precedents added near the end of the empire by Diocletian and Constantine. Not long after the death of Anthony, when Augustus was to become supreme ruler or Imperator, Emperor, he addressed members of the senate and the chief officers of State announcing his intentions, later publishing them in an edict: *'May I be privileged to build firm and lasting foundations for the Government of the State. May I also achieve the reward to which I aspire: that of being known as the author of the best possible Constitution, and of carrying with me, when I die, the hope that these foundations which I have established for the State will abide secure.'* [26]

---

[26] Ibid, p 69.

Chapter 6

Tiberius

Tiberius (b. 42 B.C., d. 37 A.D.), became emperor in 14 A.D. after the death of Augustus. The reason why Tiberius became emperor is one of the many inconsistencies and peculiarities of the new Roman Empire. Tiberius was the son of first cousins Livia, Augustus's third wife, and Tiberius Claudius Nero, who both came from the Claudian line, not the Julian. The selection of who would be the next emperor depended more upon the inclination of the emperor, with acquiescence by the Senate. Tacitus questioned Augustus' selection of Tiberius as emperor: *The more I think about history, ancient or modern, the more ironical all human affairs seem. In public opinion, expectation, and esteem no one appeared a less likely candidate for the throne than the man for whom destiny was secretly reserving it.*[1]

Tacitus speculates on why Augustus chose Tiberius to replace him instead of his only surviving grandson Agrippa Posthumus, or grandsons of his sister Octavia and Anthony, Germanicus and Claudius. Tacitus, after a review of what opinions were then being discussed about Augustus, concluded with the opinion that: *His appointment of Tiberius as his successor was due neither to personal affection nor to regard for the national interests. Thoroughly aware of Tiberius' cruelty and arrogance, he intended to heighten his own glory by the contrast with one so inferior.*[2]

The reason Tacitus gave for the selection of Tiberius to follow Augustus is supported by Seutonius. *I am also aware that, according to some writers, he* (Augustus) *so frankly disliked Tiberius' dour manner as to interrupt his own careless chatter whenever he entered; and that when*

---

[1] Tacitus, Annals, pp 127-128.

[2] Ibid, pp 37-39.

begged by Livia to adopt her son, he is suspected of having agreed the more readily because he selfishly foresaw that, with a successor like Tiberius, his death would be increasingly regretted as the years went by.[3]

Family History, early life

The story of Tiberius is frankly bizarre, especially after the death of his son Drusus. His mother Livia was reportedly only 13 years old when she gave birth to Tiberius. His father, Tiberius Claudius Nero[4], a first cousin of Livia, had supported Anthony, and the family had to flee the vengeance of Augustus. *His childhood and youth were beset with hardships and difficulties, because Nero* (Tiberius Claudius Nero) *and Livia took him wherever they went in their flight from Augustus.*[5]

After the death of his father when he was nine years old, he was raised by his mother Livia, in the household of Augustus. He, in common with all Roman rulers, had military training and experience— in Gaul, and Parthia, present Iran and Iraq, and was given a command in Pannonia, near present Hungary. He sponsored gladiatorial combats financed by Augustus.

Marital history and early career

Tiberius married Vispania, daughter of Agrippa's first wife Pomponia. A son, Drusus junior, was the only child of Tiberius and Vispania. If Tiberius had an heir it would have been Drusus, if he had survived. The death of his son would have a great influence on Tiberius.

But Tiberius was forced by Augustus to divorce Vispania and marry Julia III, daughter of Augustus, and widow of Agrippa his father-in-law. They had one child who died in infancy.

At first he lived on good terms with Julia and dutifully reciprocated her love; but gradually conceived such a loathing for her that, after their child had died in infancy at Aquileia, he broke off marital relations. On the death in Germany of his brother Drusus, senior Tiberius brought the body back to Rome, walking in front of the coffin all the way. Tiberius began a civil career as a defense lawyer and public prosecutor. *He undertook several special commissions, to reorganize the defective grain supply and to inquire into the state of slave-barracks throughout Italy.*

---

[3] Seutonius, p 125.

[4] Note. Not to be confused with the emperor Nero

[5] Seutonius, The Twelve Caesars, p 116.

Military career

Tiberius' early military career is summarized by Seutonius. *His first campaign was fought against the Cantabrians, as a colonel; next, he took an army to the east, where he restored King Tigranes of Armenia, personally crowning him on his own official dais; then he proceeded to recover the standards, captured by the Parthians from Marcus Crassus at Carrhae. For a year or so after this Tiberius governed Gallia Comata, where barbarian raids and feuds between the chieftains had caused considerable unrest. After that he fought consecutively in the Alps, Pannonia, and Germany. --- Tiberius' exploits were rewarded with an ovation, followed by a regular triumph; and it seems that what was then a novel honor had previously been conferred on him, namely triumphal regalia. He became in turn questor, praetor, and Consul, almost without an interval, and always before he was old enough to qualify officially as a candidate. A few years later he held another consulship, and was given the tribunician power for a five-year period.*

First Retirement

Yet, though in the prime of life, in excellent health, and at the height of his career, Tiberius suddenly decided to go into retirement, and withdraw as completely as possible from state affairs. His motive may have been an inveterate dislike of Julia, whom he dared not charge with adultery or divorce on any other grounds. --- At the time however, Tiberius applied for leave of absence merely on the ground that he was weary of office and needed a rest; nor would he consider either Livia's express pleas for him to stay, or Augustus' open complaints in the Senate that this was an act of desertion. On the contrary, he defeated their vigorous efforts to blunt his resolution, by a four days hunger strike. In the end he sailed off: and leaving Julia and Drusus junior, his son by Vispania, behind at Rome, hurried down to Ostia without saying a word to any of the friends who came to say goodbye.[6]

Soon afterwards, Tiberius learned that Julia had been banished (by Augustus) *for immoral and adulterous behavior, and that his name had been used by Augustus on the bill of divorce sent her. The news delighted him, but he felt obliged to send a stream of letters urging a reconciliation between Augustus and her; and well aware that Julia deserved all she got, allowed her to keep whatever presents she had at any time received from him. When the term of his tribunician power expired he asked Augustus' leave to return and visit his family, whom he greatly missed; and confessed at last that he had settled in Rhodes only because he wished to avoid the suspicion of rivalry with Gaius and Lucius. Now that both were fully-grown and the acknowledged heirs to*

---

[6] Ibid, pp 118-119.

*the throne, he explained, his reasons for keeping away from Rome were
no longer valid. Augustus, however, turned down the plea, telling him to
abandon all hope of visiting his family, whom he had been so eager to
desert.* [7]

Tiberius was about 36 years old at this time, confined to the
island of Rhodes (south west of present Turkey). Julia was exiled to the
island of Pandateria (near Naples). Both were ordered to their island
habitats by order of Augustus.

*At Rhodes Tiberius discontinued his usual exercise on
horseback and on foot in the parade grounds; wore a Greek cloak and
slippers instead of Roman dress; and for two years, or longer, grew daily
more despised and shunned— until the people of Nemausus were
encouraged to overturn his statues and busts. One day, at a private
dinner party attended by Gaius Caesar, Tiberius' name cropped up, and
a guest rose to say that if Gaius gave the order he would sail straight to
Rhodes and 'fetch back the Exile's head'— for he had come to be known
simply as 'the Exile'. This incident brought home to Tiberius that his
situation was not only worrying but perilous, and he pleaded most
urgently for a recall to Rome; Livia supported him with equal warmth,
and Augustus at last gave way.* [8]

Tiberius returns to Rome, and is given military appointments

*On his return to Rome Tiberius introduced his son Drusus to
public life, but immediately afterwards moved from the house of the
Pompeys in the 'Keels' to another residence in the Gardens of Maecenas
on the Esquiline Hill where he lived in strict retirement merely looking
after his private affairs and undertaking no official duties. Before three
years had passed, however, Gaius and Lucius Caesar were both dead*
(The heirs of Augustus, sons of Julia III); *Augustus then adopted Tiberius
as a son, along with Agrippa Postumus their* (Lucius and Gaius's) *only
surviving brother; and Tiberius was himself obliged to adopt his nephew
Germanicus. --- Yet Augustus did everything possible to advance
Tiberius' reputation, especially after having to disown Agrippa
Postumus; for by this time it had become pretty clear who the next
Emperor must be*

*Tiberius was given another three years of tribunician power,
with the task of pacifying Germany. --- There followed the Illyrian revolt,
which he was sent to suppress, and which proved to be the most bitterly
fought of all foreign wars since Rome had defeated Carthage. Tiberius
conducted it for three years at the head of fifteen legions and a
correspondingly large force of auxiliaries. --- He finally reduced the*

---

[7] Ibid, p 120.

[8] Ibid, p 121.

whole of Illyricum - a stretch of country enclosed by Italy, Noricum, The Danube, Thrace, Macedonia, and the Adriatic Sea - to complete submission.

In the following year Tiberius visited Germany and, finding that the disaster there had been due to Varus' rashness and neglect of precautions against surprise, refrained from taking any strategic decisions without the assent of his military council. This was a notable departure from habit; hitherto he had always had complete confidence in his own independent judgment, but was now relying on a large body of advisers. --- Two years after going to Germany Tiberius returned and celebrated the postponed Illyrian triumph, and with him went those generals whom he had recommended for triumphal regalia. --- The money fetched by the sale of his spoils went to restore the Temple of Concord and that of the Heavenly Twins; both buildings being rededicated in his own name and that of his dead brother Drusus.[9]

Death of Augustus

Soon afterwards the Consuls introduced a measure, which gave Tiberius joint control of the provinces with Augustus, and the task of assisting him to carry out the next five-year census. When the usual purificatory sacrifices had been completed he set off for Illyricum; but was immediately recalled by Augustus, whom he found in the throes of his last illness. Augustus died August 19, 14 A.D.

After an appropriate funeral, Augustus was declared a god and decreed a temple. But the target of every prayer was Tiberius. Addressing the senate, he offered a variety of comments on the greatness of the empire and his own unpretentiousness. Only the divine Augustus, he suggested, had possessed a personality equal to such responsibilities— he himself, when invited by Augustus to share his labors, had found by experience what hard hazardous work it was to rule the empire. Besides, he said, a State, which could rely on so many distinguished personages ought not to concentrate the supreme power in the hands of one man— the task of government would be more easily carried out by the combined efforts of a greater number.

But grand sentiments of this kind sounded unconvincing. Besides, what Tiberius said, even when he did not aim at concealment, was - by habit or nature - always hesitant, always cryptic. And now that he was determined to show no sign of his real feelings, his words became more and more equivocal and obscure. But the chief fear of the senators was that they should be seen to understand him only too well. So they poured forth a flood of tearful lamentations and prayers, gesticulating to

---

[9] Ibid, p 122-124.

heaven and the statue of Augustus, and making reverent gestures before Tiberius himself. [10]

Popular support for Germanicus as emperor

After Augustus' death and the accession of Tiberius, mutinies broke out in Illyricum and Germany. Tacitus continued, with the German mutiny: *At just about this time, and for the same reasons, the regular brigades in Germany mutinied too. They were more numerous and the outbreak was proportionately graver. Moreover they were in high hopes that Germanicus, unable to tolerate another man as emperor, would put himself at the disposal of the forces, which would then sweep all before them.*

At this time, as I have said, Germanicus was engaged upon assessments in Gaul. There he learnt that Augustus was dead. Germanicus was married to Augustus' granddaughter Agrippina and had several children by her; and since he was the son of Tiberius' brother Nero Drusus (senior) one of his grandparents was the Augusta (Livia). Yet Germanicus suffered from the fact that his grandmother and uncle hated him for reasons, which were unfair, but all the more potent. For Nero Drusus still lives on in Roman memories. It was believed that if he had obtained control of the empire, he would have brought back the free Republic. The hopes and good will thus engendered passed to his son, Germanicus. For this young man's unassuming personality and popular manner were very different from the haughty, ambiguous looks and words of Tiberius. Ill feeling among the women made things worse. The Augusta had a stepmothers's aversion to Agrippina (wife of Germanicus). *Agrippina herself was determined, and rather excitable. But she turned this to good account by her devoted faithfulness to her husband. At all events Germanicus' proximity to the summit of ambition only made him work more enthusiastically on behalf of Tiberius. After taking the oath of loyalty himself, he administered it to his immediate subordinates and to the Belgic communities. Then came the news that the army was rioting. He set out for it hurriedly.* [11] Germanicus was able to suppress the mutinies, however, only by mustering Rome's forces against the Germans and appeals to the ancestry of Germanicus.

Tiberius as emperor

The first act of Tiberius as emperor was to get rid of Agrippa Postumus. He was the oldest surviving grandson of Augustus, who had been banished on a prison island. *Tiberius revealed Augustus' death only after getting rid of young Agrippa Postumus, whom the colonel*

---

[10] Tacitus, Annals, p 39.

[11] Tacitus, Annals, pp52-53.

appointed to guard him in the prison island had received a written order to execute. So much is known, but some doubt remains whether this order was left by Augustus to be acted on when he died; or whether Livia wrote it in his name; or whether, if so, Tiberius knew anything of the matter. At all events, when the colonel arrived to report that he had done his duty, Tiberius disowned the order and threatened to make him answerable for this unauthorized execution.[12]

Seutonius provided examples illustrating the early reign of the new emperor. *Tiberius did not hesitate to exercise imperial power immediately, by calling on the Praetorians to provide him with a bodyguard; which was to be Emperor in fact and in appearance. Yet a long time elapsed before he assumed the position of Emperor. --- Tiberius accepted the title of Emperor; but hinted that he might later resign it. --- On becoming emperor, he held no more than three consulships (A.D. 18, 21, and 31). --- Such was his hatred of flatterers that he refused to let senators approach his litter, whether in greeting or on business. --- He was, moreover, quite unperturbed by abuse, slander, or lampoons on himself and his family, and would often say that liberty to speak and think as one pleases is the test of a free country.*

All this was the more noteworthy, because Tiberius showed an almost excessive courtesy when addressing individual senators, and the House as a body. Tiberius is said to address the senators:

'Let me repeat, gentlemen, that a right-minded and true-hearted statesman who has had as much sovereign power placed in his hands as you have placed in mine, should regard himself as the servant of the Senate; and often of the people as a whole; and sometimes of private citizens, too. I do not regret this view, because I have always found you to be generous, just, and indulgent masters.' [13]

Very gradually Tiberius showed that he was the real ruler of the Empire, and though at first his policy was not always consistent, he nevertheless took considerable pains to be helpful and to further the national interest. --- Tiberius cut down the expenses of public entertainments by lowering the pay of actors and setting a limit to the number of gladiatorial combats on any given festival. --- An ancient Roman custom revived by Tiberius was the punishment of married women guilty of improprieties, by the decision of a family council; so long as a public prosecutor had not intervened. --- He abolished foreign cults at Rome, particularly the Egyptian and Jewish, forcing all citizens who had embraced these superstitious faiths to burn their religious vestments and other accessories. Jews of military age were removed to unhealthy regions, on the pretext of drafting them into the army; the

---

[12] Ibid, p 126.

[13] Seutonius, pp 127-128.

others of the same race or of similar beliefs were expelled from the city and threatened with slavery if they defied the order.[14]

Death of Tiberius' son Drusus

According to Tacitus, Tiberius administered the government satisfactorily until the death of his son Drusus. *This, the year in which Tiberius' rule began to deteriorate, seems an appropriate moment to review the other branches of the government also, and the methods by which they had been administered since his accession. In the first place, public business - and the most important private business - was transacted in the senate. Among its chief men, there was freedom of discussion: their lapses into servility were arrested by the emperor himself. His conferments of office took into consideration birth, military distinction, and civilian eminence, and the choice manifestly fell on the worthiest men. The consuls and praetors maintained their prestige. The lesser offices, too, each exercised their proper authority. Moreover, the treason court excepted, the laws were duly enforced. --- Tiberius, in his ungracious fashion - grim and often terrifying as he was - maintained this policy until the death of Drusus reversed it.* [15]

Sejanus

The commander of the Guard, Sejanus, had other objectives than protection of the emperor Tiberius. Tacitus describes him: *Of audacious character and untiring physique, secretive about himself and ever ready to incriminate others, a blend of arrogance and servility, he concealed behind a carefully modest exterior an unbounded lust for power. Sometimes this impelled him to lavish excesses, but more often to incessant work. And that is as damaging as excess when the throne is its aim. ---*

Tiberius was readily amenable, praising him (Sejanus) *in conversation - and even in the senate and Assembly - as 'the partner of my labors', and allowing honors to his statues in theaters, public places, and brigade headquarters. Yet Sejanus' ambitions were impeded by the well stocked imperial house, including a son and heir, Gaius, and grown up grandchildren Nero Caesar and Drusus Caear, sons of his adoptive son Germanicus. After considering every possibility, Sejanus felt most inclined to rely on Drusus' wife Livilla, the sister of Germanicus. Unattractive in earlier years, she had become a great beauty. Sejanus professed devotion, and seduced her. Then, this first guilty move achieved - since a woman who has parted with her virtue will refuse*

---

[14] Ibid, pp 131-134.

[15] Tacitus, Annals, pp 159-160.

nothing - he incited her to hope for marriage, partnership in the empire, and the death of her husband.[16]

Drusus, junior, was the only child of Tiberius and Vispania. If Tiberius had an heir it would have been Drusus. Drusus married his first cousin Julia Livilla (daughter of Tiberius's brother Drusus, senior). But Drusus was poisoned by a servant of Drusus, at the instigation of the commander of the Guard, Sejanus, and the complicity of his wife Julia Livilla.

The death of Germanicus

The death of Germanicus was another death shrouded with conspiracy and murder, even involving Tiberius. The death of Germanicus preceded that of Drusus, as told in detail by Tacitus. Germanicus had been a popular hero as well as revered by his troops. He was the grandson of Augustus' sister Octavia, and son of the highly respected Drusus (brother of Tiberius) and Antonia. His wife Agrippina (first cousins) was the grand daughter of Augustus. Tiberius had him appointed as commander in Egypt and Cnaeus Calpurnius Piso was his assistant. *Tiberius criticized Germanicus mildly for his clothes and deportment, but reprimanded him severely for infringing a ruling of Augustus by entering Alexandria without the emperor's permission. --- Germanicus, still unaware that his expedition was frowned upon, visited the nearest of the Nile mouths, which is sacred to Hercules. --- On leaving Egypt Germanicus learnt that all his orders to divisional commanders and cities had been canceled or reversed. Between him and Piso there were violent reciprocal denunciations. Then Piso decided to leave Syria. But Germanicus fell ill, and so Piso stayed on. Then Piso left for Seleucia Pieria,* near Antioch, *to await the outcome of Germanicus' illness. He (Germanicus) had a relapse— aggravated by his belief that Piso had poisoned him.*

For a time Germanicus' condition was encouraging. But then he lost strength, and death became imminent. --- His friends touched the dying man's right hand, and swore to perish rather than leave him unavenged. Turning to his wife, Germanicus begged her - by her memories of himself and by their children - to forget her pride, submit to cruel fortune, and, back in Rome, to avoid provoking those stronger than herself by competing for their power. That was his public utterance. Privately he said more— warning her of danger (so it was said) from Tiberius. Soon afterward he died. [17]

Some time later a trial was held to determine whether or not Piso had something to do with Germanicus' death. *Tiberius was fully*

---

[16] Ibid, p 158.

[17] Tacitus, Annals, pp 110-113.

aware of the problems of the investigation and of the malignant rumors about himself. So, after listening - with the help of a few close friends - to the accusations and pleas of defense, he referred the whole case to the senate.

But for various reasons the judges were implacable— Tiberius because he had made war on the province, the senate because it remained unconvinced that Germanicus had died naturally. --- Both the emperor and Piso refused to produce private correspondence. Outside the senate-house the crowds were shouting that, if the senate spared him, they would lynch him.

Finally, pressed by his sons, he steeled himself to enter the senate again. Renewed charges, hostile cries from senators' relentless enmity everywhere, he endured. But what horrified him most was the sight of Tiberius, pitiless, passionless, adamantly close to any human feeling. Piso was carried home. --- Late at night, when his wife had left the bedroom, he ordered the door to be shut. At dawn he was found with his throat cut. A sword lay on the floor.[18]

Seutonius more or less supports Tacitus's account of Germanicus's death. *Tiberius had no paternal feelings either for his son Drusus the younger, whose vicious and dissolute habits offended him, or for his adopted son Germanicus. When Drussus died Tiberius was not greatly concerned, and went back to his usual business almost as soon as the funeral ended, cutting short the period of official mourning.*

Also he (Tiberius) described Germanicus' glorious victories as wholly ineffective, and far more than the country could afford; so little affection did he feel for him! He actually sent the Senate a letter of complaint when Germanicus hurried to Alexandria and there relieved a sudden disastrous famine, without consulting him. It is even believed that he arranged for Gnaeus Piso, the Governor of Syria, to poison Germanicus; and that Piso, when tried on this charge, would have produced his instructions had they not been taken from him when he confronted Tiberius with them, whereupon he was executed. As a result of these events, 'Give us back Germanicus!' was written on the walls throughout Rome and shouted all night. Tiberius later strengthened popular suspicion by his cruel treatment of Germanicus' wife Agrippina and her children.

At last he falsely accused her of planning to take sanctuary beside the image of her grandfather Augustus, or with the army abroad; and exiled her to the prison island of Pandateria. In punishment of her violent protests he ordered a centurion to give her a good flogging; in the course of which she lost an eye. Then she decided to starve herself to death and, that he had her jaws pried open for forcible feeding, succeeded. So he wickedly slandered her memory, persuading the senate

---

[18] Ibid, pp 125-126.

to decree her birthday a day of ill omen, and boasting of his clemency in not having her strangled and thrown out on the Stairs of Mourning. He even allowed a bill to be passed congratulating him on this pious attitude and voting a golden commemorative gift to Capitoline Jupiter. [19]

Final retirement of Tiberius and the reign of terror

Tiberius retired to Campania after the loss of his son Drusus, but oddly left Sejanus in charge of the Guard, even delegating his own authority to Sejanus. It would be much later that Tiberius would learn of Sejanus and Drusus' wife Livilla complicity in causing the death of Tiberius's son Drusus. *On eventually discovering that his own son Drusus the Younger had after all died, not as a result of his debauched habits, but from poison administered by his wife Livilla in partnership with Sejanus, Tiberius grew enraged and redoubled his cruelties until nobody was safe from torture and death.* [20]

Tacitus devoted an entire chapter to Sejanus and the death of Tiberius' son Drusus. The editor of the Annals states at the end of this chapter:

There is now a gap of two years in our manuscript of Tacitus. First Agrippina, Nero Caesar, and Drusus Caesar are exiled; and Nero Caesar dies. Then Tiberius, believing Sejanus himself (now consul) guilty of conspiracy, has him arrested in the senate and executed. Sejanus' divorced wife Apicata now reveals to Tiberius that his own son Drusus had been poisoned by Sejanus and Livilla; and Livilla too is killed or kills herself. [21]

Tacitus, from his chapter *The Reign of Terror: Frenzied with bloodshed, the emperor now ordered the execution of all those arrested for complicity with Sejanus. It was a massacre. --- Terror had paralyzed human sympathy. The rising surge of brutality drove compassion away.* [22]
Tiberius dedicated a temple in Campania and then crossed over to Capreae, off the west coast of Italy, about twenty miles south of Naples. Tiberius would spend the next ten years of his life there, never returning to Rome. The rest of the story of Tiberius is probably the most bizarre of any story most of us have ever heard of.

Prosecutions based on fabricated evidence or rumor began even before this time: *It was, indeed a horrible feature of the period that leading senators became informers even on trivial matters— some*

---

[19] Seutonius, pp 139-140.

[20] Ibid, p 145.

[21] Tacitus, Annals, p 197.

[22] Ibid, p 209.

openly, many secretly. Friends and relatives were as suspect as strangers, old stories as damaging as new. In the Forum, at a dinner-party, a remark on any subject might mean prosecution. Everyone competed for priority in marking down the victim. Sometimes this was self-defense, but mostly it was a sort of contagion, like an epidemic. Tacitus in his chapter *The First Treason Trials* cites many other examples, such as that involving a grand niece of Augusta who was charged for speaking insultingly about the divine Augustus. The madness of Tiberius is graphically depicted in Tacitus' chapter *The Reign of Terror.*

To give the reader a summary of some examples of Tiberius's conduct, the introductory statements of Seutonius are quoted.

But having found seclusion at last, and no longer feeling himself under public scrutiny, he rapidly succumbed to all the vicious passions, which he had for a long time tried, not very successfully, to disguise. I shall give a faithful account of these from the start. Even as a young officer he was such a hard drinker that his name, Tiberius Claudius Nero, was displaced by the nickname 'Biberius Caldius Mero'—meaning: 'Drinker of hot wine with no water added'.

On retiring to Capreae he made himself a private sporting house, where sexual extravagances were practiced for his secret pleasure. (The rest is too vile for this publication).

Some aspects of his criminal obscenity are almost too vile to discuss, much less to believe (and too vile to cite here).

What nasty tricks he used to play on women, even those of high rank, is clearly seen in the case of Mallonia whom he summoned to his bed. She showed such an invincible repugnance to complying with his lusts. --- Finally she left the court and went home; there she stabbed herself to death after a violent tirade against 'that filthy-mouthed, hairy, stinking old man'.

As the years went by, this stinginess turned to rapacity. It is notorious that he forced the wealthy Gnaeus Lentulus Augur to name him as his sole heir and then to commit suicide, by playing on his nervous apprehensions

Against Members of his own family.

The next paragraphs refer to Tiberius' actions against members of his own family, starting with his brother Drusus senior, then his wife Julia, ending with his mother Livia. Other examples have been mentioned above, such as his ill regard for his son Drusus and his nephew Germanicus, as well as the suspicions that he had something to do with the poisoning of Germanicus and Agrippa Postumus. In addition: *After this he made no secret of his dislike for the young pair* (the sons of Germanicus, Drusus Caesar and Nero Caesar) *and arranged that all sorts of false charges should be brought against them; --- This gave him grounds for writing the Senate so harsh a complaint that both were declared public enemies and starved to death— Nero on the island of Pontis, Drusus in a Palace cellar. Some signs of Tiberius' savage and dour character could be distinguished even in his boyhood. Theodorus the Gadarene, who taught him rhetoric, seems to have been the first to do so, since, on having occasion to reprove Tiberius, he would call him 'mud kneaded with blood!' But after he became Emperor, while he was still gaining popular favor by a pretense of moderation, there could be no doubt that Theodorus had been right.*

Executions

About this time a praetor asked Tiberius whether, in his opinion, courts should be convened to try cases of treason. Tiberius replied that the law must be enforced; and enforce it he did, most savagely, too. One man was accused of decapitating an image of Augustus. Tiberius had the witnesses examined under torture. The offender was convicted, which provided a precedent of far-fetched accusations.[23]

Soon Tiberius broke out in every sort of cruelty and never lacked for victims: these were, first, his mother's friends and even acquaintances; then those of his grandsons and daughter-in-law; finally those of Sejanus. With Sejanus out of the way his savageries increased. A detailed list of Tiberius' barbarities would take a long time to compile. I shall content myself with a few samples. Not a day, however holy, passed without an execution; he even desecrated New Year's Day. Many of his men victims were accused and punished with their children- some actually by their children - and relatives forbidden to go into mourning. Special awards were voted to the informers who had denounced them and, in certain circumstances, to the witnesses too. An informer's word was always believed. Every crime became a capital one, even the utterance of a few careless words. A poet found himself accused of slander - he had written a tragedy which presented King Agamemnon in a bad light - and a historian had made the mistake of describing Caesar's assassins, Brutus and Cassius, as 'the last of the Romans'. Both these authors were executed without delay, and their works - though once publicly read before Augustus, and accorded general praise - were called in and destroyed.

Final years and death

Much evidence is extant, not only of the hatred that Tiberius earned but of the state of terror in which he himself lived, and the insults heaped upon him.

His uneasiness of mind was aggravated, by a perpetual stream of reproaches from all sides; every one of his condemned victims either cursed him to his face or arranged for a defamatory notice to be posted

---

[23] Seutonius, Twelve Caesars, pp 135-142.

in the theater seats occupied by senators. His attitude to these reproaches varied markedly; sometimes shame made him want nobody to hear about the incident, sometimes he laughed and deliberately publicized it.

Tiberius died at age 76, March 16, 37 A.D. *The first news of his death caused such joy at Rome that people ran about yelling: 'To the Tiber with Tiberius!' --- There were also loud threats to drag his body off with a hook and fling it on the Stairs of Mourning; --- Thus the hatred of Tiberius grew hotter than ever— his cruelty, it was said, continued even after his death.*[24]

---

[24] Ibid, pp 144-151.

Chapter 7

Caligula

Gaius, or Caligula, (b. August, 12 A.D., d. January, 41), followed Tiberius as emperor in 37 A.D. and ruled to 41 A.D., when he was assassinated by the captains of his own praetorian guard. The history of Caligula, by Tacitus has been lost. No part of it apparently remains. However Seutonius provides examples for historians and students of human behavior to attempt to probe the pathology of the mind of this ruler of the Roman Empire. Josephus provides another source of information about Caligula. The last chapters of Robert Graves' historical novel *I Claudius* present the bizarre life of Caligula in a more readable form than the matter of fact presentation by Seutonius in *The Twelve Caesars*.

Family history

Gaius, later named Caligula, or 'little boots', a nickname given to him by the soldiers in his father Germanicus' army, was the son of Germanicus and Agrippina the elder. Seutonius devotes the first three pages of his chapter on Caligula to his father Germanicus. Germanicus was revered by his troops. Many people in Rome favored Germanicus to become emperor after Augustus. Germanicus died in 19 A.D. under suspicion of poisoning. The Roman people also revered Germanicus' father, Drusus senior. They were the good Claudians.

The worst Claudians were Livia, followed by his grand uncle Tiberius who preceded him and his uncle Claudius to follow Caligula. His mother Agrippina was the grand daughter of Augustus. His father Germanicus was the grandson of Augustus' sister Octavia.[1]

---

[1] See table, The Julian House.

Birth and childhood

The birthplace of Gaius is disputed. Tacitus states that Gaius' mother Agrippina accompanied Germanicus during his attempts to quell a mutiny of the army of Upper Germany. *Here were these distinguished ladies with no staff-officers or soldiers to look after them, none of the usual escort or other honors due to the supreme commander's wife. And they were off to the Treviri, to be looked after by foreigners! The men felt sorry for them, and ashamed, when they thought of her ancestry - her father was Agrippa, her grandfather Augustus, her father-in-law Nero Drusus - and of her impressive record as wife and mother. Besides, there was her baby son, Gaius, born in the camp and brought up with the regular troops as his comrades. In their army fashion they had nicknamed him 'little boots' (Caligula), because as a popular gesture he was often dressed in miniature army boots.*[2] In childhood he accompanied Germanicus and his mother in Syria. On his return he lived with his mother (Agrippina) and next, after she had been exiled, with his great-grandmother Livia. He was seven years old when his father Germanicus became ill and died of poisoning, possibly ordered by Tiberius. He gave the funeral oration for Livia when nine years old. When Gaius was eleven years old Tiberius starved his brother Drusus to death. Tiberius later murdered Caligula's mother Agrippina the Elder, and his brother Nero Caesar.

He then lived with his grandmother Antonia until Tiberius summoned him to Capreae, at the age of eighteen. He assumed his manly gown and shaved his first beard as soon as he arrived there; but this was a most informal occasion, compared with his brothers' coming of age celebrations. The courtiers tried every trick to lure or force him into making complaints against Tiberius; always, however, without success. He not only failed to show any interest in the murder of his relatives, but affected an amazing indifference to his own ill-treatment, behaving so obsequiously to his adoptive grandfather and to the entire household, that someone said of him, very neatly: 'Never was there a better slave, or a worse master!'[3]

Seutonius states that: *Gaius was, in fact, sick both physically and mentally. In his boyhood, he suffered from epilepsy; and although in his youth he was not lacking in endurance, there were times when he could hardly walk, stand, think, or hold up his head, owing to sudden faintness.*[4]

---

[2] Tacitus, Annals, p 56. (From his chapter on Tiberius)

[3] Seutonius, Twelve Caesars, pp 157-158.

[4] Ibid, p 178.

Seutonius continues his comments about his early life when on the island of Capraea: *Yet even in those days he could not control his natural brutality and viciousness. He loved watching tortures and executions; and, disguised in wig and robe, abandoned himself nightly to the pleasures of gluttonous and adulterous living. Tiberius was ready enough to indulge a passion, which Gaius had for theatrical dancing and singing, on the ground that it might have a civilizing influence on him. With characteristic shrewdness, the old Emperor had exactly gauged the young man's vicious inclinations, and would often remark that Gaius' advent portended his own death and ruin of everyone else. 'I am nursing a viper for the Roman people,' he once said.*

Gaius presently married Junia Claudilla, daughter of the distinguished Marcus Silanus; after which he was first appointed Augur, in place of his brother Drusus, and then promoted to the Priesthood, in compliment to his dutiful behavior and exemplary life. This encouraged him in the hope of becoming Tiberius' successor, because Sejanus' downfall had reduced the Court to a shadow of its former self. [5]

Death of Tiberius and accession of Caligula

According to Seutonius, after the death of Tiberius and the accession of Gaius: *He delivered a funeral speech in honor of Tiberius to a vast crowd, weeping profusely all the while; and gave him a magnificent burial. But as soon as this was over he sailed for Pandataria and the Pontian Islands to fetch back the remains of his mother and his brother Nero; --- He honored his fathers memory by renaming the month of September 'Germanicus'; and sponsored a senatorial decree which awarded his grandmother Antonia, at a blow, all the honors won by Livia Augusta in her entire lifetime. As fellow-consul he chose his uncle Claudius, who had hitherto been a mere knight; and adopted the young Tiberius Gemellus when he came of age, giving him the official title of 'Prince of the Youth'.* [6]

Gaius held several gladiatorial contests, some in Statilius Taurus' amphitheater, and others in the Enclosure; diversifying them with prize-fights between the best boxers of Africa and Campania, and occasionally allowing magistrates or friends to preside at these instead of doing so himself. Again, he staged a great number of different theatrical shows of various kinds and in various buildings - sometimes at night, with the whole city illuminated - and would scatter vouchers among the audience entitling them to all sorts of gifts, over and above the basket of food which was everyone's due. --- Many all-day games were

---

[5] Ibid, p 158.

[6] Ibid, p 159-160.

celebrated in the Circus and, between races, Gaius introduced panther-baiting and the Trojan war dance.

One of his spectacles was on such a fantastic scale that nothing like it had ever been seen before. He collected all available merchant ships and anchored them in two lines, close together, the whole way from Baiae to the mole at Puteoli, a distance of more than three and a half Roman miles. Then he had earth heaped on their planks, and made a kind of Appian Way along which he trotted back and forth for two consecutive days. On the first day he wore oak-leaf crown, sword, buckler, and cloth-of-gold cloak, and rode a gaily caparisoned charger. On the second, he appeared in the charioteer's costume driving a team of two famous horses, with a boy named Dareus, one of his Parthian hostages, displayed in the car beside him; behind came the entire Praetorian Guard, and a group of his friends mounted in Gallic chariots.

Seutonius continued with a few other achievements of the emperor Gaius, and then introduced the rest of his chapter with: *So much for the Emperor; the rest of this history must deal with the Monster.*

Proclaims that he is a God

He adopted a variety of titles: such as 'Pious', 'Son of the Camp', 'Father of the Army', 'Best and Greatest of Caesars'. --- He exclaimed, from Homer: *Nay, let there be one master, and one king!*

And he nearly assumed a royal diadem then and there, turning the semblance of a principate into an autocracy. However, after his courtiers reminded him that he already outranked any prince or king, he insisted on being treated as a god— sending for the most revered or artistically famous statues of the Greek deities (including that of Jupiter at Olympia), and having their heads replaced by his own. --- He established a shrine to himself as God, with priests, the costliest possible victims, and a life-sized golden image, which was dressed every day in clothes identical with those that he happened to be wearing.[7]

The way he treated his family

Because of Agrippa's humble origin Gaius loathed being described as his grandson, and would fly into a rage if anyone mentioned him, in speech or song, as an ancestor of the Caesars. He nursed a fantasy that his mother had been born of an incestuous union between Augustus and his daughter Julia; and not content with thus discrediting Augustus' name, canceled the annual commemorations of Agrippa's victories at Actium and off Sicily, declaring that they had proved the disastrous ruin of the Roman people. He called his great-grandmother Livia a 'Ulysses in petticoats', and in a letter to the Senate dared

---

[7] Ibid, pp 159-164.

describe her as of low birth, 'her maternal grandfather Aufidius Lurco having been a mere local senator at Fundi', although the public records showed Lurco to have held high office at Rome. When his grandmother Antonia asked him to grant her a private audience he insisted on taking Macro, the Guards Commander, as his escort. Unkind treatment of this sort hurried her to the grave though, according to some, he accelerated the process with poison and, when she died, showed so little respect that he sat in his dining-room and watched the funeral pyre burn. One day he sent a colonel to kill young Tiberius Gemellus without warning; on the pretext that Tiberius had insulted him by taking an antidote against poison— his breath smelled of it. Then he forced his father-in-law, Marcus Silanus, to cut his own throat with a razor, the charge being that he had not followed the imperial ship when it put to sea in a storm, but had stayed on shore to seize power at Rome if anything happened to himself. The truth was that Silanus, a notoriously bad sailor, could not face the voyage; and Tiberius breath smelled of medicine taken for a persistent cough which was getting worse. Gaius preserved his uncle Claudius merely as a butt of practical jokes.

It was his habit to commit incest with each of his three sisters and, at large banquets, when his wife reclined above him, placed them all in turn below him. They say that he ravished his sister Drusilla before he came of age; their grandmother Antonia, at whose house they were both staying, caught them in bed together. Later, he took Drusilla from her husband, the former Consul Lucius Cassius Longinus, openly treating her as his lawfully married wife; and when he fell dangerously ill left Drusilla all his property, and the Empire too. --- Afterwards, whenever he had to take an important oath, he swore by Drusilla's divinity, even at a public assembly or an army parade.

It would be hard to say whether the way he got married, the way he dissolved his marriages, or the way he behaved as a husband was the most disgraceful. He attended the wedding ceremony of Gaius Piso and Livia Orestilla, but had the bride carried off to his own home. After a few days, however, he divorced her, and two years later banished her, suspecting that she had returned to Piso in the interval.

Caesonia was neither young nor beautiful, and had three daughters by a former husband, besides being recklessly extravagant and utterly promiscuous; yet he loved her with a passionate faithfulness and often, when reviewing the troops, used to take her out riding in helmet, cloak, and shield. For his friends he even paraded her naked; but would not allow her the dignified title of 'wife' until she had borne him a child, whereupon he announced the marriage and the birth simultaneously. He named the child Julia Drusilla; and carried her around the temples of all the goddesses in turn before finally entrusting her to the lap of Minerva, whom he called upon to supervise his daughter's growth and education. What finally convinced him of his own paternity was her violent temper;

*while still an infant she would try to scratch her little playmates' faces
and eyes.*[8]

He had not the slightest regard for chastity, either his own or
others', and was accused of homosexual relations, both active and
passive, with Marcus Lepidus, also Mnester the comedian, and various
foreign hostages; moreover, a young man of consular family, Valerius
Catullus, revealed publicly that he had buggered the Emperor, and quite
worn himself out in the process. Besides incest with his sisters and a
notorious passion for the prostitute Pyrallis, he made advances to almost
every woman of rank in Rome; after inviting a selection of them to dinner
with their husbands he would slowly and carefully examine each in turn
while they passed his couch, as a purchaser might assess the value of a
slave, and even stretch out his hand and lift up the chin of any woman
who kept her eyes modestly cast down.[9]

Violent crimes

Often he would send for men whom he had secretly killed, as
though they were still alive, and remark off-handedly a few days later
that they must have committed suicide.

He behaved just as arrogantly and violently towards the other
orders of society. --- During gladiatorial shows he would have the
canopies removed at the hottest time of the day and forbid anyone to
leave; or take away the usual equipment, and pit feeble old fighters
against decrepit wild animals; or state comic duels between respectable
house holders who happened to be physically disabled in some way or
the other. More than once he closed down the granaries and let the
people go hungry.

The following instances will illustrate his bloodthirstiness.
Having collected wild animals for one of his shows, he found butcher's
meat too expensive and decided to feed them with criminals instead. ---
Many men of decent family were branded at his command, and sent down
the mines, or put to work on the roads, or thrown to the wild beasts.
Others were confined in narrow cages, where they had to crouch on all
fours like animals; or were sawn in half— and not necessarily for major
offences, but merely for criticizing his shows, or failing to swear by his
genius.

Gaius made parents attend their sons' executions, and when one
father excused himself on the ground of ill health, provided a litter for
him. Having invited another father to dinner just after the son's
execution, he overflowed with good-fellowship in an attempt to make him
laugh and joke.

---

[8] Ibid, pp 165-166.

[9] Ibid, p 172.

*Gaius' savage crimes were made worse by his brutal language.
--- As though mere deafness to his grandmother Antonia's good advice
were not enough, he told her: 'Bear in mind that I can treat anyone
exactly as I please!'*

*The method of execution he preferred was to inflict numerous
small wounds; and his familiar order: 'Make him feel that he is dying'
soon became proverbial. Once, when the wrong man had been killed,
owing to a confusion of names, he announced that the victim had equally
deserved death; and often quoted Accius' line: Let them hate me, so long
as they fear me.*

*Everything that he said and did was marked with equal cruelty,
even during his hours of rest and amusement and banqueting. He
frequently had trials by torture held in his presence while he was eating
or otherwise enjoying himself; and kept an expert headsman in readiness
to decapitate the prisoners brought in from gaol.*

*At one particularly extravagant banquet he bust into sudden
peals of laughter. The Consuls, who were reclining next to him, politely
asked whether they might share the joke. 'What do you think?' he
answered. 'It occurred to me that I have only to give one nod and both
your throats will be cut on the spot!'*[10]

Extravagances and the depletion of the treasury

*No parallel can be found for Gaius' far-fetched extravagances.
He invented new kinds of baths, and the most unnatural dishes and
drinks— bathing in hot and cold perfumed bath-oils, drinking valuable
pearls dissolved in vinegar, and providing his guests with golden bread
and golden meat; and would remark that a man must be either frugal or
Caesar. For several days in succession he scattered largesse from the
roof of the Julian Basilica; and built Liburnian galleys, with ten banks of
oars, jeweled sterns, multi-colored sails, and with huge baths,
colonnades, and banqueting-halls aboard— not to mention vines and
fruit trees of different varieties. In these vessels he used to take early-
morning cruises along the Campanian coast, reclining on his couch and
listening to songs and choruses. Villas and country-houses were run up
for him regardless of expense - in fact, Gaius seemed interested only in
doing the apparently impossible - which led him to construct moles in
deep, rough water far out to sea, drive tunnels through exceptionally
hard rocks, raise flat ground to the height of mountains, and reduce
mountains to the level of plains; and all at immense speed, because he
punished delay with death. But why give details? Suffice it to record that,
in less than a year he squandered Tiberius' entire fortune of 27 million
gold pieces, and an enormous amount of other treasure besides.*[11]

---

[10] Ibid, pp 167-170.

[11] Ibid, pp 172-173.

Other examples of madness

The story of his so-called invasion of England ended with the bizarre command of Caligula to his troops to gather seashells. *In the end, he drew up his army in battle array facing the Channel and moved the arrow-casting machines and together artillery into position as though he intended to bring the campaign to a close. No one had the least notion what was in his mind when, suddenly, he gave the order: 'Gather sea-shells!' He referred to the shells as 'plunder from the ocean, due to the Capitol and to the Palace', and made the troops fill their helmets and tunic-laps with them.[12]*

He worked hard to make his naturally forbidding and uncouth face even more repulsive, by practicing fearful and horrifying grimaces in front of a mirror. He was well aware that he had mental trouble, and sometimes proposed taking a leave of absence from Rome to clear his brain; Caesonia is reputed to have given him an aphrodisiac, which drove him mad. Insomnia was his worst torment. Three hours a night of fitful sleep were all that he ever got, and even then terrifying visions would haunt him— once, for instance, he dreamed that he had a conversation with an apparition of the sea. He tired of lying awake the greater part of the night, and would alternately sit up in bed and wander through the long colonades, calling out from time to time for daylight and longing for it to come.

I am convinced that this brain-sickness accounted for his two contradictory vices — over-confidence and extreme timorousness. Here was a man who despised the gods, yet shut his eyes and buried his head beneath the bedclothes at the most distant sound of thunder; and if the storm came closer, would jump out of bed and crawl underneath. ---

Gaius paid no attention to traditional or current fashions in his dress, ignoring male conventions and even the human decencies. Often he made public appearances in a cloak covered with embroidery and encrusted with precious stones, a long-sleeved tunic and bracelets; or in silk or even a woman' robe; and came shod sometimes with slippers, sometimes with buskins, sometimes with military boots, sometimes with women's shoes. Often he affected a golden beard and carried a thunderbolt, trident, or serpent-twinned staff in his hand. He even dressed up as Venus and, even before his expeditions, wore the uniform of a triumphant general, including sometimes the breastplate, which he had stolen from Alexander the Great's tomb at Alexandria. ---

To prevent Incinatus, his favorite horse, from being disturbed he always picketed the neighborhood with troops on the day before the races, ordering them to enforce absolute silence. Incinatus owned a marble table, an ivory stall, purple blankets, and a jeweled collar; also a

---

[12] Ibid, pp 176-177.

house, a team of slaves, and furniture— to provide suitable entertainment for guests whom Gaius invited in its name. It is said that he even planned to award Incitatus a consulship.[13]

Gaius, a year before his assassination, had ordered his statue to be erected in the Temple at Jerusalem, but with the advice of Herod Agrippa, this was not carried out.[14]

Caligula was assassinated, by Cassius Chaerea and other captains the guards, on January 24, A.D. 41. He ruled for almost four years.

---

[13] Ibid, pp 179-180.

[14] Josephus, The Antiquities, 19, 1-2.

Chapter 8

Claudius

Claudius (b. 10 B.C., d. A.D. 54) was emperor from 41 A.D. to 54 A.D. He was the first Roman emperor to conquer England, in 43 A.D. The invasion and conquest of England will be discussed in a later chapter. Claudius became emperor late in life, when fifty years old. He was considered unfit to hold office by Augustus and Livia, and tolerated by Tiberius and Caligula. His unusual life under these emperors is told in a remarkable historical novel *I Claudius* by Robert Graves. His life subsequently as emperor is told in a companion volume *Claudius the God.* Robert Graves was the translator of *The Twelve Caesars* by Seutonius. The *Annals of Imperial Rome* by Tacitus is also a source for the study of Claudius, however the first six years of the emperor's reign were lost, as was the reign of Caligula who preceded him and who was assassinated in A.D. 41.

The beginning of the life of Claudius was unusual and the end of his life frankly bizarre. He was handicapped with a probable birth injury and neurological deficit and considered to be retarded by his mother Antonia as well as Augustus and Livia. Yet he achieved literary accomplishments before accession. Had he remained in his scholarly pursuits, and not been thrust into the role of emperor his life may have ended sanely and even constructively had his writings survived. Claudius changed from what many regarded as the hope of the Roman Empire to its ruin in his later years. The reign of Nero and the civil wars followed. Despite the disasters he brought to the known world and the sordid end to his life, he was deified.

Family history

Claudius and his brother Germanicus, who had been favored by the people over Tiberius, and whose fame Claudius inherited, were sons of Drusus senior and Antonia. His mother Antonia was the daughter of Augustus' sister Octavia and Anthony. Claudius was the grandson of Livia and Tiberius Claudius Nero, first cousins, whose sons Tiberius and

Drusus were his uncle and father. His father Drusus and brother
Germanicus were the best of the Claudians. From Seutonius: *Drusus
commanded an army against the Raetians, and subsequently against the
Germans, while holding the successive ranks of quaestor and praetor.*
*He was the first Roman general to navigate the North Sea; and also
excavated the Drusus Canals, as they still call them (connecting the
Rhine with the Yssel). After defeating the local tribes in a series of
battles. --- These campaigns earned Drusus an ovation, with triumphal
regalia; and he became consul directly when the praetorship ended. On
resuming the war he died at his summer headquarters, in 9 B.C. --- His
body was carried to Rome by relays of leading citizens from the various
citizen municipalities and veterans' colonies which lay along the route.
--- The senate voted Drusus many honors, among them a marble arch on
the Appian Way decorated with trophies, and the surname Germanicus to
be held by himself and his descendants. Drusus was, they say, no less
eager for personal glory than devoted to republicanism. Not content with
gaining victories over the enemy, he had a long-standing ambition to win
'The Noblest Spoils' and used to chase German chieftains across the
battlefield at great risk to his life. He also openly announced that, as
soon as he came to power, he would restore the old form of
government.*[1]. No doubt the father of Claudius, as well as his brother's
fame and reputation were the basis for the hopes of Claudius as emperor.

The soldiers and the Roman people acclaimed Germanicus, his
brother, and it was hoped he would have become emperor. Germanicus
died in A.D. 19, a murder by poisoning possibly ordered by Tiberius. His
uncle Tiberius, the brother of Drusus, figured large in his own
upbringing. Both his father and grandfather died without having any
influence over his upbringing. Livia would be a great influence, not only
over Augustus and Tiberius but also over Claudius.

Early life

According to Seutonius: *He (Claudius) lost his father while he
was still a baby. Nearly the whole of his childhood and youth was so
troubled by various diseases that he grew dull-witted and had little
physical strength; and on reaching the age at which he should have won
a magistracy or chosen a private career, was considered by his family
incapable of doing either. Claudius's mother Antonia,* daughter of
Anthony and Octavia, *often called him 'a monster: a man whom Nature
had not finished but had merely begun;' and, if she ever accused anyone
of stupidity, would exclaim: 'he is a bigger fool even than my son
Claudius!' Livia, his grandmother, never failed to treat him with the
deepest scorn, and seldom addressed him personally; her reproofs came
in the form of brief, bitter letters or oral messages. When his sister*

---

[1] Seutonius, Twelve Caesars, p 185-6

Livilla heard someone predict that he would one day succeed to the throne, she prayed openly and aloud that the Roman people might be spared so cruel and undeserved a misfortune. Finally, to show what opinions, favorable and other wise, his great-uncle Augustus, held of him, I quote the following extracts from the imperial correspondence (attributed to Augustus):

My dear Livia:

As you suggested, I have now discussed with Tiberius what we should do about your grandson Claudius at the coming Games of Mars. We both agreed that a decision ought to be taken once and for all. The question is whether he has- shall I say? - full command of all his senses. If so, I can see nothing against sending him through the same degrees of office as his brother (Germanicus); *but should he be deemed physically and mentally deficient, the public (which always likes to scoff and mock at such things) must not be given a chance of laughing at him and us. I fear that we shall find ourselves in constant trouble if the question of his fitness to officiate in this or that capacity keeps cropping up. We should therefore decide in advance whether he can or cannot be trusted with offices of state.[2]*

Claudius, however, had received instruction, support and encouragement from his tutor Ahenodorus, and his brother Germanicus. Augustus, however, gave Claudius no honors except a seat in the College of Augurs (one of the four orders of the priesthood).

Claudius *applied himself seriously to literature while still a child, and published several samples of his proficiency in its various departments. This did not advance him to public office or inspire the family with brighter hopes for his future.*

Engagement and marriages

Claudius was twice betrothed while still a boy: to Augustus' great-grand-daughter Aemilia Lepida, and to Livia Medullina, surnamed Camilla, of the family of the ancient dictator Camillus. However, Aemilia Lepida's parents offended Augustus and her engagement was broken off; and Livia Medullina died of some illness on what should have been her wedding day. His first wife, Plautia Urgulanilla, whose father had won a triumph, he divorced for scandalous misbehavior and the suspicion of murder; his next, Aelia Paetina, daughter of an ex-consul, he also divorced, for slight offenses.[3] If the early marital history of Claudius seems bizarre later he would marry Messalina, whom he later executed for bigamy. He then married his niece Agrippina the younger, daughter

---

[2] Ibid, pp 188.

[3] Ibid, p187 and pp 202-203.

of his brother Germanicus.   Agrippina's son Nero (from previous marriage to Ahenobarbus) would follow him as emperor.

Early career

When his paternal uncle Tiberius succeeded Augustus, Claudius asked to be given some office of state. Tiberius sent him the consular regalia. Claudius then pressed for the duties of the office as well. Tiberius' reply ran: 'The forty gold pieces I sent you were meant to be squandered on toys during the Satunalia and Sgillaria' (gifts of little statuettes). *After that Claudius renounced all hopes of a political career, spending an obscure and idle life between his suburban mansion and a villa in Campania. Since his intimates included men of the lowest class, Claudius' reputation for stupidity was further enhanced by stories of his drunkenness and love of gambling. Yet despite this behavior, many men of distinction continued to visit him, and he never lost the people's respect.*

Literary studies

His first wife Urgulanilla may have contributed to Claudius's interest in the history of the Etruscans, since her family was able to provide him with Etruscan sources of tradition and history. The men of distinction who visited Claudius included the historian Livy who encouraged Claudius in his studies of history and other writings, none of which have survived. *While still a boy Claudius had started work on a Roman history, encouraged by Livy, and assisted by Sulpicius Flavus.* Seutonius then described a number of his writings, including an Etruscan history, a Carthaginian history *which were acknowledged by the city of Alexandria by adding a new wing to the museum called 'the Claudian' in his honor. Moreover, he wrote eight volumes of an autobiography, which are liable to criticism for their lack of taste rather than any lack of style; as well as A Defense of Cicero--- quite a learned work.* [4]

As soon as Claudius' nephew Gaius became Emperor and tried every means of gaining popularity, Claudius entered on his belated public career as Gaius' colleague in a two-months consulship; ---   He also drew lots for a second consulship, and won one that would fall due four years later. Claudius often presided as Gaius' substitute at the Games, where the audience greeted him with: 'Long live the Emperor's Uncle!' and "Long Live Germanicus' Brother!' [5]

---

[4] Ibid, p 210.

[5] Ibid, p 190.

Claudius became emperor

Caligula died at age 29 by the assassins, led by Chaerea and other commanders of the Guard. Neither the senate nor Claudius anticipated this event. The reactions of Claudius have been detailed by Seutonius.

Claudius became Emperor, at the age of fifty, (41 A.D.) *by an extraordinary accident. When the assassins of Gaius shut everyone out, pretending that he wished to be alone, Claudius went off with the rest and retired to a room called the Hermaeum; but presently heard about the murder and slipped away in alarm to a near-by balcony, where he hid trembling behind the door curtains. A Guardsman, wandering vaguely through the Palace, noticed a pair of feet beneath the curtain, pulled their owner out for identification and recognized him. Claudius dropped on the floor and clasped the soldier's knees, but found himself acclaimed Emperor. The man took him to his fellow-soldiers who were angry, confused, and at a loss what to do; however, they placed him in a litter and, because his own bearers had run off, took turns at carrying him to the Praetorian Camp. Claudius was filled with terror and despair; in his passage through the streets everyone cast him pitying glances as if he were an innocent man being hurried to execution. Once safely inside the rampart of the camp, Claudius spent the night among the sentries, confident now that no immediate danger threatened, but feeling little hope for the future since the Consuls, with the approval of the Senate and the aid of city cohorts, had seized the Forum and Capitol, and were determined to maintain public liberty (restore the Republic).*

When the tribunes of the people summoned him to visit the House and there advise on the situation, Claudius replied that he was being forcibly detained and could not come. The Senate, however, was dilatory in putting its plans into effect because of the tiresome recriminations of those who held opposing opinions. Meanwhile, crowds surrounded the building and demanded a monarchy, expressly calling for Claudius; so he allowed the Guards to acclaim him Emperor and to swear allegiance. He also promised every man 150 gold pieces, which made him the first of the Caesars to purchase the loyalty of his troops. [6]

Josephus provided an enlarged account of the assassination of Gaius. Josephus, commenting on the life of Gaius, gives us an understanding of the tyrant— that power corrupts, especially when combined with absolute immunity: *But the advantages he* (Gaius) *received from his learning did not countervail the mischief he brought upon himself in the exercise of his authority; so difficult it is for those to obtain the virtue that is necessary for a wise man, who have the absolute power to do what they please without control.* Josephus gives essentially the same account of Claudius discovery by the soldiers, as it was based in

---

[6] Ibid, p 191.

part on the accounts of Seutonius, however discusses the conflict between the senate and others who favored a restoration of the Roman Republic versus those who favored a monarchy. The importance of king Herod Agrippa in persuading Claudius to become emperor is not told by Seutonius or Tacitus. Herod Agrippa (no relation to Augustus' general Marcus Agrippa who married Julia III) was a friend of Claudius, both classmates, and a close relationship continued during Claudius's early administration and afterward. He was able to talk the troops into selecting Claudius as emperor and negotiated a settlement between the senate, other parties and Claudius and his supporting troops.

Josephus also makes it clear that Claudius came to power based on support from the soldiers. *But Claudius discoursed with the army which was there gathered together, who took oath that they would persist in their fidelity to him; upon which he gave the guards every man five thousand drachmae apiece, and proportionable quantity to their captains, and promised to give the same to the rest of the armies wheresoever they were.*

And now the consuls called the senate together --- However, a hundred, and not more were gotten together; and as they were in consultation about the present posture of affairs, a sudden clamor was made by the soldiers that were on their side, desiring that the senate would choose them an emperor, and not bring the government into ruin by setting up a multitude of rulers.[7]

The early reign of Claudius

The rule of Claudius began in A.D. 41. Claudius wasted no time in *executing a few of the colonels and centurions who had conspired against Gaius— to make an example of them and because they had, he knew, planned his own murder as well. Next, to show his family devotion, he always used 'By Augustus!' as the most sacred and frequent of his oaths; made the senate decree his grandmother Livia divine honors.*

He also never missed a chance of keeping green the fame of his brother Germanicus. --- Nor did he fail to honor Anthony; in one proclamation he begged the people 'to celebrate my father Drusus's birthday all the more heartily because it happens likewise to have been that of my maternal grandfather Anthony' --- and while annulling all Gaius's edicts, would not allow the day of his assassination to be proclaimed a public festival.[8]

Claudius held four more consulships; the first two in successive years, the others at four-yearly intervals. --- During these terms of office and indeed, at all times, Claudius was a most conscientious judge; sitting

---

[7] Josephus, The Antiquities, 19.2.5, 19.3.1-4 and 19.4.1-4.

[8] Seutonius, p 192.

in court even on his own birthday and those of his family, sometimes actually on ancient popular holidays or days of ill-omen. --- However, his behavior in hearing and deciding cases varied unpredictable; sometimes he was wise and prudent, sometimes thoughtless and hasty, sometimes down right foolish and apparently out of his senses.

The office of censor had been allowed to lapse since the days of Plancus and Paulus, sixty years previously, but Claudius assumed it; and here he proved as inconsistent in his general principles as in his particular decisions.

Claudius always interested himself in the proper upkeep of the city and the regular arrival of grain supplies. --- Once, after a series of droughts had caused a scarcity of grain, a mob stopped Claudius in the Forum and pelted him so hard with curses and stale crusts that he had difficulty in regaining the Palace by a side-door; as a result he took all possible steps to import grain, even during the winter months— insuring merchants against the loss of their ships in stormy weather.

His other achievements included magnificent public shows, gladiatorial Games, and a pageant *staged on the Campus Martius, the realistic storm and sack of a town, with a tableau of the British king's surrender, at which he presided in his purple campaigning cloak. In matters of religious ritual, civil and military customs, and the social status of all classes at home and abroad, Claudius not only revived obsolescent traditions but invented new ones.*[9]

Claudius bestowed on his friend Herod Agrippa the kingdoms in the near east which his grandfather Herod the Great had ruled. In addition he added Judea and Samaria to his provinces. Herod Agrippa had also assisted Claudius in a dispute between Greeks and Jews at Alexandria, resulting in the following decrees of Claudius: *I would grant the same rights and privileges should be preserved to the Jews which are in all the Roman empire, which I have granted to those of Alexandria. --- I will therefore be fit to permit the Jews, who are in all the world under us, to keep their ancient customs without being hindered so to do. And I do charge them also to use this my kindness to them with moderation, and not to show contempt of the superstitious observances of other nations, but to keep their own laws only.*[10]

Claudius' public works, though not numerous, were important. They included, in particular, an aqueduct begun by Gaius, the draining of Fucine Lake and the building of the harbor at Ostia. He planted a colony of soldiers at Colchester, England where a *temple erected to the divine Claudius would later become a blatant stronghold of alien rule.*[11]

[9] Ibid, pp 193-199.

[10] Josephus, The Antiquities of the Jews, 19.5.

[11] Tacitus, Annals, p 328.

Until this reign there had been two terms in the Law Courts, the summer and the winter, Claudius made them continuous. Another of his changes was to institute permanent courts, both at Rome and under the governors of the provinces, for judging fiduciary cases, instead of entrusting them to the annually appointed Roman magistrates. He canceled Tiberius' supplement to the Papian-Poppaean Law which implied that men over sixty years of age could not beget children; and sponsored a law authorizing the consuls to choose guardians for orphans; and passed another law, ruling that no person who had been exiled from province might enter the city or even Italy. --- It now became illegal for foreigners to adopt the names of Roman families, and any who usurped the rights of Roman citizens were executed in the Esquiline Field.

Augustus had been content to prohibit any Roman citizen in Gaul from taking part in the savage and terrible Druidic cult; Claudius abolished it altogether. On the other hand, he attempted to transfer the Eleusinian Mysteries from Attica to Rome; and had the ruined Temple of Venus on Mount Eryx in Sicily restored at the expense of the Public Treasury. Whenever he concluded a treaty with foreign rulers, he sacrificed a sow in the Forum, using the ancient formula of the Fetial priests. Yet all these acts, and others like them - indeed, one might say, everything that Claudius did throughout his reign - were dictated by his wives and freedmen: he practically always obeyed their whims rather than his own judgment.[12]

Messalina

The first six years of Claudius' reign (41-47 A.D.) from Tacitus' Annals were lost. His surviving three chapters are all about his last two wives, Messalina and Agrippina. *Valeria Messallina was the daughter of his cousin Messalina Barbatus* (the editor of Tacitus' Annals states Claudius married his cousin Messalina). *He had children by three of his wives. Urgulanilla bore him Drusus and Claudia; Paetina had a daughter Antonia; and Messalina presented him with Octavia and a son, first named Germanicus and then Britannicus.*

He lost Drusus just before he came of age, choked by a pear, which he had playfully thrown up and caught in his open mouth. --- Claudia's real father was Claudius' freedman Boter. Claudius disavowed paternity and, though she was born nearly five months after the divorce, had her laid her naked (exposed) outside Urgulnilla's house-door.

Antonia was twice married; first to Gnaeus Pompeius and then to Fustus Sulla, both young noblemen of the highest birth. --- Of his three

---

[12] Ibid, pp 200-202.

sons-in-law Claudius adopted only Nero; Pompeius and Sulla were put to death.[13]

The *Fall of Messalina*, the chapter from Tacitus' Annals, presents in graphic detail the sordid end of Claudius' third wife Messalina, who was secretly married to Gaius Silius when Claudius was *busy with the functions of censor.* Claudius's guardsmen demanded punishment. Silius and certain distinguished knights asked for a speedy end. The execution of accomplices was ordered. Messallina was slain by a staff officer. *Claudius was still at table when news came that Messalina had died; whether by her own hand or another's was unspecified. Claudius did not inquire. He called for more wine and went on with his party as usual.*

On the day that followed, the emperor gave no sign of hatred, satisfaction, anger distress, or any other human feeling— even when he saw the accusers exulting, and his children mourning. His forgetfulness was helped by the senate, which decreed that Messalina's name and statues should be removed from all public and private sites.[14]

We see in Claudius' administration unjust prosecutions, inhumane punishments; and corruption of lawyers and the legal establishment. *Now Suillius continued his prosecutions with unremitting ferocity. Moreover, his unscrupulousness had many imitators. For the emperor's absorption of all judicial and magisterial functions had opened up extensive opportunities for illicit gain. The most readily purchasable commodity on the market was an advocate's treachery. One distinguished knight named Samius fell on his sword at Suillius' house after paying him four hundred thousand sesterces and then finding Suillius was in collusion with the other side.*

Agrippina

From the next chapter of Tacitus' Annals, *The Mother of Nero*, we learn about the marriage of Claudius to his niece Agrippina. *Messalina's death convulsed the imperial household. Claudius was impatient of celibacy and easily controlled by his wives, and the ex-slaves quarreled about who should choose his next one. Rivalry among the women was equally fierce. Each cited their own high birth, beauty, and wealth as qualifications of this exalted marriage. The chief competitors were Lollia Paulina (who had been married to Caligula), and Germanicus' daughter Agrippina, the younger.*

Agrippina's seductiveness was a help. Visiting her uncle frequently - ostensible as a close relation - she tempted him into giving her the preference and into treating her, in anticipation, as his wife.

---

[13] Ibid, pp 203-204. Note. Nero was married to Claudius's daughter Octavia.

[14] Tacitus, Annals, p 250, 251.

Once sure of her marriage, she enlarged the scope of her plans and devoted herself to scheming for her son Lucius Domitius Ahenaobarbus (Nero), whose father was Cnaeus Domitius Ahenobarbus. It was her ambition that this boy, the future Nero, should be wedded to the emperor's daughter Octavia (who were cousins). *Rumor now strongly predicted Claudius' marriage to Agrippina; so did their illicit intercourse. But they did not yet dare to celebrate the wedding. For marriage with a niece was incestuous, and disregard of this might, it was feared, cause national disaster.* Then Vitellius, who had arranged for the death of Messalina, *untertook to arrange matters by methods of his own.* He asked Claudius if he would yield to a decree of the Assembly and the senate's recommendation. *The emperor replied that he was a citizen himself and would bow to unanimity.* Vitellius then argued before the senate the desirability of Claudius marrying Agrippina. *'We can create a precedent: the nation presents the emperor with a wife! Marriage to a niece, it may be objected, is unfamiliar to us. Yet in other countries it is regular and lawful. Here also, union between cousins, long unknown, has become frequent in course of time. Customs change as circumstances change— this innovation too will take root'.*

At this, some senators ran out of the house enthusiastically clamoring that if Claudius hesitated they would use constraint. A throng of passers-by cried that the Roman public was similarly minded. Claudius delayed no longer. After receiving the crowd's congratulations in the Forum, he entered the senate to request a decree legalizing future marriages with a brother's daughter.[15]

This story seems to us incredible. Yet it would be centuries before Mendel and the science of genetics would bring reason to bear on the matters which were the subject of marriage of an uncle to a niece, or marriage of cousins. But at the time, the emperor Claudius had the power to make the law. Nero would later rescind Claudius's edicts. *Nero annulled many of Claudius' decrees and edicts, on the ground that he had been a doddering old idiot.[16]*

Claudius becomes the mad ruler

The Roman Empire went rapidly downhill after the marriage of Claudius to Agrippina. Tacitus provides many examples. The succinct summary provided by Seutonius is quoted here:

As I mention above, Claudius fell so deeply under the influence of these freedmen and wives that he seemed to be their servant rather than their emperor; and distributed honors, army commands, indulgences or punishments according to their wishes, however

---

[15] Ibid, pp 252- 254.

[16] Seutonius, The Twelve Caesars, p 231.

capricious, seldom even aware of what he was about. I need not dwell on matters of lesser importance: how he revoked grants, canceled edicts, brazenly amended the texts of letters-patent he had issued, or even only substituted new versions for the old. Suffice it to record that he executed his father-in-law Appius Silanus, Julia, daughter of Tiberius' Son Drusus, and Julia, daughter of his own brother Germanicus— all on unsupported charges and without the right to plead in self-defense. Gnaeus Pompeius, who had married his daughter Antonia, was stabbed to death; and Lucius Silanus, whom Claudius had betrothed to his daughter Octavia, lost his praetorship and, four days later, had orders to commit suicide; this was the very New Year's day on which Claudius married Agrippina. He executed thirty-five senators and three hundred Roman knights, with so little apparent concern that once, when a centurion reported that So-and-so the ex-Consul was now duly dispatched, and Claudius denied having given any such command, his freedmen satisfied him that the soldiers had done right not to wait for instructions before taking vengeance on an enemy of the Emperor. [17]

Seutonius continues with other examples of Claudius's behavior. *No matter what time it was or where Claudius happened to be, he always felt ready for food or drink. --- It was seldom that Claudius left a dining-hall except gorged and sodden.*

His cruelty and bloodthirstiness appeared equally in great and small matters. For instance, if evidence had to be extracted under torture, or parricide punished, he allowed the Law to take its course without delay and in his own presence. --- At gladiatorial shows, whether or not they were staged by himself, he ruled that all combatants who fell accidentally should have their throats cut— above all net-fighters, so that he could gaze on their death agony. When a pair of gladiators mortally wounded each other he sent for their swords and had pocketknives made from them for his personal use. Claudius greatly enjoyed wild-beast shows and the fencing matches during the luncheon interval.

Seutonius and Tacitus describe military engagements of Claudius in England, Parthia, Germany and Gaul as well as efforts to secure grain and corn in Egypt and Africa. In England Claudius erected to himself a temple at Camulodunum. That there were continuous uprisings and wars in the states of the Roman Empire during the reigns of Augustus, Tiberius, Caligula, Claudius, and Nero is a fact of history. The invasion and conquest of England will be presented in Chapter 11, England and the Romans.

As Graves commented near the end of the life of Claudius and the accession of Nero: *To begin with, I (Claudius) knew that Nero is fated to rule as my successor, carrying on the cursed business of*

---

[17] Ibid, p 204.

monarchy, fated to plague Rome and earn everlasting hatred, to be the last of the mad Caesars. Yes, we are all mad, we Emperors. We begin sanely, like Augustus and Tiberius and even Caligula (though he was an evil character, he was sane at first) and monarchy turns our wits. [18] Claudius the God uses the personal pronoun I for Claudius.

To conclude the story of the emperor Claudius from Seutonius:

He (Claudius) declared his intention of letting Britannicus come of age because although immature, he was tall enough to wear the toga of manhood; adding 'which will at last provide Rome with a true-born Caesar.'

Soon afterwards he composed his will and made all the magistrates put their seals to it as witnesses; but Agrippina, being now accused of many crimes by informers as well as her own conscience, prevented him from going any further.

Most people think that Claudius was poisoned; but when, and by whom, is disputed. Some say that the eunuch Halotus, his official taster, administered the drug while he was dining with the priests in the Citadel; others, that Agrippina did so herself, at a family banquet, poisoning a dish of mushrooms, his favorite food.[19] Tacitus supported the idea that Claudius was poisoned by mushrooms, at the direction of Agrippina with assistance from others. Claudius died in his sixty-fourth year, and the fourteenth of his reign, on October 13, A.D. 54. Claudius, influenced by Agrippina, had selected Nero rather than his own son Britannicus to become emperor.

---

[18] Graves, Claudius the God, p 442.

[19] Seutonius, p 211.

Chapter 9

Nero

Nero, (b. A.D. 37, d. A.D. 68) was the last of the emperors descended from the Julio-Claudian line. The two families dominated Rome and the Roman Empire for over one hundred years, from the time of Julius Caesar (b. 100 B.C., d. 44 B.C.) to Nero who ruled the Roman Empire from 54 to 68 A.D.

We turn to Josephus for a brief summary of Nero. *But Claudius himself, when he had administered the government thirteen years, eight months, and twenty days, died, and left Nero to be his successor in the empire, whom he adopted by his wife Agrippina's delusions, in order to be his successor, although he had a son of his own whose name was Britannicus, by Messalina his former wife, and a daughter whose name was Octavia, whom he had married to Nero.*

Now as to the many things in which Nero acted like a madman, out of the extravagant degree of the felicity and riches which he enjoyed, and by that means used his good fortune to the injury of others; and after what manner he slew his brother, and wife, and mother, from whom his barbarity spread itself to others that were most nearly related to him and how, at last, he was so distracted that he became an actor in the scenes, and upon the theater, I omit to say any more about them because there are writers enough upon whose subjects everywhere; but I shall turn myself to those actions of his time in which the Jews were concerned.[1]

Family History

We have presented briefly, in the preceding chapter on Claudius, the life of Nero's mother Agrippina, the younger. She figured large in the reign of Nero. She determined that her son Nero instead of Brittanicus would follow Claudius. Agrippina was the youngest sister of

---

[1] Josephus, The Wars of the Jews, 2.12.8 and 2.13.1.

emperor Caligula. She was the daughter of Agrippina the elder and Germanicus, who were first cousins. Agrippina the elder was the grand daughter of Augustus. Germanicus was the grandson of Augustus's sister Octavia. The paternal line of Nero as presented by Seutonius was as follows: His grandfather *Lucius Domitius Ahenobarbus had been a famous charioteer in his youth, and gained triumphal decorations for his part in the German campaign; but was notorious for his arrogance, extravagance, and cruelty. --- The cruelty of the wild animal hunts presented by him in the Circus and elsewhere at Rome, and of a gladiatorial contest, obliged Augustus - whose private warnings he had disregarded - to issue a cautionary edict.* His father, Gnaeus *was a wholly despicable character. As a young man he served in the East on Gaius' staff, but forfeited his friendship by killing one of his own freedmen for refusing to drink as much as he was told. Yet even then he behaved no better. Once, driving through a village on the Appian Way, he whipped up his horses and deliberately ran over and killed a boy; and when a knight criticized him rather freely in the Forum he gouged out one of his eyes there and then. He was also remarkably dishonest; cheating his bankers of payment of goods he had bought and, while praetor, even swindling victorious charioteers of their prize money. --- Just before Tiberius died he was charged with treason, adultery, and incest with his sister; however, Gaius' accession saved him and he died of dropsy at Pyrgi, first formally acknowledging the paternity of Nero, his son by Germanicus' daughter Agrippina the Younger.*

Upbringing

At the age of three Nero lost his father and inherited one-third of the estate; but Gaius, who was also named in the will, not only took everything, but also banished Agrippina. Nero therefore grew up in very poor circumstances under the care of his aunt Domitia Lepida, who chose a dancer and a barber to be his tutors. However, when Claudius became Emperor, Nero had his inheritance restored to him, and a legacy from his uncle by marriage, Passienus Crispus, left him well off. His mother's recall from banishment allowed him to enjoy once more the benefits of her powerful influence.[2]

Claudius adopted Nero when he was ten years old. Claudius appointed Annaeus Seneca as his tutor. According to Tacitus, Burrus as well as Seneca were Nero's tutors: *These two men, Sextus Afranius Burrus and Luicius Annaeus Seneca, with a unanimity rare among partners in power, were, by different methods, equally influential. Burrus strength lay in soldierly efficiency and seriousness of character, Seneca's in amiable high principles and his tuition of Nero in public speaking. They collaborated in controlling the emperor's perilous adolescence;*

---

[2] Seutonius, Twelve Caesars, pp 215-216.

their policy was to direct his deviations from virtue into licensed channels of indulgence. Agrippina's violence, inflamed by all the passions of ill-gotten tyranny, encountered their united opposition. --- But from early boyhood Nero's mind, though lively, directed itself to other things – carving, painting, singing, and riding. Sometimes, too, he wrote verses, and thereby showed he possessed the rudiments of culture.[3]

From Seutonius: As a boy Nero read most of the usual humanities subjects except philosophy which, Agrippina warned him, was no proper study for a future ruler. His tutor Seneca hid the works of the early rhetoricians from him, intending to be admired himself as long as possible. So Nero turned his hand to poetry, and would dash off verses enthusiastically, without any effort. It is often claimed that he published other people's work as his own; but notebooks and papers have come into my possession, which contain some of Nero's best-known poems in his own handwriting. --- Nero also took more than an amateur's interest in painting and sculpture.[4]

Nero became emperor

After the death of Claudius, by poisoning in 54, Agrippina had Nero proclaimed emperor by the praetorian guard. Agrippina, his mother, became at least at first, an acting empress. *The first casualty of the new reign was the governor of Asia, Marcus Junius Silanus (II). Agrippina treacherously contrived his death, without Nero's knowledge. --- Equally hurried was the death of Claudius' ex-slave Narcissus. --- Imprisoned and harshly treated, the threat of imminent execution drove him to suicide. --- Other murders were meant to follow. But the emperor's tutors, Burrus and Seneca, prevented them.[5]*

At Claudius's funeral Nero's gave his first speech, composed by Seneca.

For Claudius was declared a god. A public funeral was to come first. On the day of the funeral the emperor pronounced his predecessor's praises. While he recounted the consulships and Triumphs of the dead man's ancestors, he and his audience were serious. References to Claudius' literary accomplishments too, and to the absence of disasters in the field during his reign, were favorably received. But when Nero began to talk of his stepfather's foresight and wisdom, nobody could help laughing.

Yet the speech, composed by Seneca, was highly polished— a good example of his pleasant talent, which admirably suited

---

[3] Tacitus, Annals, pp 283- 285.

[4] Seurtonius, pp 244, 245.

[5] Tacitus, Annals, pp 284.

contemporary taste. Older men, who spent their leisure in making comparisons with the past, noted that Nero was the first ruler to need borrowed eloquence.

Sorrow duly counterfeited, Nero attended the senate and acknowledged its support and the army's backing. Then he spoke of his advisers (Burrus and Seneca), *and of the examples of good rulers before his eyes. 'Besides, I bring with me no feud, no resentment of vindictiveness,' he asserted. 'No civil war, no family quarrels, clouded my early years.' Then, outlining his future policy, he renounced everything that had occasioned recent unpopularity. 'I will not judge every kind of case myself', he said, ' and give too free rein to the influence of a few individuals by hearing prosecutors and defendants behind my closed doors. From my house, bribery and favoritism will be excluded. I will keep personal and State affairs separate. The senate is to preserve its ancient functions. By applying to the consuls, people from Italy and the senatorial provinces may have access to its tribunals. I myself will look after the armies under my control.'*

Moreover, these promises were implemented. The senate decided many matters. They forbade advocates to receive fees or gifts. They excused quaestors— designate from the obligation to hold gladiatorial displays. Agrippina objected to this as a reversal of Claudius' legislation. Yet it was carried— although the meeting was convened in the Palatine, and a door built at the back so that she could stand behind a curtain unseen, and listen. Again, when an Armenian delegation was pleading before Nero, she was just going to mount the emperor's dais and sit beside him. Everyone was stupefied. But Seneca instructed Nero to advance and meet his mother. This show of filial dutifulness averted a scandal.[6]

The accomplishments of Nero's early reign were likely from the control of Nero by Burrus and Seneca. Nero was only seventeen years old when he became emperor, the youngest Roman emperor to have acceded to the throne.

Agrippina's influence over Nero became strained. Nero had married Octavia, daughter of Claudius. His mother, Agrippina, was the youngest daughter of Germanicus who was the brother of Claudius. If it had been strange that Claudius had married his niece Agrippina, it was not apparently thought unusual for Nero to have married his aunt, Octavia (by order of Claudius). But Nero fell in love with a freeborn slave Acte. Tacitus describes this whole affair as follows:

Agrippina was gradually losing control over Nero. He fell in love with a former slave Acte. His confidants were two fashionable young men, Marcus Salvius Otho (future emperor in A.D. 69), *whose father had been consul, and Claudius Senecio, son of a former imperial*

---

[6] Ibid, p 285.

slave. Nero's secret, surreptitious, sensual meetings with Acte established her ascendancy. When Nero's mother finally discovered, her opposition was fruitless. Even his older friends were not displeased to see his appetites satisfied by a common girl with no grudges. Destiny, or the greater attraction of forbidden pleasures, had alienated him from his aristocratic and virtuous wife Octavia, and it was feared that prohibition of his affair with Acte might result in seductions of noblewomen instead.

Agrippina, however, displayed feminine rage at having an ex-slave as her rival and a servant girl as her daughter-in-law, and so on. --- But her violent scoldings only intensified his affection for Acte. --- Agrippina was alarmed; her talk became angry and menacing. She let the emperor hear her say that Britannicus was grown up and was the true and worthy heir of his father's supreme position— now held, she added, by an adopted intruder, who used it to maltreat his mother.[7]

The murder of Britannicus
There followed the poisoning (A.D. 55) of Brittanicus by Nero, described by Tacitus:

Though upset by Agrippina's threats, he could not find a charge against his stepbrother or order his execution openly. Instead he decided to act secretly— and ordered poison to be prepared. --- A selected servant habitually tasted his food and drink. But the murderers thought of a way of leaving this custom intact without giving themselves away by a double death. Britannicus was handed a harmless drink. The taster had tasted it; but Britannicus found it too hot, and refused it. Then cold water containing the poison was added. Speechless, his whole body convulsed, he instantly ceased to breathe.

His companions were horrified. Some, uncomprehending, fled. Others, understanding better, remained rooted in their places, staring at Nero. He still lay back unconcernedly— and he remarked that this often happened to epileptics; that Britannicus had been one since infancy. Agrippina tried to control her features. But their evident consternation and terror showed that, like Britannicus' sister Octavia, she knew nothing. Agrippina realized that her last support was gone. And here was Nero murdering a relation. But Octavia, young though she was, had learnt to hide sorrow, affection, every feeling. After a short silence the banquet continued.[8] Britannicus died in A.D. 59.

Nero as Emperor
It would be another four years before Nero would conspire to murder his mother Agrippina. Meanwhile: *He gave an immense variety*

---

[7] Ibid, pp 288-289.

[8] Ibid, pp 290-291.

of entertainments - coming of age parties, chariot races in the circus, stage plays, a gladiatorial show - persuading even old men of consular rank, and old ladies, too, to attend the coming-of-age parties. He reserved seats for the knights and the circus, as he had done in the Theater; and actually raced four camel chariots! --- Throughout the festival all kinds of gifts were scattered to the people— 1,000 assorted birds daily, and quantities of food parcels; besides vouchers for grain, cloths, gold, silver, precious stones, pearls, paintings, slaves, transport animals, and even trained wild beasts— and finally for ships, blocks of city apartments, and farms.

Nero watched from the top of the proscenium. The gladiatorial show took place in a wooden theater, near the Campus Maritus, which had been built in less than a year; but no one was allowed to be killed during these combats, not even criminals. He did, however make 400 senators and 600 knights, some of them rich and respectable, do battle in the arena; and some had to fight wild beasts and perform various duties about the ring.[9]

About two years after his accession as emperor, he began to victimize Roman citizens in bizarre nocturnal assaults. *It might have been possible to excuse his insolent, lustful, extravagant, greedy, or cruel early practices (which were furtive and increased only gradually), by saying that boys will be boys; yet at the same time, this was clearly the true Nero, not merely Nero in his adolescence. As soon as night fell he would snatch a cap or a wig and make a round of the taverns, or prowl the streets in search of mischief— and not always innocent mischief either, because one of his games was to attack men on their way home from dinner, stab them if they offered resistance, and then drop their bodies down the sewers. He would also break into shops and rob them, afterwards opening a market at the Palace with the stolen goods, dividing them up into lots, auctioning them himself, and squandering the proceeds. During these escapades he often risked being blinded or killed— once he was beaten almost to death by a senator whose wife he had molested, which taught him never to go out after dark unless an escort of colonels was following him at an unobserved distance.*

Gradually Nero's vices gained the upper hand: he no longer tried to laugh them off, or hide, or deny them, but openly broke into more serious crime. His feasts now lasted from noon till midnight. He took an occasional break for diving into a warm bath, or if it were summer, into snow-cooled water. Sometimes he would drain the artificial lake in the Campus Martius, or the other in the Circus, and hold public dinner parties there, including prostitutes and dancing girls from all over the city among his guests. Whenever he floated down the Tiber to Ostia, or cruised past the Gulf of Baiae, he had a row of temporary brothels

---

[9] Seutonius, Twelve Caesars, pp 218-219.

erected along the shore, where married women, pretending to be innkeepers, solicited him to come ashore. He also forced his friends to provide him with dinners; one of them spent 40,000 gold pieces on a turban party, and another even more on a rose banquet.

Seutonius next described extremely bizarre sexual perversions and activities which need not be repeated here and can be summed up by quoting the ancient historian: *Nero practiced every kind of obscenity.*[10]

Nero's murders of his mother, wife, aunt and others

Nero's murder of his mother Agippina, in 59, is the critical juncture of Nero's life, after which his life becomes one of the saddest examples the human race has produced.

From Seutonius: *The over-watchful, over-critical eye that Agrippina kept on whatever Nero said or did, proved more than he could stand. He first tried to embarrass her by frequent threats to abdicate and go into retirement in Rhodes. Then, having deprived her of all honors and power, and even of her Roman and German bodyguard, he refused to have her living with him and expelled her from his Palace; after which he did everything possible to annoy her.*

From Tacitus: *Finally, however, he concluded that wherever Agrippina was she was intolerable. He decided to kill her. His only doubt was whether to employ poison, or the dagger, or violence of some other kind.*[11] There followed a plot to construct a collapsible boat, which Agrippina would use. The roof of the boat weighted down with lead was designed to collapse. The plan didn't work and Agrippina swam to shore. *Nero then dispatched an armed column, which dispersed the crowd outside the house where Agrippina had sought refuge. Anicetus surrounded her house and broke in. Arresting every slave in his path, he came to her bedroom door. Here stood a few servants— the rest had been frightened away by the invasion. Then she saw Anicetus. Behind him were a naval captain and lieutenant named Herculeius and Obaritus respectively. 'If you have come to visit me', she said, 'you can report that I am better. But if you are assassins, I know my son is not responsible. He did not order his mother's death.' The murderers closed round her bed. --- Blow after blow fell, and she died* (in A.D. 59). --- *But Nero only understood the horror of his crime when it was done. For the rest of the night, witless and speechless, he alternately lay paralyzed and leapt to his feet in terror— waiting for the dawn, which he though would be his last.*[12]

---

[10] Ibid, pp 227-229

[11] Seutonius, 231-232. Tacitus, Annals, p 313.

[12] Tacitus, Annals, pp 316-317.

From Seutonius: *Though encouraged by the congratulations which poured in from the Army, the Senate, and the people, he was never either then or thereafter able to free his conscience from the guilt of this crime.*[13]

Nero next killed his aunt Domitia Lepida, who had been his foster mother during his early childhood. *Having disposed of his mother, Nero proceeded to murder his aunt. He found her confined to bed with severe constipation. The old lady stroked his downy beard affectionately— he was already full-grown, murmuring: 'Whenever you celebrate your coming-of-age and present me with this, I shall die happy.' Nero turned to the courtiers and said laughingly: 'In that case I must shave at once.' Then he ordered the doctors to give her a laxative of fatal strength, seized her property before she was quite dead, and tore up the will so that nothing should escape him.*

Nero next disposed of Octavia, his wife, in 62 A.D. *Life with Octavia had soon bored him, and when his friends criticized his treatment of her, he retorted: 'Just being an emperor's wife ought surely to be enough to make her happy?' He tried unsuccessfully to strangle her on several occasions, but finally pronounced that she was barren, and divorced her. This act made him so unpopular and caused so great a scandal that he banished Octavia and later had her executed on a charge of adultery.*

There was no family relationship, which Nero did not criminally abuse. When Claudius' daughter Antonia refused to take Poppaea's place, he had her executed on a charge of attempted rebellion; and destroyed every other member of his family, including relatives by marriage, in the same way.[14]

Nero was no less cruel to strangers than to member of his family. --- Nero resolved on a wholesale massacre of the nobility. What fortified him in this decision, and seemed to justify it, was that he had discovered two plots against his life. --- When brought up for trial the conspirators were loaded with three sets of chains. Some, while admitting their guilt, made it seem like a favor when they claimed that by destroying a man so thoroughly steeped in evil as Nero, they would have been doing him the greatest possible service. All children of the condemned men were banished from Rome, and then starved to death or poisoned. --- After this, no consideration of selection or moderation restrained Nero from murdering anyone he pleased, on whatever pretext.[15]

---

[13]   Seutonius, p 232.

[14]   Seutonius, p 233.

[15]   Ibid, p 234.

About this time, A.D. 60, Nero expanded his activities as a performer in the theaters of Italy and Greece, while at the same time his armies were trying to suppress uprisings in England and neighboring states; as well as uprisings in Gaul, Spain and Armenia.

Rome burns

The story told and heard often that Nero fiddled while Rome burned is not quite correct. The account of Tacitus follows:

Disaster followed. Whether it was accidental or caused by a criminal act on the part of the emperor is uncertain— both versions have supporters. Now started the most terrible and destructive fire, which Rome had ever experienced. It began in the Circus, where it adjoins the Palatine and Caelian hills. Breaking out in shops selling inflammable goods, and fanned by the wind, the conflagration instantly grew and swept the whole length of the Circus. There were no walled mansions or temples, or any other obstructions, which could arrest it. First, the fire swept violently over the level spaces. Then it climbed the hills— but returned to ravage the lower ground again. It outstripped every counter-measure. The ancient city's narrow winding streets and irregular blocks encouraged its progress.

Terrified, shrieking women, helpless old and young, people intent on their own safety, people unselfishly supporting invalids or waiting for them, fugitives and lingerers alike— all heightened the confusion. When people looked back, menacing flames sprang up before them or outflanked them. When they escaped to a neighboring quarter, the fire followed— even districts believed remote proved to be involved. Finally, with no idea where or what to flee, they crowded on the country roads, or lay in the fields. Some who had lost everything - even their food for the day - could have escaped, but preferred to die. So did others, who had failed to rescue their loved ones. Nobody dared fight the flames. Attempts to do so were prevented by menacing gangs. Men crying that they acted under orders, too, openly threw in torches. Perhaps they had received orders. Or they may just have wanted to plunder unhampered.

Nero was at Antium (about thirty miles south of Rome). *He only returned to the city when the fire was approaching the mansion he had built to link the Gardens of Maecenas to the Palatine. The flames could not be prevented from overwhelming the whole to the Palatine, including his palace. Nevertheless, for the relief of the homeless, fugitive masses he threw open the Field of Mars, including Agrippa's public buildings, and even his own Gardens. Nero also constructed emergency accommodations for the destitute multitude. Food was brought from Ostia and neighboring towns, and the price of corn was cut to less than 1/4 sesterce a pound. Yet these measures, for all their popular character, earned no gratitude. For a rumor had spread that, while the city was burning, Nero had gone on his private stage and, comparing modern calamities with ancient, had sung of the destruction of Troy.*

By the sixth day enormous demolitions had confronted the raging flames with bare ground and open sky, and the fire was finally stamped out at the foot of the Esquiline Hill. But before panic had subsided, or hope revived, flames broke out again in the more open regions of the city. Here there were fewer casualties; but the destruction of temples and pleasure arcades was even worse. This new conflagration caused additional ill feeling because it started on Tigellinus' estate in the Aemilian district. For people believed that Nero was ambitious to found a new city to be called after himself.

Of Rome's fourteen districts only four remained intact. Three were leveled to the ground. The other seven were reduced to a few scorched and mangled ruins. To count the mansions, blocks, and temples destroyed would be difficult. They included shrines of remote antiquity, such as Servius Tuillius' temple of the Moon, the Great Altar and holy place dedicated by Evander to Hercules, the temple vowed by Romulus to Jupiter the Stayer, Numa's sacred residence, and Vesta's shrine containing Rome's household gods. Among the losses, too, were the precious spoils of countless victories, Greek artistic masterpieces, and authentic records of old Roman genius. All the splendor of the rebuilt city did not prevent the older generation from remembering these irreplaceable objects.[16]

Nero's end and suicide

His health was good: for all his extravagant indulgence he had only three illnesses in fourteen years, and none of them serious enough to stop him form drinking wine or breaking any other regular habit. He was entirely shameless in the style of his appearance and dress, but always had his hair set in rows of curls and, when he visited Greece, let it grow long and hang down his back. He often gave audiences in an unbelted silk dressing-gown and slippers, with a scarf round his neck.[17]

Fate made certain unexpected additions to the disasters and scandals of Nero's reign. In a single autumn 30,000 deaths from plague were registered at the Temple of Libitina. There was a British disaster, when two important garrison-towns were taken by storm, and huge numbers of Romans and allies massacred, And there was a disgraceful defeat in the east, where the legions in Armenia were sent beneath the yoke, and we almost lost Syria.[18]---

At last a series of insulting edicts signed by Vindex must have made some impression on him: in a letter to the Senate he urged them to

---

[16] Tacitus, Annals, pp 362-364.

[17] Seutonius, p 244.

[18] Ibid, p 236.

avenge himself and Rome, but pleaded an infected throat as an excuse for not appearing at the Senate House in person. --- When further urgent dispatches reached Antium in quick succession he hurried back to Rome in a state of terror. On the way, however, he happened to notice a group of monumental sculpture, which represented a beaten Gaul being dragged along, by the hair, by a mounted Roman; this lucky sign sent him into a transport of joy, and he lifted his hands in gratitude to Heaven. When he arrived in the city, he neglected to address either the Senate or the people; instead, he summoned the leading citizens to his Palace where, after a brief discussion of the Gallic situation, he devoted the remainder of the session to demonstrating a completely new type of water-organ, and explaining the mechanical complexities of several different models. He even remarked that he would have them installed in the Theatre 'if Vindex has no objection'.[19]

At last, after nearly fourteen years of Nero's misrule, the earth rid herself of him. The first move was made by the Gauls under Julius Vindex, the governor of one of their provinces. --- But when news arrived of Galba's Spanish revolt he fainted dead away and remained mute and insensible for a long while. Coming to himself, he tore his clothes and beat his forehead, crying that all was now over. --- Nero was now so universally loathed that no bad enough abuse could be found for him. --- The implications of auspices, of omens old and new, and of his own dreams, began to terrify Nero. When a dispatch bringing the news that the other armies, too, had revolted was brought him at dinner, he tore it up, pushed over the table, etc. --- He made Locusta give him some poison, which he put in a golden box; then crossed to the Servilian Gardens, where he tried to persuade the Guards officers to flee with him. --- While he hesitated, a runner brought him a letter from Phaon. Nero tore it from the man's hands and read that, having been declared a public enemy by the Senate, he would be punished 'in ancient style' when arrested. --- By this time the troop of cavalry who had orders to take him alive were coming up the road. Nero gasped: 'Hark to the sound I hear! It is hooves of galloping horses.' Then, with the help of his secretary, Epaphroditius, he stabbed himself in the throat and was already half dead when a centurion entered.[20] He died June 9, 68 A.D. He was 31 years old and had ruled for fourteen years.

His dominant characteristics were his thirst for popularity and his jealousy of men who caught the public eye by any means whatsoever. --- Nero's unreasonable craving for immortal fame made him change a number of well-known names of things and places in his own favor. The

---

[19]   Ibid, pp 238, 239.

[20]   Ibid, pp 238-243.

month of April, for instance, became Neroneus; and Rome was on the point of being renamed 'Necropolis".[21]

Nero died on the anniversary of Octavia's murder. *In the widespread general rejoicing, citizens ran through the streets wearing caps of liberty.* Galba had been proclaimed emperor by his soldiers. The civil wars followed.

---

[21] Ibid, pp 245, 246.

Chapter 10

Civil Wars and the Flavian Emperors

The examples of government and law, which the Julio Claudian emperors from Augustus to Nero had given to their successors, have been briefly reviewed. The civil wars from 68 to 69 A.D. with the brief reigns of Galba, Otho, and Vitellius followed Nero. The Romans, beginning with Julius Caesar's invasion of England in 55 and 54 B.C., and emperor Claudius's conquest of England in 43 A.D., would occupy England for the entire period of the Roman Empire in the west. The Flavian emperors Vespasian, Titus, and Domitian introduce us to the Roman expansion and occupation of England, our next chapter. The first Flavian emperor Vespasius served as a commander for the Roman armies in England. The continued expansion and conquest of England continued after Domitian during the first century A.D. The second century emperors Trajan, Hadrian and Antonius Pius left familiar landmarks in England. A listing of the Roman emperors and brief review of Rome during the second to fifth centuries provides a brief introduction to the next chapter, England and the Romans.

Tacitus and Seutonius

Since Tacitus is a primary source of the history of the Roman emperors it would be helpful to present in brief more information about this author. Tacitus was born 56 A.D. and died during the first part of Hadrian's reign, after 117. Apparently nothing is known of his early life. He began his political career as a senator under Vespasian and became a quaestor in 81 or 82, under Titus, becoming the 'questor Augusti' attending the emperor himself. He survived the reign of terror under Domitian, to become tribune in 85, praetor in 88, and consul in 97. Tacitus had extensive direct personal contact with the highest levels of government during his lifetime. He provided unique observations and commentaries on the emperors he wrote about.

Michael Grant provided a brief history of Seutonius in the forward to *The Twelve Caesars*.

Gaius Suetonius Tranquillus was born in about A.D. 70. His family probably came from Hippo Reius (Annaba in Algeria). Suetonius may have taught literature at Rome for a time. He also seems to have practiced law, and then served on the staff of Pliny the Younger, when Pliny was governor, with special powers, of Bithynia-Pontus (northern Asia Minor) in A.D. 110-112; Pliny had earlier helped to secure him a small property in Italy. Subsequently Suetonius, who was a Roman knight (eques), occupied a succession of posts at the imperial court. First he held the 'secretaryship of studies' (a studiis), of which the precise functions are uncertain. Then he became director of the imperial libraries, and was finally placed in charge of the emperor's correspondence. Probably he occupied the first two of these three offices under Trajan (98-117); the last and most important appointment dates from Hadrian (117-138). --- An allusion in his extant writings seems to indicate that he was still alive after 130. Pliny described him as a quiet and studious man, devoted to writing. He was a representative of a new generation of professional scholars who became prominent in this period.[1]

The Civil Wars

Tacitus began *The Histories with* a presentation of the emperors who followed Nero in A.D. from 68 to 69, the period of the civil wars: *From Galba, Otho, and Vitellius, I have experienced nothing either to my advantage or my hurt. I cannot deny that I owe the launching of my career to Vespasian, or that I was advanced by Titus and still further promoted by Domitian; but those who lay claim to unbiased accuracy must speak of no man with either hatred or affection. I have reserved for my old age, if life is spared to me, the reigns of the deified Nerva and of the Emperor Trajan, which afford a richer and a safer theme; for it is the rare fortune of these days that a man may think what he likes and say what he thinks.*

The story I now commence is rich in vicissitudes, grim with warfare, torn by civil strife, a tale of horror even during times of peace. Four emperors slain by the sword. Three civil wars; often entwined with these, an even larger number of foreign wars. Successes in the East, disaster in the West, disturbance in Illyricum, disaffection in Gaul. The conquest of Britain immediately given up; the rising of the Sarmatian and Suebic tribes. Dacia had the privilege of inflicting and receiving defeat at our hands, and a pretender claiming to be Nero almost deluded

---

[1] Suetonius, The Twelve Caesars, p 7.

the Parthians also into declaring war. Now too Italy was smitten with new disasters, or disasters it had not witnessed for a long period of years. Towns along the rich coast of Campania were swallowed by the earth or buried from above. The city was devastated by fires, her most ancient temples were destroyed, and the Capitol itself was fired by Roman hands. Sacred rites were grossly profaned, and there was adultery among the great. The sea swarmed with exiles, and cliffs were red with blood. Worse horrors reigned in the city. To be rich or wellborn, to hold office or refuse it, was a crime; merit of any kind meant certain ruin. Nor were the informers more hated for their crimes than for their prizes; others won administrative office and a place at the heart of power; the hatred and fear they inspired worked universal havoc. Slaves were bribed against their masters, freedmen against their patrons, and, if a man had no enemies, he was ruined by his friends.[2]

Galba

Galba was a military commander who suppressed a revolt in the Gallic provinces and Spain. Born in 3 B.C., he would have been 71 years old, when *messengers arrived from Rome with the news that Nero, too, was dead, and that the citizens had all sworn obedience to himself.*

Stories of Galba's two characteristics, cruelty and greed, preceded him; he was said to have punished townships that had been slow to receive him by levying severer taxes and even dismantling their fortifications; to have executed not only officers and imperial agents, but their wives and children too. --- Thus his power and prestige were far greater while he was assuming control of the Empire than afterwards. --- He sentenced senators and knights to death without trial on the scantiest evidence, and seldom granted applications for Roman citizenship. --- Thus he outraged almost all classes at Rome; but the most virulent hatred of him was to be found in the Army. --- The loudest grumbling came from camps in Upper Germany, where the men claimed that they had not been rewarded for their services against the Gauls and Vindex. These, the first Roman troops bold enough to withhold their allegiance, refused on January 1st to take any oath except in the name of the senate; informing the Guards, by messenger, that they were thoroughly at odds with their Spanish-appointed Emperor, and would the Guards please choose one who would be acceptable to the Army as a whole?

Galba heard about this message and, thinking that he was being criticized for his childlessness rather than his senility, singled out from the crowd at one of his morning receptions a handsome and well-bred young man, Piso Frugi Licinianus, to whom he had already shown great favor, and appointed him perpetual heir to his name and property.[3]

---

[2] Tacitus, The Histories, pp 3-4.

[3] Seutonius, The Twelve Caesars, pp 254-256.

From Tacitus: *Galba was old and ill. Of his two lieutenants, Titus Vinius was the vilest of men and Cornelius Laco the laziest. Between them, they burdened Galba with the odium of Vinius's crime, and ruined him by the disdain for Laco's inefficiency.*

His march from Spain was slow and stained with bloodshed. He executed Cingonius Varro, the consul-elect, and Petronius Turpilianus, an ex-consul, the former as an accomplice of Nymphidius, the latter as one of Nero's generals. They were both denied any opportunity of a hearing or defense, and died apparently innocent. On his arrival at Rome the butchery of thousands of unarmed soldiers gave an ill omen to his entry, and alarmed even the men who did the slaughter. --- Now that Galba was detested, everything he did, whether right or wrong, brought upon him equal detestation.

Such was the state of the Roman world when Servius Galba, consul for the second time, and Titus Vinius his colleague, inaugurated the year which was their last, and almost the last for the commonwealth of Rome.[4]

Galba's end is portrayed by Seutonius: *A rapid succession of signs, from the beginning of his reign, had been portending Galba's end in accurate detail. During his march on Rome people were being slaughtered right and left all along his route whenever he passed through a town. --- Soon afterwards, news came that Otho had seized the Guards' camp. Though urged to hurry there in person, because his rank and presence could carry the day, Galba stayed where he was, bent on rallying to his standard the legionaries scattered throughout the city. --- There a party of cavalrymen, clattering through the city streets and dispersing the mob, caught sight of him from a distance. These were his appointed assassins. They reined in for a moment, then charged at him; his followers abandoned him, and he was butchered. --- Galba was murdered beside the Curian pool, and left lying just as he fell.* The rest of the story is as graphic as Seutonius is capable of expressing in a few words. *Galba died at age of seventy-two, before he had reigned seven months.*[5]

Otho

From Seutonius, whose father had personal knowledge of the emperor: *Otho, the Emperor-to-be, was born on April 25, A.D. 32 while Arruntius Camillus and Domitius Ahenobarbus were Consuls. His early wildness earned him many a beating from his father; he is said to have been in the habit of wandering about the city at night and seizing and tossing on a blanket any drunk or disabled person who crossed his path.*

---

[4] Tacitus, The Histories, pp 6-9.

[5] Seutonius, The Twelve Caesars, pp 256-258.

After his father's death he pretended a passion for an influential freedwoman at Court, though she was almost on her last legs; with her help he insinuated himself into the position of Nero's leading favorite. This may have happened naturally enough, since Nero and Otho were birds of a feather, yet it has quite often been suggested that their relationship was decidedly unnatural. Be that as it may, Otho grew so powerful that he did not think twice before bringing one of his own proteges, a former Consul found guilty of extortion, back into the Senate House, and there thanking the senators in anticipation for the pardon that they were to grant him, having accepted an immense bribe.

As Nero's confidant he had a finger in all his schemes and secrets. --- Nero banished Ortho to Lusitania as its Governor. Otho, who held the rank of quaestor, governed Lusitania for ten years with considerable moderation and restraint. Yet he seized the earliest opportunity of revenging himself on Nero, by joining Galba as soon as he heard of the revolt; but the political atmosphere was so uncertain that he did not underrate his own chances of sovereignty.

Galba's adoption of Piso came as a shock to Otho, who had hoped from day to day to secure this good fortune himself. Resentment and a massive accumulation of debts now prompted him to revolt. His one chance of survival, Otho frankly admitted, lay in becoming Emperor. --- Otho conspired to murder Galba. *His companions hoisted him* (Otho) *on their shoulders and acclaimed him Emperor. The street crowds joined the procession as eagerly as if they were sworn accomplices, and Otho reached his headquarters to the sound of cheers and the flash of drawn swords. He then dispatched agents to murder Galba and Piso and, avoiding all promises, told the troops merely that he would welcome whatever powers they might give him, but claim no others.*

Towards evening Otho delivered a brief speech to the Senate claiming to have been picked up in the street and compelled to accept the imperial power, but promising to respect the general will. Hence he proceeded to the Palace, where he received fulsome congratulations and flattery from all present, making no protest even when the crowd called him Nero.

Meanwhile, the armies in Germany took an oath of loyalty to Vitellius. Otho heard of this and persuaded the Senate to send a deputation, urging them to keep quiet, since an Emperor had already been appointed. But he also wrote Vitellius a personal letter; an invitation to become his father-in-law and share the Empire with him. Vitellius, however, had already sent troops forward to march on Rome under their generals, and it had become clear that war was inevitable. ---

Otho immediately decided on suicide. It is more probable that his conscience prevented him from continuing to hazard lives and property in a bid for the sovereignty than that he believed his men had become demoralized and incapable of success. --- What is more, his defeated army were by no means too shattered to face further perils, and anxious to redeem their reputation, even without such assistance.

After drinking a glass of cold water and testing the points of two daggers, he put one of them under his pillow, closed the door and slept soundly. He awoke at dawn and promptly stabbed himself with a single stroke below the left breast. His attendants heard him groan and rushed in; at first he could not decide whether to conceal or reveal the wound, which proved fatal. They buried him at once, as he had ordered them to do. His age was thirty-seven; and he died in the ninety-fifth day of his reign.[6]

Vitellius

Vitellius was born A.D. 14, and succeeded Otho and Galba as emperor. *Vitellius had spent his boyhood and adolescence on Capreae, among Tiberius' male prostitutes. There he won the nickname 'Spintia', which clung to him throughout his life; by surrendering his chastity, the story goes, he secured his father's first advancement to public office. --- Vitellius who, as he grew up, was notorious for every sort of vice, became a fixture at Court. Gaius admired his skill in chariot-driving; Claudius his skill at dice; Nero not only appreciated these talents, but was indebted to him for one particular service. --- Since he was thus the favorite of three emperors, Vitellius won public offices and important priesthoods, and later served as Governor of Africa and Curator of Public works. ---*

Galba's appointment of Vitellius to the governorship of Lower Germany was a surprising one; it had been suggested that Titus Vinius arranged it. This Vinius, a man of great influence, was well disposed towards Vitellius because they were fellow-supporters of the 'Blues' in the Circus. Yet since Galba had openly stated that a glutton was the sort of rival whom he feared least, and that he expected Vitellius to cram his belly with the fruits of the province, the appointment must have been made in contempt, not approval. ---

As soon as news reached Germany of Galba's murder, Vitellius put his affairs there in order, splitting the army into two divisions, one of which stayed under his own leadership. He sent the other against Otho. --- The news of the victory at Betriacum, and of Otho's suicide, reached Vitellius before he had left Gaul. --- At the outset of his march he had himself carried through the main streets of the cities on his route, in triumphal fashion; crossed rivers in elaborately decorated barges wreathed in garlands of many kinds; and always kept a lavish supply of delicacies available.[7]

---

[6] Ibid, pp 260-265.

[7] Ibid, pp 269-272.

At last amid fanfares of trumpets, Vitellius entered Rome in general's uniform and surrounded by standards and banners. His staff also wore military cloaks, and his soldiers carried drawn swords. Paying less and less attention to all laws, human or divine, Vitellius next assumed the office of Chief Priest, and chose to do so on the anniversary of the Allia defeat, (390 B.C., a day of evil omen). On the same occasion he announced the elections for ten years ahead, and appointed himself Consul for life. Then he dispelled any doubt as to which of the Caesars was to be his model by sacrificing to Nero's ghost. ---

This was how his reign began. --- Vitellius's ruling vices were extravagance and cruelty. He banqueted three and often four times a day, namely morning, noon, afternoon, and evening - the last meal being mainly a drinking bout - and survived the ordeal well enough by taking frequent emetics. What made things worse was that he used to invite himself out to such meals at the houses of a number of different people on one and the same day; and these never cost his various hosts less than 4,000 gold pieces each. The most notorious feast of the series was given him by his brother on his entry into Rome; 2,000 magnificent fish and 7,000 game birds are said to have been served. Yet even this hardly compares in luxuriousness with a single tremendously large dish, which Vitellius dedicated to the Goddess Minerva and named 'Shield of Minerva the Protectress of the City'. The recipe called for pike-livers, pheasant-brains, flamingo-tongues, and lamprey-milt; and the ingredients, collected in every corner of the Empire right from the Parthian frontier to the Spanish Straits, were brought to Rome by naval captains and triremes. Vitellius paid no attention to time or decency in satisfying his remarkable appetite. While a sacrifice was in progress, he thought nothing of snatching lumps of meat or cake off the altar, almost out of the sacred fire, and bolting them down; and on his travels would devour cuts of meat fetched smoking hot from wayside cook shops, and even yesterday's half-eaten scraps.

His cruelty was such that he would kill or torture anyone at all on the slightest pretext— not excluding noblemen who had been his fellow-students or friends, and whom he lured to Court by promises of a share in the rule of the Empire. --- In the eighth month of Vitellius' reign the Moesian and Panonian legions repudiated him and swore allegiance to Vespasian, distant though he was; those in Syria and Judaea did the same, and took their oaths to him in person.[8]

Tacitus described the military victory of Vespasian over Vitellius on December 20, A.D. 69 and the death of Vitellius. *The scene throughout the city was cruel and distorted: on the one side fighting and wounded men, on the other baths and restaurants: here lay heaps of bleeding dead, and close at hand were harlots and their ilk. All the vice*

---

[8] Ibid, pp 272 -275.

and license of luxurious peace, and all the crime and horror of a captured town were found. You would have thought the city made with fury and riotous with pleasure at the same time. Armies had fought in the city before this, twice, when Sulla mastered Rome, once under Cinna; nor were there less horrors then. What was now so inhumane was the people's indifference. Not for one minute did they interrupt their life of pleasure. The fighting was a new amusement for their holiday. Caring nothing for either party, they enjoyed themselves in riotous dissipation and took pleasure in their country's disaster.[9]

With the points of their swords they forced Vitellius to hold up his head and face their insults, than to watch his own statues hurtling down, but above all to look at the rostra and the site of Galba's murder. At last he was thrust along to the Gemonian Steps, where the body of Flavius Sabinus had lain. Just one thing that he was heard to say had a ring of true nobility. When some tribune jeered at him, he answered, 'And yet I was once your Emperor.' After that he fell under a shower of wounds; and the mob in their perversity abused him in his death, just as they had flattered him in his lifetime.[10]

Vitellius died at the age of fifty-six; his brother and son perished with him. The senate proclaimed Vespasian emperor the following day, on December 21, 69. *At Rome the Senate decreed to Vespasian all the usual powers of the principate. They were now happy and confident. Seeing that the civil war had broken out in the provinces of Gaul and Spain, and, after causing a rebellion first in Germany and then in Illyricum, had spread to Egypt, Judea, Syria, and in fact to all the provinces and armies of the empire, they felt as if the world had been purged of guilt and that all was now over. Their satisfaction was still further enhanced by a letter from Vespasian, which at first sight seemed to be phrased as if the war was still going on. Still his tone was that of an emperor; he portrayed himself as a simple citizen, and spoke with high esteem for the state. The Senate for its part showed no lack of deference. They decreed that Vespasian himself should be consul with his son Titus for his colleague, and on Domitian they conferred the preaetorship with the powers of a consul.*[11]

THE FLAVIAN EMPERORS

Vespasian

Vespasian, Titus Flavius Vespasianus, (b. A.D. 9, d. A.D. 79), succeeded Vitellius to become emperor from 69-79. Vespasian is the

---

[9] Tacitus, The Histories, pp 167-168.

[10] Ibid, p 169.

[11] Ibid, pp 172-173.

only emperor of the Twelve Caesars praised by Seutonius. Tacitus and Josephus also speak favorably of him. *He was the first emperor who changed for the better.*[12] Vespasian was a Roman commander in England in A.D. 43, was appointed proconsulate of Africa in 63 and received a command to suppress a rebellion in Judea in 67. He subdued all Judea except Jerusalem, which was to be later conquered by his son Titus. He became emperor in 69 and brought a semblance of stability to Rome and the provinces after the devastations of his predecessors.

Family history, birth and early life

Vespasian was not a member of the patrician elite. His father, Sabinus Flavius Petro was a tax collector, later a banker. His mother, *Vespasia Polla, belonged to a good family from Nursia. Her father Vespasius Polla had three times held a colonelcy and been Camp Prefect; her brother entered the Senate as a praetor.*

Vespasian was born on 17 November, A.D. 9 in the hamlet of Falacrina, just beyond Reate, --- five years before the death of Augustus. His paternal grandmother, Tertulla, brought him up on her estate at Cosa; and as Emperor he would often revisit the house, which he kept exactly as it had always been, in an attempt to preserve his childhood memories intact.[13]

For years he postponed his candidature for the broad purple stripe of senatorial rank, already earned by his brother, Flavius Sabinus, and in the end it was his mother who drove him to take this step; not by pleading with him or commanding him by parental authority. After military service in Thrace (N.E. Greece, Turkey and S.E. Bulgaria) and a questorship in Crete, he reached, in 39, the praetorship in the earliest year allowed him by law.

Marriage

Meanwhile, Vespasian had married Flavia Domitilla, the ex-mistress of Statilius Capella, an African knight from Sabrata. Her father, Flavius Liberalis, a humble quaestor's clerk from Ferentium, had appeared before a board of arbitration and established her claim to the full Roman citizenship, in place of only a Latin one. Vespasian had three children by Flavia, namely Titus, Domitian, and Domitilla who died before he held a magistracy, and so did Flavia herself; he then took up again with Caenis, his former mistress and one of Antonia's freedwomen and secretaries, who remained his wife in all but name even when he became Emperor.[14]

---

[12] Ibid, p 32.

[13] Suetonius, Twelve Caesars, p 279.

[14] Ibid, pp 279-280.

Military experiences

Vespasian served during the reign of Claudius, under Aulus Plautius, the commander of the Roman legions in Britain, *and fought thirty battles, subjugated two warlike tribes, and captured more than twenty towns, besides the entire Isle of Vectis.* More of this story will be presented in the next chapter on England. He retired during the reign of Nero for fear that he would be punished since he had received favors from Nero's enemy Narcissus, a previous command in Germany. *In the distribution of provinces he drew Africa, where his rule was characterized by great justice and dignity.*

He toured Greece in Nero's retinue but offended him deeply, by either leaving the room during his song recitals, or staying and falling asleep. In consequence he not only lost the imperial favor but was also dismissed from Court, and fled to a small out-of-the way township, where he hid in terror of his life until finally offered a province with the command of an army.

There was an uprising of the Jews in Syria and Judea. *To crush this uprising the Romans needed a strong army under an energetic commander, who could be trusted not to abuse his considerable powers. The choice fell on Vespasian. He had given signal proof of energy and nothing, it seemed, need be feared from a man of such modest antecedents. Two legions, with eight cavalry squadrons and ten auxiliary cohorts, were therefore dispatched to join the forces already in Judea; and Vespasian took his elder son, Titus, to serve on his staff. No sooner had they reached Judea than he impressed the neighboring provinces by his prompt tightening up of discipline and his audacious conduct in battle after battle. During the assault on one enemy fortress he was wounded on the knee by a stone and caught several arrows on his shield.*[15]

Troops support Vespasian to become emperor

It is clear that Vespasian gained power by the support of the soldiers, without first attempting approval by the senate. *The move to confer the throne on Vespasian began at Alexandria, where Tiberius Alexander with great promptitude administered the oath of allegiance to his troops on 1 July. This was later celebrated as his day of accession, although it was not until the third that the Jewish army took the oath in his presence. So eager was their enthusiasm that they would not even wait for the arrival of Titus, who was on his way back from Syria, where he had been conducting the negotiations between his father and Mucianus. --- Before 15 July the whole of Syria had sworn allegiance.*

---

[15] Ibid, pp 280-281.

In Pannonia, however, the Thirteenth Legion and the Seventh Galbian had not forgotten their resentment and fury after the battle of Bedriacum. They lost no time in joining Vespasian's cause, being chiefly instigated by Antonius Primus. --- The union of the Moesian and Pannonian armies soon attracted the troops in Dalmatia to the cause. --- So the Vespasian party used all their efforts to fan every spark of discontent throughout the empire. Letters were sent to the Fourteenth Legion in Britain and to the First Legion in Spain, since both had stood for Otho against Vitellius. In Gaul too, letters were scattered broadcast. All in an instant a mighty war was in full flame. The armies of Illyricum openly revolted, and all the others were ready to follow the first sign of success.[16]

Vespasian as emperor

Vespasian received the news of the outcome of the battle of Cremona and of the death of Vitellius. He returned to Rome. *Vespasian now devoted his attention to the affairs of Italy and the capital, and received an unfavorable report of Domitian, who seemed to be trespassing beyond the natural sphere of an emperor's youthful son. He accordingly handed over the flower of his army to Titus, who was to finish off the war with the Jews.[17]*

From Suetonius: *Vespasian, still rather bewildered in his new role of Emperor, felt a certain lack of authority and impressiveness; yet both these attributes were granted him. --- Vespasian, on his return to Rome, added eight more consulships (every year from A.D. 70 to 79 except A.D. 78) to the one he had already earned. He also assumed the office of Censor, and throughout his reign made it his principal business first to shore up the State, which was virtually in a state of prostration and collapse, and then to proceed to its artistic embellishment. The troops, conceited owing to their victory, or distressed and humiliated by defeat, had been indulging in all sorts of wild excesses; and internal dissension could be noted in the provinces and free cities, as well as in certain of the client kingdoms. This led Vespasian to discharge or punish a larger number of Vitellius' men and, so far from showing them any special favor, he was slow in paying them even the rewards to which they were entitled. He missed no opportunity of tightening discipline. ---*

He reduced the free communities of Achaea, Lycia, Rhodes, Byzantium, and Samos, and the kingdoms of Tracian Cilicia and Commagene, to provincial status. He garrisoned Cappadocia as a precaution against the frequent barbarian raids, and appointed a Governor of consular rank instead of a mere knight.

---

[16] Tacitus, The Histories, pp 103-108.

[17] Ibid, p 206.

In Rome, which had been made unsightly by fires and collapsed buildings, Vespasian authorized anyone who pleased to take over the vacant sites, and build on them if the original owners failed to come forward. He personally inaugurated the restoration of the burned Capitol by collecting the first basketful of rubble and carrying it away on his shoulders; and undertook to replace the 3,000 bronze tablets which had been lost in the fire, hunting high and low for copies of the inscriptions engraved on them. Those ancient, beautifully phrased records of senatorial decrees and ordinances of the Assembly dealt with such matters as alliances, treaties, and the privileges granted to individuals, and dated back almost to the foundation of Rome.

He also started work on several new buildings; a temple of Peace near the Forum, a temple to Claudius the God on the Caelian Hill, begun by Agrippina but almost completely destroyed by Nero; and the Colosseum, or Flavian Amphitheatre, in the center of the city, on discovering that this had been a favorite project of Augustus.

He reformed the Senatorial and Equestrian Orders, weakened by frequent murders and longstanding neglect; replacing undesirable members with the most eligible Italian and provincial candidates available. --- Vespasian found a huge waiting list of law-suits: old ones left undecided because of interruptions in regular court proceedings, and new ones due to the recent states of emergency. So he drew lots for a board of commissioners to settle war compensation claims and make emergency decisions in the Centumviral Court, thus greatly reducing the number of cases. Most of the litigants would otherwise have been dead by the time they were summoned to appear. ---

In all other matters he was, from first to last, modest and lenient, and more inclined to parade, than to cast a veil over his humble origins. Indeed, when certain persons tried to connect his ancestors with the founders of Reate, and with one of Hercules' comrades whose tomb is still to be seen on the Salarian Way, Vespasian burst into a roar of laughter. He had anything but a craving for outward show; on the day of his triumph the painful crawl of the procession so wearied him, that he said frankly: 'What an old fool I was to demand a triumph, as though I owed this honor to my ancestors or had ever made it one of my own ambitions! It serves me right!' Moreover, he neither claimed the tribunician power nor adopted the title 'Father of the Country' until very late in his life; and even before the Civil War was over, discontinued the practice of having everyone who attended his morning audiences searched for concealed weapons. ---

My researches show that no innocent party was ever punished during Vespasian's reign except behind his back or while he was absent from Rome, unless by deliberate defiance of his wishes or by misinforming him about the facts in the case. He was nearly always good natured, and had a good sense of humor. He enjoyed perfect health and took no medical precautions for reserving it, except to have his throat and body massaged regularly in the ball-alley, and to fast one whole day every month.[18] *He died a natural death at age sixty-nine, after a brief febrile illness.*

Titus

Titus, (b 41 A.D., d 81), son of Vespasian, ruled from 79 to 81. Vespasian had informed the senate that *either of his sons would succeed him or no one would. He grew up at court with Britannicus, sharing his teachers and following the same curriculum. --- When Titus came of age, the beauty and talents that had distinguished him as a child grew even more remarkable. --- He had a phenomenal memory, and displayed a natural aptitude alike for almost all the arts of war and peace; handled arms and rode a horse with great skill; could compose speeches and verses in Greek or Latin with equal ease, and actually extemporized them on occasion. He was something of a musician, too; sang pleasantly, and had mastered the harp.*

Titus's reputation, while an active and efficient colonel in Germany and Britain is attested by the numerous inscribed statues and busts found in both countries. After completing his military service he pleaded in the Roman Forum as a barrister; but in order to make a reputation, not because he meant to make a career of it. The father of his first wife, Arrecina Tertulla, was only a Roman knight but commanded the Guards. When she died, Titus married the very well connected Marcia Furnilla, whom he divorced after she had bore him a daughter. When his questorship at Rome ended, he went to command one of his father's legions in Judea.[19]

Judea

Titus Caesar had been entrusted by his father with the task of completing the reduction of Judea, 69-70. While he and his father were both still ordinary citizens, Titus had, in 67-69 distinguished himself as a soldier. Now his efficiency and reputation were steadily increasing, while the provinces and armies vied with one another in their enthusiasm for him. Wishing to seem independent of his good fortune, he always showed dignity and energy in the field. His affable and friendly conversation called forth devotion. He regularly mingled with his soldiers at their duties or on the march without compromising his dignity as general. Three legions awaited him in Judea, the Fifth, Tenth, and Fifteenth, all veterans from his father's army. These were reinforced by the Twelfth from Syria, and by detachments of the Twenty-Second and the Third brought over from Alexandria. This force was accompanied by twenty

---

[18] Seutonius, pp 284-287.

[19] Ibid, pp 292-293.

auxiliary cohorts and eight regiments of cavalry; also the kings Agrippa and Sohaemus and auxiliaries for king Antiochus, a strong force of Arabs, who had the hatred for the Jews usual between neighbors, and numerous individuals who had come from Rome and the rest of Italy, each tempted by the hope of securing their first place in the Emperor's still unoccupied affections. With this force Titus entered the enemy's country; his column was drawn up in order, he sent out scouts everywhere, and held himself ready to fight. He pitched his camp not far from Jerusalem.[20]

Now the number of those that were carried captive during this whole war was collected to be ninety-seven thousand; as was the number of those that perished during the whole siege eleven hundred thousand, the greater part of whom were indeed of the same nation [with the city of Jerusalem], but not belonging to the city itself; for they were come up from all the country to the feast of the unleavened bread, and were on a sudden shut up by an army, which, at the very first, occasioned so great as traitness among them that there came a pestilential destruction upon them, and soon afterward such a famine, as destroyed them more suddenly. --- Now this vast multitude is indeed collected out of remote places, but the entire nation was now shut up by fate as in a prison, and the Roman army encompassed the city when it was crowded with inhabitants. Accordingly the multitude of those that therein perished exceeded all the destructions that either men or God ever brought upon the world; for, to speak only of what was publicly known, the Romans slew some of them, some they carried captives, and others they made search for underground, and when they found where they were, they broke up the ground and slew all they met with.[21]

Upon the completion of the conquest of Jerusalem, September 8, 70, Titus returned to Rome. *He now became his father's colleague, almost his guardian; sharing in the Judean triumph, in the Censorship, in the exercise of tribunician power, and in seven consulships. He bore most of the burdens of government and, in his father's name, dealt with official correspondence, drafted edicts, and even took over the quaestor's task of reading the imperial speeches to the Senate. Titus also assumed command of the Guards, a post which had always before been entrusted to a knight, and in which he behaved somewhat highhandedly and tyrannically.[22]*

He was believed to be profligate as well as cruel, because of the riotous parties, which he kept going with his more extravagant friends

---

[20] Tacitus, Histories, p 233.

[21] Josephus, The Wars of the Jews, 6.9.3, 9.4.

[22] Seutonius, p 294.

far into the night; and immoral, too, because he owned a troop of inverts and eunuchs, and nursed a notorious passion for Queen Berenice, to whom he had allegedly promised marriage. He also had a reputation for greed, since it was well known that he was not averse to using influence to settle his father's cases in favor of the highest bidder. --- Titus provided a most lavish gladiatorial show; he also staged a sea fight on the old artificial lake, and when the water had been let out, used the basin for further gladiatorial contests and a wild-beast hunt, 5,000 beasts of different sorts dying in a single day.[23]

Titus as emperor

Titus' reign, 79-81, was marked by a series of dreadful catastrophes— an eruption of Mount Vesuvius in Campania, in 79, (destroying Pompeii, Herculaneum, Stabiae, and Oplontis), a fire at Rome, in 80, which burned for three days and nights, and one of the worst outbreaks of plague that had ever been known. --- He set up a board of ex-consuls, chosen by lot, to relieve distress in Campania, and devoted the property of those who had died in the eruption and left no heirs to a fund for rebuilding the stricken cities. His only comment of the fire at Rome was: 'This has ruined me!' He stripped his own country mansions of their decorations, distributed these among the public buildings and temples, and appointed a body of knights to see that his orders were promptly carried out. Titus attempted to cure the plague and limit its ravages by every imaginable means, human as well as divine, resorting to all sorts of sacrifices and medical remedies.

One of the worst features of Roman life at the time was the license long enjoyed by informers and their managers. Titus had these well whipped, clubbed, and then taken to the amphitheater and paraded in the arena; where some were put up for auction as slaves and the remainder deported to the most forbidding islands. In further discouragement of any who, at any future time, might venture on similar practices, he allowed nobody to be tried for the same offence under more than one law, and limited the period during which inquiries could be made into the status of dead people.

He had promised before his accession to accept the office of Chief Priest as a safeguard against committing any crime, and kept his word. Thereafter he was never directly or indirectly responsible for a murder; and, although often given abundant excuse for revenge, he swore that he would rather die than take life.

Titus' brother Domitian took part in endless conspiracies against him, stirred up disaffection in the armed forces almost openly, and toyed with the notion of fleeing to them. Yet Titus had not the heart

---

[23] Ibid, p 295.

to execute Domitian, dismiss him from Court, or even treat him less honorably than before.

Death, however, intervened. He collapsed with fever, and complained bitterly that life was being undeservedly taken from him. Titus died at the age of forty-one, in the same country house where Vespasian had also died. It was September, A.D. 81, and he had reigned two years, two months, and twenty days.[24]

Domitian

Domitian, (b. 51, d. 96) followed Titus in 81 and ruled to 96 A.D. Some believed that Domitian may have had a hand in the death of Titus. In any case, his animosity toward his brother Titus is well established. From Suetonius: *At Vespasian's death Domitian toyed for awhile with the idea of offering his troops twice as large a bounty as Titus had given them; and stated bluntly that his father's will must have been tampered with, since it originally assigned him a half-share in the Empire. He never once stopped plotting, secretly or openly, against his brother. When Titus fell suddenly and dangerously ill, Domitian told the attendants to leave him for dead before he had actually breathed his last; and afterwards granted him no recognition at all, beyond approving his deification. In fact, he often slighted Titus's memory by the use of ambiguous terms in speeches and edicts.*

Emperor Domitian awarded his wife Domitia the title of Augusta. She had presented Domitian with a daughter during his second consulship and, in the following year with a son. He began his reign, by presenting *extravagant entertainments in the Colosseum and the Circus, by distributing a popular bounty of three gold pieces a head,* gave feasts and banquets, *scattered all kinds of gifts to be scrambled for,* etc.

Early in his reign there were constructive actions and achievements. *He restored a great many important buildings that were now gutted ruins, including the Capitol, which had now been burned down again (in 80) but allowed no names to be inscribed on them, except his own, not even the original builder's. He also raised a temple to Jupiter the Guardian on the Capitoline Hill, the Forum of Nerva (as it is now called), the Flavian Temple, a stadium, a concert hall, and the artificial lake for sea-battles— its stones laterserved to rebuild the two sides of the Great circus which had been damaged by fire.*[25]

He was most conscientious in dispensing justice, and convened many extraordinary legal sessions on the tribunals in the Forum; annulling every decision of the Centumviral court, which seemed to him unduly influenced, and continually warning the Board of Arbitrations not

---

[24] Ibid, 297-298.

[25] Ibid, pp 299-303.

to grant any fraudulent claims for freedom. It was his ruling that if a jury man were proved to have taken bribes, all his colleagues must be penalized as well as himself. He personally urged the tribunes of the people to charge a corrupt aedile with extortion, and to petition the senate for a special jury in the case; and kept such a tight hold on the city magistrates and provincial governors that the general standard of honesty and justice rose to an unprecedented high level— you need only observe how many such personages have been charged with every kind of corruption since his time![26]

His leniency and self-restraint were not, however, destined to continue long, and the cruel streak in him became apparent— rather before his avaricious traits. He executed one beardless boy, in distinctly poor health, merely because he happened to be a pupil of the actor Paris Pantomimus, and closely resembled him in his style of acting and appearance. --- Domitian put many senators to death, among them a group of ex-Consuls, three of whom, Civica Cerealis, Adilius Glabrio, and Salvidienus Orfitus, he accused of conspiracy. Cerealis was executed while governing Asia; Glabro while already in exile. Others were executed on the most trivial charges. Aelius Lamia lost his life as a result of some suspicious but old and harmless witticisms at Domitian's expense; he had been robbed of his wife by Domitian. --- Domitian was not merely cruel, but cunning a sudden into the bargain. He summoned a Palace steward to his bedroom, invited him to join him on his couch, made him feel perfectly secure and happy, condescended to share a dinner with him— yet had him crucified on the following day! --- Any charge, brought by any accuser - to have spoken or acted in prejudice of the emperor's welfare was enough - might result in the confiscation of a man's property, even if he were already dead. --- Domitian's agents collected the tax on Jews (imposed by Vespasian after the destruction of the temple of Jerusalem in A.D. 70) with a particular lack of mercy; and took proceedings not only against those who kept their Jewish origins a secret in order to avoid the tax, but against those who lived as Jews without professing Judaism. ---

A reign of terror characterized his last years, 93-96. All this made him everywhere hated and feared. Finally his friends and favoritre freedmen conspired to murder him, with the connivance of his wife Domitia. --- Domitian was such a prey to fear and anxiety that the least sign of danger unnerved him. --- As the critical day drew near his nervousness increased. The gallery where he took his daily exercise was now lined with plaques of highly-polished moonstone, which reflected everything that happened behind his back; and no imperial audiences were granted to prisoners unless Domitian were alone with them, and actually had tight hold of their fetters. To remind his staff that

---

[26] Ibid, p 303-304.

even the best of intentions could never justify a freedman's complicity in a master's murder, he executed his secretary Epaphroditius, who had reputedly helped Nero to commit suicide after everyone else had deserted him.

Domitian was murdered after retirement to his bedroom, confident from an oracle that the danger had passed. He died at the age of forty-four, on 18 September, A.D. 96, in the fifteenth year of his reign.[27]

Listing of the Roman emperors.

A listing of the Roman emperors from Augustus to Constantine helps to follow the chronology of the events to follow in the next chapter on the Roman occupation of England, following Julius Caesar's invasions in 55 and 54 B.C.

Augustus 31 B.C.- 14 A.D.
Tiberius 14 A.D.- 37 A.D.
Caligula 37-41
Claudius 41-54   Conquest of England
Nero 54-68   Revolts in England
Galba, Otho, Vitellius 68-69   Civil wars
Vespasian 69-79   Expansion to Wales, Scotland
Titus-79-81
Domitian 81-96   Civil strife   Agricola
Nerva 96-98
Trajan 98-117
Hadrian 117-138
Antonius Pius 138-161
Marcus Aurelius 161-180
Commodus 177(180)-192   Civil strife
Septimus Severus-193-211
Caracalla to 217, Elagabalus to 219, Alexander Severus to 235
Fifty years of civil strife. In the thirty-five years between Alexander Severus and Aurelian thirty-seven men were proclaimed emperors.
Aurelian 270-275
Diocletian 284-305
Constantius 305-306
Constantine 312-337
Theodosius 379-395
Justinian 527-483

We have completed a brief review of the emperors from Augustus 31 B.C. to those who ruled in the first century to Domitian (81-

---

[27] Ibid, pp 306-312.

96). The emperors who reigned during the second century, from Nerva (96-98) and Trajan (98-117) to include Hadrian of the third century, (117-138) and Antonius Pius (138-168) will be referred to in the next chapter *England and the Romans*. Since the compilation of Roman law in the Justinian Code covers laws during the time in Rome from the first century B.C. to the beginning of the third century A.D., a brief summary of the emperors Marcus Aurelius (161-180), Commodus (180-192) and Septimus Severus (193-211) will follow the second century emperors.

Nerva.

Nerva, Marcus Cocceius (b. A.D 35, d. 98), ruled from 96 to A.D.98. The first of the so-called "Good Emperors", Nerva began the reconstruction, which was made necessary by the extravagances of Domitian, who had been assassinated. Nerva's adoption of Trajan as his aide and successor in 97 pacified the military element and removed any uncertainty as to the identity of the next emperor. A program of economy brought order out of the chaos of Roman imperial finances. An old man at the time of his accession, Nerva died in Rome, Jan. 25, 98, after a reign of sixteen months.

Trajan

Trajan (b. A.D. 53, d. 117) ruled from 98 to 117. He was born in Spain and was adopted by Emperor Nerva in 97. He succeeded to the throne after Nerva's death in 98. Under Trajan the territory of Rome reached its greatest extent. His wars with the Dacians (101-106) ended with the expansion into the empire of all Dacia in the Danube Valley. His Parthian wars (114-116) carried the Roman standard to the Persian Gulf. As the result of other annexations, the kingdom of the Nabataean Arabs became the Roman province of Arabia, and provincial status was likewise accorded the defeated Armenians. While the condition of imperial finance was improved by the acquisition of the Dacian treasury and the revenue from the Dacian gold mines, an extensive public works program provided the empire with new roads and better harbor facilities. In addition to the new forum, which Trajan built at Rome, mementoes of his reign are the famous column at Rome, which commemorated his Dacian victories, and the equally well- known arch at Beneventum. Despite the lack of full and original literary sources for the reign of Trajan, it is known that he was personally popular and preserved good relations with the Senate; the army was happy and contented under this competent and successful leader.

Hadrian

Hadrian (b. A.D. 76, d. A.D. 138) ruled from 117 to 138. He was born in Rome, A.D. 76. He was a Spaniard and a distant relative of Trajan, and was chosen by him as his successor. Hadrian proved to be a great administrator. He continued Trajan's policy of friendly relations with the senate, but he also built up a permanent and powerful bureaucracy recruited from the equestrian class. Two extensive tours, the first throughout the western provinces, 121-123; and the second in the East, 123-126 amply demonstrated his sincere interest in the welfare of the empire. A wall in the north of England between Solway Firth and the Tyne River was built at Hadrian's direction about A.D. 121-122 to protect England from incursions from Scotland. It came to be known as Hadrian's Wall, and traces of it still remain. Frontier defenses were strengthened and many towns and cities improved by a government aided public works program; Hadrian also initiated the imperial post, which provided a better communication system for Italy. Other reforms included the elimination of the publican (tax farmers) and the beginnings of the codification of Roman law. Handsome, brilliant, witty, Hadrain was well educated and a great admirer of Greek culture. He was reputed to be able to write, dictate, and listen to a conversation at the same time. Expert in mathematics, music, and painting, he also wrote an autobiography, which has not survived. Toward the end of this reign Hadrian became ill and despondent and that he tried three times to commit suicide. He died July 10, 138.

Antoninus Pius

    Antoninus Pius (b. A.D. 86, d. 161) ruled from 138 to 161. Antoninus was the son of the Roman consul Aurelius Fulvus. Antoninus was a sound and careful administrator who, after years of public service, was chosen by the Emperor Hadrian to be his successor. His long and peaceful reign was marked by accord with the senate, humanitarian reforms, and the strengthening of Rome's frontier defenses. When he died after a brief illness in A.D. 161, Antoninus was succeeded by his adopted son, Marcus Aurelius.

Marcus Aurelius

    Marcus Aurelius (b. 121, d. 180) ruled from 161 to 180. He was born in Rome. Marcus was the adopted son of Antoninus Pius. Marcus Aurelius had to spend nearly his entire reign campaigning on the borders of the empire. His first war, waged with the Parthians, from A.D. 161 to 165, was a military success, but his soldiers brought back from the East a deadly plague, which swept through the empire and killed thousands of Romans. The plague was followed by many other disasters; famine, floods, and earthquakes. From 167 to 180, there was almost continuous fighting on the Danubian frontier with the Marcomanni and Quadi. The severe drain on the treasury occasioned by these wars at one time reduced the finances to such a state that Marcus Aurelius had to hold an auction of his personal possessions in the Forum; later, however, his victories provided sufficient booty for him to buy back what he had sold. The character of Marcus Aurelius, as revealed in the celebrated Meditations, is interesting. As a child, he had received careful instruction in literature, drama, music, mathematics, and oratory from the best teachers of his day. His special interest was in philosophy of a quasi-religious sort; he embraced Stoicism at the age of twelve, and his Meditations, written later, in Greek, present his more mature reflections on that philosophy. As a philosopher, Marcus Aurelius was not profound; rather, he reveals himself as a sincere, honest 'citizen of the world' struggling with familiar problems of life and death. In spite of his philosophic view of life, he was consistently hostile to Christianity, and persecution of the Christians was systematically pursued under his direction. He supported the old religion as an essential part of the imperial system and therefore considered the Christians and their teachings as a threat to the established order. In fulfillment of his conception of the duties of emperor, he paid close attention to internal administration, legal reform, and taxation. However, he was particularly blind to the faults of his son, Commodus, whom he made co-emperor in 177. This incompetent and unworthy son became emperor when Marcus Aurelius died of the plague, in 180.

Commodus
        Commodus (b. 161, d. 192) ruled from 180 to 192. He had been made co-emperor with his father, Marcus Aurelius, in A.D. 177, and became sole emperor after his father's death in 180. Dio Cassius and Herodian, historians who wrote during the first half of the third century, present the reign of Commodus in a most unfavorable light. He was criticized by his contemporaries for concluding what they considered a disgraceful peace with the German and Sarmatian tribes against whom Marcus Aurelius had fought. Relations between Commodus and the senate were far from cordial, and as early as 182, members of his own family, including his sister Lucilla, were involved in an unsuccessful conspiracy to remove Commodus from the throne. Commodus left the administration of the empire to his favorites, the praetorian prefect Perennis and the chamberlain Cleander, while he gave himself up to the pleasures of life in Rome. Early in his reign Commodus exchanged his own name, Lucius Aelius Arurelius Commodus, for that of his father, Marcus Commodus Antoninus. Later, he identified himself with the demigod Hercules and altered his name and titles to Commodus Augustus Hercules Romanus Exsuperatorius Amazonius Invictus; he also insisted that Rome should be called Colonia Commodiana (Colony of Commodus). The behavior of Commodius became increasingly irrational during the last few months of his reign. At the end of 192, a new conspiracy against Commodus was hatched in the palace; Marcia, the emperor's mistress; Eclectus, his chamberlain; and Laetus, his praetorian prefect, obtained the services of an athlete named Narcissus who obligingly strangled Commodus on Dec. 31, 192.

Septimius Severus

Septimius Severus (b. 146, d. 211) ruled from 193 to 211. He was born at Leptis Magna, Africa. Septimius Severus was the strong man who emerged as the head of the Roman state after the year of civil war following the assassination of Commodus. He had studied law at Rome and had filled the usual provincial and imperial administrative posts. In 193 he was in command of the legions stationed in Pannonia, and he marched on Rome to overthrow the puppet Emperor Julianus. The early years of the reign of Severus were spent in eliminating his rivals, Niger in the East and Albinus in the West, and in a successful war against the Parthians from 197-202. Thereafter Severus turned his attention to administrative affairs. His policy involved the concentration of executive and judicial powers in the hands of the *princeps* and his subordinates and the elevation of the provinces to a more or less equal status with Italy. He also opened the way for a progressive militarization of the imperial bureaucracy by allowing veteran officers to hold civil service posts. In 208 Severus went to Britain to undertake a series of campaigns in the Scottish highlands. After losing a large number of men and gaining very little territory, he withdrew to York, where he died Feb 4, 211. His sons, Caracalla and Geta, as co-emperors, succeeded him.

Third and Fourth Century Roman Emperors

Septimus Severus set up an autocratic rule based on the support of an army. His son Caracalla (211-217), followed. He attempted to remove the distinction between Italians and foreigners from the provinces. He was assassinated in 217. There followed Macrinus and a year later he was replaced by Heliogabalus who reigned 218-222. Heliogabalus was a mad emperor in the tradition of Nero and Commodus.

Alexander Severus, 222-235, gave Rome a brief period of good government, but the insubordination of his troops led to his murder. Fifty years of anarchy followed. There followed economic decline. Invasions of Persians, and so-called barbarian incursions of the provinces were not met by the Roman legions. Between 235 and 285 the Roman government disintegrated. Revolutions, civil wars, barbarian invasions, plagues, and famines convulsed the empire. During the middle of the third century, independent states began to gain power in Gaul and the Near East. In Rome emperors were set up and overthrown almost overnight.

Aurelian (270-275) restored order for the time being and built a wall around Rome. Aurelian was assassinated and there followed a decade of chaos when six emperors ruled. Under Diocletian, 285-305, the economy improved, and Rome's military forces were strengthened. He divided the empire into four military and administrative districts. Diocletian ruled jointly with Maximian and established two minor Caesars who were to succeed to the throne. The death of Diocletian was followed by civil wars. Constantine The Great, 306-337, suppressed the civil wars and transferred the capitol of the empire from Rome to Constantinople (formerly Byzantium). Constantine's fame was his support of Christianity, making it the state religion. Constantine, who ended the persecution of Christians, murdered his eldest son, his second wife, and his political rival Licinius.[28] Theodosius divided the empire into east and west in 395, naming his two sons as heirs and heads of the east and west empires. Alaric the Goth sacked Rome in 410. The Vandals sacked Rome in 455. As we shall see in the chapter to follow, appeals by the English for military support from Rome against the Jutes and Scots were refused in 443. The Roman legions left England in 448, never to return.

Justinian codified Roman law based on the laws developed under the Roman emperors from the first century B.C. to the beginning of the third century A.D. The compilation was ordered by Justinian, in 527 A.D and completed during the years 527-564, during the reign of Justinian.

---

[28] Michael Grant, Constantine the Great, p 226. 1998, Barnes and Noble, Inc.

Chapter 11

England and the Romans

Ancient

There are apparently no written records of the early history of England prior to the Romans. Plutarch gave one reference to England in his chapter on Caesar: *But his* (Caesar's) *expedition into Britain was the most famous testimony of his courage. For he was the first who brought a navy into the western ocean, or who sailed into the Atlantic with an army to make war; and by invading an island, the reported extent of which had made its existence a matter of controversy among historians, many of whom questioned whether it were not a mere name and fiction, not a real place, he might be said to have carried the Roman empire beyond the limits of the known world.*[1]

We shall return to The Gallic War, by Julius Caesar, to quote references of his first and second invasions of England in 55 and 54 B.C., as well as his histories of the peoples he encountered there in his Gallic Wars. Caesar's history is apparently the first written history of England. We shall quote Caesar's references to the peoples of Gaul, and to a lesser extent Germany, as well as England. It is well established in Caesar's time that these peoples had access across the narrow seas between the continent of Europe and England, the English Channel and the Strait of Dover. Historians have never appreciated the ease with which travel by water can be accomplished and it is likely that people crossed these waters long before the millennia and a half, B.C., estimated by historians. For example it is a common discovery in early childhood that some objects will float on water, like a stick or piece of wood. It is also a matter of common observation among children that objects floating on a puddle of water move when they are blown by the wind. It would not take a great leap of the imagination or a genius to figure out that these same relationships could apply to larger objects, and that use of wood for building shelters could be applied to a ship and that animal hides could

---

[1] Plutarch, Lives, v 2, p 215.

be placed on a superstructure, thus 'inventing' the first sailing vessel. In a place where there are contrary winds, or lack of wind, the use of paddles or oars would not be anything but a simple improvement over propulsion using arms and hand.

It is not necessary to delve into ancient myths regarding the first settlements of England. It is hoped that reliable archeological studies will add to our knowledge in the future. Travel by land north of England to the highlands of Scotland and back and forth across narrow bodies of water, the Irish Sea and North Channel, were probably feasible to the ancient people. Study of global climatic changes associated with the Ice Age as well as archeological studies may provide evidence that migration by land and short bodies of water were most likely accomplished by ancient peoples long before that estimated by historians.

Caesar's Invasions

Caesar had little knowledge of England but had sent Commius and Volusensus over to England to obtain advance information before his first invasion in 55 B.C. Caesar gave his reason for this invasion: *The campaign season was almost over, and because the whole of Gaul looks northwards, winter comes early in these regions. Despite these facts, Caesar changed his course to set out for Britain, aware as he was that our enemies in almost all our wars with the Gauls had received reinforcements from that quarter.* Caesar also gave another reason— to find out himself what England was like: *He considered, moreover, that even if the season left no time for a campaign, none the less, it would be a great advantage to him simply to land on the island and observe the kind of people who lived there, and the localities, harbors, and approaches. Every one of these points was unknown to almost all the Gauls. No one, except for traders, went there as a matter of course, and not even did they know anything beyond the coastline and the areas facing Gaul.*[2]

Caesar assembled eighty transport ships, including eighteen for the calvary, and distributed his warships among his quaestor, legates and prefects. He took advantage of good weather and reached England, at Dover, at about 8 or 9 A.M., August 26, 55 B.C.[3]

Caesar had to sail his ships seven miles to the west of Dover to land on a level beach. His forces encountered great difficulties landing with their heavy gear. The English were able to maneuver better and were familiar with the terrain, but Caesar's forces managed to subdue the English. Caesar was having more problems. The eighteen ships with calvary were delayed in reaching England, and had to return to port due

---

[2] Caesar, The Gallic War, p 79.

[3] Ibid, p 81 and Editors note, p 230.

to a storm that arose when the ships neared England. His warships at anchor were severely damaged by weather and very high tides. This posed a threat to the return of the forces to France. The English forces rallied but were finally subdued with the assistance of Commius and the calvary. *The enemy sent envoys to Caesar to sue for peace. Caesar doubled the number of hostages which he had previously demanded from them and ordered that they be taken to the Gallic mainland, because the autumnal equinox,* (September 24), *was at hand and he considered that as his ships were damaged the voyage should not be exposed to winter storms.*[4]

Caesar's forces returned to Gaul. He ordered to have as many ships built as possible for the invasion of England the following year. The older ships were to be altered. All were to be fitted with both sails and oars. Caesar ordered that some of the ships were to be shallower than those used in the Mediterranean and that the cargo ships were to be broader for carrying large numbers of pack animals. Caesar then left for Italy. Clearly the first invasion was preparatory for a larger invasion the following year. For this invasion, in 54 B.C., Caesar was well equipped with 600 ships ready to his specifications with five legions and 2000 calvary. His forces sailed from Bologne and landed at the same beach where they had been the previous year. *The whole fleet reached Britain at around midday, but there was no enemy visible in the area. Later, however, Caesar learned from prisoners that although a large host of them had arrived, they had panicked at the size of the fleet, which, including last year's ships and the private vessels, which certain individuals had built for their convenience was seen to number more than 800 at once. So they had left the shore and hidden themselves away on higher ground.*[5]

But another storm had severely damaged the Roman ships, which Caesar ordered to be beached and repaired. *He then pursued the English forces now led by Cassivellaunus who sent messengers to Kent (which was ruled over by four kings— Cingetorix, Carvilius, Taximagulus, and Segovax). He ordered them to muster all their forces, strike at the Roman fleet's camp without warning, and launch an assault. When they reached the camp, however, our men made a sortie. They killed a large number of the enemy, captured their aristocratic leader Lugotorix, and returned without casualties. News of this battle reached Cassivellaunus. He had suffered many defeats and his lands were ruined: he was particularly disturbed by the defection of allied states, so finally he sent envoys to Caesar through Commius the Atrebatian to surrender.*

---

[4] Ibid, p 87.

[5] Ibid, p 93.

Caesar demanded hostages, as he had done the previous year, and settled the annual tribute, which Britain must pay to the Roman people. [6]

The People of England

Caesar provided an account of the people in England: *The inland regions of Britain are inhabited by people whom the Britons themselves claim, according to oral tradition, are indigenous. The coastal areas belong to people who once crossed from Belgium in search of booty and war: almost all of these inhabitants are called by the same national names as those of the states they originally came from. After waging war they remained in Britain and began to farm the land. Population density is high, and their dwellings are extremely numerous and very like those of the Gauls.* The next part of the narrative gave inaccurate information which Caesar had of the island's geography and mineral resources and then stated: *Of all the island's inhabitants, by far the most civilized are those who live in Kent, a region which is entirely coastal. Their way of life is much the same as that of the Gauls. Inland, the people for the most part do not plant corn-crops, but live on milk and meat and clothe themselves in animal skins.* Caesar then gave his own impressions of the appearance of the Britons in battle: *All the Britons paint themselves with woad, which produces a dark color; by this means they appear more frightening in battle. They have long hair and shave their bodies, all except for the head and upper lip.* [7]

Caesar, although considering those in Britain who live inland to be indigenous, does state that the occupants in the coastal region of England came from Belgium, and elsewhere in his narrative, from other states of northern France. For example there was trade as well as military reasons for transit of people between England and the continent. Our next source of information about the early history of England and neighboring states came from Tacitus in his book Agricola, written in 98 A.D. Tacitus married the daughter of Agricola when he was a young man. Agricola (40-93 A.D.) was appointed by emperor Vespasian as a general and governor of England in 78 A.D. He had served as a military tribune in Britain from 59 to 61 and was appointed a commander in Britain in 69. His campaigns led him to successful outcomes in northern England, Wales and Scotland until 84, when he returned to Rome.

Tacitus's description of the people of Britain is as follows: *Who the first inhabitants of Britain were, whether natives or immigrants, is open to question: one must remember we are dealing with barbarians.* (The Romans of course considered all people other than themselves as barbarians). *But their physical characteristics vary, and the variation is*

---

[6] Ibid, p 99.

[7] Ibid, p 95.

suggestive. The reddish hair and large limbs of the Caledonians (upper Scotland) *proclaim a German origin; the swarthy faces of the Silures, the tendency of their hair to curl, and the fact that Spain lies opposite, all lead one to believe that Spaniards crossed in ancient times and occupied that part of the country.* (It would be many years before latitude and still later, longitude could be determined with any degree of confidence. The ancients believed that Ireland was between England and Spain). *The peoples nearest to the Gauls likewise resemble them. It may be that they still show the effect of a common origin; or perhaps it is climatic conditions that have produced this physical type in lands that converge so closely from north and south. On the whole, however it seems likely the Gauls settled in the island lying so close to their shores. In both countries you find the same ritual and religious beliefs. There is no great difference in language, and there is the same hardihood in challenging danger, the same cowardice in shirking it when it comes close.*[8] Both of these ancient authorities agree that England, at least the coastal regions across the English Channel, were populated by the Gauls.

Bede, the Father of English History, comments on England's earliest inhabitants in his *Ecclesiastical History of the English People*, written in 732 A.D., as follows: *At first the only inhabitants of the island were the Britons, from whom it takes its name, and who according to tradition, crossed into Britain from Armorica (Brittany), and occupied the southern parts. When they had spread northwards and possessed the greater part of the island, it is said that some Picts from Scythia (probably Scandinavia) put to sea in a few longships, and were driven by storms around the coasts of Britain, arriving at length on the north coast of Ireland. Here they found the nation of the Irish, from whom they asked permission to settle: but their request was refused. --- So the Picts crossed into Britain, and began to settle in the north of the island, since the Britons were in possession of the South.*[9] Thus there is agreement among these authors, Caesar, Tacitus and Bede that the earliest people of England came from the north coast of Europe. Therefore it would be of interest to know of the customs and people of Gaul at the time of Caesar.

The People of Gaul

We shall return to *The Gallic War* by Caesar which presents a good deal of information about the people of Gaul: *In the whole of Gaul two types of men are counted as being of worth and distinction. The ordinary people are considered almost as slaves. They dare do nothing on their own account and are not called to counsels. When the majority*

---

[8] Tacitus, The Agricola and The Germania, pp 61-2

[9] Bede, Ecclesisastical History of The English People, pp 45-46

are oppressed by debt or heavy tribute, or harmed by powerful men, they swear themselves away into slavery to the aristocracy, who then have the same rights over them as masters do over their slaves.[10]

Of the two types of men of distinction, however, the first is made up of the druids, and the other of the knights. The druids are involved in matters of religion. They manage public and private sacrifices and interpret religious customs and ceremonies. Young men flock to them in large numbers to gain instruction, and they hold the druids in great esteem. For they decide almost all disputes, both public and private: if some crime has been committed, if there has been murder done, if there is a dispute over an inheritance or over territory, they decide the issue and settle the rewards and penalties. If any individual or group of people does not abide by their decision, the druids ban them from sacrifices. This is their most severe punishment. Those who are banned in this way are counted among the wicked and criminal: everyone shuns them and avoids approaching or talking to them, so as not to suffer any harm from contact with them. If they seek help at law, they receive no justice, and they are never given positions of prestige. A chief druid rules over all the rest and has supreme authority among them. When such a man dies, if there is an outstanding druid among those remaining he succeeds to this position, but if there are a number of equal ability, they decide the leadership by a vote of all the druids, and sometimes even in armed combat. At a certain time of year they sit in judgment in a sacred spot in the territory of the Carnutes, in an area right in the middle of Gaul. Everyone who has a dispute comes to this place from every region, and submits to their decisions and judgments. It is believed that this institution was discovered in Britain and transferred to Gaul; and nowadays those who want to understand these matters in more detail usually travel to Britain to learn about them.[11]

It is of interest that the institution governing law as practiced in Gaul originated in Britain. We have therefore Caesar's belief that not only did settlement of England come from Gaul but that certain customs or practices in Britain were adopted in Gaul. Historians concur that the druids practiced not only in Gaul, but in England and the neighboring states.

Caesar attributed to the druids special privileges and immunities: *They do not take part in war, nor do they pay taxes like the*

---

[10] The qualification *almost* before slaves leads one to wonder just what Caesar means by this statement. It would be of interest to pursue the origins of slavery and to know just when it was introduced to Europe and England. For example, did it pass from Asia and Egypt to Rome and then to Europe several centuries B.C., or later with the Romans and Caesar?

[11] Caesar, The Gallic War, pp 127-127

rest of the people. They are exempt from military service and from all obligations. The education of the druids follows: *They are told to memorize a large number of lines of poetry, and to spend some twenty years in training. Nor do they think it proper to commit this teaching to writing, although for almost all other purposes, including public and private accounts, they use Greek characters.*

Caesar attributed the same type of education of the druids that a Roman from the nobility would follow, namely a study of the Greek poets, philosophers and oratory. Just as in Rome the next class of citizens in Gaul after the nobility (to which the Julii and Caesar belonged), are the knights, (to which Cicero's family belonged).

The second class is that composed of the knights. When necessity arises and some war flares up - which before Caesar's arrival used to happen almost every year, so that they were either on the offensive themselves or fending off attacks - they are all involved in the campaign. Each man has as many retainers and dependants about him, as is appropriate to his status in terms of his birth and resources. This is the sole form of power and influence they know.

Caesar next commented on the religion and mythology of the Gauls. Religion and mythology appear to have been as important to the laws and customs of the Gauls as to the Romans. Caesar commented that *the Gauls have practically the same views about these gods as other peoples do.*

More on the customs of the Gauls follows: *After reckoning up the sum, a husband adds to whatever sum of money he has received from his wife as a dowry a similar amount from his own goods. An account is kept of this joint sum of money and the profits are saved. Then whichever partner survives the other receives the joint portion with the accrued profits of previous years. Men have the power of life and death over their wives as over their children.*[12]

Caesar stated his opinion that the coastal areas of England were populated by people who crossed over from Belgium. Tacitus thought that the reddish hair and large limbs of the people in northern Scotland were from German origin. Caesar in *The Gallic War* gave accounts of wars involving the peoples of Belgae and wars involving German people beyond the Rhine with the Gauls. Therefore it is appropriate to give some examples of Ceasar's descriptions of the German people, from The Gallic War.

The Germans

The customs of the Germans are very different from those of the Gauls. They have no druids to preside over religious matters, nor do they concern themselves with sacrifices. The only things, which they count as

---

[12] Ibid, p 129.

gods, are things they can see and which clearly benefit them, for example, the Sun, Vulcan (fire), and the Moon. They have not even heard rumors of any others. They spend their whole life in hunting and military activity, and from childhood they are eager for hard work and endurance. Those who have remained chaste the longest win the highest praise among their own people: some believe that it makes them taller, others that it gives them greater strength and determination. They consider it a matter for shame to have sexual intercourse with a woman before reaching the age of 20— nor does the matter allow for concealment, for both sexes mingle together when they wash themselves in the rivers, and also they wear hides and skins which offer little protection, leaving most of the body naked.

They do not practice agriculture, and the majority of their food consists of milk, cheese, and meat. No one possesses a fixed area of land or estates of his own: rather, every year the magistrates and leading citizens assign each family and clan who have joined forces a tract of land of an appropriate size and location. Then after a year they oblige these men to move on. They do not have overall magistrates in peacetime, but the leaders of individual districts and settlements dispense justice among their own people and settle disputes. There is no discredit attached to acts of robbery which take place outside the borders of each state: in fact, they claim that these take place to train their young men and reduce their laziness. And besides, when one of the leaders states at an assembly that he will take command, and that those who wish to support him must declare themselves, then the men who approve him and his cause rise up, pledge their assistance, and win praise from the people. Any who pledge assistance but then do not support him are considered deserters and traitors and their word is distrusted in every respect from then on. They consider it wrong to violate the obligations of hospitality: they protect their guests from harm, whatever the reason for their presence among them, and treat them as sacrosanct. They open all their houses to such guests and share their food with them.

There was a time when the Gauls were more courageous than the Germans and took offensive military action against them. Because of their high population density and lack of land, they sent colonies across the Rhine. --- This people still dwells tn the same territory to this day, and has a fine reputation for justice and military glory. These days they endure the same state of poverty, privation, and hardship as the Germans, and have the same kind of food and clothing. The Gauls, on the other hand, live close to the Province and are familiar with imported goods, and this entails an abundant supply of items both luxurious and functional. The Gauls gradually grew accustomed to being defeated, and were beaten in many battles, so now they do not reckon themselves to be even equal in bravery to the Germans.[13]

---

[13] Ibid, pp 129-131.

Migration of People

From Caesar's accounts, which historians consider reliable, the peoples of Gaul settled in Germany, and the Germans later made numerous military incursions into Gaul and in fact were used in Caesar's armies even after Caesar had crossed the Rubicon. With the ease of travel across the Rhine, and even across the English channel it would be hard to support contentions or beliefs in the so-called purity of any race, especially of the English, Gauls or Germans. Tacitus unfortunately gave contradictory views on this subject in Chapter 4 of his work Germania, but in Chapter 28 stated:

The power of Gaul once exceeded that of Germany is recorded by that greatest of authorities, Julius Caesar; and therefore we may well believe that there were also migrations of Gauls into Germany. There was only a river between— a trifling obstacle to prevent any tribe that grew strong enough from seizing fresh lands.[14]

Tacitus considered that the peoples of northern Scotland had a German origin in view of their reddish hair and large limbs. Bede believed the first inhabitants of England came from Brittany, the north coast of France, and when they spread northward, they were met by the Picts, who originated in Scandinavia and who crossed with their longboats into northern Scotland. To return to the assumption that travel by sea took place long before that estimated by historians, it would not be unreasonable to suppose that the Germans not only crossed the English Channel to Britain, but also migrated northward into present Denmark, and made the seaward journey across the narrow waters into Scandinavia. The supposition by Bede that the Picts originated from the Scandinavians is interesting. It is well known that the Scandinavians were advanced in shipbuilding and navigation. It is also possible that sea levels changed over the period of ancient history making travel by sea, with lower sea levels less difficult.

The notion of a pure race of Germans, or anyone else in Europe, England, Ireland, Scotland and Scandinavia is most certainly ill founded. The notions of a superior race, compared to supposedly inferior people has been the source of as many wars and conflicts as has been the case for religious racism. Many examples can be cited in the history of man for these peculiar notions of racial superiority and inferiority. A seventeenth century English clergyman reported upon his return from Ireland that the inhabitants had tails. A theological debate regarding the Indians of North America focused on the question of whether they were human or animals. The slave trade was justified on the belief that the blacks were an inferior race. Incredibly, as we shall later review, even today these notions are the basis of continued conflicts, which

---

[14] Tacitus, Germania, pp 104 and 124.

supposedly rational human beings seem unable to resolve, even with the archeological evidence that all human beings had a common origin in Africa. Research should focus on modes of travel by ancient people who had the same physical and mental equipment of those to follow and had access to the same materials as we have today. Research should also focus on weather cycles corresponding to the first appearance of man, to determine whether early migrations could have been accomplished simply by using ones legs, or the construction of simple rafts, to cross shorter bodies of water than exist today.

Caesar's invasions to Claudius's conquest
It would be another hundred years before the Romans would occupy England. After 54 B.C., Caesar was occupied with the dissolution of the first triumvirate, the death of his daughter Julia, and the failure to gain political dominance over the senate. Caesar crossed the Rubicon in 49 B.C. and defeated Pompey at Pharsalia in 48. Caesar continued with military campaigns in Egypt, Pontus, Africa, and Spain from 48 to 46. Caesar was assassination in 44.Thus it was not possible to retain Roman forces in England during this period.

Augustus had no intention of invading and occupying England. An important reason why Augustus did not follow Julius Caesar by invading and occupying England is presented by Suetonius: *He (Augustus) suffered only two heavy and disgraceful defeats, both in Germany, the generals concerned being Lollius and Varus. Lollius' defeat was ignominious rather than of strategic importance; but Varus' nearly wrecked the Empire, since three legions with their general and all their officers and auxiliary forces, and the general staff, were massacred to a man. When the news reached Rome, Augustus ordered patrols of the city at night to prevent any rising; --- Indeed, it is said that he took the disaster so deeply to heart that he left his hair and beard untrimmed for months; he would often beat his head on a door shouting: 'Quintus Varus, give me back my legions!' and always kept the anniversary as a day of deep mourning.*[15] Another reason is that as long as Rome received tribute from the aristocrats in England it would not be necessary to raise the money and the forces required for an occupation.

Even in the short reign of Caligula (37-41), an invasion of England was hurriedly prepared but strangely aborted by the emperor as we learn from Suetonius: *Gaius had only a single taste of warfare, and even that was unpremeditated. --- He (Caligula) wasted no time in summoning regular legions and auxiliaries from all directions, levied troops everywhere with the utmost strictness, and collected military supplies of all kinds on an unprecedented scale. ---*

---

[15] Seutonius, The Twelve Caesars, pp 64-65.

In the end, he drew up his army in battle array facing the Channel and moved the arrow-casting machines and other artillery into position as though he intended to bring the campaign to a close. No one had the least notion what was in his mind when, suddenly, he gave the order: 'Gather sea-shells!' He referred to the shells as 'plunder from the ocean, due to the Capitol and to the Palace', and made the troops fill their helmets and tunic-laps with them; commemorating this victory by the erection of a tall lighthouse, not unlike the one at Pharos, in which fires were to be kept going all night as a guide to ships.[16]

Claudius' invasion and conquest

It was emperor Claudius, however, who, in 43 A.D., became the first to invade England since Julius Caesar, and it would be the first occupation of the island. Suetonius provided a brief description:

Claudius' sole campaign was of no great importance. The Senate had already voted him triumphal regalia, but he thought it beneath his dignity to accept these, and decided that Britain was the country where a real triumph could be most readily earned. Its conquest had not been attempted since Julius Caesar's days; and the Britons were now threatening vengeance because the Senate refused to return certain deserters. Sailing from Ostia (on the west coast of Italy, at the mouth of the Tiber River, near Rome), *Claudius was twice nearly wrecked off the Ligurian Coast,* (the northern coast of Italy), *and again near the Stoechades Islands, but made port safely at Massilis* (present Marseille). *In consequence he marched north through Gaul until reaching Gesoriacum; crossed the Channel from there; and was back in Rome six months later. He had fought no battles and suffered no casualties, but reduced a large part of the island to submission. His triumph was a very splendid one, and among those whom he invited to witness it were his provincial governors, and certain exiles as well. The emblems of this victory included the naval crown, representing the crossing and conquest, so to speak, of the ocean, which he set on the Palace gable beside the civic crown. His wife, Messalina, followed the chariot in a covered carriage, and behind her marched the generals who had won triumphal regalia in Britain.[17]*

Claudius had suppressed England's tribes in southeast England. The Britons under the command of Caractacus provided resistance to the Romans. From Tacitus: *In Britain the situation inherited by the imperial governor Publius Ostorius Scapula was chaotic. Convinced that a new commander, with an unfamiliar army and with winter begun, would not fight them, hostile tribes had broken violently into the Roman province,*

---

[16] Ibid, pp 175-177.

[17] Ibid, p 196.

But Ostorius knew that initial results are what produce alarm or confidence. So he marched his light auxiliary battalions rapidly ahead, and stamped out resistance. The enemy were dispersed and hard pressed. To prevent a rally, or a bitter treacherous peace which would give neither general nor army any rest, Ostorius prepared to disarm all suspects and reduce the whole territory as far as the Trent and Severn (in south west England).

The first to revolt against this were the Iceni (Norfolk and Suffolk counties). *We had not defeated this powerful tribe in battle, since they had voluntarily become our allies. Led by them, the neighboring tribes now chose a battlefield at a place protected by a rustic earthwork, with an approach too narrow to give access to cavalry. The Roman commander, though his troops were auxiliaries without regular support, proposed to carry these defenses. At the signal, Ostorius' infantry, placed at appropriated points and reinforced by dismounted cavalrymen, broke through the embankment. The enemy was overwhelmed, imprisoned by their own barrier.*

This defeat of the Iceni quieted others who were wavering between war and peace. The Roman army then struck against the Decangi, ravaging their territory and collecting extensive booty. The enemy did not venture upon an open engagement and, when they tried to ambush the columns, suffered for their trickery. Ostorius had nearly reached the sea facing Ireland when a rising by the Brigantes (northern England) *recalled him. For, until his conquests were secured, he was determined to postpone further expansion. The Brigantes subsided; their few peace breakers were killed, and the rest were pardoned. Next Ostorius invaded Silurian territory* (south east Wales).[18]

But neither sternness nor leniency prevented the Silures from fighting. To suppress them, a brigade garrison had to be established. (A footnote states that the site of the camp among the Silures, S.E. Wales is uncertain). *In order to facilitate the displacement of troops westward to man it, a strong settlement of ex-soldiers was established on conquered land at Camulodunum* (Colchester), about fifty miles north east of London. *Its mission was to protect the country against revolt and familiarize the provincials with law-abiding government.*

The natural ferocity of the inhabitants was intensified by their belief in the prowess of Caractacus, whose many undefeated battles - and even many victories - had made him pre-eminent among British chieftains. Caractacus was the son of Cunobelinus. *His deficiency in strength was compensated by superior cunning and topographical knowledge. Transferring the war to the county of the Ordovices* (North Wales)*, he was joined by everyone who found the prospect of a Roman peace alarming. Then Caractacus staked his fate on a battle. He selected*

---

[18] Tacitus, Annals pp 264-266.

a site where numerous factors - notably approaches and escape-routes - helped him and impeded us. On one side there were steep hills. Wherever the gradient was gentler, stones were piled into a kind of rampart. And at his front there was a river without easy crossings. The defenses were strongly manned.

The British chieftains went round their men, encouraging and heartening them to be unafraid and optimistic, and offering other stimulants to battle. Caractacus, as he hastened to one point and another stressed that this was the day that the battle would either win back their freedom or enslave them for ever. He invoked their ancestors, who by routing Julius Caesar had valorously preserved their present descendants from Roman officials and taxes, and their wives and children from defilement. These exhortations were applauded. Then, every man swore by his tribal oath that no enemy weapons would make them yield— and no wounds either.

This eagerness dismayed the Roman commander disconcerted as he already was by the river-barrier, the fortifications supplementing it, the overhanging cliffs, and the ferocious crowds of defenders at every point. But our soldiers shouted for battle, clamoring that courage could overcome everything; and their colonels spoke to the same effect, to encourage them further.

After a reconnaissance to detect vulnerable and invulnerable points, Ostorius led his enthusiastic soldiers forward. They crossed the river without difficulty, and reached the rampart. But then, in an exchange of missiles, they came off worse in wounds and casualties. However, under a roof of locked shields, the Romans demolished the crude and clumsy stone embankment, and in the subsequent fight at close quarters the natives were driven to the hilltops. Our troops pursued them closely. While light-armed auxiliaries attacked with javelins, the heavy infantry advanced in close formation. The British, unprotected by breastplates or helmets, were thrown into disorder. If they stood up to the auxiliaries, the swords and spears of the regulars cut them down, and if they faced the latter they succumbed to the auxiliaries' broadswords and pikes. It was a great victory. Caractacus' wife and daughter were captured; his brothers surrendered. He himself sought sanctuary with Cartimandua, queen of the Brigantes. But the defeated have no refuge. He was arrested, and handed over to the conquerors. The war in England was now in its ninth year, A.D. 52, which would be two years before the death of Claudius and the accession of Nero. After a review of the reputation of Caractacus, *which had spread through the provinces to Italy itself, --- then the senate met. It devoted numerous complimentary speeches to the capture of Caractacus. This was hailed as equal in glory to any previous Roman general's exhibition of a captured king.* [19]

---

[19] Ibid, pp 266-267.

Uprisings during Nero's Reign

Suetonius provides only this brief comment on the wars in England under Nero: *There was a British disaster, when two important garrison-towns* (Camulodunum or Colchester and Verulamium) *were taken by storm, and huge numbers of Romans and allies massacred.*[20] Bede provides basically the same brief summary as Suetonius: *When Nero succeeded Claudius as Emperor, he attempted no military expeditions and in consequence, apart from countless other injuries to the Roman State, he nearly lost Britain, for during his reign two most noble towns there were taken and destroyed.*[21] London was also ravaged.

Paulinas invaded the island of Mona

From Tacitus Annals: *The new imperial governor of Britain was Gaius Suetonius Paulinus* (No relation to the historian Suetonius. Paulinus will be used in the quotations to follow). *Corbulo's rival in military science, as in popular talk - which makes everybody compete - he was ambitious to achieve victories as glorious as the reconquest of Armenia. So Paulinus planned to attack the island of Mona* (presently the northwest corner of Wales, only sixty miles east of Dublin across the Irish Sea), *which although thickly populated had also given sanctuary to many refugees.*

Flat-bottomed boats were built to contend with the shifting shallows, and these took the infantry across. Then came the cavalry; some utilized fords, but in deeper water the men swam besides their horses. The enemy lined the shore in a dense armed mass. Among them were black-robed women with disheveled hair like Furies, brandishing torches. Close by stood Druids, raising their hands to heaven and screaming dreadful curses.

This weird spectacle awed the Roman soldiers into a sort of paralysis. They stood still— and presented themselves as a target. But then they urged each other (and were urged by the general) not to fear a horde of fanatical women. Onward pressed their standards and they bore down their opponents, enveloping them in the flames of their own torches. Paulinus garrisoned the conquered island. The groves devoted to Mona's barbarous superstitions he demolished. For it was their religion to drench their altars in the blood of prisoners and consult their gods by means of human entrails.

---

[20] Seutonius, The Twelve Caesars, p 236.

[21] Bede, Ecclesiastical History of the English People, p 49.

Rebellion of the Iceni

While Paulinus was thus occupied, he learnt of a sudden rebellion in the province. Prasutagus, king of the Iceni (Norfolk and Suffolk counties), *after a life of long and renowned prosperity, made the emperor co-heir with his own two daughters. Prasutagus hoped by their submissiveness to preserve his kingdom and household from attack. But it turned out otherwise. Kingdom and household alike were plundered like prizes of war, the one by Roman officers, the other by Roman slaves. As a beginning, his widow Boudicca was flogged and their daughters raped. The Icenian chiefs were deprived of their hereditary estates as if the Romans had been given the whole country. The king's own relatives were treated like slaves.*

And the humiliated Iceni feared still worse, not that they had been reduced to provincial status. So they rebelled. With them rose the Trinobantes, who lived below the Iceni, (from London to the east coast of England). *Servitude had not broken them, and they had secretly plotted together to become free again. They particularly hated the Roman ex-soldiers who had recently established a settlement at Camulodonum* (Colchester). *The settlers drove the Trinobantes from their homes and land, and called them prisoners and slaves. The troops encouraged the settlers' outrages, since their own way of behaving was the same— and they looked forward to similar license for themselves. Moreover, the temple erected to the divine Claudius* (at Colchester) *was a blatant stronghold of alien rule, and its observances were a pretext to make the natives, appointed as its priests, drain the whole country dry.*

It seemed easy to destroy the settlement; for it had no walls. That was a matter which Roman commanders, thinking of amenities rather than need, had neglected. At this juncture, for no visible reason, the statue of Victory at Camulodunum fell down— with its back turned as though it were fleeing the enemy.

Paulinus, however, was far away. So they appealed for help to the imperial agent Cautus Decianus. He sent them barely two hundred men, incompletely armed. There was also a small garrison on the spot. Reliance was placed on the temple's protection. Misled by secret pro-rebels, who hampered their plans, they dispensed with rampart or trench. They omitted also to evacuate old people and women and thus leave only fighting men behind. Their precautions were appropriate to a time of unbroken peace.

Then a native horde surrounded them. When all else had been ravaged or burnt, the garrison concentrated itself in the temple. After two days' siege, it fell by storm. The ninth Roman division, commanded by Quinus Petilius Cerialis Caesius Rufus, attempted to relieve the town, but was stopped by the victorious Britons and routed. Its entire infantry force was massacred, while the commander escaped to his camp with his cavalry and sheltered behind its defenses. The imperial agent Catus

Decianus, horrified by the catastrophe and by his unpopularity, withdrew to Gaul. It was his rapacity which had driven the province to war.

Paulinas abandoned London

But Paulinus, undismayed, marched through disaffected territory to Londinium. His town did not rank as a Roman settlement, but was an important center for businessmen and merchandise. At first, he hesitated whether to stand and fight there. Eventually, his numerical inferiority - and the price only too clearly paid by the divisional commander's rashness - decided him to sacrifice the single city of Londinium to save the province as a whole. Unmoved by lamentations and appeals, Paulinus gave the signal for departure. The inhabitants were allowed to accompany him. But those who stayed, because they were women, or old, or attached to the place, were slaughtered by the enemy. Verulamium (near Saint Albans north of London) *suffered the same fate.*

The natives enjoyed plundering and thought of nothing else. Bypassing forts and garrisons, they made for where loot was richest and protection weakest. Roman and provincial deaths at the places mentioned are estimated at seventy thousand. For the British did not take or sell prisoners, or practice other wartime exchanges. They could not wait to cut throats, hang, burn, and crucify— as though avenging, in advance, the retribution that was on its way. Paulinus collected the fourteenth brigade and detachments of the twentieth, together with the nearest available auxiliaries - amounting to nearly ten thousand armed men - and decided to attack without further delay. He chose a position in a defile with a wood behind him. There could be no enemy, he knew, except at his front, where there was open country without cover for ambushes. Paulinus drew up his regular troops in close order, with the light-armed auxiliaries at their flanks, and the cavalry massed on the wings. On the British side, cavalry and infantry bands seethed over a wide area in unprecedented numbers. Their confidence was such that they brought their wives with them to see the victory, installing them in carts stationed at the edge of the battlefield.

Boudicca

Boudicca drove round all the tribes in a chariot with her daughters in front of her. 'We British are used to woman commanders in war,' she cried. 'I am descended from mighty men! But now I am not fighting for my kingdom and wealth. I am fighting as an ordinary person for my lost freedom, my bruised body, and my outraged daughters. Nowadays Roman rapacity does not even spare our bodies. Old people are killed, virgins raped. But the gods will grant us the vengeance we deserve! The Roman division, which dared to fight, is annihilated. The others cower in their camps, or watch for a chance to escape. They will never face even the din and roar of all our thousands, much less the shock of our onslaught. Consider how many of you are fighting— and why. Then you will win this battle, or perish. This is what I, a woman, plan to do! — let the men live in slavery if they will'.

Paulinus trusted his men's bravery. Yet he too, at this critical moment, offered encouragements and appeals. 'Disregard the clamors and empty threats of the natives!' he said. 'In their ranks, there are more women than fighting men. Unwarlike, unarmed, when they see the arms and courage of the conquerors, who have routed them so often, they will break immediately. Even when a force contains many divisions, few among them win the battles— what special glory for your small numbers to win the renown of a whole army! Just keep in close order. Throw your javelins, and then carry on: use shield-bosses to fell them, swords to kill them. Do not think of plunder. When you have won, you will have everything.'

The general's words were enthusiastically received: the old battle-experienced soldiers longed to hurl their javelins. So Paulinus confidently gave the signal for battle. At first the regular troops stood their ground. Keeping to the defile as a natural defense, they launched their javelins accurately at the approaching enemy. Then, in wedge formation, they burst forward. So did the auxiliary infantry. The cavalry, too, with lances extended, demolished all serious resistance. The remaining Britons fled with difficulty since their ring of wagons blocked the outlets. The Romans did not spare even the women. Baggage animals too, transfixed with weapons, add to the heaps of dead. --- It was a glorious victory, comparable with bygone triumphs. According to one report almost eighty thousand Britons fell. Our own casualties were about four hundred dead and a slightly larger number of wounded. Boudicca poisoned herself.[22]

The Flavian emperors and Agricola

The conquest of England and neighboring states was expanded during Vespasian's reign (A.D. 69-79) while Agricola, the father- in- law of Tacitus, was governor of England. Vespasian had been commander of a Roman legion during the invasion and conquest of England in 43 A.D. under Claudius. Agricola had experience as a staff military tribune under the command of Gaius Paulinus Suetonius (referred to as Paulinus above) under emperor Nero in 61. During the civil wars of 68-69 Agricola declared for Vespasian and from 71-73 he was appointed legate of the XX legion in England. It is therefore not surprising that Vespasian, in 77, appointed Agricola, (b. 37, d, 93), governor of Britain. We turn to Tacitus work *The Agricola* which was written in 98, and which has been called a monument in praise of his father-in-law. Tacitus had married

---

[22] Tacitus, Annals, pp 327-332.

Agricola's daughter shortly before Agricola was appointed governor of Britain, where he served four years.

Tacitus began his account of Agricola in England with the following: *But when Vespasian, in the course of his general triumph, restored stable government to Britain, there came a succession of great generals and splendid armies, and the hopes of our enemies dwindled. Petilius Cerealis at once struck terror into their hearts by attacking the state of the Brigantes,* (in Yorkshire), *which is said to be the most populous in the whole province. After a series of battles,* from A.D. 71-74, - *some of them by no means bloodless - Petilius had overrun, if not actually conquered, the major part of their territory. The next commander Julius Frontinus, subdued by force of arms, 74-78, the strong and warlike nation of the Silures* (South Wales), *after a hard struggle, not only against the valor of his enemy, but against the difficulties of the terrain.*[23]

Such was the condition to which Britain had been brought by the ups and downs of warfare when Agricola crossed the Channel (in A.D. 78) *with the summer already half over. The soldiers thought they had done with campaigning for the present and were relaxing, while the enemy were looking for a chance to profit thereby. Shortly before his arrival the tribe of the Ordovices* (Wales) *had almost wiped out a squadron of cavalry stationed in their territory, and this initial stroke had excited the province. --- As the Ordovices did not venture to descend into the plain, he led his men up into the hills, marching in front himself so as to impart his own courage to the rest by sharing their danger, and cut to pieces almost the whole fighting force of the tribe.* Agricola next subdued, (in 78), the island of Anglesey, also called Mona, which Agricola had previous battle experience in 61 under Paulinus. Paulinus had been recalled during the civil wars in 68-69. Tacitus praises Agricola for his work as governor of Britain during his first year: Agricola, however, understood the feelings of the province and had learned from the experience of others that arms can effect little if injustice follows in their train. He resolved to root out the causes of rebellion. --- *By checking these abuses in his very first year of office Agricola made the Britons appreciate the advantages of peace, which, through the negligence or arbitrariness of previous governors, had been as much feared as war.*[24]

The following winter was spent on schemes of social betterment. Agricola had to deal with people living in isolation and ignorance, and

---

[23] Ibid, p 21 and 68. Tacitus fails to include dates of Agricola's campaigns and it is necessary to refer to the dates provided in the introduction to this work, The Agricola and The Germania, provided by Harold Mattingly.

[24] Ibid, pp 70-71.

therefore prone to fight; and his object was to accustom them to a life of peace and quiet by the provision of amenities. He therefore gave private encouragement and official assistance to the building of temples, public squares, and good houses. Furthermore, he educated the sons of the chiefs in the liberal arts, and expressed a preference for British ability as compared with the trained skills of the Gauls. --- And so the population was gradually led into the demoralizing temptations of arcades, baths, and sumptuous banquets. The unsuspecting Britons spoke of such novelties, as 'civilization', when in fact they were only a feature of their enslavement.[25]

Agricola advanced to the north

Agricola, in 79, advanced northwards along the western route from Chester and York and consolidated northwest England by forts and garrisons. In 80 he advanced northward along the eastern coast. *The third year of Agricola's campaigns, brought him into contact with fresh peoples; for the territory of tribes was ravaged as far north as the estuary called the Tay.* (fifty miles north of present Edinburgh). In 81, he established forts along the Forth-Clyde line (the narrow isthmus in Scotland north of Edinburgh from the Firth of Fourth to the Clyde).

In 82, *the fourth summer was spent in securing the districts already overrun; and if the valor of our army and the glory of Rome had permitted such a thing, a good place for halting the advance was found in Britain itself. The Clyde and the Forth, carried inland to a great depth on the tides of opposite seas, are separated only by a narrow neck of land. This isthmus was now firmly held by garrisons, and the whole expanse of country to the* south *was safely in our hands. The enemy had been pushed into what was virtually another island.*[26]

Agricola started his fifth campaign, (in 82), by crossing the river Annan (Southern Scotland), and in a series of successful actions subdued nations hitherto unknown. The side of Britain that faces Ireland was lined with his forces. --- Ireland, lying between Britain and Spain, and easily accessible also from the Gallic sea, might serve as a valuable link between the provinces forming the strongest part of the empire. --- An Irish prince, expelled from his home by a rebellion, was welcomed by Agricola, who detained him, nominally as a friend, in the hope of being able to make use of him. I have often heard Agricola say that Ireland could be reduced and held by a single legion with a fair-sized force of auxiliaries; and that it would be easier to hold Britain if it were

---

[25] Ibid, pp 72-73.

[26] Note. The future location of the Antonine wall, subsequently abandoned. Roman armies would retreat to Hadrian's wall, northeast from the Solway Firth. This is close to the present boundary of England and Scotland.

completely surrounded by Romans armies, so that liberty was banished from its sight.

In the summer in which his sixth year of office began (A.D. 83), *Agricola enveloped the tribes beyond the Forth.* The ninth legion was able to contain an offensive by the Caledonians. In the following year (A.D. 84), *at the beginning of the next summer Agricola suffered a grievous personal loss in the death of a son who had been born a year before. He accepted this blow without either parading the fortitude of a stoic or giving way to passionate grief like a woman. The conduct of the war was one means he used to distract his mind from its sorrow. He sent his fleet ahead to plunder at various points and thus spread uncertainty and terror; then, with an army marching light, which he had reinforced with some of the bravest of the Britons who had proved their loyalty by long years of submission, he reached Monut Graupius, which he found occupied by the enemy. The Britons were, in fact, undaunted by the loss of the previous battle, and were ready for either revenge or enslavement. They had realized at last that the common danger must be warded off by united action, and had sent round embassies and drawn up treaties to rally the full force of all their states. Already more than 30,000 men could be seen, and still they came flocking to the colors— all the young men, and famous warriors whose 'old age was fresh and green', every man wearing the decorations he had earned. At that point one of the many leaders, a man of outstanding valor and nobility named Calgacus, addressed the cole-packed multitude of men clamoring for battle.*[27]
Tacitus described the details of the battle. In brief, Agricola's troops advanced to Moray Firth, the northernmost reaches of Scotland. A crushing defeat of the Caledonians took place at Mons Graupius. He took hostages and ordered his admiral to sail round the north of Britain. He placed his troops in winter quarters.

Agricola recalled to Rome, his death

Domitian recalled Agricola in 84. Agricola spent the remaining years of his life in retirement and died in 93, possibly by poisoning. Although Tacitus lived to about 117 and Seutonius to about 130, neither Tacitus nor Seutonius provides any history of England, or Rome after the reign of Domitian (A.D. 81-96). Tacitus failed to achieve his aim *I have reserved for my old age, if life is spared to me, the reigns of the deified Nerva* (96-98) *and the emperor Trajan* (98-117). *Seutonius ended his history of the Roman emperors with Domitian,*(81-96).

Some of Agricola's Scottish forts appear to have still been held early in the reign of Trajan (98-117). In A.D. 122 and the following years

---

[27] Ibid, pp 80, 81 and 84.

Hadrian built his famous wall from the Tyne to the Solway; and in 142 Antonius Pius built a wall from the Forth to the Clyde.[28]

Bede's history, from the 2nd to 4th centuries

Bede, (b. 673-d. 735), relying on other ancient sources, provides a history of the period in England from the second to fourth centuries. In about 150 *Lucius, a British king, requested of the emperor and pope to be made a Christian. This was granted and Britons received the Faith and held it peacefully in all its purity and fullness until the time of the the emperor Diocletian.*[29]

Continuing from Bede: *In the year of our Lord 189, Severus, an African born at Leptis in the province of Tripolitania, became seventeenth emperor from Augustus and ruled seventeen years. Harsh by nature, he was engaged in almost constant warfare, and ruled the state with courage, but with great difficulty. He was victorious in the grave civil wars that troubled his reign. He was compelled to come to Britain by the desertion of nearly all the tribes allied to Rome, and after many critical and hard fought battles he decided to separate that portion of the island under his control from the remaining unconquered people. --- Severus built a rampart and ditch of this type form sea to sea* (at Hadrian's wall) *and fortified it by a series of towers. After this he was taken ill and died in Eboracum, leaving two sons, Bassianus and Geta. The latter was subsequently condemned to death as an enemy of the state, but Bassianus became emperor with the cognomen of Antoninus.*

In the year of our lord 286, Diocletian, a nominee of the army, became thirty-third in the succession of Augustus. He ruled twenty years, and chose Maximian, known as Herculius, as his co-emperor. During their reign, Carausius a man of humble birth but a capable and energetic soldier, was appointed to protect the sea-coasts, which were then being ravaged by Franks and Saxons. But he put his own interests before those of the Republic, and suspicion arose that he was deliberately permitting the enemy to raid the frontiers; any loot that he recovered from the pirates was not restored to its rightful owners, but retained for his own advantage. Maximian ordered his execution, but Carausius assumed the imperial purple and seized Britain, which he won and held for seven years with great daring. He lost his life through the betrayal of his colleague Allectius, who then held the island for three years, after which, he was defeated by Asclepiodotus, prefect of the Praetorian Guard, who thus restored Britain to the empire after ten years.

---

[28] Tacitus, The Agricola, Introduction by Mattingly, p 23.

[29] Bede, Ecclesiatical History of the English People, p 49.

Persecution of the Christians

Meanwhile Diocletian in the East and Heraculius in the West ordered all churches to be destroyed and all Christians to be hunted out and killed. This was the tenth persecution since Nero, and was more protracted and horrible than all that had preceded it. It was carried out without any respite for ten years, with the burning of churches, the outlawing of innocent people, and the slaughter of martyrs. But at length the glory of these martyrs' devoted loyalty to God was to light even Britain.[30]

There followed Bede's description of the martyrdom of Alban, later called St. Alban. *When these unbelieving Emperors were issuing savage edicts against all Christians, Alban, as yet a pagan, gave shelter to a Christian priest fleeing from his pursuers. And when he observed this man's unbroken activity of prayer and vigil, he was suddenly touched by the grace of God and began to follow the priest's example of faith and devotion. Gradually instructed by his teaching of salvation, Alban renounced the darkness of idolatry, and sincerely accepted Christ. But when the priest had lived in his house some days, word came to the ears of the evil ruler that Christ's confessor, whose place of martyrdom had not yet been appointed, lay hidden in Alban's house. Accordingly he gave order to his soldiers to make a thorough search, and when they arrived at the martyr's house, holy Alban, wearing the priest's long cloak, at once surrendered himself in the place of his guest the teacher, and was led bound before the judge.* The judge was furious that Alban had chosen Christianity above the Roman gods. He ordered Alban to be flogged by the executioners, but Alban refused to abdicate. Alban was executed despite a great crowd of men and women of all ages and conditions who came to support him.

In the same persecution suffered Aaron and Julius, citizens of the City of Legions, (possible Caerleon-on-Usk), *and many others of both sexes throughout the land. After they had endured many horrible physical tortures, death brought an end to the struggle, and their souls entered the joys of the heavenly City.*

When this storm of persecution came to an end, faithful Christians, who during the time of danger had taken refuge in woods, deserted places, and hidden caves, came into the open, and rebuilt the ruined churches. Shrines of the martyrs were funded and completed and openly displayed everywhere as tokens of victory. The festivals of the Church were observed, and its rites performed reverently and sincerely. The Christian churches in Britain continued to enjoy this peace until the time of the Arian heresy. ---

---

[30] Ibid, pp 50-51.

Devastation of Gaul and fall of Rome

At this time, Constantius, a man of exceptional kindness and courtesy, who had governed Gaul and Spain during the lifetime of Diocletian, died in Britain. His son Constantine, the child of Helena his concubine, succeeded him as ruler of Gaul. Eutropius writes that Constantine, proclaimed emperor in Britain, succeeded to his father's domains. In his time, the Arian heresy sprang up, and although it was exposed and condemned at the council of Nicaea, (in 325), the deadly poison of its false teaching nevertheless infected, as we have said, not only the continental churches, but even those of these islands.

In the year of our Lord 377, Gratian, fortieth in line from Augustus, ruled as emperor for six years from the death of Valens; he had already reigned as co-emperor with his uncle Valens and his brother Valentinian. Finding the affairs of the State in grave disorder and approaching disaster, he chose the Spaniard Theodosius to restore the empire in its need, investing him with the royal purple at Sirmium and creating him emperor of Thrace and the East.

At this juncture, however, Maximus, an able and energetic man, well fitted to be emperor, had not ambition led him to break his oath of allegiance, was elected emperor by the army in Britain almost against his will, and he crossed into Gaul at its head. Here he treacherously killed the emperor Gratian who had been dumfounded at his sudden attack, and was attempting to escape into Italy. His brother the emperor Valentinian was driven out of Italy, and took refuge in the east, where Theodosius received him with fatherly affection. Within a short time however, he regained the empire, and trapping the despot Maximus in Aquileia, he captured him and put him to death.

In the year of our Lord 394, Arcadius, son of Theodosius, forty-third in line from Augustus, became joint-emperor with his brother Honorius, and ruled for thirteen years. In his time, the Briton Pelagius spread far and wide his noxious and abominable teaching that man had no need of God's Grace. ---

In the year 407, Honorius, the younger son of Theodosius, was emperor, and the forty-forth in line from Augustus. This was two years before the invasion of Rome by Alaric, king of Goths, on which occasion the nation of the Alani, Suevi, Vandals, and many others defeated the Franks, crossed the Rhine, and devastated all Gaul. At this juncture, Gratian, a citizen of the island, set himself up as a despot and was killed. In his place Constantine, a common trooper of no merit, was chosen emperor solely on account of his auspicious name. Once he had obtained power, he crossed into Gaul, where he was hoodwinked into many worthless treaties by the barbarians and caused great harm to the commonwealth. Before long, at the orders of Honorius, Count Constantius entered Gaul with an army, besieged Constantine in the city of Arles, captured him, and put him to death. His son Constans, a monk whom he had created Caesar, was also put to death by Count Gerontius in Vienne.

Rome fell to the Goths in the 1164th year after its foundation. At the same time Roman rule came to an end in Britain, almost 470 years after the landing of Gaius Julius Caesar. The Romans had occupied the country south of the earthwork which, as I have said, Severus built across the island, as cities, forts, bridges and paved roads bear witness to this day: they also held nominal jurisdiction over the more remote parts of Britain and the islands beyond it.[31]

The Roman legions left England about A.D. 409. A desperate appeal to Rome for defense against Pict and Scot invaders was refused in A.D. 443.

The Fall of the Roman Empire

The Romans had occupied England for about four hundred years. Before continuing the next chapter *England and the Romans* with quotations from the ancient historians as well as Bede and David Hume, a few references to Gibbon's work, *The Decline and Fall of the Roman Empire*, follows:

The Greeks after their country had been reduced into a province, imputed the triumphs of Rome not to the merit but to the Fortune of the republic. The inconstant goddess, who so blindly distributes and resumes her favors, had now consented (such was the language of envious flattery) to resign her wings, to descend from her globe, and to fix her firm and immutable throne on the banks of the Tiber. ---

The arms of the republic, sometimes vanquished in battle, always victorious in war, advanced with rapid steps to the Euphrates, the Danube, the Rhine, and the ocean; and the images of gold, or silver, or brass that might serve to represent the nations and their kings were successively broken by the iron monarchy of Rome. --- Prosperity ripened the principle of decay; the causes of destruction multiplied with the extent of conquest; and as soon as time or accident had removed the artificial supports, the stupendous fabric yielded to the pressure of its own weight. ---

The emperors, anxious for their personal safety and the public peace, were reduced to the base expedient of corrupting the discipline which rendered them alike formidable to their sovereign and to the enemy; the vigor of the military government was relaxed and finally dissolved by the partial institutions of Constantine; and the Roman world was overwhelmed by a deluge of barbarians.

The decay of Rome has been frequently ascribed to the translation of the seat of empire; but this history has already shown that

---

[31] Ibid, pp 54-57.

the powers of government were divided rather than removed. --- As the happiness of a future life is the great object of religion, we may hear without surprise or scandal that the introduction, or at least the abuse, of Christianity had some influence on the decline and fall of the Roman empire. The clergy successfully preached the doctrines of patience and pusillanimity; the active virtues of society were discouraged; and the last remains of military spirit were buried in the cloister. ---

The Romans were ignorant of the extent of their danger and the number of their enemies. Beyond the Rhine and Danube the northern countries of Europe and Asia were filled with innumerable tribes of hunters and shepherds, poor, voracious, and turbulent, bold in arms and impatient to ravish the fruits of industry. The barbarian world was agitated by the rapid impulse of war, and the peace of Gaul and Italy was shaken by the distant revolutions of China. The Huns, who fled before a victorious enemy, directed their march towards the West; and the torrent was swelled by the gradual accession of captives and allies. The flying tribes who yielded to the Huns assumed in their turn the spirit of conquest; the endless column of barbarians pressed on the Roman empire with accumulated weight; and if the foremost were destroyed the vacant space was instantly replenished by new assailants. [32]

---

[32] Gibbon, pp 619-625.

Chapter 12

England from the Romans to 1066

The Roman armies left England in 409 A.D, and returned again briefly from 443 to 448 A.D. With Roman occupation since Claudius in 43 A.D., four hundred years of Roman military control of England would end. The next major conquest of England was in 1066 by William of Normandy. What developments would occur in the six hundred or so years between these major events?

After the Roman occupation by military force ended, there were invasions from the northwest by Irish (then called Scots) and Picts (from Scotland); there followed invasions from Germans (Saxons), Danes (including lower Scandinavia) and Normans.

The source for much of what follows is from Bede, known as the 'father of English history", and whose *Ecclesiastical History of The English People* will be quoted from. Bede, who was born in 673 and died in 735, presents a history of England with authority for the seventh and early eighth centuries, and relies on Roman sources, Gildas and others for late Roman and some fifth and sixth century events. He was a monk living most of his life at Jarrow, which is at the mouth of the Tyne, in Northumbria. For the late period in the ninth to eleventh centuries, and to some extent earlier, *The History of England*, by David Hume, a contemporary of Blackstone, will be used extensively. Hume's history will also be used for the years from William I, 1066, to the invasion of William III of Orange in 1688. Historians have regarded David Hume as a philosopher, however modern historians have seldom referred to his monumental work, *The History of England,* Volumes 1-6. Voltaire considered his History to be *the best written in any language* and the Earl of Chesterfield predicted that it was *the only History of England that will go down to Posterity.* Hume was appointed in 1752 as the Keeper of the Advocates Library in Edinburgh and labored over the years to produce the final edition of the work in 1778. The history is well documented.

Ancient and medieval sources are quoted throughout. Hume, with the same focus as Plutarch and Tacitus, uncovers much about human nature, including its most perverse and ailing characteristics. From the forward to Hume's work by William Todd: *Heretofore, by mere exertion of his own commanding intellect, philosopher Hume had more than once set forth what he perceived to be the 'constant and universal principles of human nature.' Now as a philosophical historian, he could ascertain from dreary chronicles all the aberrations of human behavior as there exhibited in 'wars, intrigues, factions, and revolutions.' These and other vagaries, previously recorded simply as odd phenomena, in Hume's more coherent view constituted a varied range of materials documenting the 'science of man.'*[1]

The initial stormy reception of *The History of England* was likely due to Hume's failure to give cognizance to the universal presence of religion in the lives of most people. Hume, as a scientist and humanist, often referred to the historic Roman Catholic Church as 'superstition', and referred later to the 'enthusiasm' of the opposing churches. The Bede text balances Hume's harsh regard of religion.

Irish and Picts

After the departure of the Roman armies there followed invasions by the Irish and Picts, peoples referred to as 'barbarians' by those who claim superior heritage. Many of those who invaded England after the Romans left were refuges from England, Wales and Scotland who traveled to Ireland and the remote highlands of Scotland to escape slavery, the brutality and terror of the Romans.

Henceforward, the part of Britain inhabited by the Britons, which had been hurriedly stripped of all troops and military equipment and robbed of the flower of its young men, who had been led away by ambitious despots and were never to return, lay wholly exposed to attack, since its people were untrained in the science of war. Consequently for many years this region suffered attacks from two savage extraneous races. Irish came from the northwest, and Picts from the north. I term these races extraneous, not because they came from outside Britain, but because their lands were sundered from that of Britons.[2]

Hume, relying on Gildas as well as Bede, explains further the origin of the Irish and Picts: *The Picts seem to have been a tribe of the native British race, who having been chased into the northern parts by the conquests of Agricola, had there intermingled with the ancient inhabitants: The Scots were derived from the same Celtic origin, had first been established in Ireland, had migrated to the north-west coasts of this*

---

[1] Hume, The History of England, vol 1 to 6.

[2] Bede, Ecclesiastical History of the English People, p 58.

island, and had long been accustomed, as well from their old as their new feats, to infest the Roman province by piracy and rapine.[3] The Britons appealed to Rome for help in 443. A legion was sent, and *drove the survivors out of the territory of Rome's allies. --- But as soon as the old enemies of the Britons saw that the Roman forces had left, they made a sea born invasion, breaking in and destroying wholesale, slaughtering right and left as men cut ripe corn. The Britons therefore sent more envoys to Rome with pitiful appeals for help. --- Once more a Legion was dispatched, which arrived unexpectedly in autumn and inflicted heavy casualties on the invaders, forcing all who survived to escape by sea.*

The Romans, however, now informed the Britons that they could no longer undertake such troublesome expeditions for their defense, and urged them to take up arms for their own part and cultivate the will to fight, pointing out that it was solely their lack of spirit, which gave their enemies an advantage over them. In addition, in order to assist these allies, whom they were forced to abandon, they built a strong wall of stone directly from sea to sea in a straight line between the towns that had been built as strong points, where Severus had built his earthwork, (at Hadrian's wall).[4] The Roman legion departed in 448, never to return.

On the departure of the Romans, the Picts and Irish, learning that they did not mean to return, were quick to return themselves, and becoming bolder than ever, occupied all the northern and outer part of the island up to the wall, as if it belonged to them. --- At length the Britons abandoned their cities and wall and fled in disorder, pursued by their foes.

The Britons again appealed to the Romans for help. *'To Aetius, thrice Consul, come the groans of the Britons', and in the course of the letter they describe their calamities: 'The barbarians drive us into the sea, and the sea drives us back to the barbarians. Between these, two deadly alternatives confront us, drowning or slaughter.' But even this plea could not obtain help; for at the time Aetius was already engaged in two serious wars with Blaedla and Attila, the kings of the Huns. And although Blaedla had been assassinated the previous year through the treachery of his brother Attila, the latter remained so dangerous an enemy to the State that he devastated nearly all Europe, invading and destroying cities and strongholds alike.*[5]

---

[3] Hume, History of England, vol 1, p 12. Hume provides in an extensive note the common origins of the Irish and Highlanders; that the Picts (in Scotland) originated from the Irish.

[4] Bede, p 58-59.

[5] Ibid, pp 59-61.

The Britons suffered not only the depredations of the enemy but famine. However they began a resistance and *inflicted severe losses on the enemy. --- Thereupon the Irish pirates departed to their homes unabashed, intending to return after a short interval, while the Picts remained inactive in the northern parts of the island, save for occasional raids and forays to plunder the Britons.*

When the depredations of its enemies had ceased, the land enjoyed an abundance of corn without precedent in former years; but with plenty came an increase in luxury, followed by every kind of crime, especially cruelty, hatred of truth, and love of falsehood. --- Suddenly a terrible plague struck this corrupt people, and in a short while destroyed so large a number that the living could not bury the dead. --- For they consulted how they might obtain help to avoid or repel the frequent fierce attacks of their northern neighbors, and all agreed with the advice of their king, Vortigern, to call on the assistance of the Saxon peoples across the sea.[6]

The Germans

Bede provided the result of Vortigern's call for assistance: *In the year of our Lord 449, --- the Angles or Saxons came to Britain at the invitation of King Vortigern in three longships, and were granted lands in the eastern part of the island on condition that they protect the country: nevertheless, their real intention was to subdue it. They engaged the enemy advancing from the north, and having defeated them, sent back news of their success to their homeland, adding that the country was fertile and the Britons cowardly. Whereupon a larger fleet quickly came over with a great body of warriors, which, when joined to the original forces, constituted an invincible army. These also received from the Britons grants of land where they could settle among them on condition that they maintained the peace and security of the island against all enemies in return for regular pay.*

These newcomers were from the three most formidable races of Germany, the Saxons, Angles, and Jutes.

From the Jutes are descended the people of Kent and the Isle of Wight and those in the province of the West Saxons opposite the Isle of Wight who are called Jutes to this day.

From the Saxons - that is, the country now known as the land of the Old Saxons - came the East, South, and West Saxons.

And from the Angles- that is, the country known as Angulus, which lies between the provinces of the Jutes and Saxons and is said to remain unpopulated to this day - are descended from the East and Middle Angles, the Mercians, all the Northumbrian stock (that is, those people living north of the river Humber), and the other English peoples.

---

[6] Ibid, pp 61-62.

Their first chieftains are said to have been the brothers Hengist and Horsa. The latter was subsequently killed in battle against the Britons, and was buried in east Kent, where the monument bearing his name still stands[7]

Saxon states and the heptarchy

The heptarchy included the Kingdoms of Kent, Northumbria, East Anglia, Mercia, East Saxony, South Saxony and finally Wessex. *The first Saxon state, after that of Kent, which was established in Britain, was the kingdom of South-Saxony. In the year 477, Aella, a Saxon chief, brought over an army from Germany; and landing on the southern coast, proceeded to take possession of the neighboring territory. The Britons, now armed, did not tamely abandon their possessions; nor were they expelled, till defeated in many battles by their warlike invaders. --- The Saxons, enraged by this resistance, and by the fatigues and dangers which they had sustained, redoubled their efforts against the place, and when master of it, put all their enemies to the sword without distinction. This decisive advantage secured the conquests of Aella, who assumed the name of King, and extended his dominion over Sussex and a great part of Surrey. He was stopped in his progress to the east by the kingdom of Kent: In that to the west by another tribe of Saxons, who had taken possession of that territory. These Saxons, from the situation of the country, in which they settled, were called the West-Saxons, and landed in the year 495, under the command of Cerdic, and his son Kenric.[8]* These wars between the Saxons, Cerdic with his son Kenric, against the Britons continued, even with the assistance of Arthur of legendary fame, until the deaths of Cerdic in 534 and Kenric in 560.

While the Saxons made this progress in the south, their countrymen were not less active in other quarters. In the year 527, a great tribe of adventurers, under several leaders, landed on the east coast of Britain; and after fighting many battles, of which history had preserved no particular account, they established three new kingdoms in this island. Uffa assumed the title of king of the East-Angles in 575; Creida that of Mercia in 585; and Erkenwin that of East-Saxony, or Essex, nearly about the same time; but the year is uncertain.

The Saxons, soon after the landing of Hengist, had been planted in Northumberland; but as they met with an obstinate resistance, and made but small progress in subduing the inhabitants, their affairs were in so unsettled a condition, that none of their princes for a long time assumed the appellation of king. At last in 547, Ida, a Saxon prince of great valor --- enabled the Northumbrians to carry on their conquests

---

[7] Ibid, pp 62-63.

[8] Hume, vol 1, pp 20-21.

over the Britons. He entirely subdued the county now called Northumberland, the bishopric of Durham, as well as some the southeast counties of Scotland; and he assumed the crown under the title of king of Bernicia. Nearly about the same time, Aella, another Saxon prince having conquered Lancashire, and the greater part of Yorkshire, received the appellation of king of Deiri. These two kingdoms were united in the person of Ethelfrid, grandson of Ida, who married Acca, the daughter of Aella; and expelling her brother, Edwin established one of the most powerful of the Saxon kingdoms, by the title of Northumberland. How far his dominions extended into the country now called Scotland is uncertain; but it cannot be doubted, that all the lowlands, especially the east coast of that country, were peopled in a great measure from Germany.

Thus was established, after a violent contest of nearly a hundred and fifty years, the Heptarchy, or seven Saxon kingdoms, in Britain; and the whole southern part of the island except Wales and Cornwal, had totally changed its inhabitants, language, customs, and political institutions. Hume concludes: *Hence there have been found in history few conquests more ruinous than that of the Saxons; and few revolutions more violent than that which they introduced.*[9]

Christianity

The next revolution would not be violent. It would begin by Irish monks and continue with prelates from Rome and its influence would last a thousand years or more. Bede infers that there were Christians in Britain as early as 156 A.D. and assumes that Christians in Britain were affected by emperor Diocletian who *ordered, in 303-305, all churches to be destroyed and all Christians to be hunted out and killed.*

It was recorded in 433 that; *the first Christian mission to Ireland, for which we have definite and reliable data, was that of St. Palladius. The mission however was unsuccessful. Palladius was repelled where he landed by the inhabitants of Wicklow, Ireland. He then sailed northward, and was at last driven by weather towards the Orkneys, finding harbor, eventually, on the shores of Kincardineshire* (the northernmost firth on the east coast of Scotland).[10]   Saint Patrick's teacher, Bishop Germanus, came to the Britons in 429, surviving a storm at sea. St. Germain countered the Pelagian heresy, performed miracles, and helped the Britons repel an invasion by the Saxons and Picts who had joined forces.

In the year 432 St. Patrick landed in Ireland. *It is probable that St. Patrick was born in 387, and that in 403 he was made captive in Gaul*

---

[9] Ibid, pp 22, 24.

[10] Cusack, History of Ireland, p 109.

*and carried into Ireland. He was sold as a slave, in that part of Dalriada
in the county of Antrium* (county Antrim in Northern Ireland), *to four
men, one of whom Milcho, bought up their right from the other three, and
employed him in feeding sheep or swine.* He managed to gain
passageway to Brittany, *some distance from his native place. After a
short residence at the famous monastery of St. Marin, near Tours,
founded by his saintly relative, he placed himself (probably in his
thirtieth year) under the direction of St. Germain of Auxerre.* He went to
Italy and *spent many years there, visited Lerins* (a small island off the
south coast of France) *and other islands in the Mediterranean. St.
Patrick visited Rome about the year 431, accompanied by a priest named
Segetius, who was sent with him by St. Germanus to vouch for the
sanctity of his character, and his fitness for the Irish mission. Pope
Celestine received him favorably, and dismissed him with his benediction
and approbation. St. Patrick then returned once more to his master, who
was residing at Auxerre. From thence he went into the north of Gaul,
and there receiving intelligence of the death of St. Palladius, and the
failure of his mission, he was immediately consecrated bishop by the
venerable Amato, a prelate of great sanctity.*[11]

St. Patrick landed first in Wicklow, then above Dublin; and in
County Antrim, the mouth of the Boyne, at Tara and throughout Ireland.
The See of Armagh (in Northern Ireland) *was founded about the year
455, towards the close of the great apostle's life. The saint's labors were
now drawing to a close, and the time at eternal rest was at hand. He
retired to his favorite retreat at Saull* (near Downpatrick, Northern
Ireland). --- *Here he breathed his last on Wednesday, the 17th of March,
492.*[12] Moore concludes his History of Ireland: *Unexampled, indeed, in
the whole history of the Church— was there a single drop of blood shed
on account of religion through the entire course of this mild Christian
revolution, by which, in the space of a few years, all Ireland was brought
tranquility under the dominion of the Gospel.*[13]

From Bede: *In the year of our Lord 565, when Justin the
Younger succeeded Justinian*[14] *and ruled as Emperor of Rome, a priest
and abbot named Columba, distinguished by his monastic habit and life,*

---

[11] Ibid, pp113-116.

[12] Ibid, p 126.

[13] Ibid, p 112. Thomas Moore, History of Ireland, vol 1, pp 234-258, N.Y.,
Edward Dunigan, 1858.

[14] The emperor Justinian founded the compilation of Roman law, the Justinian
Code.

came from Ireland to Britain (Scotland) to preach the word of God in the provinces of the northern Picts which are separated from those of the southern Picts by a range of steep and desolate mountains. (the Grampians). That Irish monks had come before Columba is apparent from the following: *The southern Picts, who lived on this side of the mountains, are said to have abandoned the errors of idolatry long before this date and accepted the true Faith through the preaching of Bishop Ninian. --- Columba converted that people (Picts) to the Faith of Christ by his preaching and example, and received from them the island of Iona on which to found a monastery. --- It was here that Columba died and was buried at the age of seventy-seven, some thirty-two years after he had come into Britain to preach. Before he came to Britain, he had founded a noble monastery in Ireland known in the Irish language as Dearmack the Field of Oaks, because of the oak forest in which it stands.*[15] (Durrow is located at the south border of county Laois in Ireland). Another monastery would be established at Jarrow (on the east coast of Northumbria about fifty miles south of Lindesfarne), where Bede lived most of his life.

Christian kings

During the seventh century all the kings of England among the heptarchy would be converted to Christianity. Pope Gregory in 596 sent Augustine and other monks to England. Augustine received permission from king Ethelbert to preach in Kent. King Ethelbert had already heard of the Christian religion, having a Christian wife of the Frankish royal house named Bertha.Their daughter would marry king Edwin of Northumbria, who was converted to Christianity. King Ethelbert built churches in and near London and at Canterbury. *King Ethelbert died on the twenty-fourth of February, 616, twenty-one years after embracing the Faith. --- Among the many benefits that his wisdom conferred on the nation, he introduced with the consent of his counselors a code of law inspired by the example of the Romans, which was written in English, and remains in force to this day.*[16]

Edwin

The Northumbrian people's acceptance of the Faith of Christ came about through their king's (Edwin) *alliance with the kings of Kent by his marriage to Ethelberga, known as Tata, a daughter of king Ethelbert.* Pope Boniface wrote letters to king Edwin and his wife Ethelberga admonishing the king's conversion to Christianity. *At this time, the people of the Northumbrians, the English living north of the*

---

[15]   Bede, p 148.

[16]   Ibid, pp 111-112

Humber, under Edwin their king received the Faith through the ministry of Paulinus, whom I have already mentioned. As a sign that he would come to the Faith and the heavenly kingdom, King Edwin received wide additions to the earthly realm, and brought under his sway all the territories inhabited either by English or by Britons, an achievement unmatched by any previous English king. He also brought the Isles of Anglesey and Man (at N.W. Wales and in the Irish Sea) *under English rule, in 627.*[17]

So peaceful was it in those parts of Britain under King Edwin's jurisdiction that the proverb still runs that a woman could carry her new-born babe across the island from sea to sea without any fear of harm. Such was the king's concern for the welfare of his people that in a number of places where he had noticed clear springs adjacent to the highway he ordered posts to be erected with brass bowls hanging from them, so that travelers could drink and refresh themselves. And so great was the people's affection for him, and so great the awe in which he was held, that no one wished or ventured to use these bowls for any other purpose. So royally was the king's dignity maintained throughout his realm that whether in battle or on a peaceful progress on horseback through city, town, and countryside in the company of his thegns, the royal standard was always borne before him.[18]

King Edwin was killed in 633 by a Welsh king Cadwalla who *was utterly barbarous in temperament and behavior. He was set upon exterminating the entire English race in Britain, and spared neither women nor innocent children putting them all to horrible deaths with ruthless savagery, and continuously ravaging their whole country. --- After this, for a full year, Cadwalla ruled the Northumbrian provinces, not as a victorious king but as a savage tyrant, ravaging them with ghastly slaughter until at length he also destroyed Eanfrid, who had unwisely visited him to negotiate peace accompanied only by twelve picked soldiers.*[19]

Oswald

Bede also praised King Oswald, who followed Edwin. *This king (Oswald), after the death of his brother Eanfrid, mustered an army small in numbers, but strong in the faith of Christ; and despite Cadwalla's vast forces, which he boasted of as irresistible, the infamous British leader was killed at a place known by the English as Deniseburn, that is, the Brook of Denis.*

---

[17] Ibid, pp 117, 118 and 131.

[18] Ibid, pp 134-135.

[19] Ibid, pp 140 and 144..

As soon as he became king, Oswald greatly wished that all the people whom he ruled should be imbued with the grace of the Christian Faith, of which he had received such signal proof in his victory over the heathen. So he sent to the Irish elders among whom he and his companions had received the sacrament of Baptism when in exile, asking them to send him a bishop by whose teaching and ministry the English people over whom he ruled might receive the blessings of the Christian Faith and the sacraments. His request was granted without delay, and they sent him Bishop Aidan, a man of outstanding gentleness, holiness, and moderation.

On Aidan's arrival, the king appointed the island of Lidisfarne to be his see at his own request. As the tide ebbs and flows, this place is surrounded by sea twice a day like an island, and twice a day the sand dries and joins it to the mainland. The king always listened humbly and readily to Aidan's advice and diligently set himself to establish and extend the Church of Christ throughout his kingdom. And while the bishop, who was not fluent in the English language, preached the Gospel, it was most delightful to see the king himself interpreting the word of God to his ealdorman and theigns; for he himself had obtained perfect command of the Irish tongue during his long exile. Henceforward many Irishmen arrived day by day in Britain and proclaimed the word of God with great devotion in all the provinces under Oswald's rule, while those of them who were in priest's orders ministered the grace of Baptism to those who believed. Churches were built in several places, and the people flocked gladly to hear the word of God, while the king of his bounty gave lands and endowments to establish monasteries, and the English, both noble and simple, were instructed by their Irish teachers to observe a monastic life.

For most of those who came to preach were monks, Aidan himself being a monk sent from the island of Hii (Iona) whose monastery was for a long time the principal monastery of nearly all the northern Irish and all the Picts and exercised a widespread authority. The island itself belongs to Britain, and is separated from the mainland only by a narrow strait; but the Picts living in that part of Britain (Scotland) *gave it to the Irish monks long ago, because they received the Faith of Christ through their preaching.*[20]

Bede continues his praise of Oswald: *For at length he brought under his sceptre all the peoples and provinces of Britain speaking the four languages, British, Pictish, Irish, and English. Although he reached such a height of power, Oswald was always wonderfully humble, kindly, and generous to the poor and strangers. The story is told how on the Feast of Easter one year, Oswald sat down to dine with Bishop Aidan. A silver dish of rich food was set before him, and they were on the point of*

[20] Ibid, pp 146-147.

raising their hands to bless the food, when the servant who was appointed to relieve the needs of the poor came in suddenly and informed the king that a great crowd of needy folk were sitting in the road outside begging alms of the king. Oswald at once ordered his own food to be taken out to the poor, and the silver dish to be broken up and distributed among them.

Meanwhile other kings in the heptarchy were converted to Christianity. In 635 Oswald influenced king Cynegfils of the West Saxons (later Wessex) to accept Christianity. He was baptized, by Birinius. King Sigbert of the East Angles was converted in 635, where Fursey, an Irish monk, established a monastery at Cnobhere's Town (Editor's note- abandoned by the Irish in 651). Fursey wrote a little book on his life. Bede records Furseys unusual experiences and teaching of the four fires, which were to burn and consume the world. 'One of them is Falsehood,--- the next is Covetousness,--- the next is Discord, --- and the Fourth, Cruelty'.[21] In Kent, *king Eadbald died in 640, and his son king Earconbert ruled most nobly for over twenty-four years and some months. He was the first of the English kings to give orders for the complete abandonment or destruction of idols throughout his realm, and for the observance of the Lenten fast, enforcing his decrees by suitable penalties for disobedience.*[22]

Oswald, the most Christian king of the Northumbrians, reigned for nine years. --- At the end of this period Oswald fell in a fierce battle fought at the place called in English Maserfelth (Editor's note: probably Oswestry, Shropshire) *against the heathen Mercians and their heathen king, who had also slain his predecessor Edwin. He died on the fifth of August 642, when he was thirty-eight years of age.*[23]

Oswy

Our attention must return to the kingdoms of Mercia as well as Northumbia, the largest kingdoms in central and the north of England. *When Oswald departed to the kindom of heaven, his brother Oswy, a young man of about thirty, succeeded to his earthly throne and ruled for twenty-eight troubled years. He was attacked both by the pagan Mercians, who had already killed his brother, and also by his own son*

---

[21]   Ibid, pp 172-174. Note. The miracles and miraculous events surrounding Fursey as well as elsewhere in Bede's Ecclesiastical History are omitted. It nevertheless should be pointed out that testimony, stories of miracles, and even Fursey's teaching about the end of the world are common themes in today's evangelical churches.

[22]   Ibid, pp 171 and 155.

[23]   Ibid, pp 152 and 157.

*Alchfrid and his nephew Ethelwald, son of his brother and predecessor.
In the year of our Lord 644, the second year of Oswy's reign, the most
reverend father Paulinus, formerly Bishop of York and subsequently
Bishop of Rochester, died on the tenth of October, after an episcopate
lasting nineteen years, two months, and twenty-one days.*

*Death came to Aidan when he had completed sixteen years of
his episcopate, while he was staying at a royal residence near the town
we have described* (Bamburgh). --- *Finan, who had also come from the
Irish island and monastery of Iona, succeeded him as bishop and held the
office for a considerable time. Some years later, Penda, King of the
Mercians, came into these parts, with an invading army and destroyed
everything that he found with fire and sword; and he burned down the
village and the church where Aidan had died.*[24] --- *The Mercians led by
King Penda attacked the East Angles who, finding themselves less
experienced in warfare than their enemies, asked Sigbert to go into battle
with them and foster the morale of the fighting men.* --- *But mindful of his
monastic vows, Sigbert, surrounded by a well-armed host, refused to
carry anything more than a stick, and when the heathens charged, both
he and King Egric were killed and the army scattered.*[25]

*At this period King Oswy was subjected to savage and
intolerable attacks by Penda, the above mentioned King of the Mercians,
who had slain his brother.* A savage battle at Winwaed, between Oswy
and Penda, resulted in Oswy's victory in 654. Penda was killed. The
Mercian threat to Northumbria ended.[26]

Bede's death

Bede concludes with the following summary: *At the present
time, the Picts have a treaty of peace with the English, and are glad to be
united in Catholic peace and truth to the universal Church. The Irish
who are living in Britain are content with their own territories, and do
not contemplate any raids or stratagems against the English. The Britons*
(in northwest England and southwest Scotland) *for the most part have a
national hatred for the English, and uphold their own bad customs
against the true Easter of the Catholic Church; however, they are
opposed by the power of God and man alike, and are powerless to obtain
what they want. For although in part they are independent, they have
been brought in part under subjection to the English.*

*As such peace and prosperity prevail in these days, many of the
Northumbrians, both noble and simple, together with their children, have*

---

[24] Ibid, p 169.

[25] Ibid, p 171-172.

[26] Ibid, Editors note, p 370.

laid aside their weapons, preferring to receive the tonsure and take monastic vows rather than study the arts of war. What the result of this will be the future will show.[27]

In the last chapter of the *Ecclesiastical History of the English People* Bede provided a chronological account of all the events discussed in the Ecclesiastical History, followed by a brief autobiographical account listing his numerous books as well as translations. According to a letter by Cuthbert, who later became abbot of Wearmouth and Jarrow, Bede developed frequent breathlessness, but continued cheerful and joyful to the end, while continuing with teaching and his usual duties, even working on a translation of the book of John. Bede died on May 26th, 735. He was 62 years old.

Ina and Wessex

Hume summarized the long reign of Ina, king of Wessex, who lived during the last years of the venerable Bede. *Cadwalla, at last, tired with wars and bloodshed, was seized with a fit of devotion; bestowed several endowments on the church; and made a pilgrimage to Rome, where he received baptism, and died in 689. Ina, his successor, inherited the military virtues of Cadwalla, and added to them the more valuable ones of justice, policy, and prudence. He made war upon the Britons in Somerset: and having finally subdued that province, he treated the vanquished with a humanity, hitherto unknown to the Saxon conquerors. He allowed the proprietors to retain possession of their lands, encouraged marriages and alliances between them and his ancient subjects, and gave them the privilege of being governed by the same laws. These laws he augmented and ascertained; and though he was disturbed by some insurrections at home, his long reign of thirty-seven years may be regarded as one of the most glorious and most prosperous of the Heptarchy. In the decline of his age he made a pilgrimage to Rome; and after his return, shut himself up in a cloyster, where he died* (726). [28]

Egbert

Egbert, who ruled from 802 to 839, was the sole descendant of those conquerors who subdued Britain, and who enhanced their authority by claiming a pedigree from Woden, the supreme divinity of their ancestors. The Mercians, before the accession of Egbert, had very nearly attained the absolute sovereignty in the Heptarchy: They had reduced the East-Angles under subjection, and established tributary princes in the kingdoms of Kent and Essex. Northumberland was

---

[27] Ibid, pp 324-325.

[28] Hume, vol 1, p 46.

*involved in anarchy; and no state of any consequence remained but that
of Wessex, which, much inferior in extent to Mercia, was supported
solely by the great qualities of its sovereign. Egbert led his army against
the invaders; and encountering them at Ellandun in Wiltshire, obtained a
complete victory, and by the great slaughter, which he made of them in
their flight, gave a mortal blow to the power of the Mercians.* Egbert sent
an army into Kent, conquered the East-Angles, and defeated the Mercian
king. *Thus were united all the kingdoms of the Heptarchy in one great
state* (Wessex)*, nearly four hundred years after the first arrival of the
Saxons in Britain; and the fortunate arms and prudent policy of Egbert at
last effected what had been so often attempted in vain by so many
princes. Kent, Northumberland, and Mercia, which had successively
aspired to general dominion, were now incorporated in his empire; and
the other subordinate kingdoms seemed willingly to share the same
fate.*[29]

Invasion by the Danes

But the peace described by Bede in his last days and the rise of
Egbert's power over all England was to be shattered by major invasions
from the Danes, Norwegians and Normans. Hume gives a background to
the first invasion of England in 787: *Charlemagne, though naturally
generous and humane, had been induced by bigotry to exercise great
severities upon the pagan Saxons in Germany, whom he subdued; and
besides often ravaging their country with fire and sword. He had in cold
blood decimated all the inhabitants for their revolts, and had obliged
them, by the most rigorous edicts, to make a seeming compliance with the
Christian doctrine. That religion, which had easily made its way among
the British-Saxons by insinuation and address, appeared shocking to
their German brethren, when imposed on them by the violence of
Charlemagne: and the more generous and warlike of the pagans had fled
northward into Jutland* (Denmark)*, in order to escape the fury of his
persecutions. Meeting there with a people of similar manners, they were
readily received among them; and they soon stimulated the natives to
concur in enterprises, which both promised revenge on the haughty
conqueror, and afforded subsistence to those numerous inhabitants. They
invaded the provinces of France, which were exposed by the degeneracy
and dissensions of Charlemagne' posterity; and there being known under
the general name of Normans, which they received from their northern
situation, they became the terror of all the maritime and even of the
inland countries. They were also tempted to visit England in their
frequent excursions; and being able, by sudden inroads, to make great
progress over a people, who were not defended by any naval force, who
had relaxed their military institutions, and who were sunk into a*

---

[29] Ibid, p 50.

superstition, which had become odious to the Danes and ancient Saxons, they made no distinction in their hostilities between the French and English kingdoms. Their first appearance in this island was the year 787.[30]

Viking invasions, plunder and devastation followed at the centers of learning and monasteries in Lindesfarne in 793, Jarrow in 794 and Iona in 795. In about 807 the Danes landed in the Isle of Shepey (at the mouth of the Thames), *and having pillaged it, escaped with impunity. They were not so fortunate in their next year's enterprise, when they disembarked from thirty-five ships, and were encountered by Egbert, at Charmouth in Dorsetshire. The battle was bloody; but though the Danes lost great numbers, they maintained the post, which they had taken, and thence made good their retreat to their ships. Having learned by experience, that they must expect a vigorous resistance from this warlike prince, they entered into an alliance with the Britons of Cornwal; and landing two years after in that country, made an inroad with their confederates into the county of Devon; but were met at Hengesdown by Egbert, and totally defeated. While England remained in this state of anxiety, and defended itself more by temporary expedients than by any regular plan of administration, Egbert, who alone was able to provide effectually against this new evil, unfortunately died* (839); *and left the government to this son Ethelwolf.*[31]

The invasions of the Danes continued for the next fifty years after the death of Egbert. Neither his son Ethelwolf nor his three grandsons, Ethelald, Etherlbert or Etherlred could contain the Danes. Ethelred made a treaty with the Danes to spare East Anglia, enabling the Danes to invade the kingdom of Northumbria, seizing York. In Ireland the invading Norsemen, after raiding and plundering the island monasteries in 795, *became emboldened by success, and for the first time, in 807, they marched inland; and after burning Inishmurray, they attacked Roscommon. During the years 812 and 813 they made raids in Connaught and Munster, but not without encountering stout resistance from the native forces. After this predatory and internecine warfare had continue for about thirty years, Turgesius, a Norwegian prince, established himself as sovereign of the Vikings, and made Armagh his head-quarters, A.D. 830.*[32]

Thus the invasions of Ireland, and Scotland and the northern small islands were from the Norwegians while invasions of England were from the Danes, if such differences are significant. It would appear that

---

[30] Ibid, p 56.

[31] Ibid p 57.

[32] Cusack, p 189.

most incursions of the Danes into England were from Danes who had migrated to Normandy and passed across the English Channel. Other invasions likely came across the North Sea to the east coast of England and northward.

Alfred

King Alfred, (b. 849, d. 899), and who ruled from 871 to 899, was the youngest of the grandsons of Egbert. He was the first king since Egbert to provide a unified force and resistance to repel the Danes, and subsequently the Norwegians. Alfred was the most important of the Anglo-Saxon kings during this transitional period. Alfred would repel the Danes leading to an interval or peace whereby learning could be re-established: Alfred's reign also accomplished repair of infrastructure, building of cities, the administration of government and the establishment of law. Alfred also was responsible for the translation of Bede's *Ecclesiastical History of the English People* and the *Saxon Chronicle*, often referred to as the *Anglo-Saxon Chronicle*.

Hume began his story of Alfred: *This prince gave very early marks of those great virtues and shining talents, by which, during the most difficult times, he saved his country from utter ruin and subversion. Alfred's father, Ethelwolf returned from Rome with Alfred; and Alfred, on his return home, became every day more the object of his father's affections; but indulged in all youthful pleasures, he was much neglected in his education; and he had already reached his twelfth year, when he was yet totally ignorant of the lowest elements of literature. His genius was first roused by the recital of Saxon poems, in which the queen took delight; and this species of erudition, which is sometimes able to make a considerable progress even among barbarians, expanded those noble and elevated sentiments, which he had received from nature. Encouraged by the queen, and stimulated by his own ardent inclination, he soon learned to read those compositions; and proceeded thence to acquire the knowledge of the Latin tongue, in which he met with authors, that better prompted his heroic spirit, and directed his generous views. Absorbed in these elegant pursuits, he regarded his accession to royalty rather as an object of regret than of triumph; but being called to the throne, in preference to his brother's children, as well by the will of his father, a circumstance which had great authority with the Anglo-Saxons; as by the vows of the whole nation and the urgency of public affairs, he shook off his literary indolence, and exerted himself in the defense of his people.*

He had scarcely buried his brother, when he was obliged to take the field, in order to oppose the Danes, who had seized Wilton, and were exercising their usual ravages on the countries around.[33] Alfred had few troops to engage the Danes. The Danes, who had superior numbers,

---

[33] Hume, vol 1, p 64.

feared that Alfred would gain reinforcements. An agreement was made with Alfred for the Danes to take up winter quarters in London. The Mercian king Burrhed, whose territories included London, gave the Danes money to leave London for Lincolnshire, *but the Danes had already pillaged that area and returned to Mercia, and fixing their station at Repton in Derbyshire, they laid waste the whole country desolate with fire and sword. King Burrhed fled to Rome and took shelter in a cloister. He was brother-in-law to Alfred and the last who bore the title of King in Mercia.*

The West-Saxons were now the only remaining power in England; and though supported by the vigor and abilities of Alfred, they were unable to sustain the efforts of those ravagers, who from all quarters invaded them. A new swarm of Danes came over this year under three princes. Part of them, under the command of Haldene, their chieftain, marched into Northumberland, where they fixed their quarters; part of them took quarters at Cambridge, when they dislodged in the ensuing summer, and seized Wereham, in the county of Dorset, the very center of Alfred's dominions.

Retreat of Alfred

Despite more troops and Alfred's victory over this group of Danes, a new invasion of Danes augmented by those already in England led to a victory over the English Saxons. *This last incident quite broke the spirit of the Saxons, and reduced them to despair. --- Some left their country, and retired into Wales or fled beyond sea: Others submitted to the conquerors, in hopes of appeasing their fury by a servile obedience. --- Alfred himself was obliged to relinquish the ensigns of their dignity, to dismiss his servants, and to seek shelter, in the meanest disguises, from the pursuit and fury of his enemies. He concealed himself under a peasant's habit, and lived some time in the house of a neat-herd, he had been entrusted with the care of some of his cows. Alfred, in 878, retired into the center of a bog, formed by the stagnating waters of the Thone and Parret, in Somersetshire. He here found two acres of firm ground; and building a habitation on them, rendered himself secure by its fortifications, and still more by the unknown and inaccessible roads which led to it, and by the forests and morasses, with which it was every way environed. This place he called Aethelingay, or the Isle of Nobles, and it now bears the name of Athelney.*

Alfred lay here concealed, but not inactive, during a twelve-month; when the news of a prosperous event reached his ears, and called him to the field. Hubba, the Dane, having spread devastation, fire, and slaughter, over Wales, had landed in Devonshire from twenty-three vessels, and laid siege to the castle of Kinwith, a place situated near the mouth of the small river Tau. The Earl of Devonshire, taking shelter in the castle with his followers, managed to repel the Danes. This gave Alfred hope that his subjects could successfully resist the Danes.

Return of Alfred

Alfred left his retreat and *sent emissaries to the most considerable of his subjects and summoned them to a rendezvous, attended by their warlike followers, at Brixton, on the borders of Selwood forest.*[34] *On his appearance, they received him with shouts of applause, and could not satiate their eyes with the sight of this beloved monarch, whom they had long regarded as dead, and who now with voice and looks expressing his confidence of success, called them to liberty and to vengeance. He instantly conducted them to Eddington, where the Danes were encamped: and taking advantage of his previous knowledge of the place, he directed his attack against the most unguarded quarter of the enemy. The Danes, surprised to see an army of English, whom they considered as totally subdued, and still more astonished to hear that Alfred was at their head, made but a faint resistance, notwithstanding their superiority of number; and were soon put to flight with great slaughter.*

Alfred, instead of totally destroying his enemy, *knew, that the kingdoms of East Anglia and Northumberland were totally desolated by the frequent inroads of the Danes; and he now purposed to re-people them,* in 879, *by settling there the leader of the Danes, Guthrum, and his followers. He hoped that the new planters would at last betake themselves to industry, when, by reason of his resistance, and the exhausted condition of the country, they could no longer subsist by plunder; and that they might serve him as a rampart against any future incursions of their countrymen.*

The king employed this interval of tranquility in restoring order to the state, which had been shaken by so many violent convulsions; in establishing civil and military institutions; in composing the minds of men to industry and justice; and in providing against the return of like calamities. He was, more properly than his grandfather Egbert, the sole monarch of the English, (for so the Saxons were now universally called).[35]

Alfred established a regular militia for the defense of the kingdom and provided for a naval force. He increased the shipping of his kingdom both in number and strength, and trained his subjects in the practice as well of sailing, as of naval action. His forces successfully defended new invasions of the Danes into Kent, up the Thames and into Essex.

After Alfred had subdued and had settled or expelled the Danes, he found the kingdom in the most wretched condition; desolated by the ravages of those barbarians, and thrown in disorders, which were

---

[34] Ibid, pp 66-68

[35] Ibid, pp 69-70.

calculated to perpetuate its misery. Though the great armies of the Danes were broken, the country was full of straggling troops of that nation, who, being accustomed to live by plunder, were become incapable of industry, and who, from the natural ferocity of their manners, indulged themselves in committing violence, even beyond what was requisite to supply their necessities. The English themselves, reduced to the most extreme indigence by these continued depredations, had shaken off all bands of government; and those who had been plundered to-day, betook themselves next day to a disorderly life, and from despair joined the robbers in pillaging and ruining their fellow-citizens. These were the evils, for which it was necessary that the vigilance and activity of Alfred should provide a remedy.

The administration of justice

Alfred divided England into counties. *He sub-divided the counties into hundreds, administrative and judicial units, which were further subdivided into the smallest units of ten households. Ten neighboring house-holders were formed into one corporation, who, --- were answerable for each other's conduct, and over whom one person --- was appointed to preside. Every man was punished as an outlaw who did not register. --- And no man could change his habitation, without a warrant or certificate. --- By this institution every man was obliged from his own interest to keep a watchful eye over the conduct of his neighbors.*[36]

Hume comments: *Such a regular distribution of the people, with such a strict confinement in their habitation, may not be necessary in times when men are more enured to obedience and justice; and it might perhaps be regarded as destructive of liberty and commerce in a polished state; but it was well calculated to reduce that fierce and licentious people under the salutary restraint of law and government. But Alfred took care to temper these rigors by other institutions favorable to the freedom of the citizens; and nothing could be more popular and liberal than his plan for the administration of justice.*

If a problem came up in the smallest unit, which could not be resolved, or when problems between two of these units came up, appeals were made to the hundred, which met once in four weeks for the deciding of causes. Hume comments: *Their method of decision deserves to be noted, as being the origin of juries; an institution, admirable in itself, and the best calculated for the preservation of liberty and the administration of justice, that ever was devised by the wit of man.*[37] *Twelve freeholders were chosen; who, having sworn, together with the*

---

[36] Ibid, p 76.

[37] Note, Cicero's many orations were before juries.

hundreder or presiding magistrate of that division, to administer impartial justice proceeded to the examination of that cause, which was submitted to their jurisdiction. And beside these monthly meetings of the hundred, there was an annual meeting, appointed for a more general inspection of the police of the district; for the enquiry into crimes, the correction of abuses in magistrates, and the obliging of every person to show the decennary in which he was registered. The people, in imitation of their ancestors, the ancient Germans, assembled there in arms, whence a hundred was sometimes called a wapen-take, and its court served both for the support of military discipline, and for the administration of civil justice.

The next superior court to that of the hundred was the county-court, which met twice a year, after Michaelmas (September 29) *and Easter, and consisted of the freeholders of the county, who possessed an equal vote in the decision of causes. The bishop presided in this court, together with the alderman; and the proper object of the court was the receiving of appeals from the hundred and decennaries, and the deciding of such controversies as arose between men of different hundreds.*

There lay an appeal, in default of justice, from all these courts to the king himself in council; and as the people, sensible of the equity and great talents of Alfred, placed their chief confidence in him, he was soon overwhelmed with appeals from all parts of England. --- He took care to have his nobility instructed in letters and the laws: He chose the earls and sheriffs from among the men most celebrated for probity and knowledge: He punished severely all malversation in office. And he removed all the earls, whom he found unequal to the trust; allowing only some of the more elderly to serve by a deputy, till their death would make room for more worthy successors.

The better to guide the magistrates in the administration of justice, Alfred framed a body of laws; which, though now lost, answered long as the basis of English jurisprudence, and is generally deemed the origin of what is denominated the common law.

Hume continued: *The similarity of these institutions to the customs of the ancient Germans, to the practice of the other northern conquerors, and to the Saxon laws during the Heptarchy, prevents us from regarding Alfred as the sole author of this plan of government; and leads us rather to think, that, like a wise man, he contented himself with reforming, extending, and executing the institutions, which he found previously established.*[38]

Education under Alfred

Alfred's achievements extended far beyond military, executive and judicial functions. His contributions to learning and education are

---

[38] Ibid, p 79.

noted by Hume: *When he came to the throne, he found the nation sunk into the grossest ignorance and barbarism, proceeding from the continued disorders in the government, and from the ravages of the Danes: The monasteries were destroyed, the monks butchered or dispersed, their libraries burnt; and thus the only feats of erudition in those ages were totally subverted. --- But this prince invited over the most celebrated scholars from all parts of Europe; he established schools everywhere for the instruction of his people; he founded, at least repaired, the University of Oxford, and endowed it with many privileges, revenues and immunities.* It is noteworthy that he *composed more books, than most studious men,* translated the histories of Bede and Orosius, *translated from the Greek the elegant fables of Aesop and was responsible for the Saxon Chronicle.*

    Meanwhile, this prince was not negligent in encouraging the vulgar and mechanical arts, which have a more sensible, though not a closer connection with the interests of society. He invited from all quarter, industrious foreigners to re-people his country, which had been desolated by the ravages of the Danes. He introduced and encouraged manufactures of all kinds; and no inventor or improver of any ingenious art did he suffer to go unrewarded. He prompted men of activity to betake themselves to navigation, to push commerce into the most remote countries, and to acquire riches by propagating industry among their fellow-citizens. He set apart a seventh portion of his own revenue for maintaining a number of workmen, whom he constantly employed in rebuilding the ruined cities, castles, palaces, and monasteries. Even the elegancies of life were brought to him from the Mediterranean and the Indies; and his subjects, by seeing those productions of the peaceful arts, were taught to respect the virtues of justice and industry, from which alone they could arise. Both living and dead, Alfred was regarded, by foreigners, no less than by his own subjects, as the greatest prince after Charlemagne that had appeared in Europe during several ages, and as one of the wisest and best that had ever adorned the annals of any nation.[39]

    Alfred *established his sovereignty over all the southern parts of the island, from the English channel to the frontiers of Scotland; when he died (899), in the vigor of his age and the full strength of his faculties, after a glorious reign of twenty-nine years and a half; in which he deservedly attained the appellation of Alfred the Great, and the title of Founder of the English monarchy.*[40] He died when he was fifty years old.

---

[39] Ibid, pp 80-81.

[40] Ibid, p 74.

Alfred had, by his wife, Ethelswitha, daughter of a Mercian earl, three sons and three daughters. The eldest son, Edmund died without issue, in his father's lifetime. The third, Ethelward, inherited his father's passion for letters, and lived a private life. The second, Edward, succeeded to his power; and passed by the appellation of Edward the Elder, being the first of that name who sat on the English Throne.[41]

Alfred's son, Edward, the Elder, and his grandsons, Athelstan, Edmund I, and Edred would reign for the next fifty years.

Edward the Elder

The first conflict Edward (899-924) faced was from his cousin Ethelwald, son of Alfred's older brother Ethelbert, who raised forces from Northumbria and East Anglia against Edward but was killed in battle. *The rest of Edward's reign was a scene of continued and successful action against the Northumbrians, the East-Angles, the Five-burgers* (in Mercia) *and the foreign Danes, who invaded him from Normandy and Brittanny.* Norwegians from Ireland had invaded Northumberland and took York. The Norwegians had dispatched from Dublin. Trade continued for thirty-five years between the Norwegians in York and Dublin. By this time the Norwegians had also founded Wexford, Waterford and Limerick. Edward defeated the Norwegian Reginald and his rival Sidroc. Edward died in 924. His grandsons Athelston and Edmund followed him.

Athelston and Edmund

Athelstan (924-939) ruled the English and was successful in gaining superiority over the Norwegians, Danes, Scots and defeated a Welsh king. Athelstan died in 939 and Edmund (939-946) would rule with continued difficulty from the Danes in Northumbria and Mercia. According to Hume: *Edmund was young when he came to the crown, yet was his reign short, as his death was violent. One day, as he was solemnizing a festival in the county of Gloucester, he remarked, that Leolf, a notorious robber, whom he had sentenced to banishment, and had the boldness to enter the hall where he himself dined, and to sit at table with his attendants. Enraged at this insolence, he ordered him to leave the room; but on his refusing to obey, the king, whose temper, naturally choleric, was inflamed by this additional insult, leaped on him himself, and seized him by the hair: But the ruffian, pushed to extremity, drew his dagger, and gave Edmund a wound, of which he immediately expired. The event happened in the year 946 and in the sixth year of the king's reign. Edmund left male-issue, but so young that they were*

---

[41] Ibid, p 81.

incapable of governing the kingdom; and his brother, Edred, was promoted to the throne.[42]

Edred

Edred (946-955) was confronted with rebellion of the Danes in Northumbria, and in order to quell future revolts he built garrisons in the larger English towns. He was successful in restraining the Danes and *he obliged also Malcolm, king of Scotland, to renew his homage for the lands which he held in England.* A new development was also in the making under Edred's reign. Rome and the Benedictine order of monks was gaining more control over ecclesiastics in Europe. The Pope began to promote celibacy among the priests, which several centuries later became a requirement for Catholic priests. Dunstan represented this new order and according to Hume: *He secluded himself entirely from the world; he framed a cell so small that he could neither stand erect in it, nor stretch out his limbs during his repose; and he here employed himself perpetually either in devotion or in manual labor. It is probable that his brain became gradually crazed by these solitary occupations, and that his head was filled with chimeras.* But he *gained such an ascendant over Edred, who had succeeded to the crown, as made him, not only the director of the princes's conscience, but his counselor in the most momentous affairs of government. Edred expired in 955, after a reign of nine years. His children were too young to succeed him.*[43]

Edwig

Edwig (955-959), the oldest son of Edmund I, was only sixteen or seventeen years old at the succession of power and his rule was short and came to a violent end as a result of a conflict with the church. King Edwig became passionately in love with a princess of royal blood, which was in violation of church doctrine in that she was within the degrees of affinity prohibited by the canon law. Against the advice of his counselors he married the princess, Elgiva. The conflict between Edwig and the church officials included Dunstan and Odo, the Archbishop of Canterbury. The king sent Dunstan into exile, after discovering his failure to account for funds in the public treasury. The story told by Hume to follow is an example of cruelty, which we had heretofore encountered among the Romans and Saxons, which now involved the

---

[42] Ibid, p 89.

[43] Ibid, p 92. Note. It is interesting that the story of Dunstan anticipates recent psychiatric opinions regarding the effects of isolation in small cells, such as Security Housing Units in America's prisons, causing mental disorders in many of the inmates so confined.

Roman Church. *Archbishop Odo sent into the palace a party of soldiers, who seized the queen; and having burned her face with a red hot iron in order to destroy that fatal beauty, which had seduced Edwig, they carried her by force into Ireland, there to remain in perpetual exile. Edwig, finding it in vain to resist, was obliged to consent to his divorce, which was pronounced by Odo; and a catastrophe, still more dismal, awaited the unhappy Elgiva. That amiable princess, being cured of her wounds, and having even obliterated the scars, with which Odo had hoped to deface her beauty, returned into England, and was flying to the embraces of the king, whom she still regarded as her husband; when she fell into the hands of a party, whom the primate had sent to intercept her. Nothing but her death could now give security to Odo and the monks. And the most cruel death was requisite to satiate their vengeance.*[44]
Edwig was excommunicated and died in 959.

Edgar

King Edgar (959-975), instead of waging war with the church, established harmony and a close relationship with the church, which had been initiated by his uncle king Edred (946-955). According to Hume: Edgar, who *mounted the throne in such early youth, soon discovered an excellent capacity in the administration of affairs, and his reign is one of the most fortunate that we meet with in the ancient English history. He maintained a body of disciplined troops; which he quartered in the north, in order to keep the mutinous Northumbrians in subjection, and to repel the inroads of the Scots. He built and supported a powerful navy; and that he might retain the seamen in the practice of their duty, and always present a formidable armament to his enemies, he stationed three squadrons off the coast, and ordered them to make, from time to time, the circuit of his dominions. The foreign Danes dared not to approach a country, which appeared in such a posture of defense.* He was successful in arriving at negotiations, which established his power among kings and princes of neighboring states— of Scotland, Wales, The Isle of Man, of the Orkneys and even of Ireland.[45]

But the chief means, by which Edgar maintained his authority, and preserved public peace, was the paying of court to Dunstan and the monks, who had at first placed him on the throne, and who, by their pretensions to superior sanctity and purity of manners, had acquired an ascendant over the people. --- Edgar summoned a general council of the prelates and the heads of the religious orders. He criticized the secular clergy. He was instrumental in initiating reforms and a uniformity among the clergy. In an address he gave praise to Dunstan, now

---

[44] Ibid, pp 94-95. Note. Elgiva was hung upside down.

[45] Ibid, pp 96-97.

Archbishop of Canterbury, and gave his full support to the church. It is not surprising that at his coronation in 973, when he had turned thirty, he would be anointed with holy oil and that *once the king has been consecrated he has power over the people, and they may not shake the yoke from their necks.* Edgar died in 975 leaving his son Edward to rule England, and who was only fifteen years old.

Edward the Martyr

Edward (975-979), *was anointed and crowned at Kingston; and the whole kingdom, without farther dispute, submitted to him. Edward,* later dubbed Edward the Martyr, *lived four years after his accession, and there passed nothing memorable during his reign.* He was treacherously murdered, by a servant of his stepmother and died in 979.[46] Ethelred may have had a hand in his death.

Ethelred

Ethelred (979-1016), son of Edgar's second wife, followed Edward's short reign. During his long rule, some thirty-seven years, England would be ravaged by new invasions of the Danes. Ethelred followed the advice of his Norman prelates by paying tribute to these new invaders, which only encouraged subsequent Danish and Norwegian invaders. His other recourse was to court the support of the Normans as allies against the northern invaders. He entered into an alliance with Richard I, the Duke of Normandy by marrying his daughter, Emma. Emma was the sister of Richard II (1002).

Even though the Danes had been in England longer than in France, with the similarity of their languages, there lacked the assimilation that had occurred with the Danes in Normandy. Athelstan and Edgar employed the Danes as troops, *who were quartered about the country, and committed many violences upon the inhabitants. The animosity from these repeated injuries, risen to a great height; when Ethelred, from a policy incident to weak princes, embraced the cruel resolution of massacring the latter throughout all his dominions. --- The rage of the populace, excited by so many injuries, sanctified by authority, and stimulated by example, distinguished not between innocence and guilt, spared neither sex nor age, and was not satiated without the tortures, as well as death, of the unhappy victims.*

Invasion by the Danes

Revenge from *Sweyn and his Danes followed,* in 1004. *They began to spread their devastations over the country.*[47] *Here in this year*

---

[46] Ibid, pp 104-105.

[47] Ibid, p 116.

(1005) there was the great famine throughout the English race, such that no one ever remembered one so grim before; and this year the (enemy) fleet turned from this country to Denmark, and soon returned again.

Hume provided a summary of the devastation: *It is almost impossible, or would be tedious, to relate particularly all the miseries to which the English were thenceforth exposed. We hear of nothing but the sacking and burning of towns; the devastation of the open country; the appearance of the enemy in every quarter of the kingdom; their cruel diligence in discovering any corner, which had not been ransacked by their former violence. The broken and disjointed narration of the ancient historians is here well adapted to the nature of the war, which was conducted by such sudden inroads, as would have been dangerous even to an united and well governed kingdom, but proved fatal where nothing but a general consternation, a mutual diffidence and distension prevailed. The governors of one province refused to march to the assistance of another, and were at last terrified from assembling their forces for the defense of their own province. --- And the only expedient, in which the English agreed, was the base and imprudent one, of buying a new peace for the Danes by the payment of 48,000 pounds. This measure did not bring them even that short interval of repose, which they had expected from it. The Danes, disregarding all engagement, continued their devastations and hostilities; murdered the archbishop of Canterbury in 1012. --- The English nobility found no other recourse than that of submitting everywhere to the Danish monarch, swearing allegiance to him, and delivering him hostages for their fidelity. Ethelred, equally afraid of the violence of the enemy and the treachery of his own subjects, fled into Normandy, whither he had sent before him Queen Emma, and her two sons, Alfred and Edward. Richard II received his unhappy guests with a generosity that does honor to his memory.*[48]

Death of Ethelred, rule of England by Danish kings

King Ethelred passed away on November 30, 1016. *In this way the reign of King Ethelred ended (1016) after an unhappy and inglorious reign of thirty-five years.* He had two sons by his first marriage, Edmund, and Edwy, whom Canute afterwards murdered. Queen Emma, immediately upon Ethelred's death, had conveyed into Normandy Ethelred's two sons, Alfred and Edward, by his second marriage to Emma. The only heir of Ethelred to rule in England subsequently was his son by his marriage to Emma, Edward the Confessor (1042-1066).

Canute and sons

Sweyns son, Canute I, would follow Ethelred as the first Danish king of England. Canute was chosen King after summoning a general

---

[48] Ibid, pp 117-118.

assembly of the states, and the nobles concurred. Canute and his two sons would rule England from the death of Ethelred in 1016 to 1042, the year Edward assumed the throne. Canute, who ruled from 1016 to 1035, had established himself by the terror and cruelty of his military conquests against the English. He disposed of Edmund's two sons, Edward the exile and Edgar the Atheling, by sending them to Sweden where he hoped for their death, but the Swedish king sent them to Hungary. They would never become a threat to gain the crown. Canute *put to death many of the English nobility and bestowed on his Danish colleagues the most extensive governments and jurisdictions.*He found it necessary to have Edric, who defeated Edmund at Assington, condemned as a traitor and executed. *Canute also found himself obliged, in the beginning of his reign, to load the people with heavy taxes, in order to reward his Danish followers. He exacted from them at one time the sum of 72,000 pounds; besides 11,000 pounds, which he levied on London alone. --- But these rigors were imputed to necessity; and Canute, like a wise prince, was determined that the English, now deprived of all their dangerous leaders, should be reconciled to the Danish yoke, by the justice and impartiality of his administration.* The laws during this reign were called *Danelaw. Canute restored the Saxon customs in a general assembly of the states: He made no distinction between Danes and English in the distribution of justice: And he took care, by a strict execution of law, to protect the lives and properties of all his people. The Danes were gradually incorporated with his new subjects; and both were glad to obtain a little respite from those multiplied calamities.*

He even saw fit to negotiate, with Richard II of Normandy, his marriage to Emma, formerly wed to Ethelred. *Canute saw the danger to which he was exposed, from the enmity of so warlike a people as the Normans. In order to acquire the friendship of the duke, he paid his addresses to queen Emma, sister of the prince* (Richard II). *--- The English, though they disapproved of her espousing the mortal enemy of her former husband and his family, were pleased to find at court a sovereign, to whom they were accustomed, and who had already formed connections with them: And thus Canute, besides securing, by this marriage, the alliance of Normandy, gradually acquired, by the same means, the confidence of his own subjects.*[49]

He even undertook a pilgrimage to Rome, where he resided a considerable time. --- The only memorable action, which Canute performed after his return from Rome, was an expedition against Malcolm, king of Scotland, who imposed a tax, subsequently called Danegelt, on all the lands in England. Upon Canute's appearing on the frontiers with a formidable army, Malcolm agreed, that his grandson and heir, Duncan, whom he put in possession of Cumberland, would make the

---

[49] Ibid, pp 121-126.

submission required, and that the heirs of Scotland should always acknowledge themselves vassals to England for that province.

Canute passed four years in peace after this enterprise, and he died at Shaftsbury (1035), leaving three sons, Sweyn, Harold, and Hardicanute. Sweyn, whom he had by his first marriage with Alfwen, daughter of the earl of Hampshire, was crowned in Norway: Hardicanute, whom Emma had born him was in possession of Denmark: Harold, who was of the same marriage with Sweyn, was at that time in England.[50] Canute's two sons, Harold I (1037-1040), and Hardicanute (1040-1042) would rule England, to be followed in 1042 by Edward the Confessor.

Edward the Confessor

The English, on the death of Hardicanute, saw a favorable opportunity for recovering their liberty, and for shaking off the Danish yoke, under which they had so long labored. Sweyn, king of Norway, the eldest son of Canute, was absent; and as the two last kings had died without issue, none of that race presented himself, nor any whom the Danes could support as successor to the throne.

Prince Edward, afterwards named Edward the Confessor, (b. 1002, d. 1066), *was fortunately at court on his brother's demise; and though the descendants of Edmund Ironside were the true heirs of the Saxon family, yet their absence in so remote a country as Hungary, appeared a sufficient reason for their exclusion, to a people like the English, so little accustomed to observe a regular order in the succession of their monarchs.*

The English flattered themselves, that, by the accession of Edward, who reigned from 1042 to 1066, they were delivered forever from the dominion of foreigners; but they soon found, that this evil was not yet entirely removed. The king had been educated in Normandy; and had contracted many intimacies with the natives of that country, as well as an affection for their manner. The court of England was soon filled with Normans, who, being distinguished both by the favor of Edward, and by a degree of cultivation superior to that which was attained by the English in those ages, soon rendered their language, customs, and laws fashionable in the kingdom. The study of the French tongue became general among the people. The courtiers affected to imitate that nation in their dress, equipage, and entertainments: Even the lawyers employed a foreign language in their deeds and papers. But above all, the church felt the influence and dominion of those strangers: Ulf and William, two Normans, who had formerly been the king's chaplains, were created bishops of Dorchester and London: Robert, a Norman also, was

---

[50] Ibid, p 126. Note. Harold II, son of Godwin, earl of Wessex, would become the last king of England, in 1066, after the death of Edward.

promoted to the see of Canterbury, and always enjoyed the highest favor of his master, of which his abilities rendered him not unworthy. --- the ecclesiastical preferments fell often to the share of the Normans; and as the latter possessed Edward's confidence, they had secretly a great influence on public affairs, and excited the jealousy of the English, particularly of earl Godwin.[51]

Edward and Godwin

  This powerful nobleman,(Godwin)*, besides being duke or earl of Wessex, had the counties of Kent and Sussex annexed to his government. His eldest son possessed the same authority in the counties of Oxford, Berks, Glocester, and Hereford: and Harold, his second son was duke of East-Anglia, and at the same time governor of Essex. The great authority of this family was supported by immense possessions and powerful alliances; and the abilities, as well as ambition, of Godwin himself, contributed to render it still more dangerous.*

  Edward's animosity against Godwin was grounded on personal as well as political considerations, on recent as well as more ancient injuries. The king, in pursuance of his engagements, had indeed married Editha, the daughter of Godwin; but this alliance became a fresh source of enmity between them. Edward's hatred of the father was transferred to that princess; and Editha, though possessed of many amiable accomplishments, could never acquire the confidence and affection of her husband. Edward had accused Godwin of complicity in the murder of his older brother Alfred, who died in 1036. The conflict between Edward and Godwin worsened when Godwin refused an order of the king. Edward marched his army to London and summoned a great council to judge the rebellion of Godwin and his sons. Godwin and sons retreated to Flanders. Edward confined Editha to a monastery at Werewel in Winchester. Two other sons, including Harold, took shelter in Ireland.

  The earl of Flanders permitted Godwin to purchase and hire ships within his harbors; and Godwin, having manned them with his followers, and with free-booters of all nations, put to sea, and attempted to make a descent at Sandwich. --- He sailed to the Isle of Wight, where he was joined by his son Harold with a squadron, which that nobleman had collected in Ireland. He was now master of the sea; and entering every harbor in the southern coast, he seized all the ships, and summoned his followers in those counties, which had so long been subject to his government, to assist him in procuring justice to himself, his family, and his country, against the tyranny of foreigners. Reinforced by great numbers from all quarters, he entered the Thames; and appearing before London, threw everything into confusion. The king alone seemed resolute to defend himself to the last extremity; but the

---

[51] Ibid, pp 130-132

interposition of the English nobility, many of whom favored Godwin's pretensions, made Edward hearken to terms of accommodation. --- By this treaty, the present danger of a civil war was obviated, but the authority of the crown was considerably impaired or rather entirely annihilated. [52]

Harold

Harold II, (b. 1022, d. 1066), became king of England after the death of Edward, in January 1066, and ruled to his own death in October 1066 in the battle of Hastings. *Not long after this treaty, Godwin died and his son Harold succeeded in the government of Wessex, Sussex, Kent, and Essex and gained influence in Mercia and East Anglia-the influence of Harold preponderated. The death of Siward, duke of Northumbria, made the way still more open to the ambition of that nobleman. Siward, besides his other merits, had acquired honor to England, by his successful conduct in the only foreign enterprise undertaken during the reign of Edward.*

Duncan, king of Scotland, was a prince of a gentle disposition, but possessed not the genius requisite for governing a country so turbulent, and so much infested by the intrigues and animosities of the great. Macbeth, a powerful nobleman, and nearly allied to the crown, not content with curbing of the king's authority, carried still farther his pestilent ambition: He put his sovereign to death; chased Malcolm, his son and heir, into England,; and usurped the crown. Siward, whose daughter was married to Duncan, embraced, by Edward's order, the protection of this distressed family: He marched an army into Scotland; and having defeated and killed Macbeth in battle, in 1057, he restored Malcolm to the throne of his ancestors. ---Harold's influence obtained that dukedom for his own brother Tosti.

Tosti, brother of this nobleman (Harold), who had been created duke of Northumberland, being of a violent, tyrannical temper, had acted with such cruelty and injustice, that the inhabitants rose in rebellion, and chased him from his government. Morcar, who possessed great power in those parts, confronted Harold, told him of the conduct of Tosti: He represented to Harold, that Tosti had behaved in a manner unworthy of the station to which he was advanced, and not one, not even a brother, could support such tyranny, without participating in some degree, of the infamy attending it. --- This vigorous remonstrance was accompanied with such a detail of facts, so well supported, that Harold found it prudent to abandon his brother's cause; and returning to Edward, he persuaded him to pardon the Northumbrians, and to confirm Morcar in the government. He (Harold) even married the sister of that nobleman, and by his interest procured Edwin, the younger brother, to be elected

---

[52] Ibid, pp 135-136

into the government of Mercia. Tosti in rage departed the kindgdom, and took shelter in Flanders with earl Baldwin, his father-in-law.[53]

Harold and William

Harold broke all measures with the duke of Normandy; and William clearly perceived, that he could no longer rely on the oaths and promises, which he had extorted from him. Both Harold and William had at this time intentions to gain the power of the throne to rule England. *Harold, meanwhile, proceeded, after a more open manner, increasing his popularity, in establishing his power, and in preparing the way for his advancement of the first vacancy; an event which, from the age and infirmities of the king, appeared not very distant.* Harold approached king Edward, with pretended submission to his authority, to gain permission to visit Normandy and to meet William.

On Harold's voyage to Normandy to visit William, he was driven by a storm to the territory of Guy count of Ponthieu who held Harold a prisoner for ransom; however William demanded the liberty of the prisoner and he was released. *William received him with every demonstration of respect and friendship --- and he took an opportunity of disclosing to him the great secret, of his pretensions to the crown of England, and of the will, which Edward intended to make in his favor. --- Harold was surprised at this declaration of the duke; but being sensible that he should never recover his own liberty, much less that of his brother and nephew, if he refused the demand, he feigned a compliance with William, renounced all hopes of the crown for himself, and professed his sincere intention of supporting the will of Edward, and seconding the pretension of the duke of Normandy. William, to bind him faster to his interests, besides offering him one of his daughters in marriage, required him to take an oath that he would fulfill his promises.[54]*

Harold had married the sister of Morcar, not the daughter of William, and this heralded the great battle to come between Harold and William. Meanwhile, Harold saw that almost all England was engaged in his interests. While he himself possessed the government of Wessex, Morcar had possession of Northumberland, and Edwin of Mercia. Harold now openly aspired to the succession. He insisted that it was necessary, by the confession of all, to set aside the royal family, on account of the imbecility of Edgar, the Aetheling, the sole surviving heir (descendant of Ethelred, Edmund II, and son of Edward the Exile).

---

[53] Ibid, 136-145.

[54] Ibid, pp 140-143.

Death of Edward the Confessor and Accession of Harold, January 1066

Edward, broken with age and infirmities, saw the difficulties too great for him to encounter; and though his inveterate prepossessions kept him from seconding the pretensions of Harold, he took but feeble and irresolute steps for securing the succession to the duke of Normandy. While he continued in this uncertainty, he was surprised by sickness, which brought him to his grave, on the fifth of January, 1066, in the sixty-fifth year of his age, and twenty-fifth of his reign.

According to Hume: *The most commendable circumstance of Edward's government was his attention to the administration of justice, and his compiling for that purpose a body of laws, which he collected from the laws of Ethelbert, Ina* (king of Wessex), *and Alfred. The compilation, though now lost (for the laws that pass under Edward's name were composed afterwards) was long the object of affection to the English nation.*

Harold had so well prepared matters before the death of Edward that he immediately stepped into the vacant throne; and his accession on January 5, 1066, was attended with as little opposition and disturbance, as if he had succeeded by the most undoubted hereditary title.[55] *The first symptom of danger, which the king discovered, came from abroad, and from his own brother, Tosti, who had submitted to a voluntary banishment in Flanders.* Tosti, with support from the Norwegians, invaded Northumbria and took York.

Meanwhile, William *sent ambassadors to England, upbraiding Harold with his breach of faith and summoning him to resign immediately possession of the kingdom. Harold replied to the Norman ambassadors, that the oath, with which he was reproached, had been extorted by the well-grounded fear of violence, and could never, for that reason, be regarded as obligatory.*[56]

Invasion by William and the Normans, October 1066

The Normans, as they had long been distinguished by valor among all the European nations, had at this time attained to the highest pitch of military glory. The Normans had extended their domain into Italy, at Naples and Sicily, and over the Germans and Saracens. *The situation also of Europe inspired William with hopes, that besides his brave Normans, he might employ against England the flower of the military force, which was dispersed in all the neighboring states. France, Germany, and the Low Countries, by the progress of the feudal*

---

[55] Ibid, p 146. Note. Harold was the son of Godwin, who was not related to any previous king.

[56] Ibid, p 147.

institutions, were divided and subdivided into many principalities and baronies; and the possessors, enjoying the civil jurisdiction within themselves, as well as the right of arms, acted, in many respects, as independent sovereigns, and maintained their properties and privileges, less by the authority of laws, than by their own force and valor. A military spirit had universally diffused itself throughout Europe; and the several leaders, whose minds were elevated by their princely situation, greedily embraced the most hazardous enterprises; and being accustomed to nothing from their infancy but recitals of the success attending wars and battles, they were prompted by a natural ambition to imitate those adventures.

William, by his power, his courage, and his abilities, had long maintained a pre-eminence among those haughty chieftains; and every one who desired to signalize himself by his address in military exercises, or valor in action, had been ambitious of acquiring a reputation in the court and in the armies of Normandy. Entertained with that hospitality and courtesy, which distinguished the age, they had formed attachments with the prince, and greedily attended to the prospect of the signal glory and elevation, which he promised them in return for their concurrence in an expedition against England.[57]

The emperor, Henry IV, gave all his vassals permission to embark on the invasion of England and pope Alexander II gave his support to William. William had now assembled a fleet of 3000 vessels, great and small, and had selected an army of 60,000 men, but contrary winds delayed their departure.

Harold was occupied with the revolts in Northumbria, and marching north, met the combined forces of Tosti and the Norwegians September 25, 1066. *Tosti and the Norwegian prince Halfager were slain and even the Norwegian fleet fell into the hands of Harold. But he had scarcely time to rejoice of this victory, when he received intelligence that the duke of Normandy was landed with a great army in the south of England.* William and his forces landed at Pevensey in Sussex. The English were defeated at the battle of Hastings, October 14, 1066. Harold was slain by an arrow. [58]

---

[57] Ibid, pp 149-150.

[58] Ibid, pp 153- 158.

Chapter 13

William I and sons, William II and Henry I

William I, (b 1028, d 1087), duke of Normandy, claimed the English throne based on his contacts with Edward and Harold. He invaded England and defeated Harold in 1066. Thereafter England would suffer the greatest upheaval since the Roman conquest, bringing even greater devastation than from German and Danish invasions and conquests. William I lived most of his life in Normandy. He ruled England and Normandy until 1087 when he died following an injury in Normandy. In this chapter we shall also review the reigns of his two sons who followed him, William II and Henry I. We do not have historians like the ancients who probed the depths of a person's mind and who attempt to account for their behavior such as we found in Plutarch and Tacitus. It would be more than five centuries before Shakespeare, whose historical plays provide insights into the English kings from king John to Henry VIII. It would be seven centuries before David Hume would write his monumental work, *The History of England*, which probes the mind and behavior of the English kings. Most of the following quotations are from Hume.

The Normans

The Normans were peopled by Danes, who later intermingled with the French. A Dane named Rollo was banished by the king of Denmark and was forced into Scandinavia. *Here he collected a body of troops, which, like that of all those ravagers, was composed of Norwegians, Swedes, Frisians, Danes and adventurers of all nations, who being accustomed to a roving unsettled life, took delight in nothing but war and plunder. His reputation brought his associates from all quarters.* --- The first attempt, made by Rollo, was on England, near the end of Alfred's reign (871- 899), but finding Alfred's security and defenses a deterrent, raided France, both inland and maritime provinces. The weak French king Charles granted Rollo considerable territory and gave his daughter in marriage. *Rollo, who was now in the decline of life, and was tired of wars and depredations, applied himself, with mature counsels, to the settlement of his new-acquired territory, which was thenceforth called Normandy; and he parceled it among his captains and followers.*

Family history of William I

There continues the family history of William I, going back many generations. *Rollo was followed by William, who succeeded him, governed the duchy twenty-five years; and during that time, the Normans were thoroughly intermingled with the French, had acquired their language, and had imitated their manners, and had made such progress towards cultivation, that, on the death of William, his son Richard I, though a minor, inherited his dominions: --- Richard I, after a long reign of fifty-four years, was succeeded by his son, Richard II, of the same name in the year 996, which was eighty-five years after the first establishment of the Normans in France.* This was the duke, who gave his sister, Emma, in marriage (1002) to Ethelred, king of England (979-1016).[1]

William's father Robert was the son of Richard II. *This famous prince was the natural son of Robert, duke of Normandy, by Harlotta, daughter of a tanner in Falaise, and was very early established in that grandeur, from which his birth seemed to have set him at so great a distance. While he was but nine years of age, his father had resolved to undertake a pilgrimage to Jerusalem; --- Before his departure he assembled the states of the duchy; and informing them of his design, he engaged them to swear allegiance to his natural son, William, whom, as he had no legitimate issue, he intended, in case he should die in the pilgrimage, to leave successor to his dominions.* Unfortunately, little information can be gleaned from the historical record regarding his mother. William's half- brother Odo, who later became William's most important advisor, through the years in Normandy and England, was presumably a younger son by the mother.

The Norman connection had been introduced in England by the marriage of Emma, the sister of Richard II, grandfather of William I, to Ethelred (979-1016). Edward The confessor who ruled England from was the son of Ethelred and Emma. The Norman influence became well established during the reign of their son Edward (1042-1066).

---

[1] Hume, The History of England, vol 1, pp 112-115.

Early life

    Little is known of William's early years. His father, Robert, duke of Normandy, had undertaken a pilgrimage to Jerusalem and died in this dangerous undertaking. This prince (Robert), as he had apprehended, died in his pilgrimage; and the minority of his son was attended with all those disorders, which were almost unavoidable in that situation. The licentious nobles, free from the awe of sovereign authority, broke out in personal animosities against each other, and made the whole country a scene of war and devastation.

William, duke of Normandy

    William was seven years old when his father died, and when he was fifteen (1042) began to play a role in the rule of Normandy. It would be another 24 years before William and the Normans invaded England. During this interval, William contended with uprisings of the barons in Normandy, Maine, and Anjou from 1046 to 1055. *The regency established by Robert encountered great difficulties in supporting the government under this complication of dangers; and the young prince, when he came to maturity, found himself reduced to a very low condition. But the great qualities, which he soon displayed in the field and in the cabinet, gave encouragement to his friends, and struck a terror into his enemies. He opposed himself on all sides against his rebellious subjects, and against foreign invaders; and by his valor and conduct prevailed in every action. He obliged the French king to grant him peace on reasonable terms; he expelled all pretenders to the sovereignty; and he reduced his turbulent barons to pay submission to his authority, and to suspend their mutual animosities.*[2]

    He appointed his half-brother Odo, bishop of Bayeux in 1049. From 1047 to 1052 William and his forces subdued Maine and the count of Anjou with help from an alliance with the French king Henry I. *The tranquility, which he had established in his dominions, had given William leisure to pay a visit to the king of England during the time of Godwin's banishment; and he was received in a manner suitable to the great reputation which he had acquired, to the relation by which he was connected with Edward, and to the obligations which that prince owed to his family. --- The archbishop of Canterbury had persuaded Edward to think of adopting William as his successor, a counsel, which was favored by the king's aversion to Godwin, his prepossessions for the Normans, and his esteem of the duke. That prelate, therefore, received a commission to inform William of the king's intentions in his favor; and he was the first person that opened the mind of the prince to entertain those ambitions hopes.*[3]

---

[2] Ibid, pp 139-140.

[3] Ibid, p 141.

Marriage and family

In 1052 William married Mildred, the daughter of Baldwin V of Flanders. A dispute with the pope over the possible blood relationship in this marriage was not resolved until 1059. There were three surviving sons and a daughter from this union. Robert the eldest would follow his father as duke of Normandy. He would also follow his grandfather in leaving his governance and joining the crusades. Next was William, to follow his father as king of England as well as of Normandy, and then Henry to follow William II. A daughter Adele, the youngest in the family, would be married to Stephen of Blois, and become the mother of the contested king Stephen who followed Henry I.

Conquest of England

The relationship between the Norman William and the English king Edward led to the fateful invasion of England. William also claimed that Harold assented to his aspirations for the English crown. William won the battle of Hastings, in October 14, 1066, which was to decide the fate of England. Hume provides a closing summary of the battle: *Thus was gained by William, duke of Normandy, the great and decisive victory of Hastings, after a battle which was fought from morning till sunset, and which seemed worthy, by the heroic valor displayed by both armies and by both commanders, to decide the fate of a mighty kingdom. William had three horses killed under him; and there fell near fifteen thousand men on the side of the Normans: The loss was still more considerable on that of the vanquished; besides the death of the king and his two brothers.*[4]

After the battle of Hastings, William and the Norman army took possession of Dover, Kent, and Berkhamsted, northwest of London. The nobles and Edgar Atheling, purported heir of the throne, submitted to William. *The ecclesiastics in particular, whose influence was great over the people, began to declare in his favor, and as most of the bishops and dignified clergymen were even then Frenchmen or Normans, the pope's bull, by which his enterprise was avowed and hallowed, was now openly insisted on as a reason for general submission. --- They requested him to mount their throne, which they now considered as vacant; and declared to him, that, as they had always been ruled by regal power, they desired to follow, in this particular, the example of their ancestors, and knew of no one more worthy than himself to hold the reins of government.*[5]

William was crowned, by the archbishop of York, at Westminster on December 26, 1066. He then went to Essex where he

---

[4] Ibid, pp 158-159.

[5] Ibid, pp 188-189.

received the submission of all the nobility. He had got possession of the treasure of Harold, which was considerable; and being also supplied with rich presents from the opulent men in all parts of England, who were solicitous to gain the favor of their new sovereign, he distributed great sums among his troops, and by this liberality gave them hopes of obtaining at length those more durable establishments, which they had expected from his enterprise.

He introduced into England that strict execution of justice, for which his administration had been much celebrated in Normandy; and even during this violent revolution, every disorder or oppression met with rigorous punishment. His army in particular was governed with severe discipline; and notwithstanding the insolence of victory, care was taken to give as little offence as possible to the jealousy of the vanquished. The king appeared solicitous to unite in an amicable manner the Normans and the English, by intermarriages and alliances; and all his new subjects who approached his person were received with affability and regard. No signs of suspicion appeared, not even towards Edgar Atheling, the heir of the ancient royal family, whom William confirmed in the honors of earl of Oxford, conferred on this by Harold, and whom he affected to treat with the highest kindness, as nephew to the Confessor, his great friend and benefactor.[6]

Insurrections and further conquest

This early submission to William and the Norman conquest was soon followed by rebellion. William had confiscated the estates of Harold and those who supported him at Hastings. *The king took care to place all real power in the hands of his Normans, and still to keep possession of the sword, to which, he was sensible, he had owed his advancement to sovereign authority. He disarmed the city of London and other places, which appeared most warlike and populous; and building citadels in the capital, as well as in Winchester, Hereford, and the cities best situated for commanding the kingdom, he quartered Norman soldiers in all of them, and left nowhere any power able to resist or oppose him. He bestowed the forfeited estates on the most eminent of his captains, and established funds for the payment of his soldiers. And thus, while his civil administration carried the face of a legal magistrate, his military institutions were those of a master and tyrant.*

William retired to Normandy, taking with him the chief nobles of England *to grace his court.* William secured them as hostages. *He left the administration in the hands of his uterine brother, Odo, bishop of Baieux, and of William Fitz Osberne. During his absence, discontents and complaints multiplied everywhere; secret conspiracies were entered into against the government; hostilities were already begun in many*

---

[6] Ibid, pp 191-192.

places. Hume questioned the motives of William, that in order to complete his subjugation and seizure of properties for his own appointed, he needed to goad his subjects into revolt. *In order to have a pretext for this violence, he endeavored, without discovering his intentions, to provoke and allure them into insurrections, which, he thought, could never prove dangerous, while he detained all the principal nobility in Normandy, while a great and victorious army was quartered in England, and while he himself was so near to suppress any tumult or rebellion.* Hume then added this apology: *But as no ancient writer has ascribed this tyrannical purpose to William, it scarcely seems allowable, from conjecture alone, to throw such an imputation upon him.*[7]

There were uprisings in Kent and revolts joined by Welsh princes. An important earl who supported William was put to death. *The king, informed of these dangerous discontents, hastened over to England; and by his presence, and the vigorous measures, which he pursued, disconcerted all the schemes of the conspirators. Such of them as had been more violent in their mutiny betrayed their guilt, by flying or concealing themselves; and the confiscation of their estates, while it increased the number of malcontents, both enabled William to gratify farther the rapacity of his Norman captains, and gave them the prospect of new forfeitures and attainders. The king began to regard all his English subjects as inveterate and irreclaimable enemies; and thenceforth either embraced, or was more fully confirmed in the resolution, of seizing their possessions, and of reducing them to the most abject slavery. Though the natural violence and severity of his temper made him incapable of feeling any remorse in the execution of his tyrannical purpose, he had art enough to conceal his intentions, and to preserve still some appearance of justice in his oppressions. He ordered all the English, who had been arbitrarily expelled by the Normans, during his absence to be restored to their estates: But at the same time, he imposed a general tax on the people, that of Danegelt, which had been abolished by the Confessor, and which had always been extremely odious to the nation.*

In 1068, the inhabitants of Exeter, instigated by Githa, mother to king Harold, refused to admit a Norman garrison, and betaking themselves to arms, were strengthened by the accession of the neighboring inhabitants of Devonshire and Cornwall. The king hastened with his forces to chastize this revolt; and on this approach, the wiser and more considerable citizens, sensible of the unequal contest, persuaded the people to submit, and to deliver hostages for their obedience. A sudden mutiny of the populace broke this agreement; and William, appearing before the wall, ordered the eyes of one of the hostages to be put out, as an earnest of that severity, which the rebels

---

[7] Ibid, pp 193-194.

must expect, if they persevered in their revolt. The inhabitants were anew seized with terror, and surrendering at discretion, threw themselves at the king's feet, and supplicated his clemency and forgiveness.

Final conquest

The English were now sensible that their final destruction was intended; and that, instead of a sovereign, whom they had hoped to gain by their submission, they had tamely surrendered themselves, without resistance, to a tyrant and a conqueror.[8] Many English nobles fled to foreign countries, including Edgar Atheling who escaped into Scotland with his two sisters, Margaret and Christina and were well received by Duncan, who became espoused to Margaret. *In 1069 Godwin, Edmond, and Magnus, three sons of Harold, had, immediately after the defeat at Hastings, sought a retreat in Ireland; where, having met with a kind reception from Dermot and other princes of that country, they projected an invasion on England. They hoped that all the exiles from Denmark, Scotland, and Wales, assisted by forces from these several countries, would at once commence hostilities, and rouse the indignation of the English against their haughty conquerors.* The inhabitants of York rose in arms, the Danes landed with 300 vessels, and Edgar Atheling appeared from Scotland with nobles hoping that the Northumbrians would join them in the insurrection. The English in Somerset and Dorset rose in arms, the inhabitants of Cornwal and Devon attacked Exeter, and the Welsh laid siege to Shrewsbury. *William, undismayed amidst this scene of confusion, assembled his forces, and animating them with the prospect of new confiscations and forfeitures, he marched against the rebels in the north, whom he regarded as the most formidable, and whose defeat he knew would strike a terror into all the other malcontents. --- Sensible of the restless disposition of the Northumbrians, he determined to incapacitate them ever after, from gaining him disturbance, and he issued orders for laying entirely waste that fertile country, which, for the extent of sixty miles, lies between the Humber and the Tees. The houses were reduced to ashes by the merciless Normans, the cattle seized and driven away, the instruments of husbandry destroyed; and the inhabitants compelled either to seek for a subsistence in the southern parts of Scotland, or if they lingered in England, from a reluctance to abandon their ancient habitations, they perished miserably in the woods from cold and hunger. The lives of a hundred thousand persons, are computed to have been sacrificed to this stroke of barbarous policy, which, by seeking a remedy for a temporary evil, thus inflicted a lasting wound on the power and populousness of the nation.*

All submitted to the conqueror and *the Normans became undisputed masters of the kingdom. But William, finding himself entirely*

---

[8] Ibid, pp 196-197.

master of a people, who had given him such sensible proofs of their impotent rage and animosity now resolved to proceed to extremities against all the natives of England; and to reduce them to a condition, in which they should no longer be formidable to his government. The insurrections and conspiracies in so many parts of the kingdom had involved the bulk of the landed proprietors, more or less, in the guilt of treason; and the king took advantage of executing against them, with the utmost rigor, the laws of forfeiture and attainder. Their lives were indeed commonly spared; but their estates were confiscated, and either annexed to the royal demesnes, or conferred with the most profuse bounty on the Normans and other foreigners. --- Ancient and honorable families were reduced to beggary; the nobles themselves were everywhere treated with ignominy and contempt; they had the mortification of seeing their castles and manors possessed by Normans of the meanest birth and lowest stations; and they found themselves carefully excluded from every road, which led there to riches or preferment.

Feudal laws

As power naturally follows property, this revolution alone gave great security to the foreigners; but William, by the new institutions, which he established, took also care to retain for ever the military authority in those hands, which had enabled him to subdue the kingdom. He introduced into England the feudal law, which he found established in France and Normandy, and which, during that age, was the foundation both of the stability and of the disorders, in most of the monarchial governments of Europe. He divided all the lands of England, with very few exceptions, beside the royal demesnes, into baronies; and he conferred these, with the reservation of stated services and payments, on the most considerable of his adventurers. These great barons, who held immediately of the crown, shared out a great part of their lands to other foreigners, who were denominated knights or vassals, and who paid their lord the same duty and submission in peace and war, which he himself owed to his sovereign. The whole kingdom contained about 700 chief tenants, and 60,215 knight-fees; and as none of the native English were admitted into the first rank, the few who retained their landed property, were glad to be received into the second, and under the protection of some powerful Norman.[9]

The church

William replaced the English clergy with Norman ecclesiastics, but the legate dispatched by the pope failed to establish supremacy of the church over king William. *The legate submitted to become the instrument of his tyranny; and thought.* William summoned a council of the prelates

---

[9] Ibid, pp 203-204.

and abbots at Winchester. The English archbishop of Canterbury, *Stigand, was accused of three crimes, all of which were mere pretenses, but Stigand was cast into prison, where he continued, in poverty and want, during the remainder of his life. Like rigor was exercised against the other English prelates.*

It was a fixed maxim in this reign, as well as in some of the subsequent, that no native of the island should ever be advanced to any dignity, ecclesiastical, civil, or military. --- He required that all the ecclesiastical canons, voted in any synod, should first be laid before him, and be ratified by his authority: Even bulls or letters from Rome could not legally be produced, till they received the same sanction. These regulations were worthy of a sovereign, and kept united the civil and ecclesiastical power.

The government

William had achieved conquest by military force, by the feudal laws and finally, by religion, which he had annexed to the crown. *But the English had the cruel mortification to find, that their king's authority, however acquired or however extended, was all employed in their oppression; and that the scheme of their subjection, attended with every circumstance of insult and indignity, was deliberately formed by the prince, and wantonly prosecuted by his followers, William had even entertained the difficult project of totally abolishing the English language; and, for that purpose, he ordered, that in all schools throughout the kingdom, the youth should be instructed in the French tongue, a practice which was continued from custom till after the reign of Edward III (1377), and was never indeed totally discontinued in England. The pleadings in the supreme courts of judicature were in French: The deeds were often drawn in the same language: The laws were composed in that idiom: No other tongue was used in that court.*

But amidst those endeavors to depress the English nation, the king, moved by the remonstrances of some of his prelates, and by the earnest desires of the people, restored a few of the laws of king Edward; which, though seemingly of no great importance towards the protection of general liberty, gave them extreme satisfaction, as a memorial of their ancient government, and an unusual mark of compliance in their imperious conquerors.[10]

In 1071 William would eliminate the threat from two of England's most powerful remaining earls, Morcar and Edwin. *Morcar took shelter in the Isle of Ely with the brave Hereward, who secured by the inaccessible situation of the place, still defended himself against the Normans. But this attempt served only to accelerate the ruin of the few English, who had hitherto been able to preserve their rank or fortune*

---

[10] Ibid, pp 207-208.

during the past convulsions. William employed all his endeavors to subdue the Isle of Ely; and having surrounded it with flat-bottomed boats, and made a causeway through the morasses to the extent of two miles, he obliged the rebels to surrender at discretion. Hereward alone forced his way, sword in hand, through the enemy; and still continued his hostilities by sea against the Normans, till at last William, charmed with his bravery, received him into favor and restored him to his estate. Earl Morcar and Egelwin, bishop of Durham, who had joined the malcontents, were thrown into prison, and the latter soon after died in confinement. Edwin, attempting to make his escape into Scotland, was betrayed by some of his followers; and was killed by a party of Normans. --- To complete the king's prosperity, Edgar Atheling himself, despairing of success, and weary of a fugitive life, submitted to his enemy; and receiving a decent pension for his subsistence, was permitted to live in England unmolested. But these acts of generosity towards the leaders were disgraced, as usual, by William's rigor against the inferior malcontents. He ordered the hands to by lopt off, and the eyes to be put out of many of the prisoners whom he had taken in the Isle of Ely; and he dispersed them in that miserable condition throughout the country, and monuments of his severity.[11]

There was an insurrection of Norman barons in England, which was thwarted by the wife of one of the barons, Waltheof, and who conveyed intelligence of the conspiracy to the king, and aggravated every circumstance, which, she believed would tend to incense him against Waltheof, and render him absolutely implacable. The king, who hastened over to England, in order to suppress the insurrection, found that nothing remained but the punishment of the criminals, *which he executed with great severity. Many of the rebels were hanged; some had their eyes put out; others their hands cut off.* William ordered Waltheof to be tried, condemned, and executed. *The English, who considered this nobleman, the last resource of their nation, grievously lamented his fate.*[12]

Normandy and Robert

William, ruler of Normandy in addition to England, and who spent most of his remaining years there, had to muster English forces under his command to suppress a rebellion of his oldest son Robert, created duke of Normandy. William engaged his son, who had gained the protection of the king of France, unknowingly in battle, and was wounded in his arm. Robert was conciliatory and there was a reconciliation with the intervention of his mother Matilda. In fact, William gave him a command of an army in England to march against

---

[11] Ibid, pp 209-210.

[12] Ibid, pp 213-214.

king Malcolm of Scotland. William gave his brother Odo not only the bishopric of Baieux but created him as the earl of Kent. Odo amassed considerable wealth and *aspired to the chimerical project of buying the papacy.* William ordered his arrest and his brother was detained in custody during the remainder of his reign. *Another domestic event gave the king much more concern: It was the death of Matilda, his consort, whom he tenderly loved, and for whom he had ever preserved the most sincere friendship.*

Injury and death

In 1087, he led his forces into the L'Isle de France, but was stopped by an accident. *His horse starting aside of a sudden, he bruised his belly on the pommel of the saddle; and being in a bad habit of body, as well as somewhat advanced in years, he began to apprehend the consequences, and ordered himself to be carried in a litter to the monastery of St. Bervas. He endeavored to make atonement by presents to churches and monasteries; and he issued orders, that earl Morcar, Siward Bearne and other English prisoners, should be set at liberty. He was even prevailed on, though not without reluctance, to consent, with his dying breath, to release his brother, Odo, against whom he was extremely incensed.*[13] He died September 9, 1087, from complications of his injury at age 59. William I had three sons, the oldest Robert, then William and the younger Henry. His youngest child, Adelle, would marry a French noble, Stephen of Blois. Their son Stephen would follow Henry. William left Normandy and Maine to his eldest son, Robert. He left William the crown of England.

William II

His son William II (b. 1056, d. 1100), called Rufus, (the Red), would rule England from 1087 to 1100. William acted fast upon the death of his father. He had in possession a letter from his father to the primate Lanfranc giving his recommendation that William become king of England. William secured several fortresses and got possession of the royal treasury, by which he hoped to encourage and increase his partisans. His accession violated the principle of primogeniture, wherein Robert, the eldest son would rightfully inherit the kingdom.

Revolt of Robert and the barons

The first problem that William II encountered was a threat from many earls and nobles who supported Robert as the lawful heir to the throne. *The barons, who generally possessed large estates both in England and in Normandy, were uneasy at the separation of those*

---

[13] Ibid, pp 223-224.

territories; and foresaw, that, as it would be impossible for them to preserve long their allegiance to two masters, they must necessarily resign their ancient patrimony or their new acquisitions. Robert's title to the duchy they esteemed incontestable; his claim to the kingdom plausible; and they all desired that this prince, who alone had any pretensions to unite these states, should be put in possession of both. A comparison also of the personal qualities of the two brothers led them to give the preference to the elder. The duke was brave, open, sincere, generous: Even his predominant faults, his extreme indolence and facility, were not disagreeable to those haughty barons, who affected independence, and submitted with reluctance to a vigorous administration in their sovereign.

The king, although equally brave, was violent, haughty, and tyrannical; and seemed disposed to govern more by the fear than by the love of his subjects. Robert and Henry, brothers of the late king, led the barons in a conspiracy to dethrone William II. *The king was soon in a situation to take the field; and as he knew the danger of delay, he suddenly marched into Kent; where his uncles had already seized the fortresses of Pevensy and Rochester. These places he successively reduced by famine; and though he was prevailed on by the earl of Chester, William de Warrenne, and Robert Fitz Hammon, who had embraced his cause, to spare the lives of the rebels, he confiscated all their estates, and banished them the kingdom. --- Some of them received a pardon; but the greater part were attainted and the king bestowed their estates on the Norman barons, who had remained faithful to him. William, freed from the danger of these insurrections, took little care of fulfilling his promises to the English, who still found themselves exposed to the same oppressions, which they had undergone during the reign of the Conqueror, and which were rather augmented by the violent, impetuous temper of the present monarch.* [14]

Invasion of Normandy

William's older brother Robert had neglected his rule of Normandy. *The loose and negligent administration of that prince had emboldened the Norman barons to affect a great independency; and their mutual quarrels and devastations had rendered that whole territory a scene of violence and outrage.* William gained support from some of the nobles and appeared in Normandy at the head of an army; *and affairs seemed to have come to extremity between the brothers. The nobility on both sides, strongly connected by interest and alliances, interposed and mediated an accommodation.* Meanwhile their brother Henry felt left out of the negotiations and settlements of territories in Normandy. *Robert and William with their joint forces besieged him, and had nearly reduced*

---

[14] Ibid, pp 229-230.

him by the scarcity of water. Prince Henry was obliged to capitulate; and being despoiled of all his patrimony, wandered about for some time with very few attendants, and often in great poverty.[15]

Scotland and Northumberland

Between the years 1091 and 1096 there were disorders in Scotland and England. Now that there was an alliance between William and Robert, a command was give to Robert, in 1091. *Robert here commanded his brother's army, and obliged Malcom III, (1059-1093), to accept of peace and do homage to the crown of England. This peace was not more durable. Malcom, two years after, levying an army, invaded England, and after ravaging Northumberland, he laid siege to Alnwic, where a party of Moubray's troops falling upon him by surprise, a sharp action ensued, in which Malcom was slain. This incident interrupted for some years the regular succession to the Scottish crown. William later assisted Malcom's son Duncan II, (1093-1094), to gain the Scottish crown from Malcom's brother, Donald Bane, (1093), who had advanced to the throne because of the young age of Duncan.*[16]

The Crusades

Robert sold his dominions in Normandy to William II so that he could finance an expedition to the Holy Land. From Hume: *The crusades, which now engrossed the attention of Europe, and have ever since engaged the curiosity of mankind, as the most signal and most durable monument of human folly, that has yet appeared in any age or nation.* The power of the pope and the Roman Church had increased over European nations as well as England. This would become a source of conflict between the English kings and the pope, including the reign of William II. The Seljuk Turks had seized Jerusalem in 1065, *which made the pilgrimage to Jerusalem much more difficult and dangerous to the Christians.* Pope Urban II, at the Council of Clermont, promulgated the first crusade, in 1095. Peter the Hermit preached a holy war and a massive following of crusaders resulted.

Robert, duke of Normandy, impelled by the bravery and mistaken generosity of his spirit, had early enlisted himself in the crusade; but being always unprovided with money, he found, that it would be impracticable for him to appear in a manner suitable to his rank and station, at the head of his numerous vassals and subjects, who, transported with general rage, were determined to follow him into Asia. He resolved, therefore, to mortgage or rather to sell his dominions, which he had not talents to govern; and he offered them to his brother

---

[15] Ibid, pp 231-232.

[16] Ibid, p 233.

William, for the very unequal sum of ten thousand marks. The bargain was soon concluded: The king raised the money by violent extortions on his subjects of all ranks, even on the convents, who were obliged to melt their plate in order to furnish the quota demanded of them. He was put in possession of Normandy and Maine; and Robert, providing himself with a magnificent train, set out for the Holy Land, in pursuit of glory, and in full confidence of securing his eternal salvation.[17]

Conflict with St. Anselm, archbishop of Canterbury

William II did not support the crusades. *The Normans in England did not want to abandon their homes, in quest of distant adventures. William engaged in quarrels with the ecclesiastics, particularly with Anselm, commonly called St. Anselm, archbishop of Canterbury; and it is no wonder his memory should be blackened by the historians of that order. William had undertaken an expedition against Wales, and required the archbishop to furnish his quota of soldiers for that service; but Anselm, who regarded the demand as an oppression on the church, and yet durst not refuse compliance, sent them so miserably accoutered, that the king was extremely displeased, and threatened him with a prosecution.* He appealed to Rome and obtained the king's permission to retire beyond the sea. *All his temporalities were seized; but he was received with great respect by pope Urban, who considered him as a martyr in the cause of religion, and even menaced the king, on account of his proceedings against the primate and the church, with the sentence of excommunication.*

Sudden accidental death

William II was involved in suppressing insurrections in Normandy, the surrounding territories of Anjou and the province of Maine. He was wounded in a siege and returned to England. However, his death came while hunting in the New Forest, August 2, 1100 in Hampshire, England. He was slain by an arrow. He was about forty years old and ruled England for thirteen years. He never married and left no children.

Henry I

Henry I (b. 1068, d. 1135) followed William II in 1100, but not without challenge from his older brother Robert, who was the oldest son of William I. Robert had sold his duchy of Normandy to William II so that he could obtain support for a crusade. Robert, languishing in Italy after the crusade, returned to England after Henry had already seized the treasury and had been crowned by the prelates.

---

[17] Ibid, pp 234-239.

Charter of Henry I

Soon after Henry's accession he passed a charter, *which would purportedly remedy many of the grievous oppressions, which had been complained of during the reigns of his father, William I, and his brother William II.* The charter enacted that property would not be seized by the king during the absence of the see or abbey, but be awarded to the successor. After this concession to the church, whose favor was of so great importance, he proceeded to enumerate the civil grievances. *He promised, that, upon the death of any earl, baron, or military tenant, his heir should be admitted to the possession of his estate, on paying a just and lawful relief. --- He remitted the wardship of minors, and allowed guardians to be appointed, who should be answerable for the trust: He promised not to dispose of any heiress in marriage, but by the advice of all the barons. He granted his barons and military tenants the power of bequeathing by will their money or personal estates; and if they neglected to make a will he promised that their heirs should succeed to them: He renounced the right of imposing moneyage, and of levying taxes at pleasure on the farms, which the barons retained in their own hands: He made some general professions of moderating fines; he offered a pardon for all offences; and he remitted all debts due to the crown: He required, that the vassals of the barons should enjoy the same privileges, which he granted to his own barons; and he promised a general confirmation and observance of the laws of king Edward.*

To give greater authenticity to these concessions, Henry lodged a copy of his charter in some abbey of each county; as if desirous that it should be exposed to the view of all his subjects, and remain a perpetual rule for the limitation and direction of his government: Yet it is certain that, after the present purpose was served, he never once thought, during his reign, of observing one single article of it; and the whole fell so much into neglect and oblivion, that, in the following century, when the barons, who had heard an obscure tradition of it, desired to make it the model of the great charter, which they exacted from king John, they could with difficulty find a copy of it in the kingdom.[18] All of the promises of the charter would be broken soon afterward. The charter of Henry I was used by the bishops and nobles during the reign of king John for drafting the Magna Carta.

Henry's marriage, recall of Anselm, conflict with Robert

Henry married Matilda[19], the daughter of Malcom III, king of

---

[18] Ibid, pp 252-253.

[19] There were three consecutive queens with the name Matilda. William I married Mathilda, their son Henry I married Matilida, daughter of Malcom III and their daughter Matilda was the mother of Henry II, who followed Stephen.

Scotland, and niece to Edgar Atheling, which gave him popularity among his English subjects. Henry also recalled Anselm as archbishop of Canterbury, who had been banished by William II. About one month after the death of William II, and during the time Henry I had established himself in England, Robert returned to Normandy from the Crusade and his stay in Italy. He obtained support from a number of important nobles and their forces landed at Portsmouth. They were opposed by Henry's army. *The two armies lay in sight of each other for some days without coming to action; and both princes, being apprehensive of the event, which would probably be decisive, hearkened the more willingly to the counsels of Anselm and the other great men, who mediated an accommodation between them. After employing some negotiation, it was agreed, that Robert should resign his pretensions to England, and receive in lieu of them an annual pension of 300 marks; that, if either of the princes died without issue, the other should succeed to his dominions; that the adherents of each should be pardoned, and restored to all their possessions either in Normandy or England; and that neither Robert nor Henry should thenceforth encourage, receive, or protect the enemies of the other.*

Henry was the first to violate the agreement, as he had reneged on the charter. *He confiscated the estates of Robert's supporters. Robert had allowed his province to become a scene of violence and depredation to the extent that Henry was summoned to restore order. Henry returned the following year, 1105, and was successful in conquering Normandy in 1106. Henry, besides doing great execution on the enemy, made near ten thousand prisoners; among whom was duke Robert himself, and all the most considerable barons, who adhered to his interest. This victory was followed by the final reduction of Normandy. --- He returned to England, and carried along with him the duke as prisoner. That unfortunate prince was detained in custody during the remainder of his life, which was no less than twenty-eight years. His only son, prince William was committed to the care of Helie de St. Saen, who had married Robert's natural daughter. Edgar Atheling, who had followed Robert in the expedition to Jerusalem, and who had lived with him ever since in Normandy, was another illustrious prisoner. Henry gave him his liberty, and settled a small pension on him, with which he retired; and he lived to a good old age in England, totally neglected and forgotten.*[20]

Church Controversy

Henry was involved in a great controversy with Anselm and the church over the selection of prelates by the king and homage paid to the king by the prelates. *The rite of homage, by the feudal customs, was, that*

---

[20] Ibid, pp 257-260.

the vassal should throw himself on his knees, should put his joined hands between those of his superior, and should in that posture swear fealty to him. --- Anselm had no sooner returned from banishment, than his refusal to do homage to the king raised a dispute, which Henry evaded at that critical juncture, by promising to send a messenger in order to compound the matter with Pascal II, who then filled the papal throne.[21] Henry banished Anselm for the second time, but eventually a compromise was reached. Henry would no longer select the prefects while Anselm would do homage to the king.

Death of Henry's son William

Henry, in his long reign, remained in control of England as well as Normandy, suppressing by 1120, the remaining barons who contended his rule. A disaster had occurred on Henry's return to England, followed by a vessel on which his only son William was a passenger. *William was put in a long boat, and had got clear of the ship; when hearing the cries of his natural sister, the countess of Perche, he ordered the seamen to row back in hopes of saving her: but the numbers, who then crowded in, soon sunk the boat; and the prince with all his retinue perished. Above a hundred and forty young noblemen, of the principal families of England and Normandy, were lost on this occasion. --- Henry entertained hopes, for three days, that his son had put into some distant port of England: But when certain intelligence of the calamity was brought him, he fainted away; and it was remarked, that he never after was seen to smile, nor ever recovered his wonted cheerfulness.* The marriage of Henry to his second wife failed to produce an heir. Another heir, William, son of Robert was killed in a skirmish, in 1128. Henry's daughter Matilda was the only surviving heir. Mathilda had married Henry V, who had died in 1125. Mathilda later married Geoffrey Plantagenet Count of Anjou and Maine.

Illness and death

Henry took the opportunity of paying a visit to Normandy to visit his daughter Mathilda who was always his favorite. --- An incursion of the Welsh obliged him to think of returning into England. He was preparing for the journey, but was seized with a sudden illness at St. Dennis le Forment, from eating too plentifully of lampreys. He died, in 1135, in the sixty-seventh year of his age, and the thirty-fifth year of his reign; leaving by will his daughter Matilda, heir of all his dominions, without making any mention of her husband Geoffrey Plantagenet.[22]

---

[21] Ibid, 262-263.

[22] Ibid, pp 271-276.

Chapter 14

Stephen and Henry II

Stephen

Stephen (b. 1097, d. 1154) and who ruled from 1135 to 1154 was not a direct descendant of Henry I, or of William I or William II. Stephen was count of Blois, a Frenchman. Stephen had married William I's youngest daughter Adela. Henry I's daughter Mathilda would have followed Henry were it not for Stephen's aggressive manipulation of the clergy and his military forces, which gained him the crown. Nonetheless, Stephen's reign would be characterized by contention between the forces supporting Matilda's accession as queen vs. Stephen's acquisition of the crown. As explained by Hume: *The failure, therefore, of male-heirs to the kingdom of England and duchy of Normandy, seemed to leave the succession open, without a rival, to the empress Matilda; and as Henry had made all his vassals in both states swear fealty to her he presumed, that they would not easily be induced to depart at once from her hereditary right, and from their own reiterated oaths and engagements.*

Stephen gained the crown by his rapid and forceful maneuvers. *No sooner had Henry breathed his last, than Stephen, insensible to all the ties of gratitude and fidelity, and blind to danger, gave full reins to his criminal ambition, and trust, that, even without any previous intrigue, the celerity of his enterprise and the boldness of his attempt might overcome the weak attachment, which the English and Normans in that age bore to the laws, and to the rights of their sovereign. He hastened over to England; and though the citizens of Dover, and those of Canterbury, apprized of this purpose, shut their gates against him, he stopped not till he arrived at London, where some of the lower rank, instigated by his emissaries, as well as more by his general popularity, immediately saluted him king. His next point was to acquire the good will of the clergy; and by performing the ceremony of his coronation, to put himself in possession of the throne, from which he was confident it would not be easy afterwards to expel him.[1]* Stephen had the support of the archbishop of Canterbury and was crowned on December 22, 1135.

Stephen's rule

Stephen passed a charter, like his predecessor, in which he made promises to the clergy and nobility, seized the treasury of Henry, and obtained the compliance of the nobility and clergy. He also hired, or *invited over from Brittany and Flanders, great numbers of those bravoes or disorderly soldiers, with whom every country in Europe, by reason of police and turbulent government, extremely abounded. These mercenary troops guarded the throne, by the terrors of the sword; and Stephen, that he might also overawe all malcontents by new and additional terrors of religion, procured a bull from Rome, which ratified his title, and which the pope, seeing this prince in possession of the throne, and pleased with an appeal to his authority in secular controversies, very readily granted him.*

Conditions were imposed on Stephen, by the clergy and nobles, despite the homage offered to Stephen in the manner of the feudal rights. The king was bound to defend the ecclesiastical liberties and the barons began to fortify their castles. All England was immediately filled with those fortresses, which the noblemen garrisoned either with their vassals, or with licentious soldiers, who flocked to them from all quarters. Unbounded rapine was exercised upon the people for the maintenance of these troops; and private animosities, which had with difficulty been restrained by law, now breaking out without control, rendered England a scene of uninterrupted violence and devastation. Wars between the nobles were carried on with the utmost fury in every quarter; and barons even assumed the right of coining money, and of exercising, without appeal, every act of jurisdiction; and the inferior gentry, as well as the people, finding no defense from the laws, during this total dissolution of sovereign authority, were obliged, for their immediate safety, to pay court to some neighboring chieftain, and to purchase his protection both by submitting to his exaction, and by assisting him in his rapine upon others. --- The aristocratical power, which is usually so oppressive in the feudal governments, had now risen to its utmost height, during the reign of a prince, who, though endowed with vigor and abilities, had usurped the throne, without the pretense of a title, and who was necessitated to tolerate in others the same violence, to which he himself had been beholden for his sovereignty.[2]

---

[1] Hume, vol 1, pp 280-281.

[2] Ibid, pp 282-285.

Stephen retaliated *with his mercenary soldiers, who chiefly supported his authority, having exhausted the royal treasure, subsisted by depredations; and every place was filled with the best grounded complaints against the government.* The earls and many of the barons as well as the king of Scotland challenged Stephen, but Stephen was victorious in battle. Stephen next confronted the clergy over his insistence that they provide him with soldiers and resources for his wars against the nobles. His brother Henry, bishop of Winchester, assembled a synod at Westminster, and there demanded that the king appear to defend himself. Stephen, instead of resenting this indignity, sent Aubrey de Vere to plead his cause before that assembly.

Support for Mathilda

Meanwhile in September 1139, the Empress Matilda landed in England and resided at Arundel castle, and gathered growing support by the barons who declared for her. Civil wars broke out between the supporters of Matilda versus Stephen. *It suffices to say, that the war was spread into every quarter. --- The castles of the nobility were become receptacles of licensed robbers, who sallying forth day and night, committed spoil on the open country, on the villages, and even on the cities; put the captives to torture, in order to make them reveal their treasures; sold their persons to slavery; and set fire to their houses, after they had pillaged them of everything valuable. --- The land was left untilled; the instruments of husbandry were destroyed or abandoned; and a grievous famine, the natural result of those disorders, affected equally both parties, and reduced the spoilers, as well as the defenseless people, to the most extreme want and indigence.*

Stephen taken prisoner

In a battle at Lincoln castle Stephen was taken prisoner. *Stephen's party was entirely broken by the captivity of their leader, and the barons came in daily from all quarters, and did homage to Matilda.* Matilda also gained the support of the clergy. The legate, who later instigated the Londoners to revolt, crowned her. Matilda fled to Oxford and then to Winchester. The civil wars continued in Normandy in 1146, now involving Geoffrey and the count of Anjou and Maine, who had married Matilda. Their son Henry would become the next king of England.

Death of Stephen

The story focusing on the remaining years of Stephen's reign and the ascendancy of Henry II will follow. Stephen died October 25, 1154, after a short illness. England suffered great miseries during the reign of this prince. *His advancement to the throne procured him neither tranquility nor happiness; and though the situation of England prevented the neighboring states from taking any durable advantage of her confusions, her intestine disorders were to the last degree ruinous and destructive.*[3]

Henry II

Henry II (b. 1133, d. 1189) and who ruled from 1154 to 1189 is one of the men who made the law, and his reign is important for a number of reasons. His great-grandfather, William the conqueror, could be called the first imperialist to rule England. He was of course a Norman, and by conquering England, William and the Normans extended their territory across the English Channel to occupy and control another nation. Henry II continued warfare with neighboring Wales and Scotland. He invaded and claimed Ireland to the growing empire of England and Normandy. Some modern historians credit Henry II as 'the father of common law.' His chief justice, Glanville, is thought to be the first to develop English common law. Hume scarcely mentions Glanville, except as a military commander, and attributes to Henry skills as a lawmaker, judge and administrator. Henry had attributes of a tyrant. He suppressed civil disorders with severe laws and enlarged the empire of England, the hallmarks of a great English king. His reign however was characterized by monumental conflicts between the king and the growing powers of the church. His main adversary in this conflict was Thomas Becket, having himself an astute legal mind and political acumen, and the powerful pope Alexander III. Henry had conflicts and wars involving the barons and finally civil wars against his sons, which contributed to his sad end.

Family history and early life

He was born, in 1133, in Tours in the province of Anjou, in west central France. His mother Matilda was the daughter of Henry I and the only surviving child of that king. His mother had been symbolically crowned Queen, but had been replaced by her cousin Stephen who preceded Henry II. Henry II's father was Geoffrey Plantagenet, count of Anjou and Maine, and who won the duchy from Stephen. Historians refer to the Angevins, descendants of Plantagenet, who were based in Anjou, hence the term Angevin. Little is apparently known about Henry's childhood. *At a time when Stephen was forced to submit to Rome and his nobles, --- Prince Henry, who had reached his sixteenth year, was desirous of receiving the honor of knighthood; a ceremony every gentleman in that age passed through before he was admitted to the use of arms, and which was even deemed requisite for the greatest princes. He intended to receive his admission from his great-uncle, David, king of Scotland; and for that purpose he passed through England with a great retinue, and was attended by the most considerable of his partisans. He*

---

[3] Ibid, pp 294-295.

remained some time with the king of Scotland; made incursions into England; and by his dexterity and vigor in all manly exercises, by his valor in war, and his prudent conduct in every occurrence, he roused the hopes of his party, and gave symptoms of those great qualities, which he afterwards displayed when he mounted the throne of England.

Marriage to Eleanor

Soon after his return to Normandy, he was, by Matilda's consent invested in that duchy; and upon the death of his father, Geoffrey, which happened in the subsequent year, he took possession both of Anjou and Maine, and concluded a marriage, which brought him a great accession of power, and rendered him extremely formidable to his rival. Eleanor, the daughter and heir of William, duke of Guienne, and earl of Poictou, had been married sixteen years to Lewis VII, king of France, and had attended him in a crusade, which that monarch conducted against the infidels: But having there lost the affections of her husband, and even fallen under some suspicion of gallantry with a handsome Saracen, Lewis, more delicate than politic, procured a divorce from her, and restored her those rich provinces, which by her marriage she had annexed to the crown of France. Young Henry, neither discouraged by the inequality of years, nor by the reports of Eleanor's *gallantries, made successful courtship to that princess, and espousing her six weeks after her divorce, got possession of all her dominions as her dowry.*[4]

Mathilda's Invasion of England, Stephen's demise and accession of Henry

Mathilda invaded England and faced the army of king Stephen. *A decisive action was every day expected; when the great men of both sides, terrified at the prospect of further bloodshed and confusion, interposed with their good offices, and set on foot a negotiation between rival princes. --- An accommodation was settled by which it was agreed, that Stephen should possess the crown during his lifetime, ---* and that Henry would succeed to the kingdom. Stephen died the following year, October 25, 1154

Henry was in Normandy when he received report of the death of Stephen. *He then set out on his journey, and was received in England with the acclamations of all orders of men, who swore with pleasure the oath of fealty and allegiance to him.*

Henry's rule

The first act of Henry's government corresponded to the high idea entertained of his abilities, and prognosticated the re-establishment

---

[4] Hume, vol 1, pp 293-294.

of justice and tranquility, of which the kingdom had so long been bereaved. He immediately dismissed all those mercenary soldiers, who had committed great disorders in the nation; and he sent them abroad. --- He revoked all grants made by his predecessor. He repaired the coin, which had been extremely debased during the reign of his predecessor. He was rigorous in the execution of justice, and in the suppression of robbery and violence; and that he might restore authority to the laws, he caused all the new erected castles to be demolished, which had proved so many sanctuaries to freebooters and rebels.[5]

Expansion in France

Henry returned in 1157 to Normandy and prevented his brother Geoffrey from taking possession of Anjou and Maine. Geoffrey took possession of Nantz. *Geoffrey, the king's brother, died soon after he had acquired possession of Nantz: Though he had no other title to that county, than the voluntary submission or election of the inhabitants two years before, Henry laid claim to the territory as devolved to him by hereditary right, and he went over to support his pretensions by force of arms.*

Henry's next dispute was over an attempt to acquire more territory in France, which he argued properly belonged to his wife Eleanor, who was the only child of William IV, count of Toulouse. The count, however, wished to preserve the male line and provided a disputed title to his brother, Raymond St. Giles, who obtain the support of the French king Lewis, who had been married to Eleanor. Henry had to raise a large army if he were to be successful against the French king's forces. He did not believe the feudal arrangement of raising troops would be sufficient, relying on feudal lords in his dominions to select troops, *often intractable and undisciplined.* Henry devised a new method of conscription. *He imposed, therefore, a scutage of 180,000 pounds on the knight's fees, a commutation, to which, though it was unusual, and the first perhaps to be met with in history. The military tenants willingly submitted; and with this money, he levied an army which was more under his command, and whose service was more durable and constant. --- War was now openly carried on between the two monarchs, but produced no memorable event: It soon ended in a cessation of arms, and that followed by a peace, which was not, however, attended with any confidence or good correspondence between those rival princes.* Both kings had met pope Alexander III the year before and had given him sufficient respect. The pope negotiated a truce between Henry and Lewis. *Henry, soon after he had accommodated his differences with Lewis by the pope's mediation, returned to England; where he commenced an enterprise, which, though required by sound policy, and even conducted in the main*

---

[5] Ibid, pp 300-301.

with prudence, bred him great disquietude, involved him in danger, and was not concluded without some loss and dishonor.[6]

Thomas a Becket

It may seem strange to us that the greatest threat to Henry II's control of England was the church, represented by pope Alexander III, and Thomas a Becket, whom Henry appointed as archbishop of Canterbury, and who later was accused by some of his murder.

Thomas a Becket, (b 1118, d 1170), the first man of English descent, who, since the Norman conquest, had, during the course of a whole century, risen to any considerable station, was born of reputable parents in the city of London; and being endowed both with industry and capacity, he early insinuated himself into the favor of archbishop Theobald, and obtained for that prelate some preferments and offices. By these means, he was enabled to travel for improvement to Italy, where he studied the civil and canon law at Bologna; and on his return, he appeared to have made such proficiency in knowledge, that he was promoted by his patron to the arch-deaconry of Canterbury, an office of considerable trust and profit.[7]

Henry *appointed Becket as chancellor, one of the first civil offices in the kingdom. The chancellor, in that age, besides the custody of the great seal, had possession of all vacant prelacies and abbies; he was the guardian of all such minors and pupils as were the king's tenants; all baronies which escheated to the crown were under his administration; he was entitled to a place in council, even though he were not particularly summoned; and as he exercised also the office of secretary of state, and it belonged to him to countersign all commissions, writs, and letters-patent. He was a kind of prime minister, and was concerned in the dispatch of every business of importance. Besides exercising this high office, Becket, by the favor of the king or archbishop, was made provost of Beverley, dean of Hastings, and constable of the Tower: He was put in possession of the honors of Eye and Berkham, large baronies that had escheated to the crown: and to complete his grandeur, he was entrusted with the education of Prince Henry, the king's eldest son, and heir of the monarchy. The pomp of his retinue, the sumptuousness of his furniture, the luxury of his table, the munificence of his presents, corresponded to these greater preferments; or rather exceeded any thing that England had ever before seen in any subject.*

A great number of knights were retained in his service; the greatest barons were proud of being received at his table; his house was a place of education for the sons of the chief nobility; and the king

---

[6] Ibid, pp 302-305.

[7] Ibid, pp 305-306.

himself frequently vouchsafed to partake of his entertainments. As his way of life was splendid and opulent, his amusements and occupations were gay, and partook of the cavalier spirit, which, as he had only taken deacons's orders, he did nothing unbefitting his character. He employed himself at leisure hours in hunting, hawking, gaming and horsemanship; he exposed his person in several military actions; he carried over, at his own charge, seven hundred knights to attend the king in his wars at Toulouse; in the subsequent wars on the frontiers of Normandy, he maintained, during forty days, twelve hundred knights, and four thousand of their train; and in an embassy to France, with which he was entrusted, he astonished that court by the number and magnificence of his retinue.[8]

Becket was given and assumed all the trappings of royalty. Becket, in his role in civil government, may never have given Henry any problems, but upon the death of Theobald, archbishop of Canterbury, Henry made the dreadful mistake of electing Becket archbishop of Canterbury.

Becket as Archbishop of Canterbury

No sooner was Becket installed in this high dignity, which rendered him for life the second person in the kingdom, with some pretensions of aspiring to be the first, that he totally altered his demeanor and conduct, and endeavored to acquire the character of sanctity, of which his former busy and ostentatious course of life might, in the eyes of the people, have naturally bereaved him; Without consulting the king, he immediately returned into the hands the commission of chancellor; pretending, that he must thenceforth detach himself from secular affairs, and be solely employed in the exercise of his spiritual function, but in reality, that he might break all connections with Henry, and appraise him that Becket, as primate of England, was now become entirely a new personage.

He wore sackcloth next his skin, which by his affected care to conceal it, was necessarily the more remarked by all the world. He changed it so seldom, that it was filled with dirt and vermin. His usual diet was bread. His drinking water he even rendered farther unpalatable by the mixture of unsavory herbs. He tore his back with the frequent discipline which he inflicted on it. He daily on his knees washed, in imitation of Christ, the feet of thirteen beggars, whom he afterwards dismissed with presents. He gained the affections of the monks by his frequent charities to the convents and hospitals. Every one, who made profession of sanctity, was admitted to his conversation, and returned full of panegyrics of the humility, as well as on the piety and mortification, of the holy primate. He seemed to be perpetually employed in reciting prayers and pious lectures, or in perusing religious discourses. His

---

[8] Ibid, pp 307-309.

aspect wore the appearance of seriousness, and mental recollection, and secret devotion. And all men of penetration plainly saw, that he was meditating some great design, and that the ambition and ostentation of his character had turned itself towards a new and more dangerous object.[9]

Becket soon exerted his power. He expropriated property included in the barony of the earl of Clare. *Making himself both judge and party he issued in a summary manner the sentence of excommunication against Eynsford, a military tenant of the crown, contrary to the practice established by the Conqueror, and maintained ever since by his successors, be subjected to that terrible sentence, without the previous consent of the sovereign. --- A sovereign of the greatest abilities was now on the throne. A prelate of the most inflexible and intrepid character was possessed of the primacy. The contending powers appeared to be armed with their full force, and it was natural to expect some extraordinary event to result from their conflict.*

Among their other inventions to obtain money, the clergy had inculcated the necessity of penance as an atonement for sin; and having again introduced the practice of paying them large sums as a commutation, or species of atonement, for the remission of those penances, the sins of the people, by these means, had become a revenue to the priests; and the king computed, that, by this invention alone, they levied more money upon his subjects, than flowed by all the funds and taxes, into the royal exchequer.

The ecclesiastics, in that age, had renounced all immediate subordination to the magistrate: They openly pretended to an exemption, in criminal accusations, from a trial before the courts of justice; and were gradually introducing a like exemption in civil causes: Spiritual penalties alone could be inflicted on their offences, --- and when the king demanded, that, immediately after he was degraded, he should be tried by the civil power, the primate asserted, that it was iniquitous to try a man twice upon the same accusation, and for the same offence.[10]

Henry summoned an assembly of all the prelates of England; and he put to them this concise and decisive question. Whether or not they were willing to submit to the ancient laws and customs of the kingdom? --- He required the primate instantly to surrender the honors and castles of Eye and Berkham. The bishops were terrified, and expected still farther effects of his resentment. Becket alone was inflexible, and nothing but the interposition of the pope's legate and almoner, Philip, who dreaded a breach with so powerful a prince at so unseasonable a junction, could have prevailed on him to retract the

---

[9] Ibid, pp 309-310.

[10] Ibid, pp 311-313.

saving clause, and give a general and absolute promise of observing the ancient customs.

The Constitutions of Clarendon

Henry therefore, in 1164, *deemed it necessary to define with the same precision the limits of the civil power; to oppose his legal customs to their divine ordinances; to determine the exact boundaries of the rival jurisdictions; and for this purpose, he summoned a general council of the nobility and prelates at Clarendon, to whom he submitted this great and important question. ---*

The barons were all gained to the king's party, either by the reasons which he urged, or by his superior authority: The bishops were overawed by the general combination against them: And the following laws, commonly called the Constitutions of Clarendon, were voted without opposition by this assembly.[11] The sixteen items are listed in brief as follows:

1. Suits concerning the advowson[12] and presentation of churches should be determined in the civil courts.
2. The churches, belonging to the king's fee, should not be granted in perpetuity without his consent.
3. Clerks accused of any crime, should be tried in the civil courts.
4. No person, particularly no clergyman of any rank, should depart the kingdom without the king's license.
5. Excommunicated persons should not be bound to give security for continuing in their present place of abode.
6. Laymen should not be accused in spiritual courts, except by legal and reputable promoters and witnesses.
7. No chief tenant of the crown should be excommunicated, nor his lands be put under an interdict, except with the king's consent.
8. All appeals in spiritual causes should be carried from the archdeacon to the bishop, from the bishop to the primate, from him to the king.
9. If any law-suit arose between a layman and a clergyman concerning a tenant, and it be disputed whether the land be a lay or an ecclesiastical fee, it should first be determined by the verdict of twelve lawful men to what class it belonged, and if it be found to be a lay-fee, the cause should finally be determined in the civil courts.
10. That no inhabitant in demesne[13] should be excommunicated for non-appearance in a spiritual court, till the chief officer of the place, where

---

[11] Ibid, 314-315.

[12] The right to name the holder of a church benefice.

[13] Demesne- held in one's right, not of a superior.

he resides, be consulted, that he may compel him by the civil authority to give satisfaction to the church.

11. That the archbishops, bishops, and other spiritual dignitaries should be regarded as barons of the realm; should possess the privileges and be subjected to the burthens belonging to that rank should be bound to attend the king in his great councils, and assist at all trials, till the sentence either of death or loss of members, be given against the criminal.

12. The revenue of vacant sees should belong to the king; the chapter, or such of them as he pleases to summon, should sit in the king' chapter, or such of them as he pleases to summon, should sit in the king' chapel till they made the new election with his consent, and that the bishop-elect should do homage to the crown.

13. If any baron or tenant should refuse to submit to the spiritual courts, the king should employ his authority in obliging him to make such submissions; if any of them throw off his allegiance to the king, the prelates should assist the king with their censures in reducing him.

14. Goods forfeited to the king should not be protected in churches or churchyards.

15. The clergy should no longer pretend to the right of enforcing payment of debts contracted by oath or promise; but should leave these law-suits equally with others, to the determination of the civil courts.

16. The sons of villains should not be ordained clerks, without the consent of their lord.

Henry, therefore, by reducing those ancient customs of the realm to writing, and by collecting them in a body, endeavored to prevent all future dispute with regard to them; and by passing so many ecclesiastical ordinances in a national and civil assembly, he fully established the superiority of the legislature above all papal decrees or spiritual canons, and gained a signal victory over the ecclesiastics. But as he knew, that the bishops, though overawed by the present combination of the crown and the barons, would take the first favorable opportunity of denying the authority, which had enacted these constitutions; he resolved, that they should all set their seal to them, and give a promise to observe them. Becket, finding himself deserted by all the world, even by his own brethren, was at last obliged to comply; and he promised, legally, with good faith, and without fraud or reserve, to observe the constitutions; and he took an oath to that purpose.

The church vs. the king

The king, thinking that he had now finally prevailed in this great enterprise, sent the constitutions to pope Alexander, who then resided in France; and he required that pontiff's ratification of them: But Alexander, who, though he had owed the most important obligations to the king, plainly saw, that these laws were calculated to establish the independency of England on the papacy, and of the royal power on the clergy, condemned them in the strongest terms; abrogated, annulled, and rejected them. There were only six articles, the least important, which, for the sake of peace, he was willing to ratify.

Becket renounced his oath to support Henry's laws at Clarendon. The king retaliated by calling a council to prosecute Becket. Becket refused to respond to the king's summons to appear at the king's court and was condemned as guilty of contempt of court. The king was not content with this sentence and demanded payment of three hundred pounds, and Becket after an initial protest, agreed to pay the fine. Henry demanded more payment from Becket and *required him to give in the accounts of his administration while chancellor, and to pay the balance due from the revenues of all the prelacies, abbies, and baronies, which had, during that time, been subjected to his management.* Two years passed and Becket faced a tribunal to produce the accounts which the king demanded.

After a few days spent in deliberation, Becket went to church, and said mass, where he had previously ordered the introit to the communion service should begin with these words, 'Princes sat and spake against me'; the passage appointed of the martyrdom of St. Stephen whom the primate thereby tacitly pretended to resemble in his sufferings for the sake of righteousness. He went thence to court arrayed in his sacred vestments: As soon as he arrived within the palace-gate he took the cross into his own hands, bore it aloft as his protection, and marched in that posture into the royal apartments.

Becket refused to so much as to hear the sentence against him, which the barons, sitting apart from the bishops, and joined to some sheriffs and barons of the second rank, had given upon the king's claim: He departed from the palace; asked Henry's immediate permission to leave Northampton; and upon meeting with a refusal, he withdrew secretly; wandered about in disguise for some time; and at last took shipping and arrived safely at Gravelines. Henry banished all the prelates' relations and domestics, to the number of four hundred, but the pope, when they arrived beyond sea, absolved them from their oath, and distributed them among the convents, in France and Flanders: A residence was assigned to Becket himself in the convent of Pontigny; were he lived for some years in great magnificence, partly from a pension granted him on the revenues of that abbey, partly from remittances made him by the French monarch.[14] Henry issued orders, in 1165, to his justiciaries, inhibiting, under severe penalties, all appeals to the pope or archbishop; forbidding any one to receive any mandates from them, or apply in any case to their authority; declaring it treasonable to bring from either of them an interdict upon the kingdom, and punishable in secular clergymen, by the loss of their eyes and by

---

[14] Ibid, pp320-323.

castration, in regulars by amputation of their feet, and in laymen with death; and menacing with sequestration and banishment the persons themselves, as well as their kindred, who should pay obedience to any such interdict: And he farther obliged all his subjects to swear to the observance of those orders. These were edicts of the utmost importance, affected the lives and properties of all the subjects, and even changed, for the time, the national religion, by breaking off all communication with Rome: Yet were they enacted by the sole authority of the king, and were derived entirely from his will and pleasure.[15]

Becket responded by *issuing a censure, excommunicating the king's chief ministers by name, and comprehending in general all those who favored or obeyed the constitutions of Clarendon: These constitutions he abrogated and annulled; he absolved all men from their oaths which they had taken to observe them; and he suspended the spiritual thunder over Henry himself, only that the prince might avoid the blow by a timely repentance.*

Several attempts at a reconciliation finally led in 1170 to the following compromise with Becket. *All difficulties were at last adjusted between the parties; and the king allowed Becket to return, on conditions, which may be esteemed both honorable and advantageous to that prelate. He was not required to give up any rights of the church, or resign any of those pretensions, which had been the original ground of the controversy. It was agreed, that all these questions should be buried in oblivion; but that Becket and his adherents should, without making farther submission, be restored to all their livings, and that even the possessors of such benefices as depended on the see of Canterbury, and had been filled during the primate's absence should be expelled, and Becket have liberty to supply the vacancies. In return for concessions, which entrenched so deeply on the honor and dignity of the crown, Henry reaped only the advantage of seeing his ministers absolved from the sentence of excommunication pronounced against them, and of preventing the interdict, which, if these hard conditions had not been complied with, was ready to be laid on all his dominions.[16]*

Becket returned to England, but persisted in his course of actions against the king, and *excommunicated those who assisted in the king's coronation and those who had been active in the late persecution of the exiled clergy. --- The king, though he dropped for the present, the prosecution of Becket, he still reserved to himself the right of maintaining, that the constitutions of Clarendon, the original ground of the quarrel, were both the ancient customs and the present law of the*

---

[15] Ibid, pp 323-324.

[16] Ibid, pp 328-329. An interdict for the kingdom would exclude all sacraments and privileges of the church.

realm: And though he knew, that the papal clergy asserted them to be impious in themselves, as well as abrogated by the sentence of the sovereign pontiff, he intended, in spite of their clamors, steadily to put those laws in execution.

The murder of Becket

This seeming unending conflict between Henry and Becket, despite a supposed compromise, would lead to the murder of Becket, December 29, 1170 at the hands of four knights who were members of the king's household. The king would never be the same afterward. Hume, citing a number of sources, gave the following account: *When the suspended and excommunicated prelates arrived at Baieux, where the king then resided, and complained to him of the violent proceedings of Becket, he instantly perceived the consequences; was sensible, that his whole plan of operations was overthrown; foresaw, that the dangerous contest between the civil and spiritual powers, a contest which he himself had first roused, but which he had endeavored, by all this late negotiations and concessions, to appease, must come to an immediate and decisive issue; and he was thence thrown into the most violent commotion. The archbishop of York remarked to him, that, so long as Becket lived, he could never expect to enjoy peace or tranquility: The king himself, being vehemently agitated, burst forth into an exclamation against his servants, whose want of zeal, he said, had so long left him exposed to the enterprises of the ungrateful and imperious prelate. Four gentlemen of his household, Reginald Fitz-Urse, William de Traci, Hugh de Moreville, and Richard Brito, taking these passionate expressions to be a hint of Becket's death, immediately communicated their thoughts to each other, and swearing to avenge their prince's quarrel, secretly withdrew from court. Some menacing expressions, which they had dropped, gave a suspicion of their design; and the king dispatched a messenger after them, charging them to attempt nothing against the person of the primate. But these orders arrived too late to prevent their fatal purpose. The four assassins, though they took different roads to England arrived nearly about the same time at Saltwood near Canterbury; and being there joined by some assistants, they proceeded in great haste to the archiepiscopal palace; They found the primate, who trusted entirely to the sacredness of his character, very slenderly attended; and though they threw out many menaces and reproaches against him, he was so incapable of fear, that, without using any precautions against their violence, he immediately went to St. Benedict's church, to hear vespers. They followed him thither, attacked him before the altar, and having cloven his head with many blows, retired without meeting any opposition.[17]*

---

[17] Ibid, pp 330-333.

Henry realized the dangerous consequences of Becket's murder and dispatched three bishops and five other persons to Rome to plead his innocence and total ignorance of the fact. The pope issued anathemas only against all the actors, accomplices, and abettors of Becket's murder. Two years after his death Becket was canonized by pope Alexander. *As soon as Henry found, that he was in no immediate dangers from the thunders of the Vatican, he undertook an expedition against Ireland; a design, which he had long projected, and by which he hoped to recover his credit, somewhat impaired by his late transactions with the hierarchy.*[18]

Invasion of Ireland

It is ironic that eight centuries of English domination of Ireland would have been started by a Roman pontiff, Adrian IV, who before the English invaded Ireland, in 1156, issued a bull giving Henry II the go ahead to invade and conquer Ireland. There had previously been nothing in the history of Ireland or England to support an English claim over Ireland. *Adrian IV, who then filled the papal chair, was by birth an Englishman; and being, on that account, the more disposed to oblige Henry, he was easily persuaded to act as master of the world, and to make, without any hazard or expense, the acquisition of a great island to his spiritual jurisdiction. The Irish had, by precedent from missions to the Britons, been imperfectly converted to Christianity; and, what the pope regarded as the surest mark of their imperfect conversion, they followed the doctrines of their first teachers, and had never acknowledged any subjection to the see of Rome. Adrian, therefore, in the year 1156, issued a bull in favor of Henry. --- He gave him entire right to obey him as their sovereign, and invested with full power all such godly instruments as he should think proper to employ in an enterprise, thus calculated for the glory of God and the salvation of the souls of men. Henry, though armed with this authority, did not immediately put his design in execution; but being detained by more interesting business on the continent, waited for a favorable opportunity of invading Ireland.*[19]

It was an Irishman, Dermod Mc Murrough, who invited king Henry to invade Ireland in order that he might reclaim his property and power. From Hume: *Dermot Macmorrogh, king of Leinster, had, by his licentious tyranny, rendered himself odious to his subjects, who seized with alacrity the first occasion that offered, of throwing off the yoke, which was become grievous and oppressive to them. This prince had formed a design on Dovergilda, wife of Ororic, prince of Breffny; and taking advantage of her husband's absence, who, being obliged to visit a*

---

[18] Ibid, pp337-338.

[19] Ibid, pp 340-341.

distant part of his territory, had left his wife secure, as he thought, in an island, surrounded by a bog, he suddenly invaded the place, and carried off the princess. Roderic, king of Connaught, invaded the dominions of Dermot, and expelled him his kingdom. The exiled prince had recourse to Henry, who was at this time in Guienne, craved his assistance in restoring him to his sovereignty, and offered, on that event, to hold his kingdom in vassalage under the crown of England.

Dermot supported by this authority, came to Bristol; and after endeavoring, though for some time in vain, to engage adventurers in the enterprise, he at last formed a treaty with Richard named Strongbow, earl of Strigul. This nobleman, who was of the illustrious house of Clare, had impaired his fortune by expensive pleasures; and being ready for any desperate undertaking, he promised assistance to Dermot, on condition that he should espouse Eva, daughter of that prince, and be declared heir to all his dominions. While Richard Strongbow was assembling his succors, Dermot went into Wales; and meeting with Robert Fitz-Stephens, constable of Abertivi, and Maurice Fitz-Gerald, he also engaged them in his service, and obtained their promise of invading Ireland.[20]

Fitz-Stephens first arrived in Ireland with thirty knights, sixty esquires, and three hundred archers and was joined by Maurice de Pendergail, who brought over ten knights and sixty archers to enable the siege of Wexford.[21] *Soon after, Fitz-Gerald arrived with ten knights, thirty esquires, and a hundred archers, and being joined by the former adventurers, composed a force, which nothing in Ireland was able to withstand. Roderic, the chief monarch of the island, was foiled in different actions; the prince of Ossory was obliged to submit, and give hostages for his peaceable behavior; and Dermot, not content with being restored to this kingdom of Leinster, projected the dethroning of Roderic, and aspired to the sole dominion over the Irish.*

Another force landed at Waterford and was joined by Richard Strongbow. They took Waterford and marched to Dublin, *which was taken by assault. Roderic, in revenge, cut off the head of Dermot's natural son, who had been left as a hostage in his hands; and Richard, Strongbow, marrying Eva* (daughter of Dermot), *became soon after, by the death of Dermot, in 1171, master of the kingdom of Leinster, and prepared to extend his authority over all Ireland.*

---

[20] Ibid, pp 341-342.

[21] From Cusack, *History of Ireland*, p 258, from an account of Dermod Mac Murrough's secretary, the landing took place at Bannow, near Waterford, in May, 1169. After the conquest of Wexford Fitz-Stephen received two baronies of Forth and Bargy, the first English colonies established in Ireland.

Henry in Ireland

Henry, jealous of the progress made by his own subjects, sent orders to recall all the English, and he made preparations to attack Ireland in person: But Richard Strongbow, and the other adventurers, found means to appease him, by making him the most humble submissions, and offering to hold all their acquisitions in vassalage to his crown. That monarch landed in Ireland, October 18, 1171, at the head of five hundred knights, besides other soldiers: He found the Irish so dispirited by their late misfortunes, that, in a progress which he made through the Island, he had no other occupation than to receive the homages of his new subjects; He left most of the Irish chieftains or princes in possession of their ancient territories; bestowed some lands on the English adventurers; gave Richard Strongbow the commission of seneschal of Ireland; and after a stay of a few months, returned in triumph to England; By these trivial exploits, scarcely worth relating, except for the importance of the consequences, was Ireland subdued, and annexed to the English crown.[22]

The results of Henry's invasion and conquest are given a somewhat different account by sister Mary Cusack, in her well-documented History of Ireland, first published in 1868. After discussing Henry's failure at his Synod of Cashel convened to establish influence of the clergy, Cusack gave the following summary: *Henry did not succeed much better with his administration of secular affairs. In the Curia Regis, at Lismore, he modeled Irish administration on Norman precedents, apparently forgetting that a kingdom and a province should be differently governed. --- English laws and customs were also introduced for the benefit of English settlers; the native population still adhered to their own legal observances. Henry again forgot that laws must be suited to the nation for whom they are made, and that the Saxon rules were as little likely to be acceptable to the Celt, as his Norman tongue to an English-speaking people.*

He (Henry) *therefore sailed for England from Wexford harbor, on Easter Monday, the 17th of April, 1172, and arrived the same day at Port Finnen, in Wales. We give the testimony of Cambensis, no friend to Ireland, to prove that neither clergy nor laity benefited by the royal visit. He thus describes the inauguration of that selfish system of plunder and devastation, to which Ireland has been subjected for centuries— a system which prefers the interest of the few to the rights of the many, and then scoffs bitterly at the misery it has created.*[23]

---

[22] Hume, pp 343-344.

[23] Cusack, History of ireland, pp 276-277.

Normandy and France, Henry's wars with his sons

In 1170, before his invasion of Ireland, Henry *had appointed Henry, his eldest son* (who later died in 1183), *to be his successor in the kingdom of England, the duchy of Normandy, and the counties of Anjou, Maine, and Tourraine: Richard, his second son, was invested in the duchy of Guienne and county of Poictou: Geoffrey, his third son, inherited, in right of his wife, the duchy of Brittany; and the new conquest of Ireland was destined for the appanage of John, his fourth son.*

Henry had problems with his wife Eleanor, who enlarged the conflict in the family. *Queen Eleanor, who had disgusted her first husband by her gallantries* (an affair with a Saracen), *was no less offensive to her second, by her jealousy; --- She communicated her discontents against Henry to her two younger sons, Geoffrey and Richard, persuaded them that they were also entitled to present possession of the territories assigned to them; engaged them to fly secretly to the court of France; and was meditating, herself, an escape to the same court, and had even put on a man's apparel for that purpose; when she was seized by orders from her husband, and thrown into confinement.*[24] Henry enlisted troops. Many of the nobility supported Henry's sons as did Lewis, king of France. Hostilities were first commenced by the counts of Flanders and Boulogne on the frontiers of Normandy. Neither were successful. *In another quarter, the king of France, being strongly assisted by his vassals, assembled a great army of seven thousand knights, and their followers on horseback, and a proportionable number of infantry: Carrying young Henry along with him, he laid siege to Verneuil, which was vigorously defended by Hugh de Lacy and Hugh de Beauchanp, the governors. Henry appeared with his army upon the heights above Verneuil.* Lewis desired a conference, but Henry routed the French forces. Henry pursued his other enemies and defeated the rebels. *By these vigorous measures, the insurrections were entirely quelled in Britanny; and the king, thus fortunate in all quarters, willingly agreed to a conference with Lewis, in hopes, that his enemies, finding all their mighty efforts entirely frustrated, would terminate hostilities on some moderated and reasonable conditions.* Although Henry offered promises to his sons, the conference came to an end with abrupt threats of violence.[25]

---

[24] Hume, fol 1, pp 348-349. Note. The story of Henry and his dysfunctional family is portrayed in the film classic *The Lion In Winter*.

[25] Ibid, pp 351-353.

Scotland

The king of Scotland, William, (1165-1214), made an irruption, in 1173, into Northumberland, and committed great devastations; but being opposed by Richard de Lucy, whom Henry had left guardian of the realm, he retreated into his own county, and agreed to a cessation of arms. The king of Scotland broke the truce and joined with rebellious English barons as de Lucy had marched to the south. *The king of Scotland, on the expiration of the truce, broke into the northern provinces with a great army of 80,000 men; which, though undisciplined and disorderly, and better fitted for committing devastation, than for executing any military enterprise, was become dangerous to the present factious and turbulent spirit of the kingdom. Henry, who had baffled all his enemies in France, and had put his frontiers in a posture of defense, now found England the seat of danger; and he determined by his presence to overawe the malcontents, or by his conduct and courage to subdue them. He landed at Southampton; and knowing the influence of superstition over the minds of the people he hastened to Canterbury, in order to make atonement to the ashes of Thomas a Becket. --- Next day, he received absolution; and departing for London, got soon after the agreeable intelligence of a great victory, which his general had obtained over the Scots. ---*

William, king of Scots, though repulsed before the castle of Prudhow, and other fortified places, had committed the most horrible depredations upon the northern provinces: But on the approach of Ralph de Glanville, the famous justiciary, --- seconded by other northern barons, together with the gallant bishop of Lincoln he thought proper to retreat nearer his own country, and he fixed his camp at Alnwic. --- But Glanville, informed of his situation, made a hasty and fatiguing march to Newcastle; and allowing his soldiers only a small interval for refreshments, he immediately set out towards evening for Alnwic. He marched that night above thirty miles; arrived in the morning, under cover of a mist, near the Scottish camp; and regardless of the great numbers of the enemy, he began the attack with his small, but determined body of cavalry. Hume next described the victory of the English, led by Ralph de Glanville and other northern barons, against the Scots on July 13, 1174. *This great and important victory proved at last decisive in favor of Henry, and entirely broke the spirit of the English rebels, independency of his crown as the price of his liberty.*[26]

Henry's administration and laws

Henry continued the partition of England into four divisions, and the appointment of itinerant justices to go the circuit in each

---

[26] Ibid, pp 355-356 Note. Scotland would continue as an ally of France in wars against England for another four hundred years.

division. Another important ordinance of this prince was *to decide the causes in the counties, which had a direct tendency to curb the oppressive barons, and to protect the inferior gentry and common people in their property.* Those justices were either prelates or considerable noblemen. Besides carrying the authority of the king's commission, they were able to give weight and credit to the laws.

His control over the kingdom was maintained by military and police forces. The king fixed an assize of arms, by which all his subjects were obliged to put themselves in a situation for defending themselves and the realm. Every man, possessed of a knight's fee, was ordained to have for each fee, a coat of mail, a helmet, a shield, and a lance; every free layman, possessed of goods to the value of sixteen marks, was to be armed in like manner; every one that possessed ten marks was obliged to have an iron gorget, a cap of iron, and a lance.[27]

He enacted severe penalties against robbery, murder, false coining, and arson; and ordained that these crimes should be punished by the amputation of the right hand and right foot. The pecuniary commutation for crimes, which has a false appearance of lenity, had been gradually disused; and seems to have been entirely abolished by the rigor of these statutes. The superstitious trial by water ordeal, though condemned by the church, still subsisted; but Henry ordained, that any man, accused of murder or any heinous felony by the oath of the legal knights of the county, should, even though acquitted by the ordeal, be obliged to abjure the realm.

Henry, though sensible of the great absurdity attending the trial by duel or battle, did not venture to abolish it. He only admitted either of the parties to challenge a trial by an assize or jury of twelve freeholders.[28] This latter method of trial seems to have been very ancient in England, and was fixed by the laws of king Alfred: But the barbarous and violent genius of the age had of late given more credit to the trial by battle, which had become the general method of deciding all important controversies. It was never abolished by law in England; and there is an instance of it so late as the reign of Elizabeth.

The clergy and the laity were during that age in a strange situation with regard to each other, and such as might seem totally incompatible with a civilized, and indeed with any species of government. If a clergyman were guilty of murder, he could be punished by degradation only: If he were murdered, the murderer was exposed to nothing but excommunication and ecclesiastical censure; and the crime was atoned for by penances and submission; Hence the assassins of

---

[27] Note. Hume does not mention how many of the population were villeins or slaves and if they were used in combat.

[28] Note, Hume cites Glanville. Lib ii. Cap. 7 as a reference.

Thomas a Becket himself, though guilty of the most atrocious wickedness, and the most repugnant to the sentiments of that age, lived securely in their own houses, without being called to account by Henry himself, who was so much concerned, both in honor and interest, to punish that crime, and who professed or affected on all occasions the most extreme abhorrence of it. --- But as the king, by the constitutions of Clarendon, which he endeavored still to maintain, had subjected the clergy to a trial by the civil magistrate, it seemed but just to give them the protection of that power, to which they owed obedience. It was enacted that the murderers of clergymen should be tried before the justiciary in the presence of the bishop or his official; and besides the usual punishment for murder, should be subjected to a forfeiture of their estates, and a confiscation of their goods and chattels.[29]

Hume concludes: *A certain proof how irregular the ancient feudal government was, and how near the sovereigns, in some instances, approached to despotism, though in others they seemed scarcely to possess any authority. If a prince, much dreaded and revered like Henry, obtained but the appearance of general consent to an ordinance, which was equitable and just, it became immediately an established law, and all his subjects acquiesced in it: If the prince was hated or despised; if the nobles, who supported him had small influence; if the humors of the times disposed the people to question the justice of his ordinance; the fullest and most authentic assembly had no authority. Thus all was confusion and disorder, no regular idea of a constitution; force and violence decided every thing.*[30]

Final years in conflict with family, wars with sons

Despite Henry's rule over England and conquests in Normandy and Ireland, Henry was besieged by conflicts within his own family. All four of his sons were engaged in warfare against their father in complicity with their mother, Lewis VII, king of France and his successor Philip II. King Henry had granted to his oldest son Henry the control of England, Normandy and Anjou in France. His second oldest son Geoffrey was given control of Brittany. Richard was to have his mother's inheritance, Aquitaine in France. John, the youngest, and the kings favorite, was given command of Ireland, which he mismanaged.

Wars between Richard and his older brothers over control of Normandy led to the illness and death of the king's oldest son Henry. The prince *was seized with a fever at Martel, a castle near Turenne, to which he had retired in discontents; and seeing the approaches of death, he was at last struck with remorse for his undutiful behavior towards his*

---

[29] Ibid, pp 359-360.

[30] Ibid, pp 361-362.

father.[31] Prince Henry died in 1183. He had no children. Richard carried on war against Geoffrey, who demanded that Anjou be annexed to his dominions in Brittany. Geoffrey, who had fled to the court of France, died in a tournament in 1186. Geoffrey's widow, soon after his death, delivered a son Arthur, who would follow Richard as heir to the kingdom. John, the youngest son of Henry II would follow Richard and Arthur according to the rules of primogeniture.

Death of Henry II

Henry suffered this most important defeat and he was required to submit --- to all the rigorous terms, which were imposed upon him.[32] Henry, thus defeated by his son Richard and Phillip of France in 1189, was forced to acknowledge Richard as his heir to the throne. *When king Henry demanded a list of those barons, to whom he was bound to grant a pardon for their connections with Richard, he was astonished to find, at the head of them, the name of his son John, who had always been his favorite, whose interests he had ever anxiously at heart, and who had even, on account of his ascendant over him, often excited the jealousy of Richard. The unhappy father, already overloaded with cares and sorrow, finding this last disappointment in his domestic tenderness, broke out into expressions of the utmost despair, cursed the day in which he receive his miserable being, and bestowed, on his ungrateful and undutiful children, a malediction which he never could be prevailed on to retract. The more his heart was disposed to friendship and affection, the more he resented the barbarous return, which his four sons had successively made to his parental care; and this finishing blow, by depriving him of every comfort in life, quite broke his spirit, and threw him into a lingering fever, of which he expired, at the castle of Chinon near Sumur. Henry II died July 6, 1189.*[33] His son Richard succeeded him.

---

[31]Ibid, pp 363-364.

[32] Ibid, pp 368-369.

[33] Ibid, pp 368-369.

Chapter 15

Richard I and King John

Richard and John were brothers, the surviving sons of Henry II. King Henry's eldest son prince Henry had died in 1183 leaving no children. Geoffrey died in 1186, leaving Richard the eldest surviving son of Henry II and heir to the kingdom. Richard became famous for his military ventures, not only in France against his brothers and father, but also against Islam. He spent nearly three years in the crusades and spent about fourteen months in captivity. He spent only four months of his reign in England. Geoffrey's son Arthur was the rightful heir to follow Richard. John, the youngest son, however, usurped the crown and murdered Arthur, or who was at least responsible for Arthur's death while in John's captivity. The barons and the ecclesiastics forced John to sign the Magna Carta.

Richard I

Richard I, (b. 1157, d. 1199), also known as Richard the lion-hearted, reigned from 1189 to 1199. Nothing can be cited about Richard's childhood. His mother Eleanor had been married to Lewis VII, king of France, for sixteen years. She had accompanied him on Lewis' first crusade and was divorced by the king after a gallantry with a Saracen. Richard's father Henry II married her for acquisition of territory and influence. Richard was given his mother's inheritance when he was eleven years old. Whether his mother's adventures in the crusade had anything to do with Richard's chief ambition in life can only be raised as a possibility. In any case his reign was characterized by military ventures in the crusades and his wars in France. During this period he spent only four months in England. *The king, impelled more by the love of military glory than by superstition, acted, from the beginning of his reign, as if the sole purpose of his government had been the relief of the Holy Land, and the recovery of Jerusalem from the Saracens.*

Not content with a pogrom against the Jews in London, Richard aimed for greater glory in joining a crusade against another religion, that of Islam. He joined the third crusade. Saladin had extended his own power over most of Mohammedan Syria and Mesopotamia. In 1187 his armies overran the Latin Kingdom and Jerusalem fell. The pope influenced the powers of Europe, Philip of France and emperor Fredrick Barbarossa, to recover the city of Jerusalem. Richard joined in this venture, the third crusade, from 1189 to 1192.

Richard had access to his father Henry's treasure, and put to sale the revenues and manors of the crown; the offices of greatest trust and power, even those of forester and sheriff, which anciently were so important, became venal; the dignity of chief justiciary, in whose hands was lodged the whole execution of the laws, was sold to Hugh de Puzas, bishop of Durham, for a thousand marks; --- Elated with the hopes of fame, which in that age attended no wars but those against the infidel, he was blind to every other consideration; and when some of the wiser ministers objected to this dissipation of the revenue and power of the crown he replied, that he would sell London itself could he find a purchaser. Nothing indeed could be a stronger proof how negligent he was of all future interests in comparison of the crusade, than his selling, for so small a sum as 10,000 marks, the vassalage of Scotland, together with the fortresses of Roxborough and Berwic, the greatest acquisition that had been made by his father during the course of his victorious reign.

Richard left the administration in the hands of Hugh, bishop of Durham, and of Longchamp, bishop of Ely, whom he appointed justiciaries and guardians of the realm.[1] Richard set out on the crusade September 14, 1190. He would not return to England until March 20, 1194. He had gained an alliance with Phillip, king of France; however, Phillip returned and took advantage of Richard's absence. Meanwhile Richard gloried in his military accomplishments. *The Christian adventurers under his command determined, on opening the campaign, to attempt the siege of Ascalon, in order to prepare the way for that of Jerusalem; and they marched along the seacoast with that intention. Saladin purposed to intercept their passage; and he placed himself on the road with an army, amounting to 300,000 combatants. On this occasion was fought one of the greatest battles of that age; and the most celebrated, for the military genius of the commanders, for the number and valor of the troops, and for the great variety of events which attends it. Both the right wing of the Christians commanded by d'Avesnes, and the left, conducted by the duke of Burgundy, were, in the beginning of the*

---

[1] Hume, vol 1, pp 388-389.

*day, broken and defeated; when Richard, who led on the main body,
restored the battle; attacked the enemy with intrepidity and presence of
mind; performed the part both of a consummate general and gallant
soldier; and not only gave his two wings leisure to recover from their
confusion, but obtained a complete victory over the Saracens, of whom
forty thousand are said to have perished in the field. Ascalon soon after
fell into the hands of the Christians: Other sieges were carried on with
equal success: Richard was even able to advance within sight of
Jerusalem, the object of his enterprise.[2]* The Germans, Italians, French
and Burgunians all abandoned the hope of further conquest. Richard,
therefore, *concluded a truce with that monarch Saladin; and stipulated,
that Acre, Joppa, and other seaport towns of Palestine should remain in
the hands of the Christians, and that every one of that religion should
have liberty to perform his pilgrimage to Jerusalem unmolested.* ---
Saladin died at Damascus soon after concluding this truce with the
princes of the crusade.

Capture of Richard

Richard, attempting to return to his dominions, was shipwrecked
at Aquileia, at the top of the Adriadic Sea. Richard attempted a journey in
disguise to return to Normandy, but was captured December 20, 1192,
and arrested by Leopold, duke of Austria. Emperor Henry VI ordered
Richard to be delivered to him in Germany. Richard remained in prison
in Germany until ransom was paid February 4, 1194. *The emperor, that
he might render him more impatient for the recovery of his liberty, and
make him submit to a payment of a larger ransom, treated him with the
greatest severity, and reduced him to a condition worse than that of the
meanest malefactor.* He was even produced before the diet of the empire
at Worms, and accused by Henry of many crimes and misdemeanors. ---
*Richard defended himself successfully and made such an impression on
the German princes, that they exclaimed loudly against the conduct of
the emperor; the pope threatened him with excommunication; and the
emperor found that. he had to provide for his release with payment of
150,000 marks ransom.*

Return to England

Richard returned to England March 20, 1194 with public
exultation and ordered himself crowned at Winchester. *The barons
confiscated, on account of his treason, all prince John's possessions in
England; and they assisted the king in reducing the fortresses, which still
remained in the hands of his brother's adherents. Richard, having settled
every thing in England, passed over with an army into Normandy; being
impatient to make war on Philip, and to revenge himself for the many*

---

[2] Ibid, pp 392-393.

injuries which he had received from that monarch. As soon as Philip heard of the king's deliverance from captivity, he wrote to his confederate, John, in these terms: 'Take care of yourself: The devil is broken loose'. Wars between England and France continued, with several attempted negotiations.

Richard's death

On March 28, 1199 Richard was struck in the shoulder by an arrow during an attempted siege of the castle of Chalus, near Limoges and died as a result of gangrene of the wound. It would appear that his military prowess was his highest achievement and the appellation *Coeur de Lion* was attached to his name. The spirit of the times was memorialized by the practice of placing on shields of nobles and knights a coat of arms, which henceforth would be a means of identifying wealthy families *who were proud of the pious and military enterprises of their ancestors.*[3] Richard left no heirs. He had no children by Queen Berengaria.

King John

King John, (b. 1167, d. 1216) ruled England from 1199 to 1216. Nothing seemed to go right during the reign of John. The first problem with John is that he was not the rightful heir to the crown. Arthur was the son of John's older brother Geoffrey. John was the younger brother of Richard, and youngest son of Henry II and Eleanor of Aquitaine. There is no information available about John's birth, childhood or early years. Several references in Hume indicate that he was the favorite son of Henry II. The new conquest of Ireland was destined for John. *He sent his fourth son, John, into Ireland, with a view of making a more complete conquest of the island; but the petulance and incapacity of this prince, by which he enraged the Irish chieftains, obliged the king soon after to recall him.*[4]

Richard had named Arthur, not John, as the rightful heir of the crown after Richard. John obtained support from some of the nobles and Phillip of France in a revolt against the regent, while Richard was on a Crusade.

The king's marriage

John, --- indulged his passion for Isabella, the daughter and heir of the --- count of Angouleme, a lady with whom he had become

---

[3] Ibid, p 399.

[4] Ibid, p 362.

much enamored. Isabella was married to the count de la Marche, and was already consigned to the care of that nobleman, though, by reason of her tender years, the marriage had not been consummated. The passion of John made him overlook all these obstacles: He persuaded the count of Angouleme to carry off his daughter from her husband; and having, on some pretense or other, procured a divorce from his own wife, he espoused Isabella; regardless both of the menaces of the pope, who exclaimed against these irregular proceedings, and of the resentment of the injured count, who soon found means of punishing his powerful and insolent rival.[5] John married Isabella in 1201.[6]

John assumes the crown

When Richard died in 1199, John had obtained support for the crown from the archbishop of Canterbury, the chief ministers under Richard's administration and the submission of the English barons. Arthur, however, contested John's right to the throne. He was the oldest son of Johns' older brother Geoffrey, and was the rightful heir to the throne. Some of the barons and the French king supported Arthur. Richard soon returned to France, in order to conduct the war against Philip, and to recover the revolted provinces from his nephew Arthur.

Feudal rights of Arthur as successor

The rights of primogeniture and a representation in succession arose from the feudal law; which, first introducing the right of primogeniture, made such a distinction between the families of the elder and younger brothers, that the son of the former was thought entitled to succeed to his grandfather, preferable to his uncles. But the idea of representation seems to have made, at this time, greater progress in France than in England: The barons of the transmarine provinces, Anjou, Maine, and Touraine, immediately declared in favor of Arthur's title, and applied for assistance to the French monarch as their superior lord. Philip, who desired only an occasion to embarrass John, and dismember his dominions, embraced the cause of the young duke of Britanny, took him under his protection, and sent him to Paris to be educated, along with his own son Lewis.

Normandy, John and Arthur

In 1201 John summoned together the barons of England, and required them to pass the sea under his standard, and to quell the rebels: He found that he possessed as little authority in that kingdom as in his transmarine provinces. The English barons unanimously replied that

[5] Hume, vol 1, p 410.

[6] Ibid, p 453.

they would not attend him on this expedition, unless he would promise to restore and preserve their privileges: This was the first symptom of a regular association and plan of liberty among those noblemen! But affairs were not yet fully ripe for the revolution projected. John, by menacing the barons, broke the concert; and both engaged many of them to follow him into Normandy, and obliged the rest, who stayed behind, to pay him a scutage of two marks on each knight's fee, as the price of their exemption from the service.

Arthur, the young duke of Brittany, who was now rising to man's estate, sensible of the dangerous character of his uncle, determined to seek both his security and elevation by an union with Philip and the malcontent barons. He joined the French army which had begun hostilities against the king of England: He was received with great marks of distinction by Philip; was knighted by him; espoused his daughter Mary; and was invested not only in the duchy of Britanny, but in the counties of Anjou and Maine, which he had formerly resigned to his uncle.

Young Arthur, fond of military renown, had broken in Poictou at the head of a small army; and passing near Mirebeau, he heard, that his grandmother, Queen Eleanor, who had always opposed his interest, was lodged in that place, and was protected by a weak garrison, and ruinous fortifications. He immediately determined to lay siege to the fortress, and make himself master of her person: But John, roused from his indolence by so pressing an occasion, collected an army of English and Brancons, and advanced from Normandy with hasty marches to the relief of the queen-mother. He fell on Arthur's camp before that prince was aware of the danger; dispersed his army; took him prisoner. --- The greater part of the prisoners were sent over to England; but Arthur was shut up in the castle of Falais, in Normandy.[7]

The murder of Arthur

Arthur died in the castle prison. Two versions of the story of his death are presented, one from David Hume's *The History of England* and the other from Shakespeare's historic play *King John*.

From Hume: *The king had here a conference with his nephew; represented to him the folly of his pretensions; and required him to renounce the French alliance, which had encouraged him to live in a state of enmity with all his family: But the brave, though imprudent, youth, rendered more haughty from misfortunes, maintained the justice of his cause; asserted his claim, not only to the French provinces, but to the crown of England; and in his turn, required the king to restore himself, the son of his elder brother to the possession of his inheritance. John, sensible, from these symptoms of spirit, that the young prince,*

---

[7] Ibid, pp 412-413.

though now a prisoner, might hereafter prove a dangerous enemy, determined to prevent all future peril by dispatching his nephew; and Arthur was never more heard of.[8]

The details of Arthur's murder would *be variously related by historians. But the most probable account,* according to Hume, is as follows: *The king, it is said, first proposed to William de la Braye, one of his servants, to dispatch Arthur; but William replied, that he was a gentleman, not a hangman; and he positively refused compliance. Another instrument of murder was found, and was dispatched with proper orders to Falais; but Hubert de Bourgh, chamberlain to the king, and constable of the castle, feigning that he himself would execute the king's mandate, sent back the assassin, spread the report that the young prince was dead, and publicly performed all the ceremonies of his interment: But finding, that the Bretons vowed revenge for the murder, and that all the revolted barons persevered more obstinately in their rebellion, he thought it prudent to reveal the secret, and to inform the world that the duke of Brittany was still alive, and in his custody.*

Hume ends his story, as follows: *This discovery proved fatal to the young Prince. John first removed him to the castle of Rouen; and coming in a boat, during the night time, to that place, commanded Arthur to be brought forth to him. The young prince, aware of his danger, and now more subdued by the continuance of his misfortunes, and by the approach of death, threw himself on his knees before his uncle, and begged for mercy: But the barbarous tyrant, making no reply, stabbed him with his own hands; and fastening a stone to the dead body, threw it into the Seine.*

In the Shakespeare play King John reveals his intent. John. *Do not I know thou wouldst? Good Hubert, Hubert, Hubert, throw thine eye On yon young boy: I'll tell thee what, my friend, He is a very serpent in my way; And Wheresoe'er this foot of mine doth tread, He lies before me:- doest thou understand me?* Thou art his keeper. Hubert. *And I'll keep him so that he shall not offend your majesty.* King John. *Death.* Hubert. *My lord?* King John. *A grave.* Hubert. *He shall not live.* Hubert is later characterized menacingly with a red hot iron rod threatening to burn both of Arthur's eyes out, *these eyes that never did nor never shall so much as frown on you?* After more eloquent pleadings from Arthur, Hubert finally states: *Peace; no more. Adieu! Your uncle must not know but you are dead; I'll fill these dogged spies with false reports: And, pretty child, sleep doubtless and secure, That Hubert, for the wealth of all the world, Will not offend thee.* In the Shakespeare play Arthur attempts his escape by disguising himself as a ship boy, climbed the wall of the castle prison and died after a leap.[9]

---

[8] Ibid, p 413.

[9] Ibid, pp 413-414. Shakespeare, Act III, sc 3; Act IV, sc 1.

The results were consistently disastrous, regardless of the events that caused the death of Arthur. *All men were struck with horror at this inhuman deed; and from that moment the king, detested by his subjects, retained a very precarious authority over both the people and the barons in his dominions. The Bretons, enraged at his disappointment in their fond hopes, waged implacable war against him; and fixing the succession of their government, put themselves in a posture to revenge the murder of their sovereign.*[10]

Loss of English provinces

The king of France, whose ambitious and active spirit had been hitherto confined, either by the sound policy of Henry, or the martial genius of Richard, seeing now the opportunity favorable against this base and odious prince, embraced the project of expelling the English, or rather the English king, from France, and of annexing to the crown so many considerable fiefs, which, during several ages, had been dismembered from it. With the fall of Chateau Gaillard, the most considerable fortress to guard the frontiers of Normandy, the last effort of the English failed. Philip *carried his victorious army into the western provinces; soon reduced Anjou, Maine, Touraine, and part of Pictou; and in this manner, the French crown, during the reign of one able and active prince, received such an accession of power and grandeur, as, in the ordinary course of things, it would have required several ages to attain.*[11]

Conflict with the church

In 1207 John contended with the church. With the death of Hubert Walter, archbishop of Canterbury, the monks or canons chose Reginald, their sub-prior, as his successor. He was installed and sent to Rome, all without the king's knowledge. *The king was enraged at the novelty and temerity of the attempt, in filling so important an office without his knowledge or consent.* The monks backed down and set aside his election. John nominated John de Gray, bishop of Norwich, for their primate and the election of that primate was made, but the prelates sent an agent to maintain their cause before pope Innocent. *The present controversy about the election to the see of Canterbury afforded Innocent an opportunity of claiming this right; --- and commanded the monks to choose for their primate, cardinal Langton, an Englishman by birth, but educated in France, and connected, by his interests and attachments, with the see of Rome. The monks complied with his orders, and made the election required of them.*

---

[10] Hume, vol 1, p 414.

[11] Ibid, pp 416-419.

The quarrel between the king and the see of Rome continued for some years; however, in 1209, John was excommunicated. *As the sentence of interdict had not produced the desired effect on John, and as his people, though extremely discontented, had hitherto been restrained from rising in open rebellion against him, he was soon to look for the sentence of excommunication: And he had reason to apprehend, that, notwithstanding all his precautions, the most dangerous consequences might ensure from it.*

The Pope and king Phillip of France

The next gradation of papal sentences was to absolve John's subjects from their oaths of fidelity and allegiance, and to declare every one excommunicated who had any commerce with him, in public or in private; at his table, in his council, or even in private conversation: And this sentence was accordingly, with all imaginable solemnity, in 1212, pronounced against him.[12] The pope, in order to enforce his powers, solicited Philip to obtain the property and possessions of the kingdom of England as a reward of military conquest of England. *Philip collected a fleet of 1700 vessels, great and small, in the sea-ports of Normandy and Picardy; and prepared a force, which seemed equal to the greatness of his enterprise.* John raised an army of 60,000 men. *But the people were swayed by superstition, and regarded their king with horror, as anathematized by papal censures: The barons, besides lying under the same prejudices, were all disgusted by his tyranny, and were, many of them, suspected of holding a secret correspondence with the enemy: And the incapacity and cowardice of the king himself, ill-fitted to contend with those mighty difficulties, made men prognosticate the most fatal effects from the French invasion.*

Submission to the pope

On May 13, 1212, king John submitted to the pope. *John, lying under the agonies of present terror, made no scruple of submitting to this condition. He passed a charter, in which he said, that, not constrained by fear, but of his own free will, and by the common advice and consent of his barons, he had, for remission of his own sins and those of his family, resigned England and Ireland to God, to St. Peter and St. Paul, and to pope Innocent and his successors in the apostolic chair: He agreed to hold these dominions as feudatory of the church of Rome, by the annual payment of a thousand marks; seven hundred for England, three hundred for Ireland: And he stipulated, that if he or his successors should ever presume to revoke or infringe this charter, they should instantly, except upon admonition they repented of their offence, forfeit all right to their dominion. In consequence of this agreement, John in homage to Pandolf*

---

[12] Ibid, pp 429-430.

as the pope's legate, with all the submissive rites which the feudal law required of vassals before their liege-lord and superior, he came disarmed into the legate's presence, who was seated on a throne; he flung himself on his knees before him; he lifted up his joined hands, and put them within those of Pandolf; he swore fealty to the pope; and he paid part of the tribute, which he owed for his kingdom as the patrimony of St. Peter. --- But though Pandolf had brought the king to submit to these base conditions, he still refused to free him from the excommunication and interdict, till an estimation should be taken of the losses of the ecclesiastics, and full compensation and restitution should be made them.[13]

Revolt of the Barons

If John's submissions to the church were humiliating and devastating, the revolt and victoy of the barons over king John would spell a dismal end to his life. *John, reduced to this abject situation under a foreign power* (Rome), *still showed the same disposition to tyrannize over his subjects, which had been the chief cause of all his misfortunes. One Peter of Pomfret, a hermit, had foretold, that the king, this very year, should lose his crown; and for that rash prophecy, he had been thrown into prison in Corfe-castle. --- Equally odious and contemptible, both in public and private life, he affronted the barons by his insolence, dishonored their families by his gallantries, enraged them by his tyranny, and gave discontent to all ranks of men by his endless exactions and impositions. The effect of these lawless practices had already appeared in the general demand made by the barons of a restoration of their privileges; and after he had reconciled himself to the pope, by abandoning the independence of the kingdom, he appeared to all his subjects in so mean a light, that they universally thought they might with safety and honor insist upon their pretensions.*

Origins of Magna Carta

In November 1214, Langton, the archbishop of Canterbury, who had an animosity against John, formed a plan to reform the government, which he thought would benefit the church. *Soon after, in a private meeting of some of the principal barons at London, he showed them a copy of Henry I's charter, which, he said, he had happily found in a monastery; and he exhorted them to insist on the renewal and observance of it: The barons swore, that they would sooner lose their lives than depart from so reasonable a demand. The confederacy began now to spread wider, and to comprehend almost all the barons in England; and a new and more numerous meeting was summoned by Langton at St. Edmondsbury, under the color of devotion. He again*

---

[13] Ibid, pp 432-433.

produced to the assembly the old charter of Henry; renewed his exhortations of unanimity and vigor in the prosecution of their purpose; and represented in the strongest colors the tyranny to which they had so long been subjected, and from which it now behooved them to free themselves and their posterity. The barons, inflamed by his eloquence, incited by the sense of their own wrongs, and encouraged by the appearance of their power and numbers, solemnly took an oath before the high altar, to adhere to each other, to insist on their demands, and to make endless war on the king, till he should submit to grant them. They agreed, that, after the festival of Christmas, they would prefer in a body their common petition; and in the mean time, they separated, after mutually engaging, that they would put themselves in a posture of defense, would enlist men and purchase arms and would supply their castle with the necessary provisions.[14]

On January 16, 1215, the barons asked the king to renew Henry's charter and confirm the laws of king Edward. John promised to give them a positive answer at the festival of Easter. *During this interval, John, in order to break or subdue the league of his barons, endeavored to avail himself of the ecclesiastical power, of whose influence he had, from his own recent misfortunes, had such fatal experience. He granted to the clergy a charter, relinquishing for ever that important prerogative, for which his father and all his ancestors had zealously contended; yielding to them the free election on all vacancies; reserving only the power to issue a conge d'elire, and to subjoin a confirmation of the election; and declaring, that, if either of these were with-held, the choice should nevertheless be deemed just and valid. He also made a vow to lead an army into Palestine against the infidels, --- and he sent his agent to Rome in order to appeal to the pope against the violence of his barons. The barons also sent an envoy to Rome to oblige him to restore and confirm all their just and undoubted privileges.*

About the time that the pope's letters arrived in England, the malcontent barons, on the approach of the festival of Easter, when they were to expect the king's answer to their petition, met by agreement at Stamford; and they assembled a force, consisting of above 2000 knights, besides their retainers and inferior persons without number. Elated with their power, they advanced in a body to Brackley, within fifteen miles of Oxford, the place where the court then resided; and they there received a message from the king, by the archbishop of Canterbury and the earl of Pembroke, desiring to know what those liberties were which they so zealously challenged from their sovereign. They delivered to these messengers a schedule, containing the chief articles of their demands; which was no sooner shown to the king, than he burst into a furious passion, and asked, why the barons did not also demand of him his

---

[14] Ibid, pp 438-439.

kingdom? Swearing, that he would never grant them such liberties as must reduce himself to slavery.[15]

When the barons received word of the kings reply they gathered their forces and took Bedford castle, then with support from citizens of Ware made incursions from London, and laid waste the kings parks and palaces; --- The king was left at Odiham in Surrey with a poor retinue of only seven knights; and after trying several expedients to elude the blow, after offering to refer all differences to the pope alone, or to eight barons, four to be chosen by himself, and four by the confederates, he found himself at last obliged to submit at discretion.

Runnemede and Magna Carta

A conference between the king and the barons took place at Runnemede on June 15, 1215. *The two parties encamped apart, like open enemies; and after a debate of a few days, the king, with a facility somewhat suspicious, signed and sealed the charter which was required by him.* This charter, later called Magna Carta, or great charter, will be presented in full at the conclusion of this chapter. The reader may then be able to gather an impression of the content of this charter, which involved exclusively the king and twenty-five barons. About half of this number were clergy and half earls or barons, and are included among those listed in the introduction to the charter.

John seemed to submit passively to all these regulations, however injurious to majesty. --- But he only dissembled, till he should find a favorable opportunity for annulling all his concessions. The injuries and indignities, which he had formerly suffered from the pope and the king of France, as they came from equals or superiors, seemed to make but small impression on him: But the sense of this perpetual and total subjection under his own rebellious vassals, sunk deep in his mind and he was determined, at all hazards, to throw off so ignominious a slavery. He grew sullen, silent, and reserved: He shunned the society of his courtiers and nobles: He retired into the Isle of Wight, as if desirous of hiding his shame and confusion; but in this retreat he meditated the most fatal vengeance against all his enemies. He secretly sent abroad his emissaries to enlist foreign soldiers, and to invite the rapacious Brabancons into his service, by the prospect of sharing the spoils of England, and reaping the forfeitures of so many opulent barons, who had incurred the guilt of rebellion, by rising in arms against him. And he dispatched a messenger to Rome, in order to lay before the pope the Great Charter, which he had been compelled to sign, and to complain, before that tribunal, of the violence, which had been imposed upon him.

---

[15] Ibid, pp 441-442.

Charter annulled

Innocent, considering himself as feudal lord of the kingdom, was incensed by the temerity of the barons. --- He issued, therefore, a bull, in which, --- he annulled and abrogated the whole charter, as unjust in itself, as obtained by compulsion,[16] and as derogatory to the dignity of the apostolic see. He prohibited the barons from exacting the observance of it: he even prohibited the king himself from paying any regard to it: He absolved him and his subjects from all oaths, which they had been constrained to take to that purpose: and he pronounced a general sentence of excommunication against every one who should persevere in maintaining such treasonable and iniquitous pretensions.

The king's revenge

John still found that his nobility and people, and even his clergy, adhered to the defense of their liberties, and to their combination against him: The sword of his foreign mercenaries was all he had to trust to for restoring his authority. The king laid siege to the castle of Rochester, which was reduced by famine. John had intended to have hanged the governor and all the garrison, but sacrificed only the inferior prisoners. The ravenous and barbarous mercenaries, incited by a cruel and enraged prince, were let loose against the estates, tenants, manors, houses, parks of the barons, and spread devastation over the face of the kingdom. Nothing was to be seen but the flames of villages and castles reduced to ashes, the consternation and misery of the inhabitants, the tortures exercised by the soldiery to make them reveal their concealed treasures, and reprisals no less barbarous, committed by the barons and their partisans on the royal demesnes, and on the estates of such as still adhered to the crown. The king, marching through the whole extent of England, from Dover to Berwic, laid the provinces waste on each side of him; and considered every state, which was not his immediate property, as entirely hostile and the object of military execution.[17]

The Barons invite Phillip to England

Other barons offered to acknowledge Lewis, the eldest son of Philip, for their sovereign. Philip was strongly tempted to lay hold on the rich prize which was offered to him, *but exacted from the barons twenty five hostages of the most noble birth in the kingdom; and having obtained this security, he sent over first a small army to the relief of the confederates; then more numerous forces, which arrived with Lewis himself at their head.* The foreign troops, who were from Flanders and elsewhere in France refused to fight against their monarchy and deserted

---

[16] As noted before a contract or legal agreement signed under duress is not valid.

[17] Ibid, pp 449-450.

from John. Many noblemen deserted John's party, a notable exception being Hubert de Burgh. *The earl of Salisbury and other noblemen deserted again to John's party. --- The king was assembling a considerable army, with a view of fighting one great battle for his crown; but passing from Lynne to Lincolnshire, his road lay along the sea-shore, which was overflowed at high water; and not choosing the proper time for his journey, he left in the inundation all his carriages, treasure, baggage, and regalia.*

Death of John

The affliction for this disaster, and vexation from the distracted state of his affairs, increased the sickness under which he then labored; and though he reached the castle of Newark, he was obliged to halt there, and his distemper soon after put an end to his life, in the forty-ninth year of his age, and eighteenth of his reign. King John died October 17, 1216. The oldest son of John and Isabella was Henry, then Richard and three daughters, Jane, Eleanor, and Isabella who survived him. He was succeeded by his oldest son Henry.

Summary by Hume

It is not difficult to understand why the revolt took place among the barons and ecclesiastics, which culminated in John's submission to their demands in Magna Carta, and his ultimate demise. *The character of this prince is nothing but a complication of vices, equally mean and odious; ruinous to himself, and destructive to his people. Cowardice, inactivity, folly, levity, licentiousness, ingratitude, treachery, tyranny, and cruelty, all these qualitites appear too evidently in the several incidents of his life. --- It is hard to say, whether his conduct to his father, his brother, his nephew, or his subjects, was the most culpable; or whether his crimes in these respects were not even exceeded by the baseness, which appeared in his transactions with the king of France, the pope, and the barons. His European dominions, when they devolved to him by the death of his brother, were more extensive than have ever, since his time, been ruled by any English monarch: But he first lost by his misconduct the flourishing provinces in France, the ancient patrimony of his family: He subjected his kingdom to a shameful vassalage under the see of Rome: he saw the prerogatives of his crown diminished by law, and still more reduced by faction.*[18]

---

[18] Ibid, pp 451-452.

Magna Carta

John, by the grace of God king of England, lord of Ireland, duke of Normandy and Aquitaine, count of Anjou: to the archbishops, bishops, abbots, earls, barons, justices, foresters, sheriffs, prevosts, serving men, and to all his bailiffs and faithful subjects, greetings. Know that we, by the will of God and for the safety of our soul, and of the souls of all our predecessors and our heirs, to the honor of God and for the exalting of the holy church and the bettering of our realm: by the counsel of our venerable fathers Stephen archbishop of Canterbury, primate of all England and cardinal of the holy Roman church; of Henry archbishop of Dublin; to the bishops William of London, Peter of Winchester, Jocelin of Bath and Glastonbury, Hugo of Lincoln, Walter of Worcester, William of Coventry and Benedict of Rochester; of master Pandulf, subdeacon and of the household of the lord pope; of brother Aymeric, master of the knights of the Temple in England; and of the noble men, William Marshall earl of Pembroke, William earl of Salisbury, William earl of Warren, William earl of Arundel, Alan de Galway constable of Scotland, Warin son of Gerold, Peter son of Herbert, Hubert de Burgh seneschal of Poictiers, Hugo de Neville, Matthew son of Herbert, Thomas Basset, Alan Basset, Philip d'Aubigni, Robert de Roppelay, John Marshall, John son of Hugo, and others of our faithful subjects:

1. First of all have granted to God, and, for us and for our heirs forever, have confirmed, by this our present charter, that the English church shall be free and shall have its rights intact and its liberties uninfringed upon. And thus we will that it be observed. As is apparent from the fact that we, spontaneously and of our own free will, before discord broke out between ourselves and our barons, did grant and by our charter confirm- and did cause the lord pope Innocent III, to confirm - freedom of elections, which is considered most important and most necessary to the church of England. Which charter both we ourselves shall observe, and we will that it be observed with good faith by our heirs forever. We have also granted to all free men of our realm, on the part of ourselves and our heirs forever, all the subjoined liberties, to have and to hold, to them and to their heirs, from us and from our heirs:

2. If any one of our earls or barons, or of others holding from us in chief through military service, shall die; and if, at the time of his death, his heir be of full age and owe a relief: he shall have his inheritance by paying the old relief, - the heir, namely, or the heirs of an earl, by paying one hundred pounds for the whole barony of an earl; the heir or heirs of a baron, by paying one hundred pounds for the whole barony; the heir or heirs of a knight, by paying one hundred shillings at most for a whole knight's fee; and he who shall owe less shall give less, according to the ancient custom of fees.

3. But if the heir of any of the above persons shall be under age and in wardship, - when he comes of age he shall have his inheritance without relief and without fine.

4. The administrator of he land of such heir who shall be under age shall take none but reasonable issues from the land of the heir, and reasonable customs and services; and this without destruction and waste of men or goods. And if we shall have committed the custody of any such land to the sheriff or to any other man who ought to be responsible to us for the issues of it, and he cause destruction or waste to what is in his charge: we will fine him, and the land shall be handed over to two lawful and discreet men of that fee who shall answer to us, or to him to whom we shall have referred them, regarding those issues. And if we shall have given or sold to any one the custody of any such land, and he shall have caused destruction or waste to it, - he shall lose that custody, and it shall be given to two lawful and discreet men of that fee, who likewise shall answer to us, as has been explained.

5. The administrator, moreover, so long as he may have the custody of the land, shall keep in order, from the issues of that land, the houses, parks, warrens, lakes, mills, and other things pertaining to it. And he shall restore to the heir when he comes to full age, his whole land stocked with ploughs and wainnages, according as the time of the wainnage requires and he issues of the land will reasonably permit.

6. Heirs may marry without disparagement; so, nevertheless, that, before the marriage is contracted, it shall be announced to the relations by blood of the heir himself.

7. A widow, after the death of her husband, shall straightway, and without difficulty, have her marriage portion and her inheritance, nor shall she give any thing in return for her dowry, her marriage portion or the inheritance which belonged to her, and which she and her husband held on the day of the death of that husband. And she may remain in the house of her husband, after his death, for forty days; within which her dowry shall be paid over to her.

8. No widow shall be forced to marry when she prefers to live without a husband; so, however, that she gives security not to marry without our consent, if she hold from us, or the consent of the lord from whom she holds, if she hold from another.

9. Neither we nor our bailiffs shall seize any revenue for any debt, so long as the chattels of the debtor suffice to pay the debt; nor shall the sponsors of that debtor be distrained so long as that chief debtor has enough to pay the debt. But if the chief debtor fail in paying the debt, not having the wherewithal to pay it, the sponsors shall answer for the debt. And, if they shall wish, they may have the lands and revenues of the debtor until satisfaction shall have been given them for the debt previously paid for him; unless the chief debtor shall show that he is quit in that respect towards those same sponsors.

10. If any one shall have taken any sum, great or small, as a loan from the money-lenders, and shall die before that debt is paid, - that debt shall not bear interest so long as the heir, from whomever he may hold, shall be under age. And if the debt fall into our hands, we shall take nothing save the chattel contained in the deed.

11. And if any one dies owing a debt to the moneylenders, his wife shall have her dowry, and shall restore nothing of that debt. But if there shall remain children of that dead man, and they shall be under age, the necessaries shall be provided for them, according to the nature of the dead man's holding; and, from the residue, the debt shall be paid, saving the service due to the lords. In like manner shall be done concerning debts that are due to others besides moneylenders.

12. No scutage or aid shall be imposed in our realm unless by the common counsel of our realm; except for redeeming our body, and knighting our eldest son, and marrying once our eldest daughter. And for these purposes there shall only be given a reasonable aid. In like manner shall be done concerning the aids of the city of London.

13. And the city of London shall have all its old liberties and free customs as well by land as by land as well by water. Moreover we will and grant that all other cities and buroughs, and towns and ports, shall have all their liberties and free customs.

14. And, in order to have the common counsel of the realm in the matter of assessing an aid otherwise than in the aforesaid cases, or of assessing a scutage- we shall cause, under seal through our letters, the archbishops, bishops, abbots, earls, and greater barons to be summoned for a fixed day - for a term, namely, at least forty days distant, - and for a fixed place. And, moreover, we shall cause to be summoned in general, through our sheriffs and bailiffs, all those who hold of us in chief. And in all those letters of summons we shall express the cause of the summons. And when a summons has thus been made, the business shall be proceeded with on the day appointed according to the counsel of those who shall be present, even though not all shall come who were summoned.

15. We will not allow any one henceforth to take an aid from his freemen save for the redemption of his body, and the knighting of his eldest son, and he marrying, once, of his eldest daughter; and, for these purposes, there shall only be given a reasonable aid.

16. No one shall be forced to do more service for a knight's fee, or for another free holding, than is due from it.

17. Common pleas shall not follow our court but shall be held in a certain fixed place.

18. Assizes of novel disseisin, of mort d'ancestor, and of darrein presentment shall not be held save in their own counties, and in this way: We, or our chief justice, if we shall be absent from the kingdom, shall send two justices through each county four times a year; they, with four knights from each county, chosen by the county, shall

hold the aforesaid assizes in the county, and on the day and at the place of the county court.

19. And if on the day of the county court the aforesaid assizes cannot be held, a sufficient number of knights and free tenants, from those who were present at the county court on that day, shall remain, so that through them the judgments may be suitably given, according as the matter may have been great or small.

20. A freeman shall only be amerced for a small offence according to the measure of that offence. And for a great offence he shall be amerced according to the magnitude of the offence, saving his contenement; and a merchant, in the same way, saving his merchandise. And a villein, in the same way, if he fall under our mercy, shall be amerced saving his wainnage. And none of the aforesaid fines shall be imposed save upon oath of upright men from the neighborhood.

21. Earls and barons shall not be amerced save through their peers, and only according to the measure of the offence.

22. No clerk shall be amerced for his lay tenement except according to the manner of the other persons aforesaid; and not according to the amount of his ecclesiastical benefice.

23. Neither a town nor a man shall be forced to make bridges over the rivers, with the exception of those who, from of old and of right ought to do it.

24. No sheriff, constable, coroners, or other bailiffs of ours shall hold the pleas of our crown.

25. All counties, hundreds, wapentakes, and tithings - or demensne manors being excepted - shall continue according to the old farms, without any increase at all.

26. If any one holding from us a lay fee shall die, and our sheriff or bailiff can show our letters patent containing our summons for the debt which the dead man owed to us, - our sheriff or bailiff may be allowed to attach and enroll the chattels of the dead man to the value of that debt, through view of lawful men; in such way, however, that nothing shall be removed thence until the debt is paid which was plainly owed to us. And the residue shall be left to the executors that they may carry out the will of the dead man. And, if nothing is owed to us by him, all the chattels shall go to the use prescribed by the deceased, saving their reasonable portions to his wife and children.

27. If any freeman shall have died intestate his chattels shall be distributed through the hands of his near relatives and friends, by view of the church; saving to any one the debts which the dead man owed him.

28. No constable or other bailiff of ours shall take the corn or other chattels of any one except he straightway give money for them, or can be allowed a respite in that regard by the will of the seller.

29. No constable shall force any knight to pay money for castle ward if he be willing to perform that ward in person, or — he for a reasonable cause not being able to perform it himself— through another

proper man. And if we shall have led or sent him on a military expedition, he shall be quit of ward according to the amount of time during which, through us, he shall have been in military service.

30. No sheriff nor bailiff of ours, nor any one else, shall take the horses or carts of any freeman for transport, unless by the will of that freeman.

31. Neither we nor our bailiffs shall take another's wood for castles or for other private uses, unless by the will of him to whom the wood belongs.

32. We shall not hold the lands of those convicted of felony longer than a year and a day; and then the lands shall be restored to the lords of the fiefs.

33. Henceforth all the weirs in the Thames and Medway, and throughout all England, save on the seacoast, shall be done away with entirely.

34. Henceforth the writ, which is called praecipe shall not be served on any one for any holding so as to cause a free man to lose his court.

35. There shall be one measure of wine throughout our whole realm, and one measure of ale and one measure of corn - namely, the London quart; - and one width of dyed and russet and hauberk cloths - namely, two ells below the selvage. And with weights, moreover, it shall be as with measures.

37. If any one hold of us in fee-farm, or in socage, or in burkage, and hold land of another by military service, we shall not, by reason of that fee-farm, or socage, or burkage, have the ward ship of his heir or of his land, which is held in fee from another. Nor shall we have the ward ship of that fee-farm owe military service. We shall not, by reason of some petit-serjeanty which some one holds of us through the service of giving us knives or arrows or the like, have the ward ship of his heir or of the land which he holds of another by military service.

38. No bailiff, on his own simple assertion, shall henceforth put any one to his law, without producing faithful witnesses in evidence.

. 39. No freeman shall be taken, or imprisoned, or disseized, or outlawed, or exiled, or in any way harmed - nor will we go upon or send upon him - save by the lawful judgment of his peers or by the law of the land.

40. To none will we sell, to none deny or delay right or justice.

41. All merchants may safely and securely go out of England, and come into England, and delay and pass through England, as well by land as by water, for the purpose of buying and selling, free from all evil taxes, subject to the ancient and right customs — save in time of war, and if they are of the land at war against us. And if such be found in our land at the beginning of the war, they shall be held, without harm to their bodies and goods, until it shall be known to us or our chief justice how the merchants of our land are to be treated who shall, at that time, be

found in the land at war against us. And if ours shall be safe there, the others shall be safe in our land.

42. Henceforth any person, saving fealty to us, may go out of our realm and return to it, safely and securely, by land and by water, except perhaps for a brief period in time of war, for the common good of the realm. But prisoners and outlaws are excepted according to the law of the realm; also people of a land at war against us, and the merchants, with regard to whom shall be done as we have said.

43. If any one hold from any escheat— as from the honor of Wallingford, Nottingham, Boloin, Lancaster, or the other escheats which are in our hands and are baronies— and shall die, his heir shall not give another relief, nor shall he perform for us other service than be would perform for a baron if that barony were in the hand of a baron; and we shall hold it in the same way in which the baron has held it.

44. Persons dwelling without the forest shall not henceforth come before the forest justices, through common summonses, unless they are impleaded or are the sponsors of some person or persons attached for matters concerning the forest.

45. We will not make men justices, constables, sheriffs, or bailiffs, unless they are such as know the law of the realm, and are minded to observe it rightly.

46. All barons who have founded abbeys for which they have charters of the kings of England, or ancient right of tenure, shall have, as they ought to have, their custody when vacant.

47. All forests constituted as such in our time shall straight way be annulled; and the same shall be done for river banks made into places of defense by us in our time.

48. All evil customs concerning forests and warrens, and concerning foresters and warrens, sheriffs and their servants, river banks and the guardians, shall straightway be inquired into in each count, through twelve sworn knights from that county, and shall be eradicated by them, entirely, so that they shall never be renewed, within forty days after the inquest has been made; in such manner that we shall first know about them, or our justice if we be not in England.

49. We shall straightway return all hostages and charters, which were delivered to us by Englishmen as a surety for peace or faithful service.

50. We shall entirely remove from their bailiwick the relatives of Gerard de Ahtyes, so that they shall henceforth have no bailiwick in England: Engelard de Cygnes, Andrew Peter and Gyon de Chanceles, Gyon de Cygnes, Geoffrey de Martin and his brother, Philip Mark and his brothers, and Geoffrey his nephew, and the whole following of them.

51. And straightway after peace is restored we shall remove from the realm all the foreign soldiers, crossbowmen, servants, hirelings, who may have come with horses and arms to the harm of the realm.

52. If any one shall have been disseized by us, or removed, without a legal sentence of his peers, from his lands, castles, liberties or lawful right, we shall straightway restore them to him. And if a dispute shall arise concerning this matter it shall be settled according to the judgment of the twenty-five barons who are mentioned below as sureties for the peace. But with regard to all those things of which any one was, by king Henry our father or king Richard our brother, disseized or dispossessed without legal judgment of his peers, which we have in our hand or which others hold, and for which we ought to give a guarantee: We shall have respite until the common term for crusaders. Except with regard to those concerning which a plea was moved, or an inquest made by our order, before we took the cross. But when we return from our pilgrimage, or if, by chance, we desist from our pilgrimage, we shall straightway then show full justice regarding them.

53. We shall have the same respite, moreover, and in the same manner, in the matter of showing justice with regard to forests to be annulled and forests to remain, which Henry our father or Richard our brother constitute; and in the matter of wardships of lands which belong to the fee of another - wardships of which kind we have hitherto enjoyed by reason of the fee which some one held from us in military service; - and in the matter of abbeys founded in the fee of another than ourselves - in which the lord of the fee may say that he has jurisdiction. And when we return, or if we desist from our pilgrimage, we shall straightway exhibit full justice to those complaining with regard to theses matters.

54. No one shall be taken or imprisoned on account of the appeal of a woman concerning the death of another than her husband.

55. All fines imposed by us unjustly and contrary to the law of the land, and all americaments made unjustly and contrary to the law of the land, shall be altogether remitted, or it shall be done with regard to them according to the judgment of the twenty five barons mentioned below as sureties for the peace, or according to the judgment of the majority of them together with the aforesaid Stephen archbishop of Canterbury, if he can be present, and with others whom he may wish to associate with himself for this purpose. And if he cannot be present, the affair shall nevertheless proceed without him; in such was that, if one or more of the said twenty-five barons shall be concerned in a similar complaint, they shall be removed as to this particular decision, and, in their place, for this purpose alone, others shall be substituted who shall be chosen and sworn by the remainder of those twenty-five.

56. If we have disseized or dispossessed Welshmen of their lands or liberties or other things without legal judgment of their peers, in England or in Wales, — they shall straightway be restored to them. And if a dispute shall arise concerning this, than action shall be taken upon it in the March through judgment of their peers — concerning English holdings according to the law of England, concerning Welsh holdings according to the law of Wales, concerning holdings in the March

according to the law of the March. The Welsh shall do like-wise with regard to us and our subjects.

57. But with regard to all those things of which any one of the Welsh was, by king Henry our father or king Richard our brother, disseized or dispossessed without legal judgment of his peers, which we have in our hand or which others hold, and for which we ought to give a guarantee: we shall have respite until the common term for crusaders. Except with regard to those concerning which a plea was moved, or an inquest made by our order, before we took the cross. But when we return from our pilgrimage or if, by chance, we desist from our pilgrimage, we shall straightway then show full justice regarding them, according to the laws of Wales and the aforesaid districts.

58. We shall straightway return the son of Llewelin and all the Welsh hostages, and the charters delivered to us as surety for the peace.

59. We shall act towards Alexander king of the Scots regarding the restoration of his sister, and his hostages, and his liberties and his lawful right, as we shall act towards our other barons of England; unless it ought to be otherwise according to the charters which we hold from William, his father, the former king of the Scots. And this shall be done through judgment of his peers in our court.

60. Moreover all the subjects of our realm, clergy as well as laity, shall, as far as pertains to them, observed, with regard to their vassals, all these aforesaid customs and liberties which we have decreed shall, as far as pertains to us, be observed in our realm with regard to our own.

61. Inasmuch as, for the sake of God, and for the bettering of our realm, and for the more ready healing of the discord which has arisen between us and our barons, we have made all these aforesaid concessions, — wishing them to enjoy forever entire and firm stability, we make and grant to them the following security: that the barons, namely, may elect at their pleasure twenty-five barons from the realm, who ought, with all their strength, to observe, maintain and cause to be observed, the peace and privileges which we have granted to them and confirmed by this our present charter. In such wise, namely, that if we, or our justice, or our bailiffs, or any one of our servants shall have transgressed against any one in any respect, or shall have broken some one of the articles of peace or security, and our transgression shall have been shown to four barons of he aforesaid twenty-five: those four barons shall come to us, or, if we are abroad, to our justice, showing to us our error; and they shall ask us to cause that error to be amended without delay. And if we do not amend that error, or, we being abroad, if our justice do not amend it within a term of forty days from the time when it was shown to us or, we being abroad, to our justice: the aforesaid four barons shall refer the matter to the remainder of twenty five barons, and those twenty five barons, with the whole land in common, shall distrain and oppress us in every way in their power, — namely, by taking our

castles, lands and possessions, and in every other way that they can, until amends shall have been made according to their judgment, saving the persons of ourselves, our queen and our children. And when amends shall have been made they shall be in accord with us as they had been previously. And whoever of the land wishes to do so, shall swear that in carrying out all the aforesaid measures he will obey the mandates of the aforesaid twenty five barons, and that, with them, he will oppress us to the extent of his power. And, to any one who wishes to do so, we publicly and freely give permission to swear; and we will never prevent any one from swearing. Moreover, all those in the land who shall be unwilling, themselves and of their own accord, to swear to the twenty-five barons as to distraining and oppression us with them: such ones we shall make to swear by our mandate, as has been said. And if any one of the twenty-five barons shall die, or leave the country, or in any other way be prevented from carrying out the aforesaid measures, — the remainder of the aforesaid twenty-five barons shall choose another in his place, according to their judgment, who shall been sworn in the same way as the others. Moreover, in all things entrusted to those twenty-five barons to be carried out, if those twenty-five shall be present and chance to disagree among themselves with regard to some matter, or if some of them, having been summoned, shall be unwilling or unable to be present: That which the majority of those present shall decide or decree shall be considered binding and valid, just as if all the twenty-five had consented to it. And the aforesaid twenty-five shall swear that they will faithfully observe all the foregoing, and will cause them to be observed to the extent of their power. And we shall obtain nothing from any one, either through ourselves or through another, by which any of those concessions and liberties may be revoked or diminished. And if any such thing shall have been obtained, it shall be vain and invalid, and we shall never make use of it either through ourselves or through another.

62. And we have fully remitted to all, and pardoned, all the ill-will, anger and rancor which have arisen between us and our subjects, clergy and laity, from the time of the struggle. Moreover we have fully remitted to all, clergy and laity, and - as far as pertains to us - have pardoned fully all the transgressions committed, on the occasion of that same struggle, from Easter of the sixteenth year of our reign until the re-establishment of peace. In witness of which, moreover, we have caused to be drawn up for them letters patent of lord Stephen, archbishop of Canterbury, lord Henry, archbishop of Dublin, and the aforesaid bishops and master Pandolf, regarding that surety and the aforesaid concessions.

63. Wherefore we will and firmly decree that the English church shall be free, and that the subjects of our realm shall have and hold all the aforesaid liberties, rights and concessions, duly and in peace, freely and quietly, fully and entirely, for themselves and their heirs, from us and our heirs, in all matters and in all places, forever, as has been said. Moreover it has been sworn, on our part as well as on their part of the

barons, that all these above mentioned provisions shall be observed with good faith and without evil intent. The witnesses, being the above mentioned and many others. Given through our hand, in the plain called Runnimede between Windsor and Stanes, on the fifteenth day of June, in the seventeenth year of our reign.[19]

---

[19] Note. The author(s) of the above were not noted, nor any indication that the king made any changes or originated any of the content of the charter. Since the first and last paragraphs give the English church powers, possessions and immunities, and from the history noted above, it is most likely that this document originated from the clergy under Langton archbishop of Canterbury.

Chapter 16

Henry III

The reign of Henry III, (b. 1207, d 1272), was the longest in the history of England, from 1216 to 1272, (with the exception of queen Victoria, 1837-1901). There is little written about the character and accomplishments of this king to warrant more than a brief survey. Henry III was the first king to be crowned in childhood, at the age of nine years. Descendants would rule England until the beginning of the seventeenth century. The conflicts and instability, which characterized the rule of John, would become most notable in this reign. One of the barons, the earl of Leicester, nearly usurped the crown.

Hume begins his chapter on Henry III with the following commentary: *History, being a collection of facts which are multiplying without end, is obliged to adopt such arts of abridgement, to retain the more material events, and to drop all the minute circumstances, which are only interesting during the time, or to the persons engaged in the transactions. This truth is nowhere more evident than with regard to the reign, upon which we are going to enter. What mortal could have the patience to write or read a long detail of such frivolous events as those with which it is filled, or attend to a tedious narrative which would follow, through a series of fifty-six years, the caprices and weaknesses of so mean a prince as Henry?[1]*

There were, however, important developments in English law during Henry's reign. A shorter version of Magna Carta appeared, later enacted by Edward I. Henry de Bracton, an ecclesiastic, produced *On the Laws and Customs of England*, based on Roman civil law, later considered an important contribution in the development of English common law.

---

[1] Hume, vol 2, pp 3, 4.

Family history, birth and development

Henry was the oldest son of king John and Isabella of Angouleme (west central France). Hume went into detail regarding the courtship and marriage of Henry's parents in 1201. On October 1, 1207, six years after the marriage of his parents, Henry was born at Winchester. Nothing is written or apparently considered worth commentary about Henry's early youth, associations, education, or interests.

Henry crowned

At the age of nine years of age his father king John, died, on June 15, 1016. Most of eastern England was in the hands of Louis, son of king Phillip II of France, who had invaded England with an invitation and support from the rebellious barons. Young Henry was crowned soon thereafter, but at Gloucester, away from the French forces. The earl of Pembroke, who was mareschal of England, head of the armies and head of the government at the end of king John's reign, arranged for the crowning of the youth by the bishops of Winchester and Bath. *As the concurrence of the papal authority was requisite to support the tottering throne, Henry was obliged to swear fealty to the pope, and renew that homage, to which his father had already subjected the kingdom: And in order to enlarge the authority of Pembroke, and to give him a more regular and legal title to it, a general council of the barons was soon after summoned at Bristol, where that nobleman was chosen protector of the realm.*

The barons supported the protector. Lewis and the French were expelled from the kingdom. Not long afterwards, in 1219, the earl of Pembroke died and was replaced by Peter des Roches, bishop of Winchester, and Hubert de Burgh, the justiciary. The barons, especially the earl of Albemarle challenged Hubert. *Pandolf, who was restored to his legateship, was active in suppressing this rebellion; and with the concurrence of eleven bishops, he pronounced the sentence of excommunication against Albemarle and his adherents.* More disorders broke out in London and elsewhere in England.[2]

Henry's government

This prince was nowise turbulent or factious in his disposition: His ruling passion was to amass money, in which he succeeded so well as to become the richest subject in Christendom: Yet his attention to gain threw him sometimes into acts of violence, and gave disturbance to the government. --- The character of the king, as he grew to man's estate, became every day better known; and he was found in every respect

---

[2] Hume, vol 2, pp 10-15.

unqualified for maintaining a proper sway among those turbulent barons, whom the feudal constitution subjected to his authority.

Hubert, while he enjoyed his authority, had an entire ascendant over Henry, and was loaded with honors and favors beyond any other subject. Besides acquiring the property of many castles and manors, he married the eldest sister of the king of Scots, was created earl of Kent, and by an unusual concession, was made chief justiciary of England for life: Yet Henry, in a sudden caprice, threw off his faithful minister, and exposed him to the violent persecutions of his enemies. --- He constrained him soon after to surrender himself prisoner, and he confined him in the castle of the Devises. Hubert made his escape, was expelled from the kingdom, was again received into favor, recovered a great share of the king's confidence, but never showed any inclination to reinstate himself in power and authority.

The man, who succeeded him in the government of the king and kingdom, was Peter, bishop of Winchester, a Poictevin by birth. Henry invited over a great number of Poictevins and other foreigners, who, he believed, could more safely be trusted than the English, and who seemed useful to counterbalance the great and independent power of the nobility. Every office and command was bestowed on these strangers; they exhausted the revenues of the crown, already too much impoverished; they invaded the rights of the people; and their insolence, still more provoking than their power drew on them the hatred and envy of all orders of men in the kingdom.

Peter des Roches *stirred up more dissension among the barons* and *confiscated the estates of some of the more obnoxious barons.* But the primate of the church threatened Peter des Roches with excommunication. Henry submitted and the foreigners were banished. Edmund, *the primate, who was a man of prudence, and who took care to execute the laws and observe the charter of liberties, bore the chief sway in the government.*[3]

Marriage to Eleanor of Provence and French favorites

In 1236, *the king, having married Eleanor, daughter of the count of Provence, in south France, was surrounded by a great number of strangers from that country, whom he caressed with the fondest affection, and enriched by an imprudent generosity. The bishop of Valence, a prelate of the house of Savoy, and maternal uncle to the queen, was his chief minister, and employed every art to amass wealth for himself and his relations. Peter of Savoy, a brother of the same family, was invested in the honor of Richmond, and received the rich wardship of earl Warrenne: Boniface of Savoy was promoted to the see of Canterbury:*

---

[3] Ibid, pp 16-18.

Many young ladies were invited over from Provence, and married to the chief noblemen in England, who were the king's wards.[4]

For the next twenty years of Henry's reign, there continued preference for his French in-laws over the barons. Misgovernment, and disastrous foreign entanglements followed. *The resentment of the English barons rose high at the preference given to foreigners; but no remonstrance or complaint could ever prevail on the king to abandon them, or even to moderate his attachment towards them. After the Provencals and Savoyards might have been supposed pretty well satiated with the dignities and riches which they had acquired, a new set of hungry foreigners were invited over, and shared among them those favors, which the king ought in policy to have conferred to the English nobility, by whom his government could have been supported and defended.*

Wars in France

Henry declared war against Lewis IX, in 1242, and made an expedition into Guienne, upon the invitation of his father-in-law, the count de la Marche, who promised to join him with all his forces; he was unsuccessful in his attempts against that great monarch, was worsted at Taillebourg, was deserted by his allies, lost what remained to him of Poictou, and was obliged to return, with loss of honor, into England. Henry's mother, Isabella, after the death of his father John, had been betrothed to the count de la Marche but was taken by king Lewis VIII from the count. Isabella later married the count and had four children, who visited Henry in England and were given special favors by the king. *Want of economy and an ill-judged liberality were Henry's great defects; and his debts, even before this expedition, had become so troublesome, that he sold all his plate and jewels, in order to discharge them.[5]*

Henry's foreign military enterprises had been failures, beginning early in his reign with an invasion in 1224, after which only Gascony remained of the territories captured by Henry's ancestors. By 1259, by the treaty of Paris, Henry gave up claims to Normandy, Anjou, Poitou and did homage to Louis IX for Gascony.

Rome and the promise of Sicily to Henry's son

But the grievances, which the English during this reign had reason to complain of in the civil government, seem to have been still less burdensome than those which they suffered from the usurpations and exactions of the court of Rome. --- The avarice, however, more than the ambition of the see of Rome, seems to have been in this age the ground of

---

[4] Ibid, p 19.

[5] Ibid, pp 20-22.

general complaint. The papal ministers, finding a vast stock of power amassed by their predecessors, were desirous of turning it to immediate profit, which they enjoyed at home, rather than of enlarging their authority in distant countries, where they never intended to reside. Every thing was become venal in the Romish tribunals; simony was openly practiced; no favors and even no justice could be obtained without a bribe; the highest bidder was sure to have the preference, without regard either to the merits of the person or of the cause.

But the most oppressive expedient, employed by the pope, was the embarking of Henry in a project for the conquest of Naples, or Sicily on this side of the Fare, as it was called; an enterprise, which threw much dishonor on the king, and involved him, during some years, in great trouble and expense. --- Innocent *offered the crown of Sicily for the king's second son Edmund. Henry, allured by so magnificent a present, without reflecting on the consequences, without consulting either with his brother or the parliament, accepted of the insidious proposal; and gave the pope unlimited credit to expend whatever sums he thought necessary for completing the conquest of Sicily.* --- And Henry *was surprised to find himself on a sudden involved in an immense debt, which he had never been consulted in contracting. The sum already amounted to 135,541 marks beside interest; and he had the prospect, if he answered this demand, of being soon loaded with more exorbitant expenses; if he refused it, of both incurring the pope's displeasure and losing the crown of Sicily, which he hoped soon to have the glory of fixing on the head of his son. The prelate, who resided at the court in Rome drew bills of different values, amounting to 150,540 marks on all the bishops and abbots of the kingdom, but the bishops refused to submit.* --- In the end, *the bishops and abbots, being threatened with excommunication, which made all their revenues fall into the king's hands, were obliged to submit to the exaction: And the only mitigation, which the legate allowed them, was, that the tenths, already granted, should be accepted as a partial payment of the bills. Finally, Henry began to think of breaking off the agreement, and of resigning into the pope's hands that crown, which, it was not intended by Alexander, that he or his family should ever enjoy.*[6]

Favors to foreigners and parliament's reactions

Henry continued to give favors to foreigners above the English barons, who, in 1244, *demanded that the king should give them the nomination of the great justiciary and of the chancellor, to whose hands chiefly the administration of justice was committed.* --- Four years after, *in a full parliament, when Henry demanded a new supply, he was openly reproached with the breach of his word, and the frequent violations of the charter.* --- And the king, *in answer to their remonstrance, gave the*

---

[6] Ibid, pp 25-28.

parliament only good words and fair promises, attended with the most humble submissions, which they had often found deceitful, he obtained at the time no supply; and therefore, in the year 1253, which he found himself again under the necessity of applying to the parliament, he had provided a new pretense, which he deemed infallible, and taking the vow of a Crusade, he demanded their assistance in that pious enterprise. The bishops refused to comply. The king promised redress both of ecclesiastical and civil grievances, and the parliament in return agreed to grant him a supply, a tenth of the ecclesiastical benefices, and a scutage of three marks on each knight's fee. The prelates and bishops, however, joined with the king in a ceremony, and the king responded: *'So help me God, I will keep all these articles inviolate, as I am a man, as I am a Christian, as I am a knight, and as I am a king crowned and anointed.'* *Yet was the tremendous ceremony no sooner finished, than his favorites, abusing his weakness, made him return to the same arbitrary and irregular administration; and the reasonable expectations of his people were thus perpetually eluded and disappointed.* [7]

The Provisions of Oxford

On June 11, 1258 the provisions of Oxford were dictated by the barons *who brought along with them their military vassals, and appeared with an armed force, the king who had taken no precautions against them, was in reality a prisoner in their hands, and was obliged to submit to all the terms which they were pleased to impose upon him. Twelve barons were selected from among the king's ministers, twelve more were chosen by parliament: To these twenty-four, unlimited authority was granted to reform the state; and the king himself took an oath, that he would maintain whatever ordinances they should think proper to enact for that purpose. Leicester* (earl of Leicester, Simon de Mountfort) *was at the head of this supreme council, to which the legislative power was thus in reality transferred; and all their measures were taken by his secret influence and direction. --- But the twenty-four barons, not content with the usurpation of the royal power, introduced an innovation in the constitution of parliament, which was of the utmost importance. They ordained, that this assembly should choose a committee of twelve persons, who should, in the intervals of the session, possess the authority of the whole parliament, and should attend on a summons the person of the king, in all his motions. But so powerful were these barons, that this regulation was also submitted to; the whole government was overthrown or fixed on new foundations; and the monarchy was totally subverted, without its being possible for the king to strike a single stroke in defense of the constitution against the newly erected oligarchy.* [8]

---

[7] Ibid, pp 30-32.

[8] Ibid, pp 33-38.

Revolt of the barons, the earl of Leicester

In 1263 the barons revolted in support of the earl of Leicester, *the earl of Gloucester, and Henry d'Allmaine, son of the king of the Romans. Llewellyn prince of Wales, entered into a confederacy with the earl of Leicester, and collecting all the force of his principality, invaded England with an army of 30,000 men. He ravaged the lands of Roger de Mortimer and of all the barons, who adhered to the crown; he marched into Cheshire, and committed like depredations on prince Edward's territories; every place, where his disorderly troops appeared, was laid waste with fire and sword; and though Mortimer, a gallant and expert soldier, made stout resistance, it was found necessary, that the prince himself should head the army against his invader. Edward repulsed prince Lewellyn, and obliged him to take shelter in the mountains of North Wales: But he was prevented from making further progress against the enemy, by the disorders, which soon after broke out in England.*

The Welsh invasion was the appointed signal for the malcontent barons to rise in arms; and Leicester, coming over secretly from France, collected all the forces of his party, and commenced an open rebellion. --- The violence and fury of Leicester's faction had risen to such a height in all parts of England, that the king, unable to resist their power, was *obliged to set on foot a treaty of peace, and to make an accommodation with the barons on the most disadvantageous terms. He agreed to confirm anew the provisions of Oxford, even those, which entirely annihilated the royal authority; and the barons were again re-instated in the sovereignty of the kingdom. --- They here produced a new list of twenty-four barons, to whom they proposed, that the administration should be entirely committed; and they insisted, that the authority of this junto should continue, not only during the reign of the king, but also during that of prince Edward.*

Prince Edward

Prince Edward, whose liberal mind, though in such early youth, twenty-two years of age, *had taught him the great prejudice, which his father had incurred, by his levity, inconstancy, and frequent breach of promise, refused for a long time to take advantage of this absolution; and declared that the provisions of Oxford, how unreasonable soever in themselves, and how much soever abused by the barons, ought still to be adhered to by those who had sworn to observe them. He himself had been constrained by violence to take that oath; yet was he determined to keep it. By this scrupulous fidelity, the prince, acquired the confidence of all parties, and was afterwards enabled to recover fully the royal authority, and to perform such great actions both during his own reign and that of this father.*

This prince, the life and soul of the royal party, had unhappily, before the king's accommodation with the barons, been taken prisoner by Leicester in a parley at Windsor; and that misfortune more than any other incident, had determined Henry to submit to the ignominious conditions imposed upon him. But Edward, having recovered his liberty by the treaty, employed his activity in defending the prerogatives of his family; and he gained a great part even among those who had at first adhered to the cause of the barons. Many barons, especially those on the borders of Wales and Scotland supported Edward.[9]

Prince Edward attempted to resolve the differences between the king and Leicester in Paris *at a trial and examination of the position of opposing parties. It appeared to him that the provisions of Oxford, even had they not been extorted by force, had they not been so exorbitant in their nature and subversive of the ancient constitution, were expressly established as a temporary expedient, and could not without breach of trust be rendered perpetual by the barons. He therefore annulled these provisions; restored to the king the possession of his castles, and the power of nomination to the great offices; allowed him to retain what foreigners he pleased in his kingdom, and even to confer on them places of trust and dignity; and in a word, re-established the royal power in the same condition on which it stood before the meeting of the parliament at Oxford.*

Leicester, the Battle of Lewes, surrender of king Henry and prince Edward

This equitable sentence was no sooner known in England, than Leicester and his confederates determined to reject it, and to have recourse to arms, in order to procure to themselves more safe and advantageous conditions. --- The king and prince, finding a civil war inevitable, prepared themselves for defense; and summoning the military vassals from all quarters. --- Leicester, in 1264, who possessed great talents for war, conducted his march with such skill and secrecy, that he had well nigh surprised the royalists in their quarters at Lewes in Sussex. --- He defeated with great slaughter the forces headed by the king of the Romans; and that prince was obliged to yield himself prisoner to the earl of Gloucester: He penetrated to the body, where the king himself was placed, threw it into disorder, pursued his advantage, chased it into the town of Lewes, and obliged Henry to surrender himself prisoner. --- The prince was obliged to submit to Leicester's terms.

Leicester had no sooner obtained this great advantage, and gotten the whole royal family in his power, than he openly violated every article of the treaty, and acted as sole master, and even tyrant of the kingdom. He still detained the king in effect a prisoner, and made use of

---

[9] Ibid, pp 43-48.

that prince's authority to purposes the most prejudicial to his interests, and the most oppressive of his people. He everywhere disarmed the royalists, and kept all his own partisans in a military posture. He observed the same partial conduct in the deliverance of the captives, and even threw many of the royalists into prison, besides those who were taken in the battle of Lewes: He carried the king from place to place, and obliged all the royal castles, on pretense of Henry's commands, to receive a governor and garrison of his own appointment: All the officers of the crown and of the household were named by him; and the whole authority, as well as arms of the state, was lodged in his hands. Leicester seized the estates of eighteen barons, obtained for himself the ransom of the prisoners and the spoils gained from the battle of Lewes. He gave his son a monopoly of the wool trade. *Leicester summoned a parliament, composed altogether of his own partisans, in order to rivet, by their authority, that power, which he had acquired by so much violence, and which he used with so much tyranny and injustice. An ordinance was there passed, to which the king's consent had been previously extorted, that every act of royal power should be exercised by a council of nine persons, who were to be chose and removed by the majority of three, Leicester himself, the earl of Gloucester, and the bishop of Chichester. By this intricate plan of government, the scepter was really put into Leicester's hands. ---*

The pope, still adhering to the king's cause against the barons, dispatched cardinal Guido as his legate into England, with orders to excommunicate by name the three earls, Leicester, Gloucester, and Norfolk, and all others in general, who concurred in the oppression and captivity of their sovereign

Leicester summoned a new parliament in London. He included representatives, two knights from each shire, to join the barons and prelates and this action of Leicester is credited by Hume as follows: *This period is commonly esteemed the epoch of the house of commons in England; and it is certainly the first time that historians speak of any representatives sent to parliament by the boroughs. --- Leicester, having thus assembled a parliament of his own model, and trusting to the attachment of the populace of London, seized the opportunity of crushing his rival among the powerful barons. --- Even the earl of Gloucester, whose power and influence and so much contributed to the success of the barons, but who of late was extremely disgusted with Leicester's arbitrary conduct, found himself in danger from the prevailing authority of his ancient confederate; and he retired from parliament. The known dissension gave courage to all Leicester's enemies and to the king's friends; who were now sure of protection from so potent a leader.*[10]

---

[10] Ibid, p 56.

Escape of prince Edward

Prince Edward had remained in prison since the battle of Lewes, *and as he was extremely popular in the kingdom, there arose a general desire of seeing him again restored to liberty.* An agreement was made between Leicester and prince Edward, *but instead of gaining his freedom still continued a prisoner at large. The earl of Gloucester here concerted with young Edward the manner of that prince's escape. He found means to convey to him a horse of extraordinary swiftness; and appointed Roger Mortimer, who had returned into the kingdom to be ready at hand with a small party to receive the prince, and to guard him to a place of safety. Edward pretended to take the air with some of Leicester's retinue, who were his guards; and making matches between their horses, after he thought he had tired and blown them sufficiently, he suddenly mounted Gloucester's horse, and called to his attendants, that he had long enough enjoyed the pleasure of their company, and now bid them adieu. They followed him for some time, without being able to overtake him; and the appearance of Mortimer with his company put an end to their pursuit.*

Battle of Evesham, Defeat of Leicester

The royalists, secretly prepared for this event, immediately flew to arms; and the joy of this gallant prince's deliverance, the oppressions under which the nation labored, the expectation of a new scene of affairs, and the countenance of the earl of Gloucester, procured Edward an army which Leicester was utterly unable to withstand. Prince Edward's forces captured and made prisoner Leicester's son, and in the battle of Evesham, August 4, 1265, *Leicester, his eldest son Henry, Hugh le Despenser, and about one hundred and fifty knights, and many other gentlemen of his party were slain.*

The prince finding the state of the kingdom tolerably composed, was seduced, by his avidity for glory, and by the prejudices of the age, as well as by the earnest solicitations of the king of France, to undertake an expedition against the infidels in the Holy Land. --- He sailed from England with an army; and arrived in Lewis's camp before Tunis in Africa, where he found that monarch already dead, from the intemperance of the climate and the fatigues of his enterprise.

Prince Edward, not discouraged by this event, continued his voyage to the Holy Land, where he signalized himself by acts of valor: Revived the glory of the English name in those parts: And struck such terror into the Saracens, that they employed an assassin to murder him, who wounded him in the arm, but perished in the attempt. Meanwhile, his absence from England was attended with many of those pernicious consequences, which had been dreaded from it. The laws were not executed. The barons oppressed the common people with impunity. They gave shelter on their estates to bands of robbers, whom they employed in committing ravages on the estates of their enemies.The populace of London returned to their usual licentiousness.

Death of Henry III

And the old king, unequal to the burden of public affairs, called aloud for his gallant son to return, and to assist him in swaying that scepter, which was ready to drop from his feeble and irresolute hands. At last, overcome by the cares of government, and the infirmities of age, he visibly declined, and he expired, November 16, 1272, at St. Edmondsbury in the 64th year of his age, and 56th of his reign; the longest reign that is to be met with in the English annals.[11]

Summary by Hume

The most obvious circumstance of Henry's character is his incapacity of government, which rendered him as much a prisoner in the hands of his own ministers and favorites, and as little at his own disposal, as when detained a captive in the hands of his enemies. From this source, rather than from insincerity or treachery, arose his negligence in observing his promises; and he was too easily induced, for the sake of present convenience, to sacrifice the lasting advantages arising from the trust and confidence of his people. Hence too were derived his profusion to favorites, his attachment to strangers, the variableness of his conduct, his hasty resentments, and his sudden forgiveness and return of affection. Instead of reducing the dangerous power of his nobles, by obliging them to observe the laws towards their inferiors, and setting them the salutary example in his own government; he was seduced to imitate their conduct, and to make his arbitrary will, or rather that of his ministers, the rule of his actions.--- Of all men, nature seemed least to have fitted him for being a tyrant; yet are there instances of oppression in his reign, which, though derived from the precedents, left him by his predecessors, had been carefully guarded against by the Great Charter, and are inconsistent with all rules of good government. ---

Henry left two sons, Edward his successor, and Edmund earl of Lancaster; and two daughters, Margaret queen of Scotland, and Beatrix duchess of Brittany. He had five other children, who died in their infancy.[12]

---

[11] Ibid, pp 59-63.

[12] Ibid, pp 64,65.

Chapter 17

Edward I and Edward II

Edward I, (b 1239, d 1307), reigned from 1272 to 1307, and followed the tradition of the imperialist conquerors William I (1066-1087) and Henry II (1154-1189). Edward's conquest of Wales would not be completed until the reign of Henry VIII. His attempted conquest of Scotland led to the Scots alliance with France and there followed two hundred and fifty years of wars between England and these nations. English people have regarded Edward I as an English king they could be proud of. He was *hated by his neighbors, but extremely respected and revered by his own subjects.* In common with England's conquering kings, Edward I forcefully suppressed enemies from within as well as England's foreign enemies. Edward I, even more than Henry II and Richard I, enlarged England's tradition of anti-Semitism. Mass extermination of the Jewish people, confiscation of their property and banishment followed the edicts of Edward. Edward ravaged the people and ancient traditions of Scotland. Edward, as a cruel and vicious tyrant, was aptly portrayed in the movie *Brave Heart,* a drama far more interesting, even if the history is condensed and the story embellished by romance, than the written record, which we must here pursue. The preposterous myths Edward used as a claim of being the rightful king of Scotland are evidence of disordered thinking and grandiosity even remarkable for an English king. The wars in Scotland, and the stories of William Wallace and Robert Bruce are important in Edward's reign. Edward I has been hailed by legal historians as a great innovator of government and law. He began a practice of adding to the parliament of the times the lesser nobility and representatives from the boroughs to aid him in his contest with the powerful barons, said to be an early form of the house of commons. *The most important component of government remained the king himself.* The claim that he was the Justinian of English law is not correct. *But even in the most prolific period of legislation (1275-1290) there was no attempt to codify English law in the manner of a Justinian.*[1] Nevertheless, a revised version of Magna Carta was enacted. The statutes of Westminster enacted in this reign were important early laws of England.

Edward assumes the crown

As we have presented in the story of Henry III, prince Edward was popular and effective early in his career, and was able to withstand adversity of being held prisoner by the earl of Leicester, and other hardships, while gaining favor with many of the barons. *The English were as yet so little enured to obedience under a regular government, that the death of almost every king, since the conquest, had been attended with disorders; and the council, reflecting on the recent civil wars, and on the animosities which naturally remain after these great convulsions, had reason to apprehend dangerous consequences from the absence of the son and successor of Henry. They therefore hastened to proclaim prince Edward, to swear allegiance to him, and to summon the states of the kingdom, in order to provide for the public peace in this important conjuncture.* Edward was returning from the Holy Land when he heard of the death of his father Henry and the death of an infant son, whom his princess, Eleanor of Castile, had born him at Acre in Palestine. He made his journey to London through France; and was solemnly crowned at Westminster by Robert, archbishop of Canterbury, August 19, 1274.

The king immediately applied himself to the re-establishment of his kingdom, and to the correcting of those disorders, which the civil commotions and the loose administration of his father had introduced into every part of the government. The plan of his policy was equally generous and prudent. He considered the great barons both as the immediate rivals of the crown, and oppressors of the people; and he purposed, by an exact distribution of justice, and a rigid execution of the laws, to give at once protection to the inferior orders of the state, and to diminish the arbitrary power of the great, on which their dangerous authority was chiefly founded. --- Besides enacting several useful statutes, in a parliament which he summoned at Westminster, he took care to inspect the conduct of all his magistrates and judges, to displace such as were either negligent or corrupt, to provide them with sufficient force for the execution of justice, to extirpate all bands and confederacies of robbers, and repress those more silent robberies, which were committed either by the power of the nobles, or under the countenance of public authority. By this rigid administration, the face of the kingdom was soon changed; and order and justice took the place of violence and oppression: But amidst the excellent institutions and public-spirited

---

[1] Morgan, pp 135 and 139.

plans of Edward, there still appears somewhat both of the severity of his personal character and of the prejudices of the times.

Among the various disorders, to which the kingdom was subject, no one was more universally complained of than the adulteration of the coin; and as this crime required more art than the English of that age, who chiefly employed force and violence in their iniquities, were possessed of, the imputation fell upon the Jews. --- He let loose the whole rigor of his justice against that unhappy people. Two hundred and eighty of them were hanged at once for this crime in London alone, besides those who suffered in other parts of the kingdom. --- Edward, prompted by his zeal and his rapacity, resolved some time after to purge the kingdom entirely of that hated race, and to seize to himself at once their whole property as the reward of his labor. No less than fifteen thousand Jews were at this time robbed of their effects and banished from the kingdom: Very few of that nation have since lived in England.[2]

Wales

Lewellyn, prince of Wales, had reason to entertain anxiety about his situation, and to dread the future effects of resentment and jealousy in the English monarch. --- Besides the great disproportion of force between the kingdom and the principality, the circumstances of the two states were entirely reversed; and the same intestine dissensions, which had formerly weakened England, now prevailed in Wales, and had even taken place in the reigning family. David and Roderic, brothers to Lewellyn, dispossessed of their inheritance by that prince, had been obliged to have recourse to the protection of Edward, and they seconded with all their interest, which was extensive, his attempts to enslave their native country. The Welsh prince had no resource but in the inaccessible situation of his mountains, which had hitherto, through many ages, defended his forefathers against all attempts of the Saxon and Norman conquerors; and he retired among the hills of Snowdun, resolute to defend himself to the last extremity. But Edward, equally vigorous and cautious, entering by the north with a formidable army, pierced into the heart of the country; and having carefully explored every road before him, and secured every pass behind him, approached the Welsh army in its last retreat. --- Edward trusted to the slow, but sure effects of famine, for reducing that people to subjection. --- Destitute of magazines, cooped up in a narrow corner, they, as well as their cattle, suffered all the rigors of famine; and Lewellyn, without being able to strike a stroke for his independence, was at last obliged to submit at discretion, and receive the terms imposed upon him by the victor.

The English, insolent on their easy and bloodless victory, oppressed the inhabitants of the districts which were yielded to them:

---

[2] Hume, vol 2, pp 73-76.

The lords' marchers committed with impunity all kinds of violence on their Welsh neighbors: New and more severe terms were imposed on Lewellyn himself; and Edward, when the prince attended him at Worcester, exacted a promise that he would retain no person in his principality who should be obnoxious to the English monarch. There were other personal insults, which raised the indignation of the Welsh, and made them determine rather to encounter a force, which they had already experienced to be so much superior, than to bear oppression from the haughty victors. Prince David, seized with the national spirit, made peace with his brother, and promised to concur in the defense of public liberty. The Welsh flew to arms; and Edward, not displeased with the occasion of making his conquest final and absolute, assembled all his military tenants, and advanced into Wales with an army, which the inhabitants could not reasonably hope to resist. The situation of the country gave the Welsh at first some advantage over Luke de Tany, one of Edward's captains, who had passed the Menau with a detachment; But Lewellyn, being surprised by Mortimer, was defeated and slain in an action, and 2000 of his followers were put to the sword. David, who succeeded him in the principality, could never collect an army sufficient to face the English; and being chased from hill to hill, and hunted from one retreat to another, was obliged to conceal himself under various disguises, and was at last betrayed in his lurking-place to the enemy. Edward sent him in chains to Shrewsbury; and bringing him to a formal trial before all the peers of England, ordered this sovereign prince to be hanged, drawn and quartered, as a traitor, for defending by arms the liberties of his native country, together with his own hereditary authority.

All the Welsh nobility submitted to the conqueror; the laws of England, with the sheriffs and other ministers of justice, were established in that principality; and though it was long before national antipathies were extinguished, and a thorough union attained between the people, yet this important conquest, which it had required eight hundred years fully to effect, was at last, through the abilities of Edward, completed by the English, in 1284.

The principality of Wales was fully annexed to the crown; and henceforth, after Edward had appointed his son Edward, then an infant, heir of the Welsh monarchy, gives a title to the eldest son of the kings of England.[3]

Edward's claims to Scotland

During Edward's reign there would be six invasions of Scotland, but at the end of his life Scotland would remain independent. There were also wars with France during Edward's reign but it was

---

[3] Ibid, pp 78-82.

Edward III and his oldest son the Black Prince who were responsible for the devastation in France in what later was called the one hundred years war (1290-1390). England, peopled by warlike Saxons, Danes and Normans had a penchant for insane military conflicts, in civil wars and foreign conquests, which occupy most of its history.

Edward I, as soon as he had subdued Wales, turned his attention to Scotland, where he regarded himself as heir to that kingdom. Pope Boniface, exhorted Edward to put a stop to his oppressions in Scotland and regarded Edward's purported treaty with Scotland as absurd. *The reply, which Edward made to Boniface's letter, contains particulars, no less singular and remarkable. He there proves the superiority of England by historical facts, deduced from the period of Brutus, the Trojan, who, he said, founded the British monarchy in the age of Eli and Samuel: He supports his position by all the events which passed in the island before the arrival of the Romans: And after laying great stress on the extensive dominions and heroic victories of king Arthur, he vouchsafes at last to descend to the time of Edward the elder, with which, in his speech to the states of Scotland, he had chosen to begin his claim of superiority.*[4]

The king of Scotland, Alexander III, died leaving his daughter Margaret who was married to Eric, king of Norway. Their daughter Margaret was acknowledged queen of Scotland. *The English monarch was naturally led to build mighty projects on this incident; and having lately, by force of arms, brought Wales under subjection, he attempted, by the marriage of Margaret with his eldest son Edward, to unite the whole island into one monarchy, and thereby to give it security both against domestic convulsions and foreign invasions.*

Edward and the crown of Scotland, John Baliol or Robert Bruce?

But this project, so happily formed and so amicably conducted, failed of success, by the sudden death of the Norwegian princess, who expired on her passage to Scotland, and left a very dismal prospect to the kingdom. The succession of the crown was now disputed. The controversy was to be decided by Edward, whom the Scottish parliament had given the task of deciding who the rightful heir would be from a number of contenders, chief among them John Baliol and Robert Bruce. Edward, however, informed the parliament, by the mouth of his chief justiciary, *that he was come thither to determine the right among the competitors to their crown; that he was determined to do strict justice to all parties; and that he was entitled to this authority, not in virtue of the reference made to him, but in quality of superior and liege lord of the kingdom. He then produced his proofs of his superiority, which he pretended to be unquestionable, and he required of them an acknowledgment of it. --- The Scottish parliament was astonished at so*

---

[4] Ibid, p 132.

new a pretension, and answered only by their silence. But the king, in order to maintain the appearance of free and regular proceedings, desired them to remove into their own country, to deliberate upon his claim, to examine his proofs, to propose all their objections, and to inform him of their resolution: And he appointed a plain at Upsettleton, on the northern banks of the Tweed, for that purpose.

Hume commented on the methods of the king in these deliberations with supposedly inferior people: *That neglect, almost total, of truth and justice, which sovereign states discover in their transactions with each other, is an evil universal and inveterate; is one great source of the misery to which the human race is continually exposed; and it may be doubted, whether in many instances it be found in the end to contribute to the interests of those princes themselves, who thus sacrifice their integrity to their politics.*[5]

In 1293 Edward pronounced sentence in favor of Baliol. But Edward *immediately proceded in such a manner, as made it evident, that, not content with this usurpation, he aimed also at the absolute sovereignty and dominion of the kingdom. Instead of gradually enuring the Scots to the yoke, and exerting his rights of superiority with moderation, he encouraged all appeals to England; required John Baliol himself by six different summons on trivial occasions, to come to London, refused him the privilege of defending his cause by a procurator; and obliged him to appear at the bar of his parliament as a private person. These humiliating demands were hitherto quite unknown to a king of Scotland. --- But his intention plainly was, to enrage Baliol by these indignities, to engage him in rebellion, and to assume the dominion of the state as the punishment of his treason and felony. Accordingly Baliol, though a prince of a soft and gentle spirit, returned into Scotland highly provoked at this usage, and determined at all hazards to vindicate his liberty; and the war, which soon after broke out between France and England, gave him a favorable opportunity of executing his purpose.*

Wars in France

The wars in France involved primarily the province of Gascony, in southwest France, the only territory left to England after John and Henry III's losses of Henry II's acquisitions. Philip's brother *Charles commanded the French armies and left all the Gascons prisoners at discretion, of whom about fifty were hanged by Charles as rebels: A policy, by which he both intimidated that people, and produced an irreparable breach between them and the English. --- St. Severe was more vigorously defended by Hugh de Vere, son of the earl of Oxford; but was at last obliged to capitulate, The French king, not content with these successes in Gascony, threatened England with an invasion; and by*

---

[5] Ibid, pp 133 and pp 90-91.

a sudden attempt, his troops took and burnt Dover, but were obliged soon after to retire. And in order to make a greater diversion of the English force, and engage Edward in dangerous and important wars, he formed a secret alliance with John Baliol, king of Scotland; the commencement of that strict union, which, during so many centuries, was maintained, by mutual interests and necessities, between the French and Scottish nations.[6]

Scotland

Edward received intelligence of the treaty secretly concluded between John and Philip; and though uneasy at this concurrence of a French and Scottish war, he resolved not to encourage his enemies by a pusillanimous behavior, or by yielding to their united efforts. He summoned John to perform the duty of a vassal, --- He cited John to appear in an English parliament to be held at Newcastle: And when none of these successive demands were complied with, he marched northward with numerous forces, 30,000 foot, and 4000 horse, to chastise his rebellious vassal. The Scottish nobles, including Robert Bruce, realized the superiority of the English forces and *endeavored here to ingratiate themselves with Edward, and by an early submission; and the king, encouraged by this favorable incident, led his army into the enemies' country, and crossed the Tweed without opposition at Coldstream.*

There followed Edward's assault, where 7000 of the garrison at Berwic *were put to the sword,* and in the ensuing battle at Dunbar, there was great slaughter. The loss of the Scots is said to have amounted to 20,000 men: *The castle of Dunbar, with all its garrison, surrendered next day to Edward, who, after the battle, had brought up the main body of the English, and who now proceeded with an assured confidence of success.* Edward seized the stone on which all their kings were seated at Scone; *and carried it with him to England. He gave orders to destroy the records, and all those monuments of antiquity, which might reserve the memory of the independence of the kingdom, and refute the English claims of superiority. The great seal of Baliol was broken; and that prince, John Baliol himself, was carried prisoner to London, and committed to custody in the Tower. Two years after, he was restored to liberty, and submitted to a voluntary banishment in France; where, without making any farther attempts for the recovery of his royalty, he died in a private station.*[7]

---

[6] Ibid, pp 93-99.

[7] Ibid, pp 110-111.

France

In France Philip made advances into the Low Countries and advanced upon earl of Flanders. Edward raised an army of 50,000 men, *was able to stop the career of his victories; and Philip, finding all the weak resources of his kingdom already exhausted, began to dread a reverse of fortune, and to apprehend an invasion of France itself. The king of England, --- was finding many urgent calls for his presence in England, was desirous of ending on any honorable terms a war, which served only to divert his force from the execution of more important projects. This disposition in both monarchs soon produced a cessation of hostilities for two years and engaged them to submit their differences to the arbitration of pope Boniface.*

He (Boniface) *brought them to agree, that their union should be cemented by a double marriage; that of Edward himself, who was now a widower, with Margaret,* Philip's *sister, and that of the prince of Wales, with Isabella, daughter of that monarch[8].* The treaty also led to Edward abandoning the earl of Flanders while France abandoned their treaty with the Scots. *That unhappy people, now engaged in a brave, though unequal contest for their liberties, were totally abandoned by the ally, in whom they reposed their final confidence, to the will of an imperious conqueror.[9]*

William Wallace

There was one William Wallace, of a small fortune, but descended of an ancient family, in the west of Scotland, whose courage prompted him to undertake, and enabled him finally to accomplish, the desperate attempt of delivering his native country from the dominion of foreigners. This man, whose valorous exploits are the object of just admiration, but have been much exaggerated by the traditions of his countrymen, had been provoked by the insolence of an English officer to put him to death. He fled into the woods, and offered himself as a leader to all those whom their crimes, or bad fortune, or avowed hatred of the English, had reduced to a like necessity. He was endowed with gigantic force of body, with heroic courage of mind, with disinterested magnanimity, with incredible patience, and ability to bear hunger, fatigue, and all the severities of the seasons; and he soon acquired, among those desperate fugitives, that authority, to which his virtues so justly entitled him. Beginning with small attempts, in which he was always successful, he gradually proceeded to more momentous

---

[8] Note. Isabella figures large in the story of Brave Heart, and in the reign of Edward II.

[9] Ibid, pp 123-124.

enterprises; and he discovered equal caution in securing his followers, and valor in annoying the enemy. By his knowledge of the country, he was enabled, when pursued, to ensure a retreat among the morasses of forests or mountains; and again, collecting his dispersed associated, he unexpectedly appeared in another quarter, and surprised and routed and put to the sword the unwary English.

Wallace, having, by many fortunate enterprises, brought the valor of his followers to correspond to his own, resolved to strike a decisive blow against the English government; and he concentrated the plan of attacking Ormesby at Scone, and of taking vengeance on him, for all the violence and tyranny, of which he had been guilty.

But Warrenne, collecting an army of 40,000 men in the north of England, determined to re-establish his authority. --- He suddenly entered Annandale, and came up with the enemy at Irvine. --- Many of the Scottish nobles, alarmed with their dangerous situation, here submitted to the English, renewed their oaths of fealty, promised to deliver hostages for their good behavior, and receive a pardon for past offences. --- But Wallace, whose authority over his retainers was more fully confirmed by the absence of the great nobles, persevered obstinately in his purpose; and finding himself unable to give battle to the enemy, he marched northwards, with an intention of prolonging the war, and of turning to his advantage the situation of that mountainous and barren country. When Warrenne advanced to Stirling, he found Wallace encamped at Cambuskenneth, on the opposite banks of the Forth; and being continually urged by the impatient Cressingham, who was actuated both by personal and national animosities against the Scots, he prepared to attack them in that position, --- he ordered his army to pass a bridge which lay over the Forth; but he was soon convinced, by fatal experience, of the error of his conduct. Wallace, allowing such numbers of the English to pass as he thought proper, attacked them before they were fully formed, put them to rout, pushed part of them into the river, destroyed the rest by the edge of the sword, and gained a complete victory over them[10]

Wallace, universally revered as the deliverer of his country, now received, from the hands of his followers, the dignity of regent or guardian under the captive Baliol; and finding that the disorders of war, as well as the unfavorable seasons, had produced a famine in Scotland, he urged his army to march into England, to subsist at the expense of the enemy, and to revenge all past injuries, by retaliating on the hostile nation. The Scots, who deemed every thing possible under such a leader, joyfully attended his call. Wallace, breaking into the northern counties during the winter season, laid every place waste with fire and sword; and after extending on all sides, without opposition, the fury of his ravages,

---

[10] Ibid, pp 125-127.

as far as the bishopric of Durham, he returned, loaded with spoils, and crowned with glory, into his own country.

But Edward, who received in Flanders intelligence of these events, and had already concluded a truce with France, now hastened over to England, in certain hopes, by his activity and valor, not only of wiping off this disgrace, but of recovering the important conquest of Scotland, which he always regarded as the chief glory and advantage of his reign. --- He collected the whole military force of England, Wales, and Ireland; and marched with an army of nearly a hundred thousand combatants to the northern frontiers.

The elevation of Wallace, though purchased by so great merit, and such eminent services, was the object of envy to the nobility who repined to see a private gentleman raised above them by his rank and still more by his glory and reputation. Wallace himself, sensible of their jealousy, and dreading the ruin of his country from those intestine discords, voluntarily resigned his authority, and retained only the command over that body of his followers, who being accustomed to victory under his standard, refused to follow into the field any other leader. The chief power devolved on the steward of Scotland, and Cummin of Badenoch; men of eminent birth, under whom the great chieftains were more willing to serve in defense of their country. The two Scottish commanders, collecting their several forces from every quarter, fixed their station at Falkirk, and purposed there to aide the assault of the English. Wallace was at the head of a third body, which acted under his command. The Scottish army placed their pikemen along their front: Lined the intervals between the three bodies with archers: And dreading the great superiority of the English in cavalry, endeavored to secure their front by palisadoes, tied together by ropes. In this disposition, they expected the approach of the enemy.[11]

Defeat at Falkirk, meeting of Wallace and Bruce

On July 22, 1298, at Falkirk, the English defeated the Scots. *The whole Scottish army was broken, and chased off the field with great slaughter. --- In this general rout of the army, Wallace's military skill and presence of mind enabled him to keep his troops entire; and retiring behind the Carron, he marched leisurely along the banks of that small river, which protected him from the enemy. Young Bruce, who had already given many proofs of his aspiring genius, but who served hitherto in the English army, appeared on the opposite banks; and distinguishing the Scottish chief, --- called out to him, and desired a short conference. He here represented to Wallace the fruitless and ruinous enterprise in which he was engaged; and endeavored to bend his inflexible spirit to submission under superior power and superior*

---

[11] Ibid, pp 128-129.

fortune: He insisted on the unequal contest between a weak state, deprived of its head and agitated by intestine discord, and a mighty nation, conducted by the ablest and most martial monarch of the age, and possessed of every resource either for protracting the war, or for pushing it with vigor and activity: If love of his country were his motive for perseverance, his obstinacy tended only to prolong her misery. --- To these exhortations Wallace replied, that, if he had hitherto acted alone, as the champion of his country, it was solely because no second or competitor, or what he rather wished, no leader had yet appeared to place himself in that honorable station. That the blame lay entirely on the nobility, and chiefly, on Bruce himself, who uniting personal merit to dignity of family, had deserted the post, which both nature and fortune, by such powerful calls, invited him to assume.[12] ---

The gallantry of these sentiments, though delivered by an armed enemy, struck the generous mind of Bruce: The flame was conveyed from the breast of one hero to that of another: He repented of his engagements with Edward; and opening his eyes to the honorable path, pointed out to him by Wallace, secretly determined to seize the first opportunity of embracing the cause, however desperate, of his oppressed country.

Invasion and conquest of Scotland

In 1303, they chose John Cummin for their regent; and not content with maintaining their independence in the northern parts, they made incursions into the southern counties, which Edward imagined, he had totally subdued. John de Segrave, whom he had left guardian of Scotland, led an army to oppose them; and lying at Roslin near Edinbugh, went out his forces in three divisions, to provide themselves with forage and subsistence from the neighborhood. One party was suddenly attacked by the regent and Sir Simon Fraser; and being unprepared, was immediately routed and pursued with great slaughter. It became necessary for Edward to begin anew the conquest of the kingdom. ---

The king prepared himself for this enterprise with his usual vigor and abilities. He assembled both a great fleet and a great army; and entering the frontiers of Scotland, appeared with a force, which the enemy could not think of resisting in the open field: The English navy, which sailed along the coast, secured the army from any danger of famine: Edward's vigilance preserved it from surprises: And by this prudent disposition they marched victorious from one extremity of the kingdom to the other, ravaging the open country, reducing all the castles, and receiving the submissions of all the nobility, even those of Cummin the regent.

---

[12] Ibid, pp 130-132.

Edward, having completed his conquest, in 1304, which employed him during the during the space of near two years, now undertook the more difficult work of settling the country, of establishing a new form of government, and of making his acquisition durable to the crown of England. He seems to have carried matters to extremity against the natives: He abrogated all the Scottish laws and customs: he endeavored to substitute the English in their place: he entirely razed or destroyed all the monuments of antiquity: Such records or histories as had escaped his former search were now burnt or dispersed: And he hastened, by too precipitate steps, to abolish entirely the Scottish name, and to sink it finally in the English.

Execution of Wallace

Edward, however, still deemed his favorite conquest exposed to some danger, so long as Wallace was alive; and being prompted both by revenge and policy, he employed every art to discover his retreat, and become master of his person. At last, that hardy warrior, who was determined, amidst the universal slavery of his countrymen, still to maintain his independency, was betrayed into Edward's hands by Sir John Monteith, his friend, whom he had made acquaintance with the place of his concealment. The king, whose natural bravery and magnanimity should have induced him to respect like qualities in an enemy, enraged at some acts of violence committed by Wallace during the fury of war, resolved to overawe the Scots by an example of severity: He ordered Wallace to be carried in chains to London; to be tried as a rebel and traitor, though he had never made submissions or sworn fealty to England; and to be executed on Tower-hill. This was the unworthy fate of a hero, who through a course of many years, had, with signal conduct, intrepidity, and perseverance, defended, against a public and oppressive enemy, the liberties of his native country.[13]   Wallace was executed August 23, 1305.

Robert Bruce

But the barbarous policy of Edward failed of the purpose to which it was directed. The Scots, already disgusted at the great innovations introduced by the sword of a conqueror into their laws and government, were further enraged at the injustice and cruelty exercised upon Wallace; and all the envy, which during his lifetime, had attended that gallant chief, being now buried in his grave, he was universally regarded as the champion of Scotland, and the patron of her expiring independency. The people, inflamed with resentment, were every where disposed to rise against the English government, and it was not long ere a new and more fortunate leader presented himself, who conducted them

---

[13] Ibid, pp 133-135.

to liberty, to victory, and to vengeance. Robert Bruce, who became king of Scotland, 1306-1329, *grandson of that Robert, who had been one of the competitors for the crown, had succeeded, by his grandfather's and father's death, to all their rights; and the demise of John Baliol, together with the captivity of Edward, eldest son of that prince, seemed to open a full career to the genius and ambition of this young nobleman. Bruce therefore hoped, that the Scots, so long exposed, from the want of a leader, to the oppression of their enemies, would unanimously fly to his standard, and would seat him on the vacant throne, to which he brought such plausible pretensions.*

After Bruce had been betrayed by John Cummin, and found his escape, he arrived at Dumfries, in south Scotland, where he found a number of the Scottish nobility there assembled, February 10, 1306. *The noblemen were astonished at the appearance of Bruce among them; and still more when he discovered to them the object of his journey. He told them, that he was come to live or die with them in defense of the liberties of his country, and hoped, with their assistance, to redeem the Scottish name from all the indignities, which it had so long suffered from the tyranny of their imperious masters: That the sacrifice of the rights of his family was the first injury, which had prepared the way for their ensuing slavery; and by resuming them, which was his firm purpose, he opened to them the joyful prospect of recovering from the fraudulent usurper their ancient and hereditary independence. --- The Scottish nobles declared their unanimous resolution to use the utmost efforts in delivering their country from bondage, and to second the courage of Bruce, in asserting his and their undoubted rights, against their common oppressors. Robert Bruce was crowned and inaugurated in the abbey of Scone by the bishop of St. Andrews, who had zealously embraced his cause.*[14]

Death of Edward I

On July 7, 1307, Edward suddenly expired. *Edward, vowing revenge on the whole Scottish nation, whom he deemed incorrigible in their aversion to his government, assembled a great army, and was preparing to enter the frontiers, secure of success, and determined to make the defenseless Scots the victims of his severity; when he unexpectedly sickened and died near Carlisle; enjoining with his last breath his son and successor to prosecute the enterprise, and never to desist till he had finally subdued the kingdom of Scotland. He expired in the sixty-ninth year of his age, and the thirty-fifth of his reign, hated by his neighbors, but extremely respected and revered by his own subjects. ---- Edward had by his first wife, Eleanor of Castile, four sons, but Edward, his heir and successor, was the only one that survived him.*[15]

---

[14] Ibid, pp 136-138.

[15] Ibid, pp 137-140, and 146.

The king's hopes for his son were not realized, nor would this be the end of the story of Robert Bruce.

Edward II

Edward, (b 1284, d 1327), was unsuited to rule (1307-1327). Scotland would be victorious over his forces and remain independent. *This prince was in the twenty-third year of his age, was of an agreeable figure, of a mild and gentle disposition, and having never discovered a propensity to any dangerous vice, it was natural to prognosticate tranquility and happiness from his government. But the first act of his reign blasted all these hopes, and showed him to be totally unqualified for that perilous situation, in which every English monarch, during those ages, had, from the unstable form of the constitution, and the turbulent disposition of the people, derived from it, the misfortune to be placed.*

Robert Bruce

The indefatigable Robert Bruce, though his army had been dispersed and he himself had been obliged to take shelter in the western isles, remained not long inactive; but before the death of the late king, had sallied from his retreat, had again collected his followers, had appeared in the field, and had obtained by surprise an important advantage over Aymer de Valence, who commanded the English forces. He was now become so considerable as to have afforded the king of England sufficient glory in subduing him, without incurring any danger of seeing all those mighty preparations, made by his father, fail in the enterprise. But Edward, instead of pursuing his advantages, marched but a little way into Scotland; and having an utter incapacity, and equal aversion, for all application or serious business, he immediately returned upon his footsteps, and disbanded his army. His grandees perceived from this conduct, that the authority of the crown, fallen into such feeble hands, was no longer to be dreaded, and that every insolence might be practiced by them with impunity.[16] ---

Edward *assembled forces from all quarters, with a view of finishing at one blow this important enterprise --- and assembling the whole military force of England, he marched to the frontiers with an army, which, according to the Scotch writers, amounted to a hundred thousand men.*

The victory of the Scots at Bannockburn

The army, collected by Robert, exceeded not thirty thousand combatants; but being composed of men who had distinguished themselves by many acts of valor, who were rendered desperate by their

---

[16] Ibid, p 147.

situation, and who were enured to all the varieties of fortune, they might justly, under such a leader, be deemed formidable to the most numerous and best appointed armies. The castle of Stirling, which, with Berwic, was the fortress in Scotland, that remained in the hands of the English, had long been besieged by Edward Bruce. --- Robert posted himself at Bannockburn, about two miles from Stirling; where he had a hill on his right flank, and a morass on his left: And not content with having taken these precautions to prevent his being surrounded by the more numerous army of the English; he foresaw the superior strength of the enemy in cavalry, and made provision against it. Having a rivulet in front, he commanded deep pits to be dug along its banks, and sharp stakes to be planted in them; and he ordered the whole to be carefully covered over with turf.

The English arrived in sight on the evening, and a bloody conflict immediately ensured between two bodies of cavalry. --- Early in the morning, Edward drew out his army, and advanced towards the Scots. The earl of Gloucester, his nephew, who commanded the left wing of the cavalry, impelled by the ardor of youth, rushed on the attack without precaution, and fell among the covered pits, which had been prepared by Bruce for the reception of the enemy. This body of horse was disordered: Gloucester himself was overthrown and slain. --- While the English army was alarmed with this unfortunate beginning of the action, which commonly proves decisive, they observed an army on the heights toward the left, which seemed to be marching leisurely in order to surround them; and they were distracted by their multiplied fears. This was a number of waggoners and sumpter boys, whom Robert had collected; and having supplied them with military standards, gave them the appearance at a distance of a formidable body. The stratagem took effect: A panic seized the English: They threw down their arms and fled: They were pursued with great slaughter, for the space of ninety miles, till they reached Berwic: And the Scots, besides an inestimable booty, took many persons of quality prisoners, and above 400 gentlemen, whom Robert treated with great humanity, and whose ransom was a new accession of wealth to the victorious army. The king himself narrowly escaped, by taking shelter in Dunbar.[17]

Such was the great and decisive battle of Bannockburn, which secured the independence of Scotland, fixed Bruce on the throne of that kingdom, and may be deemed the greatest overthrow that the English nation, since the conquest, has ever received. --- Robert, in order to avail himself of his present success, entered England, and ravaged all the northern counties without opposition: He besieged Carlisle; but that place was saved by the valor of Sir Andrew Harcla, the governor: He was more successful against Berwic, which he took by assault: And this

---

[17] Ibid, p 157.

prince, elated by his continued prosperity, now entertained hopes for making the most important conquests of the English. He sent over his brother Edward, with an army of 600 men, into Ireland; and that nobleman assumed the title of King of that island: He himself followed soon after with more numerous forces: The horrible and absurd oppressions, which the Irish suffered under the English government, made them, at first fly to the standard of the Scots, whom they regarded as their deliverers: But a grievous famine, which at that time desolated both Ireland and Britain, reduced the Scottish army to the greatest extremities; and Robert was obliged to return, with his forces much diminished, into his own country. His brother, after having experienced a variety of fortune, was defeated and slain near Dundalk by the English, commanded by lord Bermingham.[18]

Favorites of the King, revolt of the barons, civil war

Edward would developed relations with the French gentry, chief among them Piers Gavaston, whose close relationship and favors would enrage the powerful barons. *There was one Piers Gavaston, son of a Gascon knight of some distinction, who had honorably served the late king, and who, in reward of his merits, had obtained an establishment for his son in the family of the prince of Wales. --- He gained an ascendant over young Edward, whose heart was strongly disposed to friendship and confidence, that the late king, apprehensive of the consequences, had banished him the kingdom, and had, before he died, made his son promise never to recall him. But no sooner did he find himself master, as he vainly imagined, than he sent for Gavaston; and even before his arrival at court, endowed him with the whole earldom of Cornwall which had escheated to the crown. --- He daily loaded him with new honors and riches; married him to his own niece, sister of the earl of Gloucester; and seemed to enjoy no pleasure in his royal dignity, but as it enabled him to exalt to the highest splendor this object of his fond affections. Gavaston displayed his power and influence with the utmost ostentation; and deemed no circumstance of his good fortune so agreeable as its enabling him to eclipse and mortify all his rivals. He was vain-glorious, profuse, rapacious; fond of exterior pomp and appearance, giddy with prosperity; and as he imagined, that his fortune was now as strongly rooted in the kingdom, as his ascendant was uncontrolled over the weak monarch, he was negligent in engaging partisans, who might support his sudden and ill-established grandeur. At all tournaments, he took delight in foiling the English nobility, by his superior address: In every conversation, he made them the object of his wit and raillery: every day his enemies multiplied upon him; and naught was wanting but a little time to cement their union, and render it fatal, both to him and to his master.*

---

[18] Ibid, pp 158-159.

It behooved the king to take a journey to France, both in order to do homage for the duchy of Guienne, and to espouse the princess Isabella, to whom he had long been affianced, though unexpected accidents had hitherto retarded the completion of the marriage. Edward left Gavaston guardian of the realm, with more ample powers, than had usually been conferred; and on his return with his young queen, renewed all the proofs of that fond attachment to the favorite, of which every one so loudly complained.

Gavaston was expelled by the action among the barons to which Edward submitted and was appointed governor of Ireland. Edward received from the pope a dispensation from the oath Edward had taken to banish Gavaston. Edward *went down to Chester, to receive him* (Gavaston) *on his first landing from Ireland; flew into his arms with transports of joy; and having obtained the formal consent of the barons in parliament to his re-establishment, set no longer any bounds to his extravagant fondness and affection. Gavaston himself, forgetting his past misfortunes, and blind to their causes, resumed the same ostentation and insolence; and became more than ever the object of general detestation among the nobility.* The conflicts between the barons and the king over Gavaston finally led to Gavaston's murder in 1312. *And without any regard, either to the laws or the military capitulation, they,* the earls of Lancaster, Hereford, and Arundel, *ordered the head of the obnoxious favorite to be struck off, by the hands of the executioner.*[19]

The king's new favorite

The king's chief favorite, after the death of Gavaston, was Hugh le Despeser or Spenser, a young man of English birth, of high rank, and of a noble family. He possessed all the exterior accomplishments of person and address, which were fitted to engage the weak mind of Edward; but was destitute of that moderation and prudence, which might have qualified him to mitigate the envy of the great. Spenser persuaded the king to confer the barony of Gower on him, which precipitated a civil war. The earls of Lancaster and Hereford, supported by the Roger de Mortimer and others, gathered a formidable army and demanded that the king dismiss or confine Spenser. They seized the lands of Spenser, murdered his servants and burned his houses, then marching to London with all their forces. The king rallied and hastened with his army to the marches of Wales, the chief seat of the power of his enemies, whom he found totally unprepared for resistance. Many of the barons in those parts endeavored to appease him by submission. Their castles were seized, and their persons committed to custody. But Lancaster, in order to prevent the total ruin of his party, summoned together his vassals and retainers; declared his alliance with Scotland, which had long been suspected. The

---

[19] Ibid, pp 148, 149, and 154.

king collected an army of 30,000 and defeated Lancaster and his allies. Lancaster was executed March 23, 1322. *In those violent times, the laws were so much neglected on both sides, that, even where they might, without any sensible inconvenience, have been observed, the conquerors deemed it unnecessary to pay any regard to them. Lancaster, who was guilty of open rebellion, and was taken in arms against his sovereign, instead of being tried by the laws of his country, which pronounced the sentence of death against him, was condemned by a court-martial.[20]*

Queen Isabella

If Edward had problems with the powerful barons regarding his favorites, the queen would finally end the reign of king Edward. Isabella proposed, *that Edward should resign the dominion of Guienne to his son, now thirteen years of age; and that the prince should come to Paris, and do the homage which every vassal owed to his superior lord. This expedient, which seemed so happily to remove all difficulties, was immediately embraced: Spenser was charmed with the contrivance: young Edward was sent to Paris: And the ruin, covered under this fatal snare, was never perceived or suspected, by any of the English council.*

The queen, on her arrival in France, had there found a great number of English fugitives, the remains of the Lancastrian faction; and their common hatred of Spenser soon begat a secret friendship and correspondence between them and that princess. Among the rest was young Roger Mortimer, a potent baron in the Welsh marches, who had been obliged, with others, to make his submissions to the king, had been condemned for high treason; but having received a pardon for his life, was afterwards detained in the Tower, with an intention of rendering his confinement perpetual. He was so fortunate as to make his escape into France; and being one of the most considerable persons now remaining of the party, as well as distinguished by his violent animosity against Spenser, he was easily admitted to pay his court to queen Isabella. The graces of his person and address advanced him quickly in her affections: He became her confident and counselor in all her measures: And gaining ground daily upon her heart, he engaged her to sacrifice at last, to her passion, all the sentiments of honor and of fidelity to her husband.[21]

Edward II, deposed

The queen's conspiracies with Roger Mortimer and the king's enemies led to an invasion, led by the queen's brother, of 3000 men who *set sail from the harbor of Dort, and landed safely, and without opposition, on the coast of Suffolk. The earl of Kent was in her company:*

---

[20] Ibid, pp 160-164.

[21] Ibid, p 167.

Two other princes of the blood, the earl of Norfolk and the earl of Leicester, joined her soon after her landing with all their followers: The prelates, the bishops of Ely, Lincoln, and Hereford, brought her both the force of their vassals and the authority of their character. A popular revolt and uprising against the king followed and Edward was pursued, and was discovered in the mountains of Wales, and placed under arrest.

The queen, to avail herself of the prevailing delusion, summoned, in the king's name, a parliament at Westminster; where, together with the power of her army, and the authority of her partisans among the barons, who were concerned to secure their past treasons by committing new acts of violence against their sovereign, she expected to be seconded by the fury of the populace, the most dangerous of all instruments, and the least answerable for their excesses. A charge was drawn up against the king. --- He was accused of incapacity for government, of wasting his time in idle amusements, of neglecting public business, of being swayed by evil counselors, of having lost, by his misconduct, the kingdom of Scotland, and part of Guienne; and to swell the charge, even the death of some barons, and the imprisonment of some prelates, convicted of treason, were laid to his account. It was in vain, amidst the violence of arms and tumult of the people, to appeal either to law or to reason: The deposition of the king, without any appearing opposition, was voted by parliament, January 13, 1327: the prince, already declared regent by his party, was placed on the throne: And a deputation was sent to Edward at Kenilworth, to require his resignation, which menaces and terror soon extorted from him.

Edward II, murdered

The king, therefore was taken from his hands, and delivered over to lord Berkeley, and Mautravers, and Gournay, who were entrusted alternately, each for a month, with the charge of guarding him. While he was in the custody of Berkeley, he was still treated with the gentleness due to his rank and his misfortunes; but when the turn of Mautravers and Bournay came, every species of indignity was practiced against him, as if their intention had been to break entirely the prince's spirit. --- But as this method of laying Edward in his grave appeared still too slow to the impatient Mortimer, he secretly sent orders to the two keepers, who were at this devotion, instantly to dispatch him; and these ruffians contrived to make the manner of his death as cruel and barbarous as possible. Taking advantage of Berkeley's sickness, in whose custody he then was, and who was thereby incapacitated from attending his charge; they came to Berkeley castle, and put themselves in possession of the king's person. They threw him on a bed; held him down violently with a table, which they flung over him; thrust into his fundament a red-hot iron, which they inserted through a horn; and though the outward marks of violence upon his person were prevented by this expedient, the horrid deed was discovered to all the guards and attendants by the screams, with which the agonizing king filled the castle, while his bowels were consuming. Edward II died September 21, 1327.[22] He reigned for 20 years.

This king left four children, two sons and two daughters: Edward, his eldest son and successor; John, created afterwards earl of Cornwall, who died young at Perth; Jane, afterward married to David Bruce, king of Scotland; and Eleanor, married to Reginald, count of Gueldres.[23]

---

[22] Ibid, pp 171-172.

[23] Ibid, pp 180. 181.

Chapter 18

Edward III

Edward III, (b. 1312, d. 1377) was king of England from 1330 to 1377. Edward III followed the military and imperialistic tradition of his grandfather, Edward I. He renewed wars with Scotland and tried unsuccessfully to place Edward Baliol on the throne of Scotland. Edward claimed the crown of France in 1328 and started the hundred years war between England and France. Edward and his son the Black Prince defeated the French at Crecy and Poitiers in 1346 and 1356. The capture of Calais in 1347 and population by English settlers established a foothold for commerce and future invasions of France. His foreign military exploits bankrupted the royal treasury. The black plague in 1348, 1362 and 1369 led to loss of a third of the population and economic distress. The excessive taxation imposed on the nobles led to their final contest with the king. During the last fifteen years of his reign he suffered mental impairment. His most important legacy became the civil disturbances and wars among his descendants, the York Lancaster factions, during the reigns from Richard II to Henry VII. He declared upon the death of his eldest son Prince Edward in 1376, that his successor would be his grandson, Richard II, son of prince Edward, rather than John of Gaunt, duke of Lancaster.[1]

Invasions of Scotland

In 1327, Edward, the oldest son of Edward II, was only fifteen years old when his father was murdered. His French mother Isabella had invaded England and deposed Edward II. Edward was under the authority of Roger Mortimer and his mother Isabella. Isabella and Roger Mortimer assumed control of England, at least until 1330. But as early as 1327,

---

[1] Father of Henry IV.

Edward demonstrated his penchant for military conquest. *Young Edward, himself, burning with a passion for military fame, appeared at the head of these numerous forces; and marched from Durham, the appointed place of rendezvous, in quest of the enemy, who had already broken into the frontiers, and were laying everything waste around them.* But the Scottish forces, under the command of Murray and Douglas, nearly captured king Edward and were able to retreat from superior English forces. *The king was highly incensed at the disappointment, which he had met with, in his first enterprise, and at the head of so gallant an army. The symptoms, which he had discovered of bravery and spirit, gave extreme satisfaction, and were regarded as a sure prognostic of an illustrious reign: But the general displeasure fell violently on Mortimer, who was already the object of public odium: And every measure, which he pursued, tended to aggravate, beyond all bounds, the hatred of the nation both against him and queen Isabella.[2]*

Mortimer negotiated a peace with Robert Bruce with great disfavor among the barons. Mortimer, in order to intimidate the prince, determined to have a victim, the earl of Kent who was implicated in the murder of Edward II. *The earl was seized by Mortimer, was accused before the parliament, and condemned by those slavish, though turbulent barons, to lose his life and fortune. The queen and Mortimer, apprehensive of young Edward's lenity towards his uncle, hurried on the execution and the prisoner was beheaded the next day. But Edward, now in his eighteenth year, and feeling himself capable of governing, repined at being held in fetters by this insolent minister. --- A parliament was immediately summoned for his condemnation.* Mortimer was accused of many acts of conspiracy, and of crimes and misdemeanors. *The parliament condemned him from the supposed notoriety of the facts, without trial, or hearing his answer, or examining a witness; and he was hanged on a gibbet at the Elmes, in the neighborhood of London. It is remarkable, that this sentence was near twenty years after reversed by parliament, in favor of Mortimer's son; and the reason assigned was the illegal manner of proceeding.[3]*

Death of Robert Bruce, wars in Scotland

The wise and valiant Robert Bruce, who had recovered by arms the independence of his country, and had fixed it by the last treaty of peace with England, soon after died, and left David his son, a minor, under the guardianship of Randolf, earl of Murray, the companion of all his victories. King Edward, in the interval, secretly encouraged Baliol, who had contested with Bruce the leadership of the Scots, *connived at his*

---

[2] Hume, vol 2, pp 183-186.

[3] Ibid, pp 188-189.

assembling forces in the north; and gave countenance to the nobles, who were disposed to join in the attempt. A force of near 2,500 men was enlisted under Baliol. Lord Douglas had died in Spain during a crusade and the *earl of Murray, who had long been declining through age and infirmities, had lately died and had been succeeded in the regency by Donald earl of Marre, a man of much inferior talents. The military spirit of the Scots, though still unbroken, was left without a proper guidance and direction. The English defeated the Scots in the battle at Perth, Sept. 27, 1333. But Baliol's imprudence of his necessities making him dismiss the greater part of his English followers, he was, notwithstanding the truce, attacked of a sudden near Annan by Sir Archibald Douglas, and other chieftains of the party; he was routed; his brother John Baliol was slain; he himself was chased into England in a miserable condition; and thus lost his kingdom by a revolution as sudden as that by which he had acquired it.*[4]

Edward, ambitious of recovering that important concession made by Mortimer during his minority, threw off all scruples, and willingly accepted the offer; but as the dethroning of Baliol had rendered this stipulation of no effect, the king prepared to re-instate him in possession of the crown; an enterprise, which appeared from late experience so easy and so little hazardous. The English army was less numerous, but better supplied with arms and provisions, and retained in stricter discipline; and the king, notwithstanding the valiant defense made by Keith, had in two months reduced the garrison to extremities, and had obliged them to capitulate. The Scots were routed by the English, at Berwic, July 19, 1334.

Scots reject Baliol

If Baliol, on his first appearance, was dreaded by the Scots, as an instrument employed by England for the subjection of the kingdom, this deed confirmed all their suspicions, and rendered him the object of universal hatred. Whatever submissions they might be obliged to make, they considered him, not as their prince, but as the delegate and confederate of their determined enemy: And neither the manners of the age, nor the state of Edward's revenue permitted him to maintain a standing army in Scotland. The English forces were no sooner withdrawn, than the Scots revolted from Baliol, and returned to their former allegiance under Bruce. Sir Andrew Murray, appointed regent by the party of this latter prince, employed with success his valor and activity in many small but decisive actions against Baliol; and in a short time had almost wholly expelled him from the kingdom. Edward was obliged again to assemble an army and to march into Scotland: The Scots, taught by experience, withdrew into their hills and fastnesses: He

---

[4] Ibid, pp 191-194.

destroyed the houses and ravaged the estates of those whom he called rebels: But this confirmed them still farther in their obstinate antipathy to England and to Baliol; and being now rendered desperate they were ready to take advantage, on the first opportunity, of the retreat of their enemy, and they soon re-conquered their country for the English. Edward made anew his appearance in Scotland with like success: He found everything hostile in the kingdom, except the spot on which he was encamped: And though he marched uncontrolled over the Low Countries, the nation itself was farther than ever from being broken and subdued. Besides being supported by their pride and their calamities, by daily promises of relief from France; and as a war was now likely to break out between that kingdom and England, they had reason to expect from this incident a great diversion of that force, which had so long oppressed and overwhelmed them. [5]

Edward's claim to the crown of France

The one hundred years wars with France had their origin in Edward III's grandiose pretensions to the crown of France, which came to Edward when he was fifteen years old. Edward claimed that, since his mother Queen Isabella was the daughter of king Phillip of France, he was the true heir of the French crown. No one of any credibility seemed to regard this claim seriously inasmuch as *the last three French kings all left daughters, who were still alive, and who stood before him in the order of succession.* Moreover, the French had a well established precedent, whether rational or sensible or not, *that the crown had for nine hundred years, and for eleven generations had descended from father to son, and that no female and none who founded his title on a female had ever mounted the throne.*[6]

The remainder of Edward III's reign involved the peculiar intrigues and machinations of this king to foster his ambition to conquer and rule France. Edward enlisted the support of some of the dukes and counts in Germany and France and gained the support of the Flemmings, in the northern parts of Europe. The leader of the Flemmings *was James D'Areville, a brewer in Ghent, who governed them with a more absolute sway than had ever been assumed by any of their lawful sovereigns: He placed and displaced the magistrates at pleasure: He was accompanied by a guard, who, on the least signal from him, instantly assassinated any man that happened to fall under his displeasure: All the cities of Flanders were full of his spies; and it was immediate death to give him the smallest umbrage: The few nobles, who remained in the country, lived in continual terror for his violence: he seized the estates of all those*

---

[5] Ibid, pp 195-196.

[6] Ibid, pp 197-198.

*whom he had either banished or murdered; and bestowing a part on their
wives and children, converted the remainder to his own use.*

*Edward, by the advice of D'Arteville, in 1338, assumed, in his
commissions, the title of king of France, and, in virtue of this right
claimed their assistance for dethroning king Philip de Valois, the usurper
of his kingdom. --- From this period we may date the commencement of
that great animosity, which the English nation have ever since born to
the French, which has so visible an influence on all future transactions,
and which has been and continues to be the spring of many rash and
precipitate resolutions among them.[7] --- The English nobility and gentry
valued themselves on their French and Norman extraction: They affected
to employ the language of that country in all public transactions, and
even in familiar conversation: And both the English court and camp
being always full of nobles, who came from different provinces of
France, the two people were, during some centuries, more intermingled
together than any two distinct nations, whom we meet with in history. But
the fatal pretensions of Edward III dissolved all these connections, and
left the seeds of great animosity in both countries, especially among the
English.[8]*

War with France

Edward's first attempt to conquer France, in 1338, ended in
failure. *The king, however, entered the enemy's country, and encamped
on the fields of Vironfosse near Capelle, with an army of near 50,000
men, composed almost entirely of foreigners: Philip approached him
with an army of near double the force, composed chiefly of native
subjects; and it was daily expected that a battle would ensue. But the
English monarch was averse to engage against so great a superiority:
The French thought it sufficient if he eluded the attacks of his enemy,
without running any unnecessary hazard. The two armies faced each
other for some days: Mutual defiances were sent: And Edward, at last,
retired into Flanders, and disbanded his army.*

*Such was the fruitless and almost rediculous conclusion of
Edward's mighty preparations; and as his measures were the most
prudent, that could be embraced in his situation, he might learn from
experience in what a hopeless enterprise he was engaged. His expenses,
though they had led to no end, had been consuming and destructive: He
had contracted near 300,000 pounds of debt; he had anticipated all his
revenue; he had pawned every thing of value, which belonged to himself
or his queen; he was obliged in some measure even to pawn himself to*

---

[7] Note. All English kings since Edward III, relying on Edward's ill-founded
precedent, have claimed the crown of France, at least until 1801.

[8] Ibid, pp 200-203.

his creditors, by not sailing to England, till he obtained their permission, and by promising on his word of honor to return in person, if he did not remit their money.

Naval Victory

In 1340, Edward successfully engaged the French in a great naval battle above Flanders. *The battle was fierce and bloody: The English archers, whose force and address were now much celebrated, galled the French on their approach: And when the ships grappled together, and the contest became more steady and furious, the example of the king, and of so many gallant nobles, who accompanied him, animated to such a degree the seamen and soldiery, that they maintained every where a superiority over the enemy. The French also had been guilty of some imprudence in taking their station so near the coast of Flanders, and choosing that place for the scene of action. The Flemings, descrying the battle, hurried out of their harbors, and brought a reinforcement to the English; which, coming unexpectedly, had a greater effect than in proportion to its power and numbers. Two hundred and thirty French ships were taken: Thirty thousand Frenchmen were killed, with two of their admirals: The loss of the English was inconsiderable, compared to the greatness and importance of the victory.*

Invasion of France

The luster of this great success increased the king's authority among his allies, who assembled their forces with expedition, and joined the English army. Edward marched to the frontiers of France at the head of above 100,000 men, consisting chiefly of foreigners, a more numerous army than, either before or since has ever been commanded by any king of England. The king of France had assembled an army more numerous than the English; was accompanied by all the chief nobility of his kingdom; was attended by many foreign princes, and even by three monarchs, the kings of Bohemia, Scotland, and Navarre. The siege of Tournay, in Flanders, continued for ten weeks. --- Edward, irritated with the small progress he had hitherto made, and with the disagreeable prospect that lay before him, sent Philip a defiance by a herald; and challenged him to decide their claims for the crown of France, either by single combat, or by an action of a hundred against a hundred, or by a general engagement. A truce was concluded, which left both parties in possession of their present acquisitions and stopped all farther hostilities on the side of the Low Countries, Guiennne, and Scotland, till Midsummer next. A negotiation was soon after opened at Arrars, under the mediation of the pope's legates; and the truce was attempted to be converted into a solid peace. --- Edward himself, harassed by his numerous and importunate creditors, was obliged to make his escape by stealth into England.[9]

Domestic disturbances

Edward now found himself in a bad situation both with his own people and with foreign states; and it required all his genius and capacity to extricate himself from such multiplied difficulties and embarrassments. His unjust and exorbitant claims on France and Scotland had engaged him in an implacable war with these two kingdoms, his nearest neighbors: He had lost almost all his foreign alliances by his irregular payments: he was deeply involved in debts, for which he owed a consuming interest: His military operations had vanished into smoke; and except his naval victory, none of them had been attended even with glory or renown, either to himself or to the nation: The animosity between him and the clergy was open and declared: The people were discontented on account of many arbitrary measures, in which he had been engaged: And what was more dangerous, the nobility, taking advantage of this present necessities, were determined to retrench his power, and by encroaching on the ancient prerogatives of the crown, to acquire to themselves independence and authority.[10]

Continued wars with France

Another conflict in 1343 was averted by the mediation of the pope's legates. In 1346 *Edward invaded Normandy with a large force and in the ensuing months after destroying the ships in la Hogue, Barfleur, and Cherbourg he spread his army over the whole country, and gave them an unbounded license of burning, spoiling and plundering every place, of which they became masters. --- The intelligence of this unexpected invasion soon reached Paris; and threw Philip into great perplexity. He issued orders, however, for levying forces in all quarters, and dispatched the count of Eu, constable of France, and the count of Trancarville, with a body of troops, to the defense of Caen, a populous and commercial but open city, which lay in the neighborhood of the English Army. --- The counts of Eu and Tancarville were taken prisoners: The victors entered the city along with the vanquished, and a furious massacre commenced without distinction of age, sex, or condition. The citizens, in despair, barricaded their houses, and assaulted the English with stones, bricks, and every missile weapon: The English made way by fire to the destruction of the citizens: Till Edward, anxious to save both his spoil and his soldiers, stopped the massacre; and having obliged the inhabitants to lay down their arms, gave his*

---

[9] Ibid, pp208-210.

[10] Ibid, p 214.

troops license to begin a more regular and less hazardous plunder of the city. The pillage continued for three days: The king reserved for his own share the jewels, plate, silks, fine cloth, and fine linen; and he bestowed all the remainder of the spoil on his army. The whole was embarked on board the ships, and went over to England; together with three hundred of the richest citizens of Caen, whose ransom was an additional profit, which he expected afterwards to levy. This dismal scene passed in the presence of two cardinal legates, who had come to negotiate a peace between the kingdoms.

The king moved next to Rouen in hopes of treating that city in the same manner; but found, that the bridge over the Seine was already broken down, and that the king of France himself was arrived there with his army. He marched along the banks of that river towards Paris, destroying the whole country, and every town and village, which he met with on his road. Some of his light troops carried their ravages even to the gates of Paris; and the royal palace of St. Germans, together with Nanterre, Ruelle, and other villages, was reduced to ashes within sight of the capital.

Battle of Crecy and prince Edward

This battle, which is known by the name of the battle of Crecy, August 25, 1346, began after three o'clock in the afternoon, and continued till evening. The next morning was foggy; and as the English observed that many of the enemy had lost their way in the night and in the mist, they employed a stratagem to bring them into their power: They erected on the eminences some French standards which they had taken in the battle; and all, who were allured by this false signal were put to the sword, and no quarter given them. In excuse for this inhumanity, it was alleged that the French king had given like orders to his troops; but the real reason probably was, that the English, in their present situation, did not choose to be encumbered with prisoners. On the day of battle, and on the ensuing, there fell, by a moderate computation, 1200 French knights, 1400 gentlemen, 4000 men at arms, besides about 30,000 of inferior rank. Many of the principal nobility of France, the dukes of Lorraine and Bourbon, the earls of Flanders, Blois, Vaudemont, Aumale, were left on the field of battle. The success of the English was attributed to prince Edward. *The king, on his return to the camp, flew into the arms of the prince of Wales, and exclaimed: 'My brave son: Persevere in your honorable cause: You are my son; for valiantly have you acquitted yourself to-day: You have shown yourself worthy of empire.'*

Calais taken

The king took possession of Calais; and immediately executed an act of rigor, more justifiable than that which he had before resolved on. He knew, that, notwithstanding his pretended title to the crown of France, every Frenchman regarded him as a mortal enemy: He therefore ordered all the inhabitants of Calais to evacuate the town, and he peopled it anew with English; a policy which probably preserved so long to his successors the dominion of that important fortress. He made it the *staple of wool, leather, tin, and lead; the four chief, if not the sole commodities of the kingdom, for which there was any considerable demand in foreign markets.*[11] But of a sudden, in the following year, in 1350, *was thrown over this festivity and triumph of the court of England, by a destructive pestilence,* the black plague, *which invaded that kingdom as well as the rest of Europe; and is computed to have swept away near a third of the inhabitants in every country, which it attacked. It was probably more fatal in great cities than in the country; and above fifty thousand souls are said to have perished by it in London alone.*

The battle of Poictiers, capture of the French king John

The prince of Wales, in 1356, encouraged by the success of the preceding campaign,[12] *took the field with an army, which no historian makes amount to above 12,000 men, and of which not a third were English; and with this small body, he ventured to penetrate into the heart of France. --- The French monarch, John, provoked at the insult offered him by this incursion, and entertaining hopes of success for the young princes' temerity, collected a great army of above 60,000 men, and advanced by hasty marches to intercept his enemy. The prince, not aware of John's near approach, lost some days on his retreat before the castle of Remorantin; and thereby gave the French an opportunity of overtaking him. They came within sight at Maupertuis near Poictiers; and Edward, sensible that his retreat was now become impracticable, prepared for battle with all the courage of a young hero, and with all the prudence of the oldest most experienced commander.* --- The cardinal of Perigord attempted a negotiation but upon the king of France stipulating that *prince Edward surrender himself prisoner and ceding all the conquests, which he had made during this and the former campaign. The prince rejected the proposal.*

The prince of Wales had leisure, during the night, to strengthen, by new entrenchments, the post which he had before so judiciously chosen; and he contrived an ambush of 300 men at arms, and as many archers, whom he put under the command of the Captal de Buche, and ordered to make a circuit, that they might fall on the flank or rear of the French army during the engagement. --- John, the French king, also arranged his forces in three divisions, nearly equal. --- There was no reaching the English army but through a narrow lane, covered on each

---

[11] Ibid, pp 238-239.

[12] Note. The Scots had threatened the northern provinces but were defeated by the English.

side by hedges; and in order to open this passage, the mareschals, Andrehen and Clermont, were ordered to advance with a separate detachment of men at arms. While they marched along the lane, a body of English archers, who lined the hedges, plied them on each side with their arrows; and being very near them, yet placed in perfect safety, they coolly took their aim against the enemy, and slaughtered them with impunity. The French detachment, much discouraged by the unequal combat and diminished in their number, arrived at the end of the lane where they met on the open ground the prince of Wales himself at the head of a chosen body, ready for their reception. They were discomfited and overthrown. The division under king John, which, though more numerous than the whole English army, were somewhat dismayed with the precipitate flight of their companions. John here made the utmost efforts to retrieve, by his valor, what his imprudence had betrayed; and the only resistance made that day was by his line of battle. --- The ranks were every moment thinned around him: the nobles fell by his side, one after another: His son, scarce fourteen years of age, received a wound, while he was fighting valiantly, in defense of his father: The king himself, spent with fatigue, and overwhelmed by numbers, might easily have been slain; but every English gentleman, ambitious of taking alive the royal prisoner, spared him in the action, exhorted him to surrender, and offered him quarter. On Sept. 19. 1356, the king surrendered and his son was taken with him.[13]

Prince Edward, to be known as the Black Prince, was praised for his generous treatment of the king of France, John, and his elitist knights and entourage, also taken captive. The prince and his captives landed at Southwark May 24, 1357. The prisoner was clad in royal apparel, and mounted on a white steed, distinguished by its size and beauty, and by the richness of its furniture. The conqueror rode by his side in a meaner attire, and carried by a black palfry. In this situation, more glorious than all the insolent parade of a Roman triumph, he passed through the streets of London, and presented the king of France to his father, who advanced to meet him. Prince Edward became known as the Black Prince from the black armor he wore.

Condition of France

Meanwhile, the captivity of John, joined to the receding disorders of the French government, had produced in that country, a dissolution, almost total, of civil authority, and had occasioned confusions, the most horrible and destructive that had ever been experienced in any age or in any nation. The dauphin, now about eighteen years of age, naturally assumed the royal power during his father's captivity; but though endowed with an excellent capacity, even in

[13] Ibid, pp246-251.

such early years, he possessed neither experience nor authority sufficient to defend a state, assailed at one by foreign power and shaken by intestine faction. There were peasant revolts, which were a threat to the royal authority and the mareschals. --- *Amidst these disorders, the king of Navarre made his escape from prison, and presented a dangerous leader to the furious malcontents. --- He revived his pretensions, somewhat obsolete, to the crown of France: But while he advanced this claim, he relied entirely on his alliance with the English, --- and in all his operations, he acted more like a leader of banditti, than one who aspired to be the head of a regular government.*

Edward invaded France in November 1359. The king desired to be crowned king of France at Rheims, and carried on his attack for a period of seven weeks. *While the war was carried on in this ruinous manner, the negotiations for peace were never interrupted: But as the king still insisted on the full execution of the treaty, which he had made with his prisoner at London, and which was strenuously rejected by the dauphin, there appeared no likelihood of an accommodation. The earl, now duke of Lancaster (for this title was introduced into England during the present reign), endeavored to soften the rigor of these terms, and to finish the war on more equal and reasonable conditions. --- That his claim of succession had not from the first procured him one partisan in the kingdom; and the continuance of these destructive hostilities had united every Frenchman in the most implacable animosity against him.*

These reasons induced Edward to accept of more moderate terms of peace, on May 8, 1360. The terms of peace included the liberty of king John for a ransom of three millions of crowns of gold: That Edward should forever renounce all claim to the crown of France and the northern provinces of Normandy, Maine, Touraine and Anjou; and receive possession of the southern and western province of Aquitaine.[14]

Death of the French King John

King John died April 8, 1364 leaving the throne to his son Charles, the Dauphin. *Before Charles could think of counterbalancing so great a power as England, it was necessary for him to remedy the many disorders, to which his own kingdom was exposed. He turned his arms against the king of Navarre, the great disturber of France during that age. --- On the conclusion of the treaty of Bretigni, the many military adventurers, who had followed the standard of Edward, being dispersed into the several provinces, and possessed of strong holds, refused to lay down their arms, or relinquish a course of life, to which they were now accustomed, and by which alone they could gain a subsistence. They associated themselves with the banditti, who were already enured to the habits of rapine and violence; and under the name of the 'companies'*

---

[14] Ibid, pp 258-260.

and 'companions', became a terror to all the peaceable inhabitants. Some English and Gascon gentlemen of character, particulary Sir Matthew Gournay, Sir Hugh Calverly, the chevalier Vere, and others, were not ashamed to take the command of these ruffians, whose numbers amounted on the whole to near 40,000, and who bore the appearance of regular armies, rather than bands of robbers.

Peter, king of Castile, invasion by prince Edward

Peter, king of Castile, stigmatized by his contemporaries and by posterity, with the epithet of Cruel, had filled with blood and murder, his kingdom and his own family; and having incurred the universal hatred of his subjects, he kept, from present terror alone an anxious and precarious possession of the throne. His nobles fell every day the victims of his severity: He put to death several of his natural brothers from groundless jealousy: Each murder, by multiplying his enemies, became the occasion of fresh barbarities: And as he was not destitute of talents, his neighbors, no less than his own subjects, were alarmed at the progress of his violence and injustice. The French took arms against Peter. Peter fled from his dominions, took shelter in Guienne, and craved the protection of the prince of Wales, whom his father had invested with the sovereignty of these conquered provinces, by the title of the principality of Aquitaine.

He (Edward) *promised his assistance to the dethroned monarch; and having obtained the consent of his father, he levied a great army, and set out upon his enterprise. He was accompanied by his younger brother, John of Gaunt, created duke of Lancaster. The opposing forces were defeated. Peter, who so well merited the infamous epithet, which he bore, purposed to murder all his prisoners in cold blood; but was restrained from this barbarity by the remonstrances of the prince of Wales. All Castile now submitted to the victor: Peter was restored to the throne: And Edward finished this perilous enterprise with his usual glory. But he had soon reason to repent his connections with a man like Peter, abandoned to all sense of virtue and honor. The ungrateful tyrant refused the stipulated pay to the English forces; and Edward, finding his soldiers daily perish by sickness, and even his own health impaired by the climate, was obliged without receiving any satisfaction on this head, to return into Guienne.*

The barbarities, exercised by Peter over his helpless subjects, whom he now regarded as vanquished rebels, revived all the animosity of the Castilians against him; and on the return of Henry of Transtamare, together with du Guesclin, and some forces levied anew in France, the tyrant was again dethroned, and was taken prisoner. His brother, in resentment of his cruelties, murdered him with his own hand; and was place on the throne of Castile, which he transmitted to his posterity. The duke of Lancaster, who espoused in second marriage the eldest daughter of Peter, inherited only the empty title of that sovereignty, and, by claiming the succession, increased the animosity of the new king of Castile against England.

But the prejudice, which the affairs of prince Edward received from this splendid, though imprudent expedition, ended not with it. He had involved himself in so much debt by his preparations and the pay of his troops that he found it necessary, on his return, to impose on his principality a new tax, to which some of the nobility consented with extreme reluctance, and to which others absolutely refused to submit. This incident revived the animosity which the inhabitants bore the English, and which all the amiable qualities of the prince of Wales were not able to mitigate or assuage. They complained, that they were considered as a conquered people, that their privileges were disregarded, that all trust was given the English alone, that every office of honor and profit was conferred on the foreigners, --- and were encouraged to carry their complaints to Charles, as to their lord paramount, against these oppressions of the English government.[15]

Decline of English power in France

In 1369, the black plague, poor harvests, oppressive taxation and economic distress revisited England. *Charles --- sent to the prince of Wales a summons to appear in his court at Paris, and there to justify his conduct towards his vassals. The prince replied, that he would come to Paris; but it should be at the head of sixty thousand men.*

It soon appeared what a poor return the king had received by the distant conquests for all the blood and treasure expended in the quarrel, and how impossible it was to retain acquisitions, in an age when no regular force could be maintained sufficient to defend them against the revolt of the inhabitants, especially if that danger was joined with the invasion of a foreign enemy. --- Charles' forces invaded the southern provinces; and by means of their good conduct, the favorable dispositions of the people, and the ardor of the French nobility, they made every day considerable progress against the English. The state of the prince of Wales's health did not permit him to mount on horseback, or exert his usual activity. --- And when young Edward himself was obliged by his increasing infirmities to throw up the command, and return to his native country, the affairs of the English in the south of France seemed to be menaced with total ruin.

The king, incensed at these injuries, threatened to put to death all the French hostages, who remained in his hands, but on reflection abstained from that ungenerous revenge. After resuming, by advice of parliament, the vain title of king of France, he endeavored to send succors into Gascony; but all his attempts, both by sea and land, proved unsuccessful. The earl of Pembroke was intercepted at sea, and taken

---

[15] Ibid, pp 264-267.

prisoner with his whole army near Rochelle by a fleet, which the king of Castile had fitted out for that purpose. Edward himself embarked for Bourdeaux with another army; but was so long detained by contrary winds, that he was obliged to lay aside the enterprise. --- Sir Robert Knolles, at the head of 30,000 men, marched out of Calais, and continued his ravages to the gates of Paris, without being able to provoke the enemy to an engagement. His army was defeated by the French, and his army dispersed.

The duke of Lancaster, some time after, made a like attempt with an army of 25,000 men; and marched the whole length of France from Calais to Bourdeaux; but was so much harassed by the flying parties which attended him, that he brought into the half of his army to the place of their destination. Edward, from the necessity of his affairs was at last obliged to conclude a truce with the enemy; after almost all his ancient possessions in France had been ravished from him, except Bourdeaux and Bayonne, and all his conquests, except Calais.

The king's mental deterioration

The decline of the king's life was exposed to many mortifications and corresponded not to the splendid and noisy scenes, which had filled the beginning and the middle of it. Besides seeing the loss of his foreign dominions, and being baffled in every attempt to defend them; he felt the decay of his authority at home, and experienced, from the sharpness of some parliamentary remonstrances, the great inconstancy of the people, and the influence of present fortune over all their judgments. This prince, who during the vigor of his age, had been chiefly occupied in the pursuits of war and ambition, began, at an unseasonable period, to indulge himself in pleasure; and being now a widower, he attached himself to a lady of sense and spirit, one Alice Pierce, who acquired a great ascendant over him, and by her influence gave such general disgust, that, in order to satisfy the parliament, he was obliged to remove her from court. The indolence also, naturally attending old age and infirmities, had made him, in a great measure, resign the administration into the hands of his son, the duke of Lancaster, who, as he was far from being popular, weakened extremely the affection, which the English bore to the person and government of the king. Men carried their jealousies far against the duke; and as they saw with much regret, the death of the prince of Wales every day approaching, they apprehended, lest the succession of his son, Richard, now a minor, should be defeated by the intrigues of Lancaster, and by the weak indulgence of the old king. But Edward, in order to satisfy both the people and the prince on this head, declared in parliament his grandson heir and successor to the crown; and thereby cut off all the hopes of the duke of Lancaster, if ever had the temerity to entertain any.[16]

---

[16] Ibid, pp 269-271.

The death of prince Edward and Edward III

The above condition of the king covered the last fifteen years of the kings life. *The prince of Wales, after a lingering illness, died in the forty sixth year of his age, June 8, 1376. The king survived about a year this melancholy incident: England was deprived at once, of both these princes, its chief ornament and support: He expired,* on June 21, 1377, *in the sixty-fifth year of his age and the fifty-first of his reign.* The descendants of Edward III will be detailed in the chapters to follow.

From Hume's summary: *The English are apt to consider with peculiar fondness the history of Edward III, and to esteem his reign, as it was one of the longest, and most glorious also, that occurs in the annals of their nation. The ascendant which they then began to acquire over France, their rival and supposed national enemy, makes them cast their eyes on this period with great complacency, and sanctifies every measure, which Edward embraced for that end. But the domestic government of this prince is really more admirable than his foreign victories; and England enjoyed, by the prudence and valor of his administration, a longer interval of domestic peace and tranquility than she had been blest with in any former period, or that she experienced of many ages after.*

Hume presented a brief review of the statutes enacted in his reign, with frequent references to Magna Carta. Hume indicates that there were complaints in the house of commons against some of the king's prerogatives, not permitted in subsequent reigns as during the Tudors, *where no tyranny of abuse of power ever met with any check or opposition, or so much as a remonstrance, from parliament. --- But there was no act of arbitrary power more frequently repeated in this reign, than that of imposing taxes without consent of parliament. --- The commons made continual complaints of the multitude of robberies, murders, rapes and other disorders, which, they say, were become numberless in every part of the kingdom, and which they always ascribe to the protection of the criminals received from the great. --- Commerce and industry were certainly at a very low ebb during this period. --- The only exports were wool, skins, hides, leather, butter, tin,* and *lead. --- Parliament attempted the impracticable scheme of reducing the price of labor after the pestilence. ---* Perhaps the statute of treasons was the most lasting of Edward's statutes, at least to the time of Hume and Blackstone; *which limited the cases of high treason, before vague and uncertain, to three principal heads, conspiring the death of the king, levying war against him, and adhering to his enemies; and the judges were prohibited, if any other cases should occur, from inflicting the penalty of treason, without an application to parliament. --- Yet on the whole it appears, that the government, at best, was only a barbarous monarchy, not regulated by any fixed maxims, or bounded by any certain undisputed rights, which in practice were regularly observed. The king conducted himself by one set of principles; the barons by another; the commons by a third; the clergy by a fourth. All these systems of government were opposite and incompatible. Each of them prevailed in its turn, as incidents were favorable to it: a great prince rendered the monarchical power predominant: the weakness of a king gave reins to the aristocracy: A superstitious age saw the clergy triumphant.*

The life and the times of Edward III illustrate the problems that the historian faces in rendering an account of the age and subject. The focus of interest by the historian may be the kind of government and administration of the nation, the civil disturbances and foreign wars; or it may be a focus on the laws, statutes and peculiarities of the administration of justice; or the focus on the economic life of the times; the life and customs of the aristocracy or the elite members of society; or upon the accomplishments of the age, whether of buildings, monuments, or the arts and sciences; or upon the religious denominations and the role of the dominant church as opposed to the civil government. But least of all in importance for the historian is the fate that befalls the majority of the citizens at any given period of history. Hume ends his summary with the notation that: *The people, for whom chiefly government was instituted, and who chiefly deserve consideration, were the weakest of the whole.*[17]

---

[17] Ibid, pp 271-284.

Chapter 19

Richard II

Before telling the story of Richard II, (b. 1367, d. 1400) and who ruled from 1377 to 1399, it will be necessary to list and describe briefly the sons of Edward III, whose descendants are the subject of this story as well as the kings to follow.[1] The chaos of England from foreign wars and domestic disturbances are reflected in the intense family conflicts between Richard and his uncles. This is only a prelude to the conflicts between the houses of York and Lancaster, which defined the War of Roses. The hundred years war with France and Scotland continued but with less force during this reign. The absurdity of a hereditary monarchy is illustrated by Richard who was the second king since William I to gain the crown during his minority, at age 11, in 1377. We reviewed the first king as such in the person of Henry III, whose reign was absolutely incompetent, even more so than king John and Edward II. But we have in Richard II a tragedy involving Richard's entire family as well as the nation, the onset of the War of Roses, which can only be told by Shakespeare who documented Richard's final years before he was deposed and murdered when only 33 years old.[2] Shakespeare portrayed the York-Lancaster conflicts as an immense tragedy for England, which began with Richard II. From Shakespeare's play, *The Life and Death of King Richard II:*

---

[1] Note. See Table 2, Lancaster and York. Note also that Edward III's youngest son Thomas, duke of Gloucester should appear to the right, after Edmund. Thomas's rebellion and murder, by Richard's command, was the starting point of the York-Lancaster conflicts and wars which lasted one hundred years.

[2] Note. Of the English kings to date, only Edward I and Edward III lived past sixty years.

The bishop of Carlisle: *I speak to subjects, as a subject speaks, Stirr'd up by God, thus boldly for his king. My lord of Hereford here, whom you call king, Is a foul traitor to proud Hereford's king; and if you crown him, let me prophesy, --- The blood of English shall manure the ground, And future ages groan for this foul act; Peace shall go sleep with Turk and infidels, And in this seat of peace tumultuous wars Shall kin with kin and kind with kind confound; Disorder, horror, fear, and mutiny, Shall here inhabit, and this land be call'd The field of Golgotha and dead men's skulls. Or if you raise this house against this house, It will the woefullest division prove That ever fell upon this cursed earth, Prevent, resist it, let it not be so, Lest child, child's children, cry against you woe!*[3]

Shakespeare's historic plays can be used as valid historic sources, *where history becomes drama and drama history.* It is significant that Shakespeare's historical plays, from Richard II and Henry IV, V, VI to Richard III, and parts of Henry VIII documented accurately, except for the chronology, the conflicts and wars between the houses of York and Lancaster, with profound insights into the emotional and personal attributes of kings and aristocrats. The fraudulent attribution of William Shakesper of Stratford does nothing to embellish these great works. There is no credible evidence that William of Stratford wrote anything other than six poorly written signatures all spelled differently.[4] William had only a grammar school education, no contacts with the royal courts of England or elsewhere, lacked facility in foreign languages and even the London dialect, had no access to historical references adequate to the task, and no travel other than to London. That he could not have written the historic plays, or other plays attributed to William Shakespeare, has been documented by competent research during past decades.[5] It is well established that the works attributed to William Shakespeare were from the pen of the seventeenth earl of Oxford, Edward de Vere.[6]

---

[3] Shakespeare, King Richard II, Act IV, sc 1.

[4] See Whalen, p 18.

[5] Looney, *Shakespeare Identified*; Ogburn, *The Mysterious William Shakespeare*; Whalen, *Shakespeare: Who Was He*; Sobran, *Alias Shakespeare.*

[6] See also the classic biography: B.M. Ward, *The Seventeenth Earl of Oxford,* and Paul Altrocchi, *Most Greatly Lived,* A Biographical Novel of Edward de Vere, Seventeenth Earl of Oxford, whose pen name was William Shakespeare.

It is of interest that the earl of Oxford, Robert de Vere, figured large in the early reign of Richard II, as his best friend and confident. The seventeenth earl of Oxford, Edward de Vere was from one of the oldest aristocracies of England. Edward de Vere was a favorite of Elizabeth I, who was his life long supporter, and protector. Oxford grew up since age eleven in the household of William Cecil (lord Burghley) and later was forced to marry the daughter of the powerful lord Burghley, who became Oxford's nemesis. Burghley and the queen thought it demeaning for a favored aristocrat close to the crown to be publicly noted for writing plays and directing theatrical productions. It was also necessary for Edward de Vere to conceal the authorship of his plays and verse in view of their honest portrayal of royalty and aristocracy. Anyone who dared tell the truth about kings and aristocrats, especially lord Burghley in the reign of Elizabeth, could be tried and executed. Hume's volume 2 of *The History of England* provides an interesting companion to the Shakespeare plays.[7]

Family history

Edward III had five sons, the oldest Edward, named the Black prince due to the black armor he wore, died in 1376, just one year before the death of Edward III. Richard II was the only son or offspring of prince Edward. The second son of Edward III was Lionel who died in 1368, but who left progeny by Phillipa who married Edmund Mortimer; and whose son Roger Mortimer was the heir apparent following the death of Richard. (Edmund Mortimer was the great grandson of Roger Mortimer, who helped the queen depose Edward II). From Hume: *Of all the family, he* (Lionel) *resembled most his father and older brother in his noble qualities.* All three of the remaining sons of Edward III figured large in the story of Richard II, who were his uncles and contended for power. The oldest surviving son, John of Gaunt, who died in 1399, a year before Richard's death, is the father of Bolinbroke, who usurped the throne to become Henry IV. There followed Edmund, duke of York, who died in 1402, after being charged with the defense of Richard II against Bolinbroke. Finally, the youngest son and the one who figures large in Richard's story, was Thomas, duke of Gloucester. The author of the Shakespeare plays was most likely the author of an anonymous play, *Thomas of Woodstock*, which provides the background of Richard's ascendancy and murder of his opponents, including his uncle, Thomas,

---

[7] Note. Some of the possible references to the Shakespeare historic plays can be found in Bullough, *Narrative and Dramatic sources of Shakespeare,* Volume III.

duke of Gloucester.[8] This is the beginning of the York-Lancaster conflicts and wars. Hume stated that the details of Shakespeare's historical plays are accurate. In a footnote by Hume: *It is remarkable, that in all the historical plays of Shakespeare, where the manners and characters, and even the transactions of the several reigns are so exactly copied, there is scarcely any mention of civil Liberty.*[9]

Deaths of prince Edward and Edward III

Richard's father, prince Edward the Black Prince, died June 8, 1376. King Edward III died a year later, June 21 1377. *The prince of Wales, after a lingering illness, died in the forty-sixth year of his age; and left a character, illustrious for every eminent virtue, and from his earliest youth till the hour he expired, unstained by any blemish. His valor and military talents formed the smallest part of his merit: His generosity, humanity, affability, moderation, gained him the affections of all men; and he was qualified to throw a luster, not only on that rude age, in which he lived, and which nowise infected him with its vices, but also on the most shining period of ancient or modern history. The king survived about a year this melancholy incident. --- The decline of the king's life was exposed to many mortifications, and corresponded not to the splendid and noisy scenes, which had filled the beginning and the middle of it. Besides seeing the loss of his foreign dominions, and being baffled in every attempt to defend them; he felt the decay of his authority at home, and experienced, from the sharpness of some parliamentary remonstrances, the great inconstancy of the people, and the influence of present fortune over all their judgments.*[10]

Richard Crowned

Richard had just turned eleven years old when parliament met after Richard's ascension to the throne. *But as Edward, though he had fixed the succession to the crown, had taken no care to establish a plan of government during the minority of his grandson, it behooved the parliament to supply this defect.* The commons petitioned that the lords appoint a council of nine, *who might direct the public business. On this foot then the government stood. The administration was concluded entirely in the king's name: No regency was expressly appointed: the*

---

[8] Note. See table Lancaster and York. Thomas of Woodstock, duke of Gloucester, the youngest son of Edward III, should be to the right of Edmund duke of York.

[9] Hume, vol 4, p 368.

[10] Hume, vol 2, pp 270, 271.

nine counselors and the great officers named by the peers, did their duty, each in his respective department: And the whole system was for some years kept together, by the secret authority of the king's uncles, especially of the duke of Lancaster, who was in reality the regent.

Wars in France

In 1378, the war with France was carried on in a manner somewhat languid, and produced *no enterprise of great luster or renown, the duke of Lancaster conducted an army into Brittany, but returned without being able to perform anything memorable. In a subsequent year, 1380, the duke of Gloucester marched out of Calais with a body of 2,000 cavalry, and 8,000 infantry; and scrupled not with his small army, to enter the heart of France, and to continue his ravages till he reached his allies in the province of Brittany.*

The expenses of these armaments, and the usual want of economy attending a minority, much exhausted the English treasury, and obliged the parliament, besides making some alterations in the council, to impose a new and unusual tax of three groats on every person, male and female, above fifteen years of age.

Insurrections by the people

The commotions of the people in Flanders, the mutiny of the peasants in France, were the natural effects of this growing spirit of independence; and the report of these events, being brought into England, where personal slavery, as we learn from Froissard, was more general than in any other country in Europe, had prepared the minds of the multitude for an insurrection. One John Ball also, a seditious preacher, who affected low popularity, went about the country, and inculcated on his audience the principles of the first origin of mankind from one common stock, their equal right to liberty and to all the goods of nature, the tyranny of artificial distinctions, and the abuses which had arisen from the degradation of the more considerable part of the species, and the aggrandizement of a few insolent rulers. These doctrines, so agreeable to the populace, and so conformable to the ideas of primitive equality, which are engraved into the hearts of all men, were greedily received by the multitude; and scattered the sparks of that sedition, which the present tax raised into a conflagration.[11]

A revolt began in 1381 with a confrontation between a tax collector and a blacksmith. The people, witnessing the rape of the blacksmith's daughter, *immediately flew to arms: The whole neighborhood joined the sedition: The flame spread in an instant over the country: It soon propagated itself into that of Kent, of Herford,*

---

[11] Ibid, pp 286-290.

Surrey, Sussex, Suffolk, Norfolk, Cambridge, and Lincoln. Before the government had the least warning of the danger, the disorder had grown beyond control or opposition. The populace had shaken off all regard to their former masters: And were headed by the most audacious and criminal of their associates, who assumed the feigned names of Wat Tyler, Jack Straw, Hob Carter, and Tom Miller.

They sent a message to the king, who had taken shelter in the Tower; and they desired a conference with him. --- A great body of them quartered themselves at Mile-end; and the king, finding no defense in the Tower, which was weakly garrisoned, and ill supplied with provisions, was obliged to go out to them, and ask their demands. They required a general pardon, the abolition of slavery, freedom of commerce in market towns without toll or impost, and a fixed rent of lands instead of the services due by villeinage.[12] These requests, which, though extremely reasonable in themselves, the nation was not sufficiently prepared to receive, and which it was dangerous to have extorted by violence, were however complied with; charters to that purpose were granted them; and this body immediately dispersed and returned to their several homes.

Richard's concessions revoked by parliament

But these noble concessions on the part of Richard II, which this action may illustrate as the high point of his entire reign, although under duress, were revoked by parliament. *These charters of enfranchisement and pardon were revoked by parliament; the low people were reduced to the same slavish condition as before; and several of the ringleaders were severely punished for the late disorders. Some were even executed without process or form of law. It was pretended, that the intentions of the mutineers had been to seize the king's person, to carry him through England at their head, to murder all the nobility, gentry, and lawyers, and even all the bishops and priests, except the mendicant friars; to dispatch afterwards the king himself; and having thus reduced all to a level to order the kingdom at their pleasure.[13]*

Marriage to Anne

In 1382 king Richard, at the age of 15, was married to princess Anne of Bohemia. At this age Richard was under subjection of his uncle Thomas, the duke of Gloucester, who was the youngest son of Edward III. *The subjection, in which Richard was held by his uncles, particularly by the duke of Gloucester, a prince of ambition and genius, though it was not unsuitable to his years and slender capacity, was extremely*

---

[12] Note. Villeinage is the system of slavery that existed in England from the time even before the Romans, to the abolition of slavery in the nineteenth century.

[13] Ibid, pp 290-293.

*disagreeable to his violent temper; and he soon attempted to shake off
the yoke imposed upon him. Robert de Vere, earl of Oxford, a young man
of a noble family, of an agreeable figure, but of dissolute manners, had
acquired an entire ascendant over him; and governed him with an
absolute authority. The king set so little bounds to his affection, that he
first created his favorite marquis of Dublin, a title before unknown in
England, then duke of Ireland; and transferred to him by patent, which
was confirmed in parliament, the entire sovereignty of life of that island.
--- These public declarations of attachment turned the attention of the
whole court towards the minion: All favors passed through his hands:
Access to the king could only be obtained by his mediation: And Richard
seemed to take no pleasure in royal authority, but so far as it enabled
him to load with favors and titles and dignities this object of his
affections.*

Gloucester and the nobles versus the king

*The jealousy of power immediately produced an animosity
between the minion and his creatures on the one hand, and the princes of
the blood and chief nobility on the other; and the usual complaints
against the insolence of favorites were loudly echoed, and greedily
received, in every part of the kingdom. Moubray earl of Nottingham, the
mareschal, Fitz-Alan of Arundel, Piercy earl of Northumberland,
Montacute earl of Salisbury, Beauchamp earl of Warwic, were all
connected with each other, and with the princes, by friendship or
alliance, and still more by their common antipathy to those who had
eclipsed them in the king's favor and confidence.*[14]

*The king foresaw the tempest preparing against him and his
minister. After attempting in vain to rouse the Londoners to his defense,
he withdrew from parliament, and retired with his court to Eltham.* The
parliament, in 1386, prepared articles of impeachment against Richard's
chancellor, the earl of Suffolk. A trial was held in parliament. *Even the
proof of these articles, frivolous as they are, was found very deficient
upon the trial: It appeared, that Suffolk had made no purchase from the
crown while he was chancellor, and that all his bargains of the kind were
made before he was advanced to that dignity. It is almost needless to
add, that he was condemned, notwithstanding his defense; and that he
was deprived of his office.*

*Gloucester and his associates observed their stipulation with the
king, and attacked no more of his ministers; But they immediately
attacked himself and his royal dignity, and framed a commission after the
model of those which had been attempted almost in every reign since that
of Richard I, and which had always been attended with extreme
confusion. By this commission, which was ratified by parliament, a*

---

[14] Ibid, pp 295-296.

council of fourteen persons was appointed, all of Gloucester's faction, except Nevil, archbishop of York: The sovereign power was transferred to these men for a twelve month: The king, who had now reached the twenty-first year of his age, in 1388, was in reality dethroned: The aristocracy was rendered supreme: And though the term of the commission was limited, it was easy to foresee, that the intentions of the party were to render it perpetual, and that power would with great difficulty be wrested from those grasping hands.[15]

The king declares his power

The king, thus dispossessed of royal power, was soon sensible of the contempt, into which he was fallen. --- The king met at Nottingham with Sir Robert Tresilian, chief justice of the king's bench, and five of his judges who declared: *that the late commission was derogatory to the royalty and prerogative of the king; that those who procured it, or advised the king to consent to it, were punishable with death; that those who necessitated and compelled him were guilty of treason; that those were equally criminal who should persevere in maintaining it; that the king has the right of dissolving parliaments at pleasure; and that this assembly cannot without his consent impeach any of his ministers and judges.* ---

The duke of Gloucester, and his adherents, soon got intelligence of this secret consultation, and were naturally very much alarmed at it. They saw the king's intentions; and they determined to present the execution of them. As soon as he came to London, which, they knew, was well disposed to their party, they secretly assembled their forces, and appeared in arms at Haringay-Park, near Highgate, with a power, in which Richard and his ministers were not able to resist. A few days after, they appeared in his presence, armed and attended with armed followers; and they accused by name the archbishop of York, the duke of Ireland, the earl of Suffolk, Sir Robert Tresilian, and Sir Nicholas Brembre, as public and dangerous enemies to the state. Brembre was executed, as was Tresilian who had been discovered and taken in the interval. But these were not the only deeds of violence committed during the triumph of the party. All the other judges, who had signed the extrajudicial opinions at Nottingham, were condemned to death, and were, as a grace of favor, banished to Ireland. Lord Beauchamp of Holt, Sir James Berners, and John Salisbury, were tried and condemned to high treason; merely because they had attempted to defeat the late commission; But the life of the latter was spared. The fate of Simon Burley was more severe.

---

[15] Ibid, 297-298.

Richard's queen Anne

This execution, in 1388, more than all the others, made a deep impression on the mind of Richard; His queen, too (for he was already married to the sister of the emperor Winceslaus, king of Bohemia) interested herself in behalf of Burley: She remained three hours on her knees before the duke of Gloucester, pleading for that gentleman's life; but though she was become extremely popular by her amiable qualities, which had acquired her the appellation of the 'good queen Anne'; her petition was sternly rejected by the inexorable tyrant.[16]

An alienation of the church was attributed in part to the queen, according to Green. *Lollardy found favor in the very precincts of the court; it was through the patronage of Richard's first queen, Anne of Bohemia, that the tracts and Bible of the Reformer had been introduced into their native land, to give rise to the remarkable movement which found its earliest leaders in John Huss and Jerome of Prague.[17]* We turn to *Thomas of Woodstock:*

The queen has sold her jewels to alleviate the distress of the poor. Meanwhile the king and his minions sit in council devising strange new costumes.

Queen. I see no fault that I dare call a fault, But would your grace consider with advice What you have done unto your reverent uncles (My fears provokes me to be bold my lord) They are your noble kinsmen, to revoke the sentence were—

King. An act of folly Nan! Kings words are laws, If we infringe our word we break our law. No more of them sweet queen.[18]

The king assumed power

It might naturally be expected, that the king, being reduced to such slavery by the combination of the princes and chief nobility, and having appeared so unable to defend his servants from the cruel effects of their resentment, would long remain in subjection to them; and never would recover the royal power, without the most violent struggles and convulsions; But the event proved contrary. In less than a twelve month, Richard, who was in his twenty-third year, in 1390, declared in council, that, as he had now attained the full age, which entitled him to govern by his own authority his kingdom and household, he resolved to exercise his

---

[16] Ibid, pp 300-302.

[17] Green, p 263.

[18] Act III, sc 1, *The First part of the Reign of King Richard the Second* or *Thomas of Woodstock*, in Bullough, pp 460-491.

right of sovereignty; and when no one ventured to contradict so reasonable an intention, he deprived Fitz-Alan archbishop of Canterbury of the dignity of chancellor, and bestowed that high office on William of Wickham bishop of Winchester; the bishop of Hereford was displaced from the office of treasurer, the earl of Arundel from that of admiral; even the duke of Gloucester and the earl of Warwick were removed for a time from the council: And no opposition was made to these great changes. The history of this reign is imperfect, and little to be depended on; except where it is supported by public records: And it is not easy for us to assign the reason of this unexpected event.

The uncles of Richard— dukes of Lancaster, York and Gloucester

Richard was the only son of prince Edward, the Black Prince, who had died in 1376. The Black Prince was the eldest son of Edward III. Next oldest was Lionel duke of Clarence who had died in 1368. The surviving sons of Edward III were very concerned about the conduct of Richard and the changes he had brought about. Thomas duke of Gloucester, the youngest son of Edward III, was the most important person in Richard's government. Richard now removed him from the administration.

The duke of Lancaster returned from Spain, in 1389; *having resigned to his rival all pretensions to the crown of Castile upon payment of a large sum of money, and having married his daughter, Philippa, to the king of Portugal. The authority of this prince served to counterbalance that of the duke of Gloucester, and secured the power of Richard, who paid great court to his eldest uncle, by whom he had never been offended, and whom he found more moderate in his temper than the younger.*

Administration of government and behavior of Richard

The administration of the king, though it was not, in this interval, sullied by any unpopular act, except the seizing of the charter of London, which was soon after restored, tended not much to corroborated his authority, and his personal character brought him into contempt, even while his public government appeared, in a good measure, unexceptionable. Indolent, profuse, addicted to low pleasures; he spent his whole time in feasting and jollity, and dissipated, in idle show, or in bounties to favorites of no reputation, that revenue which the people expected to see him employ in enterprises directed to public honor and advantage. He forgot his rank by admitting all men to his familiarity; and he was not sensible, that their acquaintance with the qualities of his mind was not able to impress them with the respect, which he neglected to preserve from his birth and station. The earls of Kent and Huntingdon, his half brothers, were his chief confidants and favorites, and though he never devoted himself to them with so profuse an affection as that with which he had formerly been attached to the duke of Ireland, (Robert de

Vere), *it was easy for men to see, that every grace passed through their hands, and that the king had rendered himself a mere cipher in the government. The small regard, which the public bore to his person, disposed them to murmur against his administration, and to receive with greedy ears every complaint, which the discontented or ambitious grandees suggested to them.*[19]

Death of the queen, promise to marry Isabella

Richard's queen Anne died in 1394. There were no children by this marriage. Two years later Richard pledged to marry Isabella, although she was at the time only seven years old. A truce of twenty-five years was established between England and France. *And to render the amity between the two crowns more durable, Richard, who was now a widower, was affianced to Isabella, the daughter of Charles. This princess was only seven years of age; but the king agreed to so unequal a match, chiefly that he might fortify himself by this alliance, against the enterprises of his uncles and the incurable turbulence as well as inconstancy of his barons.*

Dissent and threat of Gloucester

Gloucester soon perceived the advantages, which this dissolute conduct gave him; and finding, that both resentment and jealousy on the part of his nephew still prevented him from acquiring any ascendant over that prince, he determined to cultivate his popularity with the nation, and to revenge himself on those who eclipsed him in favor and authority. He seldom appeared at court or in council: He never declared his opinion but in order to disapprove of the measures embraced by the king and his favorites: And he courted the friendship of every man, whom disappointment or private resentment had rendered an enemy to the administration. The long truce with France was unpopular with the English, who breathed nothing but war against that hostile nation; and Gloucester took care to encourage all the vulgar prejudices, which prevailed on this subject. Forgetting the misfortunes, which attended the English arms during the later years of Edward; he made an invidious comparison between the glories of that reign and the inactivity of the present, and he lamented that Richard should have degenerated so much from the heroic virtues by which his father and his grandfather were distinguished. The military men were inflamed with a desire of war, when they heard him talk of the signal victories formerly obtained, and of the easy prey which might be made of French riches by the superior valor of the English: The populace readily embraced the same sentiments: And all men exclaimed, that this prince, whose counsels were so much neglected, was the true support of English honor, and alone able

---

[19] Hume, vol 2, pp 304-306.

to raise the nation to its former power and splendor. His great abilities, his popular manners, his princely extraction, his immense riches, his high office of constable; all these advantages not a little assisted by his want of court-favor, gave him a mighty authority in the kingdom, and rendered him formidable to Richard and his ministers

Froissard, a contemporary writer and very impartial, but whose credit is somewhat impaired by his want of exactness in material facts, ascribes to the duke of Gloucester more desperate views, and such as were totally incompatible with the government and domestic tranquility of the nation. According to that historian, he (Gloucester) proposed to his nephew, Roger Mortimer, earl of Marche, whom Richard had declared his successor, to give him immediate possession of the throne, by the deposition of a prince, so unworthy of power and authority: and when Mortimer declined the project, he resolved to make a partition of the kingdom between himself, his two brothers, and the earl of Arundel; and entirely to dispossess Richard of the crown.[20]

Gloucester arrested, sent to Calais, imprisoned, and murdered

The king, it is said, being informed of these designs, saw that either his own ruin or that of Gloucester was inevitable; and he resolved, by hasty blow, to prevent the execution of such destructive projects.

The king's precipitate temper admitted of no deliberation. He ordered Gloucester to be unexpectedly arrested; to be hurried on board a ship which was lying in the river; and to be carried over to Calais, where alone, by reason of his numerous partisans, he could safely be detained in custody. The earls of Arundel and Warwick were seized at the same time: The malcontents, so suddenly deprived of their leaders, were astonished and overawed. And the concurrence of the dukes of Lancaster and York in those measures, together with the earls of Derby and Rutland, Aumerle, the eldest sons of these princes, bereaved them of all possibility of resistance.[21]

From *Thomas of Woodstock* it could be said that the dukes of Lancaster and York abdicated but did not concur with the actions of Richard and the arrest of Gloucester and others. The foreboding of Goucester is portrayed in Woodstock:

Adieu good York and Gaunt, farewell forever. I have a sad presage comes suddenly that I shall never see these brothers more: On earth I fear, we never more shall meet. Of Edward the Thirds seven sons we three are left To see our Fathers kingdom Ruined. I would my death might end the misery My fear presageth to my wretched country. The commons will rebel without all question, and before my God I have no

---

[20] Ibid, p 307.

[21] Ibid, pp 306-310.

*eloquence To stay this uproar. I must tell them plain We all are struck
but must not strike again.*[22]

Parliament was immediately summoned at Westminster, in
1397, and --- *the parliament passed whatever acts the king was pleased
to dictate to them.* An accusation was produced against the duke of
Gloucester, and the earls of Arundel and Warwic, as well as the
archbishop of Canterbury. The earl of Arundel was executed, the earl of
Warwick, who was also convicted of high treason, was, on account of his
submissive behavior, pardoned as to his life, but doomed to perpetual
banishment in the Isle of Man. The archbishop was protected by
ecclesiastical privileged but was banished.

*A warrant was issued to the earl Marshal, governor of Calais,
to bring over the duke of Gloucester, in order to his trial; but the
governor returned for answer, that the duke had died suddenly of an
apoplexy in that fortress. Nothing could be more suspicious from the
time, than the circumstances of that prince's death: It became
immediately the general opinion, that he was murdered by orders from
his nephew: In the subsequent reign undoubted proofs were produced in
parliament, that he had been suffocated with pillows by his keepers: And
it appeared, that the king, apprehensive lest the public trial and
execution of so popular a prince and so near a relation, might prove both
dangerous and invidious, had taken this base method of gratifying, and,
as he fancied, concealing, his revenge upon him.*

The parliament annulled and reversed the former acts of
parliament when under the influence of Gloucester and his party.
According to Hume: *The ancient history of England is nothing but a
catalogue of reversals: every thing is in fluctuation and movement: One
faction is continually undoing what was established by another: and the
multiplied oaths, which each party exacted for the security of the present
acts, betray a perpetual consciousness of their instability.*

Battles in France and Scotland

*The wars, meanwhile, which Richard had inherited with his
crown, still continued; though interrupted by frequent truces, according
to the practice of that age, and conducted with little vigor, by reason of
the weakness of all parties. The French war was scarcely heard of; the
tranquility of the northern borders was only interrupted by one inroad of
the Scots, which proceeded more from a rivalship between the two
martial families of Piercy and Douglas, than from any national quarrel:
A fierce battle or skirmish was fought at Otterborne, in which young
Piercy, sir named Hotspur, from his impetuous valor, was taken prisoner,
and Douglas slain, and the victory remained undecided. Some
insurrections of the Irish obliged the king to make an expedition into that*

---

[22] Thomas of Woodstock, Act III, sc 2, in Bullough, p 473.

country, which he reduced to obedience; and he recovered, in some degree, by this enterprise, his character of courage, which had suffered a little by the inactivity of his reign.[23]

The duke of Hereford's accusation against the duke of Norfolk, his banishment

Act 1 of Shakespeare's play *Richard II* begins with the accusation of the duke of Hereford, also known as Henry Bolinbroke, the son of John of Gaunt, against Thomas Mowbray, the duke of Norfolk. From Hume: *The duke of Herford,* (Bolinbroke, son of John of Gaunt, and future Henry IV*) appeared in parliament, and accused the duke of Norfolk of having spoken to him, in private, many slanderous words of the king, and of having imputed to that prince an intention of subverting and destroying many of his principal nobility. Norfolk denied the charge, gave Herford the lie, and offered to prove his own innocence by duel. The challenge was accepted. The time and place of combat were appointed: and as the event of this important trial by arms might require the interposition of legislative authority, the parliament thought it more suitable to delegate their power to a committee, than to prolong the session beyond the usual time which custom and general convenience had prescribed to it.*

The lists for this decision of truth and right were appointed at Coventry before the king, in 1398: All the nobility of England bandied into parties, and adhered either to the one duke or the other: The whole nation was held in suspense with regard to the event: But when the two champions appeared in the field, accoutered for the combat, the king interposed, to prevent both the present effusion of such noble blood, and the future consequences of the quarrel. By the advice and authority of the parliamentary commissioners, he stopped the duel; and to show his impartiality, he ordered, by the same authority, both the combatants to leave the kingdom, assigning one country for the place of Norfolk's exile, which he declared perpetual, another for that of Hereford, which he limited to ten years.

Hereford was a man of great prudence and command of temper; and he behaved himself with so much submission in these delicate circumstances, that the king, before his departure, promised to shorten the term of his exile four years; and he also granted him letters patent, by which he was empowered, in any case inheritance should in the interval

---

[23] Hume, pp 304-305.

accrue to him, to enter immediately in possession, and to postpone the doing of homage till his return.[24]

The weakness and fluctuation of Richard' counsels appear nowhere more evident than in the conduct of this affair. No sooner had Hereford left the kingdom, than the king's jealousy of the power and riches of that prince's family revived; and he was sensible, that, by Gloucester's death, he had only removed a counterpoise to the Lancastrian interest, which was now become formidable to his crown and kingdom. John of Gaunt, the duke of Lancaster, died Feb. 3, 1399, and Richard, with the consent of parliament *revoked his letters patent, and retained possession of the estate of Lancaster.* The banishment of Henry by Richard and the confiscation of the fortunes of his estate upon the death of John of Gaunt, duke of Lancaster, provided the basis, perhaps even more than revenge for the murder of Thomas duke of Gloucester, for the usurpation of the crown by Henry IV and the civil disturbances and wars to follow during the next one-hundred years.

Richard's expedition to Ireland

The popularity of Henry was growing among the people and opposition to Richard was increasing. *While such were the dispositions of the people, Richard had the imprudence to embark for Ireland, in order to revenge the death of his cousin, Roger earl of Marche, the presumptive heir of the crown, who had been slain in a skirmish by the natives.*[25] For more background on this visit we turn to Cusack's *History of Ireland.* It is recorded that Richard had previously visited Ireland in 1394. *The Earl of March, Edmund Mortimer, was sent to Ireland as Justiciary, with extraordinary powers. He had married Phillippa, daughter of Lionel, Duke of Clarence, by his first wife.* Edmund Mortimer earl of March died in 1381. Edmund Mortimer was succeeded by his son Roger Mortimer. Since Richard had no children, Roger Mortimer would have inherited the crown after Richard. Roger Mortimer, however, died a year before Richard's final visit to Ireland, in 1399.

On the 2nd of October, A.D. 1394, Richard II, landed on the Irish shores. The country was in its normal state of partial insurrection and general discontent; but no attempt was made to recover the chronic cause of all this unnecessary misery. --- The king's account of his reception shows that he had formed a tolerably just opinion of the political state of the country. The customs of the Irish nobles were again made a subject of ridicule, as they had been during the visit of Prince John; though one should have supposed that an increased knowledge of the world should have led to a wiser policy, if not to an avoidance of that

---

[24] Ibid, pp 311-312.

[25] Ibid, p 315.

ignorant criticism, which at once denounces everything foreign as inferior. Richard returned to England in 1395, after nine months of vain display. He appointed Roger Mortimer his viceroy. --- In 1399 king Richard paid another visit to Ireland. His exactions and oppressions had made him very unpopular in England, and it is probable that this expedition was planned to divert the minds of his subjects. If this was his object, it failed signally; for the unfortunate monarch was deposed by Parliament the same year. And was obliged to perform the act of abdication with the best grace he could. His unhappy end belongs to English history. Richard again landed in state at Waterford, and soon after marched against the indomitable MacMurrough. His main object, indeed, appears to have been the subjugation of this "rebel", who contrived to keep the English settlers in continual alarm.

Richard's army was on the verge of starvation, so he was obliged to break up his camp, and march to Dublin. Upon his arrival there, MacMurrough made overtures for peace, which were gladly accepted, and the Earl of Gloucester proceeded at once to arrange terms with him. But no reconciliation could be effected, as both parties refused to yield. When Richard heard the result, he flew into a violent passion, and swore by St. Edward he would not leave Ireland until he had MacMurrough in his hands, dead or live. How little he imagined, when uttering the mighty boast, that his own fate was even then sealed! Had he but the grace to have conciliated instead of threatened, a brave and loyal band of Irish chieftains would soon have surrounded him, and the next chapter of English history would have been less tragic. Disastrous accounts soon reached him from England, which at once annihilated his schemes of Irish conquest or revenge. His own people were up in arms, and the prescriptive right to grumble, which an Englishman is supposed to enjoy par excellence, had broken out into overt acts of violence. War was inaugurated between York and Lancaster, and for years England was deluged with blood.[26]

Henry's invasion of England

Henry, the new duke of Lancaster, had acquired, by his conduct and abilities, the esteem of the public. --- *He was connected with most of the principal nobility by blood, alliance, or friendship, and as the injury done him by the king, might in its consequence affect all of them, he easily brought them, by a sense of common interest, to take part in his resentment. The people, who must have an object of affection, who found nothing in the king's person which they could love or revere, and who were even disgusted with many parts of his conduct, easily transferred to Henry that attachment, which the death of the duke of Gloucester had left without any fixed direction. His misfortunes were lamented; the injustice,*

---

[26] Cusack, History of Ireland, pp 366-367.

which he had suffered, was complained of; and all men turned their eyes towards him, as the only person that could retrieve the lost honor of the nation, or redress the supposed abuses in the government.

Henry, embarking at Nantz, July 4, 1399, with a retinue of sixty persons, among whom were the archbishop of Canterbury and the young earl of Arundel, nephew to that prelate, landed at Ravenspur in Yorkshire; and was immediately joined by the earls of Northumberland and Westmoreland, two of the most potent barons in England. He here took a solemn oath, that he had no other purpose in this invasion, than to recover the duchy of Lancaster, unjustly detained from him; and he invited all his friends in England, and all lovers of their country, to second him in this reasonable and moderate pretension. Every place was in commotion: The malcontents in all quarters flew to arms: London discovered the strongest symptoms of its disposition to mutiny and rebellion: And Henry's army, increasing on every day's march, soon amounted to the number of 60,000 combatants.

Edmund, the duke of York, was left guardian of the realm; a place to which his birth entitled him, but which his slender abilities, and his natural connections with the duke of Lancaster, rendered him utterly incapable of filling in such a dangerous emergency. Such of the chief nobility, as were attached to the crown, and could either have seconded the guardian's good intentions or have overawed his infidelity, had attended the king into Ireland; and the efforts of Richard's friends were every where more feeble than those of his enemies. The duke of York, however, appointed the rendezvous of his forces at St. Albans, and soon assembled an army of 40,000 men, but found them entirely destitute of zeal and attachment to the royal cause, and more inclined to join the party of the rebels. He hearkened therefore very readily to a message from Henry, who entreated him not to oppose a loyal and humble supplicant in the recovery of his legal patrimony; and the guardian even declared publicly that he would second his nephew in so reasonable a request. His army embraced with acclamations the same measures; and the duke of Lancaster, reinforced by them, was now entirely master of the kingdom.[27]

Richard's return from Ireland and defeat

The king, receiving intelligence of this invasion and insurrection, hastened over from Ireland, and landed in Milford Haven with a body of 20,000 men: But even this army, so much inferior to the enemy, was either overawed by the general combination of the kingdom, or seized with the same spirit of disaffection; and they gradually deserted him, till he found that he had not above 6,000 men who followed his standard. It appeared, therefore, necessary to retire secretly from this

---

[27] Hume, pp 314,315.

small body, which served only to expose him to danger; and he fled to the isle of Anglesea, where he purposed to embark either for Ireland or France. Henry sent to him the earl of Northumberland with the strongest professions of loyalty and submission; and that nobleman, by treachery and false oaths, made himself master of the king's person, and carried him to his enemy at Flint Castle. Richard was conducted to London, by the duke of Lancaster, who was there received with the acclamations of the mutinous populace.[28]

Richard charged with felonies in Parliament, and deposed

Henry issued writs of election in the king's name, and appointed the immediate meeting of a parliament at Westminster. Henry purposed to have him solemnly deposed in parliament for his pretended tyranny and misconduct. A charge, consisting of thirty-three articles, was accordingly drawn up against him, and presented to that assembly. When the charge against Richard was presented to the parliament, though it was liable, almost in every article, to objections, it was not canvassed, or examined, nor disputed in either house, and seemed to be received with universal approbation. One man alone, the bishop of Carlisle, had the courage, amidst this general disloyalty and violence, to appear in defense of his unhappy master, and to plead his cause against all the power of the prevailing party. The speech of Carlisle before parliament in defense of Richard as portrayed in the Shakespeare play was presented on the first page of this chapter, above. After discussing the articles against Richard, Hume concluded: *The noble freedom of the bishop of Carlisle, instead of being applauded, was not so much as tolerated: He was immediately arrested, by order of the duke of Lancaster, and sent a prisoner to the abbey of St. Albans. No farther debate was attempted: Thirty-three long articles of charge were, in one meeting, voted against Richard; and voted unanimously by the same peers and prelates, who, a little before, had, voluntarily and unanimously, authorized those very acts of violence of which they now complained. That prince was deposed by the suffrages of both houses; and the throne being now vacant, the duke of Lancaster stepped forth --- and challenged the crown as his due, either by acquisition or inheritance assumed the crown. --- The whole forms such a pieced of jargon and nonsense, as is almost without example: No objection however was made to it in parliament: the unanimous voice of lords and commons placed Henry on the throne: He became king, nobody could tell how or wherefore: The title of the house of Marche, formerly recognized by parliament, was neither invalidated nor repealed, but passed over in total silence.*[29]

---

[28] Ibid, p 316.

[29] Hume, vol 2, pp 317-319.

The murder of Richard II

The circumstances and details of the murder of Richard differ among historians. The account of Hume follows: *The earl of Northumberland made a motion, in the house of peers, with regard to the unhappy prince whom they had deposed. He asked them, what advice they would give the king for the future treatment of him, since Henry was resolved to spare his life. They unanimously replied, that he should be imprisoned under a secure guard, in some secret place, and should be deprived of all commerce with any of his friends or partisans. It was easy to foresee, that he would not long remain alive in the hands of such barbarous and sanguinary enemies. Historians differ with regard to the manner in which he was murdered. It was long the prevailing opinion, that Sir Piers Exton, and others of his guards, fell upon him in the castle of Pomfret, which he was confined, and dispatched him with their halberts.[30] But it is more probable, that he was starved to death in prison; and after all sustenance was denied him, he prolonged his unhappy life, it is said, for a fortnight, before he reached the end of his miseries. This account is more consistent with the story, that the body was exposed in public, and that no marks of violence were observed upon it.[31] He died, October 23, 1399, in the thirty-fourth year of his age, and the twenty-third of his reign. He left no posterity, either legitimate or illegitimate.*

---

[30] Note. Shakespeare's story in Richard II, Act 5, sc. 5 follows this version of Hume's history, except that the murder was provoked by Richard's assault on the guards after they refused to taste the meal he had been given.

[31] Ibid, pp 323.

Chapter 20

Henry IV

Henry IV, also known as Bolinbroke, duke of Hereford, (b. 1366, d. 1413), was the first of three Lancastrian kings by the name of Henry. He usurped the throne after victory over Richard II as told in the previous chapter. Henry was the eldest son of John of Gaunt, duke of Lancaster, by his first wife, Blanche. Since Richard had no offspring, the crown rightfully descended to Phillipa, daughter of Edward III's second son Lionel, and her son Roger Mortimer.[1] When his father went to Spain, Henry was one of the lords appellant allied with Gloucester, who attacked Richard and his favorites in 1388. Henry's animosities subsided with the return of his father, duke of Lancaster from Spain. In 1397 Gloucester was banished and murdered. The following year Richard banished Henry and confiscated his estates. Henry, after the death of his father, returned to England to claim his inheritance. Henry defeated Richard and claimed the right to the throne. Henry's reign was spent for the most part in military battles to retain the crown from the insurrections, uprisings and civil wars he faced during his inglorious reign, 1399-1413. He developed a condition described as apoplexy and had 'fits' in his latter years, dying young, at age 46. Shakespeare's chronicles of Henry IV, in two plays, described the tragic events of Henry IV, interspersed and relieved with ribald tales of the friends and associates of his son Henry, prince of Wales, the future Henry V. The Shakespeare narrative closely follows, apart from the chronology, the history presented by Hume.

A contested crown, and the first Insurrection

Henry in his very first parliament had reason to see the danger, --- which he had assumed, and the obstacles which he would meet with in

---

[1] Note. See Table, Lancaster and York.

governing an unruly aristocracy always divided by faction, and at present inflamed with the resentments, consequent on such recent convulsions. The peers, on their assembling, broke out into violent animosities against each other; forty gauntlets, the pledges of furious battle, were thrown on the floor of the house by noblemen who gave mutual challenges; and 'liar' and 'traitor' resounded from all quarters. The king had so much authority with these doughty champions, as to prevent all the combats, which they threatened; but he was not able to bring them to a proper composure, or to an amicable disposition towards each other.[2]

The first insurrection, in 1400, involved members of Richard's family including the earl of Rutland, son of Edmund, duke of York. Thus we have a continuation of the civil disturbances and wars, which started with the murder of Gloucester and Richard II's disinheritance of Henry's estate leading to Henry's invasion of England and usurpation of the throne.[3] *It was not long before these passions broke into action. The earls of Rutland, Kent, and Huntingdon, and lord Spencer, who were now degraded from the respective titles of Albemarle, Surrey, Exeter, and Gloucester, conferred on them by Richard, entered into a conspiracy, together with the earl of Salisbury and lord Lumley, for raising an insurrection, and of seizing the king's person at Windsor; the treachery of Rutland gave him warning of the danger. He suddenly withdrew to London; and the conspirators, who came to Windsor with a body of 500 horse, found that they had missed this blow, on which all the success of their enterprise depended. Henry appeared, next day, at Kingston upon Thames, at the head of 20,000 men, mostly drawn from the city; and his enemies, unable to resist his power, dispersed themselves, with a view of raising their followers in the several counties, which were the seat of*

---

[2] Hume, vol 2, p 334.

[3] Note. The roses refer to the houses of York (white rose) and Lancaster (red rose). These appellations and the name War of Roses developed by historians ignored the fact that civil disputes, insurrections and wars existed for about one hundred years among the sons, grandsons and descendants of Edward III. It makes no sense to limit the one hundred year conflicts between the Yorkist and Lancaster factions to the last years, 1455 to 1485, of this series of self-destructive wars. Hume's opinion is worth quoting in full: *There is no part of English history since the Conquest, so obscure, so uncertain, so little authentic or consistent, as that of the wars between the two Roses: Historians differ about many material circumstances; some events of the utmost consequence, in which they almost all agree, are incredible and contradicted by records; and it is remarkable, that this profound darkness falls upon us just on the eve of the restoration of letters, and when the art of Printing was already known in Europe. All we can distinguish with certainty through the dark clouds, which covers that period, is a scene of horror and bloodshed.* Hume, V 2. p 469.

their interest. But the adherents of the king were hot in the pursuit, and everywhere opposed themselves to their progress. The earls of Kent and Salisbury were seized at Cirencester by the citizens; and were next day beheaded without further ceremony, according to the custom of the times. The citizens of Bristol treated Spencer and Lumley in the same manner. The earl of Huntingdon, Sir Thomas Blount, and sir Bendedict Sely, who were also taken prisoners, suffered death, with many others of the conspirators, by orders from Henry. And when the quarters of these unhappy men were brought to London, no less than eighteen bishops and thirty-two mitred abbots, joined the populace, and met them with the most indecent marks of joy and exultation.

But the spectacle the most shocking to every one, who retained any sentiment either of honor or humanity, still remained. The earl of Rutland appeared, carrying on a pole the head of lord Spencer, his brother-in-law, which he presented in triumph to Henry, as a testimony of his loyalty. This infamous man, who was soon after duke of York by the death of his father, and first prince of the blood, had been instrumental in the murder of his uncle, the duke of Gloucester; and then deserted Richard, by whom he was trusted; and conspired against the life of Henry, to whom he had sworn allegiance; had betrayed his associates, whom he had seduced into this enterprise; and now displayed, in the face of the world, these badges of his multiplied dishonor.[4]

Insurrection in Wales

The centers of rebellion were in the north, in Northumberland with invasions from Scotland; and in the west, in Wales. Henry IV, Bolinbroke, had usurped the throne by invasion and conquest of England. The heir to the throne proclaimed by king Richard II, was Edmund Mortimer, grandson of Phillipa, daughter of Edward III's eldest surviving son Lionel. An alliance between Owen Glendour of Wales, Douglas of Scotland, Henry Piercy of Northumberland and Mortimer would challenge Henry IV. Douglas invaded the north of England but was defeated by Henry Piercy, earl of Northumberland. Yet Douglas would later become the chief ally of Henry Piercy, called Hotspur the son of Northumberland. Glendour would capture Mortimer, however he would ally himself with his cause as the rightful heir to the English throne. Marriages between these families would solidify their alliances.

There was nearly a century without wars between England and Wales before the time of Owen Glendour, a powerful Welsh nobleman. Edward I had almost completely subjugated Wales by the end of the thirteenth century, however, it would not be until 1536 during the reign of Henry VIII that Wales would become annexed to England. *Owen Glendour, or Glendourduy, descended from the ancient princes of that*

---

[4] Hume vol 2, pp 334-336.

country, had become obnoxious on account of his attachment to Richard; and Reginald, lord Gray of Ruthyn, who was closely connected with the new king, and who enjoyed a great fortune in the marches of Wales, thought the opportunity favorable for oppressing his neighbor, and taking possession of his estate. Glendour, provoked at the injustice, and still more at the indignity, recovered possession by the sword: Henry sent assistance to Gray: the Welsh took part with Glendour: A troublesome and tedious war was kindled, which Glendour long sustained by his valor and activity, aided by the natural strength of the country, and the untamed spirit of its inhabitants.

As Glendour committed devastations promiscuously on all the English, he infested the estate of the earl of March; and sir Edmund Mortimer, uncle to that nobleman, led out the retainers of the family, and gave battle to the Welsh chieftain: His troops were routed, and he was taken prisoner: At the same time, the earl himself, who had been allowed to retire to this castle of Wigmore, and who, though a mere boy, took the field with his followers, fell also into Glendour's hands, and was carried by him into Wales. As Henry dreaded and hated all the family of Marche, he allowed the earl to remain in captivity; and though that young nobleman was nearly allied to the Piercies, to whose assistance he himself had owed his crown, he refused to the earl of Northumberland permission to treat of his ransom with Glendour.[5]

Douglas, the earl of Northumberland and his son Harry Piercy

In the subsequent season, Archibald earl of Douglas, at the head of 12,000 men, and attended by many of the principal nobility of Scotland, made an irruption into England, and committed devastations on the northern counties. On his return home, he was overtaken by the Piercies, at Homeldon on the borders of England, and a fierce battle ensued, where the Scots were totally routed. Douglas himself was taken prisoner, as was Mordac earl of Fife, son of the duke of Albany, and nephew of the Scottish king, with the earls of Angus, Murray, and Orkney, and many others of the gentry and nobility. When Henry received intelligence of this victory, he sent the earl of Northumberland orders not to ransom his prisoners, which that nobleman regarded as his right, by the laws of war, received in that age. The king intended to detain them that he might be able by their means to make an advantageous peace with Scotland; but by this policy he gave a fresh disgust to the family of Piercy. Douglas would become the only force in support of Hotspur in the final battle of Shrewsbury against the king and his son prince Henry.

---

[5] Ibid, pp 337-339.

Northumberland and his son resolve to overthrow king Henry

The obligations, which Henry had owed to Northumberland, were of a kind the most likely to produce ingratitude on the one side, and discontent on the other. Though Henry, on his accession, had bestowed the office of constable on Northumberland for life, and conferred other gifts on that family, these favors were regarded as their due; the refusal of any other request was deemed an injury. The impatient spirit of Harry Piercy, and the factious disposition of the earl of Worcester, younger brother of Northumberland, inflamed the discontents of that nobleman; and the precarious title of Henry tempted him to seek revenge, by overturning that throne, which he had at first established.

He entered into a correspondence with Glendour: He gave liberty to the earl of Douglas, and made an alliance with that martial chief: He roused up all his partisans to arms; and such unlimited authority at that time belonged to the great families, that the same men, who, a few years before, he had conducted against Richard, now followed his standard in opposition to Henry. When war was ready to break out, Northumberland was seized with a sudden illness at Berwic; and young Piercy, taking the command of the troops, marched towards Shrewsbury, in order to join his forces with those of Glendour.

The king had happily a small army on foot, with which he had intended to act against the Scots; and knowing the importance of celerity in all civil wars, he instantly hurried down, that he might give battle to the rebels. He approached Piercy near Shrewsbury, before that nobleman was joined by Glendour; and the policy of one leader, and impatience of the other, made them hasten to a general engagement. Neither would the earl of Worcester's army march to the battle in time.

The evening before the battle, Piercy sent a manifesto to Henry, in which he renounced his allegiance, set that prince at defiance, and in the name of his father and uncle, as well as his own, enumerated all the grievances, of which, he pretended, the nation had reason to complain. He upbraided him with the perjury, of which he had been guilty, when on landing at Ravenspur, he had sworn upon the gospels, before the earl of Northumberland, that he had no other intention than to recover the duchy of Lancaster, and that he would ever remain a faithful subject to king Richard. He aggravated his guilt in first dethroning, then murdering that prince, and in usurping on the title of the house of Mortimer, to which, both by lineal succession, and by declarations of parliament, the throne, when vacant by Richard's demise, did of right belong. He complained of his cruel policy, in allowing the young earl of Marche, whom he ought to regard as his sovereign, to remain a captive in the hands of his enemies, and in even refusing to all his friend's permission to treat of his ransom.[6]

---

[6] Ibid, pp 339-340.

The battle of Shrewsbury

The drama and background of the conflict between Northumberland, his son Piercy or Hotspur, and king Henry's forces cannot be better portrayed or told than in the historic parts of the play of Shakespeare, *King Henry IV*. The reader may elect to ignore the distractions of prince Henry and his bawdy associates, and focus on the history. The First Part of Henry IV tells of the dramatic events leading up to the battle of Shrewsbury. The overwhelming tragedy of this period of English history, perhaps requires an interlude of ribald behavior and humor to provide a distraction from the overwhelming grief, not just involving kings Richard and Henry, the members of the families of the descendants of Edward who were slain, but the entire nation embroiled in the bizarre conflicts and wars of England. It was Northumberland and his aristocratic supporters who destroyed the crown of Richard and put Henry on the throne. Yet now in this story it is Northumberland, his son Piercy and allies who conspired to dethrone Henry. Piercy was slain in battle. His army fled. The earl of Worcester, Northumberland's brother, and Douglas were captured, the former beheaded.

In the battle of Shrewsbury, July 21, 1403, *we shall scarcely find any battle in those ages, where the shock was more terrible and more constant. Henry exposed his person in the thickest of the fight: His gallant son, whose miliary achievements were afterwards so renowned, and who here performed his noviciate in arms, signalized himself on his father's footsteps, and even a wound, which he received in the face with an arrow, could not oblige him to quit the field. Piercy supported that fame, which he had acquired in many a bloody combat. And Douglas, ancient enemy and now his friend, still appeared his rival, amidst the horror and confusion of the day. This nobleman performed feats of valor, which are almost incredible: He seemed determined that the king of England should that day fall by his arm: He fought him all over the field of battle: And as Henry, either to elude the attacks of the enemy upon his person, or to encourage his own men by the belief of his presence every where, had accoutered several captains in the royal garb, the sword of Douglas rendered this honor fatal to many. But while the armies were contending in this furious manner, the death of Piercy, by an unknown hand, decided the victory, and the royalists prevailed. There are said to have fallen that day on both sides near two thousand three hundred gentlemen. About six thousand private men perished, of whom two thirds were of Piercy's army. The earls of Worcester and Douglas were taken prisoner; the former was beheaded at Shrewsbury; the latter was treated with the courtesy due to his rank and merit.*[7]

---

[7] Ibid, p 341.

Northumberland's forces conquered by the deceit of Westmoreland

Northumberland was advised of the death of his son and the victory of king Henry at Shrewsbury, as dramatically related by Shakespeare. The rest of the story of Henry IV is portrayed in the Second Part of Shakespeare's *King Henry IV.* The details of Shakespeare's history correspond to that of Hume.

From Hume: In 1405, The enemies of Henry *rose in rebellion one after the another; --- The earl of Nottingham,* (lord Mowbray) *son of the duke of Norfolk, and the archbishop of York* (Scroop), *brother to the earl of Wiltshire, whom Henry, then duke of Lancaster, had beheaded at Bristol, though they had remained quiet while Piercy was in the field, still harbored in their breast a violent hatred against the enemy of their families; and they determined, in conjunction with the earl of Northumberland to seek revenge against him. They betook themselves to arms before that powerful nobleman was prepared to join them; and publishing a manifesto in which they reproached Henry with his usurpation of the crown and the murder of the late king, they required, that the right line should be restored, and all public grievances be redressed.*

The earl of Westmoreland, whose power lay in the neighborhood, approached them with an inferior force at Shipton near York; and being afraid to hazard an action, he attempted to subdue them by a stratagem, which nothing but the greatest folly and simplicity on their part could have rendered successful. He desired a conference with the archbishop and earl between the armies: He heard their grievances with great patience. He begged them to propose the remedies: He approved of every expedient which they suggested: He granted them all their demands: he also engaged that Henry should give them entire satisfaction: And when he saw them pleased with the facility of his concessions, he observed to them, that, since amity was now in effect restored between them, it were better on both sides to dismiss their forces, which otherwise would prove an unsupportable burthen to the country. The archbishop and the earl of Nottingham immediately gave directions to that purpose: Their troops disbanded upon the field.

But Westmoreland, who had secretly issued contrary orders to his army, seized the two rebels without resistance, and carried them to the king, was advancing with hasty marches to oppress the insurrection. The trial and punishment of an archbishop might have proved a troublesome and dangerous undertaking, had Henry proceeded regularly, and allowed time for an opposition to form itself against that unusual measure: The celerity of the execution alone could here render it safe and prudent. Finding that Sir William Gascoigne, the chief justice, made some scruple of acting on this occasion, he appointed Sir William Fulthorpe for judge; who, without any indictment, trial, or defense, pronounced sentence of death upon the prelate, which was presently executed. This was the first instance in England of a capital punishment inflicted on a bishop; whence the clergy of that rank might learn, that their crimes, more than those of laic, were not to pass with impunity. The earl of Nottingham (lord Mowbray) *was condemned and executed in the same summary manner: But though many other persons of condition, such as lord Falconberg, Ralph Hastings, John Colville, were engaged in this rebellion, no others seem to have fallen victims to Henry's severity.*[8]

Final demise of the earl of Northumberland

The earl of Northumberland, on receiving this intelligence, fled into Scotland, together with lord Bardolf; and the king without opposition, reduced all the castles and fortresses belonging to these noblemen. The king thence turned his arms against Glendour, over whom his son, the prince of Wales, had obtained some advantages. But that enemy, more troublesome than dangerous, still found means of defending himself in his fastnesses, and of eluding, though not resisting, all the force of England. In a subsequent season, in 1407, *the earl of Northumberland and lord Bardolf, impatient of their exile, entered the North, in hopes of raising the people to arms; but found the country in such a posture as rendered all their attempts unsuccessful. Sir Thomas Rokesby, sheriff of Yorkshire, levied some forces, attacked the invaders at Bramham, and gained a victory, in which both Northumberland and Bardolf were slain. The death of Owen Glendour happened soon thereafter.*[9]

The last years of Henry IV

During the last two years of Henry's reign he entered into treaties with the duke of Burgandy and the duke of Orleans, however, there was little resurgence of warfare between England and France. It would be prince Henry, as Henry V, who would rekindle the imperialist flame to conquer France.

The king was so much employed in defending his crown, which he had obtained by unwarrantable means, and possessed by a bad title, that he had little leisure to look abroad, or perform any action, which might redound to the honor and advantage of the nation. His health declined some months before his death: He was subject to fits, which bereaved him, for the time, of his senses: And though he was yet in the flower of his age, his end was visibly approaching. He expired at Westminster in the forty-sixth year of his age, on March 20, 1413, *and the thirteenth of his reign.*

The crown passed to his eldest son prince Henry and the dying moments of Henry IV could not be told better than by Shakespeare.

---

[8] Ibid, pp 342-343.

[9] Ibid, pp 340-343.

Come hither, Harry, sit thou by my bed; And hear, I think, the very latest counsel That ever I shall breathe. God knows, my son, By what by-paths and indirect crook'd ways I met this crown; and I myself know well How troublesome it sat upon my head: To thee it shall descend with better quiet, Better opinion, better confirmation; for all the soil of the achievement goes With me into the earth. It seem'd in me But as an honor snatch'd with boisterous hand; And I had many living to upbraid My gain of it by their assistance; Which daily grew to quarrel and to bloodshed, Wounding supposed peace; all these bold fears Thou see'st with peril I have answered; For all my reign hath been about as a scene Acting that argument; and now my death Changes the mode; for what in me was purchas'd, Falls upon thee in a more fairer sort; So thou the garland wear'st successively.--- You won it, wore it, kept it, gave it me; Then plain and right must my possession be; Which I with more than with a common pain Gainst all the world will rightfully maintain.[10]

Hume provides a summary of his reign: *The great popularity, which Henry enjoyed before he attained the crown, and which had so much aided him in the acquisition of it, was entirely lost many years before the end of his reign; and he governed his people more by terror than by affection, more by his own policy than by their sense of duty or allegiance. When men came to reflect in cold blood on the crimes which had led him to the throne; the rebellion against his prince, the deposition of a lawful king, guilty sometimes perhaps of oppression, but more frequently of indiscretion; the exclusion of the true heir; the murder of his sovereign and near relation; these were such enormities as drew on him the hatred of his subjects, sanctified all the rebellious against him, and made the executions, though not remarkably severe, which he found necessary for the maintenance of his authority, appear cruel as well as iniquitous to the people. --- The injustice with which his predecessor had treated him, in first condemning him to banishment, then despoiling him of his patrimony, made him naturally think of revenge, and of recovering his lost rights; the headlong zeal of the people hurried him into the throne; the care of his own security, as well as his ambition, made him an usurper; and the steps have always been so few between the prisons of princes and their graves, that we need not wonder, that Richard's fate was no exception to the general rule. All these considerations make Henry's situation, if he retained any sense of virtue, much to be lamented; and the inquietude, with which he possessed his envied greatness, and the remorse, by which, it is said, he was continually haunted, render him an object of our pity, even when seated upon the throne.*[11]

---

[10] Shakespeare, Second Part, King Henry IV, Act IV, sc. 4.

[11] Hume, vol 2, pp 344-350.

Chapter 21

Henry V

Henry V, (b. 1387, d. 1422), and whose reign, 1413-1422 was characterized by suppressions of civil disorders, followed by invasions and conquest of France. The first religious uprising of any consequence, the Lollards, an early protestant sect, was brutally crushed by the king with the advice and counsel of the archbishop of Canterbury. A York vs. Lancaster uprising was met with summary executions. The archbishop encouraged Henry's claim of the crown of France and his military enterprises based on false contentions regarding French regal inheritance. Henry brought great glory to England with his victory over the French at Azincourt. *With experience of war and government as Prince of Wales, he proved a capable, fearless, and authoritarian monarch who abandoned the careful ways of his father. Even during his absences in France, his kingship was firm and energetic, enabling him to wage a war that was as much a popular enterprise as Edward III's early campaigns had been. His reign was the climax of Lancastrian England.*[1] He married Catherine, daughter of the French king Charles VI, who after the king's untimely death at age 36 married Owen Tudor, and whose grandson would become Henry VII. Henry died young, at age 36, and left his crown in the hands of his nine-month old son to become Henry VI. The conquests of Henry V would be lost during the minority of Henry VI.

Early years

Henry, after his father was sent into exile in 1398, was brought up by Richard II, at an age when he could be influenced by an errant foster father. Henry V was the oldest son of Henry IV and his first wife Mary de Bohun. It is really odd that so little is available in the historic sources regarding the early years of the kings of England, even less so

---

[1] Griffiths, in Morgan, pp 199, 200.

than we found in the ancient sources for the emperors of Rome. Three other sons, younger brothers of Henry, will be noted in this story; Thomas, duke of Clarence; John, duke of Bedford; and Humphrey, duke of Gloucester.

Youthful disorders

The Shakespeare plays portray the conduct of prince Harry and his associates interspersed with the historical narrative. The disorders of the prince are summarized by Hume: *The active spirit of young Henry, restrained from its proper exercise, broke out in extravagancies of every kind; and the riot of pleasure, the frolic of debauchery, the outrage of wine, filled the vacancies of a mind, better adapted to the pursuits of ambition, and the cares of government. This course of life threw him among companions, whose disorders, if accompanied with spirit and humor, he indulged and seconded; and he was detected in many sallies, which, to severer eyes, appeared totally unworthy of his rank and station. There even remains a tradition, that, when heated with liquor and jollity, he scrupled not to accompany his riotous associates in attacking the passengers on the streets and highways, and despoiling them of their goods; and he found an amusement in the incidents, which the terror and regret of these defenseless people produced on such occasions. This extreme of dissoluteness proved equally disagreeable to his father, as that eager application to business, which had at first given him occasion of jealousy; and he saw in this son's behavior the same neglect for decency, the same attachment to low company, which had degraded the personal character of Richard, and which, more than all his errors in government, had tended to overturn his throne.*

One of the first reforms of Henry V as king was to dissociate himself from his former companions. *He called together his former companions, acquainted them with his intended reformation, exhorted them to imitate his example, but strictly inhibited them, till they had given proofs of their sincerity in this particular, from appearing any more in his presence; and he thus dismissed them with liberal presents.*[2]

Revolt of the Lollards

One of the first conflicts of Henry's reign, in 1413, involved one of the followers of John Wickliffe. Wickliffe was an early founder of a protestant group of believers who aspired to a reformation of ecclesiastical abuses. Before presenting the uprising of lord Cobham threatening to Henry, the background of Wickliffe from Hume's chapter on Richard II is presented.

John Wickliffe, a secular priest, educated at Oxford, began in the latter end of Edward II, to spread the doctrine of reformation by his

---

[2] Hume, vol 2, pp 352-354.

discourses, sermons, and writings: and he made many disciples among men of all ranks and stations. --- The doctrines of Wickliffe, being derived from his search into the scriptures and into ecclesiastical antiquity, were nearly the same with those which were propagated by the reformers in the sixteenth century: He only carried some of them farther than was done by the more sober part of these reformers. He denied the doctrine of the real presence, the supremacy of the church of Rome, the merit of monastic vows: He maintained, that the scriptures were the sole rule of faith; that the church was dependant on the state, and should be reformed by it; that the clergy ought to posses no estates; that the begging friars were a nuisance, and ought not to be supported; that the numerous ceremonies of the church were hurtful to true piety: He asserted, that oaths were unlawful, that dominion was founded in grace, that every thing was subject to fate and destiny, and that all men were pre-ordained whether to eternal salvation or reprobation.

One of his followers, lord Cobham, leader of the Lollards, *who were every day increasing in the kingdom, and were become a formed party, which appeared extremely dangerous to the church, and even formidable to the civil authority.* Henry *found that nobleman obstinate in his opinions, and determined not to sacrifice truths of such infinite moment to this complaisance for sovereigns. Henry's principles of toleration, or rather his love of the practice, could carry him no farther; and he then gave full reins to ecclesiastical severity against the inflexible heresiarch. The primate indicted Cobham; and with the assistance of his three suffragans, the bishops of London, Winchester, and St. Davids, condemned him to the flames for his erroneous opinions.* Cobham and his Lollard followers formed a conspiracy against the king who contained the disorder. *Some were executed, the great number pardoned. Cobham, himself, who made his escape in flight, was not brought to justice, till four years after; when he was hanged as a traitor and his body was burnt on the gibbet, the execution of the sentence pronounced against him as a heretic. The parliament met and passed severe laws against the new heretics: They enacted, that whoever was convicted of Lollardy before the Ordinary, besides suffering capital punishment according to the laws formerly established, should also forfeit his lands and goods to the king; and that the chancellor, treasurer, justices of the two benches, sheriffs, justices of the peace, and all the chief magistrates in every city and borough, should take an oath to use their utmost endeavors for the extirpation of heresy.*[3]

Henry's claim of the crown of France and preparations for war

The parliament also renewed the acts of Henry IV to seize and use church revenues for the use of the king. The clergy were alarmed.

---

[3] Ibid, pp 355-356.

The archbishop of Canterbury *endeavored to divert the blow, by giving occupation to the king, and by persuading him to undertake a war against France, in order to recover his lost rights to that kingdom.* The justification of Henry's claim to the throne of France is provided in Shakespeare's play *King Henry V.* The archbishop of Canterbury provided the rational. According to the archbishop, Henry's authority derives from his great grandfather Edward III and that *there is no bar to make against your highness' claim to France.* The archbishop claimed, wrongly, that the Salic law[4] applied to Germany and not to France, Henry then asks: *May I with right and conscience make this claim?* The archbishop replies: *The sin upon my head, dread sovereign! For in the book of numbers is it writ: When a man dies, let the inheritance Descend unto the daughter. Gracious lord, stand for your own; unwind your bloody flag; Look back unto your mighty ancestors: Go, my dread lord, to your great-grandshire's tomb, From whom you claim; invoke his warlike spirit, And your great-uncle's, Edward the Black prince, who on the French ground play'd a tragedy, making defeat of the full power of France, Whiles his most mighty father on a hill Stood smiling to behold his lion's whelp Forage in blood of French nobility. O noble English, that could entertain With half their forces the full pride of France, And let another half stand laughing by, All out of work and cold for action!* [5]

York vs. Lancaster Conspiracy

But while Henry was preparing for an invasion of France and assuming the crown of France there was a flare up of the civil disorders among the descendants of Edward III. *A conspiracy to dethrone the king was detected in its infancy. The earl of Cambridge, second son of the late duke of York, having espoused the sister of the earl of Marche, had zealously embraced the interests of that family; and had held some conferences with lord Scrope of Masham, and Sir Thomas Grey of Heton, about the means of recovering to that nobleman his right to the crown of England. The conspirators, as soon as detected, acknowledged their guilt to the king; and Henry proceeded without delay to their trial and condemnation. --- A jury of commoners was summoned: The three conspirators were indicted before them: The constable of Southampton castle swore, that they had separately confessed their guilt to him: Without other evidence, Sir Thomas Grey was condemned and executed: But as the earl of Cambridge and lord Scrope, pleaded the privilege of their peerage, Henry thought proper to summon a court of eighteen barons, in which the duke of Clarence presided: the evidence, given before the jury, was read to them: The prisoners, though one of them was*

---

[4] Salic law- only descendants of males inherit the throne.

[5] Shakespeare, Henry V, Act I, sc. 2.

a prince of the blood, were not examined, nor produced in court, nor heard in their own defense; but received sentence of death upon this proof, which was every way irregular and unsatisfactory; and the sentence was soon after executed.[6]

France

Henry picked a good time to invade France. The court of France had even more contention among the dukes than was the case in England during the reigns of Richard II and Henry IV. *The death of Charles, king of France, which followed soon after that of Edward III, and the youth of his son, Charles VI put the two kingdoms for some time in a similar situation; --- The jealousies also between Charles's three uncles, the dukes of Anjou, Berri, and Burgundy, had distracted the affairs of France rather more than those between the dukes of Lancaster, York, and Gloucester. --- But the unhappy prince (Charles VI) fell suddenly into a fit of frenzy, which rendered him incapable of exercising his authority; and though he recovered from this disorder, he was so subject to relapses, that his judgment was gradually, but sensibly impaired, and no steady plan of government could be pursued by him. The administration of affairs was disputed between his brother, Lewis duke of Orleans and his cousin-german, John duke of Burgundy: --- The people were divided between these contending princes. And the king, now resuming, now dropping his authority, kept the victory undecided, and prevented any regular settlement of the state, by the final prevalence of either party.*[7]

Invasion and conquest of Harfleur

Henry put to sea, August 14, 1415, and landed near Harfleur, at the head of an army of 6,000 men at arms, and 24,000 foot, mostly archers. He immediately began the siege of that place, which was valiantly defended by d'Estouteville, and under him by de Guitri, de Gaucourt, and others of the French nobility: But as this garrison was weak, and the fortifications in bad repair, the governor was at last obliged to capitulate; and he promised to surrender the place if he received no succor before the eighteenth of September. The day came, and there was no appearance of a French army to relieve him. Henry, taking possession of the town, placed a garrison in it, and expelled all the French inhabitants, with an intention of peopling it anew with English.

King Henry's demands to the governor of Harfleur are candidly presented in *King Henry V* by Shakespeare:

---

[6] Hume, vol 2, pp 361-362.

[7] Ibid, pp 358-361.

This is the latest parley we will admit: Therefore, to our best mercy give yourselves; Or like to men proud of destruction, Defy us to our worst; for as I am a soldier, - A name that, in my thoughts, becomes me best, - If I begin the battery once again, I will not leave the half-achieved Harfleur Till in her ashes she lie buried. The gates of mercy shall be all shut up; And the flesh'd soldier, - rough and hard of heart, - In liberty of bloody hand shall range With conscience wide as hell; mowing like grass Your fresh-fair virgins and your flowering infants. What is it then to me if impious war, - Array'd in flames, like to the prince of fiends, - do, with his smirch'd complexion, all fell feats Erlink'd to waste and desolation? What is 't to me when you yourselves are cause, If your pure maidens fall into the hand Of hot and forcing violation? What rein can hold licentious wickedness When down the hill he holds his fierce career? We may as bootless spend our vain command Upon the enraged soldiers in their spoil, As send precepts to the Leviathan. To come ashore. Therefore, you men of Harfleur, Take pity of your town and of your people Whiles yet my soldiers are in my command; Whiles yet the cool and temperate wind of grace O'erblows the filthy and contagious clouds Of heady murder, spoil, and villany. If not, why, in a moment look to see The blind and bloody soldier with foul hand Defile the locks of your shrill-shrieking daughters, Your fathers taken by the silver beards, And their most reverend heads dash's to the walls; Your naked infants spitted upon pikes, Whiles the mad mothers with their howls confus'd Do break the clouds, as did the wives of Jewry at Herod's bloody hunting slaughtermen. What say you? Will you yield, and this avoid? Or, guilty in defense, be thus destroy'd?[8]

The battle of Azincour

From Hume: *The fatigues of this siege, and the unusual heat of the season had so wasted the English army that Henry could enter on no farther enterprise; and was obliged to think of returning into England. He had dismissed his transports, which could not anchor in an open road upon the enemy's coasts: And he lay under a necessity of marching by land to Calais, before he could reach a place of safety. A numerous French army of 14,000 men at arms and 40,000 foot was by this time assembled in Normandy under the constable d'Albret; a force which, if prudently conducted, was sufficient either to trample down the English in the open field, or to harass and reduce to nothing their small army,*

---

[8] Shakespeare, Henry V, Act III, sc 2. Note. Many descendants of Edward de Vere were military commanders. It was common practice of the ancient historians to prepare speeches even if no record of such could have been taken, i.e. Julius Caesar, Plutarch, Tacitus

before they could finish so long and difficult a march. Henry, therefore, cautiously offered to sacrifice his conquest of Harfleur for a safe passage to Calais; but his proposal being rejected, he determined to make his way by valor and conduct through all the opposition of the enemy.

Henry reached the Somme and was fortunate to cross the river with so many French troops on the opposite bank. *Henry then bent his march northwards to Calais; but he was still exposed to great and imminent danger from the enemy, who had also passed the Somme, and threw themselves full in his way, with a purpose of intercepting his retreat. After he had passed the small river of Ternois at Blangi he was surprised to observe from the heights the whole French army drawn up in the plains of Azincour, and so posted that it was impossible for him to proceed on his march, without coming to an engagement. Nothing in appearance could be more unequal than the battle, upon which his safety and all his fortunes now depended. The English army was little more than half the number, which had disembarked at Harfleur; and they labored under every discouragement and necessity. The enemy was four times more numerous, was headed by the dauphin and all the princes of the blood; and was plentifully supplied with provisions of every kind. Henry's situation was exactly similar to that of Edward at Cressy, and that of the Black Prince at Poictiers; and the memory of these great events, inspiring the English with courage, made them hope for a like deliverance from their present difficulties. The king likewise observed the same prudent conduct which had been followed by these great commanders: He drew up his army on a narrow ground between two woods, which guarded each flank; and he patiently expected in that posture the attack of the enemy.*

Had the French constable been able, whether to reason justly upon the present circumstances of the two armies, or to profit by past experience, he had declined a combat, and had waited, till necessity obliging the English to advance, had made them relinquish the advantages of their situation. But the impetuous valor of the nobility and a vain confidence in superior numbers brought on this fatal action, which proved the source of infinite calamities to their country. The French archers on horseback and their men at arms, crowded in their ranks, advanced upon the English archers, who had fixed pallisadoes in their front to break the impression of the enemy, and who safely plyed them, from behind that defense, with a shower of arrows, which nothing could resist. The clay soil, moistened by some rain, which had lately fallen, proved another obstacle to the force of the French cavalry: The wounded men and horses discomposed their ranks: The narrow compass, in which they were pent, hindered them from recovering any order: The whole army was a scene of confusion, terror and dismay: and Henry, perceiving his advantage, ordered the English archers, who were light and unencumbered, to advance upon the enemy, and seize the moment of victory, October 25, 1415.

No battle was ever more fatal to France, by the number of princes and nobility, slain or taken prisoners. --- The killed are computed on the whole to have amounted to ten thousand men; and as the slaughter fell chiefly upon the cavalry, it is pretended, that, of these, eight thousand were gentlemen. Henry was master of 14,000 prisoners. --- Henry interrupted not his march a moment after the battle of Azincour; he carried his prisoners to Calais, thence to England; he even concluded a truce with the enemy; and it was not till after an interval of two years that any body of English troops appeared in France.[9]

Defeat of France

But during this interruption of hostilities from England, France was exposed to all the furies of civil war; and the several parties became every day more enraged against each other. --- While France was in such furious combustion, and was so ill prepared to resist a foreign enemy, in August, 1418, *Henry, having collected some treasure, and levied an army, landed in Normandy at the head of 15,000 men; and met with no considerable opposition from any quarter. He made himself master of Falaise; Evreux and Caen submitted to him; Pont de l'Arche opened its gates; and Henry, having subdued all the lower Normandy, and having received a reinforcement of 15,000 men from England, formed the siege of Rouen, which was defended by a garrison of 4,000 men, seconded by the inhabitants, to the number of 15,000.*[10]

The king of England had, before the death of the duke of Burgundy, profited extremely by the distractions of France, and was daily making a considerable progress in Normandy. He had taken Rouen after an obstinate siege: he had made himself master of Pontoise and Gisors; He even threatened Paris, and by the terror of his arms, had obliged the court to remove to Troye: And in the midst of his successes, he was agreeably surprised, to find his enemies, instead of combining against him for their mutual defense, disposed to rush into his arms, and to make him the instrument of their vengeance upon each other. A league was immediately concluded at Arras between him and the duke of Burgundy. This prince, without stipulating any thing for himself, except the prosecution of his father's murder, and the marriage of the duke of Bedford with his sister, was willing to sacrifice the kingdom to Henry's ambition: and he agreed to every demand, made by that monarch. In order to finish this astonishing treaty, which was to transfer the crown of France to a strange,. Henry went to Troye, accompanied by his brothers, the dukes of Clarence and Gloucester; and was there met by the duke of Burgundy. The imbecility, into which Charles had fallen, made him

---

[9] Ibid, pp 363-367.

[10] Ibid, p 369.

incapable of seeing any thing but through the eyes of those who attended him; as they, on their part, saw every thing through the medium of their passions. The treaty, being already concerted among the parties, was immediately drawn, and signed, and ratified: Henry's will seemed to be a law throughout the whole negotiation: Nothing was attended to but his advantages.

The Treaty of Troye

The principal articles of the treaty of Troye, 1420, *were, that Henry should espouse the princess Catharine: That king Charles, during his lifetime, should enjoy the title and dignity of king of France: That Henry should be declared and acknowledged heir of the monarchy, and be entrusted with the present administration of the government: That kingdom should pass to his heirs general: That France and England should for ever be united under one king; but should still retain their several usages, customs, and privileges: That all the princes, peers, vassals, and communities of France, should swear, that they should both adhere to the future succession of Henry, and pay him present obedience as regent: That this prince should unite his arms to those of king Charles and the duke of Burgundy, in order to subdue the adherents of Charles, the pretended dauphin: And that these three princes should make no peace or truce with him but by common consent and agreement.*

Such was the tenor of this famous treaty; a treaty, which, as nothing but the most violent animosity could dictate it, so nothing but the power of the sword could carry into execution. It is hard to say, whether its consequences, had it taken effect, would have proved more pernicious to England or to France. It must have reduced the former kingdom to the rank of a province: It would have entirely disjointed the succession of the latter, and have brought on the destruction of every descendant of the royal family; as the houses of Orleans, Anjou, Alencon, Brittany, Bourbon, and of Burgundy itself, whose titles were preferable to that of the English princes, would on that account have been exposed to perpetual jealousy and persecution from the sovereign.

There was even a palpable deficiency in Henry's claim, which no art could palliate. For besides the insuperable objections, to which Edward III's pretensions were exposed, he was not heir to that monarchy: If female succession were admitted, the right had devolved in the house of Mortimer: Allowing, that Richard II, was a tyrant, and that Henry IV's merits, in deposing him, were so great towards the English, as to justify that nation in placing him on the throne; Richard had nowise offended France, and his rival had merited nothing of that kingdom: It could not possibly be pretended, that the crown of France was become an appendage to that of England; and that a prince, who, by any means, got possession of the latter was, without farther question, entitled to the former. So that on the whole it must be allowed, that Henry's claim to France was, if possible still more unintelligible, than the title, by which his father had mounted the throne of England.[11]   Nevertheless, *in a few days after he espoused the princess Catharine: he carried his father-in-law to Paris, and put himself in possession of that capital: he obtained from the parliament and the three estates a ratification of the treaty of Troye.*

Return to England, war with Scots

The necessity of providing supplies both of men and money obliged Henry to go over to England, in 1421; and he left the duke of Exeter, his uncle, governor of Paris, during his absence. The authority, which naturally attends success, procured from the English parliament a subsidy of a fifteenth; but, if we may judge by the scantiness of the supply, that nation was nowise sanguine on their king's victories; and in proportion as the prospect of their union with France became nearer, they began to open their eyes and to see the dangerous consequences, with which that event must necessarily be attended. It was fortunate for Henry, that he had other resources, besides pecuniary supplies from his native subjects. The provinces, which he had already conquered, maintained his troops; and the hopes of further advantages allured to his standard all men of ambitious spirits in England, who desired to signalize themselves by arms. He levied a new army of 24,000 archers, and 4,000 horsemen. And marched them to Dover, the place of rendezvous. Every thing had remained in tranquility at Paris, under the duke of Exeter; but there had happened in another quarter of the kingdom a misfortune, which hastened the kings' embarkation.

The Scots were alarmed at Henry's success in France. The regent sent a body of 7,000 men, under the command of the earl of Buchan, his second son, and were employed by the dauphin against the English. The two armies met at Bauge: the English were defeated. *This was the first action that turned the tide of success against the English; and the dauphin, that he might both attach the Scots to his service, and reward the valor and conduct of the earl of Buchan, honored that nobleman with the office of constable.*[12]

Birth of a son

And to crown all the other prosperities of Henry, his queen was delivered of a son, who was called by his father's name, and whose birth was celebrated by rejoicing no less pompous, and no less sincere at Paris than at London. The infant prince seemed to be universally regarded as the future heir of both monarchies.

---

[11] Ibid, pp 372-373.

[12] Ibid, p 375.

Death of Henry V

But the glory of Henry, when it had nearly reached the summit, was stopped short by the hand of nature; and all his mighty projects vanished into smoke. He was seized with a fistula, a malady, which the surgeons at that time had not skill enough to cure. And he was at last sensible, that his distemper was mortal, and that his end was approaching. --- He declared himself confident, that the final acquisition of France would be the effect of their prudence and valor. He left the regency of that kingdom to his elder brother John duke of Bedford; that of England to his younger, Humphrey duke of Gloucester; and the care of his son's person to the earl of Warwick. He ordered his chaplain to recite the seven penitential psalms. When that passage of the fifty-first psalm was read build thou the walls of Jerusalem; he interrupted the chaplain, and declared his serous intention, after he should have fully subdued France, to conduct a crusade against the infidels, and recover possession of the Holy Land. He expired, on August 31, 1422, *in the thirty-fourth year of his age and the tenth of his reign. --- He left by his queen, Catharine of France, only one son, not full nine months old.* Catharine, Henry's widow, married Sir Owen Tudor soon after his death. Their oldest son Edmund would father Henry VII.

Summary by Hume: *This prince possessed many eminent virtues; and if we give indulgence to ambition in a monarch, or rank it, as the vulgar are inclined to do, among his virtues, they were unstained by any considerable blemish. His abilities appeared equally in the cabinet and in the field: The boldness of his enterprises was no less remarkable than his personal valor in conducting them. He had the talent of attaching his friends by affability, and of gaining his enemies by address and clemency. The English, dazzled by the luster of his character, still more than by that of his victories, were reconciled to the defects in his title: The French almost forgot that he was an enemy: And his care in maintaining justice in his civil administration, and preserving discipline in his armies, made some amends to both nations for the calamities inseparable from those wars, in which his short reign was almost entirely occupied. That he could forgive the earl of Marche, who had a better title to the crown than himself, is a sure indication of his magnanimity; and that the earl relied so entirely on his friendship is no less a proof of his established character for candor and sincerity. There remain in history few instances of such mutual trust; and still fewer where neither party found reason to repent it.* [13]

---

[13] Ibid, pp 376-378.

Chapter 22

Henry VI

Henry VI, (b. 1421, d. 1471) was the designated king of England in 1422 when he was crowned at age 9 months. Henry was king from 1422 to 1461 and again in 1470-1471. Henry and the Lancastrian forces were defeated by Edward and the Yorkist forces in the battles of Mortimer's Cross and Touton in 1461. Edward IV was crowned. Henry became a fugitive in Scotland and was imprisoned in the Tower from 1465 to 1470, but was reinstated as king in 1470 to 1471 after victories by queen Margaret and the duke of Warwick. But Edward IV returned in 1471, captured Henry who was shortly thereafter murdered in the tower of London. This reign is one of the most confusing and bizarre periods of English history. Henry VI was the third king since the conquest to be a minority, and he was to remain in that dependent state during his lifetime. Yet he was the only king of England to be crowned king of France. The story of Henry VI, depicted by three of Shakespeare's plays and documented by Hume is bizarre. It is not possible here to present the details of the numerous persons in the time of Henry VI's reign, from 1421 to 1461 and again in 1470, including not only the royal houses of England and France; but the dukes, earls, and lords who contended for power and ended up being slain in battle, executed, or murdered. Yet we must focus on the principal characters other than the king since it was they who ruled and made the law, not the infant or minority king.

Historians have blamed Henry VI for the military conflicts during the period historians have claimed as the War of Roses, between 1455 and 1485. It has been documented, however, that the York Lancastrian wars had their origin during the reign of Richard II, even before Henry VI's grandfather Henry IV usurped the English throne in 1399. To claim only this terminal period of 1455 to 1485, rather than the origin and exacerbation of the conflicts and wars from the reign of Richard II, and in this reign of Henry VI is not reasonable. If a physician focused only on the terminal state of a patient and ignored all the preceding causes and development of the illness he would not be a responsible or competent physician. Furthermore, the time period historians have claimed for the War of Roses overlaps the reigns of Edward IV (1461 to 1483) and Richard III (1483 to 1485) to be reviewed in the chapter to follow. Another peculiarity of English history is that the wars during the time of Henry VI were supposedly caused by the insanity of Henry VI. Yet we have no details to document this supposed illness. Rather, we shall argue that Henry was simply not the person destined to control the insane conduct of the aristocrats who were at each other's throats. Henry very likely suffered a severe depressed state following the murder of his protector the duke of Gloucester and the loss of his father's territories in France. It was the unruly aristocrats who contended for power and conspired to murder or destroy the members of their own families, of the houses of York and Lancaster, all descendants of Edward III, and who were obviously responsible for these wars.

But historians could not blame Henry for the last years of the hundred years war and the defeat of the English by the French. The loss of all the possessions gained by Edward III and Henry's father Henry V were completed by 1453, when Henry was still a minority king. Many of the dukes and earls, whom we shall review below, fought for these kings and for their own glory in France. The most famous battle of Orleans, and the defeat of the English under the banner of Joan of Arc and the French king Charles VII, occurred in 1429, when Henry was only eight years old.

The duke of Bedford and the wars in France

John, Duke of Bedford (b 1389, d. 1435), was the third son of Henry IV, an uncle of Henry VI. He received the title of duke of Bedford from his elder brother Henry V. The duke of Bedford was designated by the will of Henry V to be the regent for the nine-month old Henry VI. Parliament had determined that during Bedford's absence in the wars with France his younger brother Humphrey, the Duke of Gloucester, would become regent. The duke of Bedford had assisted Henry V in his conquests in France, including Harfleur. He was in France when Henry V died in 1422. Early in the reign of Henry VI, in 1424, the English continued to make advances in France under the command of the duke of Bedford. *Though the chief seat of Charles's power lay in the southern provinces, beyond the Loire; his partisans were possessed of some fortresses in the northern, and even in the neighborhood of Paris; and it behooved the duke of Bedford first to clear these countries from the enemy, before he could think of attempting more distant conquests.* The English took a number of towns *and the united forces of England and Burgandy soon after gained a more considerable advantage.*

The battle of Verneuil, in August of 1424, was a disaster for the French and the Scots under the earl of Buchan, who had been made constable of France. Four thousand of the French, among them a considerable number of nobility perished in that battle. *The condition of the king of France now appeared very terrible, and almost desperate. He had lost the flower of his army and the bravest of his nobles in this fatal action: He had no resource either for recruiting or subsisting his troops: he wanted money even for his personal subsistence; and though all parade of a court was banished, it was with difficulty he could keep a table, supplied with the plainest necessaries for himself and his few followers: Every day brought him intelligence of some loss or misfortune: Towns, which were bravely defended, were obliged at last to surrender for want of relief or supply: He saw his partisans entirely chased from all the provinces which lay north of the Loire: And he expected soon to lose, by the united efforts of his enemies, all the territories of which he had hitherto continued to master.[1]*

Bedford had to return to England in 1426 to resolve a dispute between his brother Humphrey, duke of Gloucester, and Philip of Burgundy over a marriage between Gloucester and a cousin of the duke of Burgundy. There began contentions among the English as well as French nobles. *The duke of Burgundy was much disgusted. The duke of Brittany had entered into engagements with Charles. The French had been allowed to recover from their astonishment, into which their frequent disasters had thrown them. The count of Dunois conducted a body of 1600 men to Montgargis --- and gave a severe blow to the English. --- But the regent, soon after his arrival, revived the reputation of the English arms, by an important enterprise which he happily achieved. He secretly brought together, in separate detachments, a considerable army to the frontiers of Brittany; and fell so unexpectedly upon that province, that the duke of Brittany, unable to make resistance, yielded to all the terms required of him.*

The siege of Orleans

The city of Orleans was so situated between the provinces commanded by Henry, and those possessed by Charles, that it opened an easy entrance to either; and as the duke of Bedford intended to make a great effort for penetrating into the south of France, it behooved him to begin with this place, which, in the present circumstances, was become the most important in the kingdom. He committed the conduct of the enterprise to the earl of Salisbury, who had newly brought him a reinforcement of 6000 men from England, and who had much distinguished himself, by his abilities, during the course of the present war. --- The eyes of all Europe were turned towards this scene; where, it was reasonably supposed, the French were to make their last stand for maintaining the independence of their monarchy, and the rights of their sovereign.

---

[1] Hume, vol 2, pp 382-389.

Salisbury, commanding the English forces, attacked the fortifications, which guarded the bridge and entrance to the city, but was killed by a cannon ball. The earl of Suffolk succeeded to the command, but since it was now in the depths of winter he was content to intercept sources of supply to the city and trusted more to famine than to force for subduing the city. --- *The place was every day more and more closely invested by the English: Great scarcity began already to be felt by the garrison and inhabitants: Charles, in despair of collecting an army, which should dare to approach the enemy's entrenchments, not only gave the city for lost, but began to entertain a very dismal prospect with regard to the general state of his affairs.[2]*

Joan of Arc

Now we come to one of the most incredible stories in history, that of Joan of Arc, and the expulsion of the English from France. As we noted before in the chapter on Edward I, the movie Brave Heart provided a refreshing interlude from the readings of history. The CBS mini-series by Alliance Atlantis, *Joan of Arc*, should provide the reader with a sense of what this period of history was like. The movie closely follows the written history. The history to follow is from Hume's *The History of England*, Volume 2.

In the village of Domremi near Vaucouleurs, on the borders of Lorraine, there lived a country girl of twenty-seven years of age, called Joan d'Arc, who was servant in a small inn, and who in that station had been accustomed to tend the horses for the guests, to ride them without a saddle to the watering-place, and to perform other offices, which, in well-frequented inns, commonly fall to the share of the men servants. This girl was of an irreproachable life, and had not hitherto been remarked for any singularity, whether that she had met with an occasion to excite her genius, or that the unskillful eyes of those who conversed with her, had not been able to discern her uncommon merit.

The siege of Orleans, the progress of the English before that place, the great distress of the garrison and inhabitants, the importance of saving this city and its brave defenders, had turned thither the public eye; and Joan, inflamed by the general sentiment, was seized with a wild desire of bringing relief to her sovereign in his present distresses. --- Thinking herself destined by Heaven to this office, --- she went to Vaucouleurs; procured admission to Baudricourt, the governor; informed him of her inspirations and intentions; and conjured him not to neglect the voice of God, who spoke through her, but to second those heavenly revelations, which impelled her to this glorious enterprise. Baudricourt treated her at first with some neglect; but on her frequent return to him, and importunate solicitations, he began to remark

---

[2] Hume, vol 1, pp 390-396.

something extraordinary in the maid, and was inclined, at all hazards, to make so easy an experiment. --- But he adopted at last the schemes of Joan; and he gave her some attendants, who conducted her to the French court, which at that time resided at Chinon.[3]

It is pretended, that Joan, immediately on her admission, knew the king, though she had never seen his face before, and though he purposely kept himself in the crowd of courtiers, and had laid aside every thing in his dress and apparel which might distinguish him: That she offered him, in the name of the supreme Creator, to raise the siege of Orleans, and conduct him to Rheims to be their crowned and anointed; and on his expression doubts of her mission, revealed to him, before some sworn confidants, a secret, which was unknown to all the world beside himself, and which nothing but a heavenly inspiration could have discovered to her: And that she demanded, as the instrument of her future victories, a particular sword, which was kept in the Church of St. Catherine of Fierbois, and which, though she had never seen it, she described by all its marks, and by the place in which it had long lain neglected. --- An assembly of grave doctors and theologians cautiously examined Joan's mission, and pronounced it undoubted and supernatural. She was sent to the parliament, then residing at Poictiers; and was interrogated before that assembly: The presidents, the counselors, who came persuaded of her imposture, went away convinced of her inspiration. A ray of hope began to break through that despair, in which the minds of all men were before enveloped. Heaven had now declared itself in favor of France, and had laid bare its outstretched arm to take vengeance on her invaders.

Joan's requests were at last complied with: She was armed cap-a-pee, mounted on horseback, and shown in that martial habiliment before the whole people. Her dexterity in managing her steed, though acquired in her former occupation, was regarded as a fresh proof of her mission; and, she was received with the loudest acclamations by the spectators. The maid, as Joan was called, entered the city of Orleans and there followed the convoy of supplies and troops. *The earl of Suffolk,* who later figures large in the selection of the Queen, *was in a situation very unusual and extraordinary; and which might well confound the man of the greatest capacity and firmest temper. He saw his troops overawed, and strongly impressed with the idea of a divine influence, accompanying the maid. Instead of banishing these vain terrors by hurry and action and war, he waited till the soldiers should recover from their panic; and he thereby gave leisure for those prepossessions to sink still deeper into their minds. --- The maid called aloud, that the garrison should remain no longer on the defensive; and she promised her followers the*

---

[3] Note. Shakespeare's First Part, Henry VI, provides more detail and drama. Act I, sc 1.

assistance of heaven in attacking those redoubts of the enemy, which had so long kept them in awe, and which they had never hitherto dared to insult. The generals seconded her ardor: An attack was made on one redoubt and it proved successful: All the English who defended the entrenchments, were put to the sword or taken prisoner: And Sir John Talbot himself, who had drawn together, from the other redoubts, some troops to bring them relief, durst not appear in the open field against so formidable an enemy.[4]

By all these successes, the English were entirely chased from their fortifications on that side: They had lost above six thousand men in these different action; and what was still more important, their wonted courage and confidence was wholly gone, and had given place to amazement and despair. The maid returned triumphant over the bridge, and was again received as the guardian angel of the city.

It might prove extremely dangerous for Suffolk, with such intimidated troops, to remain any longer in the presence of so courageous and victorious an enemy; he therefore raised the siege, and retreated with all the precaution imaginable. The French resolved to push their conquests, and to allow the English no leisure to recover from their consternation. Charles formed a body of six thousand men, and sent them to attack Jergeau, whither Suffolk had retired with a detachment of his army. The siege lasted ten days; and the place was obstinately defended. Joan displayed her wonted intrepidity on the occasion. She descended into the fosse, in leading the attack; and she was confounded and beaten to the ground: But she soon recovered herself; and in the end rendered the assault successful: Suffolk was obliged to yield himself prisoner to a Frenchman call Renaud.

The remainder of the English army was commanded by Fastolfe, Scales, and Talbot, who though of nothing but of making their retreat, as soon as possible, into a place of safety; which the French esteemed the overtaking them equivalent to a victory. So much had the events, which passed before Orleans, altered every thing between the two nations! The vanguard of the French under Richemont and Xaintrailles attacked the rear of the enemy at the village of Patay. The battle lasted not a moment: The English were discomfited and fled: The brave Fastolfe himself showed the example of flight to his troops; and the order of the garter was taken from him, as a punishment for this instance of cowardice. Two thousand men were killed in this action, and both Talbot and Scales taken prisoners. This was in June of 1429.

Coronation of Charles VII

The raising of the siege of Orleans was one part of the maid's promise to Charles: The crowning of him at Rheims, July 17, 1429, was

---

[4] Hume, vol 1, pp 398-401.

the other: And she now vehemently insisted, that he should forthwith set out on that enterprise. --- Charles set out for Rheims at the head of twelve thousand men: He passed by Troye, which opened its gates to him: Chalons imitated the example: Rheims sent him a deputation with its keys, before his approach to it: And he scarcely perceived, as he passed along, that he was marching through an enemy's country. The ceremony of his coronation was here performed with the holy oil, which a pigeon had brought to king Clovis from heaven, on the first establishment of the French monarchy. The maid of Orleans stood by his side, in completed armor, and displayed her sacred banner, which had so often dissipated and confounded his fiercest enemies: And the people shouted with the most unfeigned joy, on view in such a complications of wonders. After the completion of the ceremony, the Maid threw herself at the king's feet, embraced his knees, and with a flood of tears, which pleasure and tenderness extorted from her, she congratulated him on this singular and marvelous event.

Coronation of Henry VI in France

The regent, duke of Bedford, endeavored to revive the declining state of his affairs, by bringing over the young king of England and having him crowned and anointed at Paris, in 1430. All the vassals of the crown swore allegiance and did homage to him. But this ceremony was cold and insipid, compared with the luster which had attended the coronation of Charles at Rheims; and the duke of Bedford expected more effect from an accident, which put into his hands the person that had been the author of all his calamities. Hume is referring here to the duke of Bedford's purchase of Joan from the Burgundians leading to her being burned at the stake. The crowning of Henry VI, at age nine, would seem to be the duke of Bedford's greatest legacy.[5]

The capture, trial and barbarous punishment of Joan

The maid of Orleans, after the coronation of Charles, declared to the count of Dunois, that her wishes were now fully gratified, and that she had no further desire than to return to her former condition, and to the occupations and course of life which became her sex: But that nobleman, sensible of the great advantages which might still be reaped from her presence in the army, exhorted her to persevere, till, by the final expulsion of the English, which had brought all her prophecies to their full completion. In pursuance of this advice, she threw herself into the town of Compiegne, which was at that time besieged by the duke of Burgundy, assisted by the earls of Arundel and Suffolk; and the garrison on her appearance believed themselves thenceforth invincible. But their joy was of short duration. The maid, next day after her arrival, headed a

---

[5] Ibid, pp 406, 407, and 413.

sally upon the quarters of John of Luxembourg; she twice drove the enemy from their entrenchments; finding their numbers to increase every moment, she ordered a retreat; when hard pressed by the pursuers, she turned upon them, and made them again recoil; but being here deserted by her friends, and surrounded by the enemy, she was at last, after exerting the utmost valor, taken prisoner by the Burgundians, in 1431.

The duke of Bedford fancied, that, by the captivity of that extraordinary woman, who had blasted all his successes, he should again recover his former ascendant over France; and to push farther the present advantage, he purchased the captive from John of Luxdembourg, and formed a prosecution against her, which, whether it proceeded from vengeance or policy, was equally barbarous and dishonorable.

There was no possible reason, why Joan should not be regarded as a prisoner of war, and be entitled to all the courtesy and good usage, which civilized nations practice towards enemies on these occasions. She had never, in her military capacity, forfeited, by any act of treachery or cruelty, her claim to that treatment: She was unstained by any civil crime: Even the virtues and the very decorum of her sex had ever been rigidly observed by her: And though her appearing in war, and leading armies to battle, may seem an exception, she had thereby performed such signal service to her prince, that she had abundantly compensated for this irregularity; and was on that account, the more an object of praise and admiration. It was necessary, therefore, for the duke of Bedford, to interest religion some way in the prosecution; and to cover under that cloak his violation of justice and humanity.

The bishop of Beauvais, a man wholly devoted in the English interests, presented a petition against Joan, on pretense that she was taken within the bounds of his diocese; and he desired to have her tried by an ecclesiastical court for sorcery, impiety, idolatry and magic: The university of Paris was so mean as to join in the same request: Several prelates, among whom the cardinal of Winchester was the only Englishman[6], were appointed her judges: They held their court in Rouen, where the young king of England then resided: And the maid clothed in her former military apparel, but loaded with irons, was produced before this tribunal.

She was harassed and intimidated for four months, after which she *was sentenced to be delivered to the secular arm. She then declared that she was willing to recant. But the barbarous vengeance of Joan's enemies was not satisfied with this victory. Suspecting, that the female dress, which she had now consented to wear, was disagreeable to her, they purposely placed in her apartment a suit of men's apparel; and*

---

[6] Note. Henry Beaufort, great uncle to Henry VI, bishop of Winchester later becoming cardinal, was one of the contending forces for power in England. His contention with Humphrey, duke of Gloucester will be presented below.

watched for the effects of that temptation upon her. On the sight of a dress, in which she had acquired so much renown, and which, she once believed, she wore by the particular appointment of heaven, all her former ideas and passions revived; and she ventured in her solitude to cloth herself again in the forbidden garment. Her insidious enemies caught her in that situation. Her fault was interpreted to be no less than a relapse into heresy: No recantation would now suffice, and no pardon could be granted her. She was condemned to be burned in the market place of Rouen; and the infamous sentence was accordingly executed, on June 14, 1431. The affairs of the English, far from being advanced by this execution, went every day more and more to decay.[7]

Treaty of Arras and death of Bedford

The hundred years war with France would last another twenty-five years when in 1453 all the remaining English lands in France were lost. We can only present here some of the major events leading to England's demise in France. The defection of the duke of Burgundy, following the death of the duke of Bedford's duchess, sister of the duke of Burgundy, and Bedford's sudden marriage; led to the negotiations with Charles, who made concessions favorable to the duke. *The duke of Burgundy finally determined to unite himself to the royal family of France, from which his own was descended. For this purpose, a congress was appointed at Arras under the mediation of deputies from the pope and the council of Basle.* After negotiations had been concluded, in 1435, and a treaty formed the duke sent a herald to England with a letter, in which he notified the conclusion of the treaty of Arras.

A few days after the duke of Bedford received intelligence of this treaty, so fatal to the interests of England, he died at Rouen; a prince of great abilities, and of many virtues; and whose memory, except from the barbarous execution of the maid of Orleans, was unsullied by any considerable blemish.[8] The duke of Bedford died in 1435 at the age of 46. *The fate of Henry's other brother duke of Gloucester, regent of England, was also foretold.*

The duke of Gloucester

Humphrey, duke of Gloucester, (b 1391, d. 1447) was the fourth son of Henry IV. He received his title duke of Gloucester from his brother Henry V. Parliament had declared that Humphrey, duke of Gloucester, should serve as regent for Henry VI during the absence in France of John, duke of Bedford. While the duke of Bedford had little contact with the young king except for his coronation, the duke of

---

[7] Ibid, pp 402-410.

[8] Ibid, p 413.

Gloucester was not only the protector but his good friend. We find in Shakespeare's First Part and Second Part of *King Henry VI* the bitter conflicts between Gloucester and Henry Beaufort, the bishop of Winchester. From Hume: *The violent factions, which prevailed between the duke of Gloucester and the cardinal of Winchester, prevented the English from taking the proper measures for repairing these multiplied losses in France, and threw all their affairs into confusion.* Henry had a high regard for Gloucester. The king and Gloucester were in many ways similar in character. Both were learned men and it is probable that Gloucester had a considerable influence on the king in stimulating and developing a love for learning. *According to Hume: This prince, the duke of Gloucester, is said to have received a better education than was usual in his age, to have founded one of the first public libraries in England, and to have been a great patron of learned men.*[9] Gloucester donated his library to the University at Oxford.

The Bishop of Winchester, The cardinal

Henry Beaufort, (b 1374, d 1447), was a half brother to Henry IV. He was one of the sons of John of Gaunt and his third wife Kathyrine Swineford. The bishop of Winchester, appointed cardinal in 1426 by the pope, figures large in the reign of Henry VI. We have noted above the bishop of Winchester's role in the condemnation of Joan of Arc to be burned at the stake. The bishop was enormously wealthy and used his financial resources to increase his power. The cardinal had many interests in politics and warfare, even becoming a military commander leading English forces into Normandy in a last ditch effort to retain English rule and conquests in France. His character is aptly portrayed by Shakespeare in the First Part *Henry VI*. The cardinal was a tyrant and his lust for power and domination over the king and Gloucester continued to his death. He died just weeks after he, in complicity with others, murdered Gloucester. His ambition and intention throughout his life was to usurp the power of the regent and the king, despite the will of Henry V and parliament's decision to share the powers between Henry V's brothers.

In this strange story the bishop conspired with the duke of Suffolk and his paramour, Queen Margaret, in the conspiracy to murder the duke of Gloucester. The bishop died not long after the death of Gloucester. We have the irony of a king who himself was deeply religious, sensitive to others, scholarly; and who abhorred contention, strife and bloodshed; and who contrasted markedly in character to the cardinal. It is probable that upon the death of Gloucester, the king's protector and friend, that the king suffered a severe depression augmented by the losses of his fathers kingdoms in France and the

---

[9] Ibid, p 421.

intrigues of his court. Perceived as a weak king, he would be fair game for the contending powers.

The duke of Suffolk

William de la Pole, (b 1396, d 1450), created the 1st Duke of Suffolk was an important ally of the bishop in contending for power over Gloucester and the king. His father had been killed at Agincourt and William succeeded to the earldom of Suffolk. He fought in France under Henry V and was commander of the English forces in France but had been defeated and taken prisoner by Joan of Arc until his ransom in 1431. He became important in the reign of Henry VI after the retirement of the bishop of Winchester in 1443. His most important role in history would be his arrangement of the marriage of the king with Margaret of Anjou, and his complicity in the murder of the duke of Gloucester.

As the king had now reached the twenty-third year of his age, it was natural to think of choosing him a queen; and each party was ambitious of having him receive one from their hand; as it was probable, that this circumstance would decide forever the victory between them. The duke of Gloucester proposed a daughter of the count of Armagnac; but had not credit to effect his purpose. The cardinal and his friends had cast their eye on Margaret of Anjou, daughter of Regnier, titular king of Sicily, Naples, and Jerusalem, descended from the count of Anjou, brother of Charles V, who had left these magnificent titles, but without any real power or possessions, to his posterity.

The earl of Suffolk, therefore, in concert with his associates of the English council, made proposals of marriage to Margaret, which were accepted. But this nobleman, besides preoccupying the princess's favor by being the chief means of her advancement, endeavored to ingratiate himself with her and her family, by very extraordinary concessions: Though Margaret brought no dowry with her, he ventured of himself, without any direct authority from the council, but probably with the approbation of the cardinal and the ruling members, to engage by a secret article, that the province of Maine, which was at the time in the hands of the English, should be ceded to Charles of Anjou her uncle, who was prime minister and favorite of the French king, and who had already received from his master the grant of that province as his appanage.[10]

The queen

The queen is a subject worthy of further study. She was involved from the beginning with the duke of Suffolk and the cardinal in the intrigues of the court. She, as well as the others contended for power. She also became a notable military commander during the final decade of

---

[10] Ibid, p 419.

the Lancastrian era, competing as it were for the more illustrious military exploits of Joan of Arc. She had exceptional abilities as noted by Hume. *This princess herself was the most accomplished of the age both in body and mind; and seemed to possess those qualities, which would equally qualify her to acquire the ascendant over Henry, and to supply all his defects and weaknesses. Of a masculine, courageous spirit, of an enterprising temper, endowed with solidity as well as vivacity of understanding, she had not been able to conceal these great talents even in the privacy of her father's family; and it was reasonable to expect, that, when she would mount the throne, they would break out with still superior luster.[11]*

The murder of the duke of Gloucester.

The treaty of marriage was ratified in England: Suffolk obtained first the title of marquis, then that of duke; and even received the thanks of parliament, for his services in conducting it. The princess fell immediately into close connections with the cardinal and his party, the dukes of Somerset, Suffolk and Buckingham; who, fortified by her powerful patronage, resolved on the final ruin of the duke of Gloucester.

This generous prince, worsted in all court intrigues, for which his temper was not suited, but possessing, in a high degree, the favor of the public, had already received from his rivals a cruel mortification, which he had hitherto borne without violating public peace, but which it was impossible that a person of his spirit and humanity could ever forgive. His duchess, the daughter of Reginal, lord Cobham, had been accused of the crime of witchcraft and it was pretended, that there was found in her possession a waxen figure of the king, which she and her associates, Sir Roger Bolinbroke, a priest, and one Margery Jordan of Eye, melted in a magical manner before a slow fire, with an intention of making Henry's force and vigor waste away by like insensible degrees. --- The prisoners were pronounced guilty; the duchess was condemned to do public penance, and to suffer perpetual imprisonment, the others were executed. But as these violent proceedings were ascribed solely to the malice of the duke's enemies, the people, contrary to their usual practice in such marvelous trials, acquitted the unhappy sufferers; and increased their esteem and affection towards a prince, who was thus exposed without protection, to those mortal injuries.

These sentiments of the public made the cardinal of Winchester and his party sensible, that it was necessary to destroy a man, whose popularity might become dangerous, and whose resentment they had so much causes to apprehend. In order to effect their purpose, a parliament was summoned to meet, not at London, which was supposed to be too well affected to the duke, but at St. Edmondsbury, where they expected

---

[11] Ibid, p 419.

that he would be entirely at mercy. As soon as he appeared, he was accused of treason, and thrown into prison. He was soon after found dead in his bed, on February 28, 1448. *And though it was pretended that his death was natural, and though his body, which was exposed to public view, bore no marks of outward violence, no one doubted but he had fallen a victim to the vengeance of his enemies. An artifice, formerly practiced in the case of Edward II, Richard II, and Thomas Woodstock, duke of Gloucester, could deceive nobody. The reason of this assassination of the duke seems not, that the ruling party apprehended his acquittal in parliament on account of his innocence, which, in such time, was seldom much regarded; but that they imagined his public trial and execution would have been more invidious than his private murder, which they pretended to deny.*

The cardinal of Winchester died six weeks after his nephew, whose murder was universally ascribed to him as well as to the duke of Suffolk, and which, it is said, gave him more remorse in his last moments, than could naturally be expected from a man hardened, during the course of a long life, in falsehood and in politics. What share the queen had in this guilt is uncertain; her usual activity and spirit made the public conclude with some reason, that the duke's enemies durst not have ventured on such a deed without her privity. But there happened soon after an event, of which she and her favorite, the duke of Suffolk, bore incontestably the whole odium.[12]

Suffolk impeached, banished, murdered

After the murder of the duke of Gloucester, the regent of the kingdom, there followed an action against those presumed responsible. *As the duke of Suffolk was known to have had an active hand in the crime, he partook deeply of the hatred attending it; and the clamors, which necessarily rose against him, as prime minister and declared favorite of the queen, were thereby augmented to a ten-fold pitch, and became absolutely uncontrollable. The great nobility could ill brook to see a subject exalted above them; much more one who was only great grandson to a merchant, and who was of a birth so much inferior to theirs. The people complained of his arbitrary measures; which were, in some degree, a necessary consequence of the irregular power then possessed by the prince, but which the least disaffection easily magnified into tyranny. The great acquisitions, which he daily made, were the object of envy; and as they were gained at the expense of the crown, which was itself reduced to poverty, they appeared on that account, to all indifferent persons, the more exceptionable and invidious. --- Suffolk, once become odious, bore the blame of the whole; and every grievance, in every part of the administration was universally imputed to his tyranny*

---

[12] Ibid, pp 418-422.

and injustice. Impeachment proceedings were brought against Suffolk in parliament. The commons brought many charges against him, the most relevant to the condition's complained about was *that he had, without any powers of commission, promised by treaty to cede the province of Maine to Charles of Anjou, and had accordingly ceded it; which proved the issue the chief cause of the loss of Normandy.* --- *But Suffolk maintained, with great appearance of truth, that his measure was approved of by several at the council table; and it seems hard to ascribe to it, as is done by the commons, the subsequent loss of Normandy and expulsion of the English. Normandy lay open on every side to the invasion of the French: Maine, an inland province, must soon after have fallen without any attack.*

The commons were probably sensible, that this charge of treason against Suffolk would not bear a strict scrutiny; and they, therefore, soon after, sent up, against him, a new charge of misdemeanors, which they also divided into several articles. They affirmed, among other imputations, that he had procured exorbitant grants from the crown, and embezzled the public money, had conferred on improper persons, had perverted justice by maintaining iniquitous causes, and had procured pardons for notorious offenders. The articles are mostly general, but are not improbable: And as Suffolk seems to have been a bad man and a bad minister, it will not be rash in us to think, that he was guilty, and that many of these articles could have been proved against him. Suffolk denied the charge; but submitted to the king's mercy: Henry expressed himself not satisfied with regard to the first impeachment of treason; but in consideration of the second for misdemeanors, he declared, that, by virtue of Suffolk's own submission, not by any judicial authority, in 1450, he banished him from the kingdom during five years.

A captain of a vessel was employed by his enemies to intercept him in his passage to France: he was seized near Dover; his head struck off on the side of a long boat; and his body thrown into the sea. No inquiry was made after the actors and accomplices in this atrocious deed of violence.

The duke of Somerset succeeded to Suffolk's power in the ministry, and credit with the queen; and as he was the person under whose government the French provinces had been lost, the public, who always judge by the event, soon made him equally the object of their animosity and hatred. The duke of York was absent in Ireland during all these transactions; and however it might be suspected, that his partisans had excited and supported the prosecution against Suffolk, no immediate ground of complaint could, on that account, lie against him. But there happened soon after an incident, which roused the jealousy of the court, and discovered to them the extreme danger, to which they were exposed, from the pretensions of this popular prince.[13]

Civil Disturbances, John Cade

The humors of the people, set afloat by the parliamentary impeachment, and by the fall of so great a favorite as Suffolk broke out in various commotions, which were soon suppressed, but there arose one in Kent, which was attended with more dangerous consequences. A man of low condition, one John Cade, a native of Ireland, who had been obliged to fly into France for crimes, observed, on his return to England, the discontents of the people; and he laid on them the foundation of projects, which were at first crowned with surprising success. He took the name of John Mortimer, who had been sentenced to death by parliament, and executed, in the beginning of this reign, without any trial or evidence, merely upon an indictment of high treason, given in against him. On the first mention of that popular name, the common people of Kent, the number of 20,000, flocked to Cade's standard, in 1450; and he excited their zeal by publishing complaints against the numerous abuses in government, and demanding a redress of grievances. The court, not fully sensible of the danger, sent a small force against the rioters, under the command of Sir Humphrey Stafford, who was defeated and slain in an action near Sevenoke; and Cade, advancing with his followers towards London, encamped on Black-heath. Though elated by his victory, he still maintained the appearance of moderation; and sending to the court a plausible list of grievances, he promised, that, when these should be redressed, and when lord Say, the treasurer, and Cromer, sheriff of Kent, should be punished for their malversation, he would immediately lay down his arms. The council, who observed that nobody was willing to fight against men so reasonable in their pretensions, carried the king, for the present safety, to Kenilworth; and the city immediately opened its gates to Cade, who maintained, during some time, great order and discipline among his followers. He always led them into the fields during the nighttime; and published severe edicts against plunder and violence of every kind.

But being obliged, in order to gratify their malevolence against Say and Cromer, to put these men to death without a legal trial, he found, that, after the commission of this crime, he was no longer master of their riotous disposition, and that all his orders were neglected. They broke into a rich house, which they plundered; and the citizens, alarmed at this act of violence, shut their gates against them, and being seconded by a detachment of soldiers, sent them by lord Scales, governor of the Tower, they repulse the rebels with great slaughter. The Kentishmen were so discouraged by the blow, that, upon receiving a general pardon

---

[13] Ibid, pp 431-433.

from the primate, the chancellor, they retreated towards Rochester, and there dispersed. The pardon was soon after annulled, as extorted by violence: a price was set on Cade's head, who was killed by one Iden, a gentleman of Sussex; and many of his followers were capitally punished for their rebellion. It was imagined by the court, that the duke of York had secretly instigated Cade to this attempt, in order to try, by that experiment, the dispositions of the people toward his title and family: And as the event had, so far, succeeded to this wish, the ruling party had greater reason than ever to apprehend the future consequences of his pretensions.[14]

The king

The conditions within the court of the Lancastrian king Henry VI were determined by Gloucester, the bishop of Winchester, Bedford, Suffolk and Queen Margaret. In 1450, when Henry was 29 years old, we have his first definitive action, the banishment of Suffolk. His protector and friend the duke of Gloucester had been found dead in 1448. The king's wife, queen Margaret, had become a paramour of the duke of Suffolk and contended for power by conspiring in the murder of Gloucester involving the bishop of Winchester and Suffolk. The giving away of property and wealth to the enemy of England at the time by the bishop of Winchester and the duke of Suffolk, as a condition of the marriage treaty, would alienate the landed gentry and nobles of England who expect a king to bring conquests of foreign land, wealth and booty to England, not the reverse. The odium of the loss of these lands in France and the unseemly murder of Gloucester most likely were events leading to Henry's first breakdown in 1453. Parliament appointed the duke of York as his protector. The loss of Gloucester and the loss of his father's conquests in France, together with what he may have known or suspected about Queen Margaret would certainly be enough to cause a severe depressed state. Hume makes the following observation: *Henry, in 1454, always unfit to exercise the government, fell at this time into a distemper, which so far increased his natural imbecility, that it rendered him incapable of maintaining even the appearance of royalty.*[15] The use of the word imbecility by Hume is not in keeping with the historical facts he provides or the usage of the term today.

Shakespeare provides the fullest account of the personality and character of Henry VI, which is not in keeping with most modern historical judgments about this king. The acrimonious arguments between Gloucester and the bishop of Winchester are vividly portrayed

---

[14] Ibid, pp 434-435.

[15] Ibid, p 442.

by Shakespeare. The reaction of Henry as a peacemaker, as always, follows:

Uncles of Gloucester and of Winchester, The special watchmen of our English weal, I would prevail, if prayers might prevail, To join your hearts in love and amity. O, what a scandal is it to our crown That two such noble peers as ye should Jar! Believe me, lords, my tender years can tell Civil dissension is a viperous worm That gnaws the bowels of the commonwealth.[16]

The York Lancaster conflicts were also a concern for Henry VI dramatized by two gentlemen representing the white rose and red rose factions, after which Henry comments:

Good Lord, what madness rules in brainsick men, When for so slight and frivolous a cause Such factious emulations shall arise! — Good cousins both, of York and Somerset, Quiet yourselves, I pray, and be at peace.[17]

The war between England and France was a major concern of Henry. Henry bids for peace between the realms. He asked Gloucester about a proposal for peace advanced by the pope and the Earl of Armangnac, closely related to the French king. Gloucester agrees that *peace is the only means to stop effusion of our Christian blood, and establish quietness on every side.* Henry then comments: *Ay, Marry, uncle: for I always thought it was both impious and unnatural That such inhumanity and bloody strife Should reign among professors of one faith.* Then after accepting a proposal for Henry to marry the daughter of the earl of Armagnac he dispatches the bishop of Winchester to accomplish this proposal of peace between England and France. *My lord ambassadors, your several suits Have been consider'd and debated on. Your purpose is both good and reasonable; And therefore are we certainly resolv'd To draw conditions of a friendly peace; Which by my Lord of Winchester we mean Shall be transported presently to France.[18]*

Another major conflict of the king involved his wife, Queen Margaret, whose opinion of Henry follows:

My lord of Suffolk, say, is this the guise, is this the fashion in the court of England? Is this the government of Britain's isle, And this the royalty of Albion's king? What, shall King Henry be a pupil still, Under the surly Gloucester's governance? Am I a queen in title and in style, And must be made a subject to a duke? I tell thee, Poole, when in the city of Tours Thou rann'st a tilt in honor of my love, And stol'st away the ladies' hearts of France, I thought King Henry had resembled thee In

---

[16] Shakespeare, First Part, King Henry VI, Act III, sc. 1.

[17] Ibid, Act IV, sc 1.

[18] Ibid, Act V, sc 1.

courage, courtship, and proportion; But all his mind is bent to holiness, To number Ave-Maries on his beads: His champions are, the prophets and apostles; His weapons, holy saws of sacred writ; His study is his tilt-yard, and his loves Are brazen images of canoniz'd saints. I would the college of the cardinals Would choose him pope, and carry him to Rome, and set the triple crown upon his head: — That were a state fit for his holiness.[19]

Thus we have from Shakespeare a most likely account of king Henry's character and disposition. He simply wasn't the kind of person who could rule over men such as the bishop of Winchester, the duke of Suffolk, the York Lancaster factions, his Queen; nor could he dispose of the kind of intrigues, murder, mayhem and madness that was part of the territory of the crown. Nor was Henry a military commander with a lust for power and ambition for the conquest of foreign domains. Henry exclaims, after the battle of Mortimer's Cross and his abandonment, *'Would I were dead! If God's will were so; For what is in this world but grief and woe?'* Henry's depressed state is enlarged by the scenes of insane warfare, where, after a son who had killed his father, bringing in the dead body; and a father who had killed his son, with the body in his arms, exclaims: *O pity, God, this miserable age!— What stratagems, how fell, how butcherly, Erroneous, mutinous, and unnatural, This deadly quarrel daily doth beget!* Henry exclaims: *Woe above woe! Grief more than common grief! O that my death would stay these ruthful deeds! - O pity, pity, gentle heaven, pity! - The red rose and the white are on his face, The fatal colors of our striving houses. Was ever king so griev'd for subjects woe? Much is your sorrow; mine ten times so much. Sad-hearted men, much overgone with care, Here sits a king more woeful than you are.*[20]

The duke of York

The Lancastrian kings Henry IV, V and VI were descendants of Edward III's third son, John of Gaunt and his first wife, Blanche of Lancaster. Richard Plantagenet, (b 1411, d 1460), duke of York, was the true heir to the throne. He was the son of Richard earl of Cambridge and Anne Mortimer. Henry V had executed his father in 1415 in a failed attempt to place Anne's older brother Edmund on the throne. Anne Mortimer was the great grand daughter of Edward III's second son Lionel and was the heir of the crown. The earl of Cambridge, who married Anne Mortimer, was the grandson of Edward III, son of Edward's fifth son Edmund. Their eldest son, Richard Plantagenet, by his father's marriage to Anne Mortimer, thus became the heir to the

---

[19] Shakespeare, Second Part, Act I, sc 3.

[20] Shakespeare, Third Part, Henry VI, act ii, sc 5.

throne. The York family history cannot be told better than by the words of Shakespeare attributed to Edmund Mortimer, who was the elder brother of Anne Mortimer and who died during the early reign of Henry VI, in 1425.

Therefore, good uncle, for my father's sake, In honor of a true Plantagenet, And for alliance sake, declare the cause My father, earl of Cambridge, lost his head.

Mortimer. *That cause, fair nephew, that imprisoned on'd me, And hath detain'd be all my flowering youth Within a loathsome dungeon, there to pine, Was cursed instrument of his decease*

Plantagenet. *Discover more at large what cause that was; For I am ignorant, and cannot guess.*

Mortimer. *I will, if that my fading breath permit, And death approach not ere my tale be done. Henry IV, grandfather to this king, Deposed his nephew Richard II, — Edward's son, The first-begotten, and the lawful heir Of Edward king, the third of that descent: During whose reign the Percies of the north, Finding his usurpation most unjust, Endeavour'd my advancement to the throne: The reason mov'd these warlike lords to this Was, for that, — young King Richard thus remov'd, Leaving no heir begotten of his body, — I was the next by birth and parentage; for by my mother I derived am From Lionel Duke of Clarence, the third son To King Edward the Third; whereas he From John of Gaunt doth bring his pedigree, Being but fourth of that heroic line. But Mark: as in this haughty great attempt They laboured to plant the rightful heir, I lost my liberty, and they their lives. Long after this, when Henry V, Succeeding his father Bolinbroke, did reign, Thy father, Earl of Cambridge, then deriv'd From famous Edmund Langley, Duke of York, Marrying my sister, that thy mother was, Again, in pity of my hard distress, Levied an army, weening to redeem And have install'd me in the diadem: But, as the rest, so fell that noble earl, And was beheaded. Thus the Mortimers, In whom the title rested, were suppress'd.*

Plantagenet. *Of which, my lord, your honour is the last.*

Mortimer. *True; and thou see'st that I no issue have, And my that my fainting words do warrant death: Thou art my heir; the rest I wish thee gather: But yet be wary in thy studious care.*[21]

York's supporters, Salisbury and Warwick

Richard Plantagenet, the duke of York, possessed an immense fortune from the union of so many successions, those of Cambridge and York on the one hand, with those of Mortimer on the other; Which last inheritance had before been augmented by an union of the estates of Clarence and Ulster, with the patrimonial possessions of the family of Marche. The alliances too of Richard, by his marrying the daughter of

---

[21] Shakespeare, First Part, Henry VI, Act II, sc. 5.

Ralph Neville, earl of Westmoreland, had widely extended his interest among the nobility, and had procured him many connections in that formidable order.

The family of Neville was perhaps at this time the most potent, both from their opulent possessions, and from the characters of the men, that has ever appeared in England. For besides the earl of Westmoreland, and the lords Latimer, Fauconberg, and Abergavenny; the earls of Salisbury and Warwick were of that family, and were of themselves, on many accounts, the greatest noblemen in the kingdom. Richard Neville, (b 1428, d 1471), duke of Warwick, was the son of the earl of Salisbury. The earl of Salisbury and Warwick had enormous wealth with which they could afford the tremendous costs of warfare. *No less than 30,000 persons are said to have daily lived at his board in the different manors and castles which Warwick possessed in England: The military men, allured by his munificence and hospitality, as well by his bravery, were zealously attached to his interests. His numerous retainers were more devoted to his will, than to the prince or to the laws: And he was the greatest, as well as the last, of those mighty barons, who formerly overawed the crown, and rendered the people incapable of any regular system of civil* government. But the duke of York, besides the family of Neville, had many other partisans among the great nobility.[22]

York marched to London against Somerset

The duke of York, trusting to these symptoms, raised an army of 10,000 men, with which he marched towards London; demanding a reformation of the government, and the removal of the duke of Somerset from all power and authority. Somerset, (b 1406, d. 1455) was a member of the Beaufort family, and an ally of the duke of Suffolk. Somerset had been appointed chief minister of Henry VI, but in 1453, he was sent to the tower and York was appointed lord protector. In this bizarre series of events, Somerset was released from the tower and regained the position of lord protector but not long afterward Somerset was killed in the battle of St. Albans by York's forces. These events are detailed by Hume as follows: *Salisbury and Warwic, appeared; probably with a view of mediating between the parties, and of seconding, on occasion, the duke of York's pretensions. A parley ensued; Richard still insisted upon the removal of Somerset. And his submitting to a trial in parliament: the court pretended to comply with his demands; and that nobleman was put in arrest: The duke of York was then persuaded to pay his respects to the king in his tent; and on repeating his charge against the duke of Somerset, he was surprised to see that minister step from behind the curtain, and offer to maintain his innocence. Richard now found, that he had been betrayed; that he was in the hands of his enemies; and that it*

---

[22] Hume, vol 2, p 428.

was become necessary, for his own safety, to lower his pretensions. No violence, however, was attempted against him: The nation was not in a disposition to bear the destruction of so popular a prince: He had many friends in Henry's camp: And his son, Edward, who was not in the power of the court, might still be able to revenge his death on all his enemies: He was therefore dismissed; and he retired to his seat of Wigmore on the borders of Wales[23].

Birth of prince Edward, son of king Henry and Margaret

Meanwhile the last of the English provinces in Gascony were lost in July 1453. In October of that year Queen Margaret *delivered a son, prince Edward, who provided an obstacle to York's peaceful ascension of the crown.[24] But the duke was incapable of violent counsels; and even when no visible obstacle lay between him and the throne, he was prevented by his own scruples from mounting it. Henry, always unfit to exercise the government, fell at this time into distemper, which so far increased his natural imbecility, that it rendered him incapable of maintaining even the appearance of royalty. The queen and the council, destitute of this support, found themselves unable to resist the York party; and they were obliged to yield to the torrent. They sent Somerset to the Tower; and appointed Richard lieutenant of the kingdom, with powers to open and hold a session of parliament. That assembly also, taking into consideration the state of the kingdom, created him protector during pleasure. --- Yet the duke, instead of pushing them to make further concessions, appeared somewhat timid and irresolute even in receiving the power which was tendered to him. --- This moderation of Richard was certainly very unusual and very amiable; yet was it attended with bad consequences in the present juncture, and by giving time to the animosities of faction to rise and ferment, it proved the source of all those furious wars and commotions which ensued.*

The enemies of the duke of York soon found it in their power to make advantage of his excessive caution. Henry being so far recovered from his distemper, as to carry the appearance of exercising the royal power; they moved him to resume his authority, to annul the protectorship of the duke, to release Somerset from the tower, and to commit the administration into the hands of that nobleman.[25]

---

[23] Ibid, pp 440-441.

[24] Note. Far more important than the loss of England's territories in France was the fall of Constantinople by Mohammed II and the Ottoman Turks, on May 29, 1453.

[25] Ibid, p 442.

The battle of St. Albans

  Richard, sensible of the dangers which might attend his former acceptance of the parliamentary commission, should he submit to the annulling of it, levied an army; but still without advancing any pretensions to the crown. He complained only of the king's ministers, and demanded a reformation of the government. A battle was fought at St. Albans, May 22, 1455, in which the Yorkists were superior, and without suffering any material loss, slew about 5,000 of their enemies; among him were the duke of Somerset, the earl of Northumberland, the earl of Stafford, eldest son of the duke of Buckingham, lord Clifford, and many other persons of distinction. The king himself fell into the hands of the duke of York, who treated him with great respect and tenderness: He was only obliged (which he regarded as no hardship) to commit the whole authority of the crown into the hands of his rival

  This was the first blood spilt in that fatal quarrel, which was not finished in less than a course of thirty years, which was signalized by twelve pitched battles, which opened a scene of extraordinary fierceness and cruelty, is computed to have cost the lives of eighty princes of the blood and almost entirely annihilated the ancient nobility of England.[26]

  The nation was kept some time in suspense: The vigor and spirit of queen Margaret, supporting her small power, still proved a balance to the great authority of Richard, which was checked by his irresolute temper. A parliament, which was soon after assembled, --- granted the Yorkists a general indemnity; and they restored the protectorship to the duke, who in accepting it, still persevered in all his former precautions: but at the same time they renewed their oaths of fealty to Henry, and fixed the continuance of the protectorship to the majority of his son, Edward, who was vested with the usual dignities of prince of Wales, duke of Cornwal, and earl of Chester.

  Margaret, availing herself of that prince's absence, produced her husband before the house of lords; and as his state of health permitted him at that time to act his part with some tolerable decency, he declared his intentions of resuming the government, and of putting an end to Richard's authority. Although the duke of York acquiesced, there continued suspicion and distrust among the parties. The court retired to Coventry, Richard withdrew to his castle of Wigmore: Salisbury to Middleham in Yorkshire, and Warwick to his government of Calais.[27]

The battle of Northampton

  On July 10, 1460, *Warwick landed in Kent, with the earl of Salisbury, and the earl of Marche, eldest son of the duke of York; and*

---

[26] Ibid, pp 439-443.

[27] Ibid, p 444.

being met by the primate, by lord Cobham, and other persons of distinction, he marched, amidst the acclamations of the people, to London. The city immediately opened its gates to him; and his troops increasing on every day's march. He soon found himself in a condition to face the royal army, which hastened from Coventry to attack him. The battle was fought at Northampton; and was soon decided against the royalists by the infidelity of lord Grey of Ruthin, who, commanding Henry's van, deserted to the enemy during the heat of action, and spread a consternation through the troops. The duke of Buckingham, the earl of Shrewsbury, the lords Beaumont and Egremon, and Sir William Lucie were killed in the action or pursuit: slaughter fell chiefly on the gentry and nobility; the common people were spared by orders of the earls of Warwick, and March. Henry himself, that empty shadow of a king, was again taken prisoner; and as the innocence and simplicity of his manners, which bore the appearance of sanctity, had procured him the tender regard of the people, the earl of Warwick and the other leaders took care to distinguish themselves by their respectful demeanor towards him.

Parliament and the Queen's reaction

The family history and the duke of York's rightful possession of the crown was presented in parliament October 7, 1460. Parliament had ruled that the duke of York and his heirs would hold the crown after Henry VI. Parliament had decided that the duke of York was the rightful heir to the crown but that Henry VI would continue to rule during his lifetime. At the battle of Northampton July 1460, Henry had been taken captive. The reaction of Queen Margaret to this act of parliament and the abdication of king Henry was violent in support of her title to the crown as well as her son prince Edward. *After the defeat at Northampton, she had fled with her infant son to Durham, thence to Scotland; but soon returning, she applied to the northern barons, and employed every motive to procure their assistance. Her affability, insinuation, and address, qualities in which she excelled; her caresses, her promises wrought a powerful effect on every one who approached her: The admiration of her great qualities was succeeded by compassion towards her helpless condition: the nobility of that quarter, who regarded themselves as the most warlike in the kingdom, were moved by indignation to find the southern barons pretend to dispose of the crown and settle the government: And that they might allure the people to their standard, they promised them the spoils of all the provinces, on the other side of the Trent. By these means, the queen had collected an army twenty thousand strong, with a celerity, which was neither expected by her friends, nor apprehended by her enemies.[28]*

---

[28] Ibid, pp 444-448.

Battle of Wakefield, Death of York and his eldest son

The duke of York would be killed the next month of the year, on December 24, 1460, at the battle of Wakefield in an attempt to quell an invasion of forces in the north under the command of queen Margaret, who had assumed the power of the crown during Henry's imprisonment. He was slain in battle and his body was found among the dead. *His body was found among the slain, the head was cut off by Margaret's orders, and fixed on the gates of York, with a paper crown upon it, in derision of his pretended title. His son, the earl of Rutland, a youth of seventeen, was brought to lord Clifford; and that barbarian, in revenge of his father's death, who had perished in the battle of St. Albans, murdered, in cold blood, and with his own hand, this innocent prince, whose exterior figure, as well as other accomplishments, are represented by historians as extremely amiable. The earl of Salisbury was wounded and taken prisoner, and immediately beheaded, with several other persons of distinction, by martial law at Pomfret. There fell near three thousand Yorkists in the battle.*[29] York's three surviving sons Edward, George and Richard are the subjects of the next chapter.

Battle of Mortimer's Cross

The queen, after this important victory, divided her army. She sent the smaller division under Jasper Tudor, earl of Pembroke, half brother to the king, against Edward, the new duke of York, where the earl of Warwick had been left with command of the Yorkists. Edward defeated Pembroke at Mortimer's Cross in Herfordshire, with the loss of near 4000 men: His army was dispersed; he himself escaped by flight; but his father, Sir Owen Tudor[30]*, was taken prisoner, and immediately beheaded by Edward's order. This barbarous practice, being once begun, was continued by both parties, from a spirit of revenge, which covered itself under the pretense of retaliation.*

The queen made no great advantage of this victory: Young Edward advanced upon her from the other side; and collecting the remains of Warwick's army, was soon in a condition of giving her battle with superior forces. She was sensible of her danger, while she lay between the enemy and the city of London; and she found it necessary to retreat with her army to the north.[31]

---

[29] Hume, Vol 2, pp 449-450.

[30] Grandfather of Henry VII and of the Tudor kings to follow.

[31] Ibid, p 451.

Battle of Touton

The license, in which queen Margaret had been obliged to indulge her troops, infused great terror and aversion into the city of London and all the southern parts of the kingdom; and as she there expected an obstinate resistance, she had prudently retired northwards among her own partisans.

The hostile armies met at Touton; and a fierce and bloody battle ensued, March 29, 1461. While the Yorkists were advancing to the charge.--- The sword decided the combat, which ended in a total victory on the side of the Yorkists. Edward issued orders to give no quarter. The routed army was pursued to Tadcaster, with great bloodshed and confusion; and above thirty-six thousand men are computed to have fallen in the battle and pursuit. Among these were the earl of Westmoreland, and his brother, Sir John Nevil, the earl of Northumberland, the lords Dacres and Welles, and Sir Andrew Trollop. The earl of Devonshire, who was not engaged in Henry's party, was brought a prisoner to Edward; and as soon after beheaded by martial law at York. His head was fixed on a pole erected over a gate of that city; and the head of duke Richard (York) *and that of the earl of Salisbury* (his son) *were taken down, and buried with their bodies. Henry and Margaret had remained at York during the action; but learning the defeat of their army, and being sensible, that no place in England could now afford them shelter, they fled with great precipitation into Scotland.*

Escape of Margaret, capture of king Henry

Henry and Margaret went their separate ways in Scotland. Henry stayed with friends who took him to Lancashire. He *was at last detected, delivered up to Edward, and thrown into the Tower,* where he remained from 1465 to 1470. Margaret, on the other hand, made her escape. *The fate of the unfortunate royal family, after this defeat, was singular. Margaret, flying with her son into a forest, where she endeavored to conceal herself, was beset, during the darkness of the night, by robbers, who, either ignorant or regardless of her quality, despoiled her of her rings and jewels, and treated her with the utmost indignity. The partition of this rich booty raised a quarrel among them; and while their attention was thus engaged, she took the opportunity of making her escape with her son into the thickest of the forest, where she wandered for some time over-spent with hunger and fatigue, and sunk with terror and affliction. While in this wretched condition, she saw a robber approach with his naked sword; and finding that she had no means of escape, she suddenly embraced the resolution of trusting entirely for protection to his faith and generosity. She advanced towards him; and presenting to him the young prince, called out to him, 'Here, my friend, I commit to your care the safety of your king's son'. The man, whose humanity and generous spirit had been obscured but not entirely lost by his vicious course of life, was struck with the singularity of the event, was charmed with the confidence reposed in him; and vowed, not only to abstain from all injury against the princess, but to devote himself entirely to her service. By his means she dwelt some time concealed in the forest, and was at last conducted to the sea-coast, whence she made her escape into Flanders. She passed hence into her father's court, where she had lived several years in privacy and retirement.*

This would not be the end of Margaret, Henry VI, their son and the Lancastrians. The rest of this story must be presented in the next chapter. In brief, a quarrel between the powerful Warwick, called the *king maker*, and Edward IV would lead to the restoration of Henry VI on the throne in October, 1470. This would not last long. Edward would return. Warwick was killed at the battle of Barnet April 14, 1471. Edward defeated Margaret at the battle of Teukesbury, May 4, 1471. The duke of Somerset and twenty others were beheaded. Queen Margaret was captured and sent to the tower. Their young son was murdered. *King Henry expired in that confinement a few days after the battle of Teukesbury; but whether he died a natural or violent death is uncertain. It is pretended, and was generally believed, that the duke of Gloucester killed him with his own hands: But the universal odium, which that prince has incurred, inclined perhaps the nation to aggravate his crimes without any sufficient authority. It is certain, however, that Henry's death was sudden; and though he labored under an ill state of health, this circumstance, joined to the general manners of the age, gave a natural ground of suspicion; which was rather increased than diminished, by the exposing of his body to public view. That precaution served only to recall many similar instances in the English history, and to suggest the comparison. All the hopes of the house of Lancaster seemed now to be utterly extinguished. Every legitimate prince of that family was dead: Almost every great leader of the party had perished in battle or on the scaffold.*[32] The Yorkists would rule under Edward IV.

---

[32] Ibid, pp 481-482.

Chapter 23

Edward IV and Richard III

Edward IV (b. 1442, d. 1483) followed Henry VI and reigned from 1461 to 1483 except for a brief interlude, from 1470 to 1471. Edward IV was the eldest son of Richard Plantagenet duke of York, who was killed in the battle of Wakefield by Queen Margaret's army, December 24, 1460. Edward pursued his father's claim to the throne by victories over the Lancastrians in the battle of Mortimer's Cross in 1461.

After the battle of Mortimer's cross Edward's *army was ordered to assemble in St. John's fields; great numbers of people surrounded them; an harangue was pronounced to this mixed multitude, setting forth the title of Edward and inveighing against the tyranny and usurpation of the rival family; and the people were then asked, whether they would have Henry or Lancaster for king? They unanimously exclaimed against the proposal. It was then demanded, whether they would accept of Edward, eldest son of the late duke of York? They expressed their assent by loud and joyful acclamations. A great number of bishops, lords, magistrates, and other persons of distinction were next assembled at Baynard's castle, who ratified the popular election; and the new king was on the subsequent day proclaimed in London, by the title of Edward IV, on March 5, 1461.*[1]

Edicts of king Edward and acts of parliament

On the meeting of this assembly, November 4, 1461, *Edward found the good effects of his vigorous measure in assuming the crown, as*

---

[1] Hume, vol 2, pp 451-452.

well as of his victory at Touton, by which he had secured it. The parliament no longer hesitated between the two families, or proposed any of those ambiguous decisions, which could only serve to perpetuate and inflame the animosities of party. They recognized the title of Edward, by hereditary descent, through the family of Mortimer. They annulled every grant passed during the reigns of Henry IV to Henry VI, reversed all attainders passed in previous parliaments. They passed an act of forfeiture and attainder against Henry VI, queen Margaret, and their infant son, prince Edward. Acts of forfeiture and attainder were passed against numerous earls, dukes and lords who had supported king Henry. *The parliament vested the estates of all these attainted persons in the crown; though their sole crime was the adhering to a prince, whom every individual of the parliament had long recognized, and whom that very king himself, who was now seated on the throne, had acknowledged and obeyed as his lawful sovereign.*

Executions of John de Vere, the 12 earl of Oxford, and his son Aubrey de Vere

The necessity of supporting the government established will more fully justify some other acts of violence; though the method of conducting them may still appear exceptional. John de Vere earl of Oxford and his son, Aubrey de Vere, were detected in a correspondence with Margaret. They were tried by martial law before the constable, were condemned and executed.[2] *Sir William Tyrell, Sir Thomas Tudenham, and John Montgomery were convicted in the same arbitrary court; were executed, and their estates forfeited.*[3]

King Edward marries Elizabeth (Woodville) Gray

Edward had dispatched Warwick to France to propose an engagement and marriage of Lady Bona, sister to the queen of France. But meanwhile Edward fell in love with Elizabeth Gray whose husband Sir John Gray, had been slain in the second battle of St. Albans fighting on the side of Lancaster. Edward came to pay visit after a hunting trip to her mother, who was duchess of Bedford. It was, from the story told by Hume as well as Shakespeare, love at first sight for Edward. Lady Gray had entreated Edward to take pity on her distressed condition and her impoverished children. She resisted Edward's attempt to provide relief for concessions but she refused. *His passion, irritated by opposition, and increased by his veneration for such honorable sentiments, carried him at last beyond all bounds of reason; and he offered to share his throne, as well as his heart, with the woman, whose beauty of person, and dignity*

---

[2] Note. See Shakespeare, Third Part, Henry VI, act iii, sc 3.

[3] Ibid, p 460.

of character seemed so well to entitle her to both. The marriage was privately celebrated at Grafton.[4]

Meanwhile Warwick had concluded a treaty with Lewis, king of France, for the marriage of lady Bona and king Edward. Warwick returned to England, *inflamed with rage and indignation* upon learning of the marriage, all without his knowledge. Not only had Warwick lost face in a negotiation with the king of France but Edward had awarded the new Queen's large family with offices, titles, and great wealth, in 1466. Edward next concluded an alliance with Burgundy, in 1467, and the following year Edward's sister Margaret was married to Charles the bold, duke of Burgundy. Warwick perceived all this as a threat to his own great wealth and power. *His ambitious spirit was dissatisfied, so long as he saw others surpass him in authority and influence with the king.*

What followed was an alliance of Warwick, Edward's brother the duke of Clarence, the king of France and Margaret to depose Edward and restore Henry to the throne. A number of rebellions had broken out in England to add to the confusion. In September, 1470, Warwick *seized the opportunity, and setting sail, quickly landed at Dartmouth, with the duke of Clarence, the earls of Oxford and Pemboke, and a small body of troops; while the king was in the north, engaged in suppressing an insurrection, which had been raised by lord Fitz-Hugh, brother-in-law to Warwick. The scene, which ensues, resembles more the fiction of a poem or romance than an event in true history. The prodigious popularity of Warwick, the zeal of the Lancastrian party, the spirit of discontent with which many were infected; and the general instability of the English nation, occasioned by the late frequent revolutions, drew such multitudes to his standard, that, in a very few days, his army amounted to sixty thousand men; and was continually increasing. Edward hastened southwards to encounter him; and the two armies approached each other near Nottingham, where a decisive action was every hour expected.* The only recourse for Edward was flight, which he managed on horseback to Lynne in Norfolk, where he boarded ships and made his escape to the port of Alcmaer in Holland.[5]

Henry VI restored

Immediately after Edward's flight had left the kingdom at Warwick's disposal, that nobleman hastened to London; and taking Henry from his confinement in the Tower, into which he himself had been the chief cause of throwing him, he proclaimed him king with great solemnity, in October, 1470. A parliament was summoned, in the name of that prince, to meet at Westminster; and as this assembly could pretend

---

[4] Ibid, pp 463-464.

[5] Ibid, pp 474-475.

to no liberty, while surrounded by such enraged and insolent victors, governed by such an impetuous spirit as Warwick, their votes were entirely dictated by the ruling faction. The treaty with Margaret was here fully executed: Henry was recognized as lawful kin; but his incapacity for government being avowed, the regency was entrusted to Warwick and Clarence till the majority of prince Edward. Parliament then repealed every statue made during the reign of Edward, reversed all the attainders and restored everyone of the Lancastrian cause.[6]

Edward's return

Edward returned March 25, 1471 at Ravenspur in Yorkshire. He found ready acceptance by the people of York. *Warwick assembled an army At Leicester, with an intention of meeting and giving battle to the enemy; but Edward, by taking another road, passed him unmolested, and presented himself before the gates of London. Had he been refused admittance, he was totally undone: But there were many reasons, which inclined the citizens to favor him. His numerous friends issuing from their sanctuaries, were active in his cause; many rich merchants, who had formerly lent him money, saw no other chance for their payment but his restoration. --- Edward's entrance into London, made him master not only of that rich and powerful city, but also of the person of Henry, who, destined to be the perpetual sport of fortune, thus fell again into the hands of his enemies. Edward found himself in a condition to face the earl of Warwick; who, being reinforced by his son-in-law the duke of Clarence, and his brother the marquis of Montague, took post at Barnet, in the neighborhood of London. The arrival of queen Margaret was every day expected, who would have drawn together all the genuine Lancastrians, and have brought a great accession to Warwick's forces. But the duke of Clarence, younger brother of Edward, deserted to the king in the nighttime, and carried over a body of 12,000 men along with him.[7]*

The battle of Barnett and the death of Warwick

Warwick was now too far advanced to retreat; and as he rejected with disdain all terms of peace offered him by Edward and Clarence, he was obliged to hazard a general engagement. The battle was fought with obstinacy on both sides, on April 14, 1471. The two armies, in imitation of their leaders, displayed uncommon valor: And the victory remained long undecided between them. But an accident threw the balance to the side of the Yorkists. Edward's sign was a sun; that of Warwick a star with rays; and the mistiness of the morning rendering it

---

[6] Ibid, pp 475-477.

[7] Ibid, pp 480-481.

difficult to distinguish them, the thirteenth *earl of Oxford, who fought on the side of the Lancastrians, was, by mistake, attacked by his friends, and chased off the field of battle. Warwick, contrary to his more usual practice, engaged that day on foot, resolving to show his army, that he meant to share every fortune with them; and he was slain in the thickest of the engagement. His brother, Montague, underwent the same fate: And as Edward had issued orders not to give any quarter, a great and undistinguished slaughter was made in the pursuit.*[8]

Battle of Teukesbury

The same day, on which this decisive battle was fought, queen Margaret and her son, now about eighteen years of age, and a young prince of great hopes, landed at Weymouth, supported by a small body of French forces. When this princess received intelligence of her husband's captivity, and of the defeat and death of the earl of Warwick, her courage, which had supported her under so many disastrous events, here quite left her, and she immediately foresaw all the dismal consequences of this calamity. At first she took sanctuary in the abbey of Beaulieu, but being encouraged by the appearance of Tudor, earl of Pembroke --- with other men of rank, who exhorted her still to hope for success, she resumed her former spirit, and determined to defend to the utmost the ruins of her fallen fortunes. She advanced through the counties of Devon, Somerset, and Gloucester, increasing her army on each day's march; but was at last overtaken by the rapid and expeditious Edward, at Teukesbury, on the banks of the Severne, on May 4, 1471. The Lancastrians were totally defeated: The earl of Devonshire and lord Wenlock were killed in the field: The duke of Somerset, and about twenty other persons of distinction, having taken shelter in a church, were surrounded, dragged out, and immediately beheaded: About 3000 of their side fell in battle: and the army was entirely dispersed.

Death of Henry and his son

Queen Margaret and her son were taken prisoners, and brought to the king, who asked the prince, after an insulting manner, how he dared to invade his dominions? The young prince, more mindful of his high birth than of his present fortune, replied that he came thither to claim his just inheritance. The ungenerous Edward, insensible to pity, struck him on the face with his gauntlet, and the dukes of Clarence and Gloucester, lord Hastings and sir Thomas Gray, taking the blow as a signal for farther violence, hurried the prince into the next apartment, and there dispatched him with their daggers, on May 21, 1471. Margaret was thrown into the Tower: King Henry expired in that confinement a few days after the battle of Teukesbury; but whether he died a natural

---

[8] Ibid, pp 480-481.

cause or violent death is uncertain. It is pretended, and was generally believed, that the duke of Gloucester killed him with his own hands: But the universal odium, which that prince has incurred, inclined perhaps the nation to aggravate his crimes without any sufficient authority. It is certain, however, that Henry's death was sudden; and though he labored under an ill state of health, this circumstance, joined to the general manners of the age, gave a natural ground of suspicion; which was rather increased than diminished, by the exposing of his body to public view. That precaution served only to recall many similar instances in the English history, and to suggest the comparison.[9]

Invasion of France and settlement

Parliament, after Edward was restored to the crown, once again ratified all the acts of Edward and the attainders and restorations under Henry's brief rule were reversed. *But this prince, who had been so firm, and active, and intrepid during the course of adversity, was still unable to resist the allurements of a prosperous fortune; and he wholly devoted himself, as before, to pleasure and amusement, after he became entirely master of his kingdom, and had no longer any enemy who could give him anxiety or alarm.*

But while the king was thus indulging himself in pleasure he was roused from his lethargy by a prospect of foreign conquests, which, it is probable, his desire of popularity, more than the spirit of ambition, had made him covet. Though he deemed himself little beholden to the duke of Burgundy, for the reception which that prince had given him during his exile, the political interests of their states maintained still a close connection between them; and they agreed to unite their arms in making a powerful invasion on France. A league was formed, in which Edward stipulated to pass the seas with an army, exceeding 10,000 men, and to invade the French territories: Charles promised to join him with all his forces. The king was to challenge the crown of France, and to obtain at least the provinces of Normandy and Guienne: The duke was to acquire Champaigne and some other territories, and to free all his dominions from the burthen of homage to the crown of France. ---

The prospect of a French war was always a sure means of making the parliament open their purses, as far as the habits of that age would permit. They voted the king a tenth of rents, or two shillings in the pound.

The king passed over to Calais with an army of 1500 men at arms, and 15,000 archers; attended by all the chief nobility of England, who, prognosticating future successes from the past, were eager to appear on this great theater of honor. But all their sanguine hopes were damped, when they found, on entering the French territories, that neither

---

[9] Ibid, pp 481, 482.

did the constable open his gates to them, nor the duke of Burgundy bring them the smallest assistance. --- This circumstance gave great disgust to the king, and inclined him to hearken to those advances, which the French king Lewis continually made him for an accommodation.

As Edward was now fallen into like dispositions, a truce was soon concluded on terms more advantageous than honorable to Lewis, He stipulated to pay Edward immediately 75,000 crowns, on condition that he should withdraw his army from France, and promised to pay him 50,000 crowns a year during their joint lives.

The treaty, known as the peace of Pecquigni, *did very little honor to either of these monarchs: It discovered the imprudence of Edward, who had taken his measures so ill with his allies, as to be obliged, after such an expensive armament, to return without making any acquisitions, adequate to them: It showed the want of dignity in Lewis, who, rather than run the hazard of a battle, agreed to subject his kingdom to a tribute.*[10]

Ransom of Margaret

The most honorable part of Lewis's treaty with Edward was the stipulation for the liberty of queen Margaret, who, though after the death of her husband and son she could no longer be formidable to government, was still detained in custody by Edward. Lewis paid fifty thousand crowns for her ransom; and that princess, who had been so active on the stage of the world, and who had experienced such a variety of fortune, passed the remainder of her days in tranquility and privacy, till the year 1482, when she died.

Execution of the duke of Clarence

Edward's younger brother George the duke of Clarence, would first be subject to the loss of his friends, Tyburn and Stacey, by spurious charges. *The duke of Clarence was alarmed, when he found these acts of tyranny exercised on all around him. --- But Clarence, instead of securing his own life against the present danger, by silence and reserve, was open and loud in justifying the innocence of his friends, and in exclaiming against the iniquity of their prosecutors. The king, highly offended with his freedom, or using that pretense against him, committed him to the Tower, summoned a parliament, and tried him for his life before the house of peers, the supreme tribunal of the nation.*

The duke was accused of arraigning public justice, by maintaining the innocence of men, who had been condemned in courts of judicature; and of inveighing against the iniquity of the king, who had given orders for their prosecution. --- The house of commons were no less slavish and unjust: They both petitioned for the execution of the

---

[10] Ibid, pp 485-487.

duke, and afterwards passed a bill of attainder against him. Edward's brother the duke of Clarence was executed *on* February 18, 1482, by beheading.

The duke left two children, by the elder daughter of the earl of Warwick; a son and a daughter. *Both this prince and princess were also unfortunate in their end, and died a violent death; a fate which for many years, attended almost all the descendants of the royal blood in England.*[11]

Administration

Modern historians credit Edward IV with certain advancements in finance and administration, which brought great wealth to England with establishment of trade with France, Burgundy and the Hanseatic league. It is not surprising, that with the death of so many of the most powerful barons that a mercantile class would emerge of which Edward was a part.

Death of Edward IV

While Edward was making preparations for another French war, *he was seized with a distemper, of which he expired in the forty-second year of his age, and the twenty-third of his reign: A prince more splendid and showy, than either prudent or virtuous; brave, though cruel, addicted to pleasure, though capable of activity in great emergencies. And less filled to prevent ills by wise precautions, than to remedy them, after they took place, by his vigor and enterprise.* Edward IV died April 9, 1483. *Besides five daughters this king left two sons; Edward, prince of Wales, his successor, then in his thirteen year, and Richard, duke of York, in his ninth.*[12]

Richard III

Richard III, duke of Gloucester, (b. 1452, d 1485) usurped the crown and ruled less than two years, from 1483 to 1485. The reign of Richard III was the last of the Yorkists on the throne. Richard was the youngest son of Richard Plantagenet duke of York. Richard had commanded forces in the battles of Barnet and Tewkesbury, which led to Edward's victory over the Lancastrians and title to the crown. Richard likely had a hand in the death of king Henry VI and had assisted others in the death of Henry's son Edward prince of Wales. After Edward's death the heirs to the throne were the sons of Edward IV, prince Edward and

---

[11] Ibid, pp 491-492.

[12] Ibid, pp 492-493.

Richard duke of York. Richard became protector of the realm and Edward's twelve-year old son after Edward IV's death. Richard, however, had other intentions. He would claim the crown by false testimony about his own title being superior to his older brothers Edward IV and George duke of Clarence, and would murder the sons of Edward IV to protect his crown. The persons involved in these disorders during the reign of Richard III centered about Edward IV's queen Elizabeth Woodville and her family versus Richard and his followers. The members of Elizabeth's family included her brother the earl of Rivers, her son Richard Gray, and Dorset, son by a previous marriage. Richard's allies included the duke of Buckingham, lords Hastings and Stanley.

On Edward's deathbed he exhorted these contending parties to be at peace. But Edward knew, that, though he himself had been able to overawe those rival factions, many disorders might arise from their contests during the minority of his son; and he thereafter took care, in his last illness, to summon together several of the leaders on both sides, and, by composing their ancient quarrels, to provide, as far as possible, for the future tranquility of the government. After expressing the intentions, that his brother, the duke of Gloucester, then absent in the north, should be entrusted with the regency, he recommended to them peace and unanimity during the tender years of his son; represented to them the dangers which must attend the continuance of their animosities; and engaged them to embrace each other with all the appearance of the most cordial reconciliation. But this temporary or feigned agreement lasted no longer than the king's life: He had no sooner expired, than the jealousies of the parties broke out afresh: And each of them applied, by separate messages, to the duke of Gloucester, and endeavored to acquire his favor and friendship.[13]

Arrest of the earl of Rivers

Richard, his exorbitant ambition, unrestrained by any principle either of justice or humanity, made him carry his view to the possession of the crown itself; and as this object could not be attained without the ruin of the queen and her family, he fell, without hesitation, into concert with the opposite party.

The young prince Edward, at the time of his father's death, resided in the castle of Ludlow, on the borders of Wales. --- His person was committed to the care of his uncle, the earl of Rivers, the most accomplished nobleman in England, who, having united an uncommon taste for literature to great abilities in business, and valor in the field, was entitled, by his talents, still more than by nearness of blood, to direct the education of the young monarch. The queen, anxious to preserve that ascendant over her son, which she had long maintained over her

---

[13] Hume vol 2, p 495.

husband, wrote to the earl of Rivers, that he should levy a body of forces, in order to escort the king to London, to protect him during his coronation, and to keep him from falling into the hands of their enemies.

Richard assured Elizabeth that there would be no armed conflict, hence no need of such protection. Edward was sent by another road to Stony-Stratford and Rivers met Richard at Northampton. *The earl of Rivers was received with the greatest appearance of cordiality: He passed the evening in an amicable manner with Gloucester and Buckingham: He proceeded on the road with them the next day to join the king: But as he was entering Stony-Stratford, he was arrested by orders from Richard, the duke of Gloucester: sir Richard Gray, one of the queen's sons, was at the same time put under a guard, together with sir Thomas Vaughan, who possessed a considerable office in the king's household; and all the prisoners were instantly conducted to Pomfret, on May 1, 1483.*

But the queen no sooner received intelligence of her brother's imprisonment, than she foresaw, that Gloucester's violence would not stop there, and that her own ruin, if not that of all her children, was finally determined. She therefore fled into the sanctuary of Westminster, attended by the marquis of Dorset; and she carried thither the five princesses, together with Richard, the duke of York.[14]

The earl of Rivers, Gray and Vaughan beheaded

The death of the earl of Rivers, and of the other prisoners detained in Pomfret, was first determined; and he easily obtained the consent of the duke of Buckingham, as well as of lord Hastings, to this violent and sanguinary measure. However easy it was, in those times, to procure a sentence against the most innocent person, it appeared still more easy to dispatch an enemy, without any trial or form of process; and orders were accordingly issued to Sir Richard Ratcliffe, a proper instrument in the hands of this tyrant, to cut off the heads of the prisoners.

Execution of lord Hastings

On the very day when Rivers, Gray, and Vaughan were executed, or rather murdered, at Pomfret, by the advice of Hastings, the protector summoned a council in the Tower; whither that noblemen, suspecting no design against him, repaired without hesitation. The duke of Gloucester was capable of committing the most bloody and treacherous murders with the utmost coolness and indifference. On taking his place at the council-table, he appeared in the easiest and most jovial humor imaginable. He seemed to indulge himself in familiar conversation with the counselors, before he should enter on business;

---

[14] Ibid, pp 496-498.

and having paid some compliments to Morton, bishop of Ely, on the good and early strawberries which he raised in his garden at Holborn, he begged the favor of having a dish of them, which that prelate immediately dispatched a servant to bring to him. The protector then left the council, as if called away by some other business; but soon after returning with an angry and inflamed countenance, he asked them, what punishment those deserved that had plotted against his life, who was so nearly related to the king, and was instructed with the administration of government? Hastings replied, that they merited the punishment of traitors. These traitors, cried the protector, are the sorceress, my brother's wife, and Jane Shore, his mistress, with others, their associates: See to what a condition they have reduced me by their incantations and witchcraft: Upon which he laid bare his arm, all shriveled and decayed. But the counselors, who knew that this infirmity had attended him from his birth, looked on each other with amazement; and above all, lord Hastings, who, as he had, since Edward's death, engaged in an intrigue with Jane Shore, was naturally anxious concerning the issue of these extraordinary proceedings. Hastings hesitated to agree with the king. Hastings was seized, was hurried away, and instantly beheaded on a timber-log, which lay in the court of the Tower. Lord Stanley, the archbishop of York, the bishop of Ely, and other counselors, were committed prisoners in different chambers of the Tower: And the protector, in order to carry on the farce of his accusations, ordered the goods of Jane Shore to be seized, and he summoned her to answer before the council for sorcery and witchcraft. [15]

Bizarre pretensions to the throne

The first argument of Richard was that the children of Edward IV and Elizabeth Woodville were illegitimate, in view of supposed previous relationships. Since a bill of attainder had been passed against his other brother George, duke of Clarence, his two children could not succeed to the crown. But the most preposterous claim of Richard was that his two brothers were illegitimate. Richard claimed that his mother, the duchess of York, had lovers who fathered his brothers Edward and George before her marriage to Richard Plantagenet duke of York. Only Richard was a legitimate son, according to Richard's claims. In order to give these wild assertions credibility he obtained the services of one Dr. Shaw. *The mayor, who was brother to Dr. Shaw, and entirely in the protector's interests, called an assembly of the citizens; where the duke of Buckingham, who possessed some talents for eloquence, harangued them on the protectors title to the crown, and displayed those numerous virtues, of which, he pretended, that prince possessed.* These men

---

[15] Ibid, pp 500-502.

attempted to convince enough of the people that Richard's infamous pretensions were acceptable. They then pretended that by popular acclaim Richard was the legitimate and rightful sovereign. On June 25, 1483 parliament endorsed Richard's claims and the following day he was proclaimed king.

Murders of Edward and Richard, heirs to the throne

This ridiculous farce was soon after followed by a scene truly tragical: The murder of the two young princes. Richard gave orders to Sir Robert Brakenbury, constable of the Tower, to put his nephews to death; but this gentleman, who had sentiments of honor, refused to have any hand in the infamous office. The tyrant then sent for Sir James Tyrrel, choosing three associates, Slater, Dighton, and Forest, came in the night-time to the door of the chamber where the princes were lodged; and sending in the assassins, he bade them execute their commission, while he himself stayed without. They found the young princes in bed, and fallen into a profound sleep. After suffocating them with the boltser and pillows, they showed their naked bodies to Tyrrel who ordered them to be buried at the foot of the stairs, deep in the ground, under a heap of stone. These circumstances were all confessed by the actors, in the following reign; and they were never punished for the crime: Probably, because Henry, whose maxims of government were extremely arbitrary, desired to establish it as a principle, that the commands of the reigning sovereign ought to justify every enormity in those who paid obedience to them.[16]

Execution of Buckingham

Buckingham descended by a daughter of an uncle of Richard II. By this *pedigree, he not only was allied to the royal family, but had claims for dignities as well as estates, of a very extensive nature.* Unfortunately, *Buckingham was not content with these fortunes but sought, with king Richard's help, the vast Hereford estates, which had escheated to the crown, as well as the great office of constable, which had long continued by inheritance in his ancestors of that family.* Whether the king's refusal of making restitution of the Hereford estate or other demands of Buckingham on the king, *it was impossible, that friendship could long remain inviolate between two men of such corrupt minds as Richard and the duke of Buckingham.* Buckingham was in fact largely responsible for Richard's accession of the crown. *The duke of Buckingham, --- who, by his mother, a daughter of Edmund, duke of Somerset, was allied to the house of Lancaster.*[17]

---

[16] Ibid, pp 505-506.

[17] Ibid, pp 507-509.

Richard soon received intelligence, that his enemies, headed by the duke of Buckingham, were forming some design against his authority. Richard immediately put himself in a posture of defense by levying troops in the North; and he summoned the duke to appear at court, in such terms as seemed to promise him a renewal of their former amity. But that nobleman, well acquainted with the barbarity and treachery of Richard, replied only by taking arms in Wales and giving the signal to his accomplices for a general insurrection in all parts of England. But at that very time there happened to fall such heavy rains, so incessant and continued, as exceeded any known in the memory of man; and the Severne, with the other rivers in that neighborhood, swelled to a height which rendered them impassable, and prevented Buckingham from marching into the heart of England to join his associates. The Welshmen, partly moved by superstition at this extraordinary event, partly distressed by famine in their camp, fell off from him; and Buckingham, finding himself deserted by his followers, put on a disguise, and took shelter in the house of Banister, an old servant of his family. But being detected in his retreat, he was brought to the king at Salisbury; and was instantly executed, according to the summary method practiced in that age.[18]

Murder of his wife Anne

The king was desperate to make his claim to the throne appear legitimate. He therefore decided to get rid of his wife and then proposition Elizabeth Woodville, queen of Edward IV, for the marriage of her daughter Elizabeth. But Richard seemed to ignore the fact that he had murdered princess Elizabeth's two younger brothers. Richard also seemed to be oblivious to the fact that he had murdered two of Elizabeth's uncles, the earl of Rivers and Richard Gray. *Richard had married Anne, the second daughter of the earl of Warwick, and widow of Edward prince of Wales, whom Richard himself had murdered; but this princess having born him but one son, who died about this time, he considered her as an invincible obstacle to the settlement of his fortune, and he was believed to have carried her off by poison.*[19]

The earl of Richmond, he knew, could never be formidable but from his projected marriage with the princess Elizabeth, the true heir of the crown. Richard had hoped to marry the princess, but Elizabeth Woodville had made arrangements for the marriage of Elizabeth to Henry, earl of Richmond in September 1483. *She secretly borrowed a sum of money in the city, sent it over to the earl of Richmond, required his oath to celebrate the marriage as soon as he should arrive in England, advised him to levy as many foreign forces as possible, and*

---

[18] Ibid, pp 511-512.

[19] Ibid, p 514.

promised to join him, on his first appearance, with all the friends and partisans of her family.[20]

Defection to the cause of the earl of Richmond

But the crimes of Richard were so horrid and shocking to humanity, that the natural sentiments of men, without any political or public views, were sufficient to render his government unstable; and every person of probity and honor was earnest to prevent the scepter from being any longer polluted by that bloody and faithless hand which held it. All the exiles flocked to the earl of Richmond in Brittany, and exhorted him to hasten his attempt for a new invasion, and to prevent the marriage of the princess Elizabeth, which must prove fatal to all his hopes. --- The earl of Oxford, whom Richard's suspicions had thrown into confinement, having made his escape, here joined Henry; and inflamed his ardor for the attempt, by the favorable accounts which he brought of the dispositions of the English nation, and their universal hatred of Richard's crimes and usurpation.

The battle of Bosworth

On August 7, 1485, Henry the earl of Richmond set sail from Harfleur and landed in Wales with only 2000 men. It didn't take long for Henry to gather six thousand men who had defected from Richard. On August 22, the earl of Oxford, Sir Gilbert Talbot, Sir John Savage, Henry and the earl of Pembroke decided the victory in favor of Henry earl of Richmond. *Soon after the battle began, lord Stanley, whose conduct in this whole affair discovers great precaution and abilities, appeared in the field, and declared for the earl of Richmond. This measure, which was unexpected to the men, though not to their leaders, had a proportional effect on both armies: It inspired unusual courage into Henry's soldiers; it threw Richard's into dismay and confusion.* Richard had held Stanley's son hostage with the threat to behead him if Stanley went over to the opposition.[21]

Death of Richard III

The intrepid tyrant, sensible of his desperate situation, cast his eye around the field, and descrying his rival at no great distance, he drove against him with fury, in hopes, that either Henry's death or his own would decide the victory between them. He killed with his own hands, Sir William Brandon, standard bearer to the earl: He dismounted Sir John Cheyney: He was now within reach of Richmond himself, who declined not the combat; When Sir William Stanley, breaking in with his

---

[20] Ibid, 512.

[21] Note. Stanley's son would not be executed.

troops, surrounded Richard, who fighting bravely to the last moment, was overwhelmed by numbers, and perished by a fate too mild and honorable for his multiplied and detestable enormities. --- The body of Richard was found in the field, covered with dead enemies, and all besmeared with blood: It was thrown carelessly across a horse; was carried to Leicester amidst the shouts of the insulting spectators; and was interred in Gray-Friars church of that place.[22] He died on that day, August 22, 1485 at age 32 and had reigned less than two years.

---

[22] Ibid, pp 517-518.

Chapter 24

Henry VII

Henry VII, Henry Tudor, Earl of Richmond, (b 1457, d 1509), ruled from 1485 to 1509. He defeated Richard III in the battle of Bosworth. *The victory, which Henry, the earl of Richmond, gained at Bosworth, August 22, 1485, was entirely decisive; being attended, as well with the total rout and dispersion of the royal army, as with the death of king Richard III himself. Joy for this great success suddenly prompted the soldiers, in the field of battle, to bestow on their victorious general the appellation of king, which he had not hitherto assumed; and the acclamations of 'Long live Henry the Seventh', by a natural and unpremeditated movement, resounded forth all quarters. To bestow some appearance of formality on this species of military election, Sir William Stanley brought a crown of ornament, which Richard wore in battle, and which had been found among the spoils; and he put it on the head of the victor.*[1] On October 30, after entering London with a rousing reception, cardinal Bourchier, archbishop of Canterbury crowned him.

Defective title, Family history

Henry was not an heir to the throne. Edmund Tudor, Henry's father, was the son of Owen Tudor who was captured in the battle of Mortimer's Cross in 1461 and immediately beheaded by order of Edward IV. Though Henry's descendants would be known as *Tudors* from the name of his father and grandfather, neither had any relationship to the heirs of the crown. Henry's mother, Margaret Beauford, was the great grand daughter of John of Gaunt and his third wife Catherine Swynford. Henry IV, V and VI were descendants of Blanch of Lancaster, the first wife of John of Gaunt. A matter of great importance to the Yorkists was the fact that John of Gaunt was not married to Catherine Swynford until

---

[1] Hume, vol 3, pp 3, 4.

after their children were born, including Henry's maternal grandfather. Henry VII therefore did not qualify as an heir to the Lancastrian throne. His title to the throne was based on conquest, the victory over Richard III at the battle of Bosworth August 22, 1485. He later, on January 8, 1486, married Elizabeth, daughter and only surviving heir of Edward IV. This would have presumably made him a legitimate king, or gained some support from the Yorkists. However, most of his reign, until 1499, would be threatened by York uprisings and civil war.

Early life

There is little information extant regarding the childhood and upbringing of Henry. His father Edmund Tudor had died soon after his birth. Margaret, his mother, married Henry Stafford, uncle to Buckingham, shortly after the death of his father. After the death of Stafford the mother married lord Stanley. She had no children by either of these marriages. Henry was brought up his uncle Jasper Tudor, earl of Pembroke. After the total defeat of the Lancastrians at the battle of Teukesbury, May 4, 1471, when Henry was fifteen years old, his uncle took him to live in Brittany. Henry was essentially a prisoner, however, since Edward had promised the duke of Brittany a pension to make sure that Henry would be *detained in custody.*[2] It is likely that young Henry would be influenced by the terrors and bloody conflicts during the reigns of Edward IV and Richard III. *Henry himself, who had seen most of his near friends and relations perish in battle or by the executioner, and who had been exposed in his own person to many hardships and dangers, had imbibed a violent antipathy to the York party, which no time or experience were ever able to efface.*[3]

Henry as king

The parliament being assembled at Westminster November 7, the majority immediately appeared to be devoted partisans of Henry, all persons of another disposition, either declining to stand in those dangerous times, or being obliged to dissemble their principles and inclinations. Attainders against those of the Lancastrian party were reversed, while those of the York faction were prohibited from sitting in parliament. Attainders were passed against the late king Richard, the duke of Norfolk, the earl of Surrey, Sir Humphrey Stafford, Catesby and twenty other gentlemen, who had fought on Richard's side in the battle of Bosworth. *With a parliament so obsequious, the king could not fail of obtaining whatever act of settlement he was pleased to require. He seems only to have entertained some doubt within himself on what claim he*

---

[2] Hume, Vol 2, p 510.

[3] Hume, Vol 3, pp 6-7.

should found his pretensions. In his speech to the parliament he mentioned his just title by hereditary right; but lest that title should not be esteemed sufficient, he subjoined his claim by the judgment of God, who had given him victory over his enemies.[4]

Marriage to Elizabeth

The parliament, however, conferred on him during life the duty of tonnage and poundage, which had been enjoyed in the same manner by some of his immediate predecessors. In presenting the bill of tonnage and poundage, the parliament, anxious to preserve the legal, undisputed succession to the crown, had petitioned Henry, with demonstrations of the greatest zeal, to espouse the princess Elizabeth; but they covered their true reason under the dutiful pretense of their desire to have heirs of his body. He now thought in earnest of satisfying the minds of his people in that particular. His marriage was celebrated at London, on January 8, 1486; and that with greater appearance of universal joy, than either his first entry or his coronation. Henry remarked with much displeasure this general favor born to the house of York. The suspicion, which arose from it, not only disturbed his tranquility during his whole reign; but bred disgust toward his consort herself, and poisoned all his domestic enjoyments. Though virtuous, amiable, and obsequious to the last degree, she never met with a proper return of affection or even of complaisance from her husband; and the malignant ideas of faction still, in his sullen mind, prevailed over all the sentiments of conjugal tenderness.[5]

Insurrection by Lambert Simnel

Several men pretended to be heirs of the throne even though there was ample evidence that such individuals had been executed. The first of these pretenders Lambert Simnel, *a youth of fifteen years of age, who was son of a baker, and who, being endowed with understanding above his years, and address above his condition, seemed well fitted to impersonate a prince of royal extraction.* Simnel and his supporters decided to impersonate the son of the duke of Clarence, younger brother of Edward IV. The daughters of Edward IV were still living and had greater claim to the throne, including Elizabeth. The Irish and Margaret, duchess of Burgundy, who was the sister of Richard III, supported Simnel. *After consulting with Lincoln and Lovel, she hired a body of two thousand veteran Germans, under the command of Martin Swart, a brave and experienced officer, and sent them over, together with these two noblemen, to join Simnel in Ireland. Henry was not ignorant of these*

---

[4] Ibid, pp 3-10.

[5] Ibid, pp 13-14.

intentions of his enemies; and he prepared himself for defense. He ordered troops to be levied in different parts of the kingdom, and put them under the command of the duke of Bedford, and the earl of Oxford.[6] --- The hostile armies met at Stroke in the county of Nottingham, and fought a battle, which was bloody, and more obstinately disputed than could have been expected from the inequality of their forces. --- The king's victory was purchased with loss, but was entirely decisive. Lincoln, Broughton, and Swart, perished in the field of battle, with four thousand of their followers. As Lovel was never more heard of, he was believed to have undergone the same fate. Simnel, with his tutor, Simon, was taken prisoner. Simon, being a priest, was not tried at law, and was only committed to close custody: Simnel was too contemptible to be an object either of apprehension or resentment to Henry. He was pardoned, and made a scullion in the king's kitchen.

Henry had now leisure to revenge himself on his enemies. He made a progress into the northern parts, where he gave many proofs of his rigorous disposition. A strict inquiry was made after those who had assisted or favored the rebels. The punishments were not all sanguinary: The king made his revenge subservient to his avarice. Heavy fines were levied upon the delinquents. The proceedings of the courts, and even the courts themselves, were arbitrary. Either the criminals were tried by commissioners appointed for the purpose, or they suffered punishment by sentence of a court-martial. --- But such, in this age, was the situation of the English government, that the royal prerogative, which was but imperfectly restrained during the most peaceable periods, was sure, in tumultuous, or even suspicious times, which frequently recurred, to break all bounds of law, and to violate public liberty. ---

The queen had been married near two years, but had not yet been crowned; and this affectation of delay had given great discontent to the public, and had been a principal source of the disaffection which prevailed. The king, instructed by experience, now finished the ceremony of her coronation, on November 25, 1487, and to show a disposition still more gracious, he restored to liberty the marquis of Dorset, who had been able to clear himself of all the suspicions entertained against him.[7]

Invasions of Brittany and France

Henry attempted to follow in the footsteps of Edward III and Henry V in furthering England's claims over Brittany and France. France, during the two preceding reigns, had made a mighty increase in power and greatness. *Most the great fiefs, Normandy, Champagne, Anjou, Dauphiny, Guienne, Provence, and Burgundy, had been united to*

---

[6] The Thirteenth earl of Oxford.

[7] Ibid, pp 18-22.

the crown; the English had been expelled from all their conquests. There remained the objective to annex Brittany, the last independent fief of the French monarchy.

On September 9, 1488, a small force led by Lord Woodville, brother to the queen dowager, invaded Brittany. *Woodville and all the English were put to the sword; together with a body of Bretons* by the French forces. *The duke of Orleans, the prince of Orange, and many other persons of rank were taken prisoners: And the military force of Brittany was totally broken.*[8] In 1489, Henry levied a force of 6,000 men after forming a league with emperors Maximilian and Ferdinand. The English, under lord Broke, invaded Brittany. *Lord Broke found such discord and confusion in the counsels of Brittany, that no measures could be concerted for any undertaking; no supply obtained; no provisions, carriages, artillery, or military stores procured. --- The English, disconcerted in every enterprise, by these animosities and uncertain counsels, returned home as soon as the time of their service was elapsed; leaving only a small garrison in those towns, which had been configured into their hands. During their stay in Brittany, they had only contributed still farther to waste the country; and by their departure, they left it entirely at the mercy of the enemy.*[9]

France was victorious over Brittany. The king of France then married the duchess of Brittany. Brittany was annexed to France, in 1491. On October 6, 1492, Henry invaded France after he had obtained a supply from parliament. *The nobility were universally seized with a desire of military glory; and having credulously swallowed all the boasts of the king, they dreamed of no less than carrying their triumphant banners to the gates of Paris, and putting the crown of France on the head of their sovereign. Many of them borrowed large sums, or sold off manors, that they might appear in the field with greater splendor, and lead out their followers in more complete order. The king crossed the sea, and arrived at Calais on the sixth of October, with an army of twenty-five thousand foot and sixteen hundred horse, which he put under the command of the duke of Bedford and the earl of Oxford. --- As if he had seriously intended this enterprise, he instantly marched into the enemy's country and laid siege of Bulloigne: But notwithstanding this appearance of hostility, there had been secret advances made towards peace above three months before; and commissioners had been appointed to treat of the terms. --- In order the more effectually to cover these intended measures, he secretly engaged the marquis of Dorset, together with twenty-three persons of distinction, to present him a petition for agreeing to a treaty with France. --- The demands of Henry*

---

[8] Ibid, pp 30-31.

[9] Ibid, pp 33-34.

were wholly pecuniary; and the king of France, who deemed the peaceable possession of Brittany an equivalent for any sum, and who was all on fire for his projected expedition into Italy, readily agreed to the proposals made him. He engaged to pay Henry 745,000 crowns. And he stipulated a yearly pension to Henry and his heirs of 25,000 crowns. Thus the king, as remarked by his historian Bacon, made profit upon his subjects for the war; and upon his enemies for the peace. And the people agreed, that he had fulfilled his promise, when he said to the parliament, that he would make the war maintain itself. [10]

Insurrection of Perkin Warbeck

Perkin Warbeck was the next pretender to the throne, impersonating Edward IV's younger son Richard, duke of York. There were several witnesses to Richard's murder in the tower of London, however his body, and that of his older brother Edward were never found.[11] His father Warbeck was known to Edward IV and during Warbeck's stay in London his son Perkin was born. *It was believed by some, that Edward, among his amorous adventures, had a secret commerce with Warbeck's wife; and people thence accounted for that resemblance, which was afterwards remarked between young Perkin and that monarch. Some years after the birth of this child, Warbeck returned to Tournay; where Perkin, his son, did not long remain, but by different accidents was carried from place to place, and his birth and fortunes became thereby unknown, and difficult to be traced by the most diligent inquiry. The variety and sagacity of his genius; and he seemed to be a youth perfectly fitted to act any part, or assume any character. In this light he had been represented to the duchess of Burgundy[12], who, struck with the concurrence of so many circumstances suited to her purpose, desired to be made acquainted with the man, on whom she already began to ground her hopes of success. She found him to exceed her most sanguine expectations; so comely did he appear in his person, so graceful in his air, so courtly in his* address, *so full of docility and good sense in his behavior and conversation. The lesson, necessary to be taught him, in order to his personating the duke of York, were soon learned by a youth of such quick apprehension, but, as the season seemed not then favorable for his enterprise, Margaret, in order the better to conceal him, sent him, under the care of lady Brampton, into Portugal, where he remained a year, unknown to all the world.*

---

[10] Ibid, pp 39-41.

[11] Note. During the reign of Charles I, two bodies of the same age as the princes were found.

[12] Margaret, sister of Edward IV.

Perkin was sent to Ireland, landed at Cork and proclaimed that he was Richard Plantagenet. The Irish people who had favored the York ascendancy received him with favor. Charles, at solicitation of the duchess of Burgundy, invited him to Paris. *And the whole kingdom was full of the accomplishments, as well as the singular adventures and misfortunes of the young Plantagenet. Wonders of this nature are commonly augmented at a distance. From France, the admiration and credulity diffused themselves into England: Sir George Nevil, Sir John Taylor, and above a hundred gentlemen more, came to Paris, in order to offer their services to the supposed duke of York, and to share his fortunes: And the impostor had now the appearance of a court attending him, and began to entertain hopes of final success in his undertakings.*

Henry's response

But king Henry had been informed about this imposter and had attempted to dissuade his followers by presenting evidence that Richard had been murdered. *Five persons had been employed by Richard in the murder of his nephews, or could give evidence with regard to it; Sir James Tirrel and Dighton alone were alive, and they agreed in the same story; but as the priest was dead, and as the bodies were supposed to have been remove by Richard's orders, from the place where they were first interred, and could not now be found, it was not in Henry's power to put the fact, so much as he wished, beyond all doubt and controversy.*

Henry then used intelligence to uncover and remove the threat of the imposter. *He dispersed his spies all over Flanders and England; he engaged many to pretend that they had embraced Perkin's party; he directed them to insinuate themselves into the confidence of the young man's friends; in proportions they conveyed intelligence of any conspirator he bribed his retainers, his domestic servants, nay sometimes his confessor, and by these means traced up some other confederates; Clifford himself he engaged by the hope of rewards and pardon, to betray the secrets committed to him; the more trust he gave to any of his spies, the higher resentment did he feign against them; some of them he even caused to be publicly anathematized, in order the better to procure them the confidence of his enemies.*

Almost in the same instant, he arrested Fitzwater, Mountford, and Thwaites, together with William Daubney, Robert Ratcliff, Thomas Cressenor, and Thomas Astwood. All these were arraigned, convicted, and condemned for high treason, in adhering and promising aid to Perkin. Mountford, Ratcliff, and Daubeney were immediately executed.[13]

Greater and more solemn preparations were deemed requisite for the trial of Stanley, lord chamberlain, whose authority in the nation, whose domestic connections with the king, as well as the former services,

---

[13] Ibid, pp 43-46.

seemed to secure him against any accusation of punishment. Stanley was committed to custody, and was soon after examined before the council. He denied not the guilt imputed to him by Clifford; he did not even endeavor much to extenuate it. --- And as Stanley was one of the most opulent subjects in the kingdom, being possessed of above three thousand pounds a year in land, and forty thousand marks in plate and money, besides other property of great value, the prospect of so rich a forfeiture was deemed no small motive for Henry's proceeding to extremities against him. After six week's delay, which was interposed in order to show that the king was restrained by doubts and scruple; the prisoner was brought to the trial, condemned, and presently after beheaded.[14]

The fate of Stanley made great impression on the kingdom, and struck all the partisans of Perkin with the deepest dismay. From Clifford's desertion, they found that all their secrets were betrayed; and as it appeared, that Stanley, while he seemed to live in the greatest confidence with the king, had been continually surrounded by spies, who reported and registered every action in which he was engaged, nay, every word which fell from him, a general distrust took place, and all mutual confidence was destroyed, even among intimate friends and acquaintances. The jealous and severe temper of the king, together with his great reputation of sagacity and penetration, kept men in awe, and quelled not only the movements of sedition, but the very murmurs of faction. Libels, however, crept out against Henry's person and administration; and being greedily propagated by every secret art, showed that there still remained among the people a considerable root of discontent, which wanted only a proper opportunity to discover itself

But Henry continued more intent on increasing the terrors of his people, than on gaining their affections. Trusting to the great success which attended him in all his enterprises he gave every day, more and more, a loose to his rapacious temper, and employed the arts of perverted law and justice, in order to exact fines and compositions from his people. --- The management, indeed, of these arts of chicanery, was the great secret of the king's administration. While he depressed the nobility, he exalted and honored and caressed the lawyers; and by that means both bestowed authority on the laws, and was enabled, whenever he pleased, to pervert them to his own advantage. His government was oppressive; but it was so much the less burdensome, by his extending royal authority, and curbing the nobles, he became in reality the sole oppressor in his kingdom.

Invasion by Perkin Warbeck

Having collected a band of outlaws, pirates, robbers, and necessitous persons of all nation, to the number of 600 men, he put to

---

[14] Ibid, pp 47-48.

sea, with a resolution of making a descent in England, and of exciting the common people to arms, since all his correspondence with the nobility was cut off by Henry's vigilance and severity. Information being brought him, that the king had made a progress to the north, he cast anchor on the coast of Kent, and sent some of his retainers ashore. --- The gentlemen of Kent assembled some troops to oppose him. The Kentish troops fell upon such of his retainers, as were already landed; and besides some whom they slew, they took a hundred and fifty prisoners. These were tried and condemned; and all of them executed.[15]

After Perkin was repulsed from the coast of Kent, he retired into Flanders; but as he found it impossible to procure subsistence for himself and his followers, while he remained in tranquility, he soon after made an attempt upon Ireland, which had always appeared forward to join every invader of Henry's authority. But Poynings had now put the affairs of that island in so good a posture, that Perkin met with little success. Perkin next went to Scotland where he was received by the young James IV. In 1496 James and Perkin made an inroad into England. *Perkin himself dispersed a manifesto, in which he set forth his own story, and craved the assistance of all his subjects in expelling the usurper, whose tyranny and mal administration, whose depression of the nobility by the elevation of mean persons, whose oppression of the people by multiplied impositions and vexations, had justly, he said, rendered him odious to all men.* But Perkin could not get support from the people. Meanwhile Henry summoned a parliament and they gave the king a large grant to suppress the Scots.[16]

A new rebellion

But a new rebellion erupted in the southwest. *The vote of parliament for imposing the tax was without much difficulty procured by the authority of Henry; but he found it not so easy to levy the money upon his subjects. The people, who were acquainted with the immense treasures which he had amassed, could ill brook the new impositions raised on every slight occasion; and it is probable, that the flaw, which was universally known to be in his title, made his reign the more subject to insurrections and rebellions. When the subsidy began to be levied in Cornwall, the inhabitants, numerous and poor, robust and courageous, murmured against a tax, occasioned by a sudden inroad of the Scots, from which they esteemed themselves entirely secure, and which had usually been repelled by the force of the northern counties.*

Henry had already levied an army to oppose the Scots, but ordered his armies to march south to oppose this new rebellion. *At the*

---

[15] Ibid, p 49.

[16] Ibid, pp 53-56.

battle of Blackheath, June 22, 1497, Henry's forces under the commands of the earl of Oxford, Lord Daubeney, and the earls of Essex and Suffolk defeated the rebel troops who numbered 16,000. Being tumultuary troops, ill armed, and not provided with cavalry or artillery, they were but an unequal match for the king's forces. Lord Audley, Flammoc, and Joseph, the rebel's leaders, were taken, and all three executed. The rebels, being surrounded on every side by the king's troops, were almost all made prisoners; and immediately dismissed without further punishment.

Meanwhile, Henry had made a temporary peace with Scotland. Perkin had retreated to Ireland. *Perkin next went to Cornwal where he, for the first time, took on him the name of Richard IV, king of England.* He was able to gather about 3,000 troops and landed in England. His forces increased to 7,000 but the king had mustered superior armies. *All England seemed united against a pretender, who had at first engaged their attention and divided their affections. Perkin, informed of these great preparations, immediately raised the siege of Exeter, and retired to Taunton. The Cornish rebels submitted to the king's mercy.* Perkin's wife was captured and treated with leniency by the king.

The king promised pardon to Perkin if he consented to a confession, which was authored by the king. Perkin attempted to escape from prison. *Perkin, by this new attempt, after so many enormities, had rendered himself totally unworthy of mercy; and he was accordingly arraigned, condemned, and soon after, in 1499, hanged at Tyburn.[17]*

Poynings Law

Many laws were enacted during Henry's reign. Ireland had supported both pretenders, Simmel and Perkin. *The king's authority appeared equally prevalent and uncontrolled in Ireland. Sir Edward Poynings had been sent over to that country, with an intention of quelling the partisans of the house of York, and of reducing the natives to subjection. He was not supported by forces sufficient for that enterprise: The Irish, by flying into their woods, and morasses, and mountains, for some time eluded his efforts: But Poynings summoned a parliament at Dublin, where he was more successful. He passed that memorable statute, which still bears his name, and which establishes the authority of the English government in Ireland. By this statute, all the former laws of England were made to be of force in Ireland; and no bill can be introduced into the Irish parliament, unless it previously received the sanction of the council of England.[18]*

---

[17] Ibid, pp 61-63.

[18] Ibid, p 50.

Villeinage

Villeinage went gradually into disuse throughout the more civilized parts of Europe: The interest of the master, as well as that of the slave, concurred in this alteration. The latest laws, which we find in England for enforcing or regulating this species of servitude (slavery), were enacted in the reign of Henry VII. And though the ancient statutes on this subject remain still unrepealed by parliament (as of 1778), it appears, that, before the end of Elizabeth, the distinction of villein and freeman was totally, though insensibly abolished, and that no person remained in the state, to whom the former laws could be applied.[19]

Alliances and Marriages

In 1501, Henry had now the satisfaction of completing a marriage, which had been projected and negotiated during the course of seven years, between Arthur prince of Wales and the Infanta Catherine, fourth daughter of Ferinand and Isabella; he near sixteen years of age, she eighteen. But this marriage proved in the issue unprosperous. The young prince, a few months after, sickened and died, much regretted by the nation. Henry, desirous to continue his alliance with Spain, and also unwilling to restore Catherine's dowry, which was two hundred thousand ducats, obliged his second son, Henry, whom he created prince of Wales, to be contracted to the Infanta. The prince made all the opposition, of which a youth of twelve years of age was capable; but as the king persisted in his resolution, the espousals were at length, by means of the pope's dispensation, contracted between the parties: An event, which was afterwards attended with the most important consequences.[20]

The same year, another marriage was celebrated, which was also, in the next age, productive of great events: The marriage of Margaret, the king's elder daughter, with James IV, king of Scotland.[21] This alliance had been negotiated during three years, though interrupted by several broils; and Henry hoped, from the completion of it, to remove all source of discord with that neighboring kingdom.

---

[19] Hume, The History of England, vol 2, p 524. Note. Slavery in dependent colonies and kingdoms of England, as well as the slave trade continued to well into the nineteenth century.

[20] See next chapter. Henry VIII, in a dispute with the pope over his divorce of Catherine of Aragon, would become the head of the Church of England.

[21] Note. Margaret was married to James IV. In the reign of Elizabeth, Margaret's granddaughter Mary queen of Scots, was beheaded. Her son, James VI of Scotland, succeeded Elizabeth as James I.

Death of the queen

    Amidst these prosperous incidents, the king met with a domestic calamity, which made not such impression on him as it merited: His queen, Elizabeth, daughter of Edward IV, *died in childbed, in 1503; and the infant did not long survive her. This princess was deservedly a favorite of the nation; and the general affection for her increased, on account of the harsh treatment, which it was thought, she met with from her consort.*[22]

Henry's oppressive government and laws

    All the efforts of the European princes, both in war and negotiation, were turned to Italy; and the various events, which there arose, made Henry's alliance be courted by every party, yet interested him so little as never to touch him with concern or anxiety. His close connections with Spain and Scotland ensured his tranquility; and his continued successes over domestic enemies, owing to the prudence and vigor of his conduct, had reduced the people to entire submission and obedience. Uncontrolled, therefore, by apprehension or opposition of any kind, he gave full scope to his natural propensity; and avarice, which had ever been his ruling passion, being increased by age, and encouraged by absolute authority, broke all restraints of shame or justice. He had found two ministers, Empson and Dudley, perfectly qualified to second his rapacious and tyrannical inclinations, and to prey upon his defenseless people. The instruments of oppression were both lawyers, the first of mean birth, of brutal manners, of an unrelenting temper; the second better born, better educated and better bred, but equally unjust, severe, and inflexible. By their knowledge in law, these men were qualified to pervert the forms of justice to the oppression of the innocent; and the formidable authority of the king supported them in all their iniquities.

    It was their usual practice at first to observe so far the appearance of law as to give indictments to those whom they intended to oppress: Upon which the persons were committed to prison, but never brought to trial; and were at length obliged, in order to recover their liberty, to pay heavy fines and ransoms, which were called mitigation and compositions. By degrees, the very appearance of law was neglected: The two ministers sent forth their precepts to attach men, and summon them before themselves and some others, at their private houses, in a court of commission, where, in a summary manner, without trial or jury, arbitrary decrees were issued, both in pleas of the crown and controversies between private parties. Juries themselves, when summoned proved by small security to the subject; being brow-beaten by these oppressors; nay, fined, imprisoned, and punished, if they gave

---

[22] Ibid, pp 65-66.

sentence against the inclination of the minister. The whole system of the feudal law, which still prevailed, was turned into a scheme of oppression. --- But the chief means of oppression, employed by these ministers, were the penal statutes, which, without consideration of rank, quality, or services, were rigidly put in execution against all men: Spies, informers, and inquisitors were rewarded and encouraged in every quarter of the kingdom: And no difference was made whether the statutes were beneficial or hurtful, recent or obsolete, possible or impossible to be executed. The sole end of the king and his ministers was to amass money, and bring every one under the lash of their authority.[23]

Several considerable regulations, indeed, are found among the statutes of this reign, both with regard to the police of the kingdom, and its commerce. --- Early in Henry's reign, the authority of the Star Chamber, which was before founded on common law, and ancient practice, was in some cases confirmed by act of parliament. Lord Bacon extols the utility of this court. The benefit of clergy was abridged; and the criminal, on the first offence, was ordered to be burned in the hand with a letter denoting his crime; after which he was punished capitally for any new offence. Sheriffs were no longer allowed to fine any person, without previously summoning him before their court. ---

But the most important law in its consequences, which was enacted during this reign of Henry, was that by which the nobility and gentry acquired a power of breaking the ancient entails, and of alienating their estates. By means of this law, joined to the beginning luxury and refinements of the age, the great fortunes of the barons were gradually dissipated, and the property of the commons increased in England. It is probable, that Henry foresaw and intended this consequence, because the constant scheme of his policy consisted in depressing the great, and exalting churchmen, lawyers, and men of new families, who were more dependant on him.

Sickness and death of the king

The decline of his health put an end to all such thoughts; and he began to cast his eye towards that future existence, which the iniquities and severities of his reign rendered a very dismal prospect to him. To allay the terrors, under which he labored, he endeavored, by distributing alms, and founding religious houses, to make atonement for his crimes, and to purchase, by the sacrifice of part of his ill-gotten treasures, a reconciliation with his offended maker. Remorse even seized him at intervals for the abuse of his authority by Empson and Dudley; but not sufficient to make him stop the rapacious hand of those oppressors. --- The king gave countenance to all these oppressions; till death, by its nearer approaches, impressed new terrors upon him; and he then

---

[23] Ibid, pp 66-68.

ordered, by a general clause in his will, that restitution should be made to all those whom he had injured.   He died, April 22, 1509, of a consumption at his favorite palace of Richmond, after a reign of twenty-three years and eight months, and in the fifty-second year of his age.[24]

His heirs were his eldest surviving son Henry, to become Henry VIII, and Margaret, who had married James IV.

---

[24] Ibid, p 72.

Chapter 25

Henry VIII

Henry VIII, (b 1491, d 1547) reigned from 1509 to 1547. An introduction to this complex and inscrutable person is found in Carolly Erickson's preface to the biography of Henry VIII, *Great Harry. For Henry Tudor was, as one who knew him wrote, 'undoubtedly the rarest man that lived in his time'. Even more than his exalted rank, his towering height, powerful physique and extraordinary handsomeness set Henry apart from his contemporaries. A phenomenal athlete, he seemed to draw on super-human energies as he outrode, outdanced and outfought friends and rivals both in England and abroad. These physical gifts were balanced by unfailing warmth and charm, chivalrous delicacy of feeling, and perceptive mental endowments that enabled Henry to share fully in the intellectual life of the humanists at his court and to win their respect.*

Midway in his reign darker qualities of mind emerged in Henry, growing stronger as he was continuously thwarted in his aims and in the end eclipsing his attractive nature. The radiant hero of the Battle of the Spurs became the troubled, anxious ruler of the mid-1520s, harried in mind by the fear of divine vengeance, then the fearsome murderous king of the 1530s whose wrath was fatal to those about him. The Catholic Church puts at fifty the number of martyrs whose deaths he brought about by execution or starvation. Several wives, at least a dozen blood relatives and a similar number of onetime counselors and friends lengthened the list of victims.

By the 1540's, as Henry entered his fifties, he had become a monstrous figure to his people— an inhuman tyrant of mythic proportions whose valor and integrity had dissolved under the corroding influence of adultery, sacrilege and blood lust. In actuality Henry was by this time an aging colossus plagued by agonizing pains in his legs, soured by domestic misfortunes and overburdened by governmental labors. The inner compass that had guided him to overturn the old order of English society - to undertake the reshaping of religious belief - had misled him, and he suffered in consequence.[1]

Family history

Henry was the second son of Henry VII and Elizabeth, eldest daughter of Edward IV. The family histories of his father and mother have been told in previous chapters. Henry became heir to the throne when his elder brother Arthur died in 1502, shortly after Arthur's marriage to Catherine of Aragon. After Arthur's death Henry VII decreed that his younger brother Henry would espouse and marry Catherine. His own family was complicated, to say the least, by six marriages. He had three children, each by a different wife. All would rule England during the next one hundred years. His first wife, Catherine of Aragon, was the mother of Mary (Mary I). He married Anne Boleyn, his second wife, after embroiling all Europe in controversy over the issue of the annulment of Catherine of Arragon. Elizabeth (Elizabeth I) was the only offspring of this marriage. Elizabeth's mother Anne Boleyn was beheaded by order of Henry following a fit of jealousy and a resultant accusation without evidence of infidelity. His third wife Jane Seymour died only a few days after the birth of Edward, (Edward VI), his only male heir. The marriage to his fourth wife Anne of Cleves was of short duration. An annulment was readily provided by parliament at Henry's request. Henry beheaded Catherine Howard, his fifth wife, on an accusation of infidelity. His sixth wife Catherine Parr cared for Henry during his terminal illness.

Early life

Henry's family included Margaret, Arthur, himself and his younger sister Mary. His mother Elizabeth, eldest daughter of Edward IV, had to take Henry to the tower when he was five years old for security during the civil uprisings. He was a good student. His tutor in Latin and Greek was John Skelton, a scholar praised by Erasmus. Henry was gifted in music as a youth. He was athletic and excelled in hunting, tilting and horseback. His grandmother, Margaret Beauford, the duchess of Richmond, mother of Henry VII, had an influence in his upbringing. *His father, in order to remove him from the knowledge of public business, had hitherto occupied him entirely in the pursuits of literature; and the proficiency, which he made gave no bad prognostic of his parts and capacity. Even the vices of vehemence, ardor, and impatience, to which he was subject and which afterwards degenerated into tyranny, were considered only as faults, incident to unguarded youth, which would be corrected, when time had brought him to greater moderation of*

---

[1] Erickson, Great Harry, pp 13-14.

maturity.[2] He was eleven years old when his brother Arthur died leaving Henry the undisputed heir to the throne. His father began to instruct Henry in affairs of government when he was about thirteen years old.

Henry's early reign

With the illness and death of his father in 1509 Henry acceded to the throne. He was eighteen years old. *Surrey, who had been treasurer under his father, and though few had borne a greater share in the frugal politics of the late king, knew how to conform himself to the humor of his new master; and no one was so forward in promoting that liberality, pleasure, and magnificence, which began to prevail under the young monarch. By this policy he ingratiated himself with Henry; he made advantage, as well as the other courtiers, of the lavish disposition of his master; and he engaged him in such a course of play and idleness as rendered him negligent of affairs, and willing to entrust the government of the state entirely into the hands of his ministers. The great treasures amassed by the late king, were gradually dissipated in the giddy expenses of Henry. One party of pleasure succeeded to another: Tilts, tournaments and carousals were exhibited with all the magnificence of the age: And as the present tranquility of the public permitted the court to indulge itself in every amusement, serious business was but little attended to. Or if the king intermitted the course of his festivity, he chiefly employed himself in an application to music and literature, which were his favorite pursuits, and which were well adapted to this genius. He had made such proficiency in the former art, as even to compose some pieces of church-music, which were sung in his chapel. He was initiated in the elegant learning of the ancients. And though he was so unfortunate as to be seduced into a study of the barren controversies of the Schools, which were then fashionable, and had chosen Thomas Aquinas for his favorite author, he still discovered a capacity fitted of more useful and entertaining knowledge.[3]*

Marriage with Catherine of Arragon

On June 3, 1509, Henry married Catherine of Arragon. Henry was eighteen years old. Catherine was twenty-four years old. *Her former marriage with his brother, and the inequality of their years, were the chief objections, urged against his espousing her: But on the other hand, the advantages of her known virtue, modesty, and sweetness of disposition were insisted on; the affection which she bore to the king; the large dowry to which she was entitled as princess of Wales; the interest of cementing a close alliance with Spain; the necessity of finding some*

---

[2] Hume, The History of England, vol 3, p 84.

[3] Ibid, pp 84-85.

confederate to counterbalance the power of France; the expediency of fulfilling the engagements of the late king. When these considerations were weighted, they determined the council, though contrary to the opinion of the primate, to give Henry their advice for celebrating the marriage. The countess of Richmond, who had concurred in the same sentiments with the council, died soon after the marriage of her grandson.[4]

Wolsey

Thomas Wolsey, who became a cardinal in Henry's reign and aspired to the papal crown, was Henry's lord chancellor of the kingdom. He was the dominant figure in the first twenty years of Henry's reign. We turn now to how Wolsey gained such enormous powers before reviewing the foreign affairs of Henry's early reign. *Thomas Wolsey, dean of Lincoln, and almoner to the king, surpassed in favor all his ministers, and was fast advancing towards that unrivaled grandeur, which he afterwards attained. This man was son of a butcher at Ipswich; but having got a learned education, and being endowed with an excellent capacity, he was admitted into the marquis of Dorset's family as tutor to that nobleman's children, and soon gained the friendship and countenance of his patron. He was recommended to be chaplain to Henry VII. --- The death of Henry retarded the advancement of Wolsey, and prevented his reaping any advantage from the good opinion, which that monarch had entertained of him: But thenceforth he was looked on at court as a rising man; and Fox, bishop of Winchester, cast his eye upon him as one, who might be serviceable to him in his present situation. This prelate, observing that the earl of Surrey had totally eclipsed him in favor, resolved to introduce Wolsey to the young prince's familiarity, and hoped, that he might rival Surrey in his insinuating arts, and yet be content to act in the cabinet a part subordinate to Fox himself, who had promoted him. In a little time, Wolsey gained so much on the king, that he supplanted both Surrey in his favor, and Fox in his trust and confidence. Being admitted to Henry's parties of pleasure, he took the lead in every jovial conversation, and promoted all that frolic and entertainment, which he found suitable to the age and inclination of the young monarch. Neither his own years, which were near forty, nor his character of a clergyman, were any restraint upon him, or engaged him to check, by any useless severity, the gaiety, in which Henry, who had small propensity to debauchery, passed his careless hours. During the intervals of amusement he introduced business, and insinuated those maxims of conduct, which he was desirous his master should adopt.*

Henry entered into all the views of Wolsey; and finding no one so capable of executing this plan of administration as the person who

---

[4] Ibid, p 87.

proposed it, he soon advanced his favorite, from being the companion of his pleasures, to be a member of his council; and from being a member of his council, to be his sole and absolute minister. By this rapid advancement and uncontrolled authority the character and genius of Wolsey had full opportunity to display itself. Insatiable in his acquisitions, but still more magnificent in his expense: Of extensive capacity, but still more unbounded enterprise: Ambitious of power, but still more desirous of glory: Insinuating, engaging, persuasive; and, by all turns, lofty, elevated, commanding: Haughty to his equals, but affable to his dependants; oppressive to the people, but liberal to his friends; more generous than grateful; less moved by injuries than by contempt; he was framed to take the ascendant in every intercourse with others, but exerted this superiority of nature with such ostentation as exposed him to envy, and made every one willing to recall the original inferiority or rather meanness of his fortune.[5]

The numerous enemies, whom Wolsey's sudden elevation, his aspiring character, and his haughty deportment had raised him, served only to rivet him faster in Henry's confidence; who valued himself on supporting the choice which he had made, and who was incapable of yielding either to the murmurs of the people or to the discontents of the great. That artful prelate likewise, well acquainted with the king's imperious temper, concealed from him the absolute ascendant, which he had acquired; and while he secretly directed all public councils, he ever pretended a blind submission to the will and authority of his master. By entering into the kings's pleasures, he preserved his affection; by conducting his business, he gratified his indolence; and by his unlimited complaisance in both capacities, he prevented all that jealousy, to which his exorbitant acquisitions, and his splendid ostentatious train of life should naturally have given birth. The archbishopric of York falling vacant by the death of Bambridge, Wolsey was promoted to that see, and resigned the bishopric of Lincoln. Besides enjoying the administration of Tournay, he got possession of easy leases, of the revenues of Bath, Worcester, and Hereford, bishoprics filled by Italians, who were allowed to reside abroad, and who were glad to compound for this indulgence, by yielding a considerable share of their income. He held in commendam the abbey of St. Albans, and many other church preferments. He was even allowed to unite with the see of York, first that of Durham, next that of Winchester; and there seemed to be no end of his acquisitions.

Foreign alliances and wars with France

Wolsey was the principle architect of the wars early in the reign of Henry VIII. A league of Cambray was established in 1509 by his ministers, for the conquest of the commonwealth of Venice. *Henry,*

---

[5] Ibid, pp 98-100.

without any motive from interest or passion, allowed his name to be inserted in the confederacy. In 1512, an alliance was formed with the pope, Spain and Venice against the French monarch, Lewis XII. Henry joined his father-in-law Ferdinand against France and in support of the pope. War was declared against France. Parliament *readily granted supplies for a purpose so much favored by the English nation. The war, which England waged against France, though it brought no advantage to the former kingdom, was of great prejudice to the latter; and by obliging Lewis to withdraw his forces for the defense of his own dominions, lost him that superiority, which his arms, in the beginning of the campaign, had attained in Italy.* Later that year, England invaded France. *At last, Henry, attended by the duke of Buckingham and many others of the nobility, arrived at Calais, and entered upon his French expedition, from which he fondly expected so much success and glory. The French were repelled at the battle of Guinegate. After so considerable an advantage, the king, who was at the head of a complete army of above 50,000 men, might have made incursions to the gates of Paris, and spread confusion and desolation everywhere. It gave Lewis great joy, when he heard, that the English, instead of pushing their victory, and attacking the dismayed troops of France, returned to the siege of so inconsiderable a place as Terouane. --- The Swiss at the same time had entered Burgundy with a formidable army, and laid siege to Dijon, which was in no condition to resist them. --- Scarcely ever was the French monarchy in greater danger, of less in a condition to defend itself against those powerful armies, which on every side assailed or threatened it. --- But Lewis was extricated from his present difficulties by the manifold blunders of his enemies. The Swiss entered into a negotiation and retreated. The measures of Henry showed equal ignorance in the art of war with that of the Swiss in negotiation. Tournay was a great and rich city, which, though it lay within the frontiers of Flanders, belonged to France, and afforded the troops of that kingdom a passage into the heart of the Netherlands.* Although Henry had taken Tournay, *hearing of the retreat of the Swiss, and observing the season to be far advanced, Henry thought it proper to return to England; and he carried the greater part of his army with him. --- All men of judgment, comparing the advantages of his situation with his progress, his expenses with his acquisitions, were convinced that this campaign, so much vaunted, was, in reality, both ruinous and inglorious to him.*[6]

Peace with France was arranged in 1514. The affairs of Wolsey and England in the changing European scene became more complex. Peace with France was arranged in 1514. In compliance with the treaty Henry's younger sister Mary had been sent over to France and married king Lewis XII, who died in less than three months. Mary, in 1515

---

[6] Ibid, pp 103-104.

married Charles Brandon, duke of Suffolk. Francis, duke of Angouleme, a youth of twenty-one, who had married Lewis's elder daughter, succeeded him on the throne, as Francis I.

In 1519 the emperor Maximilian died. Charles V, (Charles I of Spain, emperor of Germany), was chosen as the holy Roman emperor. Charles V *reaped the succession of Castile, of Arragon, of Austria, of the Netherlands: He inherited the conquest of Naples, of Granada; election entitled him to the empire: Even the bounds of the globe seemed to be enlarged a little before his time, that he might possess the whole treasure, as yet entire and unrifled, of the new world. But though the concurrence of all these advantages formed an empire, greater and more extensive than any known in Europe since that of the Romans, the kingdom of France alone, being close, compact, united, rich, populous, and being interposed between all the provinces of the emperor's dominions, was able to make a vigorous opposition to his progress and maintain the contest against him.* [7]

In 1520, *Henry went over to Calais with the queen and his whole court; and thence proceeded to Guisenes, a small town near the frontiers. Francis, attended in like manner, came to Ardres, a few miles distant; and the two monarchs met, for the first time, in the fields, and a place situated between these two towns, but still within the English pale: For Francis agreed to pay this compliment to Henry, in consideration of that prince's passing the sea, that he might be present at the interview. Wolsey, to whom both kings had entrusted the regulation of the ceremonial, contrived this circumstance, in order to do honor to his master. The nobility both of France and England here displayed their magnificence with such emulation and profuse expense, as procured to the place of interview the name of the 'field of the cloth of gold.'* [8]

In 1521, Emperor Charles and Francis were at war. In an attempt to negotiate a peace Wolsey was declared *an umpire between them. Wolsey's negotiations led to a new alliance of England with the pope and the emperor Charles against France. Wolsey stipulated, that England should next summer invade that kingdom with forty thousand men; and he betrothed to Charles the princess Mary, the king's only child, who had now some prospect of inheriting the crown. This extravagant alliance was prejudicial to the interests, and might have proved fatal to the liberty and independence of the kingdom.* [9] The betrothal of Mary to Charles in 1518 was set aside.

---

[7] Ibid, pp 126-128.

[8] Ibid, p 129.

[9] Ibid, p 132.

In 1522, Henry *declared war against France; and this measure was founded on so little reason, that he could allege nothing as a ground of quarrel, but Francis's refusal to submit to his arbitration, and his sending Albany into Scotland. This last step had to have been taken by the French king, till he was quite assured of Henry's resolution to attack him.* Surrey landed troops in Normandy, laid waste the country, sailed to Brittany, which he took and plundered. The French avoided a direct confrontation and harassed the English troops. Heavy rains, fatigue of the English troops and the season forced Surrey to put his troops in winter quarters. *The reason, which the war against France proceeded so slowly, on the part of England, was the want of money. All the treasures of Henry VII, were long ago dissipated; the king's habits of expense still remained; and his revenues were unequal even to the ordinary charge of government, much more to his military enterprises. Henry raised money by publishing an edict for a general tax upon his subjects, which he still called a loan. This pretended loan, as being more regular, was really more dangerous to the liberties of the people, and was a precedent for the king's imposing taxes without consent of parliament.* The French met another invasion by the king, in August of 1523, and the English had to retire in winter quarters. The major war was conducted in Italy against the French by emperor Charles, which led to the capture of Francis by the imperial forces of Charles on February 24, 1525. Francis would not be released until 1526. Henry made an alliance with France, fearing the power of the emperor, who had come into a disagreement with Wolsey.

Wolsey's riches, power and the legantine court

Wolsey's further advancement in ecclesiastical dignity served him as a pretense for engrossing still more revenues: The pope, observing his great influence over the king, was desirous of engaging him in his interests, and created him a cardinal. No churchman, under color of exacting respect to religion, ever carried to a greater height the state and dignity of that character. His train consisted of eight hundred servants, of whom many were knights and gentlemen: Some even of the nobility put their children into his family as a place of education; and in order to gain them favor with their patron, allowed them to bear offices as his servants. Whoever was distinguished by any art or science paid court to the cardinal; and none paid court in vain. Literature, which was then in its infancy, found in him a generous patron; and both by his public institutions and private bounty, he gave encouragement to every branch of erudition. Not content with this munificence, which gained him the approbation of the wise, he strove to dazzle the eyes of the populace, by the splendor of his equipage and furniture, the costly embroidery of his liveries, the luster of his apparel. He was the first clergyman in England that wore silk and gold, not only on his habit, but also on his saddles and the trappings of his horses. He caused his cardinal's hat to be borne aloft by a person of rank; and when he came to the king's chapel, would permit it to be laid on no place but the altar.[10]

The pride of Wolsey was now further increased by a great accession of power and dignity. Cardinal Campeggio had been sent as legate into England, in order to procure a tithe from the clergy, for enabling the pope to oppose the progress of the Turks. --- The clergy refused to comply with pope Leo's demand: Campeggio was recalled; and the king desired of the pope, that Wolsey, who had been joined in this commission, might alone be invested with the legantine power; together with the right of visiting all the clergy and monasteries, and even with suspending all the laws of the church during a twelve month. Wolsey, having obtained this new dignity, made a new display of that state and parade, to which he was so much addicted. On solemn feast-days, he was not content without saying mass after the manner of the pope himself: Not only he had bishops and abbots to serve him; he even engaged the first nobility to give him water and the towel. He affected a rank superior to what had ever been claimed by any churchman in England.

But Wolsey carried the matter much further than vain pomp and ostentation. He erected an office, which he called the legantine court; and as he was now, by means of the pope's commission and the king's favor, invested with all power, both ecclesiastical and civil, no man knew what bounds were to be set to the authority of his new tribunal. He conferred on it a kind of inquisitorial and censorial power even over the laity, and directed it to inquire into all matters of conscience; into all conduct which had given scandal; into all actions, which, though they escaped the law, might appear contrary to good morals. Offense was taken at this commission, which was really unbounded; and the people were the more disgusted, when they saw a man, who indulged himself in pomp and pleasure, so severe in repressing the least appearance of licentiousness in others. But to render his court more obnoxious, Wolsey made one John Allen judge in it, a person of scandalous life, whom he himself, as chancellor, had, it is said condemned for perjury: And as it is pretended, that this man either extorted fines from every one whom he was pleased to find guilty, or took bribes to drop prosecutions, men concluded, and with some appearance of reason, that he shared with the cardinal those wages of iniquity. The clergy, and in particular the monks, were exposed to this tyranny; and as the libertinism of their lives often gave a just handle against them, they were obliged to purchase an indemnity, by paying large sums of money to the legate or his judge. Not content with this authority, Wolsey pretended, by virtue of his commission, to assume the jurisdiction of all the bishop's courts; particularly that of judging of wills and testaments; and his decisions in

---

[10] Ibid, pp 113-115.

those important points were deemed not a little arbitrary. As if he himself were pope, and as if the pope could absolutely dispose of every ecclesiastical preferment, he presented to whatever priories or benefices he pleased, without regard to the right of election in the monks, or of patronage in the nobility and gentry.[11]

Execution of Buckingham

The people saw every day new instances of the uncontrolled authority of Wolsey. The duke of Buckingham, constable of England, the first nobleman both for family and fortune in the kingdom, had imprudently given disgust to the cardinal; and it was not long before he found reason to repent of his indiscretion. --- Buckingham was descended by a female from the duke of Gloucester, youngest son of Edward III; and though his claim to the crown was thereby very remote, he had been so unguarded as to let fall some expressions, as if he thought himself best entitled, in case the king should die without issue, to possess the royal dignity. He had not even abstained from threats against the king's life, and had provided himself with arms, which he intended to employ, in case a favorable opportunity should offer. He was brought to a trial; and the duke of Norfolk, whose son the earl of Surrey had married Buckingham's daughter, was created lord steward, in order to preside at this solemn procedure. The jury consisted of a duke, a marquis, seven earls, and twelve barons; and they gave their verdict against Buckingham, who was soon afer carried into execution.[12]

Anne Boleyn

No affair in history attracted more attention and importance than Henry's removal of his first wife to take another. *The queen was older than the king by no less than six years; and the decay of her beauty, together with particular infirmities and diseases, had contributed, notwithstanding her blameless character and deportment, to render her person unacceptable to him. Though she had borne him several children, they all died in early infancy, except one daughter; and he was the more struck with his misfortune, because the curse of being childless is the very threatening, contained in the Mosaic law, against those who espouse their brother's widow. The succession too of the crown was a consideration, that occurred to every one, whenever the lawfulness of Henry's marriage was called in question; and it was apprehended, that if doubts of Mary's legitimacy concurred with the weakness of her sex, the*

---

[11] Ibid, pp 124-125.

[12] Ibid, 133.

king of Scots, the next heir[13] to the throne would advance his pretensions, and might throw the kingdom into confusion. The evils as yet recent, of civil wars and convulsions, arising from a disputed title, made great impression on the minds of men, and rendered the people universally desirous of any event, which might obviate so irreparable a calamity. And the king was thus impelled, both by his private passions, and by motives of public interest, to seek the dissolution of his inauspicious, and, as it was esteemed, unlawful marriage with Catherine.

Anne Boleyn, who lately appeared at court, had been appointed maid of honor to the queen; and having had frequent opportunities of being seen by Henry, and of conversing with him, she had acquired an entire ascendant over his affections. The young lady, whose grandeur and misfortunes have rendered her so celebrated, was a daughter of Sir Thomas Boleyn, who had been employed by the king in several embassies, and who was allied to all the principal nobility in the kingdom. --- Anne herself, though then in very early youth, had been carried over to Paris by the king's sister, when the princess espoused Lewis XII, of France; and upon the demise of that monarch, and the return of his dowager into England, this damsel, whose accomplishments even in the tender years were always much admired, was retained in the service of the queen of France; and after the death of that princess, she passed into the family of the duchess of Alenson, a woman of singular merit. The exact time, when she returned to England, is not certainly known; but it was after the king had entertained doubts with regard to the lawfulness of his marriage with Catherine; if the account is to be credited, which he himself afterwards gave of that transaction.

Henry's scruples had made him break off all conjugal commerce with the queen; but as he still supported an intercourse of civility and friendship with her, he had occasion, in the frequent visits, which he paid her, to observe the beauty, the youth, the charms of Anne Boleyn. Finding the accomplishments of her mind nowise inferior to her exterior graces, he even entertained the design of raising her to the throne; and was the more confirmed in this resolution, when he found that her virtue and modesty prevented all hopes of gratifying his passion in any other manner. As every motive, therefore, of inclination and policy, seemed thus to concur in making the king desirous of a divorce from Catherine, and as his prospect of success was inviting, he resolved to make applications to Clement, and he sent Knight, his secretary, to Rome for that purpose.[14] This was in 1527, after being married 18 years to Catherine. Henry was thirty-six years old.

---

[13] Note. James IV had married Henry's sister Margaret. Their son James V would be the next heir to the throne.

[14] Ibid, pp171-173.

Henry's desire for an annulment frustrated

The politics and legality of Henry's divorce are complex, but the outcome could not be more important— the separation of the Church of England from the Church of Rome and the devastations which followed. Henry's reign would take on a new twist, especially after the death of Wolsey November 15, 1529. Henry married Anne Boleyn November 1532 and his final break with Rome came in 1534. Anne was beheaded May 19, 1537. With this long and interminable conflict over the divorce of Catherine and the marriage of Anne Boleyn, it suffices to present only a brief summary of the major events of this drama.

Pope Julian had given permission for the young king Henry, at age twelve; to marry his brother's widow Catherine of Arragon. This decision was contested by pope Clement, based on two contentions of Julian, which were not true. The first was that Henry requested the marriage. There was also the presumption that a marriage between a king of England and the Spanish emperor would ensure peace between the kingdoms. Unfortunately, with the sack of Rome by emperor Charles May 6, 1527 pope Clement was taken captive. The pope, believing his freedom would be more likely by appeasing Henry, who had formed an alliance with France and the Italian powers in opposition to Charles; granted Henry a provisional dispensation for the annulment of the marriage with Catherine and approval of the king's new marriage.

Clement, however, feared reprisals from emperor Charles, nephew to Catherine. This, no doubt, led to uncertainty and confusion regarding Clement's directives. Henry had dispatched Stephen Gardiner, secretary to Wolsey, and Edward Fox to Rome to obtain a certain dispensation from the pope. Clement, rather than deciding the case, granted a commission headed jointly by Compeggio and Wolsey, which would try the king's case May 31, 1529.

The trial of the king's marriage

Hume dramatized *The Trial of the King's Marriage*, however Catherine's appeals are portrayed with even greater drama in the Shakespeare play *Henry VIII*.[15] *From Hume: The two legates, meanwhile, opened their court at London and cited the king and queen to appear before it. They both presented themselves; and the king answered to his name, when called: But the queen, instead of answering to hers, rose from her seat, and throwing herself at the king's feet, made a very pathetic harangue, which her virtue, her dignity, and her misfortunes*

---

[15] Shakespeare, Henry VIII, Act II, sc. 4. Note. This part of the play would appear as a signature by the author of the Shakespeare works. The authorship of this play has been questioned.

rendered the more affecting. She told him, that she was a stranger in his dominions, without protection, without council, without assistance; exposed to all the injustice, which her enemies were pleased to impose upon her: That she had quitted her native country without other resource, than her connections with him and his family, and had expected, that, instead of suffering thence any violence or iniquity, she was assured in them of a safeguard against every misfortune: That she had been his wife during twenty years, and would here appeal to himself, whether her affectionate submission to his will had not merited better treatment, than to be thus, after so long a time, thrown from him with so much indignity: That she was conscious - he himself was assured - that her virgin honor was yet unstained, when he received her into his bed, and that her connections with his brother had been carried no further than the ceremony of marriage: That their parents, the kings of England and Spain, were esteemed the wisest princes of their time, and had undoubtedly acted by the best advice, when they formed the agreement for that marriage, which was now represented as so criminal and unnatural: And that she acquiesced in their judgment, and would not submit her cause to be tried by a court, whose dependence on her enemies was too visible, ever to allow her any hopes of obtaining from them an equitable or impartial decision. Having spoken these words, she rose, and making the king a low reverence, she departed from the court, and never would again appear in it.[16]

The trial focused on whether Arthur, fifteen years old at the time of his marriage to Catherine, had consummated the marriage. The king, the Spanish ambassador, and others gave testimony in opposition to the queen's testimony. *The trial was spun out till the 23d of July: and Campeggio chiefly took on him the part of conducting it. Wolsey, though the elder cardinal, permitted him to act as president of the court; because it was thought, that a trial managed by an Italian cardinal, would carry the appearance of greater candor and impartiality, than if the king's own minister and favorite had presided in it. The business now seemed to be drawing near to a period; and the king was every day in expectation of a sentence in his favor; when, to his great surprise, Campeggio, on a sudden, without any warning, and upon very frivolous pretenses, prorogued the court, till the first of October. The evocation, which came a few days after from Rome, put an end to all the hopes of success, which the king had so long and so anxiously cherished.[17]*

---

[16] Hume, Vol 3, pp 180-181,

[17] Ibid, pp 179-182.

The fall of Wolsey

The house of lords charged Wolsey with forty-four articles against him. All his great wealth and powers were taken away from him. *The king had determined to bring on the ruin of the cardinal with a motion almost as precipitate as he had formerly employed in his elevation.*[18] Campeggio had been ordered by pope Clement to delay the proceedings. Wolsey was no doubt aware of these complications and had allowed Campeggio to control the trial of the marriage. *The high opinion itself, which Henry had entertained of the cardinal's capacity, tended to hasten his downfall; which he imputed the bad success of that minister's undertaking, not to ill fortune or to mistake, but to the malignity or infidelity of his intentions. --- The dukes of Norfolk and Suffolk were sent to require the great seal from him; and on his scrupling to deliver it, without a more express warrant, Henry wrote him a letter, upon which it was surrendered, and it was delivered by the king to Sir Thomas More.*

Wolsey was ordered to depart from York-Place, a palace which he had built in London, and which, though it really belonged to the see of York, was seized by Henry, and became afterwards the residence of the kings of England, by the title of Whitehall. All his furniture and plate were also seized: Their riches and splendor befitted rather a royal than a private fortune. The walls of his palace were covered with cloth of gold or cloth of silver: He had a cupboard of plate of massy gold: There were found a thousand pieces of fine holland belonging to him. The rest of his riches and furniture was in proportion; and his opulence was probably no small inducement to the violent persecution against him.

The cardinal was ordered to retire to Asher, a countryseat which he possessed near Hampton Court. The world, that had paid him such abject court during his prosperity, now entirely deserted him on this fatal reverse of all his fortunes. He himself was much dejected with the change; and from the same turn of mind, which had made him be so vainly elated with his grandeur, he felt the stroke of adversity with double rigor.

The king *ordered him to be indicted in the Star Chamber, where a sentence was passed against him. And not content with this severity, he abandoned him to all the rigor of the parliament. Sentence was pronounced against him, 'That he was out of the king's protection; his lands and goods forfeited; and that his person might be committed to custody.'* For a time Wolsey was spared his ultimate fate but after the pope had decided against Henry and suspecting Wolsey's opposition the king pursued his prosecution against him. *The earl of Northumberland received orders, without regard to Wolsey's ecclesiastical character, to arrest him for high treason, and to conduct him to London, in order to his trial. The cardinal, partly from the fatigues of his journey, partly from*

---

[18] Ibid, pp 183-184.

the agitation of his anxious mind, was seized with a disorder, which turned into a dysentery; and he was able, with some difficulty, to reach Leicester-abbey. When the abbot and the monks advanced to receive him with much respect and reverence, he told them, that he was come to lay his bones among them; and he immediately took to his bed, whence he never rose more. He died November 28, 1530.[19] Queen Catherine would remain faithful to Henry to the end. On January 6, 1536, *Queen Catherine died at Kimbolton in the county of Huntingdon, in the fiftieth year of her age.*

Henry became head of the Church of England

Although there had been contests of power between the English kings and the Roman church there would be a growing power among the supporters of what later became known as the Protestants, among whom Martin Luther was their principal spokesman. The invention of the printing press and the availability of religious material in print for the first time, including early translations of the bible by Tindal and others, permitted those who could read to directly peruse the ancient scriptures. The growing power of the Roman church and enormous acquisitions of wealth, as exemplified in England by Wolsey, who surpassed twelfth century Becket in his worldly possessions, became a focus of further discontent. But there rose up a third force who contended for control of religion. The controversy over the king's annulment of Catherine and marriage would escalate all out of proportion and lead to Henry proclaiming himself as the supreme arbiter of all questions of religion and morality.

Henry had strong motives still to desire a good agreement with the sovereign pontiff. He apprehended the danger of such great innovations: he dreaded the reproach of heresy: He abhorred all connections with the Lutherans, the chief opponents of the papal power. Thomas Cranmer, of Cambridge College, suggested that Henry request all the chief universities in England and Europe to decide the issue of the validity of the king's marriage with Catherine. *Several universities of Europe, therefore, without hesitation, as well as without interest or reward, gave, verdict in the king's favor; not only those of France, Paris, Orleans, Bourges, Tolouse, Angiers, which might be supposed to lie under the influence of their prince, ally to Henry; but also those of Italy— Venice, Ferrara, Padua; even Bologna itself though under the immediate jurisdiction of Clement. Oxford alone and Cambridge made some difficulty; because these universities, alarmed at the progress of Lutheranism, and dreading a defection from the Holy See, scrupled to give their sanction to measures, whose consequences, they feared, would prove fatal to the ancient religion. --- The convocations of Canterbury*

---

[19] Ibid, pp 192-193.

and York, pronounced the king's marriage invalid, irregular, and contrary to the law of God, with which no human power had authority to dispense. But Clement, lying still under the influence of the emperor, continued to summon the king to appear, either by himself or proxy, before his tribunal at Rome; and the king, who knew that he could expect no fair trial there, refused to submit to such a condition, and would not even admit of any citation, which he regarded as a high insult and a violation of his royal prerogative.[20]

Parliament was convened to enforce Henry's religious claims over the kingdom. In January 1532, a fine of 118,840 pounds was imposed on members of parliament who had gone along with the legantine court. A confession was obtained by parliament that *'the king was the protector and supreme head of the church and clergy of England'.*[21] *The connections between the pope and the English clergy were, in some measure, dissolved. The next session of parliament found both the king and parliament in the same dispositions. --- The parliament showed their intention of abolishing the oath to the pope, when their proceedings were suddenly stopped by the breaking out of the plague at Westminster* in April, 1532.

Marriage to Anne Boleyn celebrated, birth of Elizabeth

Henry celebrated his marriage with Anne Boleyn November 14, 1532. At a parliament February, 1533, *Henry, finding the new queen's pregnancy to advance, publicly owned his marriage; and in order to remove all doubts with regard to its lawfulness, he prepared measures for declaring, by a formal sentence, the invalidity of his marriage with Catherine: A sentence which ought naturally to have preceded his espousing of Anne. Cranmer, archbishop of Canterbury, annulled the king's marriage with Catherine, as unlawful and invalid. By a subsequent sentence, he ratified the marriage with Anne Boleyn, who soon after was publicly crowned queen, with all the pomp and dignity suited to that ceremony. To complete the king's satisfaction on the conclusion of this intricate and vexatious affair, she was safely delivered of a daughter, who received the name of Elizabeth, and who afterwards swayed the scepter with such renown and felicity.*[22]

Henry excommunicated

When intelligence was conveyed to Rome of these transaction, so injurious to the authority and reputation of the Holy See, the conclave

---

[20] Ibid, pp 191-192.

[21] Ibid, p 195.

[22] Ibid, pp 198-200.

was in a rage, and all the cardinals of the Imperial faction urged the pope to proceed to a definitive sentence, and to dart his spiritual thunders against Henry. But Clement proceeded no further than to declare the nullity of Cranmer's sentence, as well as that of Henry's second marriage; threatening him with excommunication. There remained the possibility of reconciliation between the pope and Henry; however a courier dispatched by Henry arrived after the day appointed. On March 23, 1534, Henry was excommunicated. *News was brought to Rome that a libel had been published in England against the court of Rome, and a farce acted before the king in derision of the pope and cardinals. The pope and cardinals entered into the consistory inflamed with anger; and by a precipitate sentence, the marriage of Henry and Catherine was pronounced valid, and Henry declared to be excommunicated, if he refused to adhere to it.* Two days after, the courier arrived.

Parliament's laws against the pope, declaration of marriage to Catherine unlawful, and marriage to Anne confirmed

A parliament was assembled January 15, 1535. Laws totally destructive of the papal authority were enacted. *All provisions, bulls, dispensations, were abolished: Monasteries were subjected to the visitation and government of the king alone; the law for punishing heretics was moderated; the ordinary was prohibited from imprisoning or trying any person upon suspicion alone, without presentiment by two lawful witnesses; and it was declared that to speak against the pope's authority was no heresy: Bishops were to be appointed, from the crown. --- Campeggio and Ghinucce, two Italians, were deprived of the bishoprics of Salisbury and Worcester, which they had hitherto enjoyed. --- Convocations ought to be assembled by the king's authority only; they promise to enact no new canons without his consent; and they agree, that he should appoint thirty-two commissioners, in order to examine the old canons, and abrogate such as should be found prejudicial to his royal prerogative. An appeal was also allowed from the bishop's court to the king in chancery.*

Parliament declared the king's marriage to Catherine unlawful and the marriage of the king to Anne was established and confirmed. The crown was appointed to descend to the issue of this marriage, and failing them to the king's heirs. --- All slander against the king, queen, or their issue was subjected to the penalty of misprision of treason. --- The king found the ecclesiastical subjects as compliant as the laity. They voted that the bishop of Rome had, by the law of God, no more jurisdiction in England than any other foreign bishop; and that the authority, which he and his predecessors had there exercised, as only by usurpation and the sufferance of English princes. Four persons alone opposed this vote in the lower house, and one doubted. It passed unanimously in the upper. The bishops went so far in their complaisance, that they took out new commissions from the crown, in which all their spiritual and Episcopal authority was expressly affirmed to be derived ultimately from the civil magistrate, and to be entirely dependent on his good pleasure.[23]

Parliament conferred the king supreme head of the Church of England

Another parliament, being assembled November 3, 1534, conferred on the king the title of the only supreme head on earth of the Church of England; as they had already invested him with all the real power belonging to it. In this memorable act, the parliament granted him power, or rather acknowledged his inherent powers, 'to visit, and repress, redress, reform, order, correct, restrain, or amend all errors, heresies, abuses, offences, contempt, and enormities which fell under any spiritual authority or jurisdiction'.

Now that the king had omnipotent power over all churches and religious matters he proceeded to carry out the laws passed by parliament and whatever laws he might enact. *No prince in Europe was possessed of such absolute authority as Henry, not even the pope himself, in his own capital, where he united both the civil and ecclesiastical powers; and there was small likelihood, that any doctrine, which lay under the imputation of encouraging sedition, could ever pretend to his favor and countenance. But besides this political jealousy, there was another reason, which inspired this imperious monarch with an aversion to the reformers. He had early declared his sentiments against Luther; and having entered the lists in those scholastic quarrels, he had received, from his courtiers and theologians, infinite applause for his performance. Elated by this imaginary success, and blinded by a natural arrogance and obstinacy of temper, he had entertained the most lofty opinion of his own erudition; and he received with impatience, mixed with contempt, and contradiction to his sentiments. Luther also had been so imprudent, as to treat in a very indecent manner his royal antagonist; and though he afterwards made the most humble submissions to Henry, and apologized for the vehemence of his former expressions, he never could efface the hatred, which the king had conceived against him and his doctrines, The idea of heresy still appeared detestable as well as formidable to that prince; and whilst his resentment against the see of Rome had corrected on considerable part of his early prejudices, he had made it a point of honor never to relinquish the remainder. Separate as he stood from the Catholic Church and from the Roman pontiff, the head of it, he still valued himself on maintaining the Catholic doctrine, and on guarding, by fire and sword, the imagined purity of his speculative principles.*

Henry's ministers and courtiers were of as motley a character as his conduct; and seemed to waver, during this whole reign, between

---

[23]Ibid, pp 203-205.

the ancient and the new religion. The queen, engaged by interest as well as inclination, favored the cause of the reformers: Cromwell, who was created secretary of state, and who was daily advancing in the king's confidence, had embraced the same views; Cranmer, archbishop of Canterbury, had secretly adopted the protestant tenet; and he had gained Henry's friendship by his candor and sincerity. On the other hand, the duke of Norfolk adhered to the ancient faith; Gardiner, lately created bishop of Winchester, had enlisted himself in the same party. --- All these ministers, while they stood in the most irreconcilable opposition of principles to each other, were obliged to disguise their particular opinions, and to pretend an entire agreement with the sentiments of their master.[24]

The maid of Kent story and executions

The maid of Kent story is as bizarre as the events to follow. *Elizabeth Barton, of Aldington in Kent, commonly called the holy Maid of Kent, had been subject to hysterical fits, which threw her body into unusual convulsions; and having produced an equal disorder in her mind, made her utter strange sayings, which, as she was scarcely conscious of them during the time, had soon after entirely escaped her memory.* Several priests were involved in promulgating the revelations, which were supposedly made during these spells. The fraud associated with the miracles of the maid were exposed. *The detection of this imposture, attended with so many odious circumstances, both hurt the credit of the ecclesiastics, particularly the monks, and instigated the king to take vengeance on them. He suppressed three monasteries of the Observantine friars; and finding that little clamor was excited by this act of power, he was the more encouraged to lay his rapacious hands on the remainder. Meanwhile, he exercised punishment on individuals, who were obnoxious to him. The parliament had made it treason to endeavor depriving the king of his dignity or titles: They had lately added to his other titles, that of supreme head of the church: It was inferred, that to deny his supremacy was treason; and many priors and ecclesiastics lost their lives for this new species of guilt. It was certainly a high instance of tyranny to punish the mere delivery of a political opinion, especially one that nowise affected the king's temporal right, as a capital offence, though attended with no overt act; and the parliament, in passing this law, had overlooked all the principles, by which a civilized, much more a free people, should be governed.*

Executions of bishop Fisher and Sir Thomas More

Sir Thomas More, who succeeded Wolsey as Chancellor, is at once an object deserving our compassion, and an instance of the usual

---

[24] Ibid, pp 212-213.

progress of men's sentiments during that age. Sir Thomas More, the chancellor, foreseeing that all the measures of the king and parliament led to a breach with the church of Rome, and to an alteration of religion, with which his principles would not permit him to concur, desired leave to resign the great seal; and he descended from his high station with more joy and alacrity than he had mounted up to it. This man, whose elegant genius and familiar acquaintance with the noble spirit of antiquity, had given him very enlarged sentiments, and who had in his early years advanced principles which even at present would be deemed somewhat too free, had, in the course of events, been so irritated by polemics, and thrown into such a superstitious attachment to the ancient faith, that few inquisitors have been guilty of greater violence in their prosecution of heresy.

Bainham, accused of favoring the new opinions, was carried to More's house; and having refused to discover his accomplices, the chancellor ordered him to be whipped in his presence, and afterwards sent him to the Tower, where he himself saw him put to the torture. He was condemned as an obstinate and relapsed heretic, and was burned in Smithfield.

Many were brought into the bishops' courts for offences, which appear trivial, but which were regarded as symbols for the party. --- To harbor the persecuted preachers, to neglect the fasts of the church, to declaim against the vices of the clergy, were capital offences. Several priests who had deviated from the catholic doctrines were also condemned and burned at the stake.[25] John Fisher, bishop of Rochester, had been implicated in the Maid of Kent fraud for which he was imprisoned without consideration of his advanced age, was allowed nothing but rags while languishing in prison for twelve months. The maid of Kent was executed. *Fisher was indicted for denying the king's supremacy, was tried, condemned, and beheaded. --- The execution of this prelate was intended as a warning to More, whose compliance, on account of his great authority both abroad and at home, and his high reputation for learning and virtue, was anxiously desired by the king.[26]* Hume, vol 3, p 140. Sir Thomas More had resigned as chancellor in 1532 because he could not accept the tenets of the king and parliament that Henry was the supreme head of the church and clergy of England. --- *Rich, the solicitor general, was sent to confer with More, then a prisoner, who kept a cautious silence with regard to the supremacy: he was only inveigled to say, that any question with regard to the law, which*

---

[25] Ibid, pp 215-216.

[26] Note. More, author of Utopia, had written a treatise for king Henry opposing the position of Martin Luther for which *Henry had received the title of 'defender of the faith', an appellation still retained by the kings of England.*

established that prerogative, was a two-edged sword: If a person answer one was, it will confound his soul; if another, it will destroy his body. Nothing more was wanted to sound an indictment of high treason against the prisoner. His silence was called malicious, and made a part of his crime; and these words, which had casually dropped from him, were interpreted as a denial of the supremacy. Trials were mere formalities during this reign: The jury gave sentence against More, who had long expected this fate, and who needed no preparation to fortify him against the terrors of death. --- He was beheaded in the fifty-third year of his age. When the execution of Fisher and More was reported at Rome, especially that of the former, who was invested with the dignity of cardinal, every one discovered the most violent rage against the king; and numerous libels were published, by the wits and orators of Italy, comparing him to Caligula, Nero, Domitian, and all the most unrelenting tyrants of antiquity.

Excommunication

On August 30, 1535, Henry was excommunicated.[27]

The domestic peace of England seemed to be exposed to more hazard, by the violent innovations in religion; and it may be affirmed, that, in this dangerous conjuncture, nothing ensured public tranquility so much as the decisive authority acquired by the king, and his great ascendant over all his subjects. --- The king, conscious of his advantages, was now proceeding to the most dangerous exercise of his authority; and after paving the way for that measure by several preparatory expedients, he was at last determined to suppress the monasteries, and to put himself in possession of their ample revenues.

Suppression of lesser monasteries

Cromwell, secretary of state, had been appointed vicar-general, or viceregent, a new office, by which the king's supremacy, or the absolute, uncontrollable power, assumed over the church, was delegated to him. --- Some few monasteries, terrified with this rigorous inquisition carried on by Cromwel and his commissioners, surrendered their revenues into the king's hands; and the monks received small pensions as the reward of their obsequiousness. --- The king, though determined utterly to abolish the monastic order, resolved to proceed gradually in this great work; and he gave directions to the parliament to go no further at present, than to suppress the lesser monasteries, which possessed revenues below two hundred pounds a year. These were found to be the most corrupted, as lying less under the restraint of shame, and being exposed to less scrutiny, and it was deemed safest to begin with them, and thereby prepare the way for the greater innovations projected. By

---

[27] Ibid, pp 219-222.

this act three hundred and seventy-six monasteries were suppressed, and their revenues, amounting to thirty-two thousand pounds a year, were granted to the king; besides their goods, chattels, and plate, computed at a hundred thousand pounds more. It does not appear, that any opposition was made to this important law: So absolute was Henry's authority! A court, called the court of augmentation of the king's revenue, was erected for the management of these funds.[28]

Execution of Anne Boleyn

Meanwhile the king's jealousy laid hold of the slightest circumstance; and finding no particular object on which it could fasten, it vested itself equally on every one that came within the verge of its fury. --- The king's jealousy first appeared openly in a tilting at Greenwich, where the queen happened to drop her handkerchief; an incident probably casual, but interpreted by him as an instance of gallantry to some of her paramours. He immediately retired from the place; sent orders to confine her to her chamber. The queen was sent to the tower. The queen and her brother were tried by a jury of peers, consisting of the duke of Suffolk, the marquis of Exeter, the earl of Arundel, and twenty-three more: Their uncle, the duke of Norfolk, presided as high steward. Upon what proof or pretense the crime of incest was imputed to them is unknown: The chief evidence, it is said, amounted to no more than that Rocheford had been seen to lean on her bed before some company. --- Judgement, however, was given by the court, both against the queen and lord Rocheford: and her verdict contained, that she should be burned or beheaded at the king's pleasure. Anne Boleyn was beheaded on May 19, 1536.[29]

Marriage to Jane Seymore, birth of Edward, and death of the queen

Henry married Jane Seymour, his third wife, the day after the execution of Anne, Boleyn. Henry called a parliament three weeks later. *Henry found that the parliament was no less submissive in deeds than complaisant in their expressions, and that they would go the same lengths as the former in gratifying even his most lawless passions. His divorce from Anne Boleyn was ratified, that queen, and all her accomplices, were attainted; the issue of both his former marriages were declared illegitimate, and it was even made treason to assert the legitimacy of either of them. The crown was settled on the king's issue by Jane Seymour, or any subsequent wife. At the time of this parliament Henry established his articles of faith, and their tenets were of as motley a kind as the assembly itself, or rather as the king's system of theology.*

---

[28] Ibid, 228-230.

[29] Ibid, 233-238.

But there were uprisings and a force of 20,000 men attempted an insurrection in Lincolnshire. Other forces numbering 40,000 men were raised in the northern counties. Henry sent forces gathered at London, and the earls of Shrewsbury, Huntingdon, Derby, and Rutland suppressed the rebels. Norfolk, by command from his master, spread the royal banner, and wherever he thought proper, executed martial law in the punishment of offenders. Most were executed. On October 12, 1538, Jane Seymour delivered a son, to be later named Edward VI. The queen died a few days after giving birth to Edward.

Destruction of monasteries

But the birth of a son did not sway him from his destructive course. *There was only one particular, in which Henry was quite decisive; because he was either impelled by his avarice, or more properly speaking, his rapacity, the consequence of his profusion: This measure was the entire destruction of the monasteries. The present opportunity seemed favorable for that great enterprise, while the suppression of the late rebellion fortified and increased the royal authority: and as some of the abbots were suspected of having encouraged the insurrection, and of corresponding with the rebels, the king's resentment was further incited by that motive. A new visitation was appointed of all the monasteries in England; and a pretense only being wanted for their suppression, it was easy for a prince, possessed of such unlimited power, and seconding the present humor of a great part of the nation to find or feign one. --- On the whole, the king, at different times, suppressed six hundred and forty-five monasteries: Of which twenty-eight had abbots that enjoyed a seat in parliament. Ninety colleges were demolished in several counties; two thousand three hundred and seventy-four chanties and free chapels: A hundred and ten hospitals.*[30]

The economy

But if there were really a decay of commerce, and industry, and populousness in England, the statutes of this reign, except by abolishing monasteries, and retrenching holidays, circumstances of considerable moment, were not in other respects well calculated to remedy the evil. The fixing of the wages of artificers was attempted: Luxury in apparel was prohibited, by repeated statutes; and probably without effect. The chancellor and other ministers were empowered to fix the price of poultry, cheese, and butter. A statute was even passed to fix the price of beef, pork, mutton, and veal.

The practice of depopulating the country, by abandoning tillage, and throwing the lands into pasturage, still continued; as appears by the

---

[30] Ibid, pp 251-255.

new laws which were, from time to time, enacted against that practice.[31] *The prisoners in the kingdom, for debts and crimes, are asserted in an act of parliament, to be sixty thousand persons and above; which is scarcely credible. Harrison asserts that 72,000 criminals were executed during this reign for theft and robbery, which would amount nearly to 2000 a year.*[32]

This reign, as well as many of the foregoing and even subsequent reigns, abound with monopolizing laws, confining particular manufactures to particular towns, or excluding the open country in general. There remain still too many traces of similar absurdities. In the subsequent reign, the corporations, which had been opened by a former law, and obliged to admit tradesmen of different kinds, were again shut up by act of parliament; and every one was prohibited from exercising any trade, who was not of the corporation.[33]

Union of England and Wales, Devastations in Ireland

Henry attempted conquests of foreign territories throughout his reign. The only significant gain was the union of Wales and England. On November 3, 1534 parliament *completed the union of England and Wales, by giving to that principality all the benefit of the English laws.* On February 4, 1536, parliament *made further progress in completing the union of Wales with England and the authority of the king's courts was extended every where.*[34]

In this section, the laws of Henry, which had become the laws in Ireland, are reviewed. It is apparent that after military conquest the most important method of conquering a foreign nation is the use of laws to accomplish submission. Religion is then used to further solidify the conquest. In Ireland an attempt was made, after suppression of rebellions by military forces, to enforce Henry's new laws and at the same time change the religion of the people in compliance with the Church of England and its head, king Henry. The warfare and destruction involved the execution of priests who could not in good faith swear allegiance to Henry as the head of the Church of Ireland. The destruction of the monasteries and Catholic institutions in Ireland followed. The Irish have told stories about Henry VIII and the English tyrants to follow in front of their open fires for decades and centuries. But here we turn to written

---

[31] Ibid, p 330.

[32] Ibid, pp 328-329.

[33] Ibid, p 331.

[34] Ibid, pp 206, 230.

history by Mary Cusack, author of *The History of Ireland*, to tell the story of king Henry VIII and the Irish.

Still, until the reign of Henry VIII, the element of religious contention did not exist, and its importance as an increase source of discord, may be easily estimated by a careful consideration of its subsequent effects. Nevertheless, I believe that Irish history has not been fairly represented by a considerable number of writers, who are pleased to attribute all the sufferings and wrongs endured by the people of that country to religious grounds.

Ireland was in a chronic state of discontent and rebellion, in the eras of military violence and legal iniquity, which existed some centuries before the era of religious persecution, but, unquestionably, all the evils of the former period were enhanced and intensified, which the power which had so long oppressed and plundered, sought to add to bodily suffering the still keener anguish of mental torture.[35]

The Irish parliament was summoned in 1536; *but as a remote preparation, the Lord Deputy made a 'martial circuit' of Ireland, hoping thereby to overawe the native septs, and compel their submission to the royal will and pleasure.* They reiterated the law passed by the English parliament that *declared King Henry VIII, to be Supreme Head of the Church of Ireland;* and other acts prohibiting appeals to the pope, acts for the increase of the kings revenue, and for the suppression of abbeys and religious houses. *Some very evident proofs had been given in England, that to deny the King's spiritual supremacy was 'willfully to be dead'. With the example of Sir Thomas More before their eyes, the Anglo-Norman nobles and gentlemen, assembled in Parliament by the royal command, were easily persuaded to do the royal bidding. But the ecclesiastics were by no means so pliable.[36]*

The Archbishop of the Church of Ireland, Dr. Browne, was the person delegated to carry out the king's will. *Dr. Browne and the Lord Deputy now rivaled each other in their efforts to obtain the royal approbation, by destroying all that the Irish people held most sacred, determined to have as little cause as possible for 'the trembling in body' which the kings displeasure would effect. They traversed the land from end to end, destroying cathedrals, plundering abbeys, and burning relics. The Four Masters (ref. vol. v. p. 1445) record the work of desecration in touching and mournful strains. They tell of the heresy, which broke out in England, and graphically characterize it as 'the effect of pride, vain-glory, avarice, and sensual desire'. They mention how 'the King and Council enacted new laws and statutes after their own will.' They observe that all the property of the religious orders was seized for the*

---

[35] Cusack, The History of Ireland, pp 386-387.

[36] Ibid, pp 396-397.

King; and they conclude thus: 'They also made archbishops and bishops for themselves; and although great was the persecution of the Roman emperors against the Church, it is not probable that so great a persecution as this ever came upon the world; so that it is impossible to tell or narrate its description, unless it should be told by him who saw it.'

The era of religious persecution was thus inaugurated; and if Ireland had made no martyrs of the men who came to teach her the faith, she was not slow to give her best and noblest sons as victims to the fury of those who attempted to deprive her of that priceless deposit. Under the year 1540, the Four Master record the massacre of the Guardian and friars of the Convent at Monaghan, for refusing to acknowledge the spiritual supremacy of the King. Cornelius, Bishop of Down, a Franciscan friar, and Father Thomas FitzGerald, a member of the noble family of the Geraldines, and a famous preacher, were both killed in the convent of that Order in Dublin. Father Dominic Lopez has given a detailed account of the sufferings of the religious orders in Ireland during the reign of Henry VIII, in his rare and valuable work. I shall give two instances from this history, as a sample of the fashion in which the new doctrine of the royal supremacy was propagated. In 1539 the Prior and religious of the Convent of Atharee were commanded to take the oath of supremacy, and to surrender their property to the crown. The Superior, Father Robert, at once assembled his spiritual children, and informed them of the royal mandate. Their resolution was unanimous; after the example of the early Christians, when threatened with martyrdom and spoliation by heathen emperors, they at once distributed their provisions, clothing, and any money they had in hand amongst the poor, and concealed the sacred vessels and ornaments, so that not so much as a single emblem of our redemption was left to be desecrated by men professing to believe that they had been redeemed by the cross of Christ. Father Robert was summoned thrice to recognize the new authority. Thrice he declined; declaring that 'none had ever sought to propagate their religious tenets by the sword, except the pagan emperors in early ages, and Mahomet in a later time.' --- As for himself and his community, they were resolved that no violence should move them from the principles of truth: They recognized no head of the Catholic Church save the Vicar of Jesus Christ; and as for the King of England, they regarded him not even as a member of that holy Church, but as head of the synagogue of Satan. The conclusion of his reply was a signal for massacre. An officer instantly struck off his head with one blow. As all the prisons were already full of 'recusants', the friars were placed in confinement in private houses, some were secretly murdered, and others were publicly hanged in the market place. These events occurred on the 12th and 13th of February, 1539.[37]

---

[37] Ibid, pp 400-402.

Properties were seized for the king's coffers. All the gold and silver plate, jewels, ornaments, lead, bells etc., were reserved by special command for the King's use. The church-lands were sold to the highest bidder, or bestowed as a reward on those who had helped to enrich the royal coffers by sacrilege. Amongst the records of the sums thus obtained, we find 324 pounds, the price of divers pieces of gold and silver, of precious stones, silver ornaments, etc; also 20 pounds, the price of 1000 lbs of wax. The sum of 1710 pounds, was realized from the sale of sacred vessels belonging to thirty-nine monasteries. The profits on the spoliation of St. Mary's, Dublin realized 385 pounds. The destruction of the Collegiate Church of St. Patrick must have procured an enormous profit, as we find that Cromwell received 60 pounds for his pains in effecting the same. It should also be remembered that the value of a penny then was equal to the value of a shilling now, so that we should multiply these sums by at least by ten to obtain an approximate idea of the extent of this wholesale robbery. The spoilers now began to quarrel over the spoils. The most active or the most favored received the largest share; and Dr. Browne grumbled loudly at not obtaining all he asked for. But we have not space to pursue the disedifying history of their quarrels.[38] Other examples of the execution of priests could be cited. However, there can be no doubt that the written history provides justification for the stories the Irish have told for centuries. Henry thus followed the precedent of his father who obtained great wealth by the extractions from the injustices of the Star Chamber. Henry outdid the injustices of Wolsey's legantine court and Thomas More's inquisition.

Scotland

The wars with Scotland began early in Henry's reign. The most significant battle during this time was the battle of Flouden September 9, 1513. The king of Scotland, James IV, (b. 1488, d. 1513), who had married Henry's sister Margaret, *assembled the whole force of his kingdom; and having passed the Tweed with a brave, though a tumultuary army of above 50,000 men, he ravaged those parts of Northumberland which lay nearest that river. --- Meanwhile, the earl of Surrey, having collected a force of 26,000 men, of which 5,000 had been sent over from the king's army in France, marched to the defense of the country, and approached the Scots. On September 9, 1515, the Scots were defeated. Although equal numbers on each side were slain, about 5,000, the flower of the nobility including the king of Scotland were lost.*[39]

---

[38] Ibid, p 404.

[39] Hume, vol 3, pp 105-107.

Margaret, and their son, to be James V, who was then an infant seventeen months old, (b. 1513, d. 1542), succeeded James IV. The next heir to the crown of Scotland, son of the brother of James III, was the duke of Albany. *Albany, though first prince of the blood, had never been in Scotland, was totally unacquainted with the manners of the people, ignorant of their situation, unpracticed in their language; yet such was the favor attending the French alliance, and so great the authority of Hume, that this prince was invited to accept the reins of government. Francis, careful not to give offence to the king of England, detained Albany some time in France; but at length, sensible how important it was to keep Scotland in his interests, he permitted him to go over and take possession of the regency.*[40] In 1522 the duke of Albany attempted an invasion of northern England but the nobles failed to support him and Albany was obliged to conclude a truce with England. The duke of Albany was invited back by the king of France and remained there several years. *In 1523, Henry, that he might take advantage of the regent's absence, marched an army into Scotland under the command of Surrey, who ravaged the Merse and Teviotdale without opposition, and burned the town of Jedburgh. The Scots had neither king nor regent to conduct them: The two Humes had been put to death: Angus was in a manner banished: No nobleman of vigor or authority remained, who was qualified to assume the government.*[41] During the regent's absence the earl of Angus obtained custody of James from 1526 to 1528. James escaped from custody and later forced Angus to flee to England. James entered into a treaty with Henry in 1534. He married Mary de Guise in 1538 and thereafter entered an alliance with France against England.

The same spirit of religious innovations, which had seized other parts of Europe, had made its way into Scotland, and had begun, before this period, to excite the same jealousies, fears, and persecutions. In the fifteenth century, Wycliffe and Huss, had gained support from some of the Scottish nobles. In the sixteenth century the reformation in Europe spread to Scotland. *The clergy were at that time reduced to great difficulties not only in Scotland, but all over Europe. As the reformers aimed at a total subversion of ancient establishments, which they represented as idolatrous, impious, detestable; the priests, who found both their honor and properties at stake, thought that they had a right to resist, by every expedient, these dangerous invaders. But the most dangerous symptom for the clergy in Scotland was, that the nobility, from the example of England, had cast a wishful eye on the church revenues, and hoped, if a reformation took place, to enrich themselves by the plunder of the ecclesiastics. James himself, who was very poor, and was*

---

[40] Ibid, p 116.

[41] Ibid, pp 144-145.

somewhat inclined to magnificence, particularly in building, had been swayed by like motives; and began to threaten the clergy with the same fate that had attended them in the neighboring country. Henry also never ceased exhorting his nephew to imitate his example; and being moved both by the pride of making proselytes, and the prospect of security, should Scotland embrace a close union with him he solicited the king of Scots to meet him at York; and he obtained a promise to that purpose.

The failure of the king of Scots to meet Henry became the occasion for Henry to make preparations for war against Scotland. He employed the duke of Norfolk, whom he called the scourge of the Scots, to command in the war. James attempted to appease his uncle without success. The duke of Norfolk began to move from his camp at Newcastle; and being attended by the earls of Shrewsbury, Derby, Cumberland, Surrey, Hertford, Rutland, with many others of the nobility, he advanced to the borders. His forces amounted to above twenty thousand men; and it required the utmost efforts of Scotland to resist such a formidable armament. James had assembled his whole military force, nearly thirty thousand men. The king of Scots, inflamed with a desire of military glory, and revenge on his invaders, gave the signal for pursuing them, and carrying the war into England. But the nobles defected and James reproached them with cowardice. On November 24, 1542 the Scots were defeated at Solway Moss.

Death of James V

James V, *the king of Scots, hearing of this disaster, was astonished; and being naturally of a melancholic disposition, as well as endowed with a high spirit, he lost all command of his temper on this dismal occasion. Rage against his nobility, who, he believed, had betrayed him; shame for a defeat by such unequal numbers; regret for the past, fear of the future; all these passions so wrought upon him, that he would admit of no consolation, but abandoned himself wholly to despair. His body was wasted by sympathy with his anxious mind; and even his life began to be thought in danger. He had no issue living; and hearing that his queen was safely delivered, he asked whether she had brought him a male or female child? Being told, the latter; he turned himself in his bed: 'The crown came with a woman', he said, 'and it will go with one. Many miseries await this poor kingdom: Henry will make it his own whether by force of arms or by marriage'. A few day after he expired, in the flower of his age.*[42] James V died on December 14, 1542. The child was Mary, who later became Mary Queen of Scots. She would marry Henry Stewart, Lord Darnley. Their son James VI would become

---

[42] Ibid, pp 293-294.

king of Scotland and the first of the Stewart kings of England, as James I.[43]

Henry's last wars with France

In his final wars with France, in July, 1544, Henry led a force to Calais with 30,000 men from Flanders. The emperor led forces numbering nearly 60,000 men. Henry managed to take the city of Boulogne. *The duke of Norfolk commanded the army before Montreuil. On September 18, 1544, the emperor, after taking a number of cities, entered into peace a Crepy, where no mention was made of England. Henry, finding himself obliged to raise the siege of Montreuil, returned into England. This campaign served, to the populace, as matter of great triumph --- but all men of sense concluded that the king had, as in all his former military enterprises, made, at a great expense, an acquisition, which was of no importance.* In November 1546 Henry called his last parliament who granted expenses of the foreign wars, including a final expedition to Calais. Parliament *recognized the king to have always been, by the word of God, supreme head of the Church of England.* [44]

Henry's last years

Henry's last years were spent in persecutions, torture of his victims, executions including the beheading of his fifth wife Catherine Howard and the beheading of the earl of Surrey. His long time friend the duke of Norfolk was saved from the block by the king's death. One *Anne Ascue, a young woman of merit as well as beauty, who had great connections with the chief ladies at court, and the queen herself,* was accused by Cranmer of questioning the doctrine of transubstantiation. *She was thrown into prison. She was put to the torture in the most barbarous manner, and continued still resolute. --- She was then condemned to be burned alive; and being so dislocated by the rack, that she could not stand, she was carried to the stake in a chair. Together with her, were conducted Nicholas Belenian, a priest, John Lassels, of the king's household, and John Adams, a tailor, who had been condemned for the same crime to the same punishment. They were all tied to the stake; and in that dreadful situation the chancellor sent to inform them, that their pardon was ready drawn and signed, and would instantly be given them, if they would merit it by a recantation. They only regarded his offer as a new ornament to their crown of martyrdom; and they saw with tranquility the executioner kindle the flames, which consumed them.* [45]

---

[43] Ibid, p 309.

[44] Ibid, pp 306-308.

[45] Ibid, pp 314-315.

Death of Henry VIII

During these last years of Henry's reign further acts of religious superiority were passed by a compliant parliament. *It was enacted, this session, that any spiritual person, who preached or taught contrary to the doctrine contained in the king's book the 'Erudition of a Christian Man', or contrary to any doctrine which he should thereafter promulgated, was to be admitted on the first conviction to renounce his error; on the second, he was required to carry a faggot; which if he refused to do, or fell into a third offence, he was to be burnt.*

The king's health had long been in a declining state; but for several days all those near him plainly saw his end approaching. He was become so froward, that no one durst inform him of his condition and as some persons, during this reign, had suffered as traitors for foretelling the king's death, every one was afraid, lest, in the transports of his fury, he might, on this pretense, punish capitally the author of such friendly intelligence. At last, Sir Anthony Denny ventured to disclose to him the fatal secret, and exhorted him to prepare for the fate, which was awaiting him. He expressed his resignation; and desired that Cranmer might be sent for: But before the prelate arrived he was speechless, though he still seemed to retain his senses.[46] He died January 14, 1547, after a reign of thirty-seven years. He was fifty-six years old.

The king had made his will near a month before his demise; in which he confirmed the destination of parliament, by leaving the crown first to prince Edward, then to the lady Mary, next to the lady Elizabeth.[47]

---

[46] Ibid, p 320.

[47] Ibid, p 321.

Chapter 26

Edward VI and Mary I

Edward VI and Mary I were children of Henry VIII. Each had short reigns characterized by further religious conflicts, civil and foreign wars. The reign of Edward VI was entirely a minority rule, since the king died of tuberculosis when he was only sixteen years old.

Edward VI

Edward VI, (b 1537, d 1553) was the only son of Henry VIII and ruled from 1547 to 1553. With the rule of primogeniture Edward inherited the crown upon Henry's death, not his older sisters Mary or Elizabeth. He was only nine years old when his father died and who had set up a government of sixteen executors, chief among them Cranmer, archbishop of Canterbury and Wriothesely, chancellor. Twelve counselors were appointed who were advisory to the executors. The first act of the executors was to name a protector and the choice fell to the earl of Hertford, the king's maternal uncle. Hertford was created duke of Somerset. Wriothesely was created earl of Southampton. The council of executors removed Wriothesely from the position of chancellor and Somerset gained in power in the minority government.[1]

Somerset, as soon as the state was brought to some composure, made preparations for war with Scotland. Somerset planned that the union would be made by a marriage between the youthful Mary, queen of Scots and Edward. This would not happen. *Somerset soon perceived that the Queen dowager's attachment to France and to the Catholic religion would render ineffectual all negotiations for the intended marriage. He found himself, therefore, obliged to try the force of arms.* At the battle of Pinkey, September 10, 1547, Somerset and the English forces routed the

---

[1] Hume, vol 3, pp 333-337.

Scots. *From the field of battle to Edinburgh, for the space of five miles, the whole ground was strowed with dead bodies. The priests above all, and the monks received no quarter; and the English made sport of slaughtering men, who, from their extreme zeal and animosity, had engaged in an enterprise so ill befitting their profession. Few victories have been more decisive, or gained with smaller loss to the conquerors. There fell not two hundred of the English; and according to the most moderate computation, there perished above ten thousand of the Scots. About fifteen hundred were taken prisoners.*[2]

Parliament

The protector, on his arrival in England, summoned a parliament: And being somewhat elated with his success against the Scots, he procured from his nephew a patent, appointing him to sit on the throne, upon a stool or bench at the right hand of the king, and to enjoy the same honors and privileges, that had usually been possessed by any prince of the blood, or uncle of the kings of England. --- But if Somerset gave offence by assuming too much state, he deserves great praise on account of the laws passed this session, by which the rigor of former statutes was much mitigated, and some security given to the freedom of the constitution. All laws were repealed, which extended the crime of treason beyond the statute of the twenty-fifth of Edward III; all laws enacted during the late reign, extending the crime of felony; all the former laws against Lollardy or heresy, together with the statute of the six articles. By these repeals several of the most rigorous laws, that ever had passed in England, were annulled; and some dawn, both of civil and religious liberty, began to appear to the people. Heresy, however, was still a capital crime by the common law, and was subjected to the penalty of burning.[3]

Somerset's enlarged power was threatened by his brother, admiral Lord Seymour, a man of insatiable ambition; arrogant, assuming, implacable; and though esteemed of superior capacity to the protector, he possessed not to the same degree the confidence and regard of the people. --- the admiral's projects appeared still more dangerous to public tranquility; and as he had acquired many partisans, he made a direct attack upon his brother's authority. Somerset committed his brother to the tower. Parliament voted an attainder against lord Seymour and he was beheaded March 20, 1549.[4]

---

[2] Ibid, pp 348-352.

[3] Ibid, p 353.

[4] Ibid, pp 362-363.

Somerset's opposition and execution

It seems that no one could rise to power in England without another party rising in opposition and eventually destroying the prevailing party. *But though Somerset courted the people, the interest, which he had formed with them, was in no degree answerable to his expectations. The Catholic party, who retained influence with the lower ranks, were his declared enemies; and took advantage of every opportunity to decry his conduct. The attainder and execution of his brother bore an odious aspect. The great estate, which he had suddenly acquired, at the expense of the church and of the crown, rendered him obnoxious; and the place, which he was building in the Strand, served, by its magnificence, and still more by other circumstances which attended it, to expose him to the censure of the public. The parish church of St. Mary, with three bishops' houses, was pulled down, in order to furnish ground and materials for this structure: Not content with that sacrilege, an attempt was made to demolish St. Margaret's, Westminster, and to employ the stones to the same purpose; but the parishioners rose in a tumult, and chased away the protector's tradesmen. He then laid his hands on a chapel in St. Paul's Churchyard, with a cloister belonging to it; and these edifices, together with a church of St. John of Jerusalem, were made use of to raise his palace. What rendered the matter more odious to the people, was that the tombs and other monuments of the dead were defaced; and the bones being carried away, were buried in unconsecrated ground.*

All these imprudences were remarked, by Somerset's enemies, who resolved to take advantage of them. A conspiracy was formed including the earls of Southampton and Warwick. They obtained support from the chief nobles as assumed the whole power of the council. --- *As soon as the protector heard of the defection of the counselors, he removed the king from Hampton-court, where he then resided, to the castle of Windsor; and, arming his friends and servants, seemed resolute to defend himself against all his enemies. But, finding, that no man of rank, except Cranmer and Page, adhered to him, that the people did not rise at his summons, that the City and Tower had declared against him, that even his best friends had deserted him, he lost all hopes of success, and began to apply to his enemies for pardon and forgiveness.* He resigned the protectorship October 6, 1549. *Somerset capitulated only for gentle treatment, which was promised him.* He was, however, sent to the Tower. Two years later he was tried for treason. A jury of twenty-seven peers found insufficient evidence and acquitted him. He was accused of having an intent to assault the counselors, and a guilty verdict obtained. He was executed January 22, 1552.[5]

---

[5] Ibid, pp 375-378, 388-390.

Reformation and a new liturgy

    The day after the execution of Somerset, a session of parliament was held, in which further advances were made towards the establishment of the reformation. The new liturgy was authorized; and penalties were enacted against all those who absented themselves from public worship. The commons, after rejecting a bill renewing the rigorous statutes of treason, passed a bill *by which it was enacted, that whosoever should call the king or any of his heirs, a heretic, schismatic, tyrant, infidel or usurper of the crown, --- for the third offense, should be attainted for treason. But if any should unadvisedly utter such a slander in writing, printing, painting, carving, or graving, he was, for the first offence, to be held a traitor.*[6]

Enclosures

    During the entire reign of Edward VI there were religious conflicts generated by the clerics and nobles to the great economic and spiritual disadvantage of the people. The destruction of the monasteries had an enormous impact on people with the establishment of enclosures. *When the abbey-lands were distributed among the principal nobility and courtiers, they fell under a different management: The rents of farms were raised, while the tenants found not the same facility in disposing of the produce; the money was often spent in the capital; and the farmers, living at a distance, were exposed to oppression from their new master, or to the still greater rapacity of the stewards. --- A great demand arose for wool both abroad and at home: Pasturage was found more profitable than unskillful tillage: Whole estates were laid waste by enclosures: The tenants regarded as a useless burden, were expelled their habitations: even the cottagers, deprived of the commons, on which they formerly fed their cattle, were reduced to misery: and a decay of people, as well as a diminution of the former plenty, was remarked in the kingdom.*[7]

    The protector appointed a commission for making inquiry concerning enclosures; and issued a proclamation, ordering all late enclosures to be laid open by a day appointed, --- As this commission was disagreeable to the gentry and nobility, they stigmatized it as arbitrary and illegal; and the common people, fearing it would be eluded, and being impatient for immediate redress, could no longer contain their fury, but sought for a remedy by force of arms.

Insurrections

    The enclosures resulting from the sale of church lands to nobles and gentry led to widespread eviction, loss of livelihood, inflation of

---

[6] Ibid, pp 390-391.

[7] Ibid, pp 369-370.

prices, shortages of food and goods. In 1549, *the rising began at once in several parts of England, as if a universal conspiracy had been formed by the commonalty. The rebels in Wiltshire were dispersed by Sir William Herbert: Those in the neighboring counties, Oxford and Gloucester, by lord Gray of Wilton. Many of the rioters were killed in the field: Others were executed by martial law. The commotions in Hampshire, Sussex, Kent, and other counties, were quieted by gentler expedients; but the disorders in Devonshire and Norfolk threatened more dangerous consequences.*

The commonalty in Devonshire began with the usual complaints against enclosures and against oppressions from the gentry; but the parish priest of Sampford-Courtenay had the address to give their discontent a direction towards religion; and the delicacy of the subject, in the present emergency, made the insurrection immediately appear formidable. --- The rioters were brought into the form of a regular army, which amounted to the number of ten thousand. Lord Russel had been sent against them at the head of a small force; but finding himself too weak to encounter them in the field, he kept at a distance, and began to negotiate with them; in hopes of eluding their fury by delay, and of dispersing them by the difficulty of their subsisting in a body. Their demands were, that the mass should be restored, half of the abbey-lands resumed, the law of the six articles executed, holy water and holy bread respected, and all other particular grievances redressed. The council to whom Russel transmitted these demands, sent a haughty answer; commanded the rebels to disperse, and promised them pardon upon their immediate submission. Enraged at this disappointment, they marched to Exeter. --- The citizens of Exeter shut their gates; and the rebels, as they had no cannon, endeavored to take the place, first by scalade, then by mining, but were repulsed in every attempt. Russel meanwhile lay at Honiton, till reinforced by Sir William Herbert and lord Gray, with some German horse, and some Italian arquebusiers under Battista Spinola. He then resolved to attempt the relief of Exeter, which was now reduced to extremities. He attacked the rebels, drove them from all their posts, did great execution upon them both in the action and pursuit, and took many prisoners. Arundel and the other leaders were sent to London, tried and executed. Many of the inferior sort were put to death by martial law.

The insurrection in Norfolk rose to a still greater height, and was attended with greater acts of violence. The populace were at first excited, as in other places, by complaints against enclosures; but finding their numbers amount to twenty thousand, they grew insolent, and proceeded to more exorbitant pretensions. --- The protector affected popularity, and cared not to appear in person against the rebels: He therefore sent the earl of Warwick at the head of 6,000 men, levied for the wars against Scotland. Warwick, having tried some skirmishes with the rebels, at last made a general attack upon them, and put them to

flight. Two thousand fell in the action and pursuit.[8] Enclosures would be
a problem involving the populations in England and Ireland for centuries.
*Twenty years after the famine (mid nineteen century), Isaac Butt was still
writing, 'The vast majority of the occupiers of land in Ireland are at this
moment liable to be turned out at the pleasure of their landlord; and the
improvements carried out by the tenant continued to become the property
of the landlord.*[9]

Religious innovations and commands

*By 1549, ecclesiastical affairs were the chief object of attention
throughout the nation. A committee of bishops and divines had been
appointed by the council to compose a liturgy; and they had executed the
work committed to them. They proceeded with moderation in this delicate
undertaking: They retained as much of the ancient mass as the principles
of the reformers would permit: They indulged nothing to the spirit of
contradiction, which so naturally takes place in all great innovations:
And they flattered themselves, that they had established a service, in
which every denomination of Christians might, without scruple, concur.*
Parliament established a new form of worship. The translation of the
scriptures and form of worship was to be in English, not Latin. Celibacy
was not longer a requirement for the clergy, although it was
recommended. Confession was no longer required. The king was the
supreme head of the church. Even the council during the king's minority
reserved the right to act as the supreme head of the church and Gardiner,
who refused this allegiance was committed to the tower. Protestants who
differed from the religious doctrines of the state were severely dealt with.
*A commission by act of council was granted to the primate and some
others, to examine and search after all anabaptists, heretics, or
contemners of the book of common prayer. The commissioners were
enjoined to reclaim them, if possible; to impose penance on them; and to
give them absolution: Or if these criminals were obstinate, to
excommunicate and imprison them, and to deliver them over to the
secular arm: And in the execution of this charge, they were not bound to
observe the ordinary methods of trial; the forms of law were dispensed
with; and if any statutes happened to interfered with the powers in the
commission, they were over-ruled and abrogated by the council.* One
Joan Bocher, called Joan of Kent, expressed unorthodox opinions about
the virgin birth of Christ and was committed to the flames. Another
Dutchman, Van Paris, supporting the doctrine of Arianism, was accused
of heresy and committed to the flames. *These rigorous methods of*

---

[8] Ibid, pp 370-373.

[9] See Cecil Woodham-Smith, *The Great Hunger*, p 409, also Christopher Hill,
Liberty Against the Law, Some Seventeenth-Century Controversies.

proceeding soon brought the whole nation to a conformity, seeming or real, with the new doctrine and the new liturgy. The lady Mary alone continued to adhere to the mass, and refused to admit the established modes of worship.[10]

Mary I

Mary I, (b 1516, d 1558), followed Edward VI in a reign which lasted only five years, from 1553 to 1558. Edward VI had died from tuberculosis July 6, 1553. Mary, daughter of Henry VIII and Catherine of Aragon, would have immediately gained the crown; however, the earl of Northumberland desired that lady Jane Grey, and not Mary should be queen. He raised forces in London but was unable to meet the opposition of those who supported Mary I, who gained the crown ten days after Edward VI's death. Northumberland was executed. Mary I would be the first queen to rule England, followed shortly by her younger sister Elizabeth.

Religious commands of Mary I

Mary, in contrast to her brother Edward and sister to follow, had been brought up as a Catholic and persisted in this faith despite insistence from her father that she adopt his official tenets and the dangers during the reign of Edward VI. *Though every one besides yielded to the authority of the council, the lady Mary could never be brought to compliance; --- and remained obstinate against all this advice, and declared herself willing to endure death rather than relinquish her religion.*[11]

Mary reinstated Catholic bishops in their fees, and, *by an act of prerogative, all the preachers throughout England, except such as should obtain a particular license; and it was easy to foresee, that none but the Catholics would be favored with this privilege. --- Judge Hales, who had discovered such constancy in defending the queen's title, lost all his merit by an opposition to those illegal practices and being committed to custody, was treated with such severity, that he fell into a frenzy, and killed himself.*

Cranmer, the archbishop of Canterbury had assisted Mary during the reign of Henry, however his active part, which he had borne in promoting her mother's divorce, as well as in conducting the reformation, had made him the object of her hatred. Cranmer published a manifest in his own defense but on the publication of this inflammatory

---

[10] Ibid, pp 364-367.

[11] Ibid, p 384.

paper, Cranmer was thrown into prison, and was tried for the part, which he had acted, in concurring with the lady Jane, and opposing the queen's accession.

Parliament

In opening the parliament, October 5, 1553, the court showed a contempt of the laws, by celebrating, before the two houses, a mass of the Holy Ghost, in the Latin tongue, attended with all the ancient rites and ceremonies, though abolished by act of parliament. --- The first bill, passed by parliament, was of a popular nature, and abolished every species of treason, not contained in the statute of Edward III, and every species of felony, that did not subsist before the first of Henry VIII. The parliament next declared the queen to be legitimate, ratified the marriage of Henry with Catherine of Aragon, and annulled the divorce pronounced by Cranmer, whom they greatly blamed on that account. All the statues of king Edward, with regard to religion, were repealed by one vote. Many clauses of the riot act, passed in the late reign, were revived. --- After the parliament and convocation were dismissed, the new laws with regard to religion, though they had been anticipated, in most places, by the zeal of the Catholics, countenanced by government, were still more openly put in execution: The mass was every where re-established; and marriage was declared to be incompatible with any spiritual office. [12]

Marriage with Phillip II

Although Mary had declared her right to the choice of her husband, parliament *notwithstanding the compliance of the two houses with the queen's inclinations, they had still a reserve in certain articles; and the choice of a husband, in particular, was of such importance to the national interest, that they were determined not to submit tamely, in that respect, to her will and pleasure. --- No sooner did Charles hear of the death of Edward, and the accession of his kinswoman Mary to the crown of England, that he formed the scheme of acquiring that kingdom to their family; and he hoped, by this incident, to balance all the losses which he had sustained in Germany. His son Philip was a widower; and though he was only twenty-seven years of age, eleven years younger than the queen, this objection, it was thought, would be overlooked, and there was no reason to despair of her still having a numerous issue. The emperor, therefore, immediately sent over an agent to signify his intentions to Mary, who, pleased with the support of so powerful an alliance, and glad to unite herself more closely with her mother's family, to which she was ever strongly attached, readily embraced the proposal. Norfolk, Arundel, and Paget, gave their advice for the match. And Gardiner, who was*

---

[12] Ibid, p 410 and p 415.

become prime minister, and who had been promoted to the office of chancellor, finding how Mary's inclinations lay, seconded the project of the Spanish alliance.

The violent and sudden change of religion inspired the Protestants with great discontent; and even affected indifferent spectators with concern, by the hardships, to which so many individuals were on that account exposed. But the Spanish match was a point of more general concern, and diffused universal apprehensions for the liberty and independence of the nation. To obviate all clamor, the articles of marriage were drawn as favorable as possible for the interest and security, and even grandeur of England. --- These articles, when published, gave no satisfaction to the nation: It was universally said, that the emperor, in order to get possession of England, would verbally agree to any terms; and the greater advantage there appeared in the conditions which he granted, the more certainly might it be concluded, that he had no serious intention of observing them: That the usual fraud and ambition of that monarch might assure the nation of such a conduct; and his son Philip, while he inherited these vices from his father, added to them tyranny, sullenness, pride, and barbarity, more dangerous vices of his own. That England would become a province, and a province to a kingdom, which usually exercised the most violent authority over all her dependant dominions. The Netherlands, Milan, Sicily, Naples groaned under the burden of Spanish tyranny; and throughout all the new conquests in America there had been displayed scenes of unrelenting cruelty, hitherto unknown in the history of mankind. Philip would not arrive until July the following year, in 1555, and they were married in Westminster. The great hopes for numerous offspring, however, were never fulfilled. The queen believed she was pregnant and would deliver a child. *Her infant proved only the commencement of a dropsy, which the disordered state of her health had brought upon her.*[13]

Insurrections and the execution of lady Jane Grey

Meanwhile several insurrections resulted from Mary's religious edicts and marriage with Phillip of Spain, an even greater threat. Sir Thomas Wyatt and the duke of Suffolk had hopes of raising lady Gray to the throne to replace Mary. The duke of Suffolk, his brother lord Thomas, and lord Leonard Gray dispersed their followers and were taken prisoner. *Wyatt was at first more successful in his attempt; and having published a declaration at Maidstone in Kent, against the queen's evil counselors and against the Spanish match, without any mention of religion, the people began to flock to his standard.* The duke of Norfolk was sent against him, but his troops deserted to Wyatt. *After this proof of the dispositions of the people, especially of the Londoners, who were*

---

[13] Ibid, pp 416-425 and p 429.

mostly Protestants, Wyatt was encouraged to proceed: He led his forces to Southwark, where he required of the queen, that she should put the Tower into his hands, should deliver four counselors as hostages, and in order to ensure the liberty of the nation, should immediately marry an Englishman. --- Though he entered Westminster without resistance, his followers, finding that no person of note joined him, insensibly fell off, and he was at last seized near Temple-Bar by Sir Maurice Berkeley. Four hundred persons are said to have suffered for this rebellion: Four hundred more were conducted before the queen with ropes about their necks and falling on their knees, received a pardon, and were dismissed. Wyatt was condemned and executed.

But this rebellion proved still more fatal to the lady Jane Gray, as well as to her husband. Warning was given the lady Jane to prepare for death; a doom which she had long expected, and which the innocence of her life, as well as the misfortunes, to which she had been exposed, rendered nowise unwelcome to her. --- It had been intended to execute the lady Jane and lord Guilford together on the same scaffold at Tower-hill; but the council dreading the compassion of the people for their youth, beauty, innocence, and noble birth, changed their orders, and gave directions that she should be beheaded within the verge of the Towers. She saw her husband led to execution; and having given him from the window some token of her remembrance, she waited with tranquility till her own appointed hour should bring her to a like fate. She even saw his headless body carried back in a cart. Lady Jane Gray was beheaded February 12, 1554. The duke of Suffolk was tried, condemned, and executed soon after. Lord Thomas Gray lost his life for the same crime.[14]

Executions of Protestants

Chancellor Gardiner favored violent methods to eradicate heresy according to the new edicts of queen Mary, in 1555. *It was determined to let loose the laws in their full vigor against the reformed religion; and England was soon filled with scenes of horror, --- which prove, that no human depravity can equal revenge and cruelty, covered with the mantle of religion.*

The persecutors began with Rogers, prebendary of St. Paul's, a man eminent in his party for virtue as well as for learning. Gardiner's plan was first to attack men of that character, whom, he hoped, terror would bend to submission, and whose example, either of punishment or recantation, would naturally have influence on the multitude: But he found a perseverance and courage in Rogers, which it may seem strange to find in human nature, and of which all ages, and all sects, do nevertheless furnish many examples. --- Rogers was burnt in Smithfield.

---

[14] Ibid, pp 417-421.

Hooper, bishop of Gloucester, had been tried at the same time with Rogers; but was sent to his own diocese to be executed. This circumstance was contrived to strike the greater terror into his flock. He was burned at the stake and *was three quarters of an hour in torture, which he bore with inflexible constancy. Sanders was burned at Coventry. Taylor, parson of Hadley, was punished by fire in that place, surrounded by his ancient friends and parishioners.*

The crime, for which all the Protestants were condemned, was, their refusal to acknowledge the real presence. Gardiner, who had vainly expected, that a few examples would strike a terror into the reformers, finding the work daily multiplied upon him, devolved the invidious office on others, chiefly on Bonner, a man of profligate manners, and of a brutal character, who seemed to rejoice in the torments of the unhappy sufferers. He sometimes whipped the prisoners with his own hand, till he was tired with the violence of the exercise.

It is needless to be particular in enumerating all the cruelties practiced in England during the course of three years that these persecutions lasted. Ferrar, bishop of St. David's, was burned in his own diocese; and his appeal to cardinal Pole was not attended to. Ridley, bishop of London, and Latimer, formerly bishop of Worcester, two prelates celebrated for learning and virtue, perished together in the same flames at Oxford, and supported each other's constancy by their mutual exhortations. --- But the court, finding that Bonner, however shameless and savage, would not bear alone the whole infamy, soon threw off the mask; and the unrelenting temper of the queen, as well as of king Phillip, appeared without control. A bold step was even taken towards introducing the inquisition into England. As the bishops' courts, though extremely arbitrary, and not confined by any ordinary forms of law, appeared not to be invested with sufficient power, a commission was appointed, by authority of the queen's prerogative, more effectually to extirpate heresy. Twenty-one persons were named; but any three were armed with the powers of the whole. The commission runs in these terms; 'That since many false rumors were published among the subjects, and many heretical opinions were also spread among them, the commissioners were to inquire into those, either by presentiments, by witnesses, or any other political way they could devise, and to search after all heresies, the bringers in, the sellers, the readers of all heretical books: They were to examine and punish all misbehavior or negligence, in any church or chapel. --- 'Giving the commissioners full power to proceed, as their discretions and consciences should direct them, and to use all such means as they would invent for the searching of the premises, empowering them also to call before them such witnesses as they pleased, and to force them to make oaths of such things as might discover what they sought after.'

To bring the methods of proceeding in England still nearer to the practice of the inquisition, letters were written to lord North, and others, enjoining them, 'To put to the torture such obstinate persons as would not confess, and there to order them at their discretion'. Secret spies also and informers, were employed, according to the practice of that iniquitous tribunal.

It is computed, that in that time two hundred and seventy-seven persons were brought to the stake; besides those who were punished by imprisonment, fines, and confiscations. Among those who suffered by fire, were five bishops, twenty-one clergymen, eight lay gentlemen, eighty-four tradesmen, one hundred husbandmen, servants, and laborers, fifty-five women, and four children.[15] On March 21, 1556, during the darkest days of Mary's reign, Cranmer was accused of heresy and burned at the stake.

Foreign wars

There is no time in the history of England that we are here considering, including this brief reign of Mary, that there were no wars—religious, civil and foreign. *The great object of the queen was to engage the nation in the war, which was kindled between France and Spain; and cardinal Pole, with many other counselors, openly and zealously opposed this measure. Besides insisting on the marriage articles, which provided against such an attempt, they represented the violence of the domestic factions in England, and the disordered state of the finances; and they foreboded, that the tendency of all these measures was to reduce the kingdom to a total dependence on Spanish counsels. Philip had come to London in order to support his partisans; and he told the queen, that, if he were not gratified in so reasonable a request, he never more would set foot in England. This declaration extremely heightened her zeal for promoting his interests, and overcoming the inflexibility of her council. After employing other menaces of a more violent nature, she threatened to dismiss all of them, and to appoint counselors more obsequious; yet could she not procure a vote for declaring war with France.* After opposition proved ineffective, *war was accordingly declared against France; and preparations were everywhere made for attacking that kingdom.*

Any considerable supplies could scarcely be expected from parliament, considering the present disposition of the nation. *But though the queen owed great arrears to all her servants, besides the loans extorted from her subjects, these considerations had no influence with her; and in order to support her warlike preparations, she continued to levy money in the same arbitrary and violent manner which she had formerly practiced. She obliged the city of London to supply her with 60,000 pounds on her husband's entry; she levied before the legal time the second year's subsidy voted by parliament; she issued anew many*

---

[15] Ibid, pp 435-441.

privy seals, by which she procured loans from her people; and having equipped a fleet which she could not victual by reason of the dearness of provisions, she seized all the corn she could find in Suffolk and Norfolk, without paying any price to the owners. By all these expedients, assisted by the power of pressing, she levied an army of ten thousand men, which she sent over to the Low Countries, under the command of the earl of Pembroke.

The king of Spain had assembled an army, which, after the junction of the English, amounted to above sixty thousand men, conducted by Philibert, duke of Savoy, one of the greatest captains of the age. In the battle of St. Quintin the Spanish and English forces defeated the French. *The duke of Savoy made an attack on the French army, and put them to total rout, killing four thousand men, and dispersing the remainder. In this unfortunate action many of the chief nobility of France were either slain or taken prisoners.* Philip retired his troops into winter quarters.

But this success was to be followed by the most important loss of Calais to the French. *The duke of Guise, in eight days, during the depths of winter, made himself master of this strong fortress, that had cost Edward III a siege of eleven months at the head of a numerous army, which had, that very year, been victorious in the battle of Cressy. The English had held it above two hundred years; and as it gave them an easy entrance into France, it was regarded as the most important possession belonging to the crown. --- The English bereaved of this valuable fortress, murmured loudly against the improvidence of the queen and her council; who, after engaging in a fruitless war, for the sake of foreign interests, had thus exposed the nation to so severe a disgrace. A treasury exhausted by expenses, and burdened with debts; a people divided and dejected; a sovereign negligent of her people's welfare, were circumstances which, notwithstanding the fair offers and promises of Philip, gave them small hopes of recovering Calais. And as the Scots, instigated by French councils, began to move on the borders, they were now necessitated rather to look to their defense at home, than to think of foreign conquests.*[16]

The Scots managed to conduct only inroads on the borders. However, the most significant development in this final year of Mary's reign was the marriage of Mary Stuart, Queen of Scots, to the dauphin and an alliance with France. The wars with Scotland became more pronounced in the following reign of Elizabeth.

Death of queen Mary I

Mary had long been in a declining state of health; and having mistaken her dropsy for a pregnancy, she had made use of an improper

---

[16] Ibid, pp 451-454.

regimen, and her malady daily augmented. Every reflection now tormented her. The consciousness of being hated by her subjects, the prospect of Elizabeth's succession, apprehensions of the danger to which the Catholic religion stood exposed, dejection for the loss of Calais, concern for the ill state of her affairs, and, above all, anxiety for the absence of her husband, who, she knew, intended soon to depart for Spain, and to settle there during the remainder of his life: All these melancholy reflections prayed upon her mind, and threw her into a lingering fever, of which she died, after a short and unfortunate reign of five years, four months and eleven days.[17]   Mary I died November 17, 1558. She was forty-two years of age.

---

[17] Ibid, p 461.

Chapter 27

Elizabeth I

Elizabeth I, (b. 1533, d. 1603), was queen of England from 1558 to 1603. Her long reign was exceptional. Her personal characteristics were and always have been complex and perhaps will never be understood by historians or students of human behavior. Most historians, however, have given her great praise. Hume at the end of volume IV of The History of England, speaks very highly of her:

There are few great personages in history, who have been more exposed to the calumny of enemies, and the adulation of friends, than queen Elizabeth; and yet there scarcely is any, whose reputation has been more certainly determined, by the unanimous consent of posterity. The unusual length of her administration, and the strong features of her character, were able to overcome all prejudices; and obliging her detractors to abate much of their invectives, and her admirers somewhat of their panegyrics, have at last, in spite of political factions, and what is more, of religious animosities, produced a uniform judgment with regard to her conduct. Her vigor, her constancy, her magnanimity, her penetration, vigilance, address, are allowed to merit the highest praises, and appear not to have been surpassed by any person that ever filled a throne: A conduct less rigorous, less imperious, more sincere, more indulgent to her people, would have been requisite to form a perfect character. By the force of her mind, she controlled all her more active and stronger qualities, and prevented them from running into excess: Her heroism was exempt from temerity, her frugality from avarice, her friendship from partiality, her active temper from turbulency and a vain ambition: She guarded not herself with equal care or equal success from lesser infirmities; the rivalship of beauty, the desire of admiration, the jealousy of love, and the sallies of anger.[1]

---

[1] Hume, Vol 4, pp 351-353.

It would appear from Hume's work, the entire volume IV devoted to Elizabeth, that there was much more to her reign. Elizabeth was adept at presenting her court in an appearance of an absolute monarchy. Yet she was preoccupied with the dangers of civil uprisings and especially that of a Catholic take over, focusing on her cousin Mary, queen of Scots, whose story is as inscrutable as that of Elizabeth. It is difficult to know who really made the important decisions during her reign, herself or William Cecil, later titled Lord Burghley. Other close associates of Elizabeth, included a person of even greater influence over the centuries, Edward de Vere, author of the works attributed to William Shakespeare of Stratford. The queen never married, but had favorites including the earl of Essex, who after his beheading contributed to her melancholy and a miserable end to her life.

Family History

We have in previous chapters reviewed the life and reigns of Elizabeth's father Henry VIII, her younger brother Edward VI, and older sister Mary I. We have not presented much about the personality and background of her mother, Anne Boleyn.[2] One may assume that Anne Boleyn likely contributed a great deal to the unique characteristics of Elizabeth. From Hume: *This young lady, whose grandeur and misfortunes have rendered her so celebrated, was daughter of Sir Thomas Boleyn, who had been employed by the king in several embassies, and who was allied to all the principal nobility in the kingdom. His wife, mother to Anne, was daughter of the duke of Norfolk; his own mother was daughter of the earl of Ormond; his grandfather Sir Geoffry Boleyn, who had been mayor of London, had espoused one of the daughters and co-heirs of lord Hastings. From Erickson: At age twelve she had gone to France with her father, Henry VIII's ambassador Thomas Boleyn, and had joined the large suite for girls in the household of Frances I's queen Claude. There, under the tutelage of the ill-favored but virtuous queen, --- Anne became fluent in French, acquiring a taste for the literature and art of king Francis' gilded Renaissance court. Her pronounced musical gifts were developed; she became a skilled singer and lutenist, and may have met the reigning luminaries of French music, Josquin des Pres and Claude Mouton. Poets dedicated books and poems to her, saluting her charm and confirming the judgment of other observers that, in subtle ways, she had become a Frenchwoman. In the language of one poet, she was such a graceful maiden that no one would have believed she was English.[3]*

---

[2] See Carolly Erickson, *The First Elizabeth, Mistress Anne, and Great Harry.*

[3] Hume, vol 3, p 172-173. Erickson, Great Harry, pp 187, 188.

Early life and education

Elizabeth was born September 7, 1533, the day her father Henry VIII, married Anne Boleyn. Elizabeth was only three years old when her mother Anne was beheaded at the command of her father Henry for supposed infidelity. Although initially dispossessed of any royal heritage, Elizabeth was raised at Hatfield in Hertfordshire by a contingent of servants employed by her father. At age four her brother Edward was born and became the heir designate; however his mother, Jane Seymour, died a few days after his birth. At age six she was present at the marriage of her father's fourth wife, Anne of Cleves. This marriage would not last long, just a few months, before divorce. Shortly thereafter Henry married Catherine Howard, aunt of Elizabeth's grandmother. Catherine Howard was beheaded for infidelity when Elizabeth was nine years old. One wonders what kind of influence the bizarre violent acts of her father might have had in the life of this young girl. The life of Elizabeth, her quixotic relationships with men involving various intrigues, duplicity and vacillating emotions; and her undisputed failure to marry despite numerous proposals from various political considerations, may have been determined by these horrible early experiences. They would be followed by the extreme dangers she was exposed to, from the Catholics who regarded her as illegitimate during her father and brother's reigns, but especially during the reign of Mary I, when Elizabeth was in her early twenties.

Education

Elizabeth's foster mother at Hatfield was mistress Champernowne, who later married her mother's cousin John Ashley, known as Kat Ashley; and who provided Elizabeth's early education which included Latin, exposure to the writings of St. Gregory and other church fathers. But her upbringing was that of a protestant. Catherine Par, who followed Anne of Cleves as her father's sixth wife, when Elizabeth was ten years old, was the only queen who really became a stepmother to Elizabeth and provided further education for the next five years. Elizabeth had tutoring in the Greek and Roman classics, and received praise from Roger Ascham. It is likely that the challenges and inspiration from her scholarly education would provide a great bulwark against the hazards and great difficulties she faced in life. In 1548, when Elizabeth was fifteen years old, the plague was another terror, which took the life of one of her young tutors. Shortly after Henry's death Catherine Par married the man she was engaged to before her marriage to Henry, lord Thomas Seymour. Elizabeth would then become exposed to another terror. Thomas Seymour threatened his older brother Edward Seymour, protector during Edward VI's minority. Shortly after the death of Catherine Par, Thomas Seymour was beheaded for treason. New dangers threatened young Elizabeth with the death of Edward and the accession of Mary I in 1553 when Elizabeth was twenty years old. After the Wyatt rebellion in 1554 Elizabeth was sent to the tower, but was released two months later and kept under close custody at Woodstock.

Accession and establishment of the Protestant religion

Elizabeth was at Hatfield when she heard of her sister's death, on November 17, 1558, and after a few days she went thence to London through crowds of people, who strove with each other in giving her the strongest testimony of their affection. --- Philip, who had long foreseen this event, and who still hoped, by means of Elizabeth, to obtain that dominion over England, of which he had failed in espousing Mary, immediately dispatched orders to the duke of Ferria, his ambassador at London, to make proposals of marriage to the queen; and he offered to procure from Rome a dispensation for that purpose. But Elizabeth soon came to the resolution of declining the proposal. She saw, that the nation had entertained an extreme aversion to the Spanish alliance during her sister's reign; and that one great cause of the popularity, which she herself enjoyed, was the prospect of being free, by her means, from the danger of foreign subjection. She was sensible, that her affinity with Philip was exactly similar to that of her father with Catherine of Arragon; and that her marrying that monarch was, in effect, declaring herself illegitimate, and incapable of succeeding to the throne.

The queen, not to alarm the partisans of the Catholic religion, had retained eleven of her sister's counselors; but in order to balance their authority, she added eight more, who were known to be inclined to the protestant communion. --- With these counselors, particularly Sir William Cecil, who was named Secretary of State, she frequently deliberated concerning the expediency of restoring the Protestant religion, and the means of executing that great enterprise. Cecil told her, that the greater part of the nation had, ever since her father's reign, inclined to the reformation; and though her sister had constrained them to profess the ancient faith, the cruelties, exercised by her ministers, had still more alienated their affections from it.

The education of Elizabeth, as well as her interest, led her to favor the reformation; and she remained not long in suspense with regard to the party, which she should embrace. But though determined in her own mind, she resolved to proceed by gradual and secure steps, and not to imitate the example of Mary, in encouraging the bigots of her party to make immediately a violent invasion on the established religion. She thought it requisite, however, to discover such symptoms of her intentions as might give encouragement to the Protestants, so much depressed by the late violent persecutions. She immediately recalled all the exiles, and gave liberty to the prisoners, who were confined on account of religion.[4]

---

[4] Hume, vol 4, pp 4-7.

Parliament and the supremacy of the crown

Parliament *began the session, in 1558, with an unanimous declaration, 'that queen Elizabeth was, and ought to be, as well by the word of God, as the common and statute laws of the realm, the lawful, undoubted, and true heir to the crown, lawfully descended from the blood-royal, according to the order of succession, settled in the 35th of Henry VIII.'*

The first bill brought into parliament with a view of trying their disposition on the head of religion, was that for suppressing the monasteries lately erected, and for restoring the tenths and first fruits to the queen. This point being gained without much difficulty, a bill was next introduced, annexing the supremacy to the crown. --- By this act the crown, without the concurrence, either of the parliament or even of the convocation, was vested with the whole spiritual power; might repress all heresies, might establish or repeal all canons, might alter every point of discipline, and might ordain or abolish any religious rite or ceremony. --- In order to exercise this authority, the queen, by a clause of the act, was empowered to name commissioners, either laymen or clergymen, as she should think proper; and on this clause was afterwards founded the court of ecclesiastical commission; which assumed a large discretionary, not to say arbitrary powers, totally incompatible with any exact boundaries of the constitution, --- an act that at once gave the crown alone all the power, which had formerly been claimed by the popes.

Whoever refused to take an oath, acknowledging the queen's supremacy, was incapacitated from holding any office; whoever denied the supremacy, or attempted to deprive the queen of that prerogative, forfeited, for the first offence, all his goods and chattels; for the second, was subjected to the penalty of a premunire; but the third offence was declared treason.

A law was passed, confirming all the statutes enacted in king Edward's time with regard to religion: 'The nomination of bishops was given to the crown without any election of the chapter: The queen was empowered, on the vacancy of any see, to seize all the temporalities, and to bestow on the bishop-elect an equivalent in the impropriations belonging to the crown. --- And thus the queen, amidst all her concern for religion, followed the example of the preceding reformers, in committing depredations on the ecclesiastical revenues. --- This method of pillaging the church was not remedied till the beginning of James I. The present depression of the clergy exposed them to all injuries; and the laity never stopped, till they had reduced the church to such poverty, that her plunder was no longer a compensation for the odium incurred by it.

The Protestants ventured on the last and most important step, and brought into parliament a bill for abolishing the mass, and re-establishing the liturgy of king Edward. Penalties were enacted, as well against those who departed from this mode of worship, as against those who absented themselves from the church and the sacraments. [5]

Family history of Mary queen of Scots

Not only the wars with Scotland but the contention of Mary queen of Scots to the English throne was a major problem for Elizabeth's reign. Mary's grandfather was James IV, who in 1503 had married Margaret, older sister of Henry VIII. James IV (b 1473 d 1513) was king of Scotland from 1488 to 1513. In 1512, James took advantage of Henry's invasion of France to make inroads on northern England. James IV was defeated and killed by Henry's forces at the battle of Flodden, September 1513, which was disastrous for the Scots. James V, (b 1512, d 1542) was only 17 months old when he gained the crown of Scotland. His mother and the dukes of Albany and Angus attempted to rule Scotland. James V assumed his reign of Scotland in 1530 and entered a treaty with Henry VIII in 1534. In 1538 he married Mary of Guise, and thereafter allied Scotland with France. Once again Henry VIII was decisive in battle at Solway Moss on November 24, 1542 where the Scots were badly defeated. James V died the following month, a week before his only daughter Mary, to become queen of Scots, was born. Thus was established the next heir to the throne of England, providing Elizabeth never married or had children.

If the minority of James V at age seventeen months and his incompetent reign wasn't a sufficient disaster, the reign of Mary at one week of age, with a French noblewoman, Mary of Guise, holding the reigns of power, would bring Scotland to a disastrous civil and religious internal turmoil. The bizarre events of Mary queen of Scots would then be decisive in bringing more civil disorder in Scotland. The birth of a son to Mary was the most significant event of this period, James VI of Scotland, who later became James I of England to follow Elizabeth.

The protestant revolt in Scotland

In 1557 at Edinburgh a group of earls made a declaration of protestant beliefs and formed the *congregation of the lord. The accession of Elizabeth, which happened about this time, contributed to increase their hopes of final success in their undertaking. They ventured to present a petition to the regent, craving a reformation of the church, and of the 'wicked, scandalous, and detestable lives of the prelates and ecclesiastics.' --- They desired that the laws against heretics, should be executed by the civil magistrate alone, and that the scripture should be the sole rule in judging of heresy. They even petitioned the convocation, and insisted, that prayers should be said in the vulgar tongue, and that*

---

[5]   Ibid, pp 9-15.

bishops should be chosen with the consent of the gentry of the diocese, and priests with the consent of the parishioners.

In this critical time, John Knox arrived in Geneva, where he had passed some years in banishment, and where he had imbibed, from his commerce with Calvin, the highest fanaticism of his sect, augmented by the native ferocity of his own character. He had been invited back to Scotland by the leaders of the reformation; and mounting the pulpit at Perth, during the present ferment of men's minds, he declaimed with his usual vehemence against the idolatry and other abominations of the church of Rome, and incited his audience to exert their utmost zeal for its subversion. A priest was so imprudent after this sermon, as to open his repository of images and relics, and prepared himself to say mass. The audience, exalted to a disposition for any furious enterprise, were as much enraged as if the spectacle had not been quite familiar to them: They attacked the priest with fury, broke the images in pieces, tore the pictures, overthrew the altars, scattered about the sacred vases; and left no implement of idolatrous worship, as they termed it, entire or undefaced. They thence proceeded, with additional numbers and augmented rage, to the monasteries of the gray and black friars, which they pillaged in an instant: The Carthusians underwent the same fate: And the populace, not content with robbing and expelling the monks, vented their fury on the buildings which had been the receptacles of such abomination; and in a little time nothing but the walls of these edifices were left standing. The inhabitants of Couper in Fife soon after imitated the example.

The queen-regent, Mary of Guise, provoked at this violence, assembled an army, and prepared to chastise the rebels. She had about two thousand French under her command, with a few Scottish troops; and being assisted by such of the nobility as were well affected to her she pitched her camp within ten miles of Perth. --- The congregation, on the other hand, made preparations of defense; --- they appeared formidable from their numbers, as well as from the zeal by which they were animated. They sent an address to the regent, where they plainly insinuated, that, if they were pursued to extremities, by the cruel beasts the churchmen, they would have recourse to foreign powers for assistance; and they subscribed themselves her faithful subjects in all things not repugnant to God, assuming, at the same time, the name of the faithful congregation of Christ Jesus.

The queen regent, finding such obstinate zeal in the rebels, was content to embrace the counsels of Argyle and the prior of St. Andrews, and to form an accommodation with them. She was received into Perth, which submitted, on her promising an indemnity for past offences, and engaging not to leave any French garrison in the place. --- The congregation, inflamed with their own zeal, remained not long in tranquility. Even before they left Perth, and while as yet they had no color to complain of any violation of treaty, they had signed a new covenant, in which, besides their engagements to mutual defense, they vowed, in the name of God, to employ their whole power in destroying every thing that dishonored his holy name; and this covenant was subscribed, among others, by Argyle and the prior of St. Andrews. These two leaders now desired no better pretense for deserting the regent and openly joining their associates, than the complaints, however doubtful, or rather false, of her breach of promise. The congregation also, encouraged by this accession of force, gave themselves up entirely to the furious zeal of Knox, and renewed at Crail, Anstruther, and other places in Fife, like depredations on the churches and monasteries with those formerly committed at Perth and Couper.[6]

Elizabeth's intervention in Scotland

Cecil, secretary of State, represented to the queen, that the union of the crowns of Scotland and France, both of them the hereditary enemies of England, was ever regarded as a pernicious event; and her father, as well as protector Somerset, had employed every expedient, both of war and a negotiation, to prevent it. That the capacity, ambition, and exorbitant views of the family of Guise, who now governed the French counsels, were sufficiently known; and they themselves made no secret of their design to place their niece, Mary, queen of Scots on the throne of England.

In 1559, Elizabeth equipped a fleet, which consisted of thirteen ships of war; and giving the command of it to Winter, she sent it to the Frith of Forth: She appointed the young duke of Norfolk her lieutenant in the northern counties, and she assembled at Berwic an army of eight thousand men under the command of lord Gray. --- She concluded a treaty of mutual defense with the congregation, which was to last during the marriage of the queen of Scots with Francis and a year after; and she promised never to desist till the French had entirely evacuated Scotland. --- In January, 1560, the appearance of Elizabeth's fleet in the Frith disconcerted the French army, who were at that time ravaging the county of Fife. The Scots' fleet was dispersed by a storm. The queen regent died in the castle of Edinburgh. --- The French, who found it impossible to subsist for want of provisions, and who saw, that, the English were continually reinforced by fresh numbers, were obliged to capitulate. A settlement was made July 5, 1560. It was there stipulated, that the French should instantly evacuate Scotland; that the king and queen of France and Scotland should thenceforth abstain from bearing the arms of England, or assuming the title of that kingdom. Twelve persons, seven chosen by Mary queen of Scots, should administer Scotland in the queen's absence. *In order to hasten the execution of this important*

---

[6] Ibid, pp 19-26.

*treaty, Elizabeth sent ships, by which the French forces were transported
into their own country.*

Scottish reformers

*The subsequent measures of the Scottish reformers tended still
more to cement their union with England. --- The leaders of the
congregation, not waiting till the queen of Scots should ratify that treaty,
thought themselves fully entitled, without the sovereign's authority,
immediately to summon a parliament. --- The parliament seemed to have
been actuated by the same spirit of rage and persecution. After ratifying
a confession of faith, agreeable to the new doctrines, they passed a
statute against the mass, and not only abolished it in all the churches, but
enacted, that whoever, any where, either officiated in it or was present at
it, should be chastised, for the first offence with confiscation of goods
and corporal punishment, at the discretion of the magistrate; for the
second, with banishment; and for the third, with loss of life. A law was
also voted for abolishing the papal jurisdiction in Scotland: The
Presbyterian form of discipline was settled, leaving only at first some
shadow of authority to certain ecclesiastics, whom they called
Superintendents.[7]*

Mary, queen of Scots

The affairs in Scotland and especially involving the person of
Mary, queen of Scots, (b 1542, d 1587) would begin in the first years of
Elizabeth's reign and fear of a catholic contender for the throne would
become a constant preoccupation throughout her reign. Therefore, it is
appropriate to review the life of this important queen, who contrasts in
character to her cousin Elizabeth, but whose life appears equally complex
and inscrutable. Mary, daughter of James V and Mary of Guise, was only
a week old when James V died December 14, 1542. The family history is
above noted. Following the ravages of Henry in Scotland and the
subjection of the Scottish forces *the queen dowager,* Mary of Guise,
*called a parliament and proposed, that the young queen, for her greater
security, should be sent to France, and be committed to the custody of
that ancient ally. It was accordingly determined to send the queen to
France; and what was understood to be the necessary consequence, to
marry her to the dauphin. Villegaignon, commander of four French
gallies lying in the Frith of Forth, set sail as if he intended to return
home; but when he reached the open sea, he turned northwards, passed
by the Orkneys, and came in on the west coast at Dunbarton: an
extraordinary voyage for ships of that fabric. The young queen was there
committed to him; and being attended by the lords Ereskine and
Livingstone, she put to sea, and after meeting with some tempestuous*

---

[7] Ibid, pp 28-32.

weather, arrived safely at Brest, whence she was conducted to Paris, and soon after she was betrothed to the dauphin.[8]

Mary was five years old when she arrived in France. She was brought up in France in the royal court of Henry II and Catherine de Medicis whose family, the Guises, had great power in France. She was brought up as a Catholic and a Frenchwoman, not as a Protestant and a Scot. She was well educated in the classics and had command of several languages, however her principle language was French. She married the dauphin, Frances, son of Henry II and Catherine in April 1558, just seven months before the accession of Elizabeth.

The next heir of blood was the queen of Scots, now married to the dauphin, and the great power of that princess, joined to her plausible title, rendered her a formidable rival to Elizabeth. The king of France had secretly been soliciting at Rome a bull of excommunication against the queen. The duke of Guise, and his brothers, thinking, that it would much augment their credit, if their niece should bring an accession of England, as she had already done of Scotland, to the crown of France, engaged the king not to neglect the claim; and by their persuasion, he ordered his son and daughter-in-law to assume openly the arms as well as title of England, and to quarter these arms on all their equipages, furniture, and liveries. When the English ambassador complained of this injury, he could obtain nothing but an evasive answer; that as the queen of Scots was descended from the blood royal of England, she was entitled, by the example of many princes, to assume the arms of that kingdom.[9]

The death of Henry II in 1559 brought Francis II to the throne of France, but this weak prince and husband of Mary died the following year. *Meanwhile, the queen-mother of France, who imputed to Mary all the mortifications, which she had met with during Francis's life-time, took care to retaliate on her by like injuries; and the queen of Scots, finding her abode in France disagreeable, began to think of returning to her native country.*[10]

Mary in Scotland

In August 1561, Mary arrived in Scotland. She was nineteen years old and was ill prepared as a Frenchwoman and Catholic to handle the affairs of Scotland. *It was with great difficulty she could obtain permission for saying mass in her own chapel; and had not the people apprehended, that, if she had here met with a refusal, she would instantly*

---

[8] Hume, vol 3, pp 357-358.

[9] Hume, vol 4, p 17.

[10] Ibid, p 35.

have returned to France, the zealots never would have granted her even that small indulgence. The cry was, 'Shall we suffer that idol to be again erected within the realm?' It was asserted in the pulpit, that one mass was more terrible than ten thousand armed men landed to invade the kingdom: Lord Lindesey, and the gentlemen of Fife, exclaimed, 'That the idolater should die the death.' And if lord James, and some popular leaders, had not interposed, the most dangerous uproar was justly apprehended, from the ungoverned fury of the multitude.

John Knox

The town council of Edinburgh had the assurance, from their own authority, to issue a proclamation banishing from their district, 'all the wicked rabble of anti Christ, the pope, such as priests, monks, friars, together with adulterers and fornicators.' --- But all the insolence of the people was inconsiderable in comparison of that which was exercised by the clergy and the preachers, who took a pride in vilifying, even to her face, this amiable princess. --- The ringleader in all these insults on majesty was John Knox; who possessed an uncontrolled authority in the church, and even in the civil affairs of the nation, and who triumphed in the contumelious usage of his sovereign. His usual appellation for the queen was Jezabel; and though she endeavored, by the most gracious condescension, to win his favor, all her insinuations could gain nothing on his obdurate heart. Knox had written a book against the female accession to the crown: The title of it is, 'The first blast of the trumpet against the monstrous regiment of women.' There could be no greater contrast between the beliefs and habits of the clergy and popular following of Knox and the court of France. *The whole life of Mary was, from the demeanor of these men, filled with bitterness and sorrow.*[11]

Mary and Elizabeth

The queen of Scots, destitute of all force, possessing a narrow revenue, surrounded with a factious turbulent nobility, a bigoted people, and insolent ecclesiastics, soon found, that her only expedient for maintaining tranquility was to preserve a good correspondence with Elizabeth, who, by former connections and services, had acquired such authority over all these ranks of men. Soon after her arrival in Scotland, secretary Lidington was sent to London, in order to pay her compliments to the queen, and express her desire of friendship and a good correspondence; and he received a commission from her, as well as from the nobility of Scotland, to demand, as a means of cementing this friendship, that Mary should, by act of parliament or by proclamation, be declared successor to the crown. No request could be more unreasonable, or made at a more improper juncture. The queen replied

---

[11] Ibid, pp 40-41.

that Mary had once discovered her intention not to wait for the succession but had openly without ceremony or reserve, assumed the title of the queen of England, and had pretended a superior right to her throne and kingdom. Mary agreed, however, to the proposal that she would renounce present pretensions to the crown of England if Elizabeth would agree to declare her the successor. *But such was the jealous character of this latter princess that she never would consent to strengthen the interest and authority of any claimant, by fixing the succession; much less would she make this concession in favor of a rival queen.*[12]

Elizabeth canceled the meeting with Mary to discuss further the proposal and the two would never reach an agreement. The character of Elizabeth in rigidly refusing to consider a successor would apply not only to Mary but to attempts on the part of her counselors and parliament to propose the marriage of Elizabeth. Elizabeth was to avoid marriage, hence the appellation of *the virgin queen* affixed to her memory. Mary, with the death of her husband Frances II, and the rejection of her subjects in Scotland and her cousin the queen, would soon enter marital affairs which ultimately spelled disaster and dishonor, but which would produce Scotland's king James VI, who became England's next king as James I.

Henry Stuart, lord Darnley

After two years had been spent in evasions and artifices, in July 1564, *Mary's subjects and counselors, and probably herself, began to think it full time, that some marriage were concluded, and lord Darnley, Henry Stuart, son of the earl of Lenox, was the person, in whom most men's opinions and wishes centered.* He was Mary's first cousin, by the lady Margaret Douglas, niece to Henry VIII and who was, after her, the next heir to the crown of England. He was twenty years old and had been born and raised in England. Elizabeth, although not protesting initially, ordered that *Darnley return to England, threw the countess of Lenox and her second son into the tower, where they suffered a rigorous confinement; seized all Lenox's English estate; and though it was impossible for her to assign one single reason for her displeasure, she menaced, and protested, and complained, as if she had suffered the most grievous injury in the world. The politics of Elizabeth, though judicious, were usually full of duplicity and artifice; but never more so than in her transactions with the queen of Scots.*[13]

Mary married Darnley in 1565. *The marriage of the queen of Scots had kindled afresh the zeal of the reformers, because the family of Lenox was believed to adhere to the Catholic faith; and though Darnley,*

---

[12] Ibid, p 47.

[13] Ibid, 69-70.

who now bore the name of king Henry, went often to the established church, he could not by this exterior compliance, gain the confidence and regard of the ecclesiastics. They rather laid hold of the opportunity to insult him to his face; and Knox scrupled not to tell him from the pulpit, that God, for punishment of the offences and ingratitude of the people, was wont to commit the rule over them to boys and women. The populace of Edinburgh, instigated by such doctrines, began to meet and to associate themselves against the government. But what threatened more immediate danger to Mary's authority, were the discontents, which prevailed among some of the principal nobility. Despite the discontent of the earls and entering a confederacy for taking arms against their sovereign, queen Mary and Darnley advanced to Edinburgh at the head of their army. The rebels were obliged to retire into the south; and being pursued by a force, which now amounted to eighteen thousand men, they found themselves under a necessity of abandoning their country, and of taking shelter in England.

The marriage of the queen of Scots with lord Darnley was so natural, and so inviting in all its circumstances, that it had been precipitately agreed to by that princess and her council; and while she was allured by his youth, and beauty, and exterior accomplishments, she had at first overlooked the qualities of his mind, which nowise corresponded to the excellence of his outward figure. Violent, yet variable in his resolutions; insolent, yet credulous and easily governed by flatterers; he was destitute of all gratitude, because he thought no favors equal to his merit; and being addicted to low pleasures, he was equally incapable of all true sentiments of love and tenderness. The queen of Scots, in the first effusions of her fondness, had taken a pleasure in exalting him beyond measure. She had granted him the title of king; she had joined his name with her own in all public acts; she intended to have procured him from the parliament a matrimonial crown: But having leisure afterwards to remark his weakness and vices, she began to see the danger of her profuse liberality, and was resolved thenceforth to proceed with more reserve in the trust, which she should confer upon him. His resentment against this prudent conduct served but the more to increase her disgust; and the young prince, enraged at her imagined neglects, pointed his vengeance against every one whom he deemed the cause of this change in her measures and behavior.[14]

The murder of Mary's music teacher, David Rizzio, a Peiedmontiese, in central Italy, who became her confidant, was orchestrated and carried out by the earls, banished lords and even the father of her husband, who regarded Rizzio a threat to their interests, a papist and an enemy. A bizarre conspiracy was formed and the armed conspirators entered the dining room where Mary, Rizzio and others were

---

[14] Ibid, pp 75-76.

present. Mary was six months pregnant at the time. The conspirators tore Rizzio from Mary's protection and he was murdered in plain view of everyone. Rizzio was dispatched with some fifty-six stab wounds. *Mary was detained a prisoner in the palace; and the king dismissed all who seemed willing to attempt her rescue, by telling them, that nothing was done without his orders, and that he would be careful of the queen's safety.*[15] *The vengeance of the queen of Scots was implacable against her husband alone, whose person was before disagreeable to her, and who, by his violation of every tie of gratitude and duty, had now drawn on him her highest resentment. She engaged him to disown all connections with the assassins, to deny any concurrence in their crime, even to publish a proclamation containing a falsehood so notorious to the whole world; and having thus made him expose himself to universal contempt, and rendered it impractical for him ever to acquire the confidence of any party, she threw him off with disdain and indignation. --- He was permitted, however, to have apartments in the castle of Edinburgh, which Mary had chosen for the place of her delivery.*

Birth of James VI

Then she brought forth a son, on June 19, 1566, and as this was very important news to England, as well as to Scotland, she immediately dispatched Sir James Melvil to carry intelligence of the happy event to Elizabeth. Elizabeth was not pleased. She was able to elude, for the present, the applications of parliament. The friends of the queen of Scots multiplied every day in England. --- The most considerable men in England, except Cecil, seemed convinced of the necessity of declaring her the successor.[16]

A new confident of Mary, the earl of Bothwel, had of late acquired the favor and entire confidence of Mary; and all her measures were directed by his advice and authority. Reports were spread of more particular intimacies between them; and these reports gained ground from the continuance or rather increase of her hatred towards her husband. That young prince was reduced to such a state of desperation, by the neglects which he underwent from his queen and the courtiers, that he had once resolved to fly secretly into France or Spain, and had even provided a vessel for that purpose. Some of the most considerable nobility, on the other hand, observing her rooted aversion to him, had proposed some expedients for a divorce; and though Mary is said to have spoken honorably on the occasion, and to have embraced the proposal no farther than it should be found consistent with her own honor and her son's legitimacy.

---

[15] Ibid, pp 78-79.

[16] Ibid, pp 80-84.

Violent death of lord Darnley, the king

Meanwhile the king developed an illness and Mary came to his aid, *fitting up an apartment for him in a solitary house, at some distance from the palace, called the Kirk of Field. Mary here gave him marks of kindness and attachment; she conversed cordially with him; and she lay some nights in a room below his; but on the ninth of February, she told him, that she would pass that night in the palace, because the marriage of one of her servants was there to be celebrated in her presence. About two o'clock in the morning the whole town was much alarmed at hearing a great noise; and was still more astonished, when it was discovered that the noise came form the King's house, which was blown up by gunpowder; that his dead body was found at some distance in a neighboring field, and that no marks either of fire, contusion, or violence appeared upon it.*

No doubt could be entertained but Henry was murdered; and general conjecture soon pointed towards the earl of Bothwell as the author of the crime. But as his favor with Mary was visible, and his power great, no one ventured to declare openly his sentiments. And all men remained in silence and mute astonishment.[17]

The earl of Lenox submitted an accusation against Bothwell for the murder of his son, however, the trial court acquitted Bothwell because of the wrong date, February 9th instead of the 10th for the date of the murder, and the failure to present witnesses. Amazingly, the earl of Bothwell, apprehended the queen by his own forces on a road which she was traveling, and was accused of rape. *Some of the nobility, however, in order to put matters to further trial, sent her a private message, in which they told her that; if in reality, she lay under force, that they would use all their efforts to rescue her. Her answer, was, that she had indeed been carried to Dunbar by violence, but ever since her arrival had been so well treated, that she willingly remained with Bothwell.* In what was so far a bizarre sequence of events, it remained that Bothwell who was married, had to obtain a divorce before marriage to the queen. The divorce was presented before two different courts. The queen had to appear before the courts of judicature, to *acknowledge herself restored to entire freedom.* All this was taken care of. Craig, a minister of Edinburgh, married Bothwell, who now bore the title of the duke of Orkney, and the queen May 15, 1567, by Craig, a minister of Edinburgh.[18]

Many Scots were enraged about Mary's conduct. *Lord Hume was first in arms; and leading a body of eight hundred horse, suddenly*

---

[17] Ibid, pp 84-86.

[18] Ibid, pp 86-92.

*environed the queen of Scots and Bothwel, in the castle of Borthwic. ---
The armies met at Carberry Hill, about six miles from Edinburgh; and
Mary soon became sensible, that her own troops disapproved of her
cause, and were averse to spill their blood in the quarrel. --- She was
conducted to Edinburgh, amidst the insults of the populace; who
reproached her with her crimes, and even held before her eyes, which
way soever she turned, a banner, on which were painted the murder of
her husband, and the distress of her infant son. --- Meanwhile Bothwel,
fled unattended to Dunbar; and fitting out a few small ships, set sail for
the Orkneys, where he subsisted during some time by piracy. He was
pursued thither by Grange, and his ship was taken. Bothwel himself
escaped in a boat, and found means to get a passage to Denmark, where
he was thrown into prison, lost his senses, and died miserably about ten
years after.*[19]

Mary imprisoned and James VI, proclaimed king of Scotland

Mary became a prisoner. *The queen of Scots, seeing no
prospect of relief, lying justly under apprehensions for her life, and
believing, that no deed, which she executed during her captivity, could be
valid, was prevailed on, after a plentiful effusion of tears, to sign these
three instruments; and she took not the trouble of inspecting any one of
them. In consequence of this forced resignation, the young prince was
proclaimed king, by the name of James VI, on July 29, 1567.* He was
soon after crowned at Stirling. The earl of Murray became regent. *The
regent summoned a parliament, on December 15, which voted that Mary
was undoubtedly an accomplice in her husband's murder, condemned
her to imprisonment, ratified her demission of the crown, and
acknowledged her son for king, and Murray for regent.*

Mary had supporters who were Catholics and others who were
sympathetic. George Douglas, brother to the laird of Lochlevin was
successful in managing the escape of Mary. Mary was able to obtain
support of earls, bishops and nobles who gathered an army of six
thousand men assembled under her standard. The regent assembled
forces and a battle was fought at Langside near Glasgow, *was entirely
decisive in favor of the regent.* Mary fled southward and embraced a
resolution of taking shelter in England. *She embarked on board a fishing
boat in Galloway, and landed the same day at Wirkington in
Cumberland, about thirty miles from Carlisle, whence she immediately
dispatched a messenger to London; notifying her arrival, desiring leave
to visit Elizabeth, and craving her protection.*[20]

---

[19] Ibid, pp 94-96.

[20] Ibid, pp 96-102.

Trial of Mary, queen of Scots

Elizabeth pretended to come to the aid of Mary, but William Cecil presented arguments and warned of the danger of Mary and associates. This led to her imprisonment and trial by an English *board of commissioners* who were to hear evidence and decide her guilt or innocence. Elizabeth refused to have any contact with Mary until this issue was decided and affected an impartial position as to her guilt or innocence. Elizabeth summoned Murray and others to bring evidence to the trial. Since Carlisle was close to the border of Scotland, Mary was moved to a more secure place, at Bolton, in Yorkshire and continued in Hampton court.

Although Mary presented arguments, which were compelling in her favor, the evidence, which was presented by Murray, was devastating and remained unchallenged. *Murray, thus urged, made no difficulty in producing the proofs of his charge against the queen of Scots; and among the rest, some love-letters and sonnets of hers to Bothwell, written all in her own hand, and two other papers, one written in her own hand, another subscribed by her, and written by the earl of Huntley; each of which contained a promise of marriage with Bothwel, made before the pretended trial and acquittal of that nobleman.*

All these important papers had been kept by Bothwel in a silver box or casket, which had been given him by Mary, and which had belonged to her first husband, Francis; and though the princess had enjoined him to burn the letters as soon as he had read them, he had thought proper carefully to preserve them, as pledges of her fidelity, and had committed them to the custody of Sir James Balfour, deputy-governor of the castle of Edinburgh. --- They contained incontestable proofs of Mary's criminal correspondence with Bothwel, of her consent to the king's murder, and of her concurrence in the violence, which Bothwel pretended to commit upon her. Murray fortified this evidence by some testimonies of correspondent fact; and he added, some time after, the dying confession of one Hubert, a servant of Bothwel's who had been executed for the king's murder, and who directly charged the queen with her being accessory to that criminal enterprise.[21]

Mary's commissioners finally broke off the conferences, and never would make any reply. These papers, at least translation of them, have since been published. The objections, made to their authenticity, are in general of small force: But were they ever so specious, they cannot now be hearkened to; since Mary, at the time when the truth could have been fully cleared, did, in effect, ratify the evidence against her, by recoiling from the inquiry at the very critical moment, and refusing to give an answer to the accusation of her enemies.

---

[21] Ibid, p 113.

Orders were given for removing the queen of Scots from Bolton, a place surrounded by Catholics, to Tutbury in the county of Stafford; where she was put under the custody of the earl of Shrewsbury. --- Mary still insisted upon this alternative; either that Elizabeth should assist her in recovering her authority, or give her liberty to retire into France, and make trial of the friendship of other princes: And as she asserted, that she had come voluntarily into England, invited by many former professions of amity, she thought, that one or other of these requests could not, without the most extreme injustice, be refused her. But Elizabeth, sensible of the danger, which attended both these proposals, was secretly resolved to detain her still a captive; and as her retreat into England had been little voluntary, her claim upon the queen's generosity appeared much less urgent than she was willing to pretend.[22]

The duke of Norfolk and insurrections

In 1569 Mary had several important friends in England including the earls of Northumberland, Westmoreland and the only duke left in the kingdom— the duke of Norfolk. *The duke of Norfolk was the only peer, that enjoyed the highest title of nobility; and as there were at present no princes of the blood, the splendor of his family, the opulence of his fortune, and the extent of his influence, had rendered him without comparison the first subject in England. The qualities of his mind corresponded to his high station; Beneficent, affable, generous, he had acquired the affections of the people; prudent, moderated, obsequious, he possessed, without giving her any jealousy, the good graces of his sovereign. His grandfather and father had long been regarded as the leaders of the Catholics; and this hereditary attachment, joined to the alliance of blood, had procured him the friendship of the most considerable men of that party. --- Norfolk was at this time a widower; and being of a suitable age, his marriage with the queen of Scots had appeared so natural, that it had occurred to several of his friends and those of that princess.* The earl of Murray was involved with the making the proposal of the duke's marriage as well as the marriage of the duke's daughter to James VI. The result of these proposals was that the duke was committed to the tower upon the urging of Cecil. An insurrection followed under the leadership of the earls of Northumberland and Westmoreland. *They determined to begin the insurrection without delay; and the great credit of these two noblemen, with that zeal for the Catholic religion, which still prevailed in the north of England, soon drew together multitudes of the common people. They published a manifesto, in which they declared, that they intended to attempt nothing against the queen, to whom they vowed unshaken allegiance; and that their sole aim was to re-establish the religion of their ancestors, to*

---

[22] Ibid, pp 116-117.

remove evil counselors, and to restore the duke of Norfolk and other faithful peers to their liberty and to the queens' favor. The numbers of the malcontents amounted to four thousand foot and sixteen hundred horse; and they expected the concurrence of all the Catholics in England.[23]

The queen was not negligent in her own defense, and she had beforehand, from her prudent and wise conduct, acquired the general good will of her people, the best security of a sovereign. --- Sussex attended by the earls of Rutland, the lords Hunsdon, Evers, and Willoughby of Parham, marched against the rebels at the head of seven thousand men, and found them already advanced to the bishopric of Durham, of which they had taken possession. They retired before him to Hexham; and hearing that the earl of Warwick and lord Clinton were advancing against them with a greater body, they found no other resource than to disperse themselves without striking a blow. The common people retired to their houses: The leaders fled into Scotland. Northumberland was found skulking in that country, and was confined by Murray in the castle of Lochlevin. Westmoreland received shelter from the chieftains of the Kers and Scots, partisans of Mary; and persuaded them to make an inroad into England, with a view of exciting a quarrel between the two kingdoms. After they had committed great ravages, they retreated to their own country. This sudden and precipitate rebellion was followed soon after by another still more imprudent, raised by Leonard Dacres. Lord Hunsdon, at the head of the garrison of Berwic, was able without any other assistance, to quell these rebels. Great severity was exercised against such as had taken part in these rash enterprises. Sixty-six constables were hanged; and no less than eight hundred persons are said, on the whole, to have suffered by the hands of the executioner.[24]

The real heartbreak of the tragic borderland conflict was that it was endless. There were occasional military victories. Hunsdon engaged and defeated a large rebel force in February, and some five hundred of the rebels were killed or taken prisoner. But the battle was not decisive. The crosscurrents of Catholic against Protestant, English against Scot were too inveterate to be eradicated. The border folk, hating and hated, seemed forever poised to continue the ancient bloodbath, and the continual shifts and changes in politics on both sides of the border continued to guarantee them cause.

Elizabeth's reaction to her cousin Hunsdon's brief triumph was a trumpet-call of rejoicing. 'I doubt very much, my Harry, whether that the victory were given me more joyed me, or that you were by God appointed the instrument of my glory,' she said in a handwritten note appended to a formal letter of congratulations. 'I assure you that for my

---

[23] Ibid, pp 124-130. Note. Norfolk and the earl of Oxford were close friends.

[24] Ibid, pp 130-131.

country's good the first might suffice, but for my heart's contention the second more pleased me.' [25]

The queen released Norfolk from the tower with the promise of Norfolk that he would have no further contact with Mary. Norfolk reneged on his promise and in 1571 another conspiracy developed against the queen involving the Florentine Ridolfi together with Norfolk. The conspiracy failed, due to lack of support from Rome and Madrid. Norfolk was executed June 2, 1572. The earl of Northumberland was executed a few months later. It was about this time that another blood bath in England, based on religious differences, would this time involve further execution of Catholics. In 1570, Pope Pius V excommunicated Elizabeth and absolved her subjects from any oath of allegiance to her. In 1572 there was in France a massacre of Protestants on St. Bartholemew's Day. Fear was raised concerning the proselytizing efforts of English Jesuits returning from the mainland to England.

William Cecil, later lord Burghley

William Cecil promulgated the dangers in England of a Catholic takeover. As secretary of state and Elizabeth's chief adviser during her entire reign, in his last years as lord treasurer and chief advisor, some attention should be directed to his character and influence. Whether the reign of Elizabeth was more the result of Cecil's decisions than Elizabeth's is a question, which may be difficult to answer.

William Cecil, later lord Burghley, (b. 1520, d 1598) was educated by the best scholars of the day at Cambridge. He became secretary of state in 1550 under Edward VI, but as a protestant retreated into conformity with Catholic observances under Mary I's reign. With the accession of Elizabeth he became secretary of state.

Cecil exerted great influence in the court from the earliest years of Elizabeth's reign. *There were eighteen counselors at first; later the number was reduced to twelve. At their head was William Cecil, Elizabeth's former steward who had long since won her complete trust and reliance. --- Cecil alone combined extraordinary intelligence and ability with what Noailles called 'a sensitive understanding of his mistress.' For four decades he was to serve that mistress, and her kingdom with an indefatigable competence. Energetic man in his late thirties, Cecil seemed to take every facet of government as his personal responsibility. As royal secretary he was expected to command detailed knowledge of a wide variety of topics, from foreign and military affairs and secret intelligence to the activities of the church, royal household and local government. But this was only a beginning. Cecil desired to know, and to a remarkable extent managed to know everything of*

---

[25] Erickson, pp 250-251.

consequence that happened to anyone of importance throughout the length and breadth of England.

And he displayed that knowledge in the innumerable papers and letters and memoranda he produced— scores of thousands of documents testifying, in their bulk alone, to his tireless labors. Cecil combined the detailed conscientiousness of a meticulous clerk with the comprehensive grasp of a 'prying steward' - as one nineteenth century historian called him - overseeing the estate of England. Yet he was much more than this. He had impressive personal breadth, humanist learning, and much experience of government gained in the two previous reigns.[26] The actions of Cecil, however, must be carefully documented and assessed.

Edward de Vere, Seventeenth earl of Oxford

The most enduring contribution of Elizabeth's reign, however, may have been the seventeenth earl of Oxford, Edward de Vere, (b 1550, d 1604), who wrote under the pen name of William Shakespeare.[27] Lord Burghley was Oxford's nemesis throughout his lifetime and no doubt led to his obscurity and misjudgment in history. The conflicts, depredations and misfortunes under the power of lord Burghley, the most powerful man in the kingdom for nearly a half-century, were likely motivating factors in Oxford's great literary and dramatic productions. The Shakespeare cannon has been regarded as the most influential work of this millennium. That Oxford was the author of these works has been well documented as noted in the references to follow. Oxford *played an important role throughout queen Elizabeth's reign. From 1570 to 1580 he was perhaps second only the earl of Leicester as the chief favorite of the queen. During the same period his reputation as a man of letters was second to none.*[28] He would continue with relationships with queen Elizabeth and lord Burghley until Burghley's death in 1598 and Elizabeth's death in 1603. Elizabeth was Oxford's protector and supporter. Without her he could not have survived or written the marvelous Shakespeare cannon and other works not yet attributed to him.

The earls of Oxford go back to a time before William I. We have noted in previous chapters from Richard II to Edward IV and Richard III, their importance in the York-Lancastrian conflicts and wars. Oxford was born and spent the first years of his life at Hedingham castle. *In 1562, his father died, and Edward became the seventeenth Earl of*

---

[26] Erickson, p171.

[27] Note. See B.M. Ward, *The Seventeenth earl of Oxford* and Paul Altrocchi, *Most Greatly Lived,* A Biographical Novel of Edward de Vere, Seventeenth earl of Oxford, whose pen name was William Shakespeare.

[28] Ward, The Seventeenth Earl of Oxford, p viii.

Oxford at the age of twelve. He rode from his father's funeral to London 'with seven score horse all in black,' a fair indication of his family's wealth at the time he inherited it. At his father's death, young Oxford was sent to London to live as a royal ward under the supervision of Sir William Cecil, who was later made Lord Burghley. *This proved to be a fateful moment in his life; the strong-willed Oxford's relations with the mighty Burghley were complex, and often strained, almost until Burghley's death in 1598.*[29]

The reader may find details of Oxford's education, his remarkable abilities and wide interests ranging from music to tilting, as well as his wide literary pursuits in the references cited.[30] In 1571 Oxford married Anne Cecil, and became son-in- law to Burghley. *The wedding, held in December, was a huge social event, with the queen, the French ambassador, and other dignitaries attending. But though Oxford had been caught, he had by no means been tamed, as poor Anne was to learn.* In that year he assumed his seat in the house of lords. But in the same year he was suspected of plotting to rescue his relative, the duke of Norfolk, who was under arrest and sentence of death. *Cecil himself had prosecuted him for treason in the Ridofi plot, and Oxford and his father-in-law quarreled hotly, not for the last time.*

By his young manhood Oxford was a favorite of the queen, who nicknamed him 'my Turk'. One contemporary, Gilbert Talbot, wrote privately of him: 'My Lord of Oxford is lately grown into great credit; for the queen's majesty delighteth more in his personage, and his dancing and valiantness, than any other. --- Burghley's wife was alarmed for her daughter's sake at the warmth of the forty-year-old Elizabeth's favor for her son-in-law; Burghley himself tactfully ignored such things. --- Court gossip had it that Elizabeth and Oxford were lovers.[31]

In 1574 Oxford was again linked to a scheme to rescue Norfolk. Oxford fled to Brussels. The queen dispatched an agent to secure his return. *In 1575 Oxford, this time with Elizabeth's permission, set out on a long tour of Europe.* He was known to visit Paris, Strasbourg, Padua, Venice, Palermo, Florence and Sicily and returned by Lyons and Paris. Unfortunately, while *Oxford was in Europe he received word of the birth of a daughter and that the child may not be his. Burghley had helped spread the rumor.*

---

[29] Sobran, *Alias Shakespeare*, p 110.

[30] Looney, *Shakespeare Identified*; Ogburn, *The Mysterious William Shakespeare*; Whalen, *Shakespeare: Who Was He?*; Sobran, *Alias Shakespeare*; Ward, *The Seventeenth Earl of Oxford*; Altrocchi, *Most Greatly Lived.*

[31] Sobran, p 117.

In 1576 Oxford was embroiled in bitter accusations and controversies. Oxford, a Protestant, was accused of Catholic leanings. *At the same time, Oxford faced another personal crisis— brought on, like most of his crises, by himself. He was having an affair with one of Elizabeth's ladies in waiting, Ann Vavasor.* --- *In March 1581, Ann Vavasor gave birth to a son by him. The queen, who took lax morals among her courtiers as an affront to her majesty, was furious; she sent father, mother, and infant to the Tower of London. Oxford was released after a few weeks but remained under house arrest for months.*[32] In December that year, Oxford was reconciled to his wife. *From this point on, their marriage seems to have been peaceful at least; they had three more daughters (and an infant son who died) before Anne's death in 1588.*

There is abundant evidence for Oxford's literary accomplishments beginning with poetry in his youth. There were a number of books dedicated to him in his early twenties. *More than ever, Oxford in the 1580's was devoting his time to literature, and especially to the theater.* Several more books were dedicated to him during this period. *Oxford took over the Earl of Warwick's acting company; he soon added another company of boy actors, which performed at court for Elizabeth on one occasion.* --- *In 1584, Oxford acquired a sublease of the Blackfriars Theater, which he transferred to Lyly. He had his own company of actors at this time.*

In 1586, the queen granted Oxford a huge annual pension of 1,000 pounds. Burghley himself, with a household of eighty, received only twice that amount per year. --- *Oxford, now sad and subdued, was back in the queen's good graces in spite of everything.* --- *As England's foremost earl by birth, Oxford that year sat on the tribunal that convicted Mary, queen of Scots, of treason, a verdict that ensured her beheading. But he held no appointive office, despite his many attempts to get one. He angrily blamed Burghley for his inability to gain 'preferment'. Burghley denied the charge, saying he simply lacked the power to secure a position for Oxford; in fact Oxford had so many enemies at court that he was unable to get more than a few votes in the annual election to the Order of the Garter.* --- *Though he retained his hereditary status, he was never again able to gain advancement or exert much influence at court.* --- *During these years, Oxford suffered personal losses. Two of his children died, one an infant son who would have become the eighteenth earl of his line, the other a young daughter named Frances. Ann herself died in June 1588, a few months after giving birth to another daughter, Susan. Burghley took charge of raising the three surviving daughters.* --- *Burghley cared nothing for the theater and regarded Oxford's association with theater folk as mere slumming, disgraceful to a*

---

[32] Ibid, pp 120 and 124-126.

gentleman, let alone a great lord.[33] From 1589 onwards the life of lord Oxford becomes one of mystery. --- Poetry, the drama, and music had ever been his chief interests, and we may be sure that in them we shall find the key to his life and retirement from 1589 to 1604.[34]

There can be no doubt that Oxford had not only demonstrated exceptional talents and abilities in a wide range of activities over his lifetime, had access to the best literature and education, a unique experience with the Elizabethan court as a personal friend of Elizabeth and son-in- law of her chief long standing advisor and secretary of State Burghley, but had contacts and experience with the royal courts of Europe, and wide travel and experience with ability to converse with several languages. Who else could have command of the intricate details of the courts of the York Lancastrian families as found in Richard II, Henry IV, V, VI and Richard III other than Oxford. There is an abundant literature correlating the experiences of Oxford with the contents of the Shakespeare works.

The motivation for these creative gifts began with a man of the first standing in the social fabric of England, to a personal life of tragedy in his last twenty years, giving him thus sufficient time and opportunity to complete what were probably life long reflections and writings. In 1591, Oxford made Hedingham over to Burghley in trust for his daughters; meanwhile, he was receiving his huge annuity from the queen. At about the same time, he married Elizabeth Trentham, a maid of honor at Elizabeth's court and daughter of a wealthy knight; --- In 1593, they had a son, Henry, who inherited Oxford's title but died childless in 1625 bringing to an end the Oxford line.

In 1601, once more in his capacity as England's senior earl, Oxford was in effect foreman of the jury of twenty-five noblemen who tried the earls of Essex and Southampton for high treason after their fizzled uprising against Elizabeth. --- Oxford blamed his former friend Sir Walter Raleigh for Essex's fall. Oxford grieved for the loss of Elizabeth in 1603. The new king James I favored Oxford after his accession in 1603. Oxford died June 24, 1604. The note of record simply states, Plague.

Fear of a Catholic conspiracy

During this time period, in the 1580's, Elizabeth's court was preoccupied with the dangers of a Catholic take over of the throne. The focus centered about Mary, queen of Scots who had been under the custody of the queen since she arrived in England in 1568. *Elizabeth had reduced her to a worse captivity than that from which she had escaped*

---

[33] Ibid, pp 131-132.

[34] Ward, The Seventeenth Earl of Oxford, pp 299, and 320.

(in Scotland, 1568), --- *she found the rigors of confinement daily multiplied upon her; and at length carried to such a height that it surpassed the bounds of all human patience any longer to endure them: That she was cut off from all communication, not only with the rest of mankind, but with her only son; and her maternal fondness, which was now more enlivened by their unhappy sympathy in situation and was her sole remaining attachment to this world, deprived even of that melancholy solace, which letters or messages could give.*

The anxiety of the queen, from the attempts of the English Catholics, never ceased during the whole course of her reign. --- A conspiracy of the nobility was formed, probably with the concurrence of Elizabeth, for seizing the person of James at Ruthven, a seat of the earl of Gowry's; and the design, being kept secret, succeeded without any opposition. --- No sooner was this revolution known in England, than the queen sent Sir Henry Cary and Sir Robert Bowes to James, in order to congratulate him on his deliverance from the pernicious counsels of Lenox and Arran; to exhort him not to resent the seeming violence committed on him by the confederated lords. --- The queen of Scots had often made overtures to Elizabeth, which had been entirely neglected; but hearing of James's detention, she wrote a letter in a more pathetic and more spirited strain than usual; craving the assistance of that princess, both for her own and her son's liberty.[35]

The affairs of Scotland remained not long in the present situation. James, impatient of restraint, made his escape from his keepers; and flying to St. Andrew's, summoned his friends and partisans to attend him. --- The king of Scots, persevering in his present views, summoned a parliament; where it was enacted, that no clergyman should presume, in his sermons, to utter false, untrue, or scandalous speeches against the king, the council, or the public measures, or to meddle, in an improper manner, with the affairs of his majesty and the states. The clergy, finding that the pulpit would be no longer a sanctuary for them, were extremely offended.[36]

These revolutions in Scotland would have been regarded as of small importance to the repose and security of Elizabeth, had her own subjects been entirely united,[37] *and had not the zeal of the Catholics, excited by constraint more properly than persecution, daily threatened her with some dangerous insurrections. The vigilance of the ministers, particulary of Burghley and Walsingham, was raised in proportion to the activity of the malcontents; and many arts, which had been blameable in*

---

[35] Hume, vol 4, pp 196-199.

[36] Ibid, pp 201-202.

[37] Note. How can all people in a country have the same religious beliefs?

a more peaceful government, were employed, in detecting conspiracies, and even discovering the secret inclinations of men. Counterfeit letters were written in the name of the queen of Scots, or of the English exiles, and privately conveyed to the houses of the Catholics: Spies were hired to observe the actions and discourse of suspected persons: Informers were countenanced: and though the sagacity of these two great ministers helped them to distinguish the true from the false intelligence, many calumnies were, no doubt, hearkened to, and all the subjects, particulary the Catholics, kept in the utmost anxiety and inquietude. --- Many of these conspiracies were, with great appearance of reason, imputed to the intrigues of the queen of Scots. She was committed to the custody of Sir Amias Paulet and Sir Drue Drury, men of honor, but inflexible in their care and attentions.

Elizabeth, that she might the more discourage malcontents, by showing them the concurrence of the nation in her favor, summoned a new parliament; November 23, 1584; and she met with that dutiful attachment, which she expected. The association was confirmed by parliament; and a clause was added, by which the queen was empowered to name commissioners of the trial of any pretender the crown, who should attempt or imagine any invasion, insurrection, or assassination against her.

Execution of Catholics

A severe law was also enacted against Jesuits and popish priests: It was ordained, that they should depart the kingdom within forty days; that those who should remain beyond that time, or should afterwards return, should be guilty of treason; that those who harbored or relieved them should be guilty of felony; that those who were educated in seminaries, if they returned not in six months after notice given, and submitted not themselves to the queen, before a bishop or two justices, should be guilty of treason; and that if any, so submitting themselves, should within ten years, approach the court, or come within ten miles of it, their submission should be void. By this law, the exercise of the Catholic religion, which had formerly been prohibited under lighter penalties, was totally suppressed. Between 1577 and 1603 some 200 priests and Catholic laymen were executed.[38]

Laws against Protestants other than members of the Church of England

The queen also tried to suppress the puritans in England and members of other churches other than the Church of England of which she was the spiritual head. Parliament, the commons, in 1584, had set up a court of ecclesiastical commission and the *oath ex officio*, exacted by

---

[38] Ibid, pp 204-205, and Morgan, p 276.

that court. *The commissioners were empowered to visit and reform all errors, heresies, schisms, in a word to regulate all opinions as well as to punish all breaches of uniformity in the exercise of public worship. They were directed to make inquiry not only by the legal methods of juries and witnesses, but by all other means and ways, which they could devise; that is, by the rack, by torture, by inquisition, by imprisonment. Where they found reason to suspect any person, they might administer to him an oath, called 'ex Officio', by which he was bound to answer all questions., and might thereby be obliged to accuse himself or his most intimate friend.*[39]

Conviction of Mary queen of Scots

In September 1586, Mary queen of Scots would be tried by this same commission enacted by parliament November 1584. *Though all England was acquainted with the detection of Babingtons' conspiracy, every avenue to the queen of Scots had been so strictly guarded, that she remained in utter ignorance of the matter; and it was a great surprise to her, when Sir Thomas Gorges, by Elizabeth's orders, informed her, that all her accomplices were discovered and arrested. --- It was resolved to try Mary, not by the common statute of treason, but by the act, which had passed the former year, with a view to this very event; and the queen, in terms of that act, appointed a commission, consisting of forty noblemen and . privy-counselors, and empowered them to examine and pass sentence on Mary.* Hume reviewed the evidence and provided the following summary remarks: *But on the present trial, where the absolute power of the prosecutor concurred with such important interests and such a violent inclination to have the princess condemned; the testimony of two witnesses, even though men of character, ought to be supported by strong probabilities, in order to remove all suspicion of tyranny and injustice. ---*

The only part of the charge, which Mary positively denied, was her concurrence in the design of assassinating Elizabeth. This article indeed was the most heavy, and the only one, that could fully justify the queen in proceeding to extremities against her. In order to prove the accusation, there were produced the following evidence: Copies taken in secretary Walsingham's office of the intercepted letters between her and Babington, in which her approbation of the murder was clearly expressed; the evidence of her two secretaries, Nau and Cuirle, who had confessed, without being put to any torture, both that she received these letters from Babington, and that they had written the answers, by her order; the confession of Babington, that he had written the letters and received the answers, and the confession of Ballard and Savage, that

---

[39] Hume, vol 4, p 208.

Babington had showed them these letters of Mary written in the cipher, which had been settled between them.

It is evident, that this complication of evidence, though every circumstance corroborates the general conclusion, resolves itself finally into the testimony of the two secretaries, who alone were certainly acquainted with their mistress's concurrence in Babington's conspiracy, but who knew themselves exposed to all the rigors of imprisonment, torture, and death, if they refused to give any evidence, which might be required of them.

Having finished the trial; the commissioners adjourned from Fotheringay-castle, and met in the Star Chamber at London; where, after taking the oaths of Mary's two secretaries, who, voluntarily, without hope or reward, vouched the authenticity of those letters before produced, they pronounced sentence of death upon the queen of Scots, and confirmed it by their seals and subscriptions. Both houses of parliament unanimously ratified the sentence against Mary.[40]

Execution

Mary queen of Scots was executed February 7, 1587. Hume provided this story of her execution: *She now began, with the aid of her two women, to disrobe herself; and the executioner also lent his hand, to assist them. She smiled, and said, 'that she was not accustomed to undress herself before so large a company, nor to be served by such valets.' Her servants, seeing her in this condition, ready to lay her head upon the block, burst into tears and lamentations: She turned about to them; put her finger upon her lips, as a sign of imposing silence upon them; and having given them her blessing, desired them to pray for her. One of her maids, whom she had appointed for that purpose, covered her eyes with a handkerchief; she laid herself down, without any sign of fear or trepidation; and her head was severed from her body at two strokes by the executioner. He instantly held it up to the spectators, streaming with blood and agitated with the convulsions of death: The dean of Peterborow alone exclaimed. 'So perish all queen Elizabeth's enemies:' The earl of Kent alone replied 'Amen:' The attention of all the other spectators was fixed on the melancholy scene before them; and zeal and flattery alike gave place to present pity and admiration of the expiring princess.*[41]

Sir Francis Drake

In the late 1570's and 1580's England competed with Spain in the exploration and acquisition of territories and riches from distant

---

[40] Ibid, pp 232-237.

[41] Ibid, pp 250-251.

shores. Spain even attempted a conquest of England with their invincible armada in 1588.

Sir Francis Drake, (b, 1545? d 1596), sprung from mean parents in the county of Devon, having acquired considerable riches by depredations made in the isthmus of Panama, and having there gotten a sight of the Pacific ocean, was so stimulated by ambition and avarice, that he scrupled not to employ his whole fortune in a new adventure through those seas, so much unknown at that time to all the European nations. By means of Sir Chrisotpher Hatton, then vice-chamberlain, a great favorite of the queen's, he obtained her consent and approbation; and he set sail from Plymouth in 1577, with four ships and a pinnace, on board of which were 164 able sailors. He passed into the South Sea by the Straits of Magellan and attacking the Spaniards, who expected no enemy in those quarters, he took many rich prizes, and prepared to return with the booty, which he had acquired. Apprehensive of being intercepted by the enemy, if he took the same way homeward, by which he had reached the Pacific ocean, he attempted to find a passage by the north of California; and failing in that enterprise, he set sail for the East Indies, and returned safely this year by the Cape of Good Hope. He was the first Englishman who sailed round the Globe; and the first commander in Chief. He was knighted by Elizabeth.

In January 1586, Sir Francis Drake was admiral of *a fleet of twenty sailing ships equipped to attack the Spanish in the West-Indies. They sailed to Hispaniola; and easily making themselves master of St. Domingo by assault, obliged the inhabitants to ransom their houses by a sum of money. Carthagena fell next into their hands after some more resistance and was treated in the same manner. They burned St. Anthony and St. Helens, two towns on the coast of Florida. Sailing along the coast of Virginia, they found the small remains of a colony which had been planted there by Sir Walter Raleigh, and which had gone extremely to decay. --- He returned with so much riches as encouraged the volunteers, and with such accounts of the Spanish weakness in those countries as served extremely to inflame the spirits of the nation to future enterprises.*

Defeat of the Spanish Armada

The defeat of the Spanish armada in July 1588, was one of the most famous accomplishments in the reign of Elizabeth. The queen's vessels under the command of lord Howard of Effingham and vice-admiral Sir Francis Drake managed with smaller ships to set fire and cause confusion in the Spanish fleet. Use of long-range cannon holed the Spanish ships, and the Spanish vessels cut lines to anchors and fled. *The Spanish admiral found, in many encounters, that while he lost so considerable a part of his own navy, he had destroyed only one small vessel of the English; and he foresaw, that by continuing so unequal a combat, he must draw inevitable destruction on all the remainder. He prepared therefore to return homewards; but as the wind was contrary to this passage through the channel, he resolved to sail northwards, and making the tour of the island reach the Spanish harbors by the ocean. The English fleet followed him during some time. --- A violent tempest overtook the Armada after it passed the Orkneys: The ships had already lost their anchors, and were obliged to keep to sea: The mariners, unaccustomed to such hardships, and not able to govern such unwieldily vessels, yielded to the fury of the storm, and allowed their ships to drive either on the western isles of Scotland, or on the coast of Ireland, where they were miserably wrecked. Not a half of the navy returned to Spain; and the seamen, as well as soldiers, who remained were so overcome with hardships and fatigue, and so dispirited by their discomfiture, that they filled all Spain with accounts of the desperate valor of the English and of the tempestuous violence of that ocean which surrounds.[42]*

This victory gained the queen almost double the subsidy from parliament. But the queen would enter a state of severe melancholy, which may have been related to the execution of Mary queen of Scots, and over the behavior and final disposition of Essex who replaced her longstanding friend Leicester. If the life and character of Elizabeth remains inscrutable perhaps an understanding of her friends may aid in understanding this complex woman.

The earl of Leicester

Robert Dudley, earl of Leicester (b 1532, d 1588), was the son of the duke of Northumberland. He had attempted to put Lady Gray on the throne after the death of Edward VI and before Mary I's accession. He became a favorite of Elizabeth after her accession and was granted positions in her court. *The earl of Leicester, the great and powerful favorite of Elizabeth, possessed all those exterior qualities, which are naturally alluring to the fair sex; a handsome person, a polite address, an insinuating behavior; and by means of these accomplishments, he had been able to blind even the penetration of Elizabeth, and conceal from her the great defects, or rather odious vices, which attended his character. He was proud, insolent, interested, ambitious; without honor, without generosity, without humanity; and atoned not for these bad qualities, by such abilities or courage, as could fit him for that high trust and confidence, with which she always honored him.[43]* It was rumored that there was at least a romantic attachment between the queen and Robert Dudley. In 1560, Dudley's wife died in a suspicious fall and Leicester was thought to have murdered her in order to make way for his marriage of Elizabeth. Elizabeth rejected Dudley's proposals and with duplicity supported a dubious marriage of Dudley to Mary queen of

---

[42] Ibid, pp 270-271.

[43] Hume vol 4, p 67.

Scots, which never came about. The queen made Robert Dudley earl of Leicester. He was in good graces with the queen at least until 1581 when she was informed by an agent of the duke of Anjou, of Leicester's marriage to Lettice Knollys, widow of Walter Devereux, conducted in secret in 1578. Leicester was sent to the tower. Leicester, Hatton, and Walsingham opposed a treaty between France and England with marriage of the duke of Anjou and Elizabeth. The queen was forty-nine years old at the time. *These reflections kept the queen in great anxiety and irresolution; and she was observed to pass several nights without any sleep or repose. At last her settled habits of prudence and ambition prevailed over her temporary inclinations; and having sent for the duke of Anjou, she had a long conference with him in private, where she was supposed to have made him apologies for breaking her former engagements. He expressed great disgust on his leaving her; threw away the ring which she had given him; and uttered many curses on the mutability of women and of islanders.*[44]

Leicester failed, in 1587, to relieve the town of Sluys taken by Parma in the Netherlands. *Leicester ascribed his bad success, to the ill behavior of the Hollanders, they were equally free in reflections upon his conduct. The breach between them became wider every day: They slighted his authority, opposed his measures, and neglected his counsels; while he endeavored, by an imperious behavior, and by violence, to recover that influence which he had lost. --- But the queen, who knew the importance of her alliance with the States during the present conjuncture, was resolved to give them entire satisfaction by recalling Leicester, and commanding him to resign his government.* Leicester died in his home in 1588, cause of death unknown.

The earl of Essex

Elizabeth, in 1591, agreed in an alliance with France to send three thousand men to assist the French king who led his forces into Normandy against the Spanish. *The earl of Essex was appointed general of these forces; a young nobleman, who, by may exterior accomplishments, and still more real merit, was daily advancing in favor with Elizabeth, and seemed to occupy that place in her affections, which Leicester, now deceased, had so long enjoyed.* [45]

Robert Devereau, 2nd earl of Essex, (b 1567, d 1601) *was a cousin of Elizabeth on his mother's side. After the death of his penniless debt-ridden father, Lettice Knolly's first husband Walter Devereux, nine-year-old Essex had been brought up in Cecil's household, along with the hunchbacked boy Robert (Cecil). By age seventeen he was being*

---

[44] Hume, vol 4, pp 189-195.

[45] Ibid, pp 281-282.

advanced at court by his stepfather Leicester, and brought attention to himself by insulting Raleigh. --- He fought in the Netherlands, and later in France with considerable distinction, acquiring a reputation not only for brave and audacious soldiery but for old-fashioned chivalry as well. Duels and challenges to single combat suited his temperament perfectly, while drawing attention to his fighting ability and making him popular. But he did not entirely neglect civil for military affairs, and managed to convince Elizabeth of his statesmanship so that she appointed him a member of the council in 1593.

The queen found Essex as exasperating and delightful as a man as he had been as a boy. She called him her 'Wild Horse', and felt toward him not only a strong tie of blood - they were cousins, as Elizabeth and Lettice were - but an even stronger one of sentiment. Essex was, after all, the stepson of her lifelong love, and even before Leicester's death she was installing Essex in his court apartments. --- He was an intelligent, exuberant, extremely handsome man, good company and a brilliant escort for her, and he knew how to please and flatter her. He sat up late partnering her at cards, he sat at her side for the first performance of 'A Comedy of Errors'; he wore her favor in the tiltyard and organized athletic entertainments for her pleasure. She was in her sixties, he in his thirties, yet there was nothing grand motherly in her affection for him.

'The court is ordinarily full of discontent and factions,' De Maisse commented in his written observations (journal), 'and the queen is well pleased to maintain it so.' In 1597 the factions were very clearly defined; the Cecils, with Admiral Howard, were on one side, opposing Essex. Some of the younger men in government and the young military men favored Essex with his swashbuckling style and who had come to maturity during a decade and more of war. Between the elder Cecil and Essex there was respect and a kind of courtly mutuality, but greed corroded their relations; Essex was waiting impatiently for Cecil to die so that he could take over the latter's lucrative post as keeper of the wardrobe.

It was no wonder that the frowning queen stamped her feet in rage and lay about her with her rusty sword, for she was closing out her reign as she had begun it, in imminent peril from enemies at home and abroad. France had, as she feared, made peace with Spain in 1598, leaving England completely isolated. Under Essex's supervision, the country was being organized for semi-permanent war, with the county levies brought under the coordinated direction of military superintendents, and with new military districts designated. There was talk of compulsory military training for all men aged eighteen to fifty, and there was talk, too, of how much better off the country would be with a bold, vigorous young man to rule it.

The fall of Essex

It was undoubtedly best for all concerned that Essex was allowed early in 1599 to leave court to take on the most galling of England's immediate troubles; the rebellion in Ireland. In the latest and most grave of a series of rebellions Hugh O'Neill, earl of Tyrone, had with Spanish aid so weakened England's hold on Ireland that the situation called for an urgent and heavy counter stroke. --- Essex set out in the spring of 1599 with an army of reconquest seventeen thousand strong, yet his chance for glory was blighted by the impossible conditions he found once he arrived, as well as by his own mercurial moods and wayward judgment. Six months after he left England he was on his way back, his army reduced to a quarter of its strength and his own fighting fervor quenched by dysentery.[46]

So unexpected an issue of an enterprise, the greatest and most expensive that Elizabeth had ever undertaken, provoked her extremely against Essex; and this disgust was much augmented by other circumstances of that nobleman's conduct. --- Essex heard at once of Elizabeth's anger, and of the promotion of his enemy, Sir Robert Cecil, to the office of master of the wards, an office to which he himself aspired. --- Essex, therefore, immediately set out for England; and making speedy journeys, he arrived at court before any one was in the least apprized of his intentions. Though besmeared with dirt and sweat, he hastened up stairs to the presence chamber, thence to the privy chamber, nor stopped till he was in the queen's bed-chamber, who was newly risen, and was sitting with her hair about her face. He threw himself on his knees, kissed her hand, and had some private conference with her; where he was so graciously received, that, on his departure, he was heard to express great satisfaction, and to thank God, that, though he had suffered much trouble and many storms abroad, he found a sweet calm at home.[47]

Elizabeth took one look at Essex's muddy face and exhausted body - with typical brashness he had not stopped to think or to wash before rushing into her privy chamber at Nonsuch - and saw that he had become too weak and too unstable to be of further use to her. 'An ungovernable beast,' she remarked cryptically, 'must be stopped of his provender.' Essex was tried for misconduct, denied his court offices, and, worst of all, denied the income from his monopolies. The queen dared not do more than this, however, for the hero had grown dangerously popular, and his admirers dangerously numerous and angry.

It was not only that London was full of swaggering swordsmen who toasted Essex and sang ballads about his exploits in the tavern; he

---

[46] Erickson, The First Elizabeth, pp 386-387, 395-396.

[47] Hume, vol 4, pp 321-322.

had become the cherished idol of the impoverished, embattled populace at large. For the 1590's were a 'famine decade.' when four successive years of disastrously poor harvests brought the anxious, overtaxed people to the edge of starvation. The number of 'poor folks who died for want in the streets' was rising rapidly, and throughout the north and west the years of scarcity led to bread riots and to impassioned outbursts of violence against the royal government. Elizabeth's reign was coming to a close, not with the prosperity and contentment she might have hoped for two decades earlier, but amid groans of hunger and the rancorous shouts of protesters forced, as they said, to feed their children on 'dogs, cats and nettle roots.' Such people cried for a savior, and with very little provocation they might have been persuaded to follow Essex into rebellion.

When put to the test, however, in February of 1601, their loyalty remained with the queen. Essex, consumed by ambition and maddened by frustration, plotted to seize the court and the Tower, and then to raise the Londoners in rebellion. Elizabeth, forearmed, saw to it that her court was well defended, forcing the earl either to submit or to appeal directly to the people. --- Lacking allies on the council, deprived of the income he might have used to finance a civil war, Essex had only his soldierly rabble and the common folk to rely on. These might have been enough, had the rising been carefully timed, but without planning or preparation it could not succeed, and Essex was soon captured and executed.[48]

Elizabeth affected extremely the praise of clemency; and in every great example, which she had made during her reign, she had always appeared full of reluctance and hesitation: But the present situation of Essex called forth all her tender affections, and kept her in the most real agitation and irresolution. She felt a perpetual combat between resentment and inclination, pride and compassion, the care of her own safety and concern of her favorite; and her situation, during this interval, was perhaps more an object of pity, than that to which Essex himself was reduced. She signed the warrant for his execution; she countermanded it; she again resolved on his death; she felt a new return of tenderness. Essex's enemies told her, that he himself desired to die, and had assured her, that she could never be in safety while he lived. But what chiefly hardened her heart against him was his supposed obstinacy, in never making, as she hourly expected, any application to her for mercy; and she finally gave her consent to his execution. The execution, February 25, 1601, was private in the Tower, agreeably to his own request. --- Some of Essex's associates, Curre, Davers, Blount, Meric, and Davis, were tried and condemned, and all of these, except

---

[48] Erickson, pp 397.

Davis, were executed.[49] The earl of Southampton narrowly escaped death. He was sent to the tower and released early in the reign of James I.

Death of the queen

In 1603 Mountjoy, commissioned by the queen to suppress the rebellion in Ireland, defeated the Irish. Tyrone was in custody by Mountjoy; who intended to bring him over captive into England, to be disposed of at the queen's pleasure. *But Elizabeth was now incapable of receiving any satisfaction from this fortunate event: She had fallen into a profound melancholy; which all the advantages of her high fortune, all the glories of her prosperous reign, were unable, in any degree, to alleviate or assuage. --- She rejected all consolation: she even refused food and sustenance: And throwing herself of the floor, she remained sullen and immoveable, feeding her thoughts on her afflictions, and declaring life and existence an insufferable burden to her. Few words she uttered; and they were all expressive of some inward grief, which she cared not to reveal. But sighs and groans were the chief vent, which she gave to her despondency, and which, though they discovered her sorrows, were never able to ease or assuage them. Ten days and nights she lay upon the carpet, leaning on cushions which her maids brought her; and her physicians could not persuade her to allow herself to be put to bed, much less to make trial of any remedies, which they prescribed to her. Her anxious mind, at last, had so long preyed on her frail body, that her end was visibly approaching; and the council, being assembled, sent the keeper, admiral, and secretary, to know her will with regard to her successor. She answered with a faint voice, that, as she had held a regal scepter, she desired no other than a royal successor. --- Her voice soon after left her; her senses failed; she fell into a lethargic slumber, which continued some hours; and she expired gently, without further struggle or convulsion, in the seventieth year of her age, and forty-fifth of her reign,* on March 24, 1603.[50]

---

[49] Hume, vol 4, pp 337-338.

[50] Ibid, pp 350-351.

Chapter 28

James I

James I (b 1566, d 1625) was the first of the Stuart kings of England and reigned from 1603 to his death from illness in 1625. He was king of Scotland from his first year in 1567 and continued king of Scotland after his accession in 1603 when he became king of England. His reign contrasted from the preceding Tudor kings Henry VIII and his children Edward VI, Mary I and Elizabeth. The imperious rule during the reign of Elizabeth I would be the last example of a strong monarchical form of government to be replaced by a so-called mixed form of government with the aristocracy in the ascendant. James I was noted for favoring peace and avoiding foreign military conflicts. He was not safe from civil disorder. The gunpowder conspiracy took place only a year after his accession. However, instead of civil wars, conflicts took place primarily in parliament, where, for the first time some semblance of freedom of speech asserted itself in the house of commons. The ability of kings to make laws, which endured from one reign to another, was questioned for the first time. James was popularly known for his doctrine of the divine right of kings but parliament became skeptical of the king's claim to supremacy in all matters. The conflicts between James and parliament set the background and circumstances for his son Charles' turbulent reign, his execution; and the civil war and military dictatorship to follow. Also widely known is the translation of the bible published in 1611, called the King James Version, which ironically gave people the power to contest the throne, as well as the ecclesiastics, who each claimed they were the sole authority for truth. Religious conflicts continued despite attempts of James to establish a middle ground for the state's church, and reluctance to persecute those who deviated from his established doctrines. However, James and even more his son Charles, as Scotsmen, were regarded less than would have been the case had they been Englishmen. James, as well as Charles were tainted with the odium of Catholic inclinations, although both were Protestants. James set up the protestant plantations in Northern Ireland.

Family history

We have reviewed James's mother Mary queen of Scots in the previous chapter and her marriage to her first cousin Darnley, from the house of Stuart, along with the complications and bloody outcomes. James's father Darnley was murdered by Scot nobles and a man his mother would later marry named Bothwel. James was one year of age when his mother was removed from the throne of Scotland and who became the minority king James VI. There was no question of the hereditary right of James to the English crown. Henry VIII's children Edward, Mary and Elizabeth had no offspring. Henry VIII's sister Margaret had married James IV, and their son James V and Mary of Guise had one child, Mary queen of Scots, the mother of James VI, to become, James I.

Upbringing

James did not see his mother after his accession to the throne of Scotland at age one. Once again we have little or no information about the childhood and upbringing of an English king. The focus rather has been on political events in the life of the king, from childhood on. For James it is significant that he did not have a mother or a father during his childhood. Not found, however, are the people who did give him nurturing, care and early education. One can only guess what kind of life James might have had as a youngster by surveying the political events of the time of his youth. During his early minority, from age one, there were a succession of Scottish lords who were appointed regents, the earls of Murray, Lennox, Mar, and Morton. Morton was driven from the regency in 1578.

The earl of Morton had hitherto retained Scotland in strict alliance with the queen, and had also restored domestic tranquility to that kingdom: But it was not to be expected, that the factitious and legal authority of a regent would long maintain itself in a country unacquainted with law and order; where even the natural dominion of hereditary princes so often met with opposition and control. The nobility began anew to break into factions: The people were disgusted with some instances of Morton's avarice: And the clergy, who complained of farther encroachments on their narrow revenue, joined and increased the discontent of the other orders. The regent was sensible of his dangerous situation; and having dropped some peevish expressions, as if he were willing or desirous to resign, the noblemen of the opposite party, favorites of the young king, laid hold of this concession, and required that demission which he seemed so frankly to offer them. James was at this time but eleven years of age; yet Morton, having secured himself, as he imagined, by a general pardon, resigned his authority into the hands of the king, who pretended to conduct, in his own name, the administration of the kingdom. The regent acquired an ascendant in the council; and though he resumed not the title of regent, governed with the same authority as before. The opposite party, after holding separate conventions, took to arms, on pretense of delivering their prince from captivity, and restoring him to the free exercise of his government. Queen Elizabeth interposed by her ambassador, Sir Robert Bowes, and mediated an agreement between the factions: Morton kept possession of the government; but his enemies were numerous and vigilant, and his authority seemed to become every day more precarious.[1]

French interests favored an attempt to unite James with his mother, Mary queen of Scots, and they dispatched a count of the house of Lennox to James. *He no sooner appeared at Stirling, where James resided, than he acquired the affections of the young monarch; and joining his interests with those of James Stuart of the house of Ochiltree, a man of profligate manners, who had acquired the kings's favor, he employed himself, under the appearance of play and amusement, in instilling into the tender mind of the prince new sentiments of politics and government. He represented to him the injustice, which had been done to Mary in her deposition, and made him entertain thoughts, either of resigning the crown into her hands, or of associating her with him in the administration.*[2]

Elizabeth intervened. Lennox was accused of complicity in the murder of Darnely. James was warned against a French alliance. James was captured in 1582 by William Ruthven and forced to denounce Lennox. *The affairs of Scotland remained not long in the present situation. James, impatient of restraint, made his escape from his keepers; and flying to St. Andrew's, summoned his friends and partisans to attend him. The earls of Argyle, Marshal, Montrose, and Rothes, hastened to pay their duty to their sovereign; and the opposite party found themselves unable to resist so powerful a combination.*

James VI, king of Scotland

In 1584, James, the king of Scots, *persevering in his present views, summoned a parliament; where it was enacted, that no clergyman should presume, in his sermons, to utter false, untrue, or scandalous speeches against the king, the council, or the public measures, or to meddle, in an improper manner, with the affairs of his majesty and the states.* James would form an agreement with Elizabeth, in 1585. *The queen found no difficulty in renewing the negotiations or a strict alliance between Scotland and England; and the more effectually to gain the prince's friendship, she granted him a pension. --- A league was formed between Elizabeth and James, for the mutual defense of their dominions.*

---

[1] Hume, vol 4, pp 182-183.

[2] Ibid, pp 183-184.

--- By this league James secured himself against all attempts from abroad and opened a way for acquiring the confidence and affections of the English.[3]

In 1587 Elizabeth ordered the execution of James's mother Mary queen of Scots. James made more than a mere protest. *Elizabeth's dissimulation was so gross, that it could deceive nobody, who was not previously resolved to be blinded. --- James recalled his ambassadors from England; and seemed to breath nothing but war and vengeance. The States of Scotland, being assembled, took part in his anger; and professed that they were ready to spend their lives and fortunes in revenge of his mother's death, and in defense of his title to the crown of England. Many of his nobility instigated him to take arms. --- The Catholics took the opportunity of exhorting James to make an alliance with the king of Spain, to lay immediate claim to the crown of England. --- The queen was sensible of the danger attending these counsels; and after allowing James some decent interval to vent his grief and anger, she employed her emissaries to pacify him, and to set before him every motive of hope or fear, which might induce him to live in amity with her.[4]*

In 1589, James married Anne, the eldest daughter of the king of Denmark. And the princess embarked for Scotland; but was driven by a storm into a port of Norway. --- James made the voyage to Norway, *carried the queen thence to Copenhagen, and having passed the winter in that city, he brought her next spring to Scotland.* James VI, as king of Scotland, has been regarded as a king who ruled successfully despite the disorders and conflicts during his minority rule and that of his mother. He would continue to rule Scotland even after Elizabeth's death in 1603 as James I, king of England and Scotland.

Accession to the throne of England

James received popular acclaim as an uncontested king following the death of Elizabeth March 24, 1603. James began his reign by *bestowing knighthood on no less than 237 persons. Titles of all kinds became so common, that they were scarcely marks of distinction. --- We may presume, that the English would have thrown less blame on the king's facility in bestowing favors, had these been confined entirely to their own nation, and had not been shared out, in too unequal proportions, to his old subjects. James, who, through his whole reign, was more guided by temper and inclination than by the rules of political prudence, had brought with him great numbers of his Scottish courtiers.*

It must, however, be owned, in justice to James, that he left almost all the chief offices in the hands of Elizabeth's ministers, and

---

[3] Ibid, pp 219-220.

[4] Ibid, pp 254-255.

trusted the conduct of political concerns, both foreign and domestic, to his English subjects. Among these, secretary Robert Cecil, --- was always regarded as his prime minister and chief counselor.[5]

The gunpowder conspiracy

The Catholics were disappointed with the religious views of James. They thought he would follow his mother's beliefs. A few nobles in the north of England, among them Piercy of the house of Northumberland and Catesby, later in 1604, conspired in a plot to dig a mine under the houses of parliament. They dug the tunnel, pierced through a wall three feet thick, and placed thirty-six barrels of gunpowder in the vaults below parliament. The king, queen and prince Henry, (b 1594, d 1612) were expected to be present along with both houses of parliament. The plot was laid out in a letter delivered to Lord Monteagle by an unknown hand. Monteagle presented it to lord Salisbury, secretary of state, who showed it to the king. The vaults were inspected and the gunpowder discovered. Piercy and Catesby were killed and others of the conspiracy confessed and died by the hands of the executioner.

The first Parliament and the Millinary Petition

James's first parliament was held January 4, 1604, at Hampton court where a conference was held regarding the details of proper church doctrines and observances. The puritans had hoped that James would introduce reforms in the Church of England. A petition was prepared and introduced for changes in the church signed it was hoped by a thousand clergymen; hence the petition has been referred to as the Millenary Petition. The king himself debated the proposals brought forth by the puritans. *He was employed, in dictating magisterially to an assembly of divines concerning points of faith and discipline, and in receiving the applause of these holy men for his superior zeal and learning. --- But the king's disposition had taken strongly a contrary bias. The more he knew the puritanical clergy, the less favor he bore to them. He had remarked in their Scottish brethren a violent turn towards republicanism, and a zealous attachment to civil liberty; principles nearly allied to that religious enthusiasm, with which they were actuated. --- He dreaded likewise the popularity, which attended this order of men in both kingdoms. --- And being thus averse, from temper as well as policy, to the sect of puritans, he was resolved, if possible, to prevent its further growth in England.*

The Church of England had not yet abandoned the rigid doctrines of grace and predestination: The puritans had not yet separated themselves from the church, nor openly renounced episcopacy.

---

[5] Hume, vol 5, pp 5-6.

--- The king, it must be confessed, from the beginning of the conference, showed the strongest propensity to the established church, and frequently inculcated a maxim, which, though it has some foundation, is to be received with great limitations, NO BISHOP, NO KING. The bishops, in their turn, were very liberal of their praises towards the royal disputant; and the archbishop of Canterbury said, that undoubtedly his majesty spake by the special assistance of God's spirit. A few alterations in the liturgy were agreed to, and both parties separated with mutual dissatisfaction.[6]

Parliament and the king

The parliament was now ready to assemble; being so long delayed on account of the plague, which had broken out in London, had raged to such a degree, that above 30,000 persons are computed to have died of it in a year; though the city contained at that time little more than 150,000 inhabitants. The commons, however, agreed to make a remonstrance to the king by the mouth of their speaker; in which they maintained that, though the returns were by form made into chancery, yet the sole right of judging with regard to elections belonged to the house itself, not to the chancellor. James was not satisfied, and ordered a conference between the house and the judges, whose opinion in this case was opposite to that of the commons. This conference, he said, he commanded as an 'absolute king;' --- He added, 'that all their privileges were derived from his grant, and hoped they would not turn them against him.' --- When he compared himself with the other hereditary sovereigns of Europe, he imagined, that, as he bore the same rank, he was entitled to equal prerogatives; not considering the innovations lately introduced by them, and the military force, by which their authority was supported. In England, that power, almost unlimited, which had been exercised for above a century, especially during the late reign, he ascribed solely to royal birth and title; not to the prudence and spirit of the monarchs, nor to the conjunctures of the times. --- In his own person, therefore, he thought all legal power to be centered, by a hereditary and a divine right.[7] Thus began James's doctrine of the divine right of kings which he would repeat in every subsequent meeting of parliament, and which was contained in books he had written on the subject, *The True Law of Free Monarchies* (1598) and *Basilikon Doron* (1599) in which he expounded his own views on the divine right of kings.

---

[6] Hume vol 5, p 12.

[7] Ibid, pp 16-17.

Government and Law during the reign of Elizabeth

It would help to understand the issues and debates of parliaments from 1604 to 1621 and king James's responses by recalling some of the characteristics of Elizabeth's reign. Elizabeth did not have to proclaim the divine right of kings. She and the powerful lord Burghley ruled with methods which are described by Hume: *In order to understand the ancient constitution of England, there is not a period which deserves more to be studied than the reign of Elizabeth. The prerogatives of this princess were scarcely ever disputed, and she therefore employed them without scruple: Her imperious temper, a circumstance in which she went far beyond her successors, rendered her exertions of power violent and frequent, and discovered the full extent of her authority. --- It may not here be improper to recount some of the ancient prerogatives of the crown, and lay open the sources of that great power, which the English monarchs formerly enjoyed.*

Star Chamber

One of the most ancient and most established instruments of power was the court of Star-chamber, which possessed an unlimited discretionary authority of fining, imprisoning, and inflicting corporal punishment, and whose jurisdiction extended to all sorts of offences, contempts, and disorders, that lay not within reach of the common law. The members of this court consisted of the privy council and the judges; men, who all of them enjoyed their offices during pleasure: and when the prince himself was present, he was the sole judge, and all the others could only interpose with their advice. There needed but this one court in any government, to put an end to all regular, legal, and exact plans of liberty. For who durst set himself in opposition to the crown and ministry, or aspire to the character of being a patron of freedom, while exposed to so arbitrary a jurisdiction?

Court of High Commission

The court of High Commission was another jurisdiction still more terrible; both because the crime of heresy, of which it took cognizance, was more indefinable than any civil offence, and because its method of inquisition and of administering oaths, were more contrary to all the most simple ideas of justice and equity. The fines and imprisonments imposed by this court were frequent: the deprivations and suspensions of the clergy for nonconformity were also numerous, and comprehended at one time the third of all the ecclesiastics of England. The queen, in a letter to the archbishop of Canterbury, said expressly, that she was resolved, 'That no man should be suffered to decline either on the left or on the right hand, from the drawn line limited by authority and by her laws and injunctions.'

Martial Law

But Martial Law went beyond even these two courts in a prompt and arbitrary and violent method of decision. Whenever there was any insurrection or public disorder, the crown employed martial law; and it was during that time, exercised not only over the soldiers, but over the whole people. Any one might be punished as a rebel, or an aider and abettor of rebellion, whom the provost-martial, or lieutenant of a county, or their deputies, pleased to suspected offences.

Prison and torture

But there was a grievous punishment very generally inflicted in that age, without any other authority than the warrant of a secretary of state, or of the privy-council; and that was, imprisonment in any jail, and during any time that the ministers should think proper. In suspicious times, all the jails were full of prisoners of state; and these unhappy victims of public jealousy were sometimes thrown into dungeons, and loaded with irons, and treated in the most cruel manner. Without their being able to obtain any remedy from the law. This practice was an indirect way of employing torture: But the rack itself, though not admitted in the ordinary execution of justice, was frequently used, upon any suspicion, by authority of a warrant from a secretary or the privy-council. Even the council in the marches of Wales was empowered, by their very commission to make use of torture, whenever they thought proper.[8]

Whilst so many terrors hung over the people, no jury durst have acquitted a man, when the court was resolved to have him condemned. The practice also, of not confronting witnesses with the prisoner, gave the crown lawyers all imaginable advantage against him. And indeed, there scarcely occurs an instance, during all these reigns that the sovereign, or the ministers were ever disappointed in the issue of a prosecution. Timid juries, and judges who held their offices during pleasure, never failed to second all the views of the crown. And as the practice was anciently common of fining, imprisoning, or otherwise punishing the jurors, merely at the discretion of the court, for finding a verdict contrary to the direction of these dependant judges; it is obvious, that juries were then no manner of security to the liberty of the subject.

Sovereign power

Hume continues to provide other examples of gross injustice in this monarchical form of government where the source of law is power, and in the hands of one person, the king or queen. *The power of pressing, both for sea and land service, and obliging any person to accept of any*

---

[8] Hume, vol 4, pp 355-359.

office, however mean or unfit for him, was another prerogative totally incompatible with freedom. Although the sovereign could not impose taxes there were many other means for imposing taxes without the consent of parliament. Loans, *demands of benevolence,* customs, ship money, duties, purveyance or demand for provisions, and wardship are ways that the king could gain money. *Wardship was the most regular and legal of all these impositions by prerogative. Yet was it a great badge of slavery, and oppressive to all the considerable families. When an estate devolved on a female, the sovereign obliged her to marry any one he pleased: Whether the heirs were male or female, the crown enjoyed the whole profit of the estate during the minority. The inventions were endless, which arbitrary power might employ for the extorting of money, while the people imagined, that their property was secured by the crown's being debarred from imposing taxes. --- Embargoes on merchandise was another engine of royal power, by which the English princes were able to extort money from the people.*

The parliament pretended to the right of enacting laws, as well as of granting subsidies; but this privilege was, during that age, still more insignificant than the other. Queen Elizabeth expressly prohibited them from meddling either with state matters or ecclesiastical causes; and she openly sent the members to prison, who dared to transgress her imperial edict in these particulars. But the legislative power of the parliament was a mere fallacy; while the sovereign was universally acknowledged to possess a dispensing power, by which all the laws could be invalidated, and rendered of no effect. --- But in reality, the crown possessed the full legislative power, by means of proclamations, which might affect any matter, even of the greatest importance, and which the Star-chamber took care to see more rigorously executed than the laws themselves. --- But it is no wonder the queen, in her administration, should pay so little regard to liberty; while the parliament itself, in enacting laws, was entirely negligent of it. The persecuting statutes, which they passed against papists and puritans, are extremely contrary to the genius of freedom. --- The law of the 23rd of her reign, making seditious words against the queen capital, is also a very tyrannical statute. --- But what ensured more effectually the slavery of the people, than even these branches of prerogative, was, the established principles of the times, which attributed to the prince such an unlimited and indefeasible power, as was supposed to be the origin of all law, and could be circumscribed by none.[9]

House of Commons

The first business, in which the commons were engaged, was of the utmost importance to the preservation of their privileges; and neither

---

[9] Ibid, pp 362-367.

temper nor resolution were wanting in their conduct of it.[10] In the former periods of the English government, the house of commons was of so small weight in the balance of the constitution, that little attention had been given, either by the crown, or the people, or the house itself, to the choice and continuance of the members. The parliaments were packed with nominees of the Crown. Twenty-two new boroughs were created under Edward, fourteen under Mary; some indeed places entitled to representation by their wealth and population, but the bulk of them small towns or hamlets which lay wholly at the disposal of the royal council.[11] Elizabeth adopted the system of her two predecessors, brought in the creation of boroughs and recommendation of candidates. The practice of the chancellor appointing members of the commons gave that minister, and consequently the prince, an unlimited power of modeling at pleasure the representatives of the nation. --- The absolute authority of the queen was exerted in a manner still more open; and began for the first time to give alarm to the commons. New writs having been issued by the chancellor, when there was no vacancy, and a controversy arising upon that incident; the queen sent a message to the house, informing them, that it were impertinent for them to deal in such matters. These questions, she said, belonged only to the chancellor; and she had appointed him to confer with the judges, in order to settle all disputes with regard to elections.

The first act of the house of commons was to reverse the chancellor's sentence, of replacing a member Francis Goodwin chosen by the house. Sir John Fortescue was chosen in his place by the county. James ordered a conference between the house and the judges, whose opinion in this case was opposite to that of the commons. 'This conference he said, he commanded as an absolute king.' He added, 'That all their privileges were derived from his grant, and hoped they should not turn them against him'.

Notwithstanding this watchful spirit of liberty, which now appeared in the commons, their deference for majesty was so great, that they appointed a committee to confer with the judges before the king and council. There, the question of law began to appear, in James's eyes, a little more doubtful than he had hitherto imagined it; and in order to extricate himself with some honor, he proposed, that Goodwin and Foretescue should be set aside, and a writ be issued, by warrant of the house, for a new election. Goodwin gave his consent; and the commons embraced the expedient; but in such a manner, that while they showed their regard for the king, they secured for the future the free possession

---

[10] Hume, vol 5, p 15.

[11] Green, p 481.

of their seats, and the right, which they claimed, of judging solely in their own elections and returns.[12]

Parliament opposes Union of England and Scotland

The next parliament in 1606 was once more focused on the union of Scotland and England, in which James assumed the title of the king of Great Britain. James had been king of Scotland nearly since birth and was king of England since 1604. *The king zealously and even impatiently urged the union of the two kingdoms. He justly regarded it as the peculiar felicity of his reign, that he had terminated the bloody animosities for these hostile nations, and had reduced the whole island under one government; enjoying tranquility within itself, and security from all foreign invasions. He hoped, that, while his subjects of both kingdoms reflected on past disaster, besides regarding his person as infinitely precious, they would entertain the strongest desire of securing themselves against the return of like calamities, by a thorough union of laws, parliaments, and privileges. --- The more urgent the king appeared in promoting so useful a measure, the more backward was the English parliament in concurring with him.* Parliament however continued opposed to the union. *Except the obstinacy of the parliament with regard to the union, and an attempt on the king's ecclesiastical jurisdiction, most of their measures, during this session, were sufficiently respectful and obliging; though they still discover a vigilant spirit, and a careful attention towards national liberty.*[13]

Parliament refused to give supply to the king

The next parliament was held in 1610. *A new session was held this spring; the king full of hopes of receiving supply; the commons, of circumscribing his prerogative. The earl of Salisbury, now created treasurer after the death of the earl of Dorset, insisted on the unavoidable expense incurred, in supporting the navy, and in suppressing a late insurrection in Ireland. He mentioned three numerous courts, which the king was obliged to maintain, for himself, for the queen, and for the prince of Wales. And as the crown was now necessarily burdened with a great and urgent debt of 300,000 pounds, he thence inferred the absolute necessity of an immediate and large supply from the people. To all these reasons, which James likewise urged in a speech addressed to both houses, the commons remained inexorable. But not to shock the king with an absolute refusal, they granted him one subsidy and one fifteenth; which would scarcely amount to a hundred thousand pounds. And James received the mortification of discovering, in*

---

[12] Hume, vol 5, pp 16-18.

[13] Hume, vol 5   35-36.

vain, all his wants, and of begging aid of subjects, who had no reasonable indulgence or consideration for him. --- The prince himself began to regard an increase of pomp and splendor as requisite to support the dignity of his character, and to preserve the same superiority above his subjects, which his predecessors had enjoyed. --- Unhappily for the king, those very riches, with the increasing knowledge of the age, bred opposite sentiments in his subjects; and begetting a spirit of freedom and independence, disposed them to pay little regard, either to the entreaties or menaces of their sovereign. While the barons possessed their former immense property and extensive jurisdictions, they were apt, at every disgust, to endanger the monarch and throw the whole government into confusion. But this confusion often, in its turn, proved favorable to the monarch, and made the nation again submit to him. --- But he was a foreigner, and ignorant of the arts of popularity; they were soured by religious prejudices and tenacious of their money; and in this situation, it is no wonder, that, during this whole reign, we scarcely find an interval of mutual confidence and friendship between prince and parliament.

Complaints in parliament

There were other issues raised in this parliament. The commons voiced discontent over the king's proclamations. The king stated *that proclamations were not of equal force with laws; yet he thought it a duty incumbent on him and such a power inseparably annexed to the crown, to restrain and prevent such mischiefs and inconveniences as he saw growing on the state. --- And this prerogative, he adds, our progenitors have, in all times, used and enjoyed. --- The legality of this exertion was established by uniform and undisputed practice; and was even acknowledged by lawyers, who made, however, this difference between laws and proclamations, that the authority of the former was perpetual, that of the latter expired with the sovereign who emitted them.*

Parliament also challenged the king's prerogative, which extended to ecclesiastical affairs as had been established by Henry VIII, Edward VI and Elizabeth. *They had felt, that the Roman pontiff, in former ages, under the pretense of religion, was gradually making advances to usurp the whole civil power. They dreaded still more dangerous consequences from the claims of their own sovereign, who resided among them, and who, in many other respects, possessed such unlimited authority. They therefore deemed it absolutely necessary to circumscribe this branch of prerogative, and accordingly, in the preceding session, they passed a bill against the establishment of any ecclesiastical canons without consent of parliament. But the house of lords, as is usual, defended the barriers of the throne, and rejected the bill.*

In this session, the commons, after passing anew the same bill, made remonstrances against the proceedings of the high commission court. It required no great penetration to see the extreme danger to liberty, arising in a regal government, from such large discretionary powers, as were exercised by that court. But James refused compliance with the application of the commons. Amidst all these attacks, some more, some less violent, on royal prerogative, the king displayed, as openly as ever, all his exalted notions of monarchy and the authority of princes.[14]

The king dissolved Parliament in 1614 because parliament, instead of providing a supply to the king, *immediately resumed the subject, which had been opened last parliament, and disputed his majesty's power of levying new customs and impositions, by the mere authority of his prerogative. --- The commons applied to the lords for a conference with regard to the new impositions. --- The king seized the opportunity of dissolving immediately, with great indignation, a parliament, which had shown so firm a resolution of retrenching his prerogative, without communicating, in return, the smallest supply to his necessities. He carried his resentment so far as even to throw into prison some of the members, who had been the most forward in their opposition to his measures.*

In 1621 conflicts between parliament and the king centered on the kings negotiations with Spain for the marriage of his son Charles to the Spanish king's daughter Donna Maria. Charles's younger sister Elizabeth was married to Frederick, the protestant elector of the Palatinate in central Germany, which had been conquered by the duke of Bavaria. The English people, now overwhelmingly protestant, supported England's support of Frederick, James's son-in-law. James, however, refused to enter the conflict and planned an alliance with Spain in mediating the Thirty Years War in Germany. *Frederick now lived with his numerous family in poverty and distress. --- The zeal of the commons immediately moved them, upon their assembling, to take all these transactions into consideration. They framed a remonstrance, which they intended to carry to the king. They represented, that the enormous growth of the Austrian power threatened the liberties of Europe; that the progress of the Catholic religion in England bred the most melancholy apprehensions, lest it should again acquire an ascendant in the kingdom; that the indulgence of his majesty towards the professors of that religion had encouraged their insolence and temerity; that the uncontrolled conquest, made by the Austrian family in Germany, raised mighty expectations in the English papists; but above all that the prospect of the Spanish match elevated them so far as to hope for an entire toleration, if not the final re-establishment of their religion. The commons, therefore, entreated his majesty, that he would immediately undertake the defense of the Palatine, and maintain it by force of arms; that he would turn his*

---

[14] Ibid, pp 38-45.

sword against Spain, whose armies and treasures were the chief support of the Catholic interest in Europe; that he would enter into no negotiation for the marriage of his son but with a protestant princess; that the children of popish recusants should be taken from their parents, and be committed to the care of protestant teachers and schoolmasters; and that the fines and confiscations, to which the Catholics were by law liable, should be levied with the utmost severity.

More grievances in the house of commons

By this bold step, unprecedented in England for many years, and scarcely ever heard of in peaceable times, the commons attacked at once all the king's favorite maxims of government; his cautious and pacific measures, his lenity towards the Romish religion, and his attachment to the Spanish alliance, from which he promised himself such mighty advantages (including a lucrative dowry). --- *As soon as the king heard of the intended remonstrances of the commons, he wrote a letter to the speaker, in which he sharply rebuked the house for openly debating matters far above their reach and capacity, and he strictly forbade them to meddle with any thing that regarded his government or deep matters of state, and especially not to touch on his son's marriage with the daughter of Spain nor to attack the honor of that king or any other of his friends and confederates.*

The commons were inflamed, not terrified. Secure of their own popularity, and of the bent of the nation towards a war with the Catholics abroad, and the persecution of popery at home, they little dreaded the menaces of a prince, who was unsupported by military force, and whose gentle temper would, of itself, so soon disarm his severity. In a new remonstrance, therefore, they still insisted on their former remonstrance and advice; and they maintained, though in respectful terms, that they were entitled to interpose with their counsel in all matters of government; that to possess entire freedom of speech, in their debates on public business, was their ancient and undoubted right, and an inheritance transmitted to them from their ancestors; and that, if any member abused this liberty, it belonged to the house alone, who were witnesses of his offence, to inflict a proper censure upon him.[15]

The king's answer was sharp and prompt. He told the house, that their remonstrance was more like a denunciation of war than an address of dutiful subjects; that their pretension to inquire into all state-affairs, without exception, was such a plenipotence as none of their ancestors, even during the reign of the weakest princes, had ever pretended to. Concluding, the king said: 'Yet we are pleased to give you our royal assurance, that as long as you contain ourselves within the limits of your duty, we will be as careful to maintain and preserve your

---

[15] Ibid, pp 89-91.

lawful liberties and privileges as ever any of our predecessors were, nay, as to preserve our own royal prerogative.'

The protestation of parliament

This open pretension of the king's naturally gave great alarm to the house of commons. They framed a protestation, in which they repeated all their former claims for freedom of speech, and an unbounded authority to interpose with their advice and counsel. And they asserted, 'That the liberties, franchises, privilege, and jurisdictions of parliament, are the ancient and undoubted birth-right and inheritance of the subjects of England.'

The meeting of the house might have proved dangerous after so violent a breach. It was no longer possible, while men were in such a temper, to finish any business. The king, therefore, prorogued the parliament, and soon after dissolved it by proclamation. The leading members of the house, Sir Edward Coke, and Sir Robert Philips, were committed to the Tower; Selden, Pym, and Mallory, to other prisons. As a light punishment, Sir Dudley Digges, Sir Thomas Crew, Sir Nathaniel Rich, Sir James Perrot, joined in commissions with others, were sent to Ireland, in order to execute some business. The king, at that time, enjoyed, at least exercised, the prerogative of employing any man, even without his consent, in any branch of public service.[16]

Edward Coke

James struggled to retain the supremacy, which was exemplified by the Tudor kings and Elizabeth, but could not use the means employed by Elizabeth or lord Burghley to enforce his will. This enabled the ascendancy of the merchant class, the new aristocracy, which began to establish power and influence in the house of commons. But a new power over the influence of men became established by the lawyers and judges, exemplified by such men as Edward Coke and Francis Bacon. Coke elaborated doctrines of the so-called common law. Even laws of parliament were considered by Coke secondary to the common law he had framed. Edward Coke (b. 1552, d 1634) would have an influence over the beliefs and the practices of lawyers, prosecutors and especially judges. *Coke's ideas of supremacist judicial review conform to the tradition of the U.S. Supreme Court rather than to the subsequent history of the common law in England.[17]* Few American lawyers have read Coke's Institutes. Jefferson, as noted in the *Introduction,* had learned his

---

[16] Ibid, pp 92-93.

[17] Cantor, Imagining the law, p 306.

law from William Blackstone's *Commentaries on English Law.*[18]
Blackstone's four volume *Commentaries of the Laws of England* became
the bible of common law for American lawyers.

Edward Coke's father was a lawyer and Edward was educated
as a lawyer, entering the Inner Temple in 1572, after receiving college
education at Trinity College, Cambridge. He began practice in 1578.
Lord Burghley favored him after several decisions went in his favor. He
became a member of parliament in 1589 and became speaker of the
house of commons in 1592. The commons under Elizabeth was very
different than during the reign of James. *Elizabeth had spent more than
one million two hundred thousand pounds in Flanders and France, and
on her naval expeditions. She summoned, therefore, a parliament in
order to obtain supply: But she either thought her authority so
established, that she needed to make them no concessions in return, or
she rated her power and prerogative above money: For there never was
any parliament, whom she treated in a more haughty manner, whom she
made more sensible of their own weakness, or whose privileges she more
openly violated. When the speaker, Sir Edward Coke, made the three
usual requests, of freedom from arrests, of access to her person, and of
liberty of speech; she replied to him, by the mouth of Puckering, lord
keeper, that liberty of speech was granted to the commons, but they must
know what liberty they were entitled to; not a liberty for every one to
speak what he listeth, or what cometh in his brain to utter; their privilege
extended no farther than a liberty of Aye or No: That she enjoined the
speaker, if he perceived any idle heads so negligent of their own safety,
as to attempt reforming the church, or innovating in the commonwealth,
that he should refuse the bills exhibited for that purpose, till they were
examined by such as were fitter to consider of these things, and could
better judge of them.*[19]

Coke opposed Sir Francis Bacon for the attorney generalship in
1593. The earl of Essex supported Bacon. But Coke was appointed in
1594. As champion of the crown, Coke prosecuted the earl of Essex in
1601, and later Sir Walter Raleigh. Coke, perhaps more than any other
prosecutor, laid down the precedents for prosecutorial severity and gross
defamation of the accused. *The attorney general Coke, opened the cause
against him, and treated him with the cruelty and insolence, which that
great lawyer usually exercised against the unfortunate. He displayed in*

---

[18] Jefferson, p 37, Jefferson's only reference to Edward Coke, (*Institutes*, 4 vols),
p 735, is as follows: *I am sure, to get through old Coke this winter; for God
knows I have not seen him since I packed him up in my trunk in
Williamsburg. Well, Page, I do wish the Devil had old Coke, for I am sure I
never was so tired of an old dull scoundrel in all my life.*

[19] Hume, vol IV, pp 285-286.

the strongest colors, all the faults committed by Essex in his administration of Ireland.[20]

Coke's defamation of Sir Walter Raleigh in court was even more egregious. *Sir Edward Coke, the famous lawyer, then attorney-general, managed the cause for the crown, and threw out on Raleigh such gross abuse, as may be deemed a great reflection, not only on his own memory, but even, in some degree, on the manners of the age. Traitor, monster, viper, and spider of hell, are the terms, which he employs against one of the most illustrious men of the kingdom, who was under trial for life and fortune, and who defended himself with temper, eloquence, and courage.[21]* Raleigh spent the next thirteen years in the Tower, but was released by James for an expedition to Guiana where Raleigh claimed a rich gold mine lay unharvested. He set out on and expedition in 1617 to Guiana but no gold was found. Worse, his men, against clear orders, fought the Spanish and sacked a settlement of San Tomas, where Raleigh's son Walter was killed. When this failed expedition returned to England James arrested him. Raleigh, after a brief hearing, was executed in 1618, based on the meager findings from the trial that sent him to the Tower in 1603.

In 1613 Coke was appointed chief justice of the king's bench and became the first lord chief justice of England in 1615. His abusive behavior as a prosecutor continued while on the bench as in the trial of Somerset and Mrs. Turner. *The king, alarmed and astonished to find such enormous guilt in a man whom he had admitted into his bosom, sent for Sir Edward Coke, chief justice, and earnestly recommended to him the most rigorous and unbiased scrutiny. This injunction was executed with great industry and severity: The whole labyrinth of guilt was carefully unraveled: The lesser criminals, Sir Jervis Elvis, lieutenant of the Tower, Franklin, Weston, Mrs. Turner, were first tried and condemned: Somerset and his countess were afterwards found guilty. Northampton's death, a little before, had saved him from a like fate. It may not be unworthy of remark that Coke, in the trial of Mrs. Turner, told her, that she was guilty of the seven deadly sins: She was a whore, a bawd, a sorcerer, a witch, a papist, a felon, and a murderer. --- But the king bestowed a pardon on the principals, Somerset and the countess.[22]*

Coke was dismissed from the bench in 1616. Bacon and members of the privy council had accused him of interference with the Court of Chancery and of disrespect to the king. Coke's domestic affairs were disrupted. He had offered his fourteen-year old daughter to the

---

[20] Ibid, p 325.

[21] Hume, vol 5, p 10.

[22] Ibid, p 62.

brother of the Duke of Buckingham, in order to gain influence, to which his wife objected. Coke abducted the girl and had her married against her will to Villiers. In 1617 Coke was back in the Privy Council and Star Chamber. In 1620 Coke returned to parliament in the house of commons. We have reviewed in detail the parliament of 1621, which was largely due to the influence of Edward Coke, a leading member of commons. He was sent to the Tower by the king. He was released after nine months. His most important contributions followed in the reign of Charles I by the Petition of Right in 1628, which detailed the liberties of the members of commons with corresponding restraints upon the king. His four volume *Institutes* were completed by 1634, when he died at age 82.

Francis Bacon

Francis Bacon (b 1561, d 1626) was a contemporary of Coke, as well as Raleigh. Their lives overlapped the reigns of Elizabeth and James. Coke and Bacon continued active in the reign of Charles I. All were members of the commons, and were trained as lawyers. Both Raleigh and Bacon were enemies of Coke. Raleigh as above was accused, defamed and convicted for treason, spending thirteen years in the tower, and executed in 1618. Bacon was the son of Nicholas Bacon, keeper of the Great Seal. He attended Cambridge, studied in France, and studied law at Gray's Inn. He became a member of the commons in 1584. He was appointed solicitor general in 1607 and lord chancellor in 1618. Bacon was active in all of the debates in the house of commons until 1614. Bacon would be noted in the history books as a philosopher and an important person of the age.

Bacon, along with Coke as noted above, was involved in the trial and execution of the earl of Essex, Elizabeth's one time favorite which we have reviewed in the previous chapter. In about the year 1600, *Bacon, so much distinguished afterwards by his high offices, and still more by his profound genius of the sciences, was nearly allied to the Cecil family, being nephew to lord Burghley, and cousin to the secretary: But notwithstanding his extraordinary talent, he had met with so little protection from his powerful relations, that he had not yet obtained any preferment in the law, which was his profession. But Essex, who could distinguish merit, and who passionately loved it, had entered into an intimate friendship with Bacon; had zealously attempted, though without success, to procure him the office of solicitor-general; and in order to comfort his friend under the disappointment, had conferred on him a present of land to the value of eighteen hundred pounds. --- He was not one of the crown's lawyers; who was not obliged by his office to assist at his trial: Yet did he not scruple, in order to obtain the queen's favor, to be active in bereaving of life his friend and patron, whose generosity he had often experienced.*[23]

---

[23] Hume, vol 4, pp 326, 327.

Bacon did not participate in the debates in the 1621 parliament except for being an object of investigation by commons. *The great seal was, at that time, in the hands of the celebrated Bacon, created Viscount St. Albans; a man universally admired for the greatness of his genius, and beloved for the courteousness and humanity of his behavior. His want of economy and his indulgence to servants had involved him in necessities; and, in order to supply his prodigality he had been tempted to take bribes, by the title of presents, and that in a very open manner, from suitors in chancery. It appears, that it had been usual for former chancellors to take presents; and it is pretended, that Bacon, who followed the same dangerous practice, had still, in the seat of justice, preserved the integrity of a judge, and had given just decrees against those very persons, from whom he had received the wages of iniquity. Complaints rose the louder on that account, and at last reached the house of commons, who sent up an impeachment against him to the peers. The chancellor, conscious of guilt, deprecated the vengeance of his judges, and endeavored, by a general avowal, to escape the confusion of a stricter inquiry. The lords insisted on a particular confession of all his corruptions. He acknowledge twenty-eight articles; and was sentenced to pay a fine of 40,000 pounds, to be imprisoned in the Tower during the king's pleasure, to be for ever incapable of any office, place or employment, and never again to sit in parliament, or come within the verge of the court.*

This dreadful sentence, dreadful to a man of nice sensibility to honor, he survived five years; and being released in a little time from the Tower, his genius, yet unbroken, supported itself amidst involved circumstances and a depressed spirit, and shone out in literary productions, which have made his guilt of weaknesses be forgotten or overlooked by posterity.[24]

Further conquest of Ireland

James called himself king of Great Britain. He had pressed the commons for joining England and Scotland. Wales had become a part of England under Henry VIII. Ireland had been subject to invasions by English military forces since Henry II. According to Cusack, military conquest is the first stage in conquering a foreign nation. The second stage is the establishment of government and law in the conquered nation. Customs and even language must be uprooted and replaced. Religion and the governance of man's beliefs and opinions then completed the conquest. From Hume:

After the subjection of Ireland by Elizabeth, the more difficult task still remained; to civilize the inhabitants, to reconcile them to laws and industry, and to render their subjection durable and useful to the

---

[24] Hume, vol 5, pp 86-87.

crown of England. James proceeded in this work by a steady, regular, and well-concerted plan; and in the space of nine years, according to Sir John Davis, he made greater advances towards the reformation of the kingdom, than had been made in the 440 years, which had elapsed since the conquest was first attempted.

It was previously necessary to abolish the Irish customs, which supplied the place of laws, and which were calculated to keep that people for ever in a state of barbarism and disorder. --- After abolishing these Irish customs, and substituting English law in their place, James, having taken all the natives under his protection, and declared them free citizens, proceeded to govern them by a regular administration, military as well as civil.

A small army was maintained, its discipline inspected and its pay transmitted from England, in order to keep the soldiers from preying upon the country, as had been usual in former reigns.

All minds being first quieted by a general indemnity; circuits were established, justice administered, oppression banished, and crimes and disorders of every kind severely punished. As the Irish had been universally engaged in the rebellion against Elizabeth, a resignation of all the rights, which had been formerly granted them to separate jurisdictions, was rigorously exacted; and no authority, but that of the king and the law was permitted throughout the kingdom. ---

Plantations

The whole province of Ulster having fallen to the crown by the attainder of rebels, a company was established in London, for planting new colonies in the fertile country: The property was divided into moderated shares, the largest not exceeding 2,000 acres: Tenants were brought over from England and Scotland: The Irish were removed from the hills and fastnesses, and settled in the open country: Husbandry and the arts were taught them: a fixed habitation secured: Plunder and robbery punished: And by these means, Ulster, from being the most wild and disorderly province of all Ireland, soon became the best cultivated and most civilized.[25]

Not all shared Hume's optimism about the plantations of Northern Ireland. *James's plantation policy in Ulster, involving the dispossession of native Irish Catholic landowners and their replacement by thousands of families from England, many of them in and around Londonderry, settled by a consortium of Londoners; and, even more, from southwest Scotland, can also be counted a rather heartless short-term success, though its consequences are all-too-grimly still with us.[26]*

---

[25] Hume, vol 5, pp 47-49.

[26] Morgan, p 307.

Cusack documented not only the plantations in Northern Ireland but in other counties in Ireland preceded by enforcement of the kings edict of supremacy. *James conduct on his accession was sufficiently plain. He was proclaimed in Dublin on the 28th September 1605. A part of his proclamation ran thus: 'We hereby make known to our subjects in Ireland, that no toleration shall ever be granted by us. This we do for the purpose of cutting off all hope that any other religion shall be allowed, save that which is consonant to the laws and statutes of this realm.' The penal statutes were renewed, and enforced with increased severity. Several members of the Corporation and some of the principal citizens of Dublin were sent to prison; similar outrages on religious liberty were perpetrated at Waterford, Ross, and Limerick. In some cases these gentlemen were only asked to attend the Protestant church once, but they nobly refused to act against their conscience even once, though it should procure them freedom from imprisonment, or even from death.*

A letter to Rome says: 2,000 florins are offered for the discovery of a Jesuit, and 1,000 for the discovery of any other priest, or even of the house where he lives. Whenever the servants of any of the clergy are arrested, they are cruelly scourged with whips, until they disclose all that they know about them. Bodies of soldiers are dispersed throughout the country in pursuit of bandits and priests; and all that they seized on, they have the power, by martial law, of hanging without further trial. They enter private houses, and execute whom they please, vying with each other in cruelty.[27] Priests were executed for refusing to take the oath of supremacy.

The plan of the plantation was agreed upon in 1609. It was the old plan, which had been attempted before, though with less show of legal arrangement, but with quite the same proportion of legal iniquity. The simple object was to expel the natives, and to exterminate the Catholic religion. The six counties to be planted were Tyrone, Derry, Donegal, Armagh, Fermanagh, and Cavan. These were parceled out into portions varying from 2,000 to 4,000 acres, and the planters were obliged to build bawns and castles, such as that of Castle Monea, county Fermanagh. Sir John Hume built Tully castle on his plantation.

Plantations were established in other counties in Ireland. *It was expressly stipulated that their tenants should be English or Scotch, and Protestants; the Catholic owners of the land were, in some cases, as a special favor, permitted to remain, if they took the oath of supremacy, if they worked well for their masters, and if they paid double the rent fixed for the others. Sixty thousand acres in Dublin and Waterford, and 385,000 acres in Westmeath, Longor, Kings County, Queen's County, and Leitrim had been proportioned out in a similar manner.*[28]

---

[27] Cusack, pp 464- 465.

[28] Ibid, p 471.

Settlements in America

The first settlement in America was in 1606 resulting when James issued a charter for two settlements. Three small ships set sail from London, and in early 1607 found a colony known as Jamestown. The northern settlement in Maine did not survive more than a few months. Jamestown, located on an island, had its severe difficulties, but survived and became the capitol of Virginia from 1607 to 1698. The capitol was moved to Williamsburg, about ten miles north of Jamestown. It is fitting to add that it was here, in 1778 that a bill for establishing religious freedom was first passed by the Virginia legislature. [29] It is also appropriate to note that the first amendment to The Constitution of the United States addressed the principle concerns of those who fled England in this period and later. Freedom of religion, freedom of speech, the right to assemble, and to petition the government for redress of grievances were the chief bulwarks of liberty which continue to this day.

The next significant emigration was by the puritans who were given privilege by James, although reluctantly, to settle in America. In 1620, the *Mayflower* brought more of the Pilgrim Fathers, who had sought refuge in Holland and called Separatists, from Plymouth England to New England, a site to be named Plymouth.

George Villiers, duke of Buckingham

Buckingham had during the last two years of James' rule, 1623 to 1625, gained an influence over Charles and both asserted more power during the declining years of James. George Villiers, (b. 1592, d. 1628), was created duke of Buckingham by James in 1623. Buckingham had gained disfavor with parliament during the last two years of James' reign. *Buckingham had governed with an uncontrolled sway, both the court and nation; and could James's eyes have been opened, he had now full opportunity of observing how unfit his favorite was for the high station, to which he was raised. Some accomplishments of a courtier he possessed: Of every talent of a minister he was utterly destitute; Headlong in his passions, and incapable equally of prudence and of dissimulation: Sincere from violence rather than candor; expensive from profusion more than generosity: A warm friend, a furious enemy; but without any choice of discernment in either: With these qualities he had early and quickly mounted to the highest rank; and partook at once of the insolence, which attends a fortune newly acquired, and the impetuosity which belongs to persons born in high stations, and unacquainted with opposition.*[30] Buckingham had gained an influence over prince Charles

---

[29] Jefferson, Writings, p 40.

[30] Hume, vol 5, p 102.

and in 1623 he persuaded James to allow the prince and himself to go to Madrid to demand the Spanish Infanta, daughter of king Phillip III of Spain, to marry Charles. James had hoped to gain peace with Spain and was involved during the last three years of his reign in negotiations for the marriage of Charles to the Infanta of Spain, and had dispatched the earl of Bristol as his ambassador to Phillip IV. The negative impressions Buckingham had made with the Spanish court led to the break up of the marriage treaty between Charles and the Infanta. *But, in the same proportion, that the prince was beloved and esteemed was Buckingham despised and hated. His behavior, composed of English familiarity, and French vivacity; his sallies of passion, his indecent freedoms with the prince, his dissolute pleasures, his arrogant, impetuous temper, which he neither could, nor cared to disguise; qualities like these, could, most of them, be esteemed no where, but to the Spaniards were the objects of peculiar aversion.* Buckingham broke off the treaty with Spain. *It is not likely, that Buckingham prevailed so easily with James to abandon a project, which, during so many years, had been the object of all his wishes. --- A rupture with Spain, the loss of two million,* as a dowry, *were prospects little agreeable to this pacific and indigent monarch.*[31]

A final parliament

A parliament in 1624 was called. *The king, having broken with Spain, was obliged to concert new measures; and, without the assistance of parliament, no effectual step of any kind could be taken. The benevolence, which, during the interval, had been rigorously exacted for recovering the Palatinate, though levied for so popular an end, had procured to the king less money than ill will from his subjects. Whatever discouragements, therefore, he might receive from his ill agreement with former parliaments, there was a necessity of summoning once more this assembly; and, it might be hoped, that the Spanish alliance, which gave such umbrage, being abandoned, the commons would now be better satisfied with the king's administration.*

Buckingham delivered, to a committee of lords and commons, a long narrative, which he pretended to be true and complete, of every step taken in the negotiations with Philip: But partly by the suppression of some facts, partly by the false coloring laid on others, this narrative was calculated entirely to mislead the parliament, and to throw on the court of Spain the reproach of artifice and insincerity. Charmed with having obtained at length the opportunity, so long wished for, of going to war with papists, they little thought of future consequences; but immediately advised the king to break off both treaties with Spain, as well that which regarded the marriage, as that for the restitution of the Palatinate. The people, ever greedy of war, till they suffer by it, displayed their triumph

---

[31] Ibid, pp 108-109.

at these violent measures by public bonfires and rejoicing, and by insults to the Spanish minister. Buckingham was now the favorite of the public and of the parliament. Sir Edward Coke, in the house of commons, called him the Savior of the nation.

A treaty with France was obtained. The prospects of a conjunction with England was presently embraced, and all imaginable encouragement was given to every proposal for conciliating a marriage between Charles and princess Henrietta, daughter of Henry IV, king of France, whom Charles had met in Paris on his trip to Spain to meet the Infanta.

Parliament granted resources for a war with Spain. *Accordingly an army of six thousand men was levied in England, and sent over to Holland, commanded by four young noblemen, Essex, Oxford, Southampton and Willoughby, who were ambitious of distinguishing themselves in so popular a cause, and of acquiring military experience under so renowned a captain as Maurice. A treaty with France was obtained.*

It was determined to reconquer the Palatinate; a state lying in the midst of Germany, possessed entirely by the Emperor and duke of Bavaria, surrounded by potent enemies, and cut off from all communication with England. Count Mansfield was taken into pay; and an English army of 12,000 foot and 200 horse was levied by a general press throughout the kingdom. During the negotiations with France, vast promises had been made, though in general terms, by the French ministry; not only that a free passage should be granted to the English troops, but that powerful succors should also join them in their march towards the Palatinate. In England, all these professions were hastily interpreted to be positive engagements. The troops under Mansfelt's command were embarked at Dover; but, upon sailing over to Calais, found no orders yet arrived for their admission. The French reneged on their promises. --- Meanwhile, a pestilential distemper crept in among the English forces, so long cooped up in narrow vessels. Half the army died while on board; and the other half, weakened by sickness, appeared too small a body to march into the Palatinate.[32]

Death of James

The reign of James was now drawing towards a conclusion. This spring he was seized with a tertian fever. After some fits, he found himself extremely weakened, and sent for the prince, whom he exhorted to bear a tender affection for his wife, but to preserve a constancy in religion; to protect the Church of England; and to extend his care towards the unhappy family of the Palatine. With decency and courage, he prepared himself for his end; and he expired on the 27th of March

---

[32] Ibid, pp 112-120.

1625, after a reign over England of twenty-two years and some days; and in the fifty-ninth year of his age. His reign over Scotland was almost of equal duration with his life. --- He was only once married, to Anne of Denmark, who died on the 3rd of March 1619, in the forty-fifth year of her age, a woman eminent neither for her vices nor her virtues. --- He left only one son, Charles, then in the twenty-fifth year of his age; and one daughter, Elizabeth, married to the elector Palatine.[33]

---

[33] Ibid, p 122.

Chapter 29

Charles I

Charles I, (b 1600, d 1649), followed his father James I to the throne in 1625 and was executed in 1649. Like his father he experienced a growing escalation of conflicts with the house of commons. The commons presented in parliament grievances and the demand of what they called their ancient rights. The commons issued a Petition of Rights, which asserted certain rights of members of the new aristocracy and limitations of the powers of the king. Charles I made more compromises with parliament than previous kings, however, he never relinquished the powers of regal precedent. Although the seeds of liberty were sown, it was religious warfare, and the precedent that conflicts are to be determined by the sword, which prevailed. Failures in the commands of wars against Spain and France did not please parliament, who failed to provide the king with revenue. Members of the commons promulgated fears of a Catholic takeover, which became elaborated with the new innovations of printing into a mass insanity of fear and hatred. A massacre myth helped fuel emotions to a high pitch. The rise of Oliver Cromwell and the power of military forces led to the civil war and the beheading of Charles I, who had pleaded in his defense that *the king can do no wrong.*

Charles was the grandson of Mary Queen of Scots and the second son of James I and Anne of Denmark. His older brother Henry died in 1612. His older sister Elizabeth was married to Frederick, elector of the Palatine.[1] Upon the death of James I, March 27, 1625, Charles became the undisputed king of England.

---

[1] Note. This marriage would produce a long line of German kings to follow the Stuarts, occupying the English crown from the Georgian kings, to Queen Victoria and the present Elizabeth II.

Marriage and the duke of Buckingham

In March 1625, Charles became king and married soon afterward Henrietta Maria, daughter of king Henry IV of France and sister to the king. The duke of Buckingham assumed a dominant influence in the first years of Charles's reign, even involved with the king's marriage. *At the time, when Charles married by proxy the princess Henrietta, the duke of Buckingham had been sent to France, in order to grace the nuptials, and conduct the new queen into England. The eyes of the French court were directed by curiosity towards that man, who had enjoyed the unlimited favor of two successive monarchs, and who, from a private station, had mounted, in the earliest youth, to the absolute government of the three kingdoms. The beauty of his person, the gracefulness of his air, the splendor of his equipage, his fine taste in dress, festivals, and carousals, corresponded to the prepossessions entertained in his favor: The affability of his behavior, the gaiety of his manners, the magnificence of his expense, increased still farther the general admiration which was paid him. All business being already concerted, the time was entirely spent in mirth and entertainments; and, during those splendid scenes, among that gay people, the duke found himself in a situation, where he was perfectly qualified to excel. But his great success at Paris proved as fatal as his former failure at Madrid.[2]* Buckingham's failures were responsible for the invasions of Spain in the first year of Charles's reign and France in 1627.

War with Spain

With the failed negotiations by Buckingham and Charles for the marriage of the Infanta to Charles, there followed in Charles' reign war with Spain in October 1625. *To supply the want of parliamentary aids, Charles issued privy seals for borrowing money from his subjects. The advantage reaped by this expedient was small compensation for the disgust which it occasioned. By means, however, of that supply, and by other expedients, he was, although with difficulty, enabled to equip his fleet. It consisted of eighty vessels, great and small; and carried on board an army of 10,000 men. Sir Edward Cecil, lately created Viscount Wimbledon, was entrusted with the command. He sailed immediately for Cadiz, and found the bay full of Spanish ships of great value. He either neglected to attack these ships, or attempted it preposterously. --- But the plague having seized the seamen and soldiers, they were obliged to abandon all hopes of this prize, and return to England. Loud complaints were made against the court for entrusting so important a command to a man like Cecil, whom, though he possessed great experience, the people, judging by the event, esteemed of slender capacity.*

---

[2] Hume, vol 5, p 183.

Invasion of France

Two years later another futile foreign military venture involved an invasion of France under the command of Buckingham. *A fleet of a hundred sail, and an army of 7,000 men were fitted out for the invasion of France, and both of them entrusted to the command of the duke, who was altogether unacquainted both with land and sea service. The fleet appeared before Rochelle; but so ill-concerted were Buckingham's measures, that the inhabitants of that city shut their gates, and refused to admit allies, of whose coming they were not previously informed. All his military operations showed equal incapacity and inexperience. --- Though resolved to starve St. Martin, he guarded the sea negligently, and allowed provisions and ammunition to be thrown into it: Despairing to reduce it by famine, he attacked it without having made any breach, and rashly threw away the lives of the soldiers. --- He began to think of a retreat; but made it so unskillfully, that it was equivalent to a total rout: He was the last of the army that embarked; and he returned to England, having lost two thirds of his land forces; totally discredited both as an admiral and a general.* [3]

The first Parliament, demand for punishment of Catholics

The opposition of the house of commons to Buckingham became the focus of the first parliament, in 1625, and a major reason why commons failed to appropriate Charles' request for funds. During this session members of the house of commons, who were largely puritans, vented their fear and hatred of the Catholics. *The commons renewed their eternal complaints against the growth of popery, which was ever the chief of their grievances, and now their only one. They demanded a strict execution of the penal laws against the Catholics, and remonstrated against some late pardons, granted to priests. They attacked Montague, one of the king's chaplains, on account of a moderate book, which he had lately published, and which, to their great disgust, saved virtuous Catholics, as well as other Christians, from eternal torments. Charles gave them a gracious and a compliant answer to all their remonstrances. He was however, in his heart, extremely averse to these furious measures. Though a determined Protestant, by principle as well as inclination, he had entertained no violent horror against popery; and a little humanity, he thought, was due by the nation to the religion of their ancestors. --- The extreme rage against popery was a sure characteristic of Puritanism. The house of commons discovered other infallible symptoms of the prevalence of that party. They petitioned the king from replacing such able clergy as had been silenced for want of conformity to*

---

[3] Ibid, pp 166 and 185.

the ceremonies. They also enacted laws for the strict observance of Sunday, which the Puritans affected to call the Sabbath. --- The king, finding that the parliament was resolved to grant him no supply, and would furnish him with nothing but empty protestations of duty, or disagreeable complaints of grievances; took advantage of the plague, which began to appear at Oxford, and on that pretense, immediately dissolved them. By finishing the session with a dissolution, instead of a prorogation, he sufficiently expressed his displeasure at their conduct.[4]

The second parliament, charges against Buckingham, forced loans

The second parliament, in February 1626, led to an impeachment of Buckingham. A number of charges against Buckingham were brought forward. Most were considered without merit or incapable of proof. The matter of Buckingham's conduct in Spain was considered. However, before the matter was discussed further, Charles dismissed parliament. New grievances were voiced, even more forcefully. The war in Spain drew criticism. *Soldiers were billeted upon private houses, contrary to custom, which required, that, in all ordinary cases, they should be quartered in inns and public houses. --- The soldiers, ill-paid and undisciplined, committed many crimes and outrages; and much increased the public discontent. To prevent these disorders, martial law, so requisite to the support of discipline, was exercised upon the soldiers. --- Many too, of low condition, who had shown a refractory disposition, were pressed into the service, and enlisted in the fleet or army.* The king, denied support from the house of commons, ordered forced loans. Sheriffs and the king's men identified among the counties those who had property for the enforced loans, and a refusal to pay led to imprisonment. As many as seventy knights were imprisoned for failure to pay loans. *Five gentlemen alone, Sir Thomas Darnel, Sir John Corbet, Sir Walter Earl, Sir John Heveningham, and Sir Edmond Hambden, had spirt enough, at their own hazard and expense, to defend the public liberties, and to demand releasement, not as a favor from the court, but as their due, by the laws of their country.* Taxes on shipping or 'ship money', *a taxation, which had once been imposed by Elizabeth, but which afterwards, when carried some steps farther by Charles, created such violent discontents.* All the king's methods of procuring funds were without consent of parliament. *Passive obedience was there recommended in its full extent, the whole authority of the state was represented as belonging to the king alone, and all limitations of law and a constitution were rejected as seditious and impious.*[5]

---

[4] Ibid, pp 165-166.

[5] Ibid, pp 175-180.

The third parliament

. The third parliament, March 1628, addressed the above complaints. The Petition of Right, passed by both houses of parliament and signed by the king[6] would become the most important written document of English law since Magna Carta. The failures of the military expeditions by Charles and Buckingham had exhausted the treasury, *that they found themselves under an absolute necessity of assembling the parliament. The views of the popular leaders were much more judicious and profound. When the commons assembled, they appeared to be men of the same independent spirit with their predecessors, and possessed of such riches, that their property was computed to surpass three times that of the house of peers; they were deputed by boroughs and counties, inflamed, all of them, by the late violations of liberty; many of the members themselves had been cast into prison, and had suffered by the measures of the court; yet, notwithstanding these circumstances, which might prompt them to embrace violent resolutions, they entered upon business with perfect temper and decorum.*[7]

Edward Coke was presented in the last chapter on James I. He was an important speaker and leader in parliament and contributed to the discussions and principles of justice leading to the Petition of Rights. Other men, such as John Eliot, Dudley Digges, John Hampden, Thomas Wentworth, and John Pym deserve praise, along with the others listed above for speaking out at great expense and danger to themselves. It was more than fifteen hundred years before that Cicero, in his final book, *On Duties*, presented the moral precept that failure to do anything about known wrongs is as much a crime as the actual commitment of a crime. Therefore, it is fitting to present some of the known quotations from a few of these men who presented clearly their grievances before parliament and the king, and at great risk to their lives and fortunes. The impeachment of Buckingham and the petition of Rights to follow include example of a new kind of oratory in the house of commons reminiscent of the orations of Cicero.

Impeachment of Buckingham

If Hampden and Pym are the great figures which embody the latter national resistance, the earlier struggle for parliamentary liberty centers in the figure of Sir John Eliot. --- In the second parliament, Buckingham's impeachment was voted and carried to the lords. The

---

[6] Note. The king signed upon the threat of denial of support by parliament for his considerable expenses.

[7] Ibid, p 187.

favorite took his seat as a peer to listen to the charge with so insolent an air of contempt that one of the managers appointed by the Commons to conduct it turned sharply on him. 'Do you jeer, my lord', said Sir Dudley Digges. 'I can show you when a greater man than your lordship—as high as you in place and power and as deep in the King's favor— has been hanged for as small a crime as these articles contain.' The 'proud carriage' of the duke provoked an invective from Eliot, which marks a new era in parliamentary speech. From the first the vehemence and passion of his words had contrasted with the grave, colorless reasoning of older speakers. His opponents complained that Eliot aimed to 'stir up affections.' The quick emphatic sentences he substituted for the cumbrous periods of the day, his rapid argument, his vivacious and caustic allusions, his passionate appeals, his fearless invective, struck a new note in English eloquence.[8]

The frivolous ostentation of Buckingham, his very figure blazing with jewels and gold, gave point to the fierce attack. 'He had broken those nerves and sinews of our land, the stores and treasures of the king. There needs no search for it: It is too visible. His profuse expenses, his superfluous feasts, his magnificent buildings, his riots, his excesses, what are they but the visible evidences of an express exhausting of the State, a chronicle of the immensity of his waste of the revenues of the Crown?' With the same terrible directness Eliot reviewed the Duke's greed and corruption, his insatiate ambition, his seizure of all public authority, his neglect of every public duty, his abuse for selfish ends of the powers he had accumulated. 'The pleasure of his Majesty, his known directions, his public acts, his actions of council, the decrees of courts— all must be made inferior to this man's will. No right, no interest may withstand him. Through the power of state and justice he has dared ever to strike at his own ends.' 'My lords,' he ended, after a vivid parallel between Buckingham and Sejanus, 'you see the man! What have been his actions, what he is like, you know! I leave him to your judgment.' --- The reply of Charles was as fierce and sudden as the attack of Eliot. He hurried to the House of Peers to avow as his own the deeds with which Buckingham was charged. Eliot and Digges were called from their seats, and committed prisoners to the Tower. --- But the tide of public resistance was slowly rising.[9]

Petition of Right

In spite of Eliot's counsel, even the question of Buckingham's removal gave place to the craving for redress of wrongs done to personal liberty. 'We must vindicate our ancient liberties,' said Sir Thomas

---

[8] John Richard Green, A Short History of the English People, vol 2, pp 497, 498.

[9] Ibid, p 499.

Wentworth, in words soon to be remembered against himself: 'we must reinforce the laws made by our ancestors. We must set such a stamp upon them, as no licentious spirit shall dare hereafter to invade them.' Heedless of sharp and menacing messages from the king, of demands that they should take his 'royal word' for their liberties, the house bent itself to one great work, the drawing up a Petition of Right. The statutes that protected the subject against arbitrary taxation, against loans and benevolences, against punishment, outlawry, of deprivation of goods, otherwise than by lawful judgment of his peers, against arbitrary imprisonment without stated charge, against billeting of soldiery on the people or enactment of martial law in time of peace, were formally recited. The breaches of them under the last two sovereigns, and above all since the dissolution of the last parliament, were recited as formally.[10] --- Statutes that elaborated the above were drawn up. The lords yielded but Charles gave an evasive reply; --- Pym, Eliot and Coke were all involved in the emotional deliberations of the commons that followed. *Shouts of assent greeted the resolution to insert the Duke's name in their Remonstrance. But the danger to his favorite overcame the king's obstinacy, and to avert it he suddenly offered to consent to the Petition of Right. This was in June 1628.* --- But, like all Charles's concessions, it came too late to effect the end at which he aimed.

The murder of Buckingham

The Commons persisted in presenting their Remonstrance. Charles received it coldly and ungraciously; while Buckingham, who had stood defiantly at his master's side as he was denounced, fell on his knees to speak. 'No George!' said the king as he raised him; and his demeanor gave emphatic proof that the duke's favor remained undiminished. 'We will perish together, George,' he added at a later time, 'if thou dost.' No shadow of his doom, in fact, had fallen over the brilliant favorite, when, after the prorogation of the parliament, he set out to take command of a new expedition for the relief of Rochelle. But a lieutenant in the army, John Felton, soured by neglect and wrongs, had found in the Remonstrance some fancied sanction for the revenge he plotted, and, mixing with the throng, which crowded the hall at Portsmouth, he stabbed Buckingham to the heart. Charles flung himself on his bed in a passion of tears when the news reached him; but outside the Court it was welcomed with a burst of joy.[11]

King and parliament, increasing conflicts over taxation

---

[10] Ibid, p 501.

[11] Ibid, pp 502-503.

A new session of parliament was held January 1629, to return to the question whether funds from tonnage and poundage could be granted to the king without the consent of parliament. It was over this issue that the king refused to consider the matter and ended, or prorogued, the last session of parliament. Tonnage and poundage was a tax for the king's revenue on tons of shipping, imports as well as exports, and tax on pounds of other goods exported. Charles's first parliament in 1625 had granted the king only a year supply. Charles had terminated the next two sessions of parliament before the issue of tonnage and poundage was discussed. Charles, nonetheless, continued to collect the taxes from tonnage and poundage without the approval of parliament. Previous kings had followed this precedent of collecting taxes from tonnage or poundage, with or without the approval of parliament.

Sir John Elliot framed a remonstrance against levying tonnage and poundage without consent of parliament, and offered it to the clerk to read. It was refused. He read it himself. The question being then called for, the speaker, Sir John Finch, said, 'That he had a command from the king to adjourn, and to put no questions.'[12] *The speaker was pushed back into the chair, and forcibly held in it by Hollis and Valentine, till a short remonstrance was framed, and was passed by acclamation rather than by vote. --- The discontents of the nation ran high, on account of this violent rupture between the king and parliament. --- Sir John Elliot, Hollis, and Valentine, were summoned to their trial in the king's bench, for seditious speeches and behavior in parliament; but refusing to answer before an inferior court for their conduct, as members of a superior, they were condemned to be imprisoned during the king's pleasure, to find sureties for their good behavior, and to be fined, the two former a thousand pounds a piece, the latter five hundred. This sentence, procured by the influence of the crown, served only to show the king's disregard to the privileges of parliament, and to acquire an immense stock of popularity to the sufferers, who had so bravely, in opposition to arbitrary power, defended the liberties of their native country.* The prisoners refused to raise money for the imposed fines or even accept bail. *Because Sir John Elliot happened to die while in custody, a great clamor was raised against the administration; and he was universally regarded as a martyr to the liberties of England.*[13]

Personal rule of Charles

From 1629 to 1640 Charles ruled without parliament. Buckingham, his favorite, had been assassinated. Hume provided a

---

[12] Hume, vol 5, pp 215. The king's power of adjourning as well as proroguing the parliament, was and is never questioned.

[13] Ibid, pp 215-216.

summary of the character of the king. *When we consider Charles as presiding in his court, as associating with his family, it is difficult to imagine a character at once more respectable and more amiable. A kind husband, and indulgent father, a gentle master, a steadfast friend; to all these eulogies, his conduct in private life fully entitled him. As a monarch took in the exterior qualities, he excelled; in the essential, he was not defective. His address and manner, though perhaps inclining a little towards stateliness and formality, in the main corresponded to his high rank, and gave grace to that reserve and gravity, which were natural to him. The moderation and equity, which shone forth in his temper seemed to secure him against rash and dangerous enterprises. The good sense, which he displayed in his discourse and conversation, seemed to warrant his success in every reasonable undertaking. Other endowments likewise he had attained, which, in a private gentleman, would have been highly ornamental, and which, in a great monarch, might have proved extremely useful to his people. He was possessed of an excellent taste in all the fine arts and the love of painting was in some degree his favorite passion. Learned beyond what is common in princes, he was a good judge of writing in others, and enjoyed, himself, no mean talent in composition. In any other age or nation, this monarch had been secure of a prosperous and a happy reign. But the high idea of his own authority, which he had imbibed, made him incapable of giving way to the spirit of liberty, which began to prevail among his subjects.*

After the death of Buckingham, who had somewhat alienated Charles from the queen, she is to be considered as his chief friend and favorite. --- Charles reserved all his passion for his consort, to whom he attached himself with unshaken fidelity and confidence. --- Her religion, likewise, --- must be regarded as a great misfortune; since it augmented the jealousy, which prevailed against the court, and engaged her to procure of the Catholics some indulgences, which were generally distasteful to the nation.[14]

William Laud, archbishop of Canterbury

The men who were most important to the king during this period were Sir Thomas Wentworth who became a member of the privy counsel and later earl of Strafford, and William Laud, bishop of London, who later became archbishop of Canterbury. Laud was most determined to model the Church of England into his own creation of beliefs, ceremonies and practices to which the king agreed. Neither Laud nor the king could have anticipated that it would be religious conflicts among the Puritans in England, the Presbyterians in Scotland and the Catholics in Ireland in opposition to the Episcopal church that would bring down the government of England and lead to their own demise. *It must be*

---

[14] Ibid, pp 220-222.

confessed, that though Laud deserved not the appellation of papist, the genius of his religion was, though in a less degree, the same with that of the Romish: The same profound respect was exacted to the sacerdotal character, the same submission required to the creeds and decrees of synods and councils, the same pomp and ceremony was affected in worship, and the same superstitious regard to days, postures, meals, and vestments. No wonder, therefore, that this prelate was, every-where, among the Puritans, regarded with horror, as the forerunner of anti-Christ.[15]

Laud was a member of the notorious Star Chamber as well as the High Commission, which had ultimate authority over religious beliefs and practices permissible in the kingdom as well as in Scotland and Ireland. *Laud and his followers took care to magnify, on every occasion, the regal authority, and to treat, with the utmost disdain or detestation, all puritanical pretensions to a free and independent constitution. --- To show the greater alienation from the churches reformed after the Presbyterian model, Laud advised, that the discipline and worship of the church should be imposed on the English regiments and trading companies abroad.* The Star Chamber and High Commission were used to force compliance with the king and Laud's ecclesiastical orders. Many examples were recorded in this period of punishment of offenders by large fines, imprisonment, whippings, mutilation such as cutting off the ears of the offenders and placement in a pillory at public locations. A Scotch pamphlet writer Leighton and William Prynne, a barrister of Lincoln's Inn, writing against practices considered evil, and later libeling the archbishop, were severely punished. Laud himself, or an official went on visitations between 1634 and 1637 to the archbishoprics of Canterbury and York to determine whether the exact forms of the prayer book were used, and absolute compliance with observances ordered by the king and Laud were carried out. Offending clergymen were disciplined, brought before the court of High Commission or removed from office. *Allison had reported, that the archbishop of York had incurred the king's displeasure, by asking a limited toleration for the Catholics, and an allowance to build some churches for the exercise of their religion. For this slander against the archbishop, he was condemned in the star-chamber, to be fined 100 pounds, to be committed to prison, to be bound to his good behavior during life, to be whipped, and to be set on the pillory at Westminster and in three other towns in England. Robins, who had been an accomplice in the guilt, was condemned by a sentence equally severe.* Hume adds that *there were only five or six such instances of rigor during the course of fifteen years and that such examples were more equitable than that of most of his predecessors.* Yet Hume later details the prosecution of Williams, bishop

---

[15] Ibid, p 224.

of Lincoln, for finding letters where mention was made of *'a little great man'* and in another passage, *'a little urchin'. By inferences and constructions, these epithets were applied to Laud; and on no better foundation was Williams tried anew, as having received scandalous letters, and not discovering that private correspondence. For this offence, another fine of 8,000 pounds was levied on him.*[16]

John Lilburne

Lilburn, (b. 1614, d. 1657), deserves special mention in view of his courage in championing the freedom of speech and of the press. *Lilburne was accused before the star-chamber, of publishing and dispersing seditious pamphlets. He was ordered to be examined; but refused to take the oath, usual in that court, that he would answer interrogatories, even though they might lead him to accuse himself. For this contempt, as it was interpreted, he was condemned to be whipped, pilloried, and imprisoned. --- It was found difficult to break the spirits of men, who placed both their honor and their conscience in suffering. --- All the severities, indeed, of this reign were exercised against those who triumphed in their sufferings, who courted persecution, and braved authority.*[17]

Taxes imposed by the king

The king continued to collect taxes from tonnage and poundage without authority of parliament and declared that he had no intent of calling another parliament. *A stamp duty was imposed, a new tax, which of itself was liable to no objection; but appeared of dangerous consequence, when considered as arbitrary and illegal. --- Monopolies were revived; and oppressive method of levying money, being unlimited as well as destructive of industry. --- In 1634, ship money was now introduced. The first writs of this kind had been directed to sea-port towns only: But ship-money was at this time levied on the whole kingdom; and each county was rated at a particular sum, which was afterwards assessed upon individuals. --- As England had no military force, while all the other powers of Europe were strongly armed, a fleet seemed absolutely necessary for her security. --- And men thought a powerful fleet, though very desirable, both for the credit and safety of the kingdom, but an unequal recompense for their liberties, which, they apprehended, were thus sacrificed to the obtaining of it.*[18]

---

[16] Ibid, p 227-228, and p 242.

[17] Ibid, p 244.

[18] Ibid, p 231, 235, 242.

This year, in 1637, John Hampden acquired, by his spirit and courage, universal popularity throughout the nation, and had merited great renown with posterity, for the bold stand, which he made, in defense of the laws and liberties of his country. After the imposing of ship money, Charles, in order to discourage all opposition, had proposed this question to the judges; 'Whether, in a case of necessity, for the defense of the kingdom, he might not impose this taxation, and that he was a sole judge of the necessity?' The case was argued for twelve days, in the exchequer chamber, before all the judges of England; and the nation regarded, with the utmost anxiety every circumstance of this celebrated trial. Hampden and his lawyers argued against the king's plea of necessity*: And if such maxims and such practices prevail; what has become of national liberty? What authority is left to the great charter, to the statutes, and to that very petition of right, which, in the present reign, had been so solemnly enacted by the concurrence of the whole legislature?*

Notwithstanding these reasons, the prejudiced judges, four excepted, gave sentence in favor of the crown. Hambden, however, obtained by the trial the end, for which he had so generously sacrificed his safety and his quiet: The people were roused from their lethargy, and became sensible of the danger, to which their liberties were exposed.[19]

Settlement of America

Between the sailing of Winthrop's expedition and the assembly of the Long Parliament, in the space, that is, of ten or eleven years, two hundred emigrant ships had crossed the Atlantic, and twenty thousand Englishmen had found a refuge in the West.[20] The period referred to by Green was from 1629 to 1640, the period, which is referred to by historians as the personal rule of Charles I. If there were only five or six examples of rigor by Charles I during this period, as noted by Hume, one would need to explain why the largest emigration from England, and across the Atlantic ocean in woefully inadequate sailing vessels, had taken place during this time. There can be no doubt, however, that during the Tudor period, beginning with Henry VII and ending in Elizabeth I there were far greater atrocities towards people and greater oppression of liberties, especially religious practice and freedom of speech. The answer may lie in the possibility that the reign of terror during the Tudor age, with summary executions was a far more effective method of suppressing the liberties of the people, than public exposure of mutilated heroes in pillories. Of course one must remember that it was necessary in England to obtain permission from the king in order to leave the country. Also

---

[19] Ibid, pp 247-248.

[20] Green, p 481.

required were the ships and provisions for transporting the people across the Atlantic Ocean to America. The focus during the reign of Elizabeth was on exploration, piracy and plunder of Spanish ships laden with treasure, finding shorter trade routes, and trade in the new world. No permanent settlements followed Raleigh's three settlements in the islands off North Carolina from 1585 to 1587.

The first settlement in America was in 1606 resulting when James issued a charter for two settlements. The next significant emigration was by the puritans who were given privilege by James, although reluctantly, to settle in America. There followed in the reign of Charles I numerous settlers, establishing in 1628 Salem, north of Plymouth, and a number of other settlements in Massachusetts. John Winthrop, with some 840 settlers, established the Massachusetts Bay Company in Boston in 1630. More settlers arrived in New England, as it was called. Religion continued a source of conflict and dissenters established settlements in Exeter (1637), Portsmouth (1638), New Hampshire, and Newport (1639). Rhode Island welcomed persons of all religious views. Lord Baltimore founded The Roman Catholic colony in Maryland, in 1629, as a refuge for Catholics. It was tolerant of other religious beliefs.

Uprisings in Scotland

While the puritans fled to America the Presbyterians in Scotland had abolished the Episcopal Church of England. A Presbyterian system of church government was established. Popular uprisings and military confrontation between the Scots and Charles's forces accompanied this revolution in religious practice and government. *Charles, from the natural piety or superstition of his temper, was extremely attached to the ecclesiastics: --- He had established it as a fixed maxim of policy, to increase the power and authority of that order. The prelates, he thought, established regularity and discipline among the clergy; the clergy inculcated obedience and loyalty among the people. --- Charles great aim was to complete the work, so happily begun by his father; to establish discipline upon a regular system of canons, to introduce a liturgy into public worship, and to render the ecclesiastical government of all his kingdoms regular and uniform. The canons for establishing ecclesiastical jurisdiction were promulgated in 1635; and were received by the nation, though without much appearing opposition, yet with great inward apprehension and discontent. Men felt displeasure, at seeing the royal authority highly exalted by them, and represented as absolute and uncontrollable. They saw these speculative principles reduced to practice, and a whole body of ecclesiastical laws as established without any previous consent either of church or state. They remarked that the delicate boundaries, which separate church and state, were already passed, and many civil ordinances established by the canons, under color of ecclesiastical institutions. --- The liturgy, which the king, from his own authority, imposed on Scotland, was copied from that of England: But lest a servile imitation might shock the pride of his ancient kingdom, a few alterations, in order to save appearances, were made in it; and in that shape it was transmitted to the bishops at Edinburgh. --- As no considerable symptoms of discontent appeared, they thought that they might safely proceed in their purpose; and accordingly, in the cathedral church of St. Giles, the dean of Edinburgh, arrayed in his surplice, began the service; the bishop himself and many of the privy council being present. But no sooner had the dean opened the book, than a multitude of the meanest sort, most of them women, clapping their hands, cursing, and crying out, 'A pope! A pope! Antichrist! Stone him!' raised such a tumult, that it was impossible to proceed with the service. The bishop, mounting the pulpit, in order to appease the populace, had a stool thrown at him. --- But it being known, that the king still persevered in his intentions of imposing that mode of worship, men fortified themselves still farther in their prejudices against it; and great multitudes resorted to Edinburgh, in order to oppose the introduction of so hated a novelty. It was not long before they broke out in the most violent disorder. --- In so violent a combination of a whole kingdom, Charles had nothing to oppose but a proclamation, in February, 1638; in which he pardoned all past offences, and exhorted the people to be more obedient for the future, and to submit peaceably to the use of the liturgy. The proclamation was instantly encountered with a public protestation, presented by the earl of Hume and lord Lindesey: And this was the first time, that men of quality had appeared in any violent act of opposition. But this proved a crisis. The insurrection, which had been advancing by gradual and slow progress, now blazed up at once.[21]*

The king's concessions

Above sixty thousand people were assembled in a tumultuous manner in Edinburgh and the neighborhood. Charles possessed no regular forces in either of his kingdoms. Charles made concessions to abolish the canons, the liturgy, and the high commission court. He even gave his commissioner Hamilton the authority for the Scots to call an assembly, *which was willingly embraced by the covenanters.* In September, 1638, *the assembly met at Glasgow: And, besides a great concourse of the people, all the nobility and gentry of any family or interest were present, either as members, assessors, or spectators; and it was apparent, that the resolutions, taken by the covenanters, could here meet with no manner of opposition. --- All the acts of assembly, since the accession of James to the crown of England, were, upon pretty reasonable grounds, declared null and invalid. The acts of parliament, which affected ecclesiastical affairs, were supposed, on that very*

---

[21] Hume, vol 5, pp 254-256.

account, to have no manner of authority. And thus episcopacy, the high commission, the articles of Perth, the canons, and the liturgy, were abolished and declared unlawful: And the whole fabric, which James and Charles, in along course of years, had been reading with so much care and policy, fell at once to the ground.

War with Scotland

The king raised an army but found that the Scots had an overwhelming force. Charles signed a truce at Berwick-upon-Tweed June 18, 1639. Charles summoned the fourth parliament, which met in April 1640, later known as the short parliament, in an attempt to raise money for war against Scotland. The commons again brought up grievances. Parliament was dissolved May 5, 1640. The king continued to rely on ship money to finance the war against Scotland. The Scottish army crossed the border in August. The Scots at Newburn defeated the king's troops, August 28, 1640. *The Scots first entreated them, with great civility, not to stop them in their march to their gracious sovereign; and then attacked them with great bravery, killed several, and chased the rest from their ground. Such a panic seized the whole English army, that the forces at Newcastle fled immediately to Durham; and not yet thinking themselves safe, they deserted that town, and retreated into Yorkshire. --- Charles was in a very distressed condition. The nation was universally and highly discontented. The army was discouraged and began likewise to be discontented. --- The treasury too was quite exhausted, and every expedient for supply had been tried to the uttermost. --- In order to prevent the advance of the Scots upon him, the king agreed to a treaty, and named sixteen English noblemen, who met with eleven Scottish commissioners at Rippon.*[22]

Impeachment of Strafford and Laud

The king summoned another parliament, the long parliament, which met November 3, 1640. The men of prominence in the commons, Pym, Hampden and Oliver Cromwell, had all been ready to embark to the new world. Eight ships were lying at anchor in the Thames River. Charles denied them passage, which turned out to be a great mistake. These men and others had been the most vocal opponents of the king's supremacy. They were spokesmen in the short parliament and Charles's previous parliaments. The first order of business was not to give the king supply but to impeach his chief minister, Strafford. *The earl of Strafford was considered as chief minister, both on account of the credit, which he possessed with his master, and of his own great and uncommon vigor and capacity. By a concurrence of accidents, this man labored under the severe hatred of all the three nations, which composed the British*

---

[22] Ibid, p 279, 280.

monarchy. --- Strafford, first as deputy, then as lord lieutenant, had governed Ireland during eight years with great vigilance, activity, and prudence, but with very little popularity. In a nation so averse to the *English government and religion, these very virtues were sufficient to draw on him the public hatred. The manners too, and character of this great man, though to all full of courtesy, and to his friends full of affection, were, at bottom, haughty, rigid, and severe. His authority and influence, during the time of this government, had been unlimited; but no sooner did adversity seize him, than the concealed aversion of the nation blazed up at once, and the Irish parliament used every expedient to aggravate the charge against him. The universal discontent, which prevailed in England against the court, was all pointed toward the earl of Strafford.*

No sooner was Stafford's arrival known, than a concerted attack was made upon him in the house of commons. Pym, in a long, studied discourse, enumerated all the grievances, under which the nation labored; and, from a complication of such oppressions, inferred, that a deliberate plan had been formed of changing entirely the frame of government, and subverting the ancient laws and liberties of the kingdom. Strafford was impeached. *In the inquiry concerning grievances and in the censure of past measures, Laud could not long escape the severe scrutiny of the commons; who were led too, in their accusation of that prelate, as well as by their prejudices against his whole order, as by the extreme antipathy, which his intemperate zeal had drawn him. After a deliberation, which scarcely lasted half an hour, an impeachment of high treason was voted against this subject, the first, both in rank and in favor, throughout the kingdom. --- The capitol articles, insisted on against these two great men, was the design, which the commons supposed to have been formed of subverting the laws and constitution of England, and introducing arbitrary and unlimited authority into the kingdom. --- Thus, in a few weeks, this house of commons, not opposed, or rather seconded by the peers, had produced such a revolution in the government, that the two most powerful and most favored ministers of the king were thrown into the Tower, and daily expected to be tried for their life: Two other ministers had, by flight alone, saved themselves from a like fate: All the king's servants saw that no protection could be given them by their master: A new jurisdiction was erected in the nation; and before that tribunal all those trembled, who had before exulted most in their credit and authority. --- And the commons reaped this multiplied advantage by their vote: They disarmed the crown; they established the maxims of rigid law and liberty; and they spread the terror of their own authority.*[23] Parliament changed the impeachment of Strafford into a bill of attainder. *In March 1641 Strafford was sequestered from parliament*

---

[23] Ibid, pp 286-290.

and confined in the Tower, a committee of thirteen was chosen by the lower house, and entrusted with the office of preparing a charge against him. This committee, by direction from both houses, took an oath of secrecy; a practice very unusual, and which gave them the appearance of conspirators, more than ministers of justice. But the intention of this strictness was to render it more difficult for the earl to elude their search, or prepare for his justification. --- The articles of impeachment against Strafford are twenty-eight in number. And this species of treason, discovered by the commons, is entirely new and unknown to the laws; so is the species of proof, by which they pretend to fix that guilt upon the prisoner. They have invested a kind of accumulative or constructive evidence, by which many actions either totally innocent in themselves, or criminal in a much inferior degree, shall, when united, amount to treason, and subject the person to the highest penalties inflicted by the law. A hasty and unguarded word, a rash and passionate action, assisted by the malevolent fancy of the accuser, and tortured by doubtful constructions, is transmuted into the deepest guilt; and the lives and fortunes of the whole nation, no longer protected by justice, are subjected to arbitrary will and pleasure. The bill of attainder passed the commons with no greater opposition than that of fifty-nine dissenting votes. --- But there remained two other branches of the legislature, the king and the lords, whose assent was requisite.

The king came to the house of lords: and though he expressed his resolution, for which he offered them any security, never again to employ Strafford in any branch of public business; he professed himself totally dissatisfied with regard to the circumstance of treason, and on that account declared his difficulty in giving his assent to the bill of attainder. The commons took fire, and voted it a breach of privilege for the king to take notice of any bill; depending before the houses. --- About eighty peers had constantly attended Strafford's trial; but such apprehensions were entertained on account of the popular tumults, that only forty-five were present when the bill of attainder was brought into the house. Yet of these, nineteen had the courage to vote against it. Charles, fearing for the safety of his queen, signed the order approving the bill of attainder, but begged parliament to substitute life imprisonment for his execution. *It is certain, that strong compunction for his consent to Strafford's execution attended this unfortunate prince, during the remainder of his life; and even at his own fatal end, the memory of this guilt, with great sorrow and remorse, recurred upon him.*[24] Strafford was beheaded May 12, 1641. Laud was executed four years later.

Star Chamber and High Commission abolished

---

[24] Ibid, 312-314.

The long parliament focused on many other issues. They felt they had the power to assert themselves. They passed a bill providing that parliament should not be dissolved without its own consent. *The most unpopular of all Charles's measures, and the least justifiable, was the revival of monopolies, so solemnly abolished, after reiterated endeavors, by a recent act of parliament.*[25] *From the reports of their committees, the house daily passed votes, which mortified and astonished the court, and inflamed and animated the nation. Ship money was declared illegal and arbitrary; the sentence against Hambden canceled; the court of York abolished; compositions for knighthood stigmatized; the enlargement of the forests condemned; patents for monopolies annulled; and every late measure of administration treated with reproach and obloquy.*[26] Acts were passed abolishing the Star Chamber and High Commission. The collection of ship money was declared to be illegal. Acts were passed prohibiting taxes on tonnage and poundage without consent of parliament. Charles reluctantly signed these acts of parliament. And so began a limited monarchy and a mixed form of government with the commons in the ascendant of power.

Threat of conspiracies

It was Goring who betrayed the secret to the popular leaders. --- Pym opened the matter in the house. On the first intimation of a discovery, Piercy concealed himself and Jeremy withdrew beyond sea. This further confirmed the suspicion of a dangerous conspiracy. Goring delivered his evidence before the house; Piercy wrote a letter to his brother, Northumberland, confessing most of the particulars. --- To convey more quickly the terror and indignation at this plot the commons voted, that a protestation should be signed by all the members. It tended to increase the popular panic, and intimated what was more expressly declared in the preamble, that these blessings were now exposed to the utmost peril.

Alarms were every day given of new conspiracies: In Lancashire, great multitudes of papists were assembling: Secret meetings were held by them in caves and under-ground in Surrey: They had entered into a plot to blow up the river with gun-powder, in order to drown the city: Provisions of arms were making beyond sea: Sometimes France, sometimes Denmark, was forming designs against the kingdom.[27] Clearly, what was developing was a state of war, with the emotions of fear and hatred dominating human thinking and the course of events. The

---

[25] Ibid, p 292.

[26] Ibid, p 297.

[27] Ibid, p 322.

leaders of the commons were protestant, at the time, predominantly of the puritan faction. In August 1641 articles of pacification were formed in Scotland giving *the prospect of spreading the Presbyterian discipline in England and Ireland. Charles, despoiled in England of a considerable part of his authority, and dreading still farther encroachments upon him, arrived in Scotland, with and intention of abdicating almost entirely the small share of power, which there remained to him, and of giving full satisfaction, if possible, to his restless subjects in that kingdom.*[28]

The Irish revolt and the massacre myth

There developed in England the myth of the Irish massacre of Protestants in northern Ireland at Island Magee, (25 miles north-northwest of Belfast), in about October 1641. This provided some of the motive force for the civil war, which followed the execution of the king, and the advent of Oliver Cromwell. The massacre myth provided justification for Cromwell's depredations at Drogheda, Wexford and across Ireland.

We have already presented during the reign of Henry VIII the onset of the religious wars involving Protestants and Catholics, and which continued during the reigns of his children, Edward, Mary and Elizabeth. We have also noted during the reign of James I the establishment in the north of Ireland, plantations of English and Scots, which dislocated the Irish from their homes and land. From Hume: *There was a gentleman called Roger More, who, though of a narrow fortune, was descended from an ancient Irish family, and was much celebrated among his countrymen for valor and capacity. This man first formed the project of expelling the English, and asserting the independency of his native country. --- He observed to them, that, by the rebellion of the Scots, and factions of the English, the king's authority in Britain was reduced to so low a condition, that he never could exert himself with any favor, in maintaining the English dominion over Ireland; --- that the Scots having so successfully thrown off dependence on the crown of England, and assumed the government into their own hands, had set an example to the Irish, who had so much greater oppressions to complain of; than the English* (and Scot) *planters, who had expelled them their possessions, suppressed their religion, and bereaved them of their liberties.*[29]

An attempt was made by More and Maguire to seize the castle in Dublin which contained arms for 10,000 men. The guards who were warned in advance averted the attack. But there occurred an insurrection of Catholics against the Protestants in Ulster and the Island Magee,

---

[28] Ibid, pp 332-333.

[29] Ibid, pp 338-339.

which is portrayed as a massacre by Hume,[30] and by most Anglo-American historians.

The accounts of two Irish historians follow. From Cusack: *The king was now obliged to disband his Irish forces, and their commanders were sent orders for that purpose. They had instruction, however, to keep the men at home and together, so that they might easily be collected again if they could be made available, as strange to say, the so-called 'Irish rebels' were the only real hope which Charles had to rely on in his conflict with his disloyal English subjects. An understanding was soon entered into between these officers and the Irish party. They agreed to act in concert; and one of the former, Colonel Plunket, suggested the seizure of the Dublin castle. The 23rd of October was fixed on for the enterprise; but the attempt was frustrated by a betrayal of the plot, in consequence of an indiscretion of one of the leaders.*

The rage of the Protestant party knew no limits. The Castle was put in a state of defense, troops were ordered in all directions and proclamations were issued. In the meantime the conspirators at a distance had succeeded better, but unfortunately they were not aware of the failure in Dublin until it was too late. Sir Phelim O'Neill; was at the head of 30,000 men. He issued a proclamation, stating that he intended 'no hurt to the king, or hurt of any of his subjects, English or Scotch; but that his only object was the defense of Irish liberty.' He added that 'whatever hurt was done to any one, should be personally repaired.' The proclamation was dated and signed 23rd of October, 1641. --- *The Irish were treated with barbarous severity, especially by Sir Charles Coote; which they were most careful to avoid any bloodshed, except what was justifiable and unavoidable in war. --- The massacre of Island Magee took place about this period; and though the exact date is disputed, and the exact number of victims had been questioned, it cannot be disproved that the English and Scotch settlers at Carrickfergus sallied forth at night, and murdered a number of defenseless men, women, and children. That there was no regular or indiscriminate massacres of Protestants by the Catholics at this period, appears to be proved beyond question by the fact, that no mention of such an outrage was made in any of the letters of the Lords Justices to the Privy Council.* [31]

Another Irish historian, Seumas Mac Manus, gives the following account: *For purpose now, of inciting the English at home to wipe out the Irish --- and thus provide more estates for the covetous in Britain, there was invented a story of fearful massacre of almost all the Protestants of Ireland, on the night of the Rising. Not only did the eager*

---

[30] Note. The single reference cited by Hume to the details of the massacre is a work by Temple.

[31] Cusack, pp 479-480.

English readily believe it, but, after a while, the parties in Ireland who started the story almost came to believe it themselves. And many thousands of good, sincere Irish Protestants, and many thousands of ardent English, to this day believe the tale of a wild and indiscriminate massacre. So far went this effort to lay unbridled savagery at the doors of the Irish people, and so far succeeded, that many earnest and sincere historians, accepting the carefully prepared 'facts' put upon record for the purpose, themselves believed, and through succeeding generations and centuries perpetuated the memory of, 'the great Popish Massacre.'

The Rev. Ferdinand Warner, Protestant minister, in his 'History of the Irish Rebellion' written shortly after the event, says; 'It is easy enough to demonstrate the falsehood of the relation of every English historian of the rebellion' --- and he calculates that 4,028 Protestants were killed within the first two years of the war, and 8,000 died of ill-usage. But the Cromwellian commission appointed after the war to investigate all murders and injuries inflicted upon all the British settlers in Ireland, during the whole ten years' war --- a commission animated by plenty of healthy prejudice, and eager to accept anything in the shape of evidence against the Irish --- found 2,109 murders in the ten years of war.

Finally this long cherished and widely advertised great Popish Massacre may be disposed of in the words of the zealous, old time, Protestant historian, Rev. Dr. Taylor (in his Civil Wars of Ireland): 'The Irish massacre of 1641 has been a phrase so often repeated even in books of education that one can scarcely conceal the surprise when he learns that the tale is apocryphal as the wildest fiction of romance.' He also says: 'The stories of massacre and of horrid cruelty were circulated in England because it was to the interest of the patriot party in parliament to propagate such delusion.' [32]

The Grand Remonstrance and the king's reaction

Before pursuing the subject of the grand remonstrance in parliament, notice should be given to a very important event, the marriage of the princess Mary with William of Orange, September 9, 1641. *This was the commencement of the connections with the family of Orange: Connections, which were afterwards attended with the most important consequences, both to the kingdom and to the house of Stuart. --- It was feared, that, if the religious rage, which has seized the multitude, be allowed to evaporate, they will quickly return to the ancient ecclesiastical establishment.* It was feared that the king would garner control of the army, reverse all the gains of parliament, and return the kingdom to the papists.

---

[32] Mac Manus, pp 408-412.

In November 1641, the leaders of parliament drew up the grand remonstrance, a written document meant for popular circulation to explain the actions and plans of parliament versus the king. *To make the attack on royal authority by regular approaches, it was thought proper to frame a general remonstrance of the state of the nation; and accordingly the committee, which, at the first meeting of parliament, had been chosen for that purpose, and which had hitherto made no progress in their work, received fresh injunctions to finish that undertaking.*

The committee brought into the house that remonstrance, which had become so memorable, and which was soon afterwards attended with such important consequences. It was not addressed to the king; but was openly declared to be an appeal to the people. The harshness of the matter was equaled by the severity of the language. It consists of many gross falsehoods, intermingled with some evident truths: Malignant insinuations are joined to open invective: Loud complaints of the past, accompanied with jealous prognostications of the future. Whatever unfortunate, whatever invidious, whatever suspicious measure, had been embraced by the king from the commencement of his reign, is insisted on and aggravated with merciless rhetoric: The unsuccessful expeditions to Cadiz and the isle of Rhe, are mentioned: The sending of ships to France for the suppression of the Hugonots: The forced loans: The illegal confinement of men for not obeying illegal commands: The violent dissolution of four parliaments: The arbitrary government which always succeeded: The questioning, fining, and imprisoning of members for their conduct in the house: The levying of taxes without consent of the commons: The introducing of superstitious innovations into the church, without authority of law: In short, every thing, which, either with or without reason, had given offence, during the course of fifteen years, from the accession of the king to the calling of the present parliament

This remonstrance, so full of acrimony and violence, was a plain sign for some further attacks intended on royal prerogative, and a declaration, that the concessions, already made, however important, were not to be regarded as satisfactory. What pretensions would be advanced, how unprecedented, how unlimited, were easily imagined; and nothing less was foreseen, whatever ancient names might be preserved, than an abolition, almost total, of the monarchical government of England. The opposition, therefore, which the remonstrance met with in the house of commons, was great. For above fourteen hours, the debates as warmly managed; and from the weariness of the king's party, which probably consisted chiefly of the elderly people, and men of cool spirits, the vote was at last carried by a small majority of eleven. Some time after, the remonstrance was ordered to be printed and published, without being carried up to the house of peers, for their assent and concurrence.[33]

---

[33] Hume, vol 5, p 331, pp 351-353.

In order to obtain a majority in the upper house, the commons had recourse to the populace, who, on other occasions, had done them such important service. Amidst the greatest security, they affected continual fears of destruction to themselves and the nation, and seemed to quake at every breath or rumor of danger. They again, excited the people by never-ceasing inquiries after conspiracies, by reports of insurrections, by feigned intelligence of invasions from abroad, by discoveries of dangerous combinations at home among papists and their adherents. All stories of plots, however ridiculous, were willingly attended to, and were dispersed among the multitude, to whose capacity they were well adapted. The pulpits likewise were called in aid, and resounded with the dangers, which threatened religion, from the desperate attempts of papists and malignants. Multitudes flocked towards Westminster, and insulted the prelates and such of the lords as adhered to the crown.

The king's show of force in parliament

Charles was enraged to find that all his concessions but increased their demands; that the people, who were returning to a sense of duty towards him, were again roused to sedition and tumults; that the blackest calumnies were propagated against him, and even the Irish massacre ascribed to his counsels and machinations. --- Herbert, attorney-general, appeared in the house of peers, and, in his majesty's name, entered an accusation of high treason against lord Kimbolton and five commoners, Hollis, sir Arthur Hazlerig, Hambden, Pym, and Strode. The articles were, that they had traitorously endeavored to subvert the fundamental laws and government of the kingdom, to deprive the king of his regal power, and to impose on his subjects an arbitrary and tyrannical authority. --- These five members, at least Pym, Hambden, and Hollis, are the very heads of the popular party; and if these be taken off, what fate must be expected by their followers, who are many of them accomplices in the same treason?

The house voted all these acts of violence to be breaches of privilege, and commanded every one to defend the liberty of the members. In January 1642, the king, irritated by all this opposition, resolved next day to come in person to the house, with an intention to demand, perhaps seize in their presence, the persons whom he had accused. This resolution was discovered to the countess of Carlisle, sister of Northumberland, a lady of spirit, wit, and intrigue. She privately sent intelligence to the five members; and they had time to withdraw, a moment before the king entered. He was accompanied by his ordinary retinue to the number of above two hundred, armed as usual, some with halberts, some with walking swords. --- The commons were in the utmost disorder; and, when the king was departing, some members cried aloud, so as he might hear them, 'Privilege!, Privilege!' and the house immediately adjourned till next day.

That evening, the accused members, to show their greater apprehension, removed into the city, which was their fortress. The citizens were the whole night, in arms. --- *When the house of commons met, they affected the greatest dismay; and adjourning themselves for some days, ordered a committee to sit in Merchant-Taylors hall in the city. The committee made an exact inquiry into all circumstances attending the king's entry into the house: Every passionate speech, every menacing gesture of any, even the meanest, of his attendants, was recorded and aggravated. An intention of offering violence to the parliament, of seizing the accused members in the very house, and of murdering all who should make resistance, was inferred. And the unparalleled breach of privilege, so it was called, was still ascribed to the counsel of papists and their adherents.* --- *A letter was pretended to be intercepted, and was communicated to the committee, who pretended to lay great stress upon it. One Catholic there congratulates another on the accusation of the member; and represents that incident as a branch of the same pious contrivance, which had excited the Irish insurrection, and by which the profane heretics would soon be exterminated in England. A number of petitions were presented in commons*

The king, apprehensive of danger from the enraged multitude, had retired to Hampton-court, deserted by all the world, and overwhelmed with grief, shame, and remorse, for the fatal measures into which he had been hurried. His distressed situation he could no longer ascribe to the rigors of destiny, or the malignity of enemies: His own precipitancy and indiscretion must bear the blame of whatever disaster should henceforth befall him.[34] A number of petitions were presented in commons. One petition favored removal of the bishops from the house of peers, the Root and Branch bill. Another petition accused the bishops and others of treason for voting against the commons. The petitioners who brought favorable acts in support of the king were arrested. *The king's authority was at that time reduced to the lowest ebb.* A few days later, the king went to Yorkshire. The queen, threatened with an impeachment, retreated to France, taking with her the crown jewels, which she hoped to use to supply an army in support of the king.

Civil War

War between parliament and the king came with failure of Charles to relinquish the claims of monarchy. The outcome would be determined by the party which had superior military force in accordance with the rule of law that *the sword rules.* The king did not have a standing army. *Both houses of parliament had passed a bill that totally disarmed the crown, and had not left in any magistrate military authority, sufficient for the defense and security of the nation.* --- *A bill*

---

[34] Ibid, pp 364-369.

was introduced and passed the two houses, which restored to lieutenants and deputies the same powers, of which the votes of the commons had bereaved them; but at the same time the names of all the lieutenants were inserted in the bill; and these consisted entirely of men, in whom the parliament could confide. And for their conduct, they were accountable, by the express terms of the bill, not to the king, but to the parliament. A large magazine of arms being placed in the town of Hull, they dispatched thither Sir John Hotham, a gentleman of considerable fortune in the neighborhood, and of an ancient familty; and they gave him the authority of governor. They sent orders to Goring, governor of Portrsmouth, to obey, no commands but such as he should receive from the parliament.[35]

The king had the support of most of the nobles in the house of peers and some of the members of commons. *Charles had resolved to remove farther from London: And accordingly, taking the prince of Wales and the duke of York along with him, he arrived, by slow journeys, at York, which he determined for some time to make the place of his residence. The distant parts of the kingdom, being removed from that furious vortex of new principles and opinions, which had transported the capital, still retained a sincere regard for the church and monarchy; and the king here found marks of attachment beyond what he had before expected. From all quarters of England, the prime nobility and gentry, either personally, or by messages and letters, expressed their duty towards him; and exhorted him to save himself and them from that ignominious slavery, with which they were threatened. The magazine of Hull contained the arms of all the forces levied against the Scots; and Sir John Hotham, the governor, refused to receive the king, and shut the gates. Charles immediately, proclaimed him traitor, and complained to the parliament of his disobedience. --- The county of York levied a guard for the king of 600 men. --- The queen, disposing of the crown-jewels in Holland, had been enabled to purchase a cargo of arms and ammunition. Part of these, after escaping many perils, arrived safely to the king.*

Demands of parliament

That the king might despair of all composition, the parliament sent him the conditions, on which they were willing to come to an agreement. Their demands, contained in nineteen propositions amounted to a total abolition of monarchical authority. They required, that no man should remain in the council, who was not agreeable to parliament; that no deed of the king's should have validity, unless it passed the council, and was attested under their hand; that all the officers of state and principal judges should be chosen with consent of parliament, and enjoy their offices for life; that none of the royal family should marry without

---

[35] Ibid, pp 374-375.

consent of parliament or council; that the laws should be executed against Catholics; that the votes of popish lords should be excluded; that the reformation of the liturgy and church-government should have place, according to advice of parliament; that the ordinance with regard to the militia, be submitted to; that the justice of parliament pass upon all delinquents; that a general pardon be granted, with such exceptions as should be advised by parliament; that the forts and castles be disposed of by consent of parliament, and that no peer be made but with consent of both houses.

The king's rejection and war

The king rejected these proposals. *The king and all his counselors esteemed war on any terms, preferable to so ignominious a peace. Charles accordingly resolved to support his authority by arms. 'His towns,' he said, 'were taken from him, his ships, his arms, his money; but there still remained to him a good cause, and the hearts of his loyal subjects, which, with God's blessing, he doubted not, would recover all the rest.' Collecting therefore some forces, he advanced southwards; and at Nottingham, August 25, 1642, he erected his royal standard, the open signal of discord and civil war throughout the kingdom.*[36]

In this manner the civil war started. Only a few highlights and issues of the civil war can here be presented. The first confrontation of significance was the battle of Edgehill, October 23, 1642. *At the conclusion, 5,000 men are said to have been found dead on the field of battle; and the loss of the two armies, as far as we can judge by the opposite accounts, was nearly equal.* Soon after this battle, negotiations between parliament and the king were held at Oxford early in 1643. The king refused again the nineteen articles and the power of parliament to assert itself. There were a number of battles fought in 1643, with the balance in favor of the king. Hampden was killed in battle and in 1643 Pym died.

Scots and parliament defeat the king

In September 1643, an agreement between the English parliament and the Scots was established. *The English parliament was, at that time, fallen into great distress, by the progress of the royal arms; and they gladly sent to Edinburgh commissioners, with ample power, to treat of a nearer union and confederacy with the Scottish nation.* The Solemn League and Covenant was framed at Edinburgh, which effaced all former restraints and vows taken in both kingdoms; and long maintained its credit and authority. The subscribers of the covenant vowed to preserve the reformed religion established in the Church of

---

[36] Ibid, pp 382-385.

Scotland; but by the artifice of Vane, no declaration more explicit was made with regard to England and Ireland, than that these kingdoms should be reformed, *according to the word of God and the example of the purest churches.* --- *Great were the rejoicings among the Scots, that they should be the happy instruments of extending their mode of religion, and dissipating that profound darkness, in which the neighboring nations were involved.*[37]

The Scots, early in 1644, entered the war, crossed the border into England and won several battles. The battle of Marston-moor July 2, 1644, was the largest battle in the war fought between the royalist and parliament forces supported by the Scots. *This action was obstinately disputed between the most numerous armies, that were engaged during the course of these wars; nor were the forces on each side much different in number. Fifty thousand British troops were led to mutual slaughter; and the victory seemed long undecided between them. Prince Rupert, who commanded the right wing of the royalists, was opposed to Cromwell, who conducted the choice troops of the parliament. --- After a sharp combat, the cavalry of the royalists gave way; and such of the infantry, as stood next them, were likewise borne down, and put to flight.*[38] The general leading the parliament forces in the battle of Marston-moor was Oliver Cromwell.

Presbyterians and Independents

Cromwell represented the Independents (Congregationalists) who were opposed by the Presbyterians. The Independents developed in England while the Presbyterians flourished in Scotland, before their ascendancy in England. The Presbyterians derived their doctrines and beliefs from the Swiss reformer John Calvin. As noted in the last two chapters, John Knox was an avid promulgator of the Presbyterian doctrines. There was little influence of the Presbyterians on the Church of England during the reigns of Elizabeth and James. In 1640, Charles was forced to accept a bill, removing bishops from all civil offices. In 1643 the Westminster Assembly convened, *consisting of 121 divines and 30 laymen, celebrated in their party for piety and learning.* Their advice and recommendations were not approved by parliament or by the king. In the summer of 1644, parliament had carried out its plan of calling an assembly of Puritan clergymen to meet at Westminster. The Westminster Assembly opposed church rule by bishops and episcopacy. Both houses of parliament voted that the Church of England become Presbyterian in its organization. The Westminster Confession was adopted.[39] The use of

---

[37] Ibid, pp 422-423.

[38] Ibid, p 436.

[39] Note. Still in use today by the Presbyterian churches.

the book of common prayer was forbidden. Altars and crucifixes were destroyed. Stained glass windows and religious artifacts were destroyed. Presbyteries took the place of bishoprics. The Assembly took the place of the king and High Commission. The Presbyterians imposed their religion on all others. This was accepted by the English parliament in 1648.

The Independents, of which Oliver Cromwell was the head, *rejected all ecclesiastical establishments, and would admit of no spiritual courts, no government among pastors, no interposition of the magistrate in religious concerns, no fixed encouragement annexed to any system of doctrines or opinions. According to their principles, each congregation, united voluntarily and by spiritual ties, composed, within itself, a separate church, and exercised a jurisdiction, but one destitute of temporal sanctions, over its own pastor and it own members. The election alone of the congregation was sufficient to bestow the sacerdotal character; and all essential distinction was denied between the laity and the clergy.*[40]

The new model army and the battle of Naseby

Presbyterians and Independents were not only different in belief and practice but became hostile forces one against another. The Presbyterians had obtained concessions from the king and believed the king would accept the proposals of parliament, without further conflict. The Independents wished to continue the war to achieve a complete victory over the king. A new model army under the command of Fairfax and Cromwell was formed. The battle of Naseby, June 14, 1645, led to the defeat of the king's army. Letters from the king to the queen were intercepted which showed that the king planned to bring a foreign army into England. The king's forces suffered more defeats later that year and Charles retreated to Oxford. Oxford was surrounded and in April 1646, Charles escaped to Newark where Charles surrendered to the Scotch army May 5, 1646.

The king seized by the Independents

On June 3, 1647 the king was seized. *A party of five hundred horse appeared at Holdenby, conducted by one Joyce.* Protests from the king and parliamentary commissioners were met by Joyce who said *'the king must immediately go with me'. --- The king, after protracting the time as long as he could, went into his coach; and was safely conducted to the army near Cambridge. The parliament, informed of this event by their commissioners, were thrown into the utmost consternation. Fairfax himself was no less surprised at the king's arrival. That bold measure, executed by Joyce, had never been communicated to the general. The orders were entirely verbal; and no body avowed them. And, while every*

---

[40] Ibid, p 442.

one affected astonishment at the enterprise, Cromwell, by whose counsel it had been directed, arrived from London, and put an end to their deliberations.

The parliament, though at present defenseless, was possessed of many resources; and time might easily enable them to resist that violence, with which they were threatened. Without further deliberation, therefore, Cromwell advanced the army upon them, and arrived in a few days at St. Albans. --- There being no signs of resistance, the army, in order to save appearances, removed, at the desire of the parliament, to a greater distance from London, and fixed their headquarters at Reading. They carried the king along with them in all their marches. Attempts of Cromwell to negotiate with the king were unsuccessful. The king said on several occasions: *'You cannot be without me. You cannot settle the nation but by my assistance.'* [41] Cromwell marched to London with the king. *It behooved the parliament to submit. The army marched in triumph through the city; but preserved the greatest order, decency, and appearance of humility. They conducted to Westminster the two speakers, who took their seats as if nothing had happened. The eleven impeached members, being accused as authors of the tumult, were expelled; and most of them retired beyond the sea: Seven peers were impeached: The mayor, one sheriff, and three aldermen, sent to the Tower: Several citizens and officers of the militia were committed to prison. Every deed of the parliament annulled, from the day of the tumult till the return of the speakers: The lines about the city leveled: The militia restored to the independents.*

The leaders of the army, having established their dominion over the parliament and city, ventured to bring the king to Hampton-Court; and he lived, for some time, in that palace, with an appearance of dignity and freedom. --- Intelligence being daily brought to the king of menaces thrown out by the agitators; he began to think of retiring from Hampton-Court, and of putting himself in some place of safety. [42] The king escaped with three assistants and arrived at Tichfield. His escape to France was prevented and the king fled to the Isle of Wight. The governor there, Hampton, was entirely dependent on Cromwell. The army framed four proposals, which they brought to the king. The king was required to give control of the military to parliament, to recall all his proclamations and declarations against the parliament; that he was to annul all the acts and appointment of peers, renounce the power of making peers without consent of parliament, and allow both houses of parliament to adjourn as they thought proper. *No sooner had the king refused his assent to the four bills, than Hammond, by orders from the army, removed all his*

---

[41] Ibid, pp 497- 505.

[42] Ibid, pp 508-509.

servants, cut off his correspondence with his friends, and shut him up in close confinement.

The second civil war

 The advance of the army to London, the subjection of the parliament, the seizing of the king at Holdenby, his confinement at Carlsbroke-castle, (on the Isle of Wight), *were so many blows, sensibly felt by that nation; as threatening the final overthrow of Presbytery, to which they were so passionately devoted.* The parliament of Scotland had voted appropriations to arm 40,000 men in support of the king's authority. --- *While the Scots were making preparations for the invasion of England, every part of that kingdom was agitated with tumults, insurrections, conspiracies, and discontents. --- And having gained a complete victory over the crown, they found themselves loaded with a multiplicity of taxes, formerly unknown; and scarcely an appearance of law and liberty remained in the administration. The Presbyterians, who had chiefly supported the war, were enraged to find the prize, just when it seemed within their reach, snatched by violence, from them. The royalists, disappointed in their expectations, by the cruel treatment, which the king now received from the army, were strongly animated to restore him to liberty, and to recover the advantages, which they had unfortunately lost. All orders of men were inflamed with indignation at seeing the military prevail over the civil power, and king and parliament at once reduced to subjection by a mercenary army.*[43]

 In July 1648 uprisings took place in favor of the king in Kent, Essex, Surrey, Wales as well as Scotland. Cromwell and the military council prepared themselves with vigor and conduct for defense. The establishment of the army was, at this time, 26,000 men. Colonel Horton first attacked the revolted troops in Wales, and gave them a considerable defeat. The remnants of the vanquished threw themselves into Pembroke, and were there closely besieged, and soon after taken, by Cromwell. Lambert was opposed to Langdale in the north, and gained advantages. Sir Michael Livesey defeated the earl of Holland at Kingston, and pursuing his victory, took him prisoner at St. Neots. Fairfax, having routed the Kentish royalists at Maidstone, followed the broken army: And when they joined the royalists of Essex, and threw themselves into Colchester; he laid siege to that place. --- Hamilton, having entered England with a numerous, though undisciplined, army durst not unite his forces with those of Langdale; because the English royalists had refused to take the convenant; and the Scottish Presbyterians, though engaged of the king, refused to join them on any other terms.

 Cromwell feared not to oppose 8,000 men, to the numerous armies of 20,000, commanded by Hamilton and Langdale. He attacked

---

[43] Ibid, 520-521.

the later by surprise, near Preston in Lancashire; and, though the royalists made a brave resistance, yet, not being succored in time by their confederates, they were almost entirely cut in pieces. Hamilton was next attacked, put to rout, and pursued to Utoxeter, whether he surrendered himself prisoner. Cromwell followed his advantage; and marching into Scotland with a considerable body, Joined Argyle, who was also in arms; and having suppressed the moderate Presbyterians, he placed power entirely in the hands of the violent party.

Purge of parliament

A fresh remonstrance from the council of officers called for the election of a new parliament; for electoral reform; for the recognition of the supremacy of the houses in all things; for the change of kingship, should it be retained, into a magistracy elected by the parliament, and without veto on its proceedings. Above all, they demanded that 'the capital and grand author of our troubles, by whose commissions, commands, and procurement, and in whose behalf and for whose interest only, of will and power, all our wars and troubles have been, with all the miseries attending them, may be specially brought to justice for the treason, blood, and mischief he is therein guilty of.' The demand drove the houses to despair. Their reply was to accept the king's concessions, unimportant as they were, as a basis of peace. The step was accepted by the soldiers as a defiance: Charles was again seized by a troop of horse, and carried off to Hurst Castle, while a letter from Fairfax announced the march of his army upon London. 'We shall know now,' said Vane, as fresh troops took their post round the houses of parliament, 'who is on the side of the king, and who on the side of the people.' But the terror of the army proved weaker among the members than the agonized loyalty, which strove to save the monarchy and the Church, and a large majority in both houses still voted for the acceptance of the terms which Charles had offered.

The next morning saw Colonel Pride at the door of the house of commons with a list of forty members of the majority in his hands. The council of officers had resolved to exclude them, and as each member made his appearance he was arrested, and put in confinement. 'By what right do you act?' a member asked, 'By the right of the sword,' Hugh Peters is said to have replied. The house was still resolute, but on the following morning forty more members were excluded, and the rest gave way. The sword had fallen; and the two great powers which had waged this bitter conflict, the parliament and the monarchy, suddenly disappeared. The expulsion of one hundred and forty members, in a word of the majority of the existing house, reduced the commons to a name. The remnant who remained to co-operate with the army were no longer representative of the will of the country; in the course imagery of popular speech they were but the 'rump' of a parliament. While the house of commons dwindled away to a sham, the house of lords passed away altogether.[44]

The trial and execution of the king

A court of High Commission was appointed by the rump parliament consisting of one hundred and fifty commissioners. *The solicitor, in the name of the commons, represented, that Charles Stuart, being admitted king of England, and entrusted with a limited power; yet nevertheless from a wicked design to erect an unlimited and tyrannical government, had traiterously and maliciously levied war against the present parliament, and the people, whom they represented, and was therefore impeached as a tyrant, traitor, murderer, and a public and implacable enemy to the commonwealth. After the charge was finished, the president directed his discourse to the king, and told him that the court expected his answer.*

The king, though long detained a prisoner, and now produced as a criminal, sustained, by his magnanimous courage, the majesty of a monarch. With great temper and dignity, he declined the authority of the court, and refused to submit himself to their jurisdiction. He represented, that, having been engaged in treaty with his two houses of parliament, and having finished almost every article, he had expected to be brought to his capital in another manner, and ere this time, to have been restored to his power, dignity, revenue, as well as to his personal liberty: That he could not now perceive any appearance of the upper house, so essential a member of the constitution; and had learned, that even the commons, whose authority was pretended, were subdued by lawless force, and were bereaved of their liberty: That he himself was their native hereditary king; nor was the whole authority of the state, though free and united, entitled to try him, who derived his dignity from the Supreme Majesty of Heaven: --- That those, who arrogated a title to sit as his judges, were born his subjects, and born subject to those laws, which determined, 'That the king can do no wrong.'

Three times was Charles produced before the court, and as often declined their jurisdiction. On the fourth, the judges having examined some witnesses, by whom it was proved, that the king had appeared in arms against the forces commissioned by the parliament, they pronounced sentence against him.

It is confessed, that the king's behavior, during this last scene of his life, does honor to his memory; and that, in all appearances before his judges, he never forgot his part, either as a prince or as a man. Three days were allowed the king between his sentence and his execution. This interval he passed with great tranquility, chiefly in reading and devotion. All his family, that remained in England, were allowed access to him. It

---

[44] Green, vol 2, pp 433-434.

consisted only of the princess Elizabeth and the duke of Gloucester, for the duke of York had made his escape. Gloucester was little more than an infant. The princess, notwithstanding her tender years, showed an advanced judgment and the calamities of her family had made a deep impression upon her. After many pious consolations and advice, the king gave her in charge to tell the queen, that, during the whole course of his life, he had never once, even in thought, failed in his fidelity towards her; and that his conjugal tenderness and his life should have an equal duration. ---

It must be observed, that no reader, almost of any party or principle, was ever shocked, when he read, in ancient history, that the Roman senate voted Nero, their absolute sovereign, to be a public enemy, and, even without trial, condemned him to the severest and most ignominious punishment; a punishment, from which the meanest Roman citizen, was, by the law, exempted. The crimes of that bloody tyrant are so enormous, that they break through all rules; and extort a confession, that such a dethroned prince is no longer superior to his people, and can no longer plead, in his own defense, laws, which were established for conducting the ordinary course of administration. But when we pass from the case of Nero to that of Charles, the great disproportion, or rather total contrariety, of character immediately strikes us: and we stand astonished, that, among a civilized people, so much virtue could ever meet with so fatal a catastrophe. --- But, it must be confessed, that these events furnish us with another instruction, no less natural, and no less useful, concerning the madness of the people, the furies of fanaticism, and the danger of mercenary armies.

At one blow was his head severed from his body. A man in a vizor performed the office of executioner: Another, in a like disguise, held up to the spectators, the head, streaming with blood, and cried aloud, 'This is the head of a traitor!' [45] *The king left six children; three males, Charles, born in 1630, James, duke of York, born in 1633, Henry, duke of Gloucester, born in 1641; and three females, Mary princess of Orange, born in 1631, Elizabeth, born in 1635, and Henrietta, afterwards duchess of Orleans, born at Exeter 1644.*

---

[45] Hume, vol 5, pp 537-540.

Chapter 30

The Interregnum
and
Oliver Cromwell

The interregnum is the period from the death of Charles I in 1649, to the restoration of the monarchy by Charles II in 1660. The Commonwealth is the period referred to by most historians from 1649 to 1653, while the Protectorate is referred to as the period from 1653 to 1660. Yet it is clear that the interregnum was really a government by a military dictatorship. The army led by Oliver Cromwell had gained complete control of England. In the previous chapter the military victories by the army and Cromwell at Marston-Moor, 1644, and Naseby, 1645, over the king were noted. The army and Cromwell, in 1649, eliminated the house of peers and retained only the rump parliament made up of men who went along with the army. Under the army and Cromwell, Charles I was tried and beheaded January 30. 1649.

Oliver Cromwell, (b 1599, d 1658), *was born at Huntingdon, the last year of the former century, of a good family; though he himself, being the son of a second brother, inherited but a small estate from his father. In the course of his education he had been sent to the university; but his genius was found little fitted for the calm and elegant occupations of learning; and he made small proficiencies in his studies. He even threw himself into a dissolute and disorderly course of life; and he consumed, in gaming, drinking, debauchery, and country riots, the more early years of his youth, and dissipated part of his patrimony. All of a sudden, the spirit of reformation seized him; he married, affected a grave and composed behavior, entered into all the zeal and rigor of the puritanical party, and offered to restore to every one whatever sums he had formerly gained by gaming.* Cromwell had married, in 1620, Elizabeth, daughter of Sir James Bourchier, a wealthy merchant in London. *The same vehemence of temper, which had transported him into the extremes of pleasure, now distinguished his religious habits. His house was the resort of all the zealous clergy of the party; and his hospitality, as well as his liberalities to the silenced and deprived ministers, proved as chargeable as his former debaucheries. Though he had acquired a tolerable fortune by a maternal uncle, he found his affairs so injured by his expenses, that he was obliged to take a farm at St. Ives, and apply himself, for some years, to agriculture as a profession. But this expedient served rather to involve him in farther debts and difficulties. From accident and intrigue he was chosen by the town of Cambridge member of the long parliament. His domestic affairs were then in great disorder; and he seemed not to posses any talent, which could qualify him to rise in that public sphere, into which he was now at last entered. His person was ungraceful, his dress slovenly, his voice untunable, his elocution homely, tedious, obscure, and embarrassed. The fervor of his spirit frequently prompted him to rise in the house; but he was not heard with attention. His name, for above two years, is not to be found oftener than twice in any committee; and those committees, into which he was admitted, were chosen for affairs, which would more interest the zealots than the men of business. In comparison of the eloquent speakers and fine gentlemen of the house, he was entirely overlooked; and his friend Hambden alone,* his near kinsman, *was acquainted with the depth of his genius, and foretold, that, if a civil war should ensue, he would soon rise to eminence and distinction. He was no less than forty-three years of age, when he first embraced the military profession; and by force of genius, without any master, he soon became an excellent officer. --- He raised a troop of horse; fixed his quarters in Cambridge. --- His troop of horse he soon augmented to a regiment; and he first instituted that discipline and inspired that spirit, which rendered the parliamentary armies in the end victorious.*[1]

Hambden's judgment of Cromwell proved to be correct. His talents as a military man and religious leader of his troops were exemplified by his major role in the defeat of the king at Marston-Moor, as well as the defeat of the royalists at Naseby, in June 1645. These victories were a prelude to the ascendancy of Cromwell's power. The purge of parliament and the execution of the king fulfilled Cromwell and the Independent party's objectives to get complete victory over their opponents. The rump parliament appointed a council of state, thirty-eight in number, to administer the nation backed by the army. Cromwell was appointed as the first chairman of the council of state. On May 19, 1649, commons abolished the office of king and the house of lords. What remained of the house of commons declared that *the people of England were a Commonwealth and Free State, by the supreme authority of this nation.* Opposition by other political parties such as the Levellers, who insisted on an equal distribution of power and property; and the

---

[1] Hume, vol 6, pp 55-56.

Millenarians or fifth-monarchy men, who believed that government itself should be abolished, were suppressed.

Invasion and decimation of Ireland

The people of Ireland had declared for Charles II upon the execution of the king. Ireland was an opponent to be eliminated as a threat to the new establishment of power in England. *When the English commonwealth was brought to some tolerable settlement, men began to cast their eyes towards the neighboring island. After the execution of the king, Cromwell himself began to aspire to a command, where so much glory, he saw, might be won, and so much authority acquired. In his absence, he took care to have his name proposed to the council of state; and both friends and enemies concurred immediately to vote him into that important office.* Cromwell made preparations for the invasion of Ireland.[2]

Cromwell and his army reached Ireland August 14, 1649. *The most famous of the parliamentary generals— his son Henry, Monk, Blake, Ireton, Waller, Ludlow, and others accompanied him. He brought with him, for the propagation of the gospel and the commonwealth, the 200,000 pounds in money, eight regiments of foot, six of horse, several troops of dragoons, a large supply of bibles, and a corresponding provision of ammunition and scythes.*[3]

The lord lieutenant of Ireland was Ormonde, a native Irishman, who had declared for Charles II. *Ormonde had garrisoned Drogheda,* about 40 miles north of Dublin, *with 3,000 of his choicest troops. They were partly English, and were commanded by a brave loyalist, Sir Arthur Aston. This was really the most important town in Ireland; and Cromwell, whose skill as a military general cannot be disputed, at once determined to lay siege to it. He encamped before the devoted city on the 2nd of September, and in a few days had his siege guns posted on the hill and still known as Cromwell's fort. Two breaches were made on the 10th, and he sent in his storming parties about five o'clock in the evening. The besieged at last wavered; quarter was promised to them, and they yielded; but the promise came from men who knew neither how to keep faith or to show mercy. The brave governor, Sir Arthur Aston, retired with his staff to an old mill on an eminence, but they were disarmed and slain in cold blood. The officers and soldiers were first exterminated, and then men, women, and children were put to the sword. The butchery occupied five entire days.*

---

[2] Ibid, p 11.

[3] *The scythes and sickles were to cut down the corn, that the Irish might be starved if they could not be conquered.* Cusack, History of Ireland, p 500,

A number of the townspeople fled for safety to St. Peter's church, on the north side of the city, but every one of them was murdered, all defenseless and unarmed as they were; others took refuge in the church steeple, but it was of wood, and Cromwell himself gave orders that it should be set on fire, and those who attempted to escape the flames were piked. The principal ladies of the city had sheltered themselves in the crypts. It might have been supposed that this precaution would be unnecessary, or, at least, that English officers would respect their sex; but, alas for common humanity it was not so. When the slaughter had been accomplished above, it was continued below. Neither youth nor beauty was spared. Thomas Wood, who was one of these officers, and brother to Anthony Wood, the Oxford historian, says he found in these vaults 'the flower and choicest of the women and ladies belonging to the town; amongst whom, a most handsome virgin, arrayed in costly and gorgeous apparel, kneeled down to him with tears and prayers to save her life.' Touched by her beauty and her entreaties, he attempted to save her, and took her out of the church; but even his protection could not save her. A soldier thrust his sword into her body; and the officer, recovering from his momentary fit of compassion, 'flung her down upon the rocks,' according to his own account, but first took care to possess himself of her money and jewels. This officer also mentions that the soldiers were in the habit of taking up a child, and using it as a buckler, when they wished to ascend the lofts and galleries of the church, to save themselves from being shot.[4]

Green gave an account consistent with that of Cusack. *The storm of Drogheda by Cromwell was the first of a series of awful massacres. The garrison fought bravely, and repulsed the first attack; but a second drove Aston and his force back to the Mill-Mount. 'Our men getting up to them,' read Cromwell's terrible despatch, 'were ordered by me to put them all to the sword. And indeed, being in the heat of action, it forbade them to* spare *any that were in arms in the town, and I think that night they put to death about two thousand men.' A few fled to St. Peter's church, whereupon I ordered the steeple to be fired, where one of them was heard to say in the midst of the flames: 'God damn me, I burn, I burn.' 'In the church itself nearly one thousand were put to the sword. I believe all their friars were knocked on the head promiscuously but two.' --- Of the remnant who were driven to yield at last through hunger, when they submitted, their officers were knocked on the head, every tenth man of the soldiers killed, and the rest shipped for the Barbadoes* (as slaves). *'I am persuaded,' the dispatch ends, 'that this is a righteous judgment of God upon these barbarous wretches who have imbued their hands in so much innocent blood, and that it will tend to prevent the effusion of blood for the future.' A detachment sufficed to relieve Derry,*

---

[4] Ibid, pp 501-502.

and to quiet Ulster; and Cromwell turned to the south, where as stout a defense was followed by as terrible a massacre at Wexford.[5]

Cusack described the massacre at Wexford: *These savage butcheries had the intended effect. The inhabitants of all the smaller towns fled at his approach, and the garrisons capitulated. Trim, Dundalk, Carlingford, and Newry, had yielded; but Wexford still held out. The garrison amounted to about 3,000 men, under the command of Colonel Sinnot, a brave loyalist. After some correspondence on both sides, a conference took place between four of the royalists and Cromwell, at which he contrived to bribe Captain Stafford, the governor of the castle. --- As soon as he found that Stafford could be bribed, he denounced the proposals of the garrison as abominable and impudent. The traitor opened the castle-gates, and the parliamentary troops marched in. The besieged were amazed and panic-stricken; yet, to their eternal credit, they made what even Cromwell admits to have been a 'stiff resistance.' The massacre of Drogheda was renewed with all its horrors, and the treacherous general held in his hand all the time the formal offer of surrender, which had been made by the townspeople and his own reply. He informs the parliament that he did not intend to destroy the town, but his own letter reveals the treachery; and he congratulates his correspondents and the 'unexpected providence' which had befallen them. He excuses the massacre on the plea of some outrages which had been offered to the 'poor Protestants' forgetting what incomparably greater cruelties had been inflicted by the Protestants on the Catholics, both for their loyalty and for their religion. MacGeoghegan mentions the massacre of two hundred women, who clung to the market-cross for protection. His statement is not corroborated by contemporary authority; but there appears no reason to doubt that it may have taken place, from what has already been recorded at Drogheda on unquestionable authority.*[6]   Cromwell and his forces marched through Ireland subduing New Ross, October 18, 1649, and Cork, Youghal, Kinsale, and Bandon. In January 1650, his forces set out for Limerick, taking castles and other towns on the way, Cashel, Kilkenny, Clonmel, and Ross. *Pressing demands were now made by the parliament for his return to England, where the royalists had also to be crushed and subdued; and after committing the command of his army to Ireton, he sailed from Youghal, on the 20ᵗʰ of May, leaving, as a legacy to Ireland, a name which was*

---

[5] Green, A Short History of the English People, p 575.

[6] Cusack, p 503. Note. There stands in the market place at the center of Wexford a statue of an Irish defender. The Irish even today tell stories of men, women and children piked by English soldiers while attempting to escape along the roads leading to the bull ring. On the other hand, history is told differently by most modern Anglo-American writers who justify Cromwell' massacres by the Irish revolt of 1641 and the supposed massacre of the Protestants by the Catholics.

only repeated to be cursed, and an increase of miseries which already had seemed incapable of multiplication. [7]

Charles II and Cromwell in Scotland

While Cromwell proceeded with such uninterrupted success in Ireland, which in the space of nine months he had almost entirely subdued, fortune was preparing for him a new scene of victory and triumph in Scotland.

Charles II's hopes for Irish support were dashed by Cromwell's victories. Charles's negotiations with the Scots were sorely influenced by the defeat of royalist Montrose and his execution May 21, 1650. *The king, in consequence of his agreement with the commissioners of Scotland, set sail for that country; and being escorted by seven Dutch ships of war, which were sent to guard the herring fishery, he arrived in the Frith of Cromarty. Before he was permitted to land, he was required to sign the covenant; and many sermons and lectures were made him, exhorting him to persevere in that holy confederacy. None of his English friends, who had served his father, were allowed to remain in the kingdom. The king himself found, that he was considered as a mere pageant of state, and that the few remains of royalty, which he possessed, served only to draw on him the greater indignities.* [8]

Fairfax having resigned his commission, it was bestowed on Cromwell, who was declared captain-general of all the forces in England. This command, in a commonwealth, which stood entirely by arms, was of the utmost importance; and was the chief step, which this ambitious politician had yet made towards sovereign power. He immediately marched his forces, and entered Scotland with an army of 16,000 men. At the battle of Dunbar, September 3, Cromwell defeated the Scots. *The Scots, though double in number to the English, were soon put to flight, and pursued with great slaughter. The chief, if not only resistance was made by one regiment of Highlanders, that part of the army, which was the least infected with fanaticism. No victory could be more complete than this, which was obtained by Cromwell. About 3,000 of the enemy were slain, and 9,000 taken prisoners. Cromwell pursued his advantage and took possession of Edinburgh and Leith. The remnant of the Scottish army fled to Sterling.*

The battle of Worcester September 3, 1650, secured Cromwell's victory in Scotland. *With an army of about 30,000 men, Cromwell fell upon Worcester; and attacking it on all sides, and meeting with little resistance except from duke Hamilton and general Middleton, broke in upon the disordered royalists. The streets of the city were strowed with*

---

[7] Ibid, pp 504-505.

[8] Hume, vol 6, pp 16, 25.

dead: Hamilton, a nobleman of bravery and honor, was mortally wounded; Massey wounded and taken prisoner; the king himself, having given many proofs of personal valor, was obliged to fly. The whole Scottish army was either killed or taken prisoners. The escape of Charles from Scotland was an incredible journey, which took him in disguise to many remote quarters, eventually sailing from Shoreham in Sussex to Fescamp in Normandy. *No less than forty men and women had at different times been privy to his concealment and escape.*[9]

Cromwell and Parliament

A contest between the powers of the army and parliament developed. Parliament insisted on the retention of its powers and the right of choosing representatives. *A conference took place between the leaders of the commons and the officers of he army, who resolutely demanded not only the omission of these clauses, but that the parliament should at once dissolve itself, and commit the new elections to the council of state.* On April 20, 1653, Cromwell brought his army to parliament and closed down what had remained of the rump parliament. Cromwell's voice could be heard in broken sentences. *'It is not that you should sit here any longer! You should give place to better men! You are no parliament.' thirty musketeers entered at a sign from their general, and the fifty members present crowded to the door. --- The door of the house was locked at last, and the dispersion of the parliament was followed a few hours after by that of its executive committee, the council of state. Cromwell himself summoned them to withdraw.*[10] *The dispersion of parliament and of the council of state left England without a government, for the authority of every official ended with that of the body from which his power was derived. --- The army formed a provisional council of state, consisting of eight officers of high rank and four civilians, with Cromwell as their head.* A convention was formed *putting the largest construction on its commission, and boldly undertook the whole task of constitutional reform. --- With a remarkable energy it undertook a host of reforms, for whose execution England has had to wait to our own day. The frenzied alarm which these bold measures aroused among the lawyer class was soon backed by that of the clergy, who saw their wealth menaced by the establishment of civil marriage, and by proposals to substitute the free contributions of congregations for the payment of tithes. The 'barebones parliament' as the assembly was styled in derision, was charged with a design to ruin property, the church, and the law, with enmity to knowledge, and a blind and ignorant fanaticism. --- Cromwell himself shared the general uneasiness at its proceedings. ---*

---

[9] Ibid, pp 35-38.

[10] Green, A Short History of the English People, p 581.

The dissolution of the convention by Cromwell in December 1653, replaced matters in the state in which its assembly had found them; but there was still the same general anxiety to substitute some sort of legal rule for the power of the sword.[11]

In 1654 a new *instrument of government was drawn up by the army wherein Cromwell became the lord protector and ruler of the three nations of the British Empire, England, Scotland, and Ireland with the advice and help of a council of state and a parliament, which was to be called every three years.*

Foreign affairs, Wars with Holland and Spain

Cromwell's use of military force in Ireland, Scotland and England to accomplish his ends impressed European powers with the might of the new administration and the emergence of a new British empire. The Navigation Act, which had been passed by parliament in 1651, was designed to drive Dutch merchants from the field of commerce which it had dominated. According to the Navigation Act goods transported from foreign ports in Asia, Africa, or America could land in England only in English merchant vessels. The Dutch protested. In 1652 war was declared between Holland and England. The English admiral Blake defeated the best Dutch admiral Tromp and his successor De Ruyter. A treaty was signed in 1654. In 1652, Blake's victory over a French fleet had led to the capture of Dunkirk.

The defeat of the Dutch had left England the chief sea power of the world; and before the dissolution of the parliament, two fleets put to sea with secret instructions. The firsts, under Blake, appeared in the Mediterranean, exacted reparation from Tuscany for wrongs done to English commerce, bombarded Algiers, and destroyed the fleet with which its pirates had ventured through the reign of Charles to insult the English coast. The thunder of Blake's guns, every Puritan believed, would be heard in the castle of St. Angelo, and Rome itself would have to bow to the greatness of Cromwell.

Jamaica

In May 1655 Cromwell sent an expedition to the Spanish West Indies. *Though Blake sailed to the Spanish coast, he failed to intercept the treasure fleet from America; and the second expedition, which made its way to the West Indies, was foiled in a descent on St. Domingo. Its conquest of Jamaica, important as it really was in breaking through the monopoly of the New World in the south which Spain had till now enjoyed, seemed at the time but a poor result for a vast expenditure of blood and money.* [12] For the next 150 years the West Indies were

---

[11] Ibid, pp 582-583.

[12] Ibid, p 593.

important to the prosperity of England. Jamaica was the center of the slave trade, first supplying slaves for other Caribbean Islands and most significantly for the southern colonies in America.[13] Cromwell renewed The East Indies Company's charter for a monopoly on trade in October 1657. This would lead to England's plunder of India.

Ireland

In Ireland the work of conquest had been continued by Ireton, and completed after his death by general Ludlow, as mercilessly as it had begun. Thousands perished by famine or the sword. Shipload after shipload of those who surrendered were sent overseas for sale into forced labor in Jamaica and the West Indies. More than forty thousand of the beaten Catholics were permitted to enlist for foreign service, and found a refuge in exile under the banners of France and Spain. The work of settlement, which was undertaken by Henry Cromwell, the younger and abler of the protector's sons, turned out to be even more terrible than the work of the sword. It took as its model the colonization of Ulster, the fatal measure, which had destroyed all hope of a united Ireland and had brought inevitably in its train the massacre and the war. The people were divided into classes in the order of their assumed guilt. All who after fair trial were proved to have personally taken part in the massacre were sentenced to banishment or death. The general amnesty, which free 'those of the meaner sort' from all questions, --- was far from extending to the landowner. Catholic proprietors, who had shown goodwill to the parliament, even though they had taken no part in the war, were punished by the forfeiture of a third of their estates. All who had borne arms were held to have forfeited the whole, and driven into Connaught, where fresh estates were carved out for them from the lands of the native clans. No such doom had ever fallen on a nation in modern times as fell upon Ireland in its new settlement. Among the bitter memories which part Ireland from England the memory of the bloodshed and confiscation, which the puritans wrought remains the bitterest; and the worst curse an Irish peasant can hurl at his enemy is 'the curse of Cromwell.'[14]

Final Dissolution of parliament

The government of the protector had become a simple tyranny, but it was impossible for him to remain content with the position of a tyrant. He was as anxious as ever to give a legal basis to his administration; and he seized on the war as a pretext for again

---

[13] Franklin, From Slavery to Freedom, pp 46-55, Chapter IV, Seasoning in the Islands.

[14] Green, p 589-590.

summoning a parliament, in 1657. *But he no longer trusted, as in the parliament of 1654, to perfect freedom of election. The sixty members sent from Ireland and Scotland were simply nominees of the government. Its whole influence was exerted to secure the return of the more conspicuous members of the council. All Catholics, and all royalists who had actually fought for the king, were still disqualified from voting. It was calculated that of the members returned one-half were bound to the government by ties of profit or place. But Cromwell was still unsatisfied. A certificate of the council was required from each member before admission to the house; and a fourth of the whole number returned - one hundred in all, with Haselrig at their head - were by this means excluded on grounds of disaffection or want of religion. --- In his opening address Cromwell boldly took his stand in support of the military despotism wielded by the major generals. 'It hath been more effectual towards the discountenancing of vice and settling religion than anything done these fifty years. I will abide by it,* he said, *with singular vehemence.'* Cromwell had, in early 1655, divided England into eleven districts, each under command by a major general. There followed debate in parliament and the introduction of a bill in support of the major generals. *One of the members of parliament wrote to his son Henry 'What makes me fear the passing of this Act, is that thereby His Highness' government will be more founded in force, and more removed from that natural foundation which the people in parliament are desirous to give him, supposing that he will become more theirs than now he is.'* The bill was rejected and Cromwell bowed to the feeling of the nation by withdrawing the powers of the major generals.

It was no mere pedantry, still less was it vulgar flattery, which influenced the parliament in their offer to Cromwell the title of king. The experience of the last few years had taught the nation the value of the traditional forms under which its liberties had grown up. A king was limited by constitutional precedents. 'The kings prerogative,' it was well urged, 'is under the courts of justice, and is bounded as well as any acre of land, or anything a man hath.' A protector, on the other hand, was new in our history, and there were no traditional means of limiting his power. 'The one office being lawful in its nature,' said Glynne, 'known to the nation, certain in itself, and confined and regulated by the law, and the other not so— that was the great ground which the parliament did so much insist on this office and title.' Under the name of monarchy, indeed, the question really at issue between the party headed by the officers and the party led by the lawyers in the commons was that of the restoration of constitutional and legal rule. An overwhelming majority carried the proposal, but a month passed in endless consultation between the parliament and the protector.[15]

---

[15] Ibid, pp 594-595.

Cromwell's real concern throughout was with the temper of the army. To Cromwell his soldiers were no common swordsmen. They were 'godly men, men that will not be beaten down by a worldly and carnal spirit while they keep their integrity;' men in whose general voice he recognized the voice of God.'They are honest and faithful men,' he urged, 'true to the great things of the government.' --- A petition from the officers to parliament demanded the withdrawal of the proposal to restore the monarchy, 'in the name of the old cause for which they had bled.' Cromwell had at once anticipated the coming debate on this petition, a debate, which might have led to an open breach between the army and the commons, by a refusal of the crown. 'I cannot undertake this government,' he said, 'with that title of king; and that is my answer to this great and weighty business.'

Parliament met again after a period of six months, but in February 1658, Cromwell dissolved parliament. Cromwell had shown signs to the parliament that he was not well or even rational. *'God knows,' he burst out a little time before to the parliament, 'I would have been glad to have lived under my woodside, and to have kept a flock of sheep, rather than to have undertaken this government.' --- 'I have some infirmities upon me,' he owned twice over in this speech at the opening of the parliament; and his feverish irritability was quickened by the public danger. No supplies had been voted, and the pay of the army was heavily in arrears, while its temper grew more and more sullen at the appearance of the new constitution and the reawakening of the royalist intrigues. The continuance of the parliamentary strife threw Cromwell at last, says an observer at this court, 'into a rage and passion like unto madness.' Summoning his coach, by a sudden impulse, the protector drove with a few guards to Westminster; and summoned the two houses to his presence. 'I do dissolve this parliament,' he ended a speech of angry rebuke, 'and let God be judge between you and me.' [16]*

Death of Cromwell

The last days of Cromwell were not happy or peaceful to say the least. On the one hand the royalists threatened him. He was also fearful of conspiracies by the millenarians in the army and by an active agitator of the Levellers. *The protector might better have supported those fears and apprehensions, which the public distempers occasioned, had he enjoyed any domestic satisfaction, or possessed any cordial friends of his own family, in whose bosom he could safely have unloaded his anxious and corroding cares. But Fleetwood, his son-in-law, actuated by the wildest zeal, began to estrange himself from him. His eldest daughter, married to Fleetwood, had adopted republican principles so vehement, that she could not with patience behold power lodged in a single person,*

---

[16] Ibid, pp 596-597.

even in her indulgent father. His daughter Elizabeth died August 6, 1658, only a few weeks before his final demise. His other daughters were no less prejudiced in favor of the royal cause, and regretted the violence and iniquities, into which, they thought, their family had so unhappily been transported.

Overwhelmed with the load of public affairs, dreading perpetually some fatal accident in his distempered government, he saw nothing around him but treacherous friends or enraged enemies. --- Each action of his life betrayed the terrors under which he labored. The aspect of strangers was uneasy to him: With a piercing and anxious eye he surveyed every face, to which he was not daily accustomed. He never moved a step without strong guards attending him: He wore armor under his clothes, and farther secured himself by offensive weapons, a sword, falchion, and pistols, which he always carried about him He returned from no place by the direct road, or by the same way which he went. Every journey he performed with hurry and precipitation. Seldom he slept above three nights together in the same chamber. And he never let it be known beforehand what chamber he intended to choose, nor entrusted himself in any, which was not provided with back doors, at which sentinels were carefully placed. Society terrified him, which he reflected on his numerous, unknown, and implacable enemies.[17]

But it would not be an assassin who would kill him. *His body also, from the contagion of his anxious mind, began to be affected; and his health seemed sensibly to decline. He was seized with a slow fever, which changed into a tertian ague. At length, the fever increased, and he himself began to entertain some thoughts of death, and to cast his eye toward that future existence, whose idea had once been intimately present to him. --- Meanwhile all the symptoms began to wear a more fatal aspect, and the physicians were obliged to break silence, and to declare that the protector could not survive the next fit, with which he was threatened. The council was alarmed, A deputation was sent to know his will with regard to his successor. His senses were gone, and he could not now express his intentions. They asked him whether he did not mean, that his eldest son, Richard, should succeed him in the protectorship. A simple affirmative was, or seemed to be, extorted from him. Soon after, on the 3rd of September 1658, he expired. Cromwell was in the fifty-ninth year of his age when he died. He left two sons, Richard and Henry; and three daughters; one married to general Fleetwood, another to Lord Fauconberg, a third to lord Rich.[18] His wife Elizabeth died in 1672.*

---

[17] Hume, vol 6, p 105.

[18] Ibid, pp 105-107, 110.

Chapter 31

Charles II and James II

Charles II, (b. 1630, d 1685) was the first king of the restoration of the monarchy, which followed the military dictatorship of the army and Cromwell. Charles II ruled from 1660 and died from an unexpected illness in 1685 at age 55. The Romans had detested monarchy ever since the tyrannical reign of Superbus nearly five hundred years B.C. Members of the senate assassinated Julius Caesar because he had taken upon himself the powers of a king. Yet England could not be governed except by a monarchy. Cicero in his widely read dialogues, *The Republic* and *The Laws*, had presented arguments against monarchy as well as a government ruled by an aristocracy. Those who espouse government by monarchy, an aristocracy or a mixed form of government have always, even today, never believed that democracy could be anything but mob rule. People, including the landed aristocracy, the wealthy merchant class, and the protestant factions became disgusted with government by the army and Cromwell. The army and Cromwell who had removed from power the king and the aristocracy was sufficient proof to them that a so-called republic could not govern itself. But there never had been established in England any of the conditions or requirements for a democratic form of government. The natural aspirations of men were easily suppressed once more by the power of the sword. Most Englishmen were anxious for a return of government by king and parliament.

Parliament in this reign attempted to assert its power over the king. Charles's character and reign differed from that of his father in that he was a master of the political arts of his time, in contrast to the imperious, distant and haughty Charles I. Charles II attempted to woo parliament using devious methods of wit, charm, dissimulation and dishonesty, but in the last three years his reign was tyrannical, as a prelude to his brother James II's rule. Of the many bills that were passed by parliament during his reign, only a few survived the kings prerogative and his final resolve to continue the rights and privileges of monarchy.

The exception was parliament's passage of the act of habeas corpus in 1679. This act became the most important landmark of liberty for the English people since Magna Carta and the Petition of Right.

Background of Charles II

Charles II was the oldest surviving son of Charles I and Henrietta Maria, daughter of the French king Henry IV. He was born in London and his earliest years witnessed the conflicts of his father Charles I while opposed to parliament. There followed the civil war. His father sent him, *at age fifteen to the west, with the title of general, and had given orders, if he were pressed by the enemy, that he should make his escape into a foreign country, and save one part of the royal family from the violence of the parliament.*[1] The following year he left under the king's orders to join his mother in Paris.

Charles in Scotland

After the execution of his father in 1649, Charles was proclaimed king of Scotland as Charles II. However, Charles had to compromise with the Scot commissioners and sign the covenant, which had been proclaimed by the Scots in 1640 to safeguard their protestant beliefs. The covenant required: *that he should bind himself by his royal promise to take the covenant; that he should ratify all acts of parliament, by which Presbyterian government, the directory of worship, the confession of faith, and the catechism were established; and that in civil affairs he should entirely conform himself to the direction of parliament, and in ecclesiastical affairs to that of the assembly.* The queen mother, and Charles's brother in law, the prince of Orange, convinced him that he should not refuse a kingdom *merely from regard to episcopacy.* Charles landed in Scotland June 28, 1650. --- *The king himself found that he was considered as a mere pageant of state, and that the few remains of royalty, which he possessed, served only to draw on him the greater indignities.*[2] Charles issued a proclamation, which condemned his father opposing the reformation, and the covenant of his mother's Catholic beliefs. The Scots required *that Charles pass through a public humiliation, and do penance before the whole people. They sent him twelve articles of repentance, which he was to acknowledge; and the king had agreed, that he would submit to this indignity. --- Charles in the mean time found his authority entirely annihilated, as well as his character degraded. He was consulted in no public measure. He was not called to assist at any councils.*

---

[1] Hume, vol 5, pp 475, 477.

[2] Hume, vol 6, pp 20, 25.

Charles became a fugitive, to France and Spain

   Under Cromwell, Charles became a fugitive after a futile effort to march into England but was defeated by Cromwell at the battle of Worcester September 3, 1951. Charles made his dramatic escape after assuming many disguises. *After one and forty days concealment, he arrived safely at Fescamp in Normandy*, in October 1651.[3] *The queen of England and her son, Charles, during these commotions, passed most of their time at Paris; and notwithstanding their near connection of blood, received but few civilities, and still less support, from the French court. The French ministers treated Charles with such affected indifference that he thought it more decent to withdraw, and prevent the indignity of being desired to leave the kingdom. He went first to Spain, thence he retired to Cologne; where he lived two years, on a small pension, about 6,000 pounds a year, paid him by the court of France, and on some contributions sent him by his friends in England. --- Sir Edward Hyde, created lord-chancellor, and the marquess of Ormond, were his chief friends and confidants. In February 1658, Charles formed a league with Philip of Spain, removed his small court to Bruges in the Low Countries, and raised four regiments of his own subjects, whom he employed in the Spanish service. The duke of York,* the future James II, *who had, with applause, served some campaigns in the French army, and who had merited the particular esteem of marshal Tureen, now joined his brother, and continued to seek military experience under Don John of Austria and the prince of Conde.*[4]

The restoration of the monarchy

   The Presbyterians, the royalists, being united, formed the voice of the nation, which, without noise, but with infinite ardor, called for the king's restoration. --- Harassed with convulsions and disorders, men ardently longed for repose, and were terrified at the mention of negotiations or delays, which might afford opportunity to the seditious army still to breed new confusion. The passion too for liberty, having been carried to such violent extremes, and having produced such bloody commotions, began, by a natural movement, to give place to a spirit of loyalty and obedience; and the public was less zealous in a cause, which was become odious, on account of the calamities, which had so long attended it. --- Above all the general was averse to the mention of conditions; and resolved, that the crown, which he intended to restore, should be conferred on the king entirely free and unencumbered.[5]

---

[3] Ibid, pp 35- 38.

[4] Ibid, pp 46, 55.

[5] Ibid, pp 135-136.

Charles, who was in Holland at Breda, signed a declaration in which the king agreed to settle property disputes, pay and disband the army, provide amnesty, and provide an offer of religious toleration. The new parliament, on May 1, 1660, received the king's declaration favorably and on May 8 both houses of parliament *voted a committee to invite the king to return and take possession of the government.* Charles II landed at Dover, and entered London on the 29ᵗʰ of May. Parliament passed an act of indemnity, which pardoned all but those who sat on the high court of justice who had condemned Charles I to the block, as well as some members of the long parliament such as Harry Vane, who were beheaded and quartered. Even the bodies of such prominent men such as Oliver Cromwell, his son-in-law and second in command Ireton, Pym, the leader in the commons, Blake, the naval commander, and others were dug up from their graves at Westminster and thrown into a common grave. Money was levied to pay the soldiers in the army, who were then disbanded. *No more troops were retained than a few guards and garrisons, about 1,000 horse, and 4,000 foot.*

Acts passed by parliament

Not a voice demanded the restoration of the Star Chamber, or of monopolies, or of the court of High Commission; no one disputed the justice of the condemnation of ship-money, or the assertion of the sole right of parliament to grant supplies to the crown. The militia, indeed, was placed in the king's hands; but the army was disbanded, though Charles was permitted to keep a few regiments for his guard. The revenue was fixed at 1,200,000 pounds; and this sum was granted to the king for life.[6] Another act had been passed in 1661, which required all government officials to attend the rites of the Church of England. In 1664, the 'Conventicle Act' was passed, which prohibited religious assembly, of more than four persons, not in conformity with the established church. Catholics were excluded, permanently (until 1832), from any office of government in England. To all of these acts of parliament the king consented.

Request for religious toleration denied, Act of Uniformity

But the religious problems remained. A parliament, which met in 1661, was opposed to any semblance of religious toleration. Thereafter the assemblage of the commons and lords could not arrive at any rational accommodation to Charles's request for religious toleration. Religious fears and hatreds, which had been fomented since the reign of Henry VIII, and which reached a state of mass insanity in the civil war and the military dictatorship under Cromwell, would continue to plague England. It was as important to control of the minds as well as the bodies of all

---

[6] Green, pp 618-619.

men. A conference between bishops and some Presbyterian ministers was held at Savoy palace, March 25, 1661, as James at Hampton Court had previously attempted, in 1604, with the puritans. No agreement could be made in view of the mutual hostilities between Episcopalians and Presbyterians. Both were opposed to all dissenters representing other denominations. All of the above were violently opposed to any toleration whatsoever of the Catholics. On May 8, 1661, *an act was passed for the security of the king's person, and government. --- Charles expressed much satisfaction, when he gave his assent to the act for that purpose. It is certain, that the authority of the crown, as well as that of the church, was interested in restoring the prelates to their former dignity.* In 1662, an act of uniformity was passed by parliament. *The bill of uniformity was a pledge of their sincere attachment to the Episcopal hierarchy, and of their antipathy to Presbyterianism.*[7] This required every clergyman and every schoolmaster to express consent to everything in the official prayer book of the Episcopalian church. The Presbyterians became 'dissenters', along with the Independents, Baptists, Quakers and other sects.

Marriage of the king

During the interval between parliaments, Charles was married to Catherine of Portugal, on May 19, 1662. The marriage brought to England Tangier and Bombay. There were no children by this marriage. Catherine is seldom mentioned, except that she would later be accused of complicity with the popish plot, simply because she was a Catholic.

Character of the king

That Charles had great natural parts no one doubted. In his earlier days of defeat and danger he showed a cool courage and presence of mind, which never failed him in the many perilous moments of his reign. His temper was pleasant and social, his manners perfect, and there was a careless freedom and courtesy in his address, which won over everybody who came into his presence. His education indeed had been so grossly neglected that he could hardly read a plain Latin book; but his natural quickness and intelligence showed itself in his pursuit of chemistry and anatomy, and in the interest he showed in the scientific inquiries of the Royal Society. Like Peter the Great his favorite study was that of naval architecture, and he piqued himself on being a clever ship-builder. He had some little love too for art and poetry, and a taste for music. But his shrewdness and vivacity showed itself most in his endless talk. He was fond of telling stories, and he told them with a good deal of grace and humor. His humor indeed never forsook him; even on his death-bed he turned to the weeping courtiers around and whispered an apology for having been so unconscionable a time in dying. He held his

---

[7] Ibid, pp 163-175.

own fairly with the wits of his Court, and bandied repartees on equal terms with Sedley or Buckingham. Even Rochester in his merciless epigram was forced to own that Charles 'never said a foolish thing.' --- But courage and wit and ability seemed to have bestowed on him in vain. Charles hated business. He gave to other observers no sign of ambition. The one thing he seemed in earnest about was sensual pleasure, and he took his pleasure with a cynical shamelessness, which roused the disgust even of his shameless courtiers. Mistress followed mistress, and the guilt of a troop of profligate women was blazoned to the world by the gift of titles and estates. The royal bastards were set amongst English nobles. The ducal house of Grafton springs from the king's adultery with Barbara Palmer, whom he created duchess of Cleveland. The Dukes of St. Albans owe their origin to his intrigue with Nell Gwynn, a player and a courtesan. Loise de Querouaille, a mistress sent by France to win him its interests became Duchess of Portsmouth and ancestress of the house of Richmond. An earlier mistress, Lucy Walters, was mother of a boy whom he raised to the dukedom of Monmouth, and to which the dukes of Buccleuch trace their line; but there is good reason for doubting whether the king was actually his father. But Charles was far from being content with these recognized mistresses, or with a single form of self-indulgence. Gambling and drinking helped to fill up the vacant moments when he could no longer toy with his favorites to bet at Newmarket. No thought of remorse or of shame seems ever to have crossed his mind. 'He could not think God would make a man miserable,' he said once, 'only for taking a little pleasure out of the way.' From shame indeed he was shielded by his cynical disbelief in human virtue. Virtue he regarded simply as a trick by which clever hypocrites imposed upon fools. Honor among men seemed to him as mere a pretense as chastity among women. Gratitude he had none, for he looked upon self-interest as the only motive of men's actions, and though soldiers had died and women had risked their lives for him, he 'loved others as little as he thought they loved him.' But if he felt no gratitude for benefits he felt no resentment for wrongs. He was incapable either of love or of hate. The only feeling he retained for his fellow-men was that of an amused contempt.[8]

Foreign affairs

      The duplicity of Charles was shown in the confused foreign affairs of England with Holland and France. Parliament, with Charles' consent, had banished his able adviser, Edward Hyde earl of Clarendon. *He retired into France, where he lived in a private manner. He survived his banishment six years; and he employed his leisure chiefly in reducing into order the History of the Civil Wars, for which he had before*

---

[8] Green, p 630-631.

collected materials.[9] Charles became involved himself in foreign affairs. The navigation act under Cromwell had led to war between England and Holland with the defeat of the Dutch by Blake and his successor. Blake had captured Dunkirk from the French in 1652. In 1662 Charles ceded Dunkirk to Louis XIV for 200,000 pounds.

The old commercial jealousy between the Dutch and English, which had been lulled by a formal treaty in 1662, but which still lived on in petty squabbles at sea, was embittered by the cession of Bombay - a port which gave England an entry into the profitable trade with India - and by the establishment of a West Indian Company in London which opened a traffic with the Gold Coast of Africa. The quarrel was fanned into a war. Parliament voted a large supply unanimously; and the king was won by hopes of the ruin of the Dutch Presbyterian and republican government, and by his resentment at the insults he had suffered from Holland in his exile.[10] War between England and Holland led to severe losses on both sides. England's naval forces led to the capture of New York from the Dutch in 1664.

In 1668, a triple alliance, an agreement between England, Holland and Sweden was formed to contain the threat of France under Louis XIV. Charles, however, had loyalties more to France than Holland. His mother Henrietta Maria, was sister of Louis XIII, and Charles had spent part of his exile with his mother in France. Charles, notwithstanding his inclinations, entered upon the Triple Alliance after the urging of his ambassador Sir William Temple. In 1670, Charles made a secret treaty with Louis XIV, the treaty of Dover, to assist France in its war with Spain. Charles promised English troops to help France in the event of a war between Holland and France. Charles had violated the Triple Alliance. His dealings with the French were kept secret from the parliament as was the payment of 100,000 pounds per year along with a payment of 1,600,000 pounds for Charles to postpone another session of parliament.

War against Holland

Charles issued a declaration of war on March 17, 1672 against Holland following an attack of the Dutch fleet by English ships under Robert Holmes. William III, prince of Orange was appointed both general and admiral. De Ruyter was sea commander of a fleet of ninety-one ships of war opposed by the duke of York, the future James II. *The loss sustained by the fleets of the two maritime powers was nearly equal,*

---

[9] Hume, p 215. Hume adds: *The performance does honor to his memory; and except Whitlock's memorials, is the most candid account of those times, composed by any contemporary author.*

[10] Green, p 628.

if it did not rather fall heavier on the English. The French suffered very little, because they had scarcely been engaged in the action; and as this backwardness is not their national character, it was concluded, that they had received secret orders to spare their ships, while the Dutch and English should weaken each other by their mutual animosity. Almost all the other actions during the present war tended to confirm this suspicion. The French under Lewis subdued the Dutch under prince William. *Charles still persisted in his alliance with France; and the combined fleets approached the coast of Holland, with an English army on board. - -- It is pretended that an unusual tide carried them off the coast. Very tempestuous weather, it is certain, prevailed all the rest of the season; and the combined fleets either were blown to a distance, or durst not approach a coast, which might prove fatal to them. Lewis, finding that his enemies gathered courage behind their inundations, and that no farther success was likely for the present to attend his arms had retired to Versailles.[11]* In the forthcoming parliament February 4, 1673, Charles found that he could expect no supply from the commons *for carrying on a war, so odious to them.* After a number of sea battles during the summer and early fall Charles resolved *to make a separate peace with the Dutch, on the terms, which they had proposed through the channel of the Spanish ambassador.[12]*

Changes in the ministry

Charles had replaced the earl of Clarendon with five ministers, lords Clifford, Ashley, Buckingham, Arlington, and Lauderdale. From the first letter of each of these ministers there formed the name *cabal,* which has since had an odious connotation. Ashley and Buckingham shared in the knowledge of the king's secret treaty with France. Ashley, the earl of Shaftesbury, was dismissed for favoring the test act. He would later become the chief proponent of the exclusion bill, which declared that Charles's brother James, a Catholic, could not inherit the crown.

Charles created Thomas Osborne earl of Danby and appointed him lord treasurer. He was impeached by the commons for obtaining money from the French, but it was the king who had acquired large retainers from Lewis, not Danby. Charles covered up his own involvement by sending him to the tower.

Tories and Whigs

Meanwhile, parliament underwent new changes. For the first time political parties had emerged which represented different beliefs about government— which have been known ever since as Tories and

---

[11] Hume, vol 6, pp 261-262, pp 271-272.

[12] Ibid, 272-275, p 281-282.

Whigs. The Tories were largely composed of the landed gentry and the clergy, while the wealthy merchants and some of the lords made up the Whig party. The Tories supported monarchy and the Church of England. The Whigs, originally called Petitioners or Whigamores, presented in parliament a number of petitions to the king. Charles dissolved parliament in 1679 after petitions favoring the exclusion bill had been presented. Ashley the earl of Clarendon, in 1682, had fled to Holland to avoid prosecution for treason. Other members of the cabal left the service of the king or were dismissed. A system of bribery had been developed by the leaders of both parties to influence members to vote in their favor. In 1682 Charles began to contest the power of London to retain its charter. The crown's judges ruled against the city's charter. Charles named the new members of the government who were Tories replacing the Whigs. The system of contest between political parties in parliament in a sense mirrored the practices in the courts, with its opposing sides of controversy and conflict. *Underlying everything was a continued propulsion of faction and violence between two contending powers.*

Habeas corpus

After a long struggle the act, which is known as the habeas corpus act passed finally in 1679. By this great statute the old practice of the law was freed from all difficulties and exceptions. Every prisoner committed for any crimes, treason or felony was declared entitled to his writ even in the vacations of the courts, and heavy penalties were enforced on judges or gaolers who refused him this right. Every person committed for felony or treason was entitled to be released on bail, unless indicted at the next session of gaol delivery after his commitment, and to be discharged if not indicted at the sessions, which followed. It was forbidden under the heaviest penalties to send a prisoner into any places or fortresses beyond the seas.[13]

The popish plot

A series of events known as the *popish plot* soon developed into a mass fear and hatred of an implacable enemy, that of the Catholics. *The English nation, ever since the fatal league with France, had entertained violent jealousies against the court; and the subsequent measures, adopted by the king, had tended more to increase than cure the general prejudices. Some mysterious design was still suspected in every enterprise and profession: Arbitrary power and popery were apprehended as the scope of all projects: Each breath or rumor made the people start with anxiety: Their enemies, they thought, were in their very bosom, and had gotten possession of their sovereign's confidence. While in this timorous, jealous disposition, the cry of a plot all on a sudden*

---

[13] Green, p 662.

struck their ears: They were wakened from their slumber; and like men frightened and in the dark, took every figure for a specter. The terror of each man became the source of terror to another. And a universal panic being diffused, reason and argument and common sense, and common humanity lost all influence over them. From this disposition of men's minds we are to account for the progress of the popish plot.

Rumors of the plot was spread by *a doctor Tongue, a divine of the church of England,; a man active, restless, full of projects, void of understanding. He presented forty-three articles to the king, who requested further examination. Tongue admitted that he had not written the articles but that they were placed under his door.* Titus Oates was determined to be the author of this intelligence. According to Oates, who presented this material to the council and to parliament, the pope had declared that he was entitled to *the possession of England and Ireland on account of the heresy of prince and people, and had accordingly assumed the sovereignty of these kingdoms.* The Jesuits were delegated to accomplish these objectives. The churches were to be filled by Spanish priests and other Jesuits who were to be distributed all over England. *The king was to be solemnly tried and condemned as a heretic; and a resolution taken to put him to death. Thousands were promised to a person who would kill the king, ten thousand pounds to George Wakeman, the queen's physician.* More intelligence was forthcoming. The great fire of London had been the work of the Jesuits. --- *Besides these assassinations and fires; insurrections, rebellions, and massacres were projected by that religious order in all the three kingdoms. There were twenty thousand Catholics in London, who would rise in forty-and-twenty hours or less; and Junison, a Jesuit, said, that they might easily cut the throats of a hundred thousand Protestants. Eight thousand Catholics had agreed to take arms in Scotland. Ormond,* in Ireland, *was to be murdered by four Jesuits; a general massacre of the Irish Protestants was concerted; and forty thousand black bills were already provided for that purpose. Coleman had remitted two hundred thousand pounds to promote the rebellion in Ireland; and the French king was to land a great army in that island.* --- *After all this havoc, the crown was to be offered to the duke of York, but on the following conditions; that he receive it as a gift from the pope; that he confirm all the papal commissions for offices and employment; that he ratify all past transactions, by pardoning the incendiaries, and the murders of his brother and of the people; and that he consent to the utter extirpation of the protestant religion.*[14]

Oates, the informer of this dreadful plot, was himself the most infamous of mankind. He was the son of an Anabaptist preacher, chaplain to colonel Pride; but having taken orders in the church, he had

---

[14] Hume, pp 332-333.

been settled in a small living by the duke of Norfolk. He had been indicted for perjury; and by some means had escaped. He was afterwards a chaplain on board the fleet; whence he had been dismissed on complaint of some unnatural practices, not fit to be named. He then became a convert to the Catholics; but he afterwards boasted, that his conversion was a mere pretense, in order to get into their secrets and to betray them. He was sent over to the Jesuits' college at St. Omers, and though above thirty years of age, and he lived some time among the students. He was dispatched on an errand to Spain; and thence returned to St. Omers; where the Jesuits, heartily tired of their convert, at last dismissed him from their seminary. It is likely, that, from resentment of this usage, as well as from want and indulgence, he was induced, in combination with Tongue, to contrive that plot, of which he accused the Catholics.

This abandoned man, when examined before the council, betrayed his impostures in such a manner, as would have utterly discredited the most consistent story, and the most reputable evidence. --- Notwithstanding these objections, great attention was paid to Oates's evidence, and the plot became very soon the subject of conversation, and even the object of terror to the people. The violent animosity, which had been excited against the Catholics in general, made the public swallow the grossest absurdities when they accompanied an accusation of those religionists: And the more diabolical any contrivance appeared, the better it suited the tremendous idea entertained of a Jesuit. Danby likewise, who stood in opposition to the French and Catholic interest at court, was willing to encourage every story, which might serve to discredit that party. By his suggestion, when a warrant was signed for arresting Coleman, there was inserted a clause for seizing his papers; a circumstance attended with the most important consequences. --- His correspondence, during the years 1674, 1675, and part of 1676, was seized, and contained many extraordinary passages. In particular he said to la Chaise, 'We have here a mighty work upon our hands, no less than the conversion of three kingdoms, and by that perhaps the utter subduing of a pestilent heresy, which has a long time domineered over a great part of this northern world. There were never such hopes of success, since the days of queen Mary, as now in our days. God has given us a prince,' meaning the duke of York.[15]

Green concurs with the above account by Hume and continues. *Oates would have been dismissed indeed with contempt but for the seizure of Coleman's correspondence. His letters gave a new color to the plot. Danby himself, conscious of the truth that there were designs which Charles dared not avow, was shaken in his rejection of the disclosures, and inclined to use them as weapons to check the king in his Catholic*

---

[15] Ibid, pp 337-339.

policy. But a more dexterous hand had already seized on the growing panic. Shaftesbury, released after a long imprisonment and hopeless of foiling the king's policy in any other way, threw himself into the plot. 'Let the treasurer cry as loud as he pleases against popery, 'he laughed, 'I will cry a note louder.' But no cry was needed to heighten the popular frenzy from the moment when Sir Edmondsbury Godfrey, the magistrate before whom Oates had laid his information, was found in a field near London with his sword run through his heart. His death was assumed to be murder, and the murder to be an attempt of the Jesuits to 'stifle the plot.' A solemn funeral added to public agitation; and the two houses named committees to investigate the charges made by Oates.

In this investigation Shaftesbury took the lead. Whatever his personal ambition may have been, his public aims in all that followed were wise and far-sighted. He aimed at forcing Charles to dissolve parliament and appeal to the nation. He aimed at driving Danby out of office and at forcing on Charles a ministry, which should break his dependence of France and give a constitutional turn to his policy. He saw that no security would really avail to meet the danger of a Catholic sovereign, and he aimed at excluding James from the throne. But in pursuing these aims he rested wholly on the plot. He fanned the popular panic by accepting without question some fresh depositions in which Oates charged five Catholic peers with part in the Jesuit conspiracy. The peers were sent to the Tower, and two thousand suspected persons were hurried to prison. A proclamation ordered every Catholic to leave London. The trainbands were called to arms, and patrols paraded through the streets, to guard against the Catholic rising, which Oates declared to be at hand. Meanwhile Shaftesbury; turned the panic into political account by forcing through parliament an exclusion *bill which excluded Catholics from a seat in either house. The exclusion remained in force for a century and a half; but it had really been aimed against the Duke of York, and Shaftesbury was defeated by a provision which exempted James from the operation of the bill.*[16]

A national hysteria

A national hysteria followed in the wake of the popish plot. Informers came forth to give perjured testimony. Executions and murders of many innocent persons, chiefly owing to their religious beliefs, resulted. That there was no foundation whatsoever for the popish plot would appear most certain to most of us today, yet man is capable of almost any belief if it follows his emotional state, especially those emotions of fear and anger. *The popish plot passed for incontestable; and had not men soon expected with certainty the legal punishment of these criminals, the Catholics had been exposed to the hazard of an universal*

---

[16] Green, pp 650-651.

massacre. The torrent indeed of national prejudices ran so high, that no one, without the most imminent danger, durst venture openly to oppose it; nay, scarcely any one, without great force of judgment, could even secretly entertain an opinion contrary to the prevailing sentiment. The loud and unanimous voice of a great nation had mighty authority over weak minds; and even later historians are so swayed by the concurring judgment of such multitudes, that some of them have esteemed themselves sufficiently moderate, when they affirmed, that many circumstances of the plot were true, though some were added, and others much magnified. But it is an obvious principle, that a witness, who perjures himself in one circumstance, is credible in none: That the authority of the plot, even to the end of the prosecutions, stood entirely upon witnesses.[17]

Besides the general interest of the country party to decry the conduct of all the king's ministers, *the prudent and peaceable administration of Ormand,* in Ireland, *was in a particular manner displeasing to them. In England, where the Catholics were scarcely one to a hundred, means had been found to excite an universal panic, on account of insurrections and even massacres, projected by that sect; and it could not but seem strange that in Ireland, where they exceeded the Protestants six to one, there should no symptoms appear of any combination or conspiracy. Such an incident, when duly considered, might even in England shake the credit of the plot, and diminish the authority of those leaders, who had so long, with such industry, inculcated the belief of it on the nation. Rewards, therefore, were published in Ireland to any that would bring intelligence or become witnesses; and some profligates were sent over to that kingdom, with a commission to seek out evidence against the Catholics. Under pretense of searching for arms or papers, they broke into houses, and plundered them: They threw innocent men into prison, and took bribes for their release: And after all their diligence, it was with difficulty, that country, commonly fertile enough in witnesses, could furnish them with any fit for their purpose.* Several men were found, *who were immediately sent over to England; and though they possessed neither character sufficient to gain belief even for truth, nor sense to invent a credible falsehood, they were caressed, rewarded, supported and recommended by the earl of Shaftesbury. Oliver Plunket, the titular primate of Ireland, a man of peaceable dispositions, was condemned and executed upon such testimony.*[18]

---

[17] Hume, p 347.

[18] Ibid, pp 411-412.

Reactions against parliament and support for the king

Shaftesbury threw himself more and more on the support of the Plot. The prosecution of its victims was pushed recklessly on. Three Catholics were hanged in London. Eight priests were put to death in the country. Pursuivants and informers spread terror throughout every Catholic household. He counted on the reassembling of the parliament to bring all this terror to bear upon the king. But Charles had already marked the breach, which the earl's policy had made in the ranks of the country party. He saw that Shaftesbury was unsupported by any of his colleagues save Russell. --- It was with their full support therefore that Charles deprived Shaftesbury of his post of lord president of the council. The dismissal was the signal for a struggle to whose danger Charles was far from blinding himself. --- The perjury of Oates proved too much at last for the credulity of juries; and the acquittal of four of his victims was a sign that the panic was beginning to ebb.

Acts of yet greater daring showed the lengths to which Shaftesbury was ready to go. He had grown up amidst the tumults of civil war, and, gray headed as he was, the fire and vehemence of his early days seemed to wake again in the singular recklessness with which he drove on the nation to a struggle in arms. Early in 1680 he formed a committee for promoting agitation throughout the country; and the petitions which it drew up for the assembly of the parliament were sent to every town and grand jury and sent back again with thousands of signatures. Monmouth, in spite of the king's orders, returned at Shaftesbury's call to London; and a daring pamphlet pointed him out as the nation's leader in the coming struggle 'against popery and tyranny.' So great was the alarm of the council that the garrison on every fortress was held in readiness for instant war. But the danger was really less than it seemed. The tide of opinion had fairly turned. Acquittal followed acquittal. A reaction of horror of a remorse at the cruelty which had hurried victim after victim to the gallows succeeded to the pitiless frenzy which Shaftesbury had fanned into a flame. --- The memory too of the civil war was still fresh and keen, and the rumor of an outbreak of revolt rallied men more and more round the king.

The first act of the house on meeting in October 1680, was to vote that their care should be 'to suppress popery and prevent a popish successor.' Commons passed the measure but the lords were not in favor. --- Shaftesbury's course, in fact, went wholly on a belief that the penury of the treasury left Charles at his mercy, and that a refusal of supplies must wring from the king his assent to the exclusion. But the gold of France had freed the king from his thraldom. He had used the parliament simply to exhibit himself as a sovereign whose patience and conciliatory temper was rewarded with insult and violence; and now that his end was accomplished, he no sooner saw the exclusion bill re-introduced, than he suddenly dissolved the houses after a month's sitting, and appealed in a royal declaration to the justice of the nation at large.

The appeals met by an almost universal burst of loyalty. The church rallied to the king; his declaration was read from every pulpit; and the Universities solemnly decided that 'no religion, no law, no fault, nor forfeiture,' could avail to bar the sacred right of hereditary succession. The arrest of Shaftesbury on a charge of suborning false witnesses to the plot marked the new strength of the crown. London indeed was still true to him; the Middlesex grand jury ignored the bill of his indictment; and his discharge from the tower was welcomed in every street with bonfires and ringing of bells. --- William of Orange too visited England to take advantage of the turn of affairs to pin Charles to the policy of the Alliance; but the king met both counsels with evasion. He pushed boldly on in his new course. He confirmed the loyalty of the church by a renewed persecution of the nonconformists, which drove Penn from England and thus brought about the settlement of Pennsylvania as a refuge for his fellow Quakers. He was soon strong enough to call back James to court. Monmouth who had resumed his progresses through the country as a means of checking the tide of reaction, was arrested.[19]

Monmouth, Russell, and the other conspirators, were, during some time, in apprehensions, lest despair should push him into some dangerous measure; when they heard, that, after a long combat between fear and rage, he, Shaftesbury, had at last abandoned all hopes of success, and had retired into Holland. --- A council of six was erected, consisting of Monmouth, Russell, Essex, Howard, Algernon Sidney, and John Hambden, grandson of the great parliamentary leader. --- Their common hatred of the duke of York and the present administration united them in one party; and the dangerous experiment of an insurrection was fully resolved on.

The Rye House plot

Another conspiracy had been formed later known as the Rye House plot. One of the conspirators had a farm called Rye House *which lay on the road to Newmarket whither the king commonly went once a year, for the diversion of the races.* The plan was to overturn the kings cart on the road and to make their escape through the fields. An accident at Newmarket delayed the king in his usual journey. The conspiracy was detected. Lengthy trials of Russel and Sidney followed and they were found guilty of treason and executed. Essex was found in the tower with his throat cut. Suicide was determined by the coroner's inquest to be the cause of death. Charles ordered Monmouth, his father, to leave the kingdom.[20]

---

[19] Green, pp 655-657.

[20] Hume, pp 426-440.

The severities, exercised during this part of the present reign, were much contrary to the usual tenor of the king's conduct; and though those who studied his character more narrowly, have pronounced, that toward great offences he was rigid and inexorable, the nation were more inclined to ascribe every unjust or hard measure to the prevalence of the duke, into whose hands the king had, from indolence, not from any opinion of his brother's superior capacity, resigned the reins of government. The crown indeed gained a great advantage from the detection of the conspiracy and lost none by the rigorous execution of the conspirators: The horror entertained against the assassination-plot which was generally confounded with the project for an insurrection, rendered the whole party unpopular, and reconciled the nation to the measures of the court. [21]

Illness and death of Charles II

On February 6, 1685, Charles *was seized with a sudden fit, which resembled an apoplexy; and though he was recovered from it by bleeding, he languished only for a few days, and then expired, in his fifty-fifth year and in the twenty-fifth of his reign. He was so happy in a good constitution of body, and had ever been so remarkably careful of his health, that his death struck as great a surprise into his subjects, as if he had been in the flower of his youth. --- During the few days of the king's illness, clergymen of the Church of England attended him; but he discovered a total indifference towards their devotions and exhortations. Catholic priests were brought, and he received the sacrament from them, accompanied with the other rites of the Romish church.*

Charles had no surviving heirs. He was succeeded by his brother James.

James II

James II, the duke of York, brother of Charles II, (b. 1634, d 1701) became king by right of hereditary descent upon the death of Charles II. James's short rule, from 1685 to 1688, was tyrannical and led to the military conquest of the crown by William at the invitation of the leading powers in parliament. Fears of a take over by James and the Catholics were realized early by James's conduct in Scotland, in 1682, some three years before the death of Charles II. *As the king was master in England, and no longer dreaded the clamors of the country party, he permitted the duke of York to pay him a visit; and was soon after prevailed on to allow of his return to England, and of his bearing a part in the administration. The duke went to Scotland, in order to bring up his family, and settle the government of that country.*

---

[21] Ibid, p 441.

The duke, during his abode in Scotland, had behaved with great civility towards the gentry and nobility; and by his courtly demeanor had much won upon their affections: But his treatment of the enthusiasts was still somewhat rigorous; and in many instances he appeared to be a man of a severe, if not an unrelenting temper. It is even asserted, that he sometimes assisted at the torture of criminals, and looked on with tranquility, as if he were considering some curious experiment. --- Every man was bound to declare to the government his suspicion against every man, and to avoid the company of traitors: To fail in this duty was to participate in the treason: The conclusion on the whole was, 'You have conversed with a rebel; therefore you are yourself a rebel.' --- The Presbyterians, alarmed with such tyranny, from which no man could deem himself safe, began to think of leaving the country; and some of their agents were sent to England, in order to treat with the proprietors of Carolina for a settlement in that colony. Any condition seemed preferable to the living in their native country, which, by the prevalence of persecution and violence, was become as insecure to them as a den of robbers. Above two thousand persons were outlawed on pretense of their conversing with rebels, and they were continually hunted in their retreat by soldiers, spies, informers, and oppressive magistrates.[22]

Accession

The first words of James on his accession February, 1685, his promise 'to preserve the government both in church and state as it is now by law established,' were welcomed by the whole country with enthusiasm. All the suspicions of a Catholic sovereign seemed to have disappeared. --- It was necessary to summon a parliament, for the royal revenue ceased with the death of Charles, but the elections, swayed at once by the tide of loyalty and by the command of the boroughs which the surrender of their charters had given to the crown, sent up a house of commons in which James found few members who were not to his mind. A revenue of nearly two millions was granted to the king for life.

Uprisings in Scotland

The question of religious security was waived at a hint of the royal displeasure. All that was wanted to rouse the loyalty of the country into fanaticism was supplied by a rebellion in the North, and by another under Monmouth in the West. The hopes of Scotch freedom had clung ever since the restoration to the house of Argyll. The great Marquis, indeed, had been brought to the block at the king's return. His son, the earl of Argyll, --- was at last convicted of treason in 1682 on grounds at which every English statesman stood aghast. --- The earl escaped however to Holland, and lived peacefully there during the last years of

---

[22] Hume, vol 6, pp 416-418.

the reign of Charles. Monmouth had found the same refuge at the Hague, where a belief in the king's purpose to recall him secured him a kindly reception from William of Orange. But the accession of James was a death blow to the hopes of the duke, while it stirred the fanaticism of Argyll to a resolve of wresting Scotland from the rule of a Catholic king. The two leaders determined to appear in arms in England and the North, and the two expeditions sailed within a few days of each other. Argyll's attempt was soon over. His clan of the Campbells rose on his landing in Cantyre, but the country had been occupied for the king, and quarrels among the exiles who accompanied him robbed his effort of every chance of success. His force scattered without a fight; and Argyll, arrested in an attempt to escape, was hurried to a traitor's death.[23]

Tyranny of the king

James was, in fact, resolved on a far more terrible vengeance; and the chief justice Jeffreys, a man of great natural powers but of violent temper, was sent to earn the seals by a series of judicial murders, which have left his name a byword for cruelty. Three hundred and fifty rebels were hanged in the 'Bloody Circuit,' as Jeffreys made his way through Dorset and Somerset. More than eight hundred were sold into slavery beyond sea. A yet larger number were whipped and imprisoned. The queen, the maids of honor, the courtiers, even the judge himself, made shameless profit from the sale of pardons. What roused pity above all were the cruelties wreaked upon women. Some were scourged from market town to market town. Mrs. Lisle, the wife of one of the regicides, was sent to the block at Winchester for harboring a rebel. Elizabeth Gaunt, for the same act of womanly charity, was burned at Tyburn. Pity turned into horror when it was found that cruelty such as this was avowed and sanctioned by the king.[24]

Never king mounted the throne of England with greater advantages than James; nay, possessed greater facility, if that were any advantage, of rendering himself and his posterity absolute: But all these fortunate circumstances tended only, by his own misconduct, to bring more sudden ruin upon him. The nation seemed disposed of themselves to resign their liberties, had he not, at the same time, made an attempt upon their religion: And he might even have succeeded in surmounting at once their liberties and religion, had he conducted his schemes with common prudence and discretion. Openly to declare to the parliament, so early in his reign, his intention to dispense with the tests, struck an universal alarm throughout the nation; infused terror into the church, which had

---

[23] Green, pp 664-665.

[24] Ibid, 665-666.

hitherto been the chief support of monarchy; and even disgusted the army, by whose means alone he could now purpose to govern.[25]

James dismissed his two ministers, Halifax and Sunderland, who would not support him in reversing the test act, which had prohibited Catholics from holding any public office. James, using the prerogative of an absolute monarch dispensed with the acts which parliament had passed. He was *filling his fresh regiments with Catholic officers. He met with parliament with a haughty declaration that whether legal or not, his grant of commissions to Catholics must not be questioned, and with a demand of supplies for his new troops. Loyal as was the temper of the houses, their alarm for the church, their dread of a standing army, was yet stronger than their loyalty. The commons by the majority of a single vote deferred the grant of supplies till grievances were redressed, and demanded in their address the recall of the illegal commissions. The lords took a bolder tone; and the protest of the bishops against any infringement of the Test Act was backed by the eloquence of Halifax. But both houses were at once prorogued. The king resolved to obtain from the judges what he could not obtain from parliament. He remodeled the bench by dismissing four judges who refused to lend themselves to his plans. --- The principle laid down by the new judges asserted the right of the king to dispense with penal laws, according to his own judgment. --- Catholics were admitted into civil and military offices without stint, and four Catholic peers were sworn as members of the privy council. The laws forbidding the presence of Catholic priests in the realm, or the open exercise of Catholic worship, were set at nought.*

The ecclesiastical commission

Meanwhile James had begun a bold and systematic attack upon the Church of England. *He regarded his ecclesiastical supremacy as a weapon providentially left to him for undoing the work, which it had enabled his predecessors to do. Under Henry and Elizabeth it had been used to turn the Church of England from Catholic to Protestant. Under James it should be used to turn it back again from Protestant to Catholic. The High Commission indeed had been declared illegal by an act of the long parliament, and this act had been confirmed by the parliament of the restoration. But it was thought possible to evade this act. --- With this reserve, seven commissioners were appointed for the government of the church, with Jeffreys at their head; and the first blow of the commission was at the bishop of London.*[26]

Amongst all the engines of authority formerly employed by the crown, none had been more dangerous or even destructive to liberty than

---

[25] Hume, vol 6, p 468.

[26] Green, p 668.

the court of High Commission, which, together with the Star Chamber, had been abolished in the reign of Charles I by act of parliament; in which a clause was also inserted, prohibiting the erection, in all future times, of that court. James deemed this law no obstacle; and an ecclesiastical commission was anew issued, by which seven commissioners were vested with full and unlimited authority over the Church of England. On them were bestowed the same inquisitorial powers, possessed by the former court of High Commission.

Charles had assumed a power of issuing a declaration of general indulgence, and of suspending at once all the penal statutes, by which a conformity was required to the established religion. --- James, more imprudent and arbitrary than his predecessor, issued his proclamations, suspending all the penal laws in ecclesiastical affairs, and granting a general liberty of conscience of all his subjects. --- In order to procure a better reception for his edict of toleration, the king, finding himself opposed by the church, began to pay court to the dissenters; and he imagined, that, by playing one party against another, he should easily obtain the victory over both; a refined policy which it much exceeded his capacity to conduct. --- To the surprise of the harassed and persecuted Presbyterians, they heard the principles of toleration every where extolled, and found that full permission was granted to attend conventicles; an offence, which, even during this reign, had been declared no less than a capital enormity. --- It is likewise remarkable, that the king declared in express terms, 'that he had thought first, by his sovereign authority, prerogative royal, and 'absolute' power, which all his subjects were to obey 'without reserve', to grant this royal toleration.' [27]

The next measure of the court, in 1688, was an insult still more open on the ecclesiastics, and rendered the breach between the king and that powerful body fatal, as well as incurable. --- The king published a second declaration of indulgence, almost in the same terms with the former; and he subjoined an order, that, immediately after divine service, it should be read by the clergy in all the churches. As they were known universally to disapprove of the use made of the suspending power, this clause, they thought, could be meant only as an insult upon them; and they were sensible, that, by their compliance, they should expose themselves, both to public contempt, on account of their tame behavior, and to public hatred, by their indirectly patronizing so obnoxious a prerogative.

---

[27] Ibid, pp 481-482.

Six bishops to the tower

In order to encourage them in this resolution, six prelates --- met privately with the primate, and concerted the form of a petition to the king. They there represent in few words, that, --- they could not, in prudence, honor, in conscience, so far make themselves parties as the distribution of it all over the kingdom would be interpreted to amount to. They therefore besought the king that he would not insist upon their reading that declaration. The king ordered the six bishops to the tower, *and the crown lawyers received directions to prosecute them for the seditious libel, which it was pretended, they had composed and uttered.* There were great crowds gathered, including the wealthy merchants and noblemen, outside the tower and Westminster where the bishops were tried. *The jury took several hours to deliberate, and kept, during so long a time, the people in the most anxious expectation. But when the wished for verdict, not guilty, was at last pronounced, the intelligence was echoed throughout the hall, was conveyed to the crowds without, was carried into the city, and was propagated with infinite joy throughout the kingdom.*[28]

A few days before the acquittal of the bishops, on June 10, 1688, *an event happened, which, in the king's sentiments, much overbalanced all the mortifications, received on that occasion. The queen,* Mary of Modena, James's second wife, *was delivered of a son, who was baptized by the name of James. This blessing was impatiently longed for, not only by the king and queen, but also by all the zealous Catholics both abroad and at home.* Since this was the only male heir to the throne, the plan of William and Mary to succeed James II was threatened.

Invasion of William

On the same day the bishops had been acquitted a group of nobles, bishops, and some members of parliament, both Whigs and Tories, had invited William to come to England to replace the tyrannical king. On November 5, 1688, William landed at Tor Bay with his Dutch army. William's wife Mary, James's eldest daughter, was the heir to the throne prior to the birth of James just days earlier. William marched to London and met James's forces. Those supporting James largely abandoned him in defeat. James negotiated with William for safe passage of the queen and infant son to France. James left the kingdom on December 18, 1688 for France to join his wife and son.

William called a convention of members of parliament who passed a bill offering the crown to William and Mary as joint sovereigns.

---

[28] Ibid, pp 489-493.

Chapter 32

William III and Mary

William III, or William of Orange, (b. 1650, d 1702), and Mary (b. 1662) reigned jointly from 1688 until Mary's death in 1694. William III continued to be king of Great Britain and the Netherlands until his death in 1702. The nobles and bishops reacted to the Catholic threat of James II and his tyrannical rule. They invited William to come over to England and replace James. William and his Dutch forces landed at Torbay November 15, 1688. James II fled to France and joined his wife and son. Parliament in January 1689 declared, in James's absence, William to rule England jointly with Mary. The reign of William and Mary was most notable in establishing the precedent of rule by parliament over the king. The protestant supremacy and rule by parliament have been called the Revolution, or second Revolution in England, the first being that following Oliver Cromwell. William was the first and only Dutchman to rule England. Mary and Anne were the last of the Stuarts. Neither would play much of a role as queens.

Family background

The heir to the throne after James II would have been the infant son of James by his second wife, Mary of Modena. James Francis Edward was named the *'Old Pretender'* by parliament. He was Catholic and therefore excluded from inheriting the crown. Parliament invited William to England to replace James II, and he gained the crown by military as well as parliamentary supremacy. Mary II, wife of William, was the eldest daughter of James II and Anne Hyde, his first wife. Her younger sister Anne would follow her on the throne. William's father was William II, prince of Orange who died eight days before William's birth. His mother was Mary, younger sister of Charles II and James II, and who were children of Charles I and Henrietta Maria (daughter of the French king Henry IV). William and Mary were therefore first cousins, grandchildren of Charles I. They had no children.

Life of William of Orange before he gained the crown of England

William's mother died when he was ten years old. His grandmother and his uncle, the elector of Brandenburg, became his guardians. He was tutored in part by Johan De Witt, with an emphasis on politics and government. *De Witt was murdered, August 1672, in a popular tumult, and his fall called William, the Prince of Orange, to the head of the Dutch Republic. Though the new Statdholder had hardly reached manhood, his great qualities at once made themselves felt. His earlier life had schooled him in a wonderful self-control. He had been left fatherless and all but friendless in childhood, he had been bred among men who looked on his very existence as a danger to the State, his words had been watched, his looks noted, his friends jealously withdrawn. In such an atmosphere the boy grew up silent, wary, self-contained, grave in temper, cold in demeanor, blunt and even repulsive in address. He was weak and sickly from his cradle, and manhood brought with it an asthma and consumption, which shook his frame with a constant cough; his face was sullen and bloodless and scored with deep lines, which told of ceaseless pain. But beneath this cold and sickly presence lay a fiery and commanding temper, an immoveable courage, and a political ability of the highest order. William was a born statesman. Neglected as his education had been in other ways, for he knew nothing of letters or of art, he had been carefully trained in politics by John De Witt; and the wide knowledge with which in his first address to the States-General the young Stadholder reviewed the general state of Europe, the cool courage with which he calculated the chances of the struggle at once won him the trust of his countrymen. Their trust was soon rewarded. Holland was saved, and province after province won back from the arms of France, by William's dauntless resolve.[1]*

Parliament declares William and Mary to be king and queen of England

William and his Dutch armies landed at Torbay on November 5, 1688. William III defeated the army of James and on December 18, 1688 James II departed for France. A convention of members of parliament was established, and a declaration of rights on February 13, 1689 *recited the misgovernment of James II; condemned James's establishment of an ecclesiastical commission and forming an army without parliament's sanction as illegal; denied the right of any king to suspend or dispense with laws, or to exact money, save by consent of parliament. It asserted the right of a subject to petition, to a free choice of representatives, in parliament, and to a pure and merciful administration of justice. It declared the right of both houses to liberty of debate. It demanded securities for the free exercise of their religion by all Protestants, and*

---

[1] Green, pp 675-676.

bound the new sovereign to maintain the Protestant religion and the law and liberties of the realm; and declared William and Mary, prince and princess of Orange, king and queen of England.[2]

English Bill of Rights

Parliament passed the English Bill of Rights in 1689, reviewed by Green as follows:

1. The right of the people through its representatives to depose the king, to change the order of succession, and to set on the throne whomever they would, was now established. All claim of Divine Right, or hereditary right independent of the law, was formally put an end to by the election of William and Mary.

2. That the king no longer had the power to dispense with laws or executing the laws.

3. Parliament had the absolute power over taxation. An annual vote of supplies by parliament was established.

4. A standing army was prohibited during times of peace.

5. A Mutiny Act was established which provided for discipline of the army and an annual vote of supplies by parliament.

6. Election of members of parliament ought to be free.

7. Freedom of speech, debates, or proceedings in parliament ought not to be impeached or countered in any court or jurisdiction outside parliament.

8. Excessive bail ought not be required nor excessive fines, or cruel and unusual punishment.

9. That parliaments should be held frequently for redressing grievances, for strengthening and preserving of the laws.

James II and William III in Ireland, battle of the Boyne

William's primary interest in gaining the crown of England was to gain an important ally for his European wars against Lewis XIV of France thus securing the integrity of the territories of Holland. However, parliament was interested in rooting out the last remnants of Catholicism, to reliever them of the danger of James II or his infant son regaining the crown. Ireland had been a repository not only of people adhering to the Catholic faith but who had supported Catholic kings, at least in part, including James II. After the accession of James II, colonel Richard Talbot became the earl of Tyrconnel and was appointed chief of the armed forces. Catholics were now admitted to the army, to the bar, and to the senate. Most of the counties in Ireland declared for James with the exception of Charlemont and Carrickfergus in the county of Ulster. Tyrconnel went to France and invited James to Ireland. James landed at Kinsale, on March 12, 1689, and met with Tyrconnel in Cork. James

---

[2] Ibid, p 683.

proceeded to Dublin where he summoned a parliament and issued proclamations. *The parliament passed in all thirty-five acts with due deliberation and the advice of counsel. The most memorable are: The act that declared the parliament of England could not bind Ireland, --- and sentences given in Ireland could not be brought to England: The act for the repeal of the act of settlement that had confirmed the Cromwellian settlers in their possession of the lands they had seized: The act for liberty of conscience: the act relating to the army --- the act of supply for the army empowered the king to raise 20,000 pounds a month by land tax distributed over the counties and towns according to their abilities.*[3]

William, with many nobles and experienced officers arrived June 11, 1689 at Carrickfergus. William drove to Belfast, *and was received by acclamations, and loud shouts of 'God bless the Protestant king!' There were bonfires and discharges of cannon at the various camps of the Williamites. The army comprised a strange medley of nationalities. More than half were foreigners; and on these William placed his principal reliance, for at any moment a reaction might take place in favor of the lawful king. The Williamite army was well supplied, well trained, admirably commanded, accustomed to war, and amounted to between forty and fifty thousand. The Jacobite force,* led by James, *only consisted of twenty thousand, and of these a large proportion were raw recruits.*[4]

The famous battle of the Boyne led to the victory of the Protestants over the Catholics and William III over James II. The hostile forces confronted each other for the first time on the banks of the Boyne, July 1, 1689. *James did all that was possible to secure a defeat. At one moment he decided to retreat, at the next he would risk a battle; then he sent his baggage and six of his field-pieces to Dublin, for his own special protection; and while thus so remarkably careful of himself, he could not be persuaded to allow the most necessary precaution to be taken for the safety of his army. Tyrconnel's valor could not save the day for Ireland against fearful odds. --- When the enemy had crosed the ford at Oldbridge, James ordered Lauzan to march in a parallel direction to Dulek. Tyrconnel followed. The French infantry covered the retreat in admirable order, with the Irish cavalry. --- The retreat was again resumed; and at the deep defile of Naul the last stand was made. --- Thus ended the famous battle of the Boyne. England obtained thereby a new governor and a national debt; Ireland, fresh oppression, and an intensification of religious and political animosity, unparalleled in the history of nations.*[5] Protestants in Northern Ireland still celebrate the

---

[3] McManus, p 439.

[4] Ibid, pp 562-563.

[5] Ibid, p 564-565.

battle of the Boyne every year, on July 12. They assemble in a large force dressed in ritual garb, beating huge drums, while they march through a Catholic section of Belfast.

James fled to Dublin, *left the armies in command to Tyrconnel who led his armies to Limerick. James embarked in a small French vessel for Kinsale, from thence he sailed to France.* William entered Dublin Sunday, July 7th and was received with acclamations by the Protestants. Drogheda, Kilkenny, Duncannon, and Waterford, capitulated to the victorious army, the garrisons marching to Limerick, towards which place William now directed his course. --- William's forces entered Limerick on August 20. A fierce battle ensued. --- A council of war was held; William whose temper was not the most amiable at any time, was unusually morose. He had lost 2,000 men between the killed and the wounded, and he had not taken the city. On Sunday, August 31, the siege was raised. William returned to England, where his presence was imperatively demanded. The miliary command was confided to the count de Solmes, who was afterwards succeeded by De Ginkel. Lauzan returned to France with Tyrconnel, and the Irish forces were confided to the care of the Duke of Berwick, a youth of twenty, with a council of regency and a council of war to advise him.

The famous *Marlborough appeared before Cork with an army of 1,500 men, and on September 22 the garrison were made prisoners of war after a brief and brave resistance; but the conditions on which they surrendered were shamefully violated. Kinsale was next attacked. In January Tyrconnel returned to Ireland with a small force and supplies. Hostilities began June 7th with the siege of Ballymore Castle, in Westmeath. The governor surrendered, and Athlone was next attacked.* Ginkel led the English forces of 20,000 men against the Irish, whose embattled forces numbered 15,000. *The loss on both sides was immense, and can never be exactly estimated. Many of the dead remained unburied, and their bones were left to bleach in the storms of winter and the sun of summer.* --- Tyrconnel died at Limerick, of apoplexy, while he was preparing to put the city into a state of defense. The Irish defending Limerick surrendered and a treaty was signed October 3, 1691. *The Irish who surrendered were given the choice whether they would serve under William III or the French. An Ulster battalion, and a few men in each regiment, in all about 1,000, entered the service of the government; 2,000 received passes to return home; 11,000, with all the cavalry, volunteered for France, and embarked for that country in different detachments, under their respective officers.* The treaty of Limerick was later violated.

The penal laws

In 1695, the penal laws were established by the Protestant Irish parliament, under the viceroy lord Capel. These laws were totally inconsistent with the provisions of the Bill of Rights established by the

English parliament. Cusack enumerates the penal laws of Ireland as follows:

1. The Catholic peers were deprived of their right to sit in parliament.

2. Catholic gentlemen were forbidden to be elected members of parliament.

3. It denied all Catholics the liberty of voting, and it excluded them from all offices of trust, and indeed from all remunerative employment, however insignificant.

4. They were fined 60 pounds a month for absence from the Protestant form of worship.

5. They were forbidden to travel five miles from their houses, to keep arms, to maintain suits at law, or to be guardians or executors.

6. Any four justices of the peace could, without further trial, banish any man for life if he refused to attend the Protestant service.

7. Any two justices of the peace could call any man over sixteen before them, and if he refused to abjure the Catholic religion, they could bestow his property on the next of kin.

8. No Catholic could employ a Catholic schoolmaster to educate his children; and if he sent his child abroad for education, he was subject to a fine of 100 pounds, and the child could not inherit any property either in England or Ireland.

9. Any Catholic priest who came to the country should be hanged.

10. Any Protestant suspecting any other Protestant of holding property in trust for any Catholic, might file a bill against the suspected trustee, and take the estate or property from him.

11. Any Protestant seeing a Catholic tenant-at-will on a farm, which, in his opinion, yielded one-third more than the yearly rent, might enter on that farm, and, by simply swearing to the fact, take possession.

12. Any Protestant might take away the horse of a Catholic, no matter how valuable, by simply paying him 5 pounds.

13. Horses and wagons belonging to Catholics, were in all cases to be seized for the use of the militia.

14. Any Catholic gentleman's child who became a Protestant, could at once take possession of his father's property. [6]

Scotland, The massacre of Glencoe

In England not a sword had been drawn for James. In Scotland his tyranny had been yet greater than in England, and so far as the Lowlands went the fall of his tyranny was as rapid and complete. No sooner had he called his troops southward to meet William's invasion than Edinburgh rose in revolt. The western peasants were at once up in

---

[6] Cusack, pp 376-377.

arms, and the Episcopalian clergy who had been the instruments of the Stuart misgovernment ever since the Restoration were rabbled and driven from their parsonages in every parish. The news of these disorders forced William to act, though he was without a show of legal authority over Scotland. On the advice of the Scotch Lords present in London, he ventured to summon a Convention similar to that, which had been summoned in England, and on his own responsibility to set aside the laws which excluded Presbyterians from the Scotch parliament. This convention resolved that James had forfeited the crown by misgovernment, and offered it to William and Mary. The offer was accompanied by a claim of right framed on the model of the Declaration of Rights, to which they had consented in England, but closing with a demand for the abolition of prelacy. Both crown and claim were accepted, and the arrival of the Scotch regiments, which William had brought from Holland, gave strength to the new government.

In the Highlands nothing was known of English government or misgovernment: All that the revolution meant to a Highlander was the restoration of the house of Argyll. To many of the clans it meant the restoration of lands which had been granted them on the earl's attainder; and the MacDonalds, the Macleans, the Camerons, were as ready to join Dundee in fighting the Campbells and the government which upheld them as they had been ready to join Montrose in the same cause forty years before. They were soon in arms. As William's Scotch regiments under general Mackay climbed the pass of Killiecrankie, Dundee charged them at the head of three thousand clansmen and swept them in headlong rout down the glen. But his death in the moment of victory broke the only bond, which held the Highlanders together, and in a few weeks the host, which had spread terror through the Lowlands melted helplessly away. In the next summer Mackay was able to build the strong post of Fort William in the very heart of the disaffected country, and his offers of money and pardon brought about the submission of the clans.

Sir John Dalrymple, the master of stair, in whose hands the government of Scotland at this time mainly rested, had hoped that a refusal of the oath of allegiance would give grounds for a war of extermination, and free Scotland forever from its terror of the Highlanders. He had provided for the expected refusal by orders of a ruthless severity. 'Your troops,' he wrote to the officer in command, 'will destroy entirely the country of Lochaber, Lochiel's lands, Keppoch's, Glengarry's, and Glencoe's. Your powers shall be large enough. I hope the soldiers will not trouble the government with prisoners.' But his hopes were disappointed by the readiness with which the clans accepted the offers of the government.

All submitted in good time save Macdonald of Glencoe, whose pride delayed his taking of the oath till six days after the latest date fixed by the proclamation. Foiled in his larger hopes of destruction, Dalrymple seized eagerly on the pretext given by Macdonald, and an order 'for the extirpation of that sect of robbers' was laid before William and received the royal signature. 'The work,' he wrote the master of stair to colonel Hamilton who undertook it, 'must be secret and sudden.' The troops were chosen from among the Campbells, the deadly foes of the clansmen of Glencoe, and quartered peacefully among the Macdonalds for twelve days, till all suspicion of their errand disappeared. At daybreak they fell on their hosts, and in a few moments thirty of the clansfolk lay dead on the snow. The rest, sheltered by a storm, escaped to the mountains to perish for the most part of cold and hunger. 'The only thing I regret,' said the master of stair when the news reach him, 'is that any got away.' Whatever horror the massacre of Glencoe had roused in later days, few save Dalrymple knew of it at the time.[7]

France and Europe

William III had throughout his lifetime the objective of defeating Lewis XIV of France. *In 1690, when the wars in Ireland and Scotland were taking place, the French sent a fleet of eighty vessels to attack England in support of James II. They gained a victory over the Dutch and English fleets. They burned part of the town of Teignmouth. So urgent was the need for his presence abroad that William left, as we have seen, his work in Ireland undone, and crossed in the spring of 1691 to Flanders. It was the first time since the days of Henry VIII that an English king had appeared on the continent at the head of an English army. But the slowness of the allies again baffled William's hopes. He was forced to look on with a small army while a hundred thousand Frenchmen closed suddenly around Mons, the strongest fortress of the Netherlands, and made themselves masters of it in the presence of Lewis.*

In the beginning of 1692 an army of thirty thousand troops was quartered in Normandy in readiness for a descent on the English coast. There followed a naval battle considered to be the greatest since the Armada. The English and Dutch fleets defeated this time the French navy. The battle continued three days. The French fleet was scattered, and England saved from invasion. *France ceased from that moment to exist as a great naval power; for though her fleet was soon recruited to its former strength, the confidence of her sailors was lost, and not even Tourville ventured again to tempt in battle the fortune of the seas.*[8]

Battles followed on the border between France and Holland with William in command of the forces of the alliance, which had been formed against France. France was victorious in most of the battles but William reorganized his forces that were supplied by the grants of the

---

[7] Green, pp 385-386.

[8] Ibid, pp 695-696.

English parliament. In 1695 William defeated the French and captured the French fortress of Namur in Holland. A treaty, the 'peace of Ryswick,' was signed in 1697.

Government

The revolution of 1689 was enacted by a convention of parliament in the declaration of rights and elaborated by parliament in the Bill of Rights later that year. The monarchy of England had been altered to a mixed form of monarchy and aristocracy with parliament in the ascendancy. The power in parliament, however, had shifted from the hereditary peers, nobles and landed aristocracy; to the commons who were representatives of the growing wealthy merchant class. The revolution had also permanently dispossessed the Catholics from power and established some form of settlement of the Protestants by the toleration act of 1689.

After more than six hundred years of conflict, since William I, between king and aristocracy some semblance of accommodation had been made between king and parliament, not however without protests from the king. In fact, there were growing tensions and differences between parliament and the king throughout William's reign. Mary was little more than window dressing in this reign, having claim to the throne as eldest daughter of James II, even though James II and his son were the legitimate heirs to the crown. In 1701 James II died while in exile in France. Louis XIV proclaimed James's son, who the English called the *old Pretender,* king of England.

Parliament, by the act of settlement in 1701, would now determine who would inherit the crown.[9] There were other changes in government during this period. The development of the two political parties, Tories and Whigs, formed the basis of selection of ministers and would determine for the most part how the nation would be ruled. The development of these political parties during the reign of Charles II was introduced in the last chapter. The parties had by now become established. The Tories wanted continued control of the established Church of England, retention of the power of the landed aristocracy and peace abroad. The Whigs, mostly wealthy merchants, who were the majority throughout most of William's reign, favored the support of the army and the foreign wars, as well as amelioration of the contention among the Protestant sects. The party system determined who would be the ministers of the king after 1694 at the urging of Sunderland who dismissed the Tories and selected ministers from the Whig party.

---

[9] Note. The kings who usurped the throne by military force instead of hereditary right were William I, Stephen, John, Edward III, Henry IV, Richard III, Henry VII, and William III.

However, bribery became a noted feature of the system to favor votes in parliament. The party who became the majority of parliament thus gained control of the ministry and influence over the king. During the reign of William several of the ministers, called the Whig junto, were the special advisors of the king. This replaced the privy council whose members had been selected and dismissed at the kings command. The origins of the cabinet were thus established. In 1694 the Bank of England was established to provide loans to the government to satisfy a growing national debt. The bank was established by a group of wealthy merchants who formed a company whose charter was granted by the government. A permanent national debt began in 1692, augmented by the expenses of foreign wars.

Death of William III

During the final year of William's life, the war of the Spanish succession was immanent. The king of Spain was inept to govern, had no children and died November 1700. France and England now had an opportunity for gaining the Spanish possessions abroad. A grand alliance between England, Holland, and the Austrians was formed to counter the claims of France to the Spanish territories. Parliament appropriated sufficient funds for raising 40,000 men and refurbishing the navy. William had appointed John Churchill, earl of Marlborough, general and head of the English and Dutch forces.

William died in March 1702 after injuries from a fall from his horse. Anne, younger sister of Mary and James II, succeeded him.

Chapter 33

Anne and Marlborough

Anne, Queen of England, (b. 1665, d. 1714), shared the power of government with her minister, Marlborough, (b. 1650, d. 1722) from 1702 to 1714. Anne's husband, prince George of Denmark really played no role in government. Anne was selected by parliament, in accordance with the Act of Settlement, 1701, because she was raised as a Protestant as opposed to James II's son, a Catholic. Anne was the younger sister of Mary, daughter of James II and Anne Hyde. Anne's selection of Marlborough came through her own personal contacts with the wife of John Churchill, later earl and duke of Marlborough, in the court of William III. During his last days William had selected Marlborough to head the military command opposing Louis XIV of France. This reign corresponded to the years of the Wars of the Spanish Succession, from 1702 to 1713, also known as Queen Anne's War, as it involved territories in America. The queen's ministers and the parliament held the power of the crown. The Tories and Whigs contended for supremacy. Marlborough was of greater influence until late in the reign when he and the Whigs were ousted from power and replaced by the Tories. Of long term consequence was the union of England and Scotland in 1707. England also extended its empire in the Mediterranean and the Americas. The treaty of Utrecht in 1713 ended the war of Spanish succession and helped establish English power in the colonies and eventual conquest of Canada. The English gained possessions in the Caribbean, which assured continued wealth from the slave trade.

Anne and Sarah Jennings (Marlborough)

Luckily he (Marlborough) *had now found a new groundwork for his fortunes in the growing influence of his wife over the king's second daughter, Anne; and at the crisis of the revolution the adhesion of Anne to the cause of Protestantism was of the highest value. No sentiment of gratitude to his older patron hindered Marlborough from sympathy to William's effort, or from deserting the ranks of James's army when it faced William in the field. His desertion proved fatal to the royal cause; but great as this service was it was eclipsed by a second. It was by his wife's persuasion that Anne was induced to forsake her father and take refuge in Danby's camp. Unscrupulous as his conduct had been, the services, which he rendered to William were too great to miss their reward. He became earl of Marlborough; he was put at the head of a force during the Irish war where his rapid successes won William's regard; and he was given high command in the army of Flanders. But the sense of his power over Anne soon turned Marlborough from plotting treason against James to plot treason against William. Great as was his greed of gold, he had married Sarah Jennings, a penniless beauty of Charles's court, in whom a violent and malignant temper was strangely combined with a power of wining and retaining love. --- It was on his wife's influence over her friend that the earl's ambition counted in its designs against William. His plan was to drive the king from the throne by backing the Tories in their opposition to the war as well as by stirring to frenzy the English hatred of foreigners, and to seat Anne in his place. The discovery of his designs roused the king to a burst of unusual resentment. 'Were I and my lord Marlborough private persons,' William exclaimed, 'the sword would have to settle between us.' As it was, he could only strip the earl of his offices and command, and drive his wife from St. James's. Anne followed her favorite, and the court of the princess became the center of the Tory opposition; while Marlborough opened a correspondence with James. So notorious was his treason that on the eve of the French invasion of 1692 he was one of the first of the suspected persons sent to the Tower.*

The death of Mary forced William to recall Anne, who became by this event his successor; and with Anne the Marlboroughs returned to court. The king could not bend himself to trust the earl again; but as death drew near he saw in him the one man whose splendid talents fitted him, in spite of the baseness and treason of his life, to rule England and direct the grand alliance in his stead. He employed Marlborough therefore to negotiate the treaty of alliance with the emperor, and put him at the head of the army in Flanders. But the earl had only just taken the command when a fall from his horse prove fatal to the broken frame of the king 'There was a time when I should have been glad to have been delivered out of my troubles,' the dying man whispered to Portland, 'but I own I see another scene, and could wish to live a little longer.' He knew, however, that the wish was vain, and commended Marlborough to Anne as the fittest person to lead her armies and guide her counsels, Anne's zeal needed not quickening. Three days after her accession the earl was named captain-general of the English forces at home and abroad, and entrusted with the entire direction of the war. His supremacy over home affairs was secured by the construction of a purely Tory administration with Lord Godolphin, a close friend of Marlborough's, as lord Treasurer at its head. The queen's affection for

*his wife ensured him the support of the crown at a moment when Anne's
personal popularity gave the crown a new weight with the nation.[1]*

War in Europe and the new world

The war of the Spanish succession, from 1702 to 1713, cannot
here be reviewed. Marlborough was head of the allied forces against
French forces in the Netherlands, Germany, Italy and Spain. The major
victory was at Blenheim in 1704, which resulted in forcing the French
out of Germany. *After a few marches the armies met on the north bank of
the Danube, near --- the village of Blenheim --- one of the most
memorable battles in the history of the world. In one respect the struggle
which followed stands almost unrivaled, for the whole of the Teutonic
race was represented in the strange medley of Englishman, Dutchmen,
Hannoverians, Danes, Wurtembergers and Austrians who followed
Marlborough and Eugene. --- The center, however, which the French
believed to be unassailable, had been chosen by Marlborough for the
chief point of attack; and by making an artificial road across the morass
he was at last enabled to throw his eight thousand horsemen on the
French cavalry which occupied this position. --- The French center was
flung back on the Danube and forced to surrender. --- Of the defeated
army only twenty thousand escaped. Twelve thousand were slain,
fourteen thousand were captured. Germany was finally freed from the
French.[2]* For this victory Marlborough was given the royal manor of
Woodstock built for him at public expense. His campaigns in the
Netherlands in the borders between France and Holland from 1706 to
1709 led to the Treaty of Utrecht in 1713. Under the terms of this treaty
England retained Gibraltar and Minorca, which the English fleet had
captured during this war. In America England obtained claims to Nova
Scotia, Newfoundland, the land around Hudson Bay, and one of the West
Indian Islands. England obtained concessions from Spain to take Negro
slaves from Africa to the Spanish West Indies. This gave England a
monopoly of the slave trade with the Spanish colonies. The islands in the
Caribbean were the training grounds (seasoning) for sale of slaves to the
Colonies, South America and Cuba. John Franklin Hope described the
monstrous treatment of these people.[3] England after the War of the
Spanish Succession had now the strongest naval fleet in the world. Spain
had never recovered and Holland could not support the long and
expensive wars to protect themselves against Louis XIV and the French.
The French could not afford the costs of the wars and the maintenance of
her navies.

---

[1] Green, pp 706-708.

[2] Green, pp 711, 712.

[3] Hope, pp 50-51.

Union of Scotland

Soon after Anne came to the throne, in 1702, commissioners were appointed from England and Scotland to arrange the terms of a union. In 1707, the union was agreed upon the following conditions. *The act of union provided that the two kingdoms should be united into one under the name of Great Britain, and that the succession to the crown of this United Kingdom should be ruled by the provisions of the English Act of Settlement. The Scotch church and the Scotch law were left untouched: but all rights of trade were thrown open, and a uniform system of coinage adopted. A single parliament was henceforth to represent the United Kingdom, and for this purpose forty-five Scotch members were added to the five hundred and thirteen English members of the house of commons, and sixteen representative peers to the one hundred and eight who formed the English house of lords.*[4] The union jack, by uniting the square red cross of England with the Scots' diagonal white cross of St. Andrew, was at the same time adopted as the flag of the United Kingdom. The established churches were unchanged, with the Presbyterian church in Scotland and the Episcopalian Church in England. There remained differences in the statute and common law, the money and banking systems, the universities and other institutions.

Conflicts between Tories and Whigs

Anne was at heart a Tory, and her old trust in Marlborough died with his submission to the Whig demands. The growing opposition of the Tories to the war threw the duke more and more on the support of the Whigs, and the Whigs sold their support dearly. The wars in Europe decided the outcome, especially the *terrible slaughter, which bears the name of the battle of Malplaquet, in the Netherlands in 1709. The French had lost twelve thousand men, but forcing their lines of entrenchment had cost the allies a loss of double that number. Horror at such a 'deluge of blood' increased the growing weariness of the war; and the rejection of the French offers was unjustly attributed to a desire on the part of Marlborough of lengthening out a contest, which brought him profit and power.*

A storm of popular passion burst suddenly on the Whigs. Its occasion was a dull and silly sermon in which a high church divine, Dr. Sacheverell, maintained the doctrine of non-resistance at St. Paul's. His boldness challenged persecution; but in spite of the warning of Marlborough and of Somers the Whig ministers resolved on his impeachment before the lords, and the trial at once widened into a great party struggle. An outburst of popular enthusiasm in Sacheverell's favor showed what a storm of hatred had gathered against the Whigs and the

---

[4] Green, pp 714-715.

war. The most eminent of the Tory churchmen stood by his side at the bar, crowds escorted him to the court and back again while the streets rang with cries of 'The church and Dr. Sacheverell.' A small majority of the peers found the preacher guilty, but the light sentence they inflicted was in effect an acquittal, and bonfires and illuminations over the whole country welcomed it as a Tory triumph. At the opening of 1712 the Whig majority in the house of lords was swamped by the creation of twelve Tory peers. Marlborough was dismissed from his command, charged *with* misuse of public funds, *and condemned as guilty by a vote of the house of commons. The duke at once withdrew from England, and with his withdrawal all opposition to the peace was at and end.*[5]

Illness and death of the queen

The failure of the queen's health made the succession the real question of the day, and it was a question, which turned all politics into faction and intrigue. Threat of civil war erupted when the Tories began negotiations for the return of the Old Pretender if he converted to the Church of England. In the beginning of 1714 the Whigs had made ready for a rising on the queen's death, and invited Marlborough from Flanders to head them, in the hope that his name would rally the army to their cause. But events moved faster than their plans. Anne was suddenly struck with apoplexy. The act of settlement had been established by parliament in 1701, providing that the crown after the death of Anne would go to her second cousin Sophia, granddaughter of James I. James's daughter Elizabeth had married Frederick V, Elector Palatine. Their daughter Sophia was married to Ernest Augustus, elector of Hanover. The privy council at once assembled. *The right of the house of Hanover was at once acknowledged.*[6]

---

[5] Ibid, pp 716-719.

[6] Ibid, p 720.

Chapter 34

George I, George II,
Walpole and Pitt

George I, (b. 1660, d. 1727), was elector of Hanover from 1698 to 1727 and king of England from 1714 to 1727. He followed Anne without contest after the death of Anne in 1714. According to parliament's act of settlement in 1701, George's Protestant mother Sophia was declared heir to the crown upon Anne's death instead of James II's son, a Catholic. George's mother Sophia died in 1714 and George became heir to the throne. The German connection began with the marriage of Elizabeth, eldest daughter of Charles I, to Frederick V, elector Palatine. Their daughter Sophia married Ernest Augustus, elector of Hanover.[1]

George I

George was never popular in England. He never learned to speak English and could not communicated with his ministers or parliament. He stopped attending cabinet meetings. His only apparent interest in government was related to his native lands in Germany. George married his cousin Sophia Dorothy of Celle in 1682. This marriage produced George II. In 1694 George accused Sophia of infidelity and she was condemned to a prison where she died 32 years later. George's primary qualification for the crown, apart from the

---

[1] Note. The 'four Georges' followed in succession and sat on the crown during the remaining eighteenth and the first part of the nineteenth centuries. George III reigned during the American independence. Five generations of Hanoverian kings, all marrying German princesses, produced Queen Victoria and her grandson George V whose son Edward VIII was named the duke of Windsor to conceal the German lineage.

hereditary linkage with the Stuarts, was his Protestant background and his inveterate fear and hatred of the Catholics. This led to his exclusion of the Tories whom he suspected of loyalties to James's son, the *Old Pretender*. During this reign, England's first prime minister Walpole managed the civil and foreign affairs of government. Twenty years of peace and the avoidance of foreign and domestic warfare were the most notable achievement during Walpole's administration. *At home, the new king's accession was followed by striking political results. Under Anne the throne had regained much of the older influence which it lost through William's unpopularity; but under the two sovereigns who followed Anne, the power of the crown lay absolutely dormant. They were strangers, to whom loyalty in its personal sense was impossible; and their character as nearly approached insignificance, as it is possible for human character to approach it.*[2]

Uprising

In 1715 a Jacobite uprising resulted when James, the *Old Pretender*, roused in Scotland the earl of Mar and the Highlanders to restore the Stuart claim to the throne. Anne did not support James before her death. Louis XIV had died in the same year. *Six thousand highlanders joined Mar at Perth, but his cowardice or want of conduct kept his army idle, till Argyll had gathered forces to meet it in an indecisive engagement at Sheriffmuir. The Pretender, who arrived too late for the action, proved a yet more sluggish and incapable leader than Mar; and at the close of 1715 the advance of fresh forces drove James over-sea again and dispersed the clans to their hills. In England the danger passed away like a dream. The accession of the new king had been followed by some outbreaks of riotous discontent; but at the talk of Highland risings and French invasions Tories and Whigs alike rallied round the throne; while the army went for king George. The suspension of the Habeas Corpus Act, and the arrest of their leader, Sir William Wyndham, cowed the Jacobites; and not a man stirred in the west when Ormond appeared off the coast of Devon, and called on his party to rise. Oxford alone, where the university was a hotbed of Jacobitism, showed itself restless; and a few of the Catholic gentry rose in Northumberland, under lord Derentwater and Mr. Forster. The arrival of two thousand Highlanders who had been sent to join them by Mar spurred them to a march into Lancashire, where the Catholic party was strongest; but they were soon cooped up in Preston, and driven to surrender.*[3]

---

[2] Green, p 721.

[3] Ibid, p 725.

The Men Who Made the Law

Walpole

Robert Walpole, (b. 1676, d. 1745), has been regarded as England's first prime minister. *Walpole entered parliament two years before William's death as a young Norfolk landowner of fair fortune, with the tastes and air of the class from which he sprang. His big square figure, his vulgar good-humored face were those of a common country squire. And in Walpole the squire underlay the statesman to the last. He was ignorant of books, he 'loved neither writing nor reading,' and if he had a taste for art, his real love was for the table, the bottle, and the chase. He rode as hard as he drank. Even in moments of political peril, the first dispatch he would open was the letter from his gamekeeper. There was the temper of the Norfolk fox-hunter in the 'doggedness' which Marlborough noted as his characteristic, in the burly self-confidence which declared 'If I had not been prime minister I should have been archbishop of Canterbury,' in the stubborn courage which conquered the awkwardness of his earlier efforts to speak, or meet single-handed at the last the bitter attacks of a host of enemies. There was the same temper in the genial good-humor which became with him a new force in politics. No man was ever more fiercely attacked by speakers and writers, but he brought in no 'gagging act' for the press; and though the lives of most of his assailants were in his hands through their intrigues with the Pretender, he made little use of his power over them. --- He saw the value of the political results, which the revolution had won, and he carried out his 'revolution principles' with a rare fidelity through years of unquestioned power. But his prosaic good sense turned skeptically away from the poetic and passionate sides of human feeling. Appeals to the loftier or purer motives of action he laughed at as 'school-boy flights.' Your young members who talked of public virtue or patriotism he had one good-natured answer: 'You will soon come off that and grow wiser.*[4]

Walpole entered the house of commons, and under Anne was a member of the council which controlled the affairs of the navy during the Wars of the Spanish Succession. In 1708 he was promoted to secretary at war and in 1710 to treasurer of the navy. During these years he established himself as a member of the Whig party. However, with the rise of the Tories, Walpole was impeached in 1712 for corruption and sent to the Tower. Following the death of Anne and with the accession in 1714 of George a Whig majority was obtained. Walpole was appointed as chairman of a committee, which led to the impeachment of his Tory enemies. Walpole became first lord of the Treasury and chancellor of the Exchequer in October, 1715.

---

[4] Ibid, p 724.

The South Sea Bubble

The stock market crash of 1720 enhanced the power and influence of Townshend and Walpole. *The sudden increase of English commerce begot at this moment the mania of speculation. Ever since the age of Elizabeth the unknown wealth of Spanish America had acted like a spell upon the imagination of Englishmen; and Harley gave countenance to a South Sea Company, which promised a reduction of the public debt as the price of a monopoly of the Spanish trade. Spain however clung jealously to her old prohibitions of all foreign commerce; and the Treaty of Utrecht only won for England the right of engaging in the Negro slave trade, and of despatching a single ship to the coast of Spanish America. But in spite of all this, the company again came forward, offering in exchange for new privileges to pay off the national debt and burdens, which amounted to nearly a million a year. It was in vain that Walpole warned the ministry and the country against this 'dream.' Both went mad; and in 1720 bubble company followed bubble company, till the inevitable reaction brought a general ruin in its train. The crash brought Stanhope to the grave. Of his colleagues, many were found to have received bribes from the South Sea Companies to back its frauds. Craggs, the secretary of state, died of terror at the investigation; Aislabie, the chancellor of the Exchequer, was sent to the Tower; and in the general wreck of his rivals Walpole mounted again into power. In 1721 he became first lord of the treasury while Townshend returned to his post of secretary of state.*[5]

Walpole as statesman and financier

If no minister has fared worse at the hands of poets and historians, there are few whose greatness has been more impartially recognized by practical statesmen. The years of his power indeed are years without parallel in our history for political stagnation. His long administration of more than twenty years is almost without a history. All legislative and political activity seemed to cease with his entry into office. Year after year passed by without a change. In the third year of his ministry there was but one division in the house of commons. The Tory members were so few that for a time they hardly cared to attend its sittings; and in 1722 the loss of bishop Atterbury of Rochester, who was convicted of correspondence with the Pretender, deprived of his bishopric and banished by act of parliament deprived the Jacobites of their only remaining leader. Walpole's one care was to maintain the quiet, which was reconciling the county to the system of the revolution. But this inaction fell in with the temper of the nation at large. It was popular with the class, which commonly presses for political activity. The energy of the trading class was absorbed in the rapid extension of

---

[5] Ibid, p 728.

commerce and accumulation of wealth. So long as the country was justly and temperately governed the merchant and shopkeeper were content to leave government in the hands that held it. All they asked was to be let alone to enjoy their new freedom, and develop their new industries.

Walpole was the first and he was the most successful of our peace ministers. --- Peace indeed was hard to maintain. The emperor Charles VI had issued a pragmatic sanction, by which he provided that his hereditary dominions should descend unbroken to his daughter, Maria Theresa. --- Spain, still resolute to regain her lost possessions, and the old monopoly of trade with her American colones, seized the opportunity of detaching the emperor from the alliance of the four powers, which left her isolated in Europe. Spain had secret negotiations for taking Gibralter and Minorca from England, securing lands in Italy and increased trading privileges in America. --- The moderation of Walpole alone averted a European war. While sending British squadrons to the Baltic, the Spanish coast, and America, he succeeded by diplomatic pressure in again forcing the emperor to inaction; Spain was at last brought to sign the treaty of Seville, and to content herself with a promise of the succession of a Spanish prince to the Duchies of Parma and Tuscany; and the discontent of Charles at this concession was allayed in 1731 by giving the guarantee of England to the pragmatic sanction.

As Walpole was the first of our peace ministers, so he was the first of our financiers. He was far indeed from discerning the powers which later statesmen have shown to exist in a sound finance, but he had the sense to see, what no minister had till then seen, that the wisest course a statesman can take in presence of a great increase in national industry and national wealth is to look quietly on and let it alone. --- The wisdom of Walpole was rewarded by a quick upgrowth of prosperity. Our exports, which were six millions in value at the beginning of the century, had doubled by the middle of it. The rapid development of the Colonial trade gave England a new wealth.[6]

In 1724 George relied completely on Walpole and Townsend. In 1727 George I, while on a trip to Hanover, died from complications of a stroke. His son George II succeeded him.[7]

---

[6] Ibid, p 730.

[7] Note. His daughter Sophia, wife of king Frederick William I of Prussia, was the mother of Frederick the Great.

George II

George II, (b. 1683, d. 1760) inherited the crown from his father. He held the crown from 1727 to 1760. When George was eleven years old his father, George I, had accused his mother of infidelity and she spent the remaining years of her life in prison. There was intense conflict between father and son throughout. During Walpole's service with George I, the prince met with Walpole's opponents and other dissident Whigs at his London residence, Leicester house. George married, in 1705, Caroline of Brandenburgh-Ansbach, a gifted and intelligent woman.

The government

The accession of George II in 1727 gave a fatal shock to Walpole's power; for the new king was known to have hated his father's minister hardly less than he had hated his father. But hate Walpole as he might, the king was absolutely guided by the adroitness of his wife, Caroline of Anspach; and Caroline had resolved that there should be no change in the ministry. The years which followed were in fact those in which Walpole's power reached its height. He gained as great an influence over George II as he had gained over his father. His hold over the house of commons remained unshaken. The country was tranquil and prosperous. The prejudices of the landed gentry were met by a steady effort to reduce the land-tax. The church was quiet. The Jacobites were too hopeless to stir. A few trade measures and social reforms crept quietly through the houses. An inquiry into the state of the gaols showed that social thought was not utterly dead. A bill of great value enacted that all proceedings in courts of justice should henceforth be in the English language. Only once did Walpole break this tranquility by an attempt at a great measure of statesmanship. No tax had from the first moment of its introduction been more unpopular than the excise for tobacco and wine. --- *The necessaries of life and the raw materials of manufacture were in Walpole's plan to remain absolutely untaxed. The scheme was an anticipation of the principles, which have guided English finance since the triumph of free trade; but in 1733 Walpole stood ahead of his time. A violent agitation broke out; riots almost grew into revolt; and in spite of the Queen's wish to put down resistance by force, Walpole withdrew the bill. 'I will not be the minister,' he said with noble self-command, 'to enforce taxes at the expense of blood.' What had fanned popular prejudiced into a flame during the uproar was the violence of the so-called Patriots.*[8]

---

[8] Ibid, pp 730-731.

Opposition to Walpole, war with Spain

Walpole's excise bill, even though withdrawn was the focus of opposition in parliament. Despite influential peers in opposition, Walpole and Newcastle were able to win their ministries by a small majority in 1734. Bribery and corruption had entered politics since the reign of Charles II but it had flourished under Walpole. *'All these men have their price,'* he once said to a friend. Rather than raise taxes, the sinking fund, a fund established to reduce the national debt, was raided year after year for increasing amounts. In 1736, Frederick, prince of Wales, quarreled violently with his father George II. This was poorly handled by Walpole and a court of opposition arose at Leicester house. In 1737 Walpole's chief support, Caroline, died. Walpole resigned in George II's reign to be followed by opposition forces and the most important minister of this period, William Pitt, who rallied England's commercial classes to aggressive trade practices, world conquest and modern imperialism.

The prospect of war involving England was raised by the alliance between France and Spain. The Spanish resented the privileges, which England gained from the treaty of Utrecht— the monopoly of the slave trade to the West Indies and trading rights to Vera Cruz. Another wave of hysteria was generated. *The ill-humor of the trading classes rose to madness in 1738 when a merchant captain named Jenkins told at the bar of the house of commons the tale of his tortures by the Spaniards, and produced an ear which, he said, they had cut off with taunts at the English king. It was in vain that Walpole strove to do justice to both parties, and that he battled stubbornly against the cry for an unjust and impolitic war. --- But it was not till he stood utterly alone that Walpole gave way and that he consented in 1739 to a war against Spain. 'They may ring their bells now.' the great minister said bitterly, as peals and bonfires welcomed his surrender; 'but they will soon be wringing their hands.'* [9] An English fleet was sent on a worldwide voyage of plunder and exploration. After four years its gain was the plunder of a Spanish fort on the coast of Peru, the capture of a Spanish galleon on the way to Manila, and seizure of some Spanish colonies and ships in the Indies. The vessels returned to Portsmouth with gold and silver. Elsewhere the fleet suffered heavy losses.

War of the Austrian Succession

The involvement of England and the royals in European politics is of interest, but cannot here be more than briefly alluded to. The War of the Austrian Succession, 1740 to 1748, contributed to Walpole's resignation in 1742. The principle contenders in this war were Maria Theresa of Austria and Frederick the Great of Prussia, who was the nephew of George II. Charles VI of Austria had decreed that his daughter

---

[9] Ibid, pp 733-734.

Maria Theresa would inherit his dominions. Frederick of Prussia, upon Charles's death seized part of the lands of Maria Theresa, who formed an alliance with other nations including England. Frederick formed an alliance with France. In 1743, however, another alliance formed of England, Hanover, Prussia, Austria and Holland, all joined against France. George II, in his singular moment of glory, formed an invasion of France and entered the field at Dettingen, with a small victory. In 1745 the English and their allies were defeated in the battle of Fontenoy in Holland, aided by the Irish brigade. The war between France and England extended to India. There appeared to be no gains by any of the parties in this war. A peace was made in 1748 at Aix la Chapelle where conditions at the outset of the war were secured.

Rebellion in Scotland

But there was one last threat of the Catholics taking over. The Scots had suffered from the union with England. Prosperity came to the wealthy landowners and some of the Glasgow merchants, but there was increasing poverty for the highlanders and small craftsmen in the Lowlands. The Scottish aristocracy resented the way they were treated by the English. Charles Edward Stuart, grandson of James II, was the last in the Tudor line. *In 1745, the young adventurer again embarked with but seven friends in a small vessel and landed on a little island of the Hebrides. For three weeks he stood almost alone; but on the 29th of August the clans rallied to his standard in Glenfinnan, and Charles found himself at the head of fifteen hundred men. His force swelled to an army as he marched through Blair Athol on Perth, entered Edinburgh in triumph, and proclaimed 'James the Eighth' at the Town Cross; and two thousand English troops who marched against him under Sir John Cope were broken and cut to pieces on the 21st of September by a single charge of the clansmen at Preston Pans. Victory at once doubled the forces of the conqueror. The prince was now at the head of six thousand men; but all were still Highlanders, for the people of the Lowlands held aloof from his standard, and it was with the utmost difficulty that he could induced them to follow him to the south. His tact and energy however at last conquered every obstacle, and after skillfully evading an army gathered at Newcastle he marched through Lancashire, and pushed on the 4th of December as far as Derby. But here all hope of success came to an end. Hardly a man had risen in his support as he passed through the districts where Jacobitism boasted of its strength. The people flocked to see his march as if to see a show. Catholics and Tories abounded in Lancashire, but only a single squire took up arms. Manchester was looked on as the most Jacobite of English towns, but all the aid it gave was an illumination and two thousand pounds. From Carlisle to Derby he had been joined by hardly two hundred men. The policy of Walpole had in fact secured England for the house of Hanover. The long peace, the prosperity of the country, and the clemency of the government, had done their work.*[10]

Trade, Conquest and William Pitt

Twenty years of peace under Walpole came to an end with the rise of a new group of Patriots. Their spokesman and leader was William Pitt. It was William Pitt who produced the rallying cry which propelled the nation into war *'When Trade is as stake it is your last retrenchment; you must defend it, or perish.* Walpole had stood for the interests of men of substance who gained from security and low taxation in contrast to the rash commercial adventurers. Pitt would lead the nation into a new era of extended commercial ventures and world conquests. The controversies over the church had laid dormant. There arose a new group of Protestants led by John Wesley and his brother, which gave birth to a new religious sect. John and Charles Wesley held the first Methodist conference in 1744. Although they separated from the established church there was no resulting conflict. In fact, the Anglican ministers adopted some of the ways of the Methodists in their enthusiasm for preaching and this became the 'evangelical movement' within the Anglican Church.

William Pitt, the Elder, (b. 1708, d. 1778), was the grandson of Thomas Pitt, governor of the East India company's enterprise at Madras, India. 'Diamond Pitt', as the grandfather was called had made a fortune in his commercial ventures. He believed that the wealth and greatness of England depended on men like himself, ready to fight for a fortune in foreign countries. William grew up with his grandfather's beliefs that England's greatness and prosperity depended on aggression, on seizing and holding on to the world's trade. Pitt entered parliament in 1735 and headed the younger 'Patriots' in their attack on Walpole. Carteret had been a member of this group. Pitt was supported by a wealthy noble, lord Cobham, and in 1737 was given a grant by George II's son Frederick Louis, prince of Wales, who opposed his father and Walpole. With the fall of Walpole in 1742 this group, called the Patriots, opposed the new ministers Pelham and Newcastle.

England became embroiled in European wars under the king's new minister Carteret. Pitt and his group opposed Carteret's policy of forming a coalition of German states protecting the electorate of Hanover. Carteret's policies led only to increase in government expenses and taxes. The French defeated the English at Fontenoy. Carteret's failures and the influence of the new prime minister, Henry Pelham, led to William Pitt entering the government in 1746. He was appointed as vice-treasurer for Ireland and a few months later paymaster general of the forces. He remained in this position for nine years. He received a large gift from the duchess of Marlborough and in 1754, at age 46, married

---

[10] Ibid, p 743.

Lady Hester Grenville. Her fortune and wise handling of money provided Pitt with the means for a grand display in his glorious years as statesman during the seven years war against France, from 1756 to 1763. Pelham had died in 1754 and was succeeded by his brother the duke of Newcastle. Pitt became secretary of state under George II in 1756. In 1757 Pitt became chief advisor of foreign affairs and leader of the house of commons. Under his leadership Great Britain extended its empire from India, Africa Germany, the West Indies and Canada to the American colonies. The key to Pitt's foreign policy was to gather support for waging war against England's old enemy, France. *But it was the capture of trade which haunted his imagination and which to him and his City supporters made the whole struggle a matter of life and death for England. Trade was wealth and power. The only rival was France.*

There were four theaters of trade— North America, the West Indies, Africa, and India. North America meant the control of fur, fish, and naval supplies. The strategy of attack had been worked out many years previously in consultation with American merchants. The capture of Quebec and Montreal was sufficient to capture the trade of Canada. Louisburg, northeast Nova Scotia, was reduced by Wolfe in 1758. Canada was open to attack. James Cook was sent to make a detailed survey of the St. Lawrence River— a survey carried out with superb efficiency and thoroughness. Nothing illustrates Pitt's grasp as the realities of naval war better than this survey of Cook's, for without the knowledge which it brought, Wolfe's task would have been doubly difficult.

Elsewhere there was equal success but except in Africa, less unity of purpose. About the West Indies, the City was divided. Bedford, the city millionaire, who was one of Pitt's most ardent supporters, regarded the capture of French sugar islands as likely to produce a glut of sugar, and reduce the price. Pitt believed that America could easily absorb the surplus, once the trade between Guadeloupe and the American colonies had been freed. Pitt got his way, and he was right. Guadalupe was captured, and within a year Guadalupe's customs duties had risen by 50 per cent and paid for the expedition sent against it. In these years everything Pitt touched seemed to bring victory and profit. Dakar, with the gum and slave trade of Africa, was captured in 1759. Eyre Coote and Clive were winning such massive victories in India that Pitt left them to their own devices and concentrated on capturing the channels of oriental trade. At Mauritius, an island east of Madagascar, Pitt had his one failure, but this was wiped out by the brilliant attack on Manila, perhaps the greatest naval and military achievement of the war, and one which brought the control of the China trade in tea.[11]

---

[11] Plumb, England in the Eighteenth Century, pp 112-113.

The Glory of Pitt and British Imperialism

The defeat of the French fleets brought celebrations in England. Church bells rang and crowds swarmed to Westminster Abbey and St. Paul's to honor their heroes and their dead. Green, a clergyman, also gives great praise to Pitt's military achievements. Green devoted several pages in praise of Pitt, yet we can only provide selected events illustrating this man's foreign ministry, which was responsible for the trade and military policies of the British Empire, which even today is reflected in world politics. Pitt would become a model for future statesmen by his oratory, dramatic presentations and ability to motivate the merchants to his causes of trade, conquest and profit. *In the year which followed the peace of Paris two English ships were sent on a cruise of discovery to the Straits of Magellan; three years later Captain Wallis reached the coral reefs of Tahiti; and in 1768 Captain Cook traversed the Pacific from end to end, and wherever he touched, in New Zealand, in Australia, he claimed the soil for the English Crown, and opened a new world for the expansion of the English race. Statesmen and people alike felt the change in their country's attitude. --- Its people, steeped in the commercial ideas of the time, saw in the growth of their vast possessions, the monopoly of whose trade was reserved to the mother country, a source of boundless wealth. The trade with America alone was in 1772 nearly equal to that England carried on with the whole world at the beginning of the century. To guard and preserve so vast and lucrative a dominion became from this moment not only the aim of British statesmen but the resolve of the British people.[12]*

The Poor and the Irish

The glory of England was not reflected in the poor of England who were dispossessed of their homes and livelihood from the enclosures, which brought wealth to the landed gentry. The Bill of Rights during the reign of William III did not apply to the poor or the Catholics. The penal laws, following the military conquests of William III, had devastated Ireland. During the reigns of Anne and the Georges Ireland remained under a merciless cruel subjection by the English. Cusack describes the plight of Ireland at the transition from George I to George II. *The country was suffering at this period from the most fearful distress. There were many causes for this state of destitution, which were quite obvious to all but those who were interested in maintaining it. The poorer classes, being almost exclusively Catholics, had been deprived of every means of support. Trade was crushed, so that they could not become traders; agriculture was not permitted, so that they could not become agriculturists. There was, in fact, no resource for the majority but to emigrate, to steal, or to starve. To a people whose religion always*

---

[12] Green, p 758.

had a preponderating influence on their moral conduct, the last alternative only was available, as there were not the same facilities for emigration then as now. The cultivation of the potato had already become general; it was indeed, the only way of obtaining food left to these unfortunates. They were easily planted, easily reared; and to men liable at any moment to be driven from their miserable holdings, if the attempted to effect 'improvement,' or to plant such crops as might attract the rapacity of their landlords, they were an invaluable resource. The man might live who eats nothing but potatoes all the year round, but he could scarcely be envied or ejected for his wealth. In 1739 a severe frost destroyed the entire crop, and a frightful famine ensued, in which it was estimated that 400,000 persons perished of starvation.[13]

The plight of the slaves

Neither was the glory of England reflected in the slave trade and the way these people were managed. John Franklin Hope described the plight of the slaves during this period. It will be recalled that the English had a monopoly of the slave trade following the Treaty of Utrecht. The 'seasoning' of the slaves brought from Africa by British merchant ships was preparatory for their sale to the colonists in the southern plantations. *Perhaps it was the slave codes and their enforcement that did more than anything else to carry forward the process of seasoning the slaves in the island. --- In 1724 there were thirty-two thousand Negroes and fourteen thousand whites. The influence of the planters in England made possible the passage, in 1667, of the act to regulate the Negroes on the British Plantations. It referred to the Negroes in the Caribbean as 'of wild, barbarous, and savage nature to be controlled only with strict severity.' One important ingredient in the seasoning process was the overseer's lash. A typical one was made of plaited cowhide. In the hands of a stern overseer it could draw blood through the breeches of a slave. One visitor in Jamaica fell ill at his first sight of a common flogging. At times the floggings were so sever as to inflict wounds so large that a man's finger could be inserted in them. Another favorite type of punishment was to suspend the slave from a tree by ropes and the iron weights around his neck and waist. Still another was to crop the slave's ears and to break the bones of his limbs. If these punishments would seem to shorten life and to reduce efficiency, it must be remembered that Negroes were being*

---

[13] Cusack, pp 582-583. The famine and starvation of the Irish at this time should not be confused with the great famine a century or so later. The basic causes of both famines were essentially the same. See Woodham-Smith, *The Great Hunger.*

brought in at an increasing rate down past the opening of the nineteenth century and there was, consequently, no great inclination to preserve life. Furthermore, it was extremely important in a society where Negroes outnumbered whites that the Negroes be continuously impressed with the superior strength of the whites and their willingness to exercise it in all its fury whenever necessary.[14]

The statutory recognition of slavery in Virginia came in 1661. At first the Negro population of Virginia grew quite slowly. In 1625 there were only 23 Negroes in the colony; and as late as the middle of the century scarcely 300 could be counted. With the chartering of the Royal African Company in 1672 the shipment of slaves into the colony was accelerated. By the end of the century they were being brought in at the rate of more than 1,000 per year. It was in the eighteenth century that the Negro population grew at what some Virginians began to view as an alarming rate. In 1708 there were 12,000 Negroes and 18,00 whites. By 1756 there were 120,156 Negroes and 173,316 whites in Virginia with Negroes outnumbering whites in many communities.

The Virginia slave code, borrowing heavily from practices in the Caribbean had served as a model for other mainland codes, was comprehensive if it was anything at all. Slaves were not permitted to leave the plantations without the written permission of their master. Slaves wandering about without such permits were to be taken up and returned to their masters. Slaves found guilty of murder or rape were to be hanged. For major offenses, such as robbing a house or a store, slaves were to receive sixty lashes and be placed in the pillory, where their ears were to be cut off. For petty offenses, such as insolence and associating with whites or free Negroes, they were to be whipped, branded, or maimed. The docility of the slaves, about which many masters boasted, was thus achieved through the enactment of a comprehensive code containing provisions for punishment designed to break even the most irascible blacks in the colony. With the sheriffs, the courts, and even the slaveless whites on their side, the masters should have experienced no difficulty in maintaining peace among their slaves.

The number of slaves in other colonies increased during the reign of the Georges. *In Maryland by 1750 there were forty thousand blacks as compared with a hundred thousand whites. --- It was a foregone conclusion that slaves would be introduced into the Carolinas as soon as it was feasible. After all, four of the proprietors of the colony were members of the Royal African Company and fully appreciated the profits that could come from the slave trade decades to come.*

Georgia, which was named after king George II, *was the only important New World colony to be established by England in the eighteenth century,* in 1733. *By 1760 there were six thousand whites and*

---

[14] Hope, From Slavery to Freedom, pp 51-52.

three thousand blacks. In 1773, when the last estimate was made before the War for Independence, the white population had increased to eighteen thousand, while the black population numbered some fifteen thousand. Much of Georgia's slave code, adopted in 1755, was taken from the South Carolina code, and it reflected South Carolina's experience rather than Georgia's. For example, the interdiction against more than seven Negroes being out together without a white chaperon indicated South Carolina's general fear of Negro uprisings. Between Saturday evening and Monday morning, not even those slaves who were authorized to possess firearms were permitted to carry them on their persons. Under no conditions were Negroes to be taught to read and write.[15]

Death of George II

George had little interest in the affairs of government, but was a direct participant against the French in 1743. George died suddenly, on October 25, 1760. His son Frederick had died in 1751. The crown passed to his grandson, George III.

---

[15] Ibid, pp 56-62.

Chapter 35

George III and
American Independence

George III, George Wilhelm Friedrich, (b. 1738, d. 1820), also elector and king of Hanover, is notable for fostering the conditions in England and America which led to the Declaration of Independence July 4, 1776 and the victory of the American forces over the English, in 1782 with a treaty of Peace signed September 3, 1783. George III succeeded his grandfather George II in 1760 and, although retaining the crown until his death in 1820, his son George IV replaced him in 1811 due to a condition of mental instability and incompetence, which ended his administrative rule. As with all histories the scope of one's interest must select a few events of the many and in this work the focus is on the men who made the law. Blackstone (b 1723 d 1780) published the commentaries on English Law, the first volume in 1765 and the remaining three volumes by 1769. David Hume (b 1711 d 1776) was a contemporary of Blackstone. *The History of England,* the edition used in this book, was published in 1778. We can only here touch on some of the results of George's rule during the first twenty years of his administration, which led to the American Revolution and to the attempted Irish revolution, as well as the subjection of India to Imperial rule. In contrast to the administration under the feeble kings, George I and George II, we must focus more attention on George III since he attempted to regain regal powers lost since the 1689 English revolution. For the first twenty years there was a succession of ministers and prime ministers none of whom lasted very long under the king's command. Although parliament had enacted sufficient legislation to limit the powers of the king it became clear, early after the ascendancy of George III, that the English government and established laws were ineffective in controlling the new king. The wars with France, the French revolution, Napoleon and the associated War of 1812 between England and the United States, will not be a subject of this review. These events were in a period of English history, which took place after the American independence.

Family history and upbringing.

About the only advantage this king had over George I and George II is that he was brought up in England and spoke English, although at the late age of eleven years. There is of course no reliable documentation of what was wrong with George, or even what led to his father's death in 1751 when George was twelve years old. His father's death was 'sudden and unexpected.' His mother, princes Augusta of Saxe-Gotha, the third German princess in succession, brought George up to be a *true king*. The violent conflicts between George I and George II, and especially the violence between George II and his father prince Frederick, no doubt had an effect on young George. George was considered slow in mental development, the cause unknown. No one could at that time anticipate the importance of selecting a competent leader at this crucial juncture of English history and in the nation, which would later become the most powerful empire in the world.

The reign of George III

To check this republican spirit, to crush all dreams of severance, and to strengthen the unity of the British Empire was one of the chief aims of the young sovereign who mounted the throne on the death of his grandfather in 1760. For the first and last time since the accession of the house of Hanover England saw a king who was resolved to play a part in English politics; and the part which George III succeeded in playing was undoubtedly a memorable one. In ten years he reduced government to a shadow, and turned the loyalty of his subjects at home into disaffection. In twenty he had forced the American colonies into revolt and independence, and brought England to what then seemed the brink of ruin. Work such as this has sometimes been done by very great men, and often by very wicked and profligate men; but George was neither profligate nor great. He had a smaller mind than any English king before him save James II. He was wretchedly educated, and his natural powers were of the meanest sort. Nor had he the capacity for using greater minds than his own by which some sovereigns have concealed their natural littleness. On the contrary, his only feeling towards great men was one of jealousy and hate. He longed for the time when 'decrepitude or death' might put an end to Pitt; and even when death had freed him from 'this trumpet of sedition,' he denounced the proposal for a public monument to the great statesman as 'an offensive measure to me personally.' But dull and petty as his temper was, he was clear as to his purpose and obstinate in the pursuit of it. And his purpose was to rule. 'George,' his mother, the princess of Wales, had continually repeated to him in youth, 'George be king.' He called himself always ' a Whig of the Revolution,' and he had no wish to undo the work, which he believed the revolution to have done. But he looked on the subjection of his two predecessors to the will of their ministers as no real part of the work of the revolution, but as a usurpation of that authority which the revolution had left to the crown. And to this usurpation he was determined not to submit. His resolve was to govern, not to govern against the law, but simply to govern, to be freed from the dictation of parties and ministers, and to be in effect the first minister of the State.

How utterly incompatible such a dream was with the parliamentary constitution of the country as it had received its final form from Sunderland, it is easy to see; but George was resolved to carry out his dream. And in carrying it out he was aided by the circumstances of the time. The spell of Jacobitism was broken by the defeat of Charles Edward, the young pretender, *and the later degradation of his life wore finally away the thin coating of disloyalty, which clung to the clergy and the squires. They were ready again to take part in politics, and in the accession of a king who, unlike his two predecessors, was no stranger but an Englishmen, who had been born in England and spoke English; they found the opportunity they desired. From the opening of the reign Tories gradually appeared again at court. It was only slowly indeed that the party as a whole swung round to a steady support of the government; but their action told at once on the complexion of English politics. Their withdrawal from public affairs had left them untouched by the progress of political ideas since the revolution of 1688, and when they returned to political life it was to invest the new sovereign with all the reverence, which they had bestowed on the Stuarts.*[1]

George and his ministers, foreign affairs

George III acceded to the crown at mid point in the Seven Years War (1756-1763) against France. It was Pitt, the elder, who devised the strategy of the war while George II merely looked on, and then died in 1760. *Had Pitt and Newcastle* (Pelham) *held together, supported as the one was by the commercial classes and public opinion, the other by the Whig families and the whole machinery of parliamentary management, George must have struggled in vain. But the ministry was already disunited. The Whigs, attached to peace by the traditions of Walpole, dismayed at the enormous expenditure, and haughty with the pride of a ruling oligarchy, were in silent revolt against the war and the supremacy of the Great Commoner* (Pitt the elder). *It was against their will that Pitt rejected proposals of peace from France on the terms of a desertion of Prussia. In 1761 Pitt urged a new war with Spain. --- His colleagues shrank from the plans so vast and daring; and Newcastle was spurred to revolt by the king and backed in it by the rest of the Whigs. It was in vain that Pitt enforced his threat of resignation by declaring himself*

---

[1] Green, pp 761-762.

responsible to 'the people,' or that the Londoners hung after his dismissal from office on his carriage wheels, hugged his footman, and even kissed his horses. The fall of the great statesman in October changed the whole look of European affairs. 'Pitt disgraced,' wrote a French philosopher— 'It is worth two victories to us!' Frederick, on the other hand, was almost driven to despair.[2]   George saw in the great statesman's fall nothing but an opening for peace. He quickly availed himself of the weakness and unpopularity in which the ministry found itself involved after Pitt's departure to drive the duke of Newcastle from office by a series of studied mortifications, and to place the Marquis of Bute at its head. Bute was a mere court favorite, with the abilities of a gentlemen usher, but he was willing to do the king's will, and the king's will was to end the war. Frederick, who still held his ground stubbornly against fate, was brought to the brink of ruin in the spring of 1762 by the withdrawal of the English subsidies. --- Pitt's policy had been vindicated by a Spanish declaration of war three weeks after his fall; and the surrender of Cuba and the Philippines to a British fleet brought about the Peace of Paris in September 1763. England restored Martinique, the most important of her west Indian conquests, to France, and Cuba and the Philippines to Spain in return for the cession of Florida. Her real gains were in India and America. In the first the French abandoned all right to any military settlement. From the second they wholly withdrew. To England they gave up Canada, Nova Scotia, and Louisiana as far as the Mississippi, while they resigned the rest of that province to Spain, in compensation for its surrender of Florida to the British crown.[3]

George's government and the Bribery of Electors

In September 1761 George married Charlotte Sophia of Mecklenburg-Strelitz, a German princess selected by Bute. *The anxiety, which the young king showed for peace abroad, sprang simply from his desire to begin the struggle for power at home. So long as the war lasted, Pitt's return to office and the union of the Whigs under his guidance was an hourly danger. But with peace the king's hands were free. He could count on the dissensions of the Whigs, on the new-born loyalty of the Tories, on the influence of the crown patronage which he had taken into his own hands; but what he counted on most of all was the character of the house of commons. At a time when it had become all-powerful in the state, when government hung simply on its will, the house of commons had ceased in any real and effective sense to represent the commons at all. The changes in the distribution of seats which were*

---

[2] Note. George II and Pitt had supported Frederick II, or Frederick the Great, who led Prussia to new conquests. Frederick was the nephew of George II.

[3] Ibid, p 764.

called for by the natural shifting of population and wealth since the days of Edward I had been recognized as early as the Civil Wars; but the reforms of the long parliament were canceled at the restoration. From the time of Charles II to that of George III not a single effort had been made to meet the growing abuses of our parliamentary system. Great towns like Manchester or Birmingham remained without a member, while members still sat for boroughs, which, like Old Surum, had actually vanished from the face of the earth.

The effort of the Tudor sovereigns to establish a court party in the house by a profuse creation of boroughs, most of which were mere villages then in the hands of the crown, had ended in the appropriation of these seats by the neighboring landowners, who bought and sold them as they sold their own estates. Even in towns which had a real claim to representation, the narrowing of municipal privileged ever since the fourteenth century to a small part of the inhabitants, and in many cases the restriction of electoral rights to the members of the governing corporation, rendered their representation a mere name. The choice of such places hung simply on the purse or influence of politicians. Some were 'the king's boroughs,' others were 'close boroughs' in the hands of jobbers like the duke of Newcastle, who at one time returned a third of all the borough members in the house. The counties and the great commercial towns could alone be said to exercise any real right of suffrage, though the enormous expense of contesting such constituencies practically left their representation in the hands of the great local families. But even in the counties the suffrage was ridiculously limited and unequal. Out of a population in fact of eight millions of English people, only a hundred and sixty thousand, were electors at all. How far such a house was from really representing English opinion we see from the fact that in the height of his popularity Pitt could hardly find a seat in it.

Purchase was becoming more and more the means of entering parliament. Seats were bought and sold in the open market at a price which rose to four thousand pounds, and we can hardly wonder that reformers could allege without a chance of denial, 'This house is not a representative of the people of Great Britain. It is the representative of nominal boroughs, of ruined and exterminated towns, of noble families, of wealthy individual, of foreign potentates.' The meanest motives naturally told on a body returned by such constituencies, cut off from the influence of public opinion by the secrecy of parliamentary proceedings, and yet invested with almost boundless authority. Walpole and Newcastle had made bribery and borough-jobbing the base of their power. George III seized it in his turn as a base of the power he proposed to give to the crown. The royal revenue was employed to buy seats and to buy votes. Day by day George himself scrutinized the voting-list of the two houses, and distributed rewards and punishments as members voted according to his will or no. Promotion in the civil service, preferment in the church, rank in the army, was reserved for 'the king's friends.' Pensions and court places were used to influence debates. Bribery was employed on a scale never known before. Under Bute's ministry an office was opened at the Treasury for the purchase of members, and twenty-five thousand pounds are said to have been spent in a single day.[4]

Opposition and Criticism

The result of these measures was soon seen in the tone of the parliament. Till now it had bowed beneath the greatness of Pitt; but in the teeth of his denunciation the provisions of the Peace of Paris were approved by a majority of five to one. 'Now indeed,' cried the princess dowager, 'my son is king.' But the victory was hardly won which king and minister found themselves battling with a storm of popular ill will such as never since the overthrow of the Stuarts assailed the throne. Violent and reckless as it was, the storm only marked a fresh advance in the re-awakening of public opinion. By this time several publications and newspapers had formed and greater interest in the affairs of government had developed. The parliament indeed had become supreme, and in theory the parliament was a representative of the whole English people. But in actual fact the bulk of the English people found itself powerless to control the course of English government. For the first and last time in our history parliament was unpopular and its opponents sure of popularity. The house of commons was more corrupt than ever, and it was the slave of the king. The king still called himself a Whig, yet he was reviving a system of absolutism, which Whiggism had long made impossible. His minister was a mere favorite, and in Englishmen's eyes a foreigner. The masses saw this, but they saw no way of mending it. They had no means of influencing the government they hated save by sheer violence. They came therefore to the front with their old national and religious bigotry, their long-nursed dislike of the Hanoverian Court, their long-nursed habits of violence and faction, their long nursed hatred of parliament, but with no means of expressing them save riot and uproar. Bute found himself the object of a sudden and universal hatred; and in 1763 he withdrew from office as a means of allying the storm of popular indignation.

Bute was replaced by George Grenville, its nominal chief, but its measures were still secretly dictated by the favorite. Charles Townshend and the duke of Bedford, the two ablest of the Whigs who had remained with Bute after Newcastle's dismissal, refused to join it. --- Townshend and Bedford remained apart from the main body of the Whigs, and both sections held aloof from Pitt. George had counted on the divisions of the opposition in forming such a ministry; and he counted on the weakness of the ministry to make it the creature of his will. ---

---

[4] Ibid, pp 764-765.

Grenville's one aim was to enforce the supremacy of parliament over subject as over king. He therefore struck fiercely at the new force of opinion, which had just shown its power in the fall of Bute. The opinion of the country no sooner found itself unrepresented in parliament than it sought an outlet in the press. In spite of the removal of the censorship after the revolution, the press had been slow to attain any political influence. Under the first two Georges its progress had been hindered by the absence of great topics for discussion, the worthlessness of the writers, and above all the lethargy of the time. It was in fact not till the accession of George III that the impulse, which Pitt had given to the national spirit, and the rise of a keener interest in politics, raised the press into a political power.

John Wilkes

The nation found in it a court of appeal from the houses of parliament. The journals became organs for that outburst of popular hatred which drove lord Bute from office; and in the 'North Briton' John Wilkes led the way by denouncing the cabinet and the Peace of Paris with peculiar bitterness and venturing to attack the hated minister by name. --- He woke the nation to a conviction of the need for parliamentary reform by his defense of the rights of constituencies against the despotism of the house of commons. He took the lead in the struggle, which put an end to the secrecy of parliamentary proceedings. He was the first to establish the right of the press to discuss public affairs. --- In 'Number 45' of the 'North Briton' Wilkes had censured the speech from the throne at the opening of parliament. A general warrant by the secretary of state was issued against the 'authors, printers, and publishers of this seditious libel.' [5] John Wilkes's arrest was declared illegal by one of the judges because of absolute immunity as a member of parliament, but the house expelled him and ordered his newspaper to be 'burned by the hangman.' He was convicted of libel but went to France. He returned to England and became a popular hero but was sent to prison. Upon popular acclaim he was released from prison and became mayor of London and received praise, later publishing critical comments against the government signing them as 'Junius' instead of his own name.

George's government and the American colonies

Pitt had waged war with characteristic profusion, and he had defrayed the cost of the war by enormous loans. At the time of the Peace of Paris the public debt stood at a hundred and forty million pounds. The first need therefore which met Bute after the conclusion of the Peace was that of making provision for the new burdens, which the nation had

---

[5] Ibid, pp 766-768.

incurred, and as these had been partly incurred in the defense of the American colonies it was the general opinion of Englishmen that the colonies should bear a share of them. In this opinion Bute and the king concurred, but their plans went further than mere taxation. The new minister declared himself resolved on a rigorous execution of the Navigation laws, laws which a monopoly of American trade was secured to the mother-country, on the raising of a revenue within the colonies for the discharge of the debt, and above all on impressing upon the colonists a sense of their dependence upon Britain. The direct trade between America and the French or Spanish West Indian islands had hitherto been fettered by prohibitory duties, but these had been easily evaded by a general system of smuggling. The duties were now reduced, but the reduced duties were rigorously exacted, and a considerable naval force was dispatched to the American coast with a view of suppressing the clandestine trade with the foreigner.

The stamp tax

The revenue, which was expected from this measure, was to be supplemented by an internal Stamp Tax, a tax on all legal documents issued within the colonies. Grenville pursued a rigid enforcement of the Navigation laws. The excise or stamp duty, which Walpole's good sense had rejected— was another order from his schemes for suppressing the contraband traffic. Unlike the system of the Navigation Acts, it was a gigantic change in the whole actual relations of England and its colonies. They met it therefore in another spirit. Taxation and representation, they asserted, went hand in hand. America had no representatives in the British parliament. Benjamin Franklin was dispatched to England. *Grenville had no mind to change his plans without an assurance, which Franklin could not give, of a union of the colonies to tax themselves; and the Stamp Act was passed through both houses with less opposition than a turnpike bill.*

With the influence of Edmund Burke, secretary to lord Rockingham, parliament repealed the Stamp Act, in February 1766. Pitt had returned to the ministry and accepted the earldom of Chatham and a seat in the house of lords, *but a painful and overwhelming illness, the result of nervous disorganization, withdrew him from public affairs, and his withdrawal robbed his colleagues of all vigor or union. --- George III was able to set Chatham's policy disdainfully aside, and to plunge into a contest far more disastrous than his contest with the press. In all the proceedings of the last few years, what had galled him most had been the act, which averted a war between England and her colonies. To the king the Americans were already 'rebels,' and the great statesman whose eloquence had made their claims irresistible was a 'trumpet of sedition.' George deplored in his correspondence with his ministers the repeal of the Stamp Acts. 'All men feel,' he wrote, 'that the fatal compliance in 1766 has increased the pretensions of the Americans to absolute independence.' --- No sooner had the illness of lord Chatham removed him in 1767 from any real share in public affairs, than the wretched administration which bore his name suspended the Assembly of New York on its refusal to provide quarters of English troops, and resolved to assert British sovereignty by levying import duties of trivial amount at American ports. The Assembly of Massachusetts was dissolved on a trifling quarrel with its governor, and British soldiers occupied Boston for a time. The remonstrances of the legislatures of Massachusetts and Virginia, however, coupled with a fall in the funds, warned the ministers of the dangerous course on which they had entered; and in 1769 the troops were withdrawn, and all duties, save one, abandoned.*

The Boston tea party

But the king insisted on retaining the duty on tea; and its retention was enough to prevent any thorough restoration of good feeling. A series of petty quarrels went on in almost every colony between the popular assemblies and the governors appointed by the crown, and the colonists persisted in the agreement to import nothing from the mother country. But the king was now supreme. The attack of Chatham (Pitt) in 1770 had completed the ruin of the ministry. Those of his adherents who still clung to it resigned their posts; and were followed by the duke of Grafton. All that remained were the Bedford faction and the dependents of the king; these were gathered under the former chancellor of the exchequer, lord North, into a ministry which was in fact a mere cloak for the direction of public affairs by George himself. --- His fixed purpose was to seize on the first opportunity of undoing the 'fatal compliance of 1766.' A trivial riot gave him the handle he wanted. In December 1773 the arrival of some English ships laden with tea kindled fresh irritation in Boston, where the non-importation agreement was strictly enforced. A mob in the disguise of Indians boarded the vessels and flung their contents into the sea. The outrage was deplored alike by the friends of America in England and by its own leading statesmen; and both Washington and Chatham were prepared to support the government in its looked for demand of redress. But the thought of the king was not of redress but of repression, and he set roughly aside the more conciliatory proposal of lord North and his fellow-ministers. They had already rejected as 'frivolous and vexatious' a petition of the Assembly of Massachusetts for the dismissal of two public officers whose letters home advised the withdrawal of free institutions from the colonies. They now seized on the riot as a pretext for rigorous measures. A bill introduced in the parliament in the beginning of 1774 punished Boston by closing its port against all commerce. Another punished the state of Massachusetts by withdrawing the liberties it had enjoyed ever since the Pilgrim Fathers landed on its soil. Its charter was altered. The choice of its council was transferred from the people to the crown, and the nomination of its judges was transferred to the English governor.

In the governor, too, by a provision more outrageous than even these, was vested the right of sending all persons charged with a share in the late disturbances to England for trial. To enforce these measures of repression troops were sent to America, and general Gage, the commander in chief there, was appointed governor of Massachusetts. The king's exultation at the prospect before him was unbounded. 'The die,' he wrote triumphantly to his minister, 'is cast.' 'The colonies must either triumph or submit. Four regiments would be enough to bring the Americans to their senses.' Unluckily, the blow at Massachusetts was received with anything but meekness. The jealousies between state and state were hushed by the sense that the liberties of all were in danger. If the British parliament could cancel the charter of Massachusetts and ruin the trade of Boston, it could cancel the charter of every colony and ruin the trade of every port from the St. Lawrence to the coast of Georgia. All therefore adopted the cause of Massachusetts; and all their legislatures, save that of Georgia, sent delegates to a congress which assembled on the 4th of September, 1774, in Philadelphia.[6]

A Boston town meeting had discussed and decided not to permit the landing of British goods in their harbor. There had been meetings in other towns in the colonies. After the outrageous actions of the British government the leaders of the Boston Town Meeting appealed to the other colonies and this First Continental Congress was held in Philadelphia September 4, 1774. The congress adopted the Association, an agreement, which provided that all goods from Britain would not be imported in America and all goods exported from all the colonies would not be exported to Britain. In Massachusetts, the provincial congress met in defiance of general Gage and made preparations for war. In April 1775, general Gage sent troops to Lexington and Concord. War with the colonial militia began. At the Second Continental Congress, George Washington was made commander in chief, June 1775. The Declaration of Independence was adopted July 4, 1776, and six weeks later all members of congress had signed this document. The rest is history. Cornwallis surrendered at Yorktown October 17, 1782. A Treaty of Peace was signed September 3, 1783. The first written Constitution in the history of nations was adopted in 1787 and the Bill of Rights was ratified in 1791.The full text of The Declaration of Independence is printed at the end of this chapter. Comments by Jefferson on its formation as well as the significant parts of Jefferson's original document, which were deleted, are also provided, in particular the important paragraph dealing with the slave trade.

---

[6] Ibid, pp 769-778.

The beginnings of British commercial ventures and imperialism were noted in the last chapter in the founding of Madras, on the south east coast of India in 1640 during the reign of Charles I. 'Diamond Pitt', grandfather of William Pitt, provided William with the belief that England's greatness and prosperity depended on seizing and holding on to the world's trade. Charles II leased Bombay, on the north west coast of India, to the East India Company in 1668. Charles II had leased Calcutta in Bengal at the north east coast of India to the East India Company in 1690. Other European powers contended for this new opportunity for trade and wealth. The most important were the French settlements, which had been established close to the above British settlements. These were all trading companies, however, national wars of conquest between England and France over these territories developed. Robert Clive, an employee of the British East India Company who had developed military skills defeated the French on the south east coast near Madras in 1751. He went to London in triumph and later returned in 1754 with the first deployment of British royal troops. The victory of Clive at the battle of Plassey, in Bengal, in 1757 over the French was considered a major victory for the English. *With the victory of Plassey began in fact the empire of England in the east.*[7] In 1763, the provisions of the Peace of Paris, at the end of the Seven Years War, prohibited the French from maintaining military bases in India.

British military forces remained in India. Warren Hastings, from 1773 to 1785, extended the East India Company's government over much of northern and central India. *His intention was to make British rule paramount in India. It was easy to show that the administration of Bengal, reformed by Hastings, was both more efficient and more just, if no less expensive, than the native rule which had preceded it. But the impeachment of Warren Hastings raised issues far deeper than the specific charges of cruelty and extortion for which he was tried. Clive had become an empire builder by accident. Hastings was an empire builder by design. His policy was to build up a strong British India, to extend its territories, when opportunity arose, and to knit to this paramount power, independent Indian princes by offering them military protection against their enemies. It was a policy of war and imperial expansion. The Company floundered in hopeless difficulties. --- The Company possessed a monopoly on all opium grown in Bengal. It was smuggled into China in return for silver. The profits were so great that, by 1815, Chinese bullion was one of the major supports of British administration in Bengal. The necessity of these transactions was not debated. The end justified the means; without the China trade there was*

---

[7] Green, p 754.

a danger of the whole British rule in India collapsing, and the collapse of British rule would mean a return to anarchy and civil war.

In earlier days, and even in the days of Clive and Hastings, Englishmen had mixed in a free social intercourse with the natives, learnt their language, and appreciated native culture. That attitude withered and died rapidly during the governor-generalships of Cornwallis and Wellesley. Cornwallis excluded all natives from the high posts in government service and discontinued the honors customarily paid to Indian nobles. Wellesley carried the process further and excluded all Indians and Eurasians from the regular entertainment at Government House. Such an attitude came even more naturally to the cantonments, for a successful army usually despises its victim, while exiled wives of army officers were intent on preserving their insular standards and by the assumption of social arrogance, attempted to dispel the fear aroused by the alien and incalculable environment. The more English society in India isolated itself from native life, the more bigoted became its attitude. This bigotry was encouraged by the growing evangelism amongst the English middle classes, for the missionaries and chaplains who flocked to India at the end of the century were horrified by many native customs which they made no attempt to understand. The attitude of moral righteousness was again strengthened, for obviously a race wallowing in such abominable heathenism was unfit to rule. Lord Hastings, in 1773, had written the following:

> *The Hindoo appears a being nearly limited to mere animal functions and even in them indifferent. Their proficiency and skill in the several lines of occupation to which they are restricted, are little more than the dexterity which any animal with similar conformation but with no higher intellect than a dog, an elephant, or a monkey, might be supposed to be capable of attaining. It is enough to see this in order to have full conviction that such a people can at no period have been more advanced in civil policy.*[8]

Ireland

We last noted briefly an account of the conditions in Ireland following the defeat of the Irish at the battle of the Boyne by William III and subsequent devastations across Ireland. The penal laws enacted to totally suppress Irish agriculture, industry, religion and participation in government continued in force. The history of Ireland under the conquest and domination of England does not enhance the credibility of English government and rule of law in their dependent conquered colonies. Ireland, with the cities of Dublin and Waterford, was first invaded by Henry II and the first plantation established near present Wexford, in

---

[8] Plumb, pp 175-178.

south east Ireland. Henry VII dispatched his general Sir Edward Poynings to Ireland in response to the threat of Yorkist pretenders to the throne, Lambert Simmel and Perkin Warbveck. The king declared that all offices in Ireland were to be held at the king's pleasure. *Poynings Law*, first established in Dublin, enforced the law that no Irish parliament might meet without the king's consent, no bills could be introduced by the Irish parliament without the kings permission; and all existing English laws were to be enforced in Ireland. Religious racism was introduced in Ireland by Henry VIII. England had long established precedents of fear, hatred and prejudice beginning with the crusades in the reigns after William's invasion and conquest of England, the expulsion of the Jewish people beginning with Henry II, and by the destructive slave trade escalating in the seventeenth to nineteenth centuries. The mass insanity of religious racism continued during the reigns of Mary I, Edward VI, Elizabeth I and Oliver Cromwell. The plantations of English and Scottish settlers in Ireland were established by Cromwell's soldiers and during the reigns of the Stuarts, especially James I.

After William III's conquests and the penal laws, the Irish were reduced to a condition, which Cusack recommended should be included in the history of the middle ages. *Three quarters of Irish land belonged to Englishmen or to Anglo-Irish Protestant families. By the middle of the* Eighteenth *century three quarters of a million pounds in rent was leaving Ireland each year for the pockets of the absentee landlords living in England, no wool was allowed to be exported except to England; its manufacture was absolutely forbidden. Irish ships were not allowed to trade with the colonies, although economically Ireland was extremely dependent on America. In consequence, Irish economy was forced into a course, which was fatal to a fast-growing population. The raising of sheep for wool, and of cattle for beef, whose free export to Europe was permitted, led to the growth of vast grazing grounds and consequent depopulation. The peasantry was driven to find a precarious subsistence on a potato patch, frequently no larger than a garden. Famine was endemic.*[9]

It is bitter but true that the English were responsible. They had invaded Ireland, conquered it, and, in spite of repeated rebellion, mastered it. Each rebellion had been followed by harsh retribution. The land had been taken away to compensate the victims and to pay for the alien administration, which the conquerors had imported. Its economy had been rigidly and absolutely subordinated to England's. Whatever the causes, each rebellion appeared as a Roman Catholic revolt against a Protestant government, so every pacification brought harsher laws against Catholic priests or Catholic laymen, who were deprived of the

---

[9] Plumb, p 179.

few rights of citizenship which eighteenth-century governments accorded to their people. In consequence, the institutions of government in Ireland were all in the hands of a small Protestant minority. --- Its boroughs were rotten by English standards; elections scarcely took place— in the reign of George II the same parliament sat for thirty-three years. No Catholics, of course, were allowed to hold a seat.[10]

The American war commenced in 1775, and the English parliament at once resolved to relieve Ireland of some of her commercial disabilities. Some trifling concessions were granted, just enough to show the Irish that they need not expect justice except under the compulsion of fear, and not enough to benefit the country. --- When the independence of the American States was acknowledge by France, a bill for the partial relief of the Catholics passed unanimously through the English parliament. Catholics were now allowed a few of the rights of citizens. They were permitted to take and dispose of leases, and priests and schoolmasters were no longer liable to prosecution.[11]

Henry Grattan had entered parliament in the year 1775. In 1779 he addressed the house on the subject of a free trade for Ireland; and on the 19th of April 1780, he made his famous demand for Irish independence. His address, his subject, and his eloquence were irresistible. 'I wish for nothing,' he exclaimed, 'but to breathe in this our land, in common with my fellow-subjects, the air of liberty. I have no ambition, unless it be the ambition to break your chains and to contemplate your glory. I never will be satisfied as long as the meanest cottager in Ireland has a link of the British chain clinging to his rags. He may be naked, but he shall not be in irons.[12]

In 1783 the British government had reluctantly given way: Poynings' Law, which had controlled Anglo-Irish relations since the reign of Henry VII, was swept away and the Act of Renunciation declared 'the exclusive right of the parliament and courts of Ireland in matters of legislation and judicature.' And yet no true solution had been achieved. Although the legislature was independent, it was venal. The executive remained English, appointed and dominated by London. Gratton realized that the Irish parliament must be reformed if a solution was ever to be found for Ireland's gravest problems— the problems of

---

[10] Ibid, pp 180-181.

[11] Note. More than two hundred years later, in Northern Ireland, eight Catholic churches were burned and two Catholic elementary schools destroyed, yet the American press scarcely reported that one Catholic Church was burned.

[12] Cusack, pp 589-590.

religious liberty, of absentee landlords, of a depressed peasantry, and a dependent commerce. ---

With America in revolt and the volunteers in arms Whitehall had capitulated before Irish demands. The wars with revolutionary France provided another golden opportunity for Ireland to force its demands by an implied or overt act of rebellion. The United Irishmen were formed by Wolfe Tone and reluctantly the threat was recognized, but again the English capitulation was half-hearted. The Catholic vote was conceded, but Catholics were denied membership of the Irish lords or commons. The United Irishmen entered into an alliance with France and made a bid for independence. The situation was exacerbated by the viceroy, Fitzwilliam, exceeding his powers and promising full Catholic emancipation. When he was recalled in 1795, the bitterness was intense. The country was swept into disorder. The Protestants, fearful of full emancipation, especially in Ulster, reorganized the Orange Society and harried the Catholics. The United Irishmen plotted with the French and attempted to organize resistance. Between 1796 and 1798 they were overborne and broken up with extreme brutality; complete license was given the troops to torture and to kill, to drive home a bloody lesson on the Irish. Maddened by these excesses, and hopeful of help from France, the Catholics rose in 1798.[13]

Cusack devotes a number of pages to the extreme cruelty inflicted on the Catholics prior to the famous battle of Vinegar Hill to which an entire volume is devoted.[14] The battle of Vinegar Hill in 1798 concluded the attempts of the Irish to gain independence from England. *The camp on Vinegar Hill as now beset on all sides by the royal troops, an attack was planned by general Lake, with 20,000 men and a large train of artillery. General Needham did not arrive in time to occupy the position appointed for him; and after an hour and a half of hard fighting; the Irish gave way, principally from want of gunpowder. The soldiers now indulged in the most wanton deeds of cruelty. The hospital at Enniscorthy was set on fire, and the wounded men shot in their beds. At Wexford, general More prevented his troops from committing such outrages; but when the rest of the army arrived, they acted as they had done at Enniscorthy. Court-martials were held, in which the officers were not even sworn, and victims were consigned to execution with reckless atrocity. The bridge of Wexford, where a Catholic priest had saved so many Protestant lives, was now chosen for the scene of slaughter; and all this in spite of a promise of amnesty. --- The Irish were never once accused of having offered the slightest insult to a woman; the military, besides shooting them indiscriminately with the men, treated*

---

[13] Plumb, p 184-185.

[14] Byrne, Battle of Vinegar Hill, Enniscorthy, County Wexford, Ireland.

them in a way which cannot be described, and under circumstances which added a more than savage inhumanity to their crime.

The inhuman treatment of Catholics was noted by quotations of Cusack from the *Annals of Ballilore*, written by a member of the Society of Friends. *Her account of '98, being the annals of a family and a village, is, perhaps, almost a work comprising a more extended range of observation; and yet what was suffered in Ballitore was comparatively trifling when compared with the sufferings of other villages and towns. The first trial was the quartering of the yeomen, 'from whose bosom,' writes this gentle lady, 'pity seemed banished.' The Suffolk Fencibles and the Ancient Britons were next quartered on the unfortunate inhabitants. They commenced the cruel torturing, for which the yeomen and militia obtained an eternal reprobation; the public floggings, of which she writes thus— 'the torture was excessive, and the victims were long in recovering, and in almost every case it was applied fruitlessly;' yet these demons in human form never relaxed their cruelty. 'The village, once so peaceful, exhibited a scene of tumult and dismay; and the air ran with the shrieks of the sufferers, and the lamentations of those who beheld them suffer.' --- The most cruel scene of all was the murder of the village doctor, a man who had devoted himself unweariedly to healing the wounds of both parties; but because he attended the 'rebels,' and showed them any acts of common humanity, he was taken before a court-martial, and 'hacked to death' by the yeomen with their swords. 'He was alone and unarmed when seized,' writes Mrs. Leadbeater, 'and I believe had never raised his hand to injure any one.'*

The French allies of Irish insurgents appear to have a fatality for arriving precisely when their services are worse than useless. On the 22nd of August 1798, Humbert landed at Killala with a small French force, who, after a number of engagements, were eventually obliged to surrender at discretion.[15]

Declaration of Independence

The full text of the Declaration of Independence approved by congress follows. Not commonly known are some of the events, which led to this document. Jefferson was chairman of a committee to draft the declaration. The members of the committee included John Adams, Dr. Franklin, Roger Sherman, Robert R. Livingston and Jefferson. Jefferson was admirably suited for this task in view of his wide knowledge of history, law, and government. He had participated in the response of the colonists to the recent acts of the English parliament. Jefferson had furthermore presented his resolve before congress with his paper *A Summary view of the Rights of British America*, written in 1774, to be presented to king George III. In that document, Jefferson cited numerous

---

[15] Cusack, pp 628-631.

acts of the British parliament from the reigns of Charles II, William and Mary, William III, Anne, George II and George III. Jefferson appealed to the ability and right of the king to veto acts involving the colonies, which were in direct conflict with those in England. *It is now, therefore, the great office of his majesty, to resume the exercise of his negative power, and to prevent the passage of laws by any one legislature of the empire, which might bear injuriously on the rights and interests of another. Yet this will not excuse the wanton exercises of this power, which we have seen his majesty practice on the laws of the American* legislatures. *For the most trifling reasons, and sometimes for no conceivable reason at all, his majesty has rejected laws of the most salutary tendency.*[16]

In his autobiography Jefferson stated: *In 1769, I became a member of the legislature by the choice of the county in which I live, and continued in that until it was closed by the revolution. I made one effort in that body for the permission of the emancipation of slaves, which was rejected; and indeed, during the regal government, nothing liberal could expect success. Our minds were circumscribed within narrow limits by an habitual belief than it was our duty to be subordinate to the mother country in all matters of government, to direct all our labors in subservience to her interest, and even to observe a bigoted intolerance for all religions but hers. The difficulties with our representatives were of habit and despair, not of reflection and conviction.*[17]

Many of the grievances, which form the version of the Declaration of Independence, prepared by Jefferson, are found in *A Summary View of the Rights of British America*. Of particular interest are Jefferson's statements on slavery. Jefferson's statement on slavery in his *A Summary View of the Rights of British America* presented to congress in 1774 follows: *The abolition of domestic slavery is the great object of desire in those colonies where it was unhappily introduced in their infant state. But previous to the enfranchisement of the slaves we have, it is necessary to exclude all further importations from Africa; yet our repeated attempts to effect this by prohibitions, and by imposing duties which might amount to a prohibition, have been hitherto defeated by his majesty's negative: Thus preferring the immediate advantages of a few African corsairs to the lasting interests of the American state, and to the rights of human nature, deeply wounded by this infamous practice.*[18]

The congressional committee deleted Jefferson's statements on slavery from his original draft of the *Declaration of Independence*. The deleted statements of Jefferson follow: *He has waged cruel war against*

---

[16] Jefferson, Writings, p 115.

[17] Ibid, p 5.

[18] Ibid, pp 115-116.

human nature itself, violating its most sacred rights of life and liberty in the persons of a distant people who never offended him, captivating and carrying them into slavery in another hemisphere, of to incur miserable death in their transportation thither. This piratical warfare, the opprobrium of INFIDEL powers, is the warfare of the CHRISTIAN king of Great Britain. Determined to keep open a market where MEN should be bought and sold, he had prostituted his negative for suppressing every legislative attempt to prohibit or to restrain this execrable commerce. And that this assemblage of horrors might want no fact of distinguished die, he is now exciting those very people to rise in arms among us, and to purchase that liberty of which he had deprived them, by murdering the people on whom he also obtruded them; thus paying off former crimes committed against the LIBERTIES of one people, with crimes which he urges them to commit against the LIVES of another.[19]

The full text of the Declaration of Independence adopted by the committee follows.

---

[19] Ibid, p 22.

The Declaration of Independence
July 4, 1776

When in the Course of human events, it becomes necessary for one people to dissolve the political bands which have connected them with another, and to assume among the Powers of the earth, the separate and equal station to which the Laws of Nature and Nature's God entitle them, a decent respect for the opinions of mankind requires that they should declare the causes which impel them to the separation.

We hold these truths to be self-evident, that all men are created equal, that they are endowed by their Creator with certain unalienable Rights, that among these are Life, Liberty and the pursuit of Happiness. That to secure these rights, Governments are instituted among Men, deriving their just powers from the consent of the governed. That whenever any Form of Government becomes destructive of these ends, it is the Right of the People to alter or abolish it, and to institute new Government, laying its foundation on such principles and organizing its powers in such form, as to them shall seem most likely to effect their Safety and Happiness.

Prudence, indeed, will dictate that Governments long established should not be changed for light and transient causes; and accordingly all experience hath shown, that mankind are more disposed to suffer, while evils are sufferable, than to right themselves by abolishing the forms to which they are accustomed. But when a long train of abuses and usurpations, pursuing invariably the same Object evinces a design to reduce them under absolute Despotism, it is their right, it is their duty, to throw off such Government, and to provide new Guards for their future security.

Such has been the patient sufferance of these Colonies; and such is now the necessity which constrains them to alter their former Systems of Government. The history of the present King of Great Britain is a history of repeated injuries and usurpations, all having in direct object the establishment of an absolute Tyranny over these States. To prove this, let Facts be submitted to a candid world.

He has refused his Assent to Laws, the most wholesome and necessary for the public good.

He has forbidden his Governors to pass Laws of Immediate and pressing importance, unless suspended in their operation till his Assent should be obtained; and when so suspended, he has utterly neglected to attend to them. He has refused to pass other laws for the accommodation of large districts of people, unless those people would relinquish the right of Representation in the Legislature, a right inestimable to them and formidable to tyrants only.

He has dissolved Representative Houses repeatedly, for opposing with manly firmness his invasions of the rights of the people.

He has refused for a long time, after such dissolutions, to cause others to be elected; whereby the Legislative Powers, incapable of Annihilation, have returned to the People at large for their exercise; the State remaining in the meantime exposed to all the dangers of invasion from without, and convulsions within.

He has endeavored to prevent the population of these States; for that purpose obstructing the Laws for Naturalization of Foreigners; refusing to pass others to encourage their migration hither, and raising the conditions of new Appropriations of Lands.

He has obstructed the Administration of Justice, by refusing his Assent to Laws for establishing Judiciary Powers.

He has made Judges dependent on his Will alone, for the tenure of their offices, and the amount and payment or their salaries.

He has erected a multitude of New Offices, and sent hither swarms of Officers to harass our People, and eat out their substance.

He has kept among us, in times of peace, Standing Armies without the Consent of our legislature.

He has affected to render the Military independent of and superior to the civil Power.

He has combined with others to subject us to a jurisdiction foreign to our constitution, and unacknowledged by our laws; giving his Assent to their acts of pretended Legislation:

For quartering large bodies of armed troops among us:

For protecting them, by a mock Trial, from Punishment of any Murders which they should commit on the Inhabitants of these States:

For cutting off our Trade with all parts of the world:

For imposing taxes on us without our Consent:

For depriving us in many cases, of the benefits of Trial by Jury:

For transporting us beyond Seas to be tried for pretended offenses:

For abolishing the free System of English Laws in a neighboring Province, establishing therein an Arbitrary government, and enlarging its Boundaries so as to render it at once an example and fit instrument for introducing the same absolute rule into these Colonies:

For taking away our Charters, abolishing our most valuable Laws, and altering fundamentally the Forms of our Governments:

For suspending our own Legislature, and declaring themselves invested with Power to legislate for us in all cases whatsoever.

He has abdicated Government here, by declaring us out of his Protection and waging War against us.

He has plundered our seas, ravaged our Coasts, burnt our towns, and destroyed the lives of our people.

He is at this time transporting large armies of foreign mercenaries to complete the works of death, desolation and tyranny, already begun with circumstances of Cruelty and perfidy scarcely paralleled in the most barbarous ages, and totally unworthy of the Head of a civilized nation.

He has constrained our fellow Citizens taken Captive on the high Seas to bear Arms against their Country, to become the executioners of their friends and Brethren, or to fall themselves by their Hands.

He has excited domestic insurrections amongst us, and has endeavored to bring on the inhabitants of our frontiers, the merciless Indian Savages, whose known rule of war-fare, is and undistinguished destruction of all ages, sexes and conditions.

In every stage of these Oppressions We have Petitioned for Redress in the most humble terms: Or repeated Petitions have been answered only by repeated injury. A Prince, whose character is thus marked by every act which may define a Tyrant, is unfit to be the ruler of a free People.

Nor have We been wanting in attention to our British brethren. We have warned them from time to time of attempts by their legislature to extend an unwarrantable jurisdiction over us. We have reminded them of the circumstances of our emigration and settlement here. We have appealed to their native justice and magnanimity, and we have conjured them by the ties of our common kindred to disavow these usurpations, which would inevitably interrupt our connections and correspondence. They too have been deaf to the voice of justice and of consanguinity. We must, therefore, acquiesce in the necessity, which denounces our Separation, and hold them, as we hold the rest of mankind, Enemies in War, in Peace Friends.

We therefore, the representatives of the united States of America, in General congress, Assembled, appealing to the Supreme Judge of the world for the rectitude of our intentions, do, in the Name and by Authority of the good People of these Colonies, solemnly publish and declare, That these United Colonies are, and of Right ought to be Free and Independent States; that they are Absolved from all Allegiance to the British Crown, and that all political connection between them and the State of Great Britain, is and ought to be totally dissolved; and that as Free and independent States, they have full Power to levy War, conclude Peace, contract Alliances, establish Commerce, and to do all other acts and Things which Independent States may of right do. And for the support of this Declaration, with a firm reliance on the Protection of Divine providence, we mutually pledge to each other our lives, our Fortunes and our sacred Honor.

Chapter 36

Conclusion

This book is meant as an introduction to the study of government and law and for use as a companion book to the author's *Critical Commentaries on Blackstone*. The writer, like most Americans, had little exposure in school to history and the men here studied. With the new technologies available to us, it is possible to learn by writing. Inter-library loans and the Internet provide opportunities for self-education while at home. There also has been a resurgence of interest in historical studies in documentaries presented on educational television. The motivation to study history has been rejuvenated by the historical novel. The writer has been motivated and influenced by all these sources of information. However, the writer has selected histories written by what the writer considers the greatest literary masterpieces of history.

The study of history is a requirement for the study of law. Nearly half of Blackstone's *Commentaries on the Laws of England* contains historical references to the laws of England. Blackstone elaborated what he considered the foundation of law in Section II of his Introduction, volume I. LAW--- *is prescribed by some superior, and which the inferior is bound to obey.*[1] The reader will have to judge whether the actions of the emperors and kings herein reviewed are *superior people*. Many Americans will react, as I did by reading about the actions of these men, with negative feelings, even disgust and abhorrence. The despicable lives and actions of these men are not cause to lose faith in humanity. On the contrary, the fact that people have survived the atrocities brought to this world by the worst of these men gives hope for mankind. The great majority of human beings in all parts of the world have been able to lead lives, which are constructive and had moments of love, toleration, and beneficence to their fellow human

---

[1] Blackstone, *Commentaries on the Law of England*, vol 1, p 38.

beings. Most people have a sense of fairness and know the difference between right and wrong. It remains to decide whether these men studied, the men who made the law, are in fact superior and whether it makes sense in a democratic nation such as the United States for *laws to be made by superior people for inferior people to follow.*

That the men who founded this nation were very different from the Roman emperors and English kings is evident from the historical record. Few would argue against the proposition that the origins of this country and the hope of people around the world were inspired by the founders of this nation who created the Declaration of Independence and the Constitution of the United States with the first ten Amendments, the Bill of Rights. Few people realize that this was the first written constitution to appear among all nations. England, for example, has never had a written constitution. The U.S. Constitution and Bill of Rights and the intent of its founders remain the basis of law in this country, even more today than ever before. That *the object of government is justice,* was proclaimed by James Madison, and later emblazoned in the opening words of the U.S. constitution *We the people of the United States, in order to form a more perfect union, establish justice.*

The object of government is justice. This should be remembered as a guide to our responsibilities as citizens to oversee the actions of men in our government. As Jefferson advised— *I am persuaded myself that the good sense of the people will always be found to be the best army. They may be led astray for a moment, but will soon correct themselves. The people are the only censors of their governors: and even their errors will tend to keep these to the true principles of the institution. --- If once they become inattentive to the public affairs, you and I, and congress and assemblies, judges and governors shall all become wolves.*[2]

Blackstone provided his own views about government, living as he did in England during the reign of George III. He quoted Cicero and then Tacitus, *who treats this notion of a mixed government, formed out of them all, and partaking of the advantages of each as a visionary whim; and one that, if effected could never be lasting or secure.* Blackstone then countered with: *But happily for us of this island, the British constitution has long remained, and I trust will long continue, a standing exception to the truth of this observation. For, as with the executive power of the laws is lodged in a single person, they have all the advantages of strength and dispatch, that are to be found in the most absolute monarchy; and as the legislature of the kingdom is entrusted to three distinct powers, entirely independent of each other; first, the king; secondly, the lords spiritual and temporal, which is an aristocratical assembly or persons selected for their piety, their birth, their wisdom, their valor or their property; and, thirdly, the house of commons, freely chosen by the people from among*

---

[2] Jefferson, pp 880-881.

themselves, which makes it a kind of democracy.[3] The question is whether our system of government and law should follow that of the laws established in England before and after the American revolutionary war? The Declaration of Independence made it quite clear that the intent of those who fought to gain independence from England was to separate the new nation from English kings and parliament, and that included a separation from the way England was governed and ruled. Nothing in the Constitution of the United States and the amendments to follow established English common law as the basis of law in the United States. Neither is there anything in the constitution supporting judge made rules of judicial supremacy and absolute immunity.

It is not possible to summarize the grave concerns many citizens have of the justice system as it now functions in the United States. Only one example will be given here. The most recent U.S. Supreme Court decision, Bush v. Gore (2000), orchestrated by chief justice William Rehnquist, demonstrated the absolute failure of our present justice system. It fostered the continued racism that infects this nation, and violated the basic foundations of democracy, which reads that *We the people --- establish justice.* It was also the intent of the founders of our nation to have a system of checks and balances between branches of government. This decision, not the people or the voters, decided who would be the president of the United States. Bush v. Gore, however, contrasted with the opinion given by chief justice Taney and six other concurring justices of the United States Supreme in the Dred Scott decision (1856)[4] when it was decided that all black people are merely property and have no rights whatsoever as citizens. At least the name of the justice was given who delivered the opinion of the court as well as the concurring justices. Bush v. Gore also contrasts with the devastating U.S. Supreme Court decision Plessy v. Ferguson (1896)[5] in that at least the name of the justice who delivered the opinion of the court is stated, *Justice Brown.* The U.S. Supreme court in *Plessy v. Ferguson* established the practice of segregation in the south, which apparently still rules as far as voting is concerned.

No one would use the machines in Florida, which counted the votes of blacks and other minorities, for medical, scientific or even consumer research. No one knows who wrote the decision for the court in Bush v. Gore. Nor was it certain who signed on to the per curiam (the

[3] Blackstone, pp vi, 50-51.

[4] Dred Scott v Sandford, 60 U.S. 393; 1856 Lexis 472; 15 L. Ed. 691; 19 HOW 393.

[5] Plessy v Ferguson, 163 U.S. 537; 16 S.Ct. 1138; 1896 U.S. Lexis 3390; 41 L.Ed 256.

whole court) decision. Nor was it argued that the only justices concurring with Rehnquist, Thomas and Scalia, had compelling reasons to recuse themselves in view of conflicts of interest involving close family members. Nor were the opinions of justices O'Connor or Kennedy, ever revealed or disclosed. But one thing is certain. The whole court decision was not a decision of the whole court. Justices Souter, Stevens, Ginsburg and Breyer presented at the end of Bush v. Gore dissenting opinions, which clearly differed from the whole court opinion. All this, and much more, without a whimper of protest from congress, excepting twelve members who walked out of congress the day the Florida electoral votes were certified, with Al Gore presiding. No doubt this decision will be discussed for the next one hundred years, along with Dred Scott and Plessy v Ferguson.

Most Americans are unaware that the U.S. Supreme court has given absolute immunity to legislators, judges, and prosecutors; and finally, the death of truth and justice in this nation's courts, the most recent (in 1983) decision stating that police, social workers, psychologists and in fact all witnesses can lie with impunity on the witness stand.[6] In the last two decisions justice William Rehnquist voted approval. Stevens and O'Connor joined Rehnquist in the 1983 decision. The people will have to decide whether these persons should not only have enormous power but also have absolute immunity *regardless of behavior*, no matter what they say or do in court. Should anyone in a democracy have absolute immunity? Who has the right to give anyone such privileges?

Another motivation for this book rests in the need to develop an understanding of the nature and character of the tyrant. The book *Modern Tyrants* by Daniel Chirot was an eye opener for the writer. The major tyrants of the twentieth century were presented. Should we also not look for the men around us who could be tyrants? The writer had originally intended this work to be a study of tyrants, comparing the ancient, medieval, and early modern tyrants to those in modern times. As we have seen in the above chapters none of the emperors or kings were alike. Not all were tyrants. Their behavior cannot be explained simply due to *human nature,* or the times in which they lived. People often make the mistake of using words as if they were certain realities— to groups of people, such as people on welfare, the mentally ill, illegal aliens, prisoners, tyrants or terrorists. The above words can be used with invectives of disapproval, derogation, censure or even hatred and justification for denial of benefits or rights, punishment, removal from society, or even extermination. Therefore it is important to remember that each person in

---

[6] Legislators, Tenney v. Brandhove, 341 US 367 (1951; Judges, Pierson v. Ray 386 US 547 (1967); Prosecutors, Imbler v. Pachtman, 424 US 409 (1976); Witnesses, Brisco v. LaHue, 460 US 325 (1983).

one of the above groups is, in his own way, a unique person. Yet, on the other hand, there is a need to study people to determine how they might be like other persons, and such things as their probable outcome, response or need for treatment, and alternative methods of management.

The author studied a broad sample of patients, hospitalized and outpatients, who had various appellations of *mental illness* affixed to them.[7] Historical data, a number of neurological and other performance variables were entered into a computer. A cluster analysis program then boiled down some ninety variables into five clusters, which accounted for 92% of the correlations of the data. The patients were then scored on each of the five clusters. Some eleven clusters of patients were then formed from this computer program and their relations to each other were shown. From computer comparisons of follow up data, the groups had significant differences of outcome adjustment, regardless of the so-called *diagnoses* they had been given. It was hoped that the same user oriented computer programs could be used for a study of modern tyrants of all sorts, and then compared to ancient, medieval and early modern tyrants here studied. To the author's dismay the user friendly program no longer existed and it was thus necessary to alter the objectives of this work and focus on *The Men Who Made the Law*.

But should it not be the right of the people to know something about the people who have great power and could be like the tyrants of old, such as chief justice Rehnquist, and president George W. Bush? What can we find out about Rehnquist? In a news article a young attorney in Arizona who was a member of the Republican party's so-called Flying Squad went to the precincts to test the ability of black and Latino voters *to comply with the law that you had to read English and interpret what you read. A passage of the constitution was read and people who spoke broken English were ordered to interpret it to prove they had the language skills to vote.* That attorney was William Rehnquist who presented as a bully, racist and budding tyrant in this nasty, sneaky disenfranchisement of minority voters. What about the make up of president George W. Bush? Does he have some of the same characteristics as George III? If so, this country is in deep trouble.

With all the universities and brilliant people attending, and all the availability of computers and access to information, one wonders why there is at present little interest in studying the makeup of tyrants? A basic tenet of the neurologist is that *the brain is the organ of behavior*. The brain of man has not changed during the time of written history. Study of the tyrants of history is therefore a prelude to a study of today's tyrants. In this book a preliminary review of the ancient, medieval and modern Roman emperors and English kings to George III was based on historians and writers such as Cicero, Plutarch, Tacitus, Hume and

---

[7] Harman, Computer Prediction of Chronic Psychiatric Patients, 1970.

Shakespeare. These historians wrote what they believed to be the true characteristics of these men, whether good or bad, and did not hesitate to call an emperor or king a tyrant.

The study of tyrants should also be directed to a study of the people who go along with the tyrants, not only the bureaucrats and functionaries of governments but the people who are subjected to their power. It remains for those interested in the fields of history and the social sciences to provide to citizens knowledge about the tyrants among the men in power and great influence. How can tyrants be identified and compared? What factors give rise to the tyrant? What happens to some men when they are given absolute power and absolute immunity? Unfortunately, psychiatrists from the mid eighteenth to twentieth centuries focused on a study of poor people who were in asylums or state hospitals, instead of the wealthy men in positions of power and influence. The primary responsibility rests with the historians and others to document accurately the facts about these men. From this data, those in the social sciences can provide empirical studies, which are worthy of the name science. Modern computers can handle enormous quantities of data and can handle sophisticated user oriented statistical programs for empirical analysis of data.

The most challenging task remains for studies of law and the justice system, which are worthy of the name of science. Law students and lawyers, since the 1880's at Harvard, are trained to focus on the written reports of judges in court cases. This is called research! Rather a first step in any research would be a compilation of all the laws generated by statutes and court decisions, federal, state, and local. This enormous compilation could be handled by modern computers and would involve far less effort that went into the compilation of the *Corpus Juris Civilis* including the *Digest of Justinian* during the reign of emperor Justinian in the sixth century. Consistency of the laws should be the initial focus followed by comparisons with federal and state constitutions. Compilations of American federal and state cases and statutes where English law has been used as a precedent would not be a formidable task. More than one group of capable, conscientious and motivated persons, independent of government and the lawyer establishment, should be actively pursuing this research.

Research should also be conducted, worthy of the name science and independent of political influence, to determine what happens to people in the justice system. Again massive amounts of data can be handled and computer programs could be employed for empirical studies, which include outcome data and predictive formulations.

Of great importance is the application of knowledge from these studies to political processes. People must follow up on the advice of Jefferson to watch over government, and courts, at all levels. A reform party to become truly a people's party must focus on reforms in government including the fields of law and the justice system.

THE JULIAN HOUSE

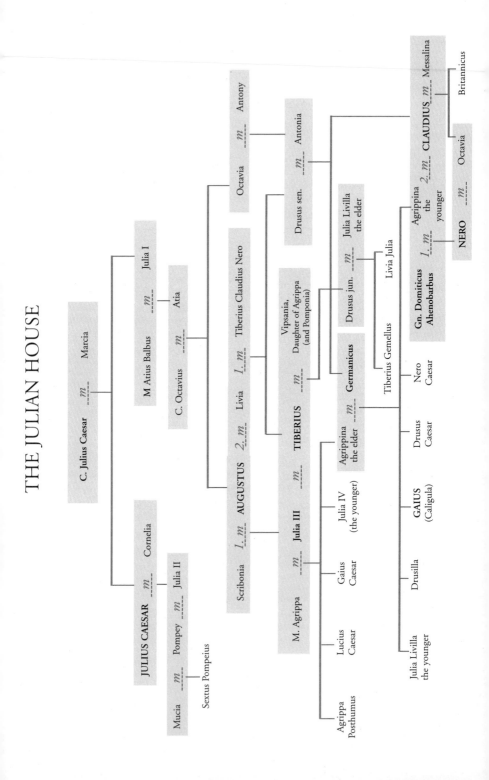

LANCASTER AND YORK

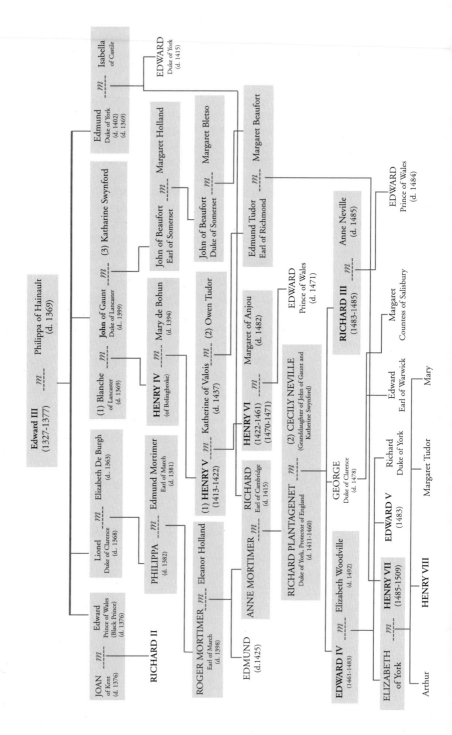

Bibliography

Altrocchi, Paul Hemenway, *Most Greatly Lived*, Xlibris Corporation, www.Xlibris.com, 2000.

The Anglo Saxon Chronicle, New York: Routledge, 1998.

Bede, *Ecclesiastical History of the English People*, London: Penguin Books, 1990.

Bentham, *A Bentham Reader*, Edited by Mary Peter Mack, New York, Pegasus, 1969.

Blackstone, William, *Commentaries on the Laws of England*, Volumes I-IV, Chicago and London: The University of Chicago Press, 1765 to 1769, 1979.

Bullough, Geoffrey, *Narrative and Dramatic Sources of Shakespeare*, Volume III, London: Routledge and Kegan Paul, New York: Columbia University Press, 1966.

Caesar, Julius, *The Gallic War*, Oxford, New York: Oxford University Press, 1996.

_____ *The Civil War*, Oxford, New York: Oxford University Press, 1998.

Cantor, Norman F., *Imagining the Law*, New York: Harpers Perennial, 1997.

Chirot, Daniel, *Modern Tyrants*, Princeton, New Jersey: Princeton University Press, 1994.

Cicero, Marcus, *The Republic and the Laws*, Oxford, New York: Oxford University Press, 1998.

_____ *On Duties*, Cambridge, New York: Cambridge University Press, 1991.

_____ *Selected Political Speeches*, London: Penguin Books, 1989.

_____ *Selected Works*, London: Penguin Books, 1971.

Cusack, Mary Frances, *History of Ireland*, London: Bracken Books, 1868, 1995.

The Debate on the Constitution, Part I and Part II, New York: The Library of America, 1992.

Erickson, Carolly, *The First Elizabeth*, New York: St. Martin's Griffin, 1983.

_____ *Great Harry*, New York: St. Martin'Griffin, 1980.

Franklin, John Hope, *From Slavery to Freedom*, New York: Alfred A. Knopf, 1974.

Gibbon, Edward, *The Decline and Fall of the Roman Empire*, Abridged, London, Penguin Books, 1985.

Graves, Robert, *I, Claudius*, New York: Vintage Books, 1989.

_____ *Claudius the God*, New York, Vintage International, 1989.

Green, John Richard, *A short History of the English People*, New York, American Book Company, Revised from the 1874 Edition.

Harman, Charles, *Critical Commentaries on Blackstone*, Brookings, Old Court Press, 2002.

_____Computer Prediction of Chronic Psychiatric Patients, J. Nerv. and Ment. Dis. Vol. 1 50:590-603, 1970.

Hume, David, *The History of England*, Volumes I-VI, Indianapolis: Liberty Fund, 1778, 1983.

James, Lawrence, *The Rise and Fall of the British Empire*, New York, St. Martin's Griffin, 1994.

Jefferson, Thomas, *Writings*, New York: Library of America, 1984.

Josephus, *The Complete Works*, Nashville: Thomas Nelson Publishers, 1998.

Justinian, *The Digest of Justinian*, Volumes I and II, Philadelphia: University of Pennsylvania Press, 1885.

Justinian's Institutes, Ithaca, New York, Cornell University Press, 1987.

Locke, John, *Two Treatises of Government*, Cambridge, Cambridge University Press, 1997.

Looney, Thomas J., *Shakespeare Identified*, New York, Frederick A. Stokes Company, 1920, Reprinted by Oxenford Press, 1996

MacManus, Seumas, *The Story of the Irish Race*, Old Greenwich, Connecticut: The Devin-Adair company, 1966.

Montesquieu, Baron De, *The Spirit of the Laws*, New York, The Hafner Press, 1949.

Morgan, Kenneth O., *The Oxford Illustrated History of Britain,* Oxford, New York, Oxford University Press, 1986.

Ogburn, Charlton, *The Mysterious William Shakespeare*, McLean, Virginia: EPM Publications, 1992.

Plumb, J.H., *England in the Eighteenth Century,* London: Penguin Books, 1969.

Plutarch, *Plutarch's Lives*, Volumes I and II, New York: Modern Library, 1992.

Seutonius, *The Twelve Caesars*, London: Penguin Classics, 1989.

Shakespeare, William, *The Complete Works*, New York: Gramercy Books, 1975.

Sobran, Joseph, Alias Shakespeare, New York: The Free Press, 1997.

Tacitus, *The Agricola and the Germania*, London: Penguin Classics, 1970.

_____*The Annals of Imperial Rome*, London: Penguin Classics, 1996.

_____*The Histories,* Oxford, N.Y.: Oxford University Press, 1997.

Trevelyan, G.M. *A Shortened History of England*, London, Penguin Books, 1987.

Ward, B.M., *The Seventeenth Earl of Oxford,* London: John Murray, 1928.

Whalen, Richard F., *Shakespeare: Who Was He?,* Westport, Connecticut, London: Praeger, 1994.

Woodham-Smith, Cecil, *The Great Hunger*, New York: Old Town Books, 1962.

Index